FIRST CANADIAN EDITION

# Promoting Community Change

## Making It Happen in the Real World

**HENRY PARADA**
*Ryerson University*

**LISA BARNOFF**
*Ryerson University*

**KEN MOFFATT**
*Ryerson University*

**MARK S. HOMAN**
*Pima Community College*



NELSON EDUCATION

NELSON EDUCATION

**Promoting Community Change: Making It Happen in the Real World, First Canadian Edition**

by Henry Parada, Lisa Barnoff, Ken Moffat, Mark S. Homan

**Vice President, Editorial Director:**
Evelyn Veitch

**Editor-in-Chief, Higher Education:**
Anne Williams

**Acquisitions Editor:**
Anne-Marie Taylor

**Marketing Manager:**
Ann Byford

**Developmental Editor:**
Theresa Fitzgerald

**Photo Researcher:**
Kristiina Paul

**Permissions Coordinator:**
Kristiina Paul

**Content Production Manager:**
Christine Gilbert

**Production Service:**
MPS Limited, a Macmillan Company

**Copy Editor:**
Wendy Thomas

**Proofreader:**
Dianne Fowlie

**Indexer:**
David Luljak

**Production Coordinator:**
Ferial Suleman

**Design Director:**
Ken Phipps

**Managing Designer:**
Franca Amore

**Interior Design:**
Carianne Sherriff

**Cover Design:**
Liz Harasymczuk

**Cover Image:**
All four images Courtesy of Habitat for Humanity Canada

**Compositor:**
MPS Limited, a Macmillan Company

**Printer:**
RR Donnelly



Printed and bound in The United States of America
1 2 3 4 13 12 11 10

For more information contact Nelson Education Ltd., 1120 Birchmount Road, Toronto, Ontario, M1K 5G4. Or you can visit our Internet site at http://www.nelson.com



**Library and Archives Canada Cataloguing in Publication**

Promoting community change : making it happen in the real world / Henry Parada ... [et al.].
– 1st Canadian ed.
American eds. written by Mark. S. Homan.

Includes bibliographical references and index.
ISBN 978-0-17-610430-6

1. Community development—Textbooks. 2. Community organization—Textbooks.
I. Parada, Henry, 1959-

HN110.C6P76 2010
307.1'4 C2010-902595-4

ISBN-13: 978-0-17-610430-6
ISBN-10: 0-17-610430-5

*We dedicate this book to all the communities and organizations that have allowed us to work with them and to learn from them about what is important about community change.*

# ABOUT THE AUTHORS

**HENRY PARADA** is an Associate Professor in the School of Social Work, Ryerson University. He has also taught social work at the Autonomous University of Santo Domingo, Dominican Republic; National Autonomous University of Nicaragua, Estelí Campus; and La Plata University, Argentina. He spent over ten years in direct practice within child protection as a front-line social worker and supervisor. His research interests include analysis of institutional practices, social work epistemology, and methodology. Henry has published in the area of the governance of workers and clients in child protection, institutional ethnography, the construction of subject locations, community education, and Latin American social work. Henry has been leading a six-year university-community development project in the Dominican Republic (Tier 2 CIDA-UPCD). He recently finished an institutional ethnography of the national Child Protection System practices in the Dominican Republic. He is also leading two research projects dealing with the sexual commercial exploitation of children in the Dominican Republic and is co-leading a third one in Nicaragua. His projects have received funds from Canadian International Development Agency, Latin America and Caribbean Exchange Grant, Canadian Institutes of Health, UNICEF, Ryerson International Initiative Funds, and the Social Sciences and Humanities Research Council (SSHRC-International).

**LISA BARNOFF** is an Associate Professor in the School of Social Work, Ryerson University. The focus of her research and writing is on the implementation of anti-oppressive practices within community-based social service agencies. Lisa's teaching experience includes courses on social work theory and practice, anti-oppression, violence against women, family violence, and sexual diversity. Lisa's practice experience is in the women's services sector. She has worked on the front line and in management positions in agencies working with communities of women facing issues related to violence, poverty, homelessness, and experience with the mental health system. At Ryerson University, Lisa has engaged in administration, most recently acting as the Associate Director, Field Education.

**KEN MOFFATT** is an Associate Professor in the School of Social Work, Ryerson University. His research interests include community practice in the context of diversity, post-structural understandings of subjectivity, the influence of technique and technology on human relations and human/personal change, and cultural studies. He has recently become engaged in collaborative art-based projects and writing that focus on the critical analysis of symbol creation in the context of globalization. He has taught courses in community work, critical perspectives on marginalization, queer theory, identity and diversity, anti-oppression and social work practice. Ken has worked in the field of social work as a child welfare worker, program management officer, and community worker. In the past, he has worked in administration as the Graduate Programme Director at York University and Ryerson University Schools of Social Work.

**MARK S. HOMAN** is a full-time faculty member (since 1978) and former chair of the Social Services Department at Pima Community College. In addition to these duties, Mark has served as an adjunct faculty member in the Department of Sociology and Social Work at Northern Arizona University; the Graduate School of Social Work at Arizona State University; and the Counseling, Deafness, and Human Services Department at the University of Tennessee. He has also been a guest lecturer at other colleges, universities, and training consortia in the United States, Russia, and Sweden. He received his master's degree in social work from Arizona State University in 1975 and is certified as an Independent Social Worker by the State of Arizona.

Mark is a strong advocate of community empowerment and uses his own very active involvement in the community to contribute to its improvement and to increase his own learning. For 30 years he has worked with diverse populations in urban, rural, and reservation communities on a broad range of issues, including neighbourhood stabilization and empowerment, hunger, reproductive rights, children with special health care needs, community mental health, family planning, community health work, capital punishment, public schools and community development, political campaign organizing, foster care, and adoption. In addition to his roles as organizer, lobbyist, consultant, and teacher, Mark has developed and directed several human services programs. He has also been a founding member of many community organizations and agencies and has served on numerous community boards and councils.

Mark is the author of *Rules of the Game: Lessons from the Field of Community Change*, a concise guide that offers practical wisdom, including 135 "rules" that demystify the community change process. He conducts workshops and delivers numerous presentations dealing with various aspects of community building and community power. He is frequently asked by public and private organizations to assist them in increasing their effectiveness.

Mark also serves on the Editorial Board of two national publications: *Human Service Education*, the journal of the National Organization of Human Service Education; and *Frontline Initiative*, the publication of the National Alliance for Direct Support Professionals, published by the University of Minnesota. He has been the recipient of numerous awards, including the Outstanding Faculty Award from Pima Community College, Outstanding Field Faculty award from Arizona State University School of Social Work, and the President's Award and the Lenore McNeer Award given by the National Organization for Human Service Education.

At this stage of his career Mark has come to accept the fact that he will not be playing shortstop for the San Francisco Giants.

CONTENTS

## 4 Relating Community Change to Agency Work and Professional Practice 68



# PART TWO Putting the Pieces Together 87

## 5 Power 89



## 6 Knowing Your Community 113



## 7 Powerful Planning 142

## 15 Lobbying for Change 362

# PREFACE

How is it that the idea of transforming communities and building the power of people affected by social conditions gets missed too often in social work education and practice? How is it that graduating social work students might know about techniques for dealing with individuals and so little about techniques for improving the communities in which these individuals live? And why is it that these are still so often considered completely separate areas anyway?

The answers are probably many. Perhaps the profession rewards work that engages in individual situations but not situations that affect groups, made up of individuals. Perhaps our professional culture is informed by a larger culture that prefers to keep people who are in need unorganized and dependent, their combined strengths unrecognized and underutilized. Perhaps as social workers we see more clearly the individual faces of anguish and want so much to do what we can to bring relief quickly without touching the structural and oppressive conditions that brought the anguish in the first place. No doubt some combination of these and several other factors explain why many social workers who work with people have not been expected to know much about communities before they graduate. The skills related to community change may have been taken for granted, as if it were sufficient that they be learned on the fly—if they needed to be learned at all.

We believe there is now a renewed recognition of the role strengthened communities can play in preventing problems and producing solutions to problems that individuals and families experience. Healthy communities nurture the health of their members. In the fields of social work, social services, and health care, we are taking steps to provide students with intentional training in how to organize people to deal constructively and powerfully with the oppressive conditions they face. Promoting community change is not something students should study and discuss only in theory. It is something they should learn how to do, which is what this book emphasizes. Part 1 looks at the need for community change and considers how community change activities relate to the change agent's professional life.

Part 2 gives clear, practical direction on how to go about the business of promoting change. Each of these chapters concentrates on a specific issue with which a successful change agent needs to be familiar.

Part 3 offers more detailed insights into three common arenas of change. These chapters help the reader understand typical settings where change can occur. Building on principles and techniques described in earlier chapters, the reader is introduced to particular knowledge and skills that apply to these circumstances.

## Key Changes for the First Canadian Edition

In preparing this first Canadian edition, we have benefited from feedback from editors, reviewers, and readers alike. We have largely maintained the structure of the original text, but have adopted the book to better fit in a Canadian context. We have introduced perspectives and ideas on community work that have emerged from Canadian scholars, and we have drawn on Canadian examples throughout the book. New and updated Canadian material has been added to each chapter to build on the ideas of previous editions.

Attention to different forms of oppression and to anti-oppressive practices has been introduced, with a particular emphasis on understanding the oppressive practices that affect marginalized communities and how introducing those anti-oppressive frameworks into the work of community change is an essential aspect of Canadian community practice. Drawing from this framework, we have extended the discussion of privilege, forms of oppression—racism, classism, and homophobia among others—and we have kept the discussion of *global perspectives*. Each chapter includes a Global Perspectives feature that presents the views of citizens, activists, and scholars from around the world. We have emphasized the importance of diversity by race, class, sexuality, and gender in considering the complexities of Canadian communities.

A change agent grounded in theory will be much more effective than one who makes up action from one adventure to the next. In this first Canadian edition, we provide the reader with an effective *framework for action*. Several theoretical frameworks—system theory, multicultural approaches, anti-oppressive theories, Aboriginal world views and critical reflective work—are described along with a theory of community change to help in understanding how theory can undergird organized action. Further, the discussion of social capital has been expanded and linked to a more thorough examination of other forms of *community capital*.

## Tried and True Features

We have drawn extensively from our experiences and have benefited from the work and writing of other change agents and scholars. Certainly, a number of students will work at the community level, and the first Canadian edition provides these students with a strong foundation for understanding the elements of community change within the Canadian context and offers practical approaches for taking action. However, many other students envision primary professional roles that lead them to work more at the individual and family level, and the material is oriented to the real-world experiences these workers will encounter as well so that they can imagine and integrate community influences and possibilities in their practice.

Community change is interesting, exciting, and demanding work, and we hope you get a flavour of this in our descriptions of the subject. We approach the reader as a potential change agent and a partner in discovery. Several features of the book support this approach. Introductory questions to begin each chapter orient the reader to key areas to be covered in the chapter. From time to time, we ask readers to Take a Moment to Discover, inviting the reader to consider how the material relates to his or her own experiences, or we suggest a simple activity that can help the reader solidify understanding of the topic. Change Agent Tips offer specific tricks of the trade that deal with typical situations or problems. Fundamental ideas are clarified or defined in brief Capturing Concepts sections, and Did You Know? features provide additional information on topics under discussion.

This book is written for all those students and professionals who truly want to make a difference. We hope you find inspiration, direction, and confidence in the following pages. You will certainly find challenges in the real world. With your sense of purpose and the knowledge you gain from this book, you will be well prepared to face those challenges.

We learn a lot from our students and from the members of communities with whom we work. We would like to learn from you as well. So this is an invitation for you to send us feedback as well as stories—discoveries you have made or challenges you have faced. You can send them to the first author, Henry Parada, at Ryerson University, School of Social Work, 350 Victoria Street, Toronto, Ontario, M5B 2K3.

## Acknowledgments

Many members of the Nelson Education team contributed their expertise to this edition. Three deserve particular mention. First, Anne Williams for inviting us to take on this project and for working closely with us in the initial stages. She trusted that we could accomplish this task and was unwavering in her support of our work. Theresa Fitzgerald was also instrumental in assisting us in getting this book to production. Theresa was extremely patient and was consistently helpful as we engaged in the writing process and prepared the manuscript for publication. Wendy Thomas worked diligently with us on the copy-editing process, and we are appreciative of the thoroughness and thoughtfulness of her work.

We must thank our faculty colleagues in the School of Social Work at Ryerson University, who provide a space for critical analysis and encouragement to engage in anti-oppressive approaches to social work. We especially want to thank Dr. Akua Benjamin for her leadership in community and her unflagging support of our teaching and research.

We thank the reviewers of this text who provided valuable suggestions that improved the content of the book, especially as it relates to the Canadian context of community work. They are Carolyn Anderson, Mount Royal University; Tom Brenner, University of Waterloo; Philip Durrant, Niagara College; Cheryl Higgs, Durham College; and Sandra Preston, McMaster University.

Our respective family members deserve much credit for the completion of this book. Their constant support and encouragement for our work is foundational to our success. In particular, Henry would like to thank B. M. McLeod. Lisa would like to thank her partner, Bonnie Levine; their daughter, Edie Levine-Barnoff; and her parents, Dorothy and Philip Barnoff. Ken would like to thank his partner, George Rallis, and his niece Tasha Rabinowitz.

Finally, we wish to acknowledge our own group process as co-authors. While at times it was not easy, we maintained our commitment to each other and to this project and we have come to learn a great deal about each of our strengths.

Henry Parada, Lisa Barnoff, and Ken Moffatt

*Mark Homan would like to thank a number of people for assistance on the American edition of this book:*

It is hard to capture in just a few words the many gifts I have received from my mentor, Dr. Ann Nichols of Arizona State University. Her thoughtful critique of my work and the ready offerings from her wealth of knowledge have refined my thinking and enriched the book.

Jo Namsick, Pima Community College librarian, deserves special recognition; her ability to mine the resources of the library provided me with ready access to information troves from around the world. No request was too trivial or too demanding for her timely attention. She is a gem. Jean Lewis, Tucson-Pima Public Library reference librarian, patiently guided me through the workings of the Foundation Center Collection and helped unlock the vault of the Grants and Nonprofit Information Center.

Dr. Alf Ronnby, from the University of Goteborg in Sweden, offered numerous insights on theoretical principles and helped to expand my awareness of views from other parts of our world.

I put my ideas to the test through my own work to promote community change. Lee Hunter from the Arizona Department of Health Services has been an insightful partner in much of my work and learning. Parent Leaders who partner with us in our work through the Office of Children with Special Health Care Needs have inspired me and taught me more than they can ever imagine.

Butch Melser, Information Technology Supervisor at Pima Community College, did his best to see that my understanding of information and communication technology stayed on line. Jan Lesher's political acumen and public relations expertise sharpened my views of these aspects of community work. The ongoing support of my colleagues at Pima Community College, especially Alvin Lewis, Shay Kelly, Tommie Miller, Diana Montano, Sheila Hughes, and Mike Curry, has been especially important.

I benefit so much from the students who continue to teach me. Their willingness to challenge themselves, their communities, and their teacher bring both inspiration and lessons.

Finally, my beautiful family. Any catalogue of the gifts you have given me would be incomplete. I feel your love in so many ways, and I am a better man for it.

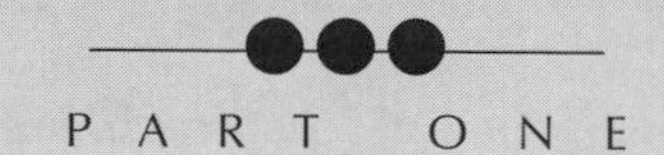

PART ONE

# Responding to the Need for Community Change

Part 1 introduces you to the idea of promoting community change—the idea that you do not have to contribute to the presence of problems by inattention and inaction. We believe you should look at, not look away from, problems that go beyond the individual and be willing to confront those problems with the knowledge and skills at your disposal. You cannot take sole responsibility for the problems you see, nor can you tackle them all, but you can make a conscious decision to help change policies and improve conditions that affect the lives of people in your community. Further, you have the opportunity to bring people together to discover community assets that may lie hidden from view. With community members you can figure out how to use these resources to strengthen the community and improve the lives of its members. It is important to acknowledge this as a legitimate, if not fundamental, part of your role as a social worker.

As in any significant aspect of your life, being a community change agent requires a sense of conviction and balance. This is not to be confused with being devoid of passion—far from it! Your strong feelings that the rights of the people you serve be acknowledged and fully granted provide a necessary fuel to your involvement. A spirit of principle should infuse your actions, but your passion should not substitute for purpose.

Four chapters make up Part 1. In Chapter 1, Introduction to Understanding Change, we provide an overview of the process of community change. You will glimpse the range of community conditions you may confront as a professional working in the social services field. Further, we explore some of the fundamental issues involved in working to promote change, including the critical importance of understanding oppressive practices that may affect community members. This discussion will help you see the community itself, not just its individual members, as an arena for change. We will describe a number of ways your work can help engage your community. Finally, in this chapter we recognize the value of idealism as a source of strength and clarity.

In Chapter 2, Theoretical Frameworks for Community Dynamics, we present theoretical frameworks that provide the basis for understanding how you can promote action to change conditions that affect people. Having a strong theoretical base for your actions will help you to analyze what is occurring and therefore to know how to move forward in your work. In this chapter we discuss a range of different frameworks including systems theory, multiculturalism, anti-oppression, Aboriginal world views, and critical reflection.

In Chapter 3, Understanding Community Change, we describe the role community change plays in the provision of support and service. Perhaps you are not sure how community change fits with your picture of what people working in social services do. This is a common reservation. Many social workers do not have a clear understanding of community change, so it is difficult to recognize its importance to their work. In this chapter we also survey approaches used by Canadian social service professionals working in community change. All this is closely linked to the social work profession's ethical values. Your professional preparation gives you the theoretical knowledge as well as ethical and practical skills that you can put to use in the context of community change.

In Chapter 4, Relating Community Change to Agency Work and Professional Practice, we focus on you as a change agent. To help explore this relationship between community change and professional practice, we examine three views of Canadian social welfare. We discuss the developmental approaches that build on strengths, identifying resources within the community that can be cultivated and utilized; the emphasis is on potential, not problems and the importance of partnership development. We encourage you to look at the difference between a more traditional individual service approach and one that builds on and develops combined strengths to make a sustained difference in community participation. We continue exploring the social work values that support community work.

Working to promote community change is an exciting endeavour that will energize you and make your decision to become a professional in the field of social services more meaningful. Some of the changes you make may seem relatively minor, but they represent a new direction that over time will account for meaningful improvement of a situation. Some of your efforts may start small, but you will see them grow to secure significant changes. Perhaps you will even initiate actions that substantially alter the balance of power in your community, producing significant, permanent change. All these opportunities are open to you as a community worker. All of them result in a situation that is better for your having acted. All give you the chance to help eliminate problems.

We invite you to consider these opportunities more fully in the following pages.

CHAPTER ONE

# Introduction to Understanding Change

**This chapter will help you better understand the following questions:**

- What are the "community-based" issues?
- Why are community-based issues important for social workers?
- Why is the promotion of community change an important social work activity?
- What are some of the key concepts relevant to community practice?
- Why are some individuals and communities resistant to change?
- Why are issues of discrimination and oppression important to community practice?
- What are some of the targets of community change?

## WHAT IS GOING ON OUT THERE?

Saul Alinsky made these observations on social workers:

> They come to the people of the slums not to help them rebel and fight their way out of the muck . . . most social work does not even reach the submerged masses. Social work is largely a middle class activity and guided by a middle class psychology. In the rare instances where it reaches the slum dwellers it seeks to get them adjusted to their environment so they will live in hell and like it. A higher form of social treason would be difficult to conceive. (as quoted in Meyer, 1945)

Strong words, are they not? How do they apply to the way in which you plan to provide social services? Will you address only the singular problems of individuals, or will you reflect occasionally on the bigger picture? Will you look beyond the immediate situation to understand the fundamental barriers and broader social structures that your clients face? Will you shake your head and wring your hands, or will you do something about it? What kind of a social service worker do you intend to be?

### What You Will See If You Look

If you look carefully around you, beyond your immediate reality, and try to see carefully what is happening in your city, community, or neighbourhood, you will notice many issues that should concern you as people living in Canada. Let us discuss two issues that you can see evidence of each day, right now.

#### Poverty

Statistics Canada's low-income cut-off (LICO) is a measure of poverty that is used to identify low-income families. A family is considered to be poor according to this measure if the family devotes a larger share of its income to the necessities of food, shelter, and clothing than an average family would. For example, a family on welfare uses approximately 50 to 60 percent of its income on housing (Raphael, 2007). According to the National Council of Welfare, an alarming number of people living in Canada live below the LICO. The numbers of Canadians whose income is less than 50 percent of the LICO grew from 143,000 families and 287,000 individuals in 1989 to 277,000 families and 456,000 individuals in 1997 (Hick, 2002). The overall percentage of Canadians living in poverty was 11.9 percent in 1997 (Hick, 2002). Statistics Canada's 2001 census revealed that 10.8 percent of children in a family with two parents live in poverty. That is, one in every ten children in two-parent families lives in poverty! This percentage jumps to 45.5 percent for children living in a single-parent family. That is almost half of all children in single-parent families (Hick, 2002)! See Table 1.1.

A number of factors contribute to poverty, such as unemployment, underemployment, and dependence on inadequate social assistance. In addition, another factor that increases the risk of living in poverty is being a member of a marginalized community, which includes the following groups: Aboriginal communities, women, racialized people, people with disability, and recent immigrants (Galabuzi, 2006; Raphael, 2007). These communities are more likely to live in poverty due to unemployment, reliance on part-time work, and lower wages.

The poverty of these communities is related to the experience of multiple forms of discrimination, including colonialism and racism (Galabuzi, 2006; Raphael, 2007). The World Health Organization (2002) tells us that more than 1.2 billion people in the world, half of them children, live on less than $1 a day. Is this acceptable to you?

## Food insecurity

Another issue that is evident in Canada is that of insecurity of the food supply. According to the World Food Summit, food security exists when "all people, at all times, have physical and economic access to sufficient, safe and nutritious food that meets their dietary needs and food preferences for an active and healthy life" (FAO, 2009). A survey conducted between 1998 and 1999 by the Applied Research Branch of Human Resources Development Canada (Brink, 2001) reported

**TABLE 1.1** Low-Income Cut-Off (1992 Base) After Tax, 2008

| | Community size | | | | |
|---|---|---|---|---|---|
| | | Urban areas | | | |
| | Rural areas | Less than 30,000 | 30,000 to 99,999 | 100,000 to 499,999 | 500,000 and over |
| Size of family unit | Dollars | | | | |
| 1 person | 12,019 | 13,754 | 15,344 | 15,538 | 18,373 |
| 2 persons | 14,628 | 16,741 | 18,676 | 18,911 | 22,361 |
| 3 persons | 18,215 | 20,845 | 23,255 | 23,548 | 27,844 |
| 4 persons | 22,724 | 26,007 | 29,013 | 29,378 | 34,738 |
| 5 persons | 25,876 | 29,614 | 33,037 | 33,453 | 39,556 |
| 6 persons | 28,698 | 32,843 | 36,640 | 37,100 | 43,869 |
| 7 or more persons | 31,519 | 36,072 | 40,241 | 40,747 | 48,181 |

Source: Statistics Canada. Table 202-0801—Low income cut-offs before and after tax for rural and urban areas, by family size, current dollars, annual, CANSIM (database). http://cansim2.statcan.gc.ca/cgi-win/cnsmcgi.exe?Lang=E&CNSM-Fi=CII/CII_1-eng.htm (accessed: September 7, 2009).

**TABLE 1.2** Toronto Families Living Below the Low-Income Cut-Off (LICO), 2007

| Communities | Percentage living below poverty line (LICO) |
|---|---|
| European | 11% |
| South Asian | 21% |
| East Asian | 19% |
| South and Central American | 20% |
| African | 39% |
| Arab and West Asian | 30% |
| Caribbean | 22% |

Source: The Colour of Poverty. Fact Sheet No. 6, *Understanding the Racialization of Poverty in Ontario in Income Levels and Social Assistance in 2007*. Reprinted by permission.

approximately 10.2 percent of the population in Canada lived in a household that had experienced an episode of food insecurity in the previous year. When a family experiences food insecurity, it means it cannot guarantee its next meal or that its members have gone without food that is necessary for proper nutrition. These episodes increase particularly those who live below the poverty line (LICO). See Table 1.2. The report states that those families with at least one child experienced high instances of food insecurity. Families with children less than five years old had increased chances of 13.6 percent of experiencing food insecurity, and families with children younger than twelve years old became vulnerable to experiencing food insecurity by 12.8 percent. The same study also found that food insecurity is more prevalent among lone-parent families (26.6 percent) than two-parent families, as well as among young adults (12.5 percent of 18- to 34-year-olds) (Brink, 2001). According to the Canadian Association of Food Banks (CAFB, 2007), an estimated 720,231 people used Canadian food banks in March 2007, including single parents, two-parent families, children, and seniors. A little over 50 percent of the households that used the services of food banks were families with at least one child, and 38.7 percent of food bank clients are children.

Health Canada's (2007) report on income-related household food security in Canada for the year 2004 indicated that 1.1 million Canadian households (9.2 percent) were moderately or severely food insecure. Off-reserve Aboriginal households experienced higher levels of food

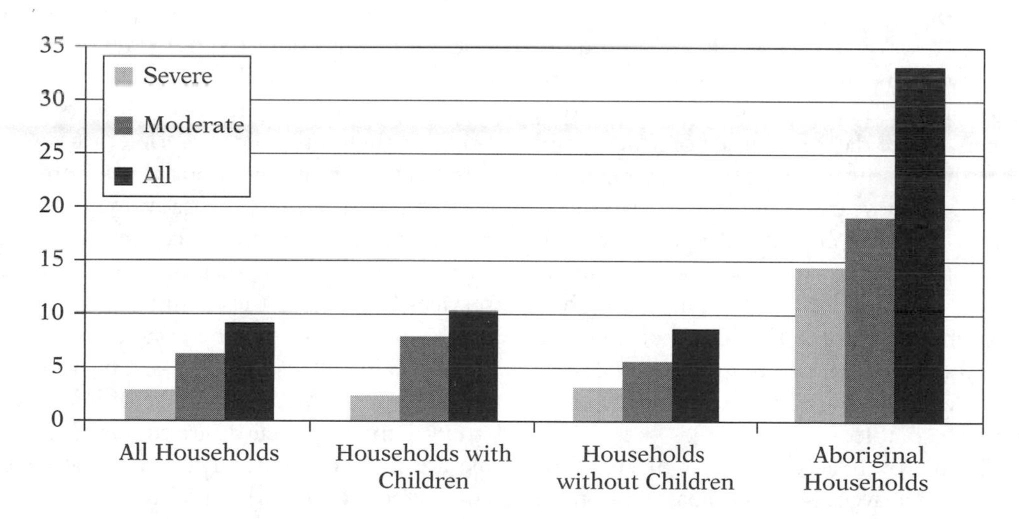


**FIGURE 1.1** Challenges for Social Works in Providing Services

Source: Based on Health Canada. (2007). Canadian Community Health Survey Cycle 2.2, Nutrition (2004), Income-Related Household Food Security in Canada. Ottawa: Office of Nutrition Policy and Promotion, Health Products and Food Branch.

insecurity. Thirty-three percent of all Aboriginal household experience food insecurity—14.4 percent severe insecurity and 19 percent moderate insecurity (Health Canada, 2007). See Figure 1.1.

## Institutional Context of Community Practice

In recent years, Canadian governments have taken a neo-liberal approach to politics, meaning that the state's involvement in people's affairs is minimized (Lee & Todd, 2007). In their initiatives to balance budgets, governments have changed funding policies (CCSD, 2003), and this shift in the way that government funds are distributed has resulted in significant cuts to funds allocated to social service agencies (Ilcan & Basok, 2004). As a consequence, these agencies have been forced to reduce staff and cut many of their services. In the face of these cuts, nonprofit, community, and public social service agencies are struggling to provide services. This struggle makes it difficult for agencies to develop innovative services that are responsive to the communities they serve (Barnoff, George, & Coleman, 2006).

You will see evidence of other challenges in social work and community work on a daily basis as you work in social services. Community members who use social services often have to wait too long for an appointment, wait too long to be seen on the day of their appointment, and have too little time with you or other professionals when they are finally seen. The forms they must complete are often lengthy and confusing. Some agency staff can be insensitive, unhelpful, or downright rude. Taken together, these practices reinforce the idea that community members who have to use these services are unworthy and lack dignity. Are these conditions you find acceptable?

Will you grow to accept a system that employs denial and defensiveness as its primary responses? Will you care if workers and agencies are isolated from the day-to-day lives of the people they serve? Will you ignore the needs of chronically underserved or unreached populations? Will you tolerate mediocrity as the standard of your profession and keep silent about a "service" system that lives in fear of being found out?

Many of us do not like to be confronted with these questions. We hope they will just go away. At times, we hope that someone else will deal with these issues, and we cope by more narrowly defining our responsibilities to those who use our services. Through community practice, we begin to face squarely some of these issues and stop avoiding responsibility.

Most of you are not going to work for community change as your primary professional role. But all of you will be confronted, from time to time, with the challenge to promote change. All of you will face barriers to your practice. All of you will have your professional ethics tested. Rather than looking away, we need to develop strategies to respond.

### Beyond a consideration of problems

An honest reflection on the many local, provincial, national, and international problems that exist can be intimidating, even discouraging. You may look at our provision of social services in the face of so many needs and conclude that people just do not care about each other. Do we assume that we—including you—just do not care? That could be, but frankly, we doubt it. Take another look.

People are burdened by their fears and held back by their prejudices. People are also confused by their myths about the nature of our society and the paths to a disadvantaged life. This is undeniable. Fear, prejudice, and myths about society play a part in shaping the availability of services. But just as these limitations are facts of life, so too is the genuine concern that we feel for those in distress. People are moved by suffering, emboldened in the face of injustice, and strengthened by their desire to contribute. People are touched by their altruistic desire to be connected to each other and to help.

If you believe that people have an interest in and the capacity for good, you will act to take advantage of those beliefs. If you do not, your cynicism will quickly lead to burnout. Your belief in goodness will be tested—sometimes to the point where you fail to see others acknowledge it and sometimes because it does not seem effective—but you will pass these tests. You will find strength and energy when you convert the power of caring and common decency into an active force to counter those influences that flaw the system in which you work as a professional. Good will and altruism are not enough. We need to reflect on how we can put these positive forces into practice. But even with the best of intentions, we at times reinforce those prejudicial and marginalizing forces that so hurt the communities with which we work.

You care enough to think about your own involvement in social services. Do you think it is possible that you are the *only one* who feels this way? Probably not. We need to think about how to come together and form partnerships with others who care, especially those who share a different social experience from ourselves.

## CAN YOU REALLY DO ANYTHING ABOUT ALL THOSE PROBLEMS?

Perhaps a better and more realistic question is this: Can you do anything about *any* of the problems you encounter? You will have to leave many problems for other people, but you can tackle a fair share of your own quite well. Some thought, some planning, some common sense, some interest, a sense of purpose, and a touch of luck are the basic ingredients. Add some understanding of how social processes affect people's sense of agency—the ability to make decisions and have control of their own life—some skill in determining tactics, some creativity, and you have a potent combination that will definitely produce results. These are the elements of effective community practice, and you can accomplish a great deal with them. All these components are available to any social worker.

You can provide significant leadership in bringing people together in order to make change, although you may not be the only leader or even the most "important" one. You can make a difference in your own community even if you have other primary professional responsibilities. But remember this fundamental principle: any problem that involves more than one person requires the involvement of more people than just you to resolve it. In other words, do not try to do everything by yourself. We often use the word *you*, but, in general, we mean not only you as an individual but also those with whom you are working.

Community problems, like personal problems, provide opportunities for growth as well as for setbacks. Persistent patterns of denial or withdrawal harm the community or service agency just as they harm the individual. Half-hearted or poorly managed attempts at solving problems can prove discouraging. However, purposeful, organized efforts—even less than perfect ones—yield results that can improve present conditions and set the stage for effectively confronting future challenges. Recognizing and confronting problems creates the possibility that social situations will be different, most likely better.

When problems are accepted as permanent, opportunities for change are missed.

## SOME BASIC ISSUES THAT DESERVE YOUR ATTENTION

As you begin to think about confronting some of the problems you will routinely encounter as a social worker, consider the following themes: empowerment, resistance to working for change, working with community issues, and understanding values affecting community practice.

### Empowerment

Working with others to promote change does not mean you become a leader with others merely following. To be successful, you will be working with others in a cooperative fashion so that your shared work has a powerful influence on both community members and people such as politicians and bureaucrats who can influence the well-being of communities. People can come to feel more capable through the skills they acquire, but it is through their connections with

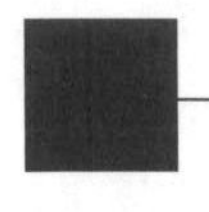

## CAPTURING CONCEPTS

### Community, Community Problems, and Community Change

Throughout this book, you will be encouraged to consider concerns that affect communities of people and that can be addressed through the actions of a community of people working together. But what exactly is a community? For our purposes, a **community** is based on relationships (Lee & Todd, 2007) and consists of a number of people with something in common that connects them in some way and that distinguishes them from others. This common connection most often is associated with identity. That is, people identify with each other as a group. Identity can be organized around social characteristics that result in particular social opportunities and social issues. Some common markers of identity are race, class, ability, gender, sexuality, national identity, and country of origin. Identity could also be associated with where a person lives—a city and/or a neighbourhood (Lee, 1999; McGrath, George, Lee, & Moffatt, 2007). It may be an activity, like a job, that provides the connection. When we use the term *community*, we do not presuppose any particular size or number of people.

Some communities are fully developed, recognizing certain common interests and working to provide mutual benefits. Members of other communities may barely even notice any common bond or characteristic among themselves. Communities are usually made up of sets of smaller communities in the same way that cities have different neighbourhoods, and universities have different colleges and departments. Communities are not uniform groups. They are always heterogeneous, made up of members who are diverse in multiple ways (Moffatt, George, Lee, & McGrath, 2005).

So when we refer to "your" community, we mean any of those sets of people with whom you are connected in some way (or could become connected to) and whose interests or actions are important enough for you to be concerned about them (Lee, McGrath, Moffatt, & George, 1996).

Communities have needs that include the health of their members, economic vitality, or effective policymaking. When these needs are not adequately met and discomfort to members results, **community problems** exist. If circumstances remain the same, the problems and the discomfort will persist. The only way to get rid of the problems or to reduce them is for people to do things differently. That is what **community change** is all about.

Community change also occurs through **community development** when members recognize and strengthen their interrelationships, build on their strengths, and increase resources in a community through collaboration (Lee & Todd, 2007). **Community change** is the process of producing modification or innovation in attitudes, policies, or practices in the community to reduce (or eliminate) problems, provide for general improvements in the manner in which needs are met, or develop resources for the benefit of its members. Community change is not just about working within the community but it is about working sometimes with and sometimes against institutions such as the state and the market that impact the health of the community (Lee et al., 1996; Lee & Todd, 2007). Community practices that aim to bring change often focus on individuals and communities that have been marginalized. Alleviating the marginalized status of community members is not only a goal; it is incorporated into community approaches to practice.

others that they become more powerful. You will assist your community partners in developing stronger beliefs in their own personal power, the power of interpersonal interactions, and the power of your organized group. When people feel a greater sense of worth and personal control, they recognize that they can participate with others to influence conditions that affect them. This process and its outcome are known as *empowerment* (Bishop, 1994, 2002; DuBois & Krogsrud Miley, 2000; Gutíerrez, 1995; Mancoske & Hunzeker, 1994).

The empowerment of those participating in an effort to effect change depends on six factors:

- Personal interest or investment in the project—a feeling of being an important part of things
- Belief in the possibility of a successful outcome
- Development and recognition of individual and group resources
- Opportunity to take action and to make meaningful contributions
- Recognition of common interests and common risk-taking while acknowledging the ever-present diversity within every community
- Knowing that it is not always the fault of the individual who has health and well-being difficulties but that social factors influence well-being.

By keeping four simple points in mind, you can further the process of empowerment considerably.

1. Provide community members with opportunities for making decisions and performing tasks. Community leaders need to spread these opportunities around.
2. Offer encouragement to one another. This should be done in a way that communicates a belief in each community member's capabilities.
3. Recognize members' contributions and their results, as well as the overall progress that is taking place. This will keep the focus on productivity and accomplishment. It will also build members' beliefs in their capabilities.
4. Act as a group whenever possible. Also share stories about how social influences are limiting the community and how to overcome them. This will give community members an experience of united power and will also reinforce an awareness of common commitment and shared risk-taking.

At the same time, do not forget that within every community, there are always a multitude of diversities that must be acknowledged, discussed, and taken into account in every action plan.

Some specific techniques for helping members discover their own power are discussed later in the book. However, if you remember only these basic elements of empowerment and the strategies promoting them, you will find you are not doing things all by yourself. In fact, one of

### Take a Moment to Discover

Why do people, especially social service professionals, not take up the banner for change more readily and more often? The best answer is probably found by questioning yourself: "When I see something that needs to be changed or fixed, why do I not act?" How do any of these responses fit your reactions?

- I am afraid of what might happen.
- I really do not know enough about the situation.
- I am afraid that people will not like me, especially my friends or colleagues—or people that I think are more important than I am.
- I do not think that anyone really sees the situation in the same way that I do.
- I really do not have the right to make changes.
- I really do not deserve for things to be better.
- I really do not know what to do.
- I am too busy . . . with more important matters.
- It is too big, and I am only one person.
- It is not my job.

Choose any one of these responses and think about it for a minute. What arguments could you devise to challenge this statement?

the most important things that you can do to promote community change is to work toward developing leadership and a sense of ownership within the communities themselves.

## Resistance to Working for Change

A good insight into resistance is provided by Filley, House, and Kerr (1976), who describe the phenomenon of "sunk costs" to explain a source of opposition to change. Many people, or at least enough people in a position to make a difference, have made a significant investment in either shaping the current situation or learning how to function within it. Change suggests that the time, energy, skill, or experience that these people have invested is no longer relevant or needed. Change implies that these investments were either poorly spent or are no longer of value. Considered from this standpoint, the introduction of a new invention or a new procedure may threaten individuals' investments in their own experiences and may even jeopardize their careers. Furthermore, people who have invested an extraordinary amount of time and effort to master the game as it is currently played may well be unreceptive to playing it differently. It is important to note that very often the status quo (that is, the way things currently are) benefits some people within communities so they have an interest in maintaining that status quo.

Perhaps the most profound source of resistance to change is simply what we tell ourselves. People who hold on to problems frequently send themselves messages that rob them of their power by stating and confirming current limitations—both real and imagined—in a way that implies that constraints are forever fixed. People who act to improve problem conditions acknowledge current limitations but they also acknowledge current assets. They are willing to use these assets to test the limitations and break them down.

If you take the risk to rethink how you think about community problems (and community strengths) and if you take assertive action, you will receive some direct benefits. You will feel better about yourself and be more highly regarded by others who have taken part in the experience, sometimes even including your opponents.

Change can cause discomfort and provoke fear. Even little changes can cause discomfort. Surprisingly, even changes that are beneficial can cause discomfort, simply because they are new. Major changes are often accompanied by even more significant discomforts. These are often times of anxiety and anger. It is difficult for people in power such as a mayor and city councillors to share their power when they are used to communities being docile or quiet. Those who have always been favoured in community decisions do not like others receiving attention. Those who want change do not even act until their discomfort with present conditions provokes them to act. Someone will always feel uncomfortable in some way when change is under way. Attempts to prevent or quiet this discomfort are powerful sources of resistance.

Change means that things are no longer predictable. This can be scary as uncertainty is frightening for most of us. Uncertainty causes tension. A child caught alone in a candy store when the lights suddenly go out knows that there are treats all around, but the darkness may hide monsters as well. Danger may lurk behind what we do not see or do not know.

There is nothing wrong with feeling some trepidation about promoting change. It is fairly natural. Here are some steps that you can take to overcome your hesitancy:

- *Confront the source of your concerns.* If time is a concern, see how you can better organize the things you have to do. If uncertainty about the outcome or the success of the effort bothers you, take stock of your assets, including the things you know how to do, the support you currently have, and other factors that work in your favour. Knowing that you can improve the odds in your favour may help you to accept

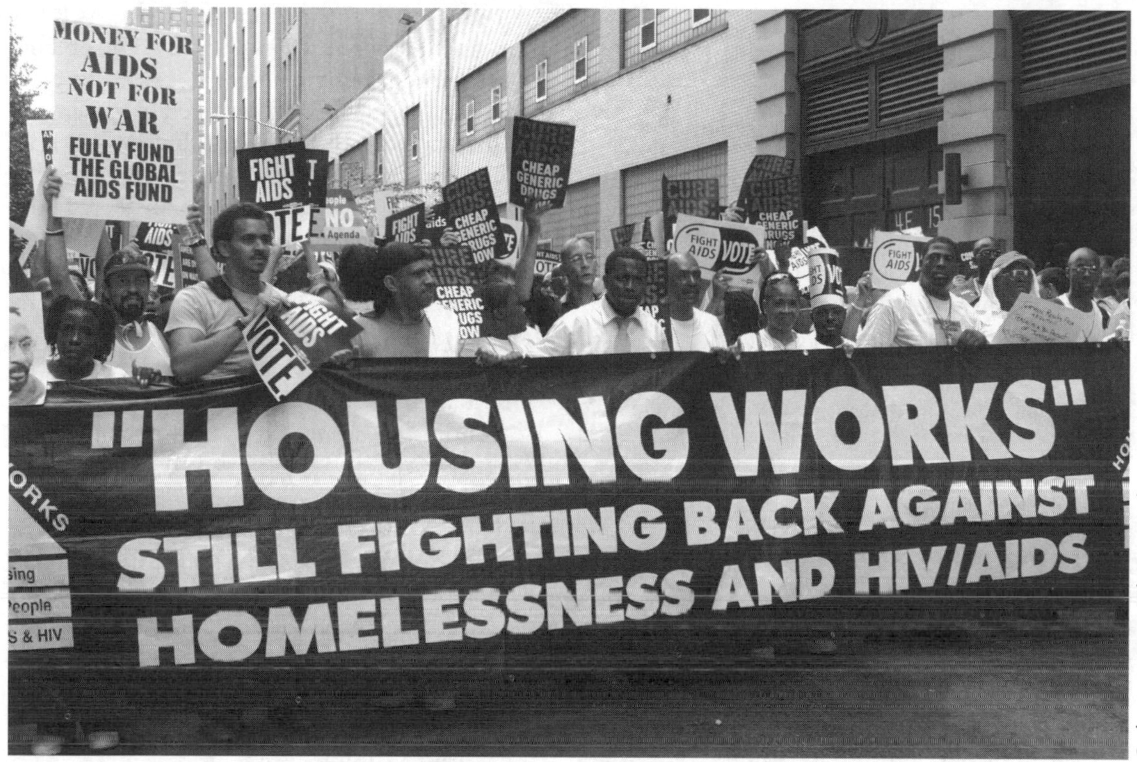


Catherine Jones / Shutterstock

**Engaging in collective action to bring about change in the community is an important element of your social work practice.**

a lack of certainty as a condition of working for change.

• *Develop support.* Act in concert with others so you can share the work, receive encouragement, and benefit from group problem-solving efforts. Purposefully cultivate support and increase communication with others who have promoted change. This will go a long way toward building your confidence and overcoming resistance.

• *Remind yourself of why the change is important.* If you keep in touch with the feelings that provoked your interest in the first place, you will have a strong source of motivation. Consider what the consequences of inattention will be.

• *Take advantage of training opportunities.* Participate in workshops, classes, or in-service training programs in order to increase your knowledge and skills in program development or community change. This will strengthen your sense of personal capability.

• *Identify a simple starting point.* Feelings of being overwhelmed can undermine your willingness to take action. Look for small ways to get started.

• *Decide to act.* "Sort of" doing things will lead to mediocre results and discontent. Make a clear decision to act.

• *Take it a step at a time.* If big changes are too intimidating at times, it might be best to take a step in the right direction and then reconsider how it feels for you. Keep your plan in place but reflect on how you feel at various steps along the way.

## Take a Moment to Discover

Imagine yourself walking into a room filled with people who are similar to one another but very different from you.

- What are you feeling?
- Can you identify the source of your feelings?
- What feelings would you like to have in this situation?
- How will you act on this intention?
- What do these people look like?
- What does this picture of whom you select as "different" tell you about yourself?

## Working with Community Issues

Something has to demand your interest and grab the attention of others. Something must spark a surge of effort in order to overcome the many reasons not to bother to make things different. Something must sustain your drive and give meaning and purpose to your use of power. Issues are what provoke action. Issues give you energy and a reason to move.

Issues help us to see and to get a handle on the problems or conditions that we face. Issues are often rooted in controversy (Williams, 1989) and disagreement (Kettner, Daley, & Nicolas, 1985). At times issues are defined through the recognition of shared experience. We begin to realize that an experience is not one that is our own but find there are others who share the experience. By defining issues, we can focus on a proposed solution to a problem (Staples, 1984) or underscore the consequences of not acting. Issues bring an undesirable situation into focus in a way that can lead to action. An issue is tied to something specific; it is not just a general dissatisfaction with the way things are. Issues serve to crystallize feelings by attaching them to a specific circumstance, condition, or set of behaviours. Issues give people something specific to work on.

Issues are different from problems. As Robinson and Hannah (1994) explain, "Problems are common gripes which are discussed in general terms, characterized by overall agreement that they need to be addressed, but in fact, lead to no action. Issues, on the other hand, are specific, selected aspects of a concern dissected into manageable parts of solutions that can be acted upon" (p. 82).

Issues are developed by people in order to attack a problem. They come in layers—from superficial indications of things gone awry to fundamental sources of chronic destructive conditions. Issues have a number of basic elements.

- Issues are a way to define, perceive, understand, or give focus to a situation.
- Issues are an expression of dissatisfaction about a situation.
- Issues are produced by either obstacles or resistance to improvement.
- Issues imply action or contain proposed solutions to difficulties.
- Issues shape people's responses to the situation and serve as rallying points.

An example of a community defining an issue can be seen in Springwater Township, Simcoe County, near Barrie, Ontario, where a coalition of Aboriginal persons, particularly women from Christian Island, provided leadership along with local farmers, townspeople from towns such as nearby Elmvale and Wyevale, and cottagers who banded together to protest the opening of a landfill that threatened to contaminate local waters. These residents defined that issue as an environmental concern using political pressure such as meetings with politicians, signs of protest, and petitions; media consultations; employing expert consultants; and making sure they had members on the community advisory board of the project. The local community groups also engaged a national-level organization, the Council of Canadians, to increase the profile of the issue. They engaged in creative strategies such as creating an encampment across the road from the site. The purpose of this activity, led by the Aboriginal women, was to witness the degradation of the site as it began construction. Other strategies included rallies and shows at the encampment site, as well as protests, such as a large caravan of tractors and hay wagons that snaked its way through the local fields to the site. Ultimately, community members were willing to engage in civil disobedience by blocking the entrance to the dump site for construction vehicles. For example, this protest led to the arrest of senior citizens who were members of a local church who blocked trucks. Construction of the dump site was stopped by the county, which had previously been pushing forward with construction in spite of community members' and Aboriginal persons' concerns of those community members who were organizing against it. This community action was successful partially due to the fact that a large and diverse group of people became involved in a variety of community actions but always focused on a single issue: water and environmental degradation. The above is an example of a successful issued-based community initiative. Though issues may contain the seeds to solutions, they also hold some traps for the unwary problem-solver. You must understand that the way in which you analyze a problem will always suggest particular methods for solving it. Sometimes by defining too big an issue for action, you can feel overwhelmed. You can overcome this potential shortcoming by discovering how other people see the issue. It also helps to have a clear understanding of the kind of issue you are working on.

### Take a Moment to Discover

Think back to a time when you confronted an issue or volunteered your time to help out with something. Perhaps it was a simple issue like not getting the correct change from a cashier. Maybe it was more substantial, like helping out on an elementary school fundraiser. Whatever it was, you refused to ignore the matter. You did something.

Reflect on this situation, and answer the following questions:

Why did you act?
What prompted your involvement?
What interests were at stake?
What does this suggest to you about what motivates people to respond?

## Types of Issues

Not all issues have equal significance. There are various types that serve various purposes. Though you will be more concerned with developing particular issues for the direct purpose of generating action, issues also commonly describe extensive concerns. Certain *fundamental issues* can provide the starting point for consideration and action. Hunger or poverty as outlined above, for example, circumscribes a set of problems or questions. They provide the broad context for action and speak to basic concerns that we have as citizens. Because they are so broad, they often demand broad actions, such as political organizing. In addition, they do provide the foundation on which more specific issues can be built. They give us a framework we can use to identify, examine, and give meaning to these more specific matters.

*Specific issues* are those clearly identifiable sources of frustration or barriers to accomplishment that call for purposeful, distinct action. They are compelling and exciting (Staples, 1984). Specific issues fit into three categories: mobilizing or recruitment issues, long-range issues, and maintenance issues.

*Mobilizing* or *recruitment issues* strike people's self-interest and attract people to the organization (Staples, 1984). They seize attention, generate dissatisfaction with current conditions, and spur people to action. These mobilizing issues help to illustrate the problem and motivate people to do something about it. They act like a magnet by showing people that joining with others is a good way to work on the things that bother them. These issues tend to be immediate and pressing. Acting on them can produce direct results in a relatively short period of time.

An example of a mobilizing and recruitment issue can be seen in Vancouver, British Columbia, where a grassroots organization has sprung up to combat poverty within the Vancouver community. Community members have created mobilemovement.tv, a website that informs the public and provides an opportunity for community members to voice their concerns through posting. The website also allows people to donate money to the cause. Donations go to many projects that combat poverty within Canadian communities (Hill, 2009).

*Long-range issues* require sustained effort on several fronts over a span of time. Although they are still specific, people are less inclined to jump on board either because the payoff is too far in the future or because the challenge just seems too big or too difficult. Still, these issues are important to nourish the organization and help it achieve more significant benefits for the community it serves.

Mobilizing or recruitment issues can be used as building blocks for achieving success on a long-range issue. It is important to help people understand both broad issues that will be dealt with in the long term as well as specific issues that can be dealt with in the short term. Often, broad and specific issues support each other in helping people to define direction.

An example of a long-range issue can be seen in Hamilton, Ontario. Here, members of the Hamilton Roundtable for Poverty have presented a policy called Bill 152 to the Ontario government. Bill 152 is a long-term act aimed at reducing poverty in Ontario by investing in communities that are most vulnerable to poverty in the future. The members of the Hamilton Roundtable for Poverty have taken the legislative route to ensure that poverty is reduced in the long term (Weaver, 2009).

*Maintenance issues* are aimed not so much at drawing people out or resolving a particular matter as they are directed to promoting the organization itself. For example, a maintenance issue may involve taking a strong public position on a community controversy or endorsing another group's stand. These issues can provide mileage by establishing new allies, increasing visibility and credibility, and developing new skills (Staples, 1984).

The actions of a group called Solidarity with the Six Nations provide an example of the use of maintenance issues. This group seeks to illuminate the public on the issue of Aboriginal peoples' struggle over land claims in Canada. The group has specifically taken an interest in the controversial issue of Caledonia land claims in Ontario, and seeks to unite the Six Nations people through online discussions to increase the visibility and credibility of the Caledonian people (Six Nations Reclamation, nd).

If you are working on the fundamental issues of hunger and poverty, you may have a long-range issue involving low-income security benefit levels (welfare) in different provinces or your own province. You may find you have to tackle unnecessarily exasperating application procedures, and demanding the elimination of a ridiculous application form becomes a mobilizing issue. A good maintenance issue would be your public endorsement of a civil rights group's report that changes patterns of racism in the operation of a particular welfare office.

## Issues and Organizations

What kind of issue is used and how it is used will depend on the kind of organization promoting the change. Management of the issue will vary with the purpose of the organization, its intended longevity, and its stage of development. Take a look at some different types of organizing efforts and their resulting relationship to issues.

*Temporary, Single-Issue Organizations.* Some organized efforts are temporary ones. They deal with a particular situation and bring about a distinct and limited change. This is a fairly typical approach to promoting change. Once the issue that has prompted a group to form has been resolved, there is nothing to keep the group active, and people return to their routine activities. Most temporary, single-issue groups do not give much thought to developing the organization beyond the resolution of their particular problem.

*Ongoing, Single-Issue Organizations.* Some groups work on a rather large "single" issue over a long period of time. Usually, this is a more fundamental issue like hunger or education. They are not so much single-issue organizations as they are organizations with a limited focus restricted to a set of related issues. Their primary purpose is to deal with a persistent community problem, with less intention on empowering the organization itself. They draw people interested in this one issue and make no real effort to attract people with other interests. Since they intend to be around for a while, they must address two distinct continuing goals. First, they must accomplish the purpose of the organization, which is to rectify certain community problems. Second, they must build and solidify the organization itself in the process. Their use of issues must further both these ends.

An example of a community coming together for a single ongoing issue can be seen in the crises of Darfur in Sudan. Many Canadian groups are asking the public to call on the Prime Minister's Office to exhort the government of Sudan to stop the genocide in Darfur. These groups are loosely connected through the Internet and share the goal of stopping the genocide of Darfur. They are not focused on developing an organization to stop future genocides but rather on ending the current atrocities being committed in Darfur (Rahman, 2008).

*Multi-Issue, Power-Based Organizations.* Even though multi-issue organizations attract a lot of attention in the literature on community change, they are probably less frequently developed than other types of organizations. They are established to contend with an array of issues affecting people in a similar constituency. Multi-issue organizations cast their nets much farther than single-issue groups, hoping to snag a broader array of issues and bring in people who are attached to them. These organizations use issues as a way to achieve progress by improving conditions while at the same time attracting new members. Alinsky (1972) has said that "[this] organization is born out of the issues and the issues are born out of the organization" (p. 121). Issues are beneficial in building the organization so that it can confront other issues in the future and strengthen its ability to be an ongoing community influence. Although these groups confront a range of issues, at any given moment they are likely to have a particular focus. In addition to improving specific community conditions, these organizations intend to alter the established balance of power in the community. They are concerned not only with firming up the organization but also with expanding the power base by attracting new members and giving those members a real feeling of power.

An example of a multi-issue power-based organization is the Kitchener Downtown Community Health

> Centre in Ontario. The Community Health Centre seeks to address the well-being of people in the Kitchener community. The Community Health Centre accomplishes this by working with the homeless, elderly, new immigrants, and refugees on their health issues. By incorporating such a wide range of conditions, the Community Health Centre attracts many volunteers interested in bettering the Kitchener community. The range of issues Kitchener health centre addresses, its main concern remains the health of the members of the Kitchener community (KWMC, 2009).

However, these are usually only starting points to deal with more social community-based concerns, and people can be encouraged to develop more inclusive, broader-ranging concerns and issues as they go along.

## Understanding and Working against Discrimination

As a community worker and a promoter of community change, it is vital that you understand how discrimination and oppression operate within communities. Why? Because you will find that many of the issues that face community members, even those that at first glance might appear to be problems of individual people, are in fact rooted in social relations of oppression such as racism, sexism, classism, and homophobia operating in the wider society. These terms and others are described in the Capturing Concepts box and are discussed further in Chapter 2. Because these social relations of oppression play a role in many of the issues facing community members, you will need to pay them some attention when you are naming and working on issues, as well as planning your strategies of action (Bishop, 1994, 2002; McGrath et al., 2007).

Racism, sexism, homophobia, classism, and ableism, as well as other social relations of discrimination, allow for the fear and consequent dislike of others simply because they are members of different groups. These biases are central issues facing community workers today. This fear and exercise of power brings oppression (Lee & Todd, 2007; Lee et al., 1996). The fear is further aggravated by the perception that there is a limited set of resources over which groups must fight rather than an expanding (or potentially expanding) set of resources that can be shared. For example, a number of Canadian scholars have argued that the basic myth of Canadian capitalism is that any attempt by one group to better its position must necessarily come at the expense of another (Carniol, 2005; Mullaly, 2002).

The idea that we must be in competition with each other as individuals and communities over limited power and resources is simply a belief. However, it is true that resources are limited and tend to be concentrated within dominant groups. Dominant groups are those groups that have the most access to resources and systems of power. The actions and ideas of the dominant group have an influence on the well-being and opportunities of marginalized groups. At times, dominant groups or persons use their influence to intentionally disadvantage certain groups or communities and to encourage them to compete against each other. The group in the most advantaged position must respond to the system that grants them their resources and the privileges that follow. When those well-entrenched arrangements are challenged—when equal accommodations are sought by a less advantaged group, or when one group seems to be thwarted in its efforts to improve its lot—conflict heightens the fears and divisions (Lee et al., 1996; Mullaly, 2002; Wharf, 2002).

The dominant group, in many overt or subtle ways, demands allegiance to its own culture in exchange for social and economic benefits (Lee, 1999). One of the questionable strategies members of marginalized groups can use to gain access to opportunities and resources is to deny their own culture in favour of adopting attributes of the dominant group. For example, the children

## CAPTURING CONCEPTS

The following concepts are important in working with communities. These definitions are not necessarily universally accepted, and you will learn throughout the book that these concepts need to be situated within a context in order to be properly understood.

**Oppression:** According to Mullaly (2002), oppression is determined by whether a person or group is blocked from opportunities to "self-development, is excluded from full participation in society, does not have equal access to rights that the dominant group take for granted, [and] is assigned to second-class citizenship because it belongs to . . . a category of people" (p. 28). There are many forms of oppression that operate simultaneously in any given context, including, for example, racism, sexism, classism, ableism, heterosexism, and so on (p. 28).

**Privilege:** Privilege refers to the unearned benefits that accrue to one group of people as a result of the oppression of another group of people (Yee & Dumbrill, 2003). Carniol (2005) indicates that those benefits are received due to "the way power is organized in society" (p. 7). Carniol (2005) further describes different forms of privileges, such as colonial privileges, racial privileges, class privileges, and male privileges.

**Racism:** Racism is a system in which one group of people exercises power over another on the basis of the socially constructed category of race. The concept of race has been used to classify humankind according to physical characteristics such as skin colour, hair texture, and facial features. Race is also used to differentiate groups based on common ancestry (Galabuzi, 2006, 251–252).

**Sexism:** Sexism is a "system of male dominance that advantages men and disadvantages women in all areas of public and private life, . . . [that is] built into the way society is organized and structures the world, . . . [and] that centres around male points of view and needs" (Barnoff & Coleman, 2007, p. 32).

**Homophobia and Heterosexism:** Homophobia is a fear of gay persons. It manifests itself as acts of prejudice, discrimination, harassment, or violence against sexual minorities, including lesbians, gay men, bisexual, transsexual, and transgender (LGBTT) persons. Heterosexism is based on the assumption that individuals, families, and communities are made up only of heterosexuals. This makes the successes, issues, and mistreatment of LGBTT persons invisible and therefore difficult to deal with (Schneider, 1997; Warner, 2002).

**Classism:** Classism is discrimination based on socioeconomic position. Class relations (like all other power relations) are clearly tied up with other systems of oppression, such as those based on race and gender. For example, many people talk about "the feminization of poverty" or the "racialization of poverty" to refer to the fact that women and racialized people are overrepresented among those living in poverty.

**Ableism:** Ableism is a social relation of oppression that maintains a power imbalance between able-bodied people and people with disabilities. An understanding of ableism shows that "disabilities" do not reside within individuals, but rather involve a social process. In other words, it is the organization of our physical and social environment that dis-ables people from full and equitable inclusion (Barnoff, 2001; Carniol, 2005).

of second-generation immigrants living in Canada might distance themselves from the customs and traditions of their parents in order to immerse themselves in the mainstream Canadian society. When marginalized groups are "forced" to act in ways that are more similar to the norms of the dominant culture, the potential the marginalized groups have to threaten the status quo is weakened. Some members of marginalized groups resist this control by undermining or attacking the interests of the dominant group. The group or community members can also develop alternative cultures that are not interested in belonging to the dominant group (Moffatt et al., 2005).

For example, many in the LGBTT communities have supported the fight for equal marriage because it became an important battle for the future of gay rights in Canada. Others, such as Croteau, Lark, and Lance (2005), criticized how gay community leaders feel comfortable using the same notion of "family" that has been used by conservatives who opposed same-sex marriage. Family is not a word of inclusiveness, and they further state that "not everybody wants marriage." They further stated that the LGBTT community seems to be losing its pride in diversity and the acceptance of differences (Croteau et al., 2005). The belief is that you need to be careful taking on the norms and language of the dominant group because you lose pride and a sense of agency in your own community. In Canada, there has been a long struggle to define whether the family and marriage are useful concepts in the LGBTT community or whether they are heterosexist terms that obscure strong community links (Warner, 2002).

As an agent of change, you may see behaviours and ways of organizing that seem to be counterproductive to you, but in fact, they make sense for the group or community that is resisting dominance. For example, you may observe and notice that Black communities or Aboriginal communities express distrust and sometimes open hostility toward police and the judicial systems. It could appear to you that their distrust and hostility is counterproductive to the safety of their communities. But before you form an opinion, try to understand the "racial profiling process" that Black and Aboriginal communities experience regularly. Remember that over 50 percent of African Canadians reported to have been stopped by the police compared to 23 percent of Whites and 11 percent of Asians. Of African Canadians who had not been involved in any criminal activities, 34 percent claimed they had been stopped by the police on two or more occasions in the previous two years, compared to 4 percent of White Canadians (Wortley & Tanner, 2003). Smith (2006) argues that "the most glaring evidence of racism in the criminal justice is found in inquiries and research which consistently shows Aboriginal people are heavily overrepresented in correctional facilities across Canada" (p. 81). In Saskatchewan, Aboriginal people have been incarcerated at almost ten times the provincial rate. In Manitoba, 61 percent of inmates were Aboriginals; in Alberta, it was over 35 percent (p. 81).

When you are working with the group or community, it is important to understand how cultures and behaviours, as well as systems of community, may be rooted in acts of resistance to social relations that hurt the community (Lepishchak & Moffatt, 2007). You need to understand how particular communities experience oppression.

Forms of discrimination and oppression, such as racism, homophobia, ableism, and gender inequity, are rooted in our institutions, norms, and traditions. They divide people and lead to differences in well-being. Many problems that you will see as a worker are expressions of these fears and divisions. And as a worker, your own relationship with the community you are trying to help may be influenced by racism as well as other forms of discrimination. Devaluing those who are different or keeping somebody who is different from getting ahead means that opportunities for mutual gain are squandered and many people are left behind (Carniol, 2005; Lundy, 2004; Mullaly, 2002).

At times, communities and their members succumb to hopelessness and despair due to experiences of discrimination and oppression. Community members may take personal responsibility for the broad social relations that hurt them—which can lead to self-harm (Alphonse, George, & Moffatt, 2008). In worst-case scenarios, community members may exploit each other or simply give up trying to participate, since it seems impossible to do so. Other community members may give up their cultural identity for economic gain. This move can be accompanied by deep-seated resentment for what they lost—sometimes community, sometimes their identity—in order to get ahead. Actions such as these result in loss for all groups involved (Devore & Schlesinger, 2000). The danger for you as an agent of change occurs when, to try to keep a semblance of peace and keep people focusing on working together to bring about change, you may act as if these troubling actions are not taking place. Instead, your actions will be much more equitable (and much more effective overall) if you can find a way to allow community members to find their voice, to discuss their differences, to rethink their relations to each other, and to resist the ways oppression affects their interactions with each other and their actions and strategies to bring about community change (Lee & Todd, 2007).

Oppression has consequences for everyone who is involved in an effort to effect community change. A group that has directly suffered from racism may need to confront not only the immediate issue at hand but also the racist conditions that led to it and continue to support it. A group whose practices have limited another group's freedom and choice may need to examine whether its desired course of action in a particular circumstance perpetuates these practices. A multiracial group that shares a common aspect that sets it apart, such as gender, sexuality, or class, may need to face the strain of a history of racial divisiveness within the group and to find a way to honour each other (Barnoff & Moffatt, 2007). A big part of working with any group is the ability to understand not only how that group is positioned in relation to power but also the multifaceted impact that power has on the diverse members within that group. For effective, equitable community change to occur, we must not gloss over our differences but instead must always focus attention on these aspects of our identities.

Difficulties can arise when members of different cultural groups interact with one another. Some misunderstandings can be expected when groups have different cultural norms, rituals, and belief systems. However, when one group historically has politically, economically, and culturally discriminated against another and thus limited that group's opportunities and expressions, the undercurrents of tension and anxiety are bound to be present and can be profound. The burden becomes even heavier when members of the offending group are ignorant of this history or deny it altogether (Lee, 2008; Wesley-Esquimaux, 2009).

As an agent of change, you need to be aware of how limited resources affect the opportunities for certain communities. But you also need to remember that sometimes the competition for resources is a way for dominant communities to retain their power. As an agent of change, you can imagine that by working together we can create resources together. You can also be aware that tension and even conflict, at times, in community work can be acceptable as long as you can continue to work toward a common good. Good community practice must always include and value every member of the community, no matter who they are.

## TARGETS FOR COMMUNITY CHANGE

Where can you start? How can you begin to make an impact on your community? Your desire to improve community conditions can take you into five basic arenas of action. In addition to being active in the community itself, you can have a considerable effect by making efforts to improve the service delivery system, directing attention to your own agency, working in the political field, or taking action through the courts. Throughout this book we will go into much greater detail in each of these areas.

### Community Involvement

There are many forms of community activities. Here are some of the activities you might be involved in:

1. *Neighbourhood empowerment* helps people within a particular geographic area to develop their resources and lay claim to their right to control their own destinies. After the

family, the neighbourhood is the first building block of the community. Helping people in a neighbourhood band together to determine their own living conditions is a primary strategy for improving the quality of a community.

2. *Community problem-solving* is another approach for bringing people together. Using this method, you bring together various, even apparently competing, interests within a community in order to creatively resolve a particular problem that affects them all. Crime, transportation, education, or environmental concerns could be the focus of such an effort. Though no permanent organization for redistributing community power is likely to be put in place, this approach is liable to stimulate a discovery of underlying community issues that may be the focus of future problem-solving efforts. Further, members of the community gain experience working with one another, an outcome may have benefits beyond the resolution of the particular problem being tackled at the moment.

3. *Developing community support systems* is another way to promote community change efforts. This approach counters the painful aspect of living in a community of strangers. People who do not feel they are part of the community live in numbing isolation: they struggle alone against problems that can overwhelm them. A community is a rich source of sustenance that can offer practical assistance and psychological support, but people need to find each other amid the noise and confusion. Developing community support systems provides the means for community members to be in routine contact with one another in a climate of giving and receiving. Parents grappling with the challenges of caring for children with mental illnesses, teens struggling with the consequences of pregnancy, social service workers feeling separated from the ideals that originally brought them to their profession—all could gain strength from a system of mutual assistance and support.

4. *Community education* is a basic means for assisting the community by bringing matters to the community's attention and preparing it for knowledgeable action. Keeping the community from ignoring the needs of its citizens or from relying on myths to guide its direction is a steady challenge.

5. *Developing a broad-based community organization* that wields power and works to redistribute community resources and access to community decision making is a meaningful approach for producing far-reaching change. The presence of such an organization establishes a new force to recognize within the community, one that can take sustained action on issues that affect people other than the rich and powerful. These organizations activate many members of the community to press for a clearly articulated issue agenda. They often use the strength (including the financial support) of significant community institutions, such as religious congregations, as critical building blocks. In larger communities, these organizations mobilize thousands of people. Unless you intend to specialize in the practice of community organization and development, you will probably not serve as the lead organizer of such a group. However, there will be many important leadership roles within this type of organization that you can fill.

## Improving the Service Delivery System

At least five opportunities await you if you want to make improvements in the services that community members receive:

- Change program regulations.
- Improve program delivery.
- Encourage cooperation between agencies.
- Develop a new program.
- Empower service users.

Public program regulations, believe it or not, are not always developed with a keen eye for discerning the most effective manner of benefiting program participants. Sometimes those who establish the rules are looking out for other interests (Fabricant, 1985; Lipsky, 1984). You will face regulations that frustrate at least as much as they help. You can join the chorus

### Take a Moment to Discover

Why do we put so much energy into developing shelters for the homeless instead of getting rid of homelessness? Why do we feel so good about food banks providing emergency food instead of taking steps to eliminate hunger and the widespread need for emergency food? Are these problems too big for a nation like ours to solve? Hardly, though we can constrict ourselves into thinking so.

Let's look at some of the reasons that community problems remain despite the fact that we are well aware of them.

- We believe that we have no time to do the job well.
- The problems are hopelessly complex. Where do we start?
- It is too much work.
- It is better to smooth things over than to cause disruption.
- The people who would be disturbed by changing things are more important than the people who are hurting now.
- Some groups of people are benefiting from the way things are now.
- The people who are feeling the problem are not worth the trouble.
- Significant intervention costs too much.
- We would rather cover up things that we do not want to look at.
- We fear the possibility that things are out of control, or will be.
- It is just a bad habit.
- It is easier to shut up those who feel the problem than it is to challenge those in authority because those in need are less threatening and are appreciative of any help we can give them.
- We need to feel we are at least doing something.

Consider this list. Is this the way that a nation or a community responds? How might this list guide your actions as an agent of community change?

of those who would rather complain than act, or you can start your own choir, giving voice to the need for change. Confronting regulations that hinder your work will make life easier for you and for those who use your services. Many workers simply conclude that "those are the rules and we can't change them." They are wrong. Yes, some regulations (for example, those established by the federal government) are more difficult to change than others (for example, regulations generated by local authorities), but any and all regulations are always subject to scrutiny and modification. A well-organized group, perhaps working in alliance with other groups, can make great improvements in services simply by changing regulations, thereby helping a program to work better.

Similarly, remaining attentive to opportunities for program improvement can lead you to helpful changes in the way that services are provided. Experimenting with program design and service methods can result in significant benefits for both the sponsoring agency and those who use services. By capitalizing on a desire by both line staff and management to do a better job more easily, you can accomplish some significant gains. Old habits and other barriers to innovation exist, but forces for program improvement also exist in most situations.

Cooperation between social service agencies is not always the way things work in certain communities. Sometimes we find not only that agencies are not working together, but in fact they are working to undermine one another's efforts. Often, this is because the context in which agencies are working is one that creates a culture of competitiveness between them. For example, as funding opportunities dwindle, agencies increasingly are having to compete with one another in order to be awarded the limited funds that still exist. Also, funding is often associated with a single project or activity so it is difficult at times to imagine broader community needs. When agencies must compete with each other constantly, it can make it difficult for them to also maintain healthy partnerships (Barnoff,

George, & Coleman, 2006). Helping agencies to develop their skills in networking and coalition building in the current competitive environment can be a very significant intervention, potentially setting the stage for future collaborative efforts. Developing a new social service program or agency to add to the community's arsenal of resources is an exciting and productive endeavour. This kind of activity sparks the creative interest of people who not only like the prospect of providing a needed service but also enjoy the process of bringing an idea to life.

Organizing community members who use the services of an organization is an often underused approach to upgrade community services. Social service workers do not routinely and systematically involve service users in planning, developing, and refining services in a way that vests them with real authority. We as social workers profess through our statement of ethics that service users have a right to self-determination and to recognize and assume responsibility for important aspects of their lives, so the involvement of service users would seem to be almost automatic. Unfortunately, it is not. Paternalistic attitudes regarding what is best for the community often remain unchallenged in the arena of service delivery. This state of affairs offers a wonderful opportunity fo  social service workers who seek fundamental changes in the manner in which services are provided. Certainly, such an approach must include an awareness of the risks. Altering the perception of service users as powerless and dependent is a challenge in itself. Regarding service users as relatively powerless and dependent sustains the interests of many individuals, both inside and outside the social service system. You must understand that those interests will feel threatened when you work to increase the abilities of service users to participate in decision making.

## Making Improvements Within Your Own Agency

You will not often need to look beyond your own agency to recognize situations that call for change. Much of what you can do to improve the social service system in your community applies just as well to the organization for which you work. Needed changes in agency regulations, policies, or procedures may demand your attention. You will have the opportunity to create new programs or to improve existing ones to better serve people in need. Developing more cooperative working relationships among members of the staff and volunteers may well be necessary. Finally, helping service users to have a legitimate say over the services that they receive will undoubtedly be both a challenge and an opportunity. Few organizations are created perfectly; it is always possible to make things better. This is as true for your own agency as it is for any other.

## Political Involvement

Your participation in the political process occurs in two fundamental areas. The first and most obvious one is electing people to office in the first place. In this instance, you will be working in a political campaign. The second involves dealing with the people who have been elected, working to influence them as they perform the duties of their office. This work is generally referred to as lobbying. (Although lobbying is most often directed at elected officials, it is not limited to them. Other policymakers, such as regulators, can be the focus of lobbying activities.) Lobbying involves your use of argument and political power to help shape the development of public policy, usually by refining and promoting the passage of inclusive, non-oppressive policies or by blocking the advancement of exclusive, oppressive ones.

Working to elect or to influence government officials at local, provincial, or federal levels is a powerful means of affecting policies that regulate behaviour, as well as those that shape how existing resources are distributed and who has access to those being developed. The efforts of an organized, dedicated group of people can have a tremendous impact here.

## Using the Courts

Shaping laws through the political process may contribute to improving conditions in your community, but using the laws currently in place may have far-reaching consequences as well. You may well find that the rights of the people you serve are being ignored and, in practice, denied. Litigation can secure the action that community members require. Getting powerful interests in the community to apply rights and protections equally to all of its citizens may take more than good intentions. The courts may have to step in to hold individuals, or even the public at large, accountable. In Canada, the Charter of Rights and Freedoms has been an important mechanism by which community members have challenged the state to be more responsive and guarantee the safety and rights of community members.

Opportunities for taking part in the process of strengthening your community are plentiful. Through your participation, you may gain experience in a wide variety of change venues. Much like different games, each arena will hold its special appeal and unique challenges. You will come to appreciate the impact you can have regardless of where you perform.

## ● CONCLUSION: RETAIN YOUR IDEALISM

No matter what role you play in community work, you will recognize opportunities to determine a new direction in furthering human growth. Sometimes it will not be enough to tackle problems one at a time or to tolerate inefficiencies or abuses that are an affront to human dignity. You will not allow ignorance to keep problems alive, and you will no longer accept community problems as inevitable or unsolvable.

You will acknowledge that there are a number of sources of community problems, but that there is also a huge reservoir of concern and resources to deal with them. You will recognize that others share your capacity to care and to act.

You will come to believe that you can make a contribution in a fundamental way. You will learn how to overcome your own and others' resistance to change. You will combine your talents and actions with others' in ways that increase your belief in your abilities and your potential to make a difference. As a community worker, you can point out the many successes no matter how small.

You will come to see that problems are not isolated phenomena that touch individuals only. You will see how they affect a community of people, and you will work with that community to solve them. You will recognize and respect the different cultural perspectives on the issues that all of you face. You will learn how the unique strengths of different cultures add vitality to your overall effort. You will become competent in building respectful relationships with people whose culture is different from yours. As a community worker, you can point out the many successes and strengths that occur by working together in community. As well, you can point out to community members the strengths of their existing culture and social relations.

You will learn different ways to express your interest in making things better. You may work to help a neighbourhood develop or utilize its resources. You may start a new program in response to a community need. You may help to elect an ally to office. Or you may work to determine a greater role for service users in shaping the services that can improve the quality of their lives. Remember and remind others in the communities that learning to think differently is one of the beautiful aspects of community work.

You will hold to your ideals, and you will act on them. You will have understood well the challenge to change. Sometimes you will be a member of the community you are working with and therefore you will hold on to the ideals with much conviction and emotion (Lee et al., 2002). Never give up on those broad ideas and concepts that motivate you—concepts such as belonging, equality, justice, kindness, and humanity.

Most real progress occurs when individuals and communities take hold of the idea that there is a better, more humane, or more just way. Change occurs when we believe in ourselves, in community members, and in our affairs with one another.

Idealism is the belief that things could be better, that they should be better, and that an individual can play a part in making them better. This is not easy. Idealism requires spirit, faith, commitment, and courage. In Canada, idealism has been a key historical element of community practice and change. Idealism has been both a motivation and a vision for change (Moffatt, 2001). People are not willing to settle for mediocrity or meanness but rather are interested in equality and social justice. Change agents and community members are most effective when they are idealists.

Idealism is not to be confused with naïveté. Idealism is a purposeful, powerful belief. A real idealist is willing to take a hard, uncompromising look at the world and reckon with it, trusting it. Idealists trust in their own power, the strength of decency, and others who share those convictions. An idealist simply refuses to bend to the limits of existing social situations and is willing to imagine relations that do not yet exist. Francisco Sagasti (1990) has said, "At least we have the capacity to imagine a better situation than the one we are in at present . . . . The basis of our optimism is being able to link imagination, visions of what can be better, what can work . . . to existing situations . . . and work out from them."

Someone may say to you, "You are an idealist." Take it as a compliment.

## HELPFUL WEBSITES

**Canadian Association of Social Workers (CASW)**

www.casw-acts.ca

A federation of nine provincial and one territorial social work organizations, the CASW provides a national role in strengthening and advancing the social work profession in Canada. CASW promotes social justice and well-being for all Canadian residents.

**Housing New Canadians**

www.hnc.utoronto.ca

Housing New Canadians is a research partnership focused on housing access and discrimination in the Toronto area, where about 40 percent of all newcomers to Canada settle.

**Community Foundations of Canada (CFC) Social Justice Philanthropy**

www.cfc-fcc.ca/socialjustice/index.cfm

CFC works to establish communities where all citizens have economic opportunity, equal access to high-quality education and health care, cultural voices, safety, and the respect of their fellow citizens. They are working to establish communities that are environmentally healthy and that treat their citizens fairly and equitably.

**Metro Toronto's Changing Communities: Innovative Responses Canada, Community Participation and Urban Governance**

www.vcn.bc.ca/citizens-handbook/unesco/most/usa9.html

The site says, "Changes in Metro Toronto's communities have led to new strategic directions and policies in the government of Metropolitan Toronto. These, in turn, have resulted in new ways to plan, design, and deliver services in the Community Services Department. The 'Best Practice' document submitted to the United Nations last summer describes ways that the Department has approached the areas of organizational change, governance and participation, service delivery, program development, service planning, and development and community supports.

"The examples provided within the Best Practices document describe partnerships between Metro Toronto and other levels of government, the community service sector, service users, and political representatives. They reflect Metropolitan Toronto's political and corporate commitment to respond to the needs of our diverse communities."

CHAPTER TWO

# Theoretical Frameworks for Community Dynamics

**This chapter will help you better understand the following questions:**

- How does systems theory explain community dynamics and community change?
- What does a multiculturalism approach have to offer to community work?
- What is cultural competence and what are some of the pros and cons of this approach?
- What is an anti-oppression approach to community work?
- What are the foundational beliefs of an Aboriginal world view in relation to community work?
- Why is critical reflection important for community work?

The theoretical frameworks for action presented in this chapter provide differing foundational theories and organizing models that you can draw on to shape your efforts to promote change. Although no set of theories can describe all dimensions of human interaction, there are several theoretical frameworks that inform work for community change. In this chapter, we discuss a range of frameworks, including systems theory, those that take culture into consideration, anti-oppression theories, Aboriginal world views, and critical reflection.

## SYSTEMS THEORY AND COMMUNITIES

### Understanding Systems

According to systems theory, each organism—a city, a neighbourhood, an individual—is a system that requires ongoing input in the form of care and energy. The system takes in energy to grow, produce, and sustain life, as well as to maintain its equilibrium. Maintaining equilibrium or balance is one of the core concerns of any system. A system acts when it feels out of balance. It will take radical action when that imbalance has achieved the level of crisis.

A number of authors have helped to create an understanding of systems, among them Anderson, Carter, and Lowe (1999); Cowan and Egan (1979); Brill (1998); Senge, Kleiner, Roberts, Ross, and Smith (1994); Dubois and Krogsrud-Miley (2000); Johnson and Schwartz (1997); Kirst-Ashman and Hull (2001); Lumsden and Lumsden (2000); Napier and Gershenfeld (1999); and Schmolling, Youkeles, and Burger (1997). The notion of systems theory is consistent with the ecological perspective of human interaction. All systems act to meet their needs for survival, if not growth. When a need is felt, the system experiences a kind of imbalance, which leads to action in order to meet the need.

Those outside of the system may recognize or point out needs and may influence the system by trying to affect those needs. But change will happen only when those within the system recognize the problem and take purposeful action. Actions may be taken by community members in response to intervention from someone or something outside the systems. This can be useful, but at times these actions may be superficial if they are designed primarily to please another party (system). At times, community members can get off track by responding to people or systems outside their community, and this can take away from the resources needed to maintain the system or to resist threats to the community system. At times, persons outside the system (or community in this case) wilfully engage in activities to disrupt the system and make it less effective, humane, or safe for people.

An important aspect of systems theory is the idea that all systems operate in relationships with other systems. Furthermore, each particular system is part of a larger set of systems and is itself made up of smaller sets of systems. For example, a neighbourhood is part of a city, which is part of a county, which is part of a province, and so on. Within the neighbourhood itself are several streets, and on each street live a number of households, and within each household are individuals. Even individuals are made up of various smaller systems, such as a respiratory system, a skeletal system, and so on. In addition there can be subsystems within the neighbourhood such as parents of children within the local school, or neighbours who share identities such as country of origin, age, culture, or language or identities such as race and sexuality.

Another important aspect of systems theory is the idea that each system always has to respond to external influences (other systems). The idea that there are multiple systems operating simultaneously means that social reality can become quite complex, and there are always a multitude of factors that enable or constrain the possibility of action in any given community. For example, systems of governance and policy can interact with a low-income community so that the members are treated with disrespect and are treated individually rather than as a self-respecting holistic community. Welfare is an example of how, rather than providing resources for the whole community that respect the systems in place within the community, the government instead provides welfare to each individual, who then behaves as if they are the whole system in themselves and are therefore to blame for their poverty.

Systems theory focuses on the interaction between systems, arguing that a change in any one part of a system (large or small) will necessarily have an impact on the entire system overall. In this way, systems theory helps us to understand how the actions of a group of people within the community can positively or negatively affect the health of the community and its members, resulting in an opportunity or a risk. It can also help us to see how actions that occur outside of the community itself also affect community health. Here, too, are conditions of opportunity or risk. Each system interprets the reactions it receives from the broader environment and makes adjustments, thus operating as a thermostat in an attempt to regulate itself and maintain social balance.

Think about some of the systems in which you operate. In addition to your primary system—your self—you also routinely participate in four broader levels of systems, described by Healy (2005). *Microsystems,* or personal settings, are the small immediate systems of our everyday lives. These include our family, friendship groups, work settings, and classrooms. The *mesosystem*, or network of personal settings, involves interaction of our immediate systems with one another. What happens in one personal system has an impact on other systems. For example, what happens in your family can affect your participation in the classroom. The *exosystem,* made up of the larger institutions of our society, does not directly and immediately envelop us but does influence our personal systems and our network of personal systems. The exosystem includes government agencies, religious organizations, and the economic system. These systems also interact with one another while they influence our more immediate systems. The *macrosystem*, or culture, influences all the other systems of our lives and includes our common beliefs, acceptable forms of behaviour and social relationships, and our expectations.

Consider a community agency that exploits its workers, demanding high caseloads and paying low salaries. It is likely to suffer from high turnover, low morale, and poor productivity. If that same agency is uncooperative with other agencies and misrepresents how it uses its money, it may suffer a loss of its reputation in the community, losing opportunities for collaborative partnerships, and even possibly seeing its funding terminated. In this way, it has negatively affected the systems within the agency and within the community.

A healthy community takes care of its component parts while conducting transactions with larger systems in order to get what it needs and being aware of how larger systems actively work against the community at times. An agent of change can use this understanding to help a community take care of itself, perhaps by encouraging a group within the community to assert its rights in order to get the attention it needs or by helping a number of groups within the community to work together for their mutual benefit. At a broader level, an agent of change can help to provoke a response from the wider community (including government), compelling it to fulfill its responsibilities to smaller communities or to change a tactic or system that is hurtful to the community. This may take the form of providing direct resources (such as money), technical assistance, legal protection, or other types of support that a smaller community needs in order to truly flourish.

# MULTICULTURAL APPROACHES

Multiculturalism is a theory but it is also an important symbol and organizing principle in a diverse country such as Canada. The use of the term *multiculturalism* implies that Canada is a country that recognizes, values, and celebrates ethnic and cultural differences and is one in which cultural exchange and harmony are encouraged. Canadian multiculturalism differs from the "melting pot" approach in the United States of America. In the "melting pot" model, each cultural group is expected to give up those aspects of their culture that make them different from what is considered to be "the norm" in the United States and to assimilate into broader American culture. In the logic of the melting pot, differences between ethnic groups are meant to eventually disappear. All groups eventually "melt way" into one "pot" that is "American society." Rather than encouraging this type of assimilation, the official Canadian policy of multiculturalism is one that highlights Canada's ethnic diversity and where some attempt is made to respect and support a variety of cultural communities (Srivastava, 2007).

There are many examples of multiculturalism across Canada. These expressions often take the form of festivals in cities where local residents celebrate their different origins by gathering together to share cultural foods and dances with one another. Halifax, Nova Scotia, for example, is just one of the many cities that annually celebrate the ethnic and cultural differences within the community through a multicultural festival. Keep your eyes open to see when your community takes part in a multicultural festival (Kublick, 2009).

## The Need for Cultural Awareness, Respect, and Reflection

When you are doing the work of community change, you will notice that everything happens through relationships. These relationships generate and use the investment of time as well as the varied perspectives and skills of many people. Two fundamental elements of any relationship are communication and trust.

Cultural differences between a community worker and community members, as well as between community members themselves, can provide challenges to communication and the development of trust. The success of relationships in this context often requires a broadening of perspectives and the use of a wide variety of skills. Ignorance of the different ways people experience the world and the different ways people express that experience can lead to mistakes in understanding each other. Without communication and trust in relationships, you will have limited access to the many abilities and competencies of community members and your change efforts are not likely to be successful. Community workers sometimes make mistakes by thinking that things that are different are not reliable because they are considered to be less predictable. Uncertainty can also produce fear and anxiety, which will certainly become barriers to the development of trust. In addition, a history of experiences of mistreatment will often result in a lack of trust among community members or of the community worker when there are cultural differences. In these instances, you as a community worker will need to think of creative ways to engage in actions that can help you establish trust with community members. You will also need to think a lot about how you might be creating barriers to building trusting relationships because you are either afraid of or poorly understand the differences between you and members of the community (Lee, 1999; Moffatt, 1996; Moffatt, George, Lee, & McGrath, 2005).

Effective community workers as change agents understand that issues of trust and possibilities for miscommunication are always present in relationships. You need to remember that this will be especially true when people from various cultural backgrounds are working together on a change effort. The degree of difficulty will be heightened when conflict or power imbalances have characterized the history of interactions between groups (even if these conflicts or power imbalances do not seem to you to be operating in the present moment). In other words, as a community worker not only must you acknowledge what is going on right now, but you must also think about the historical patterns of the relationships that have existed between and among communities. These patterns often have to be investigated and confronted before community members can move forward together (Barnoff & Moffatt, 2007; Mullaly, 2002).

## What Is Cultural Competence?

Cultural competence is the capacity to respond appropriately to the various cultural environments in which we may participate. Having cultural competence enables us to strengthen our relationships and accomplish our mutual purposes. Cultural competence is both a value and an essential set of skills in our diverse society.

Cross, Bazron, Dennis, and Isaacs (1989) argue that cultural competence should include the capacity to

- Value diversity
- Conduct self-assessment
- Recognize and relate effectively to the dynamics of difference
- Acquire and institutionalize cultural knowledge
- Develop adaptations to programs and services that will resonate with the cultural contexts of the individuals and communities served.

Understanding differences between groups is central to an appreciation of human diversity. Johnson (2001) points out, "Though there are common human needs, people fulfill those needs in different ways" (p. 9). Behaviour can never be understood apart from the cultural context in which it occurs. As Johnson explains, affirming human diversity means that we understand that "normal" behaviour depends on the social situation of the person. This social situation can be the interpersonal relationship, the cultural setting, or an organization's policies and practices. A whole range of social relations affects what we think

## DID YOU KNOW?

### Standards for Practice in Social Work

The Canadian Association of Social Workers has prepared a code of ethics for those engaged in this work. Section 1.2, entitled "Demonstrate Cultural Awareness and Sensitivity," recommends that

- Social workers strive to understand culture and its functions in human behaviours and society, recognizing the strengths that exist in all cultures
- Social workers acknowledge the diversity within and among individuals, communities, and cultures
- Social workers acknowledge and respect the impact that their own heritage, values, beliefs, and perspectives can have on their practice and on clients whose background and values may be different from their own
- Social workers seek a working knowledge and understanding of clients' racial and cultural affiliation and identities, values, beliefs, and customs
- Where possible, social workers provide and secure social work services in the language chosen by the client. When using an interpreter, when possible, social workers should preferentially secure an independent and qualified professional interpreter.



of as "normal" or how we behave. Behaviour is always "appropriate or inappropriate relative to the social situation in which a person is operating. What may be appropriate in one situation may be inappropriate in another" (p. 9). Diversity affects how we understand situations as well as how we might choose to intervene. Understanding diversity is important in community work.

The first step in working with any group of people is to assume that you have much to learn about them and they about you. Trying to take a so-called objective or scientific approach to communities will not help you to see the complexities of cultural difference and historical experience. This is especially true when past experiences have involved a history of prejudice or marginalization (Moffatt et al., 2005). You must learn about the factors that influence your relationship with communities and never assume that you know what is best for them. It is important that you reflect on this idea, particularly in situations in which you are working with people whose culture and life experiences are different from your own (Boushell, 2000). If you remain culturally insensitive, you risk acting in ways that can be seen as offensive. You may even contribute to systems of prejudice that are currently in place. This is true even if you are well intentioned.

What should you know to work with culturally diverse groups? A general understanding of the cultures involved is a necessary first step (Nelson-Jones, 1992). Important cultural factors include values; ways of relating to other persons, the physical world, and the spiritual world; family structure and the nature of family relationships; history, including the meaning attached to change and development; communication patterns, including nonverbal aspects; community life and structure; and coping mechanisms (Johnson & Yanca, 2001). It is also important to understand the experience of the minority group with the dominant culture (Corey & Corey, 1998; Devore & Schlesinger, 2000; Gutiérrez & Lewis, 1995; Johnson & Yanca, 2001; Rivera & Erlich, 1998). Dominant culture is the culture that has most access to means of communication, such as the media, and to resources, such as education and money, that allow the culture to be expressed openly and widely. Dominant groups have undue influence over minority groups and their opportunities (Yee & Dumbrill, 2003).

Some important questions to ask include these:

- What is the history of this group?
- How much and what type of interaction has there been between this group and other groups?
- What similarities and differences exist between the groups?
- How have group members reacted to efforts by the dominant group to control them?
- What impact have these experiences had on each group?

By answering questions like these, you will begin to develop an awareness of the sources of harmony and tension that are likely to affect the ways in which members of different groups will (at least initially) work together. It will help you to understand some tensions that might exist and that you need to attempt to overcome between you, the change agent, and the community. This is especially true if you are considered by community members to be part of a dominant culture or dominant group.

Rivera and Erlich (1998, pp. 13–17) list a number of important considerations when working with diverse communities of colour:

- Become familiar with customs, traditions, social networks, and values.
- Learn the language and subgroup slang.
- Understand leadership styles and development.
- Know who has power and recognize sources of mediating influences between ethnic communities and wider communities.
- Review past organizing strategies and analyze their strengths and limitations.
- Acquire skills in conscientization (developing a critical consciousness) and empowerment.
- Acquire skills in assessing community psychology.
- Be aware of your personal strengths and limitations.

Of all the things you need to know, perhaps the most important is to know yourself. Question the biases you hold, your fears, assumptions, expectations, intentions, desire and capability to learn, and the limitations of your own experiences. An honest appraisal will increase your self-awareness and give you confidence in gaining a better awareness of others. You will never master it all, not because it is hopeless, but because it is a lifelong process of learning. Accept the simple fact that you can never fully understand another's experience and perspective. You can, however, develop greater and greater levels of understanding (Moffatt et al., 2005).

If you do not know something you need to know, do not be afraid to ask. You will not be expected to know everything. An important aspect of working with any community is your ability to gather information to increase your understanding.

No one can provide you with a checklist of the key factors you need to know about every single group with whom you might be working. You will have to determine these things for yourself. Do be skeptical about anyone who tells you that they are experts about any group or claims to know everything about a community. For example, there are many First Nations communities in Canada, and there are often significant differences between them (Smylie, 2009). It would be a mistake to generalize your understanding of one nation and apply it to all nations (Edwards & Edwards, 1995). Members of groups with a common identity often share beliefs, but there are always distinct and important differences. Given this, what can you do? You can go to workshops, read, participate in community events, reflect on what does and does not work, talk to people, and perhaps most importantly, listen actively.

With all this emphasis on differences, do not lose sight of the fact that there are also many similarities among people. By focusing only on our differences, we run the risk of overemphasizing our separateness (Corey & Corey, 1998). This can make it difficult for people of different cultures to acknowledge their ability to work together.

It is also a mistake to regard all individuals solely in terms of the general traits of their culture. Shulman (1991) warns of the dangers of "teaching culturally specific techniques that are then implemented without regard to within-group heterogeneity" (p. 227). This can result in new stereotypes that reduce members of the group to simple categories. Cormier and Hackney (1993) caution that knowing something about a culture does not mean you know everything about each of its individual members. Remember that we all have multiple identities, and our cultural identity is but one of these. Members of any one cultural group will also vary in the extent of their identification with specific cultural characteristics.

Not every member of a cultural group will necessarily embrace or adopt the dominant values of that cultural group. Acknowledging the potential for differences within any one cultural group will help you to avoid stereotypes.

Recognizing the diversities that exist within any one group is important. If you do not keep this at the forefront of your mind, there is a serious risk that under the guise of "cultural competence" (presumably a good thing), you could instead be operating in problematic ways that are based on unfounded assumptions. It is a fine line: the concept of culture is definitely very important, and for change agents differences between cultures are important to understand; at the same time, though, you must be careful not to make too many assumptions or to operate on the basis of stereotypes and generalizations about groups of people (Sakmoto 2007; Sakamoto & Pitner, 2005).

Remember this: everyone you work with is going to have cultural and life experiences that are different from yours. This is true even when you are working with people with whom you share a cultural identity, because membership in a particular cultural group is only one aspect of identity. You need to always be thinking about how group members who share a culture are also different with regard to their race, class, gender, sexuality, ability, religion, country of origin, and other such factors. Because of this multiplicity of identities, members of a cultural group will have diverse and unique experiences (Dominelli & Campling, 2002; Jeffery, 2007).

As well as recognizing the diversity in every group, in order to successfully work with any community, you will need to have some idea about how people in that community see and relate to the world. Other people will perceive the world in a way that is different from your perceptions. Respecting those differences shows that you value the differences and are not trying to gloss over them or pretend they do not exist. There may be times when it will be important for you to admit that you are having difficulty understanding how they see the world, and to ask for more guidance and education. This will help you to develop a relationship of trust.

An excellent example of cultural community work can be seen in the work of an organization called Tungasuvvingat Inuit in Ottawa. Tungasuvvingat Inuit's goal is to empower and enhance the lives of Inuit people living in Ontario and other parts of Canada. The organization accomplishes its goals through advising other agencies throughout Canada about Inuit culture and values. Tungasuvvingat Inuit assists Inuit people to establish a life in Southern Ontario and ensures that Northern Inuit receive services that might not be widely available in the north, such as surgery and specialists, providing translation when necessary. Information regarding the Inuit culture is vital in ensuring that social work agencies in Ontario and across Canada respect the Inuit culture in addition to becoming culturally competent and sensitive (Tungasuvvingat, 2009).

## CAPTURING CONCEPTS

### Developing Cultural Sensitivity

The term **culture** gets tossed around pretty freely and has been defined broadly. Rivera and Erlich (1998) describe culture as "a collection of behaviours and beliefs that constitute standards for deciding what is, standards for deciding what can be, standards for deciding how one feels about it, standards for deciding what to do about it, and standards for deciding how to go about doing it" (p. 8). Barker (1999) defines culture as "the customs, habits, skills, technology, arts, values, ideology, science, and religious and political behaviour of a group of people in a specific time period" (p. 114).

Notions of culture are not limited to readily identifiable ethnic groups. Many groups have developed standards or customs for interpreting the world and acting in it (Longres, 2000). Employees of large public welfare agencies experience the culture of their organizations. Police officers have a special language and established codes of behaviour that reflect their perception of their uniqueness. Regardless of the cultural group you are addressing, cultural knowledge, cultural awareness, and cultural sensitivity are necessary to smooth your way.

When you take the time to familiarize yourself with selected cultural characteristics, such as the history, values, belief systems, and behaviours of the members of another ethnic group, you are acquiring **cultural knowledge** (Adams, 1995).

You can use this knowledge to develop sensitivity and understanding of an ethnic group. **Cultural awareness** usually involves internal changes in attitudes and values that emphasize the qualities of openness and flexibility that people develop in relation to others. Cultural awareness must be supplemented with cultural knowledge (Adams, 1995).

Knowing that cultural differences as well as similarities exist, without assigning values (better or worse, right or wrong) to those cultural differences, is a sign of **cultural sensitivity**.

"**Cultural competence** is a set of congruent behaviours, attitudes, and policies that come together in a system, agency, or among professionals, and enables that system, agency, or those professionals to work effectively in cross-cultural situations" (Cross et al., 1989, p. 13). The Center for Effective Collaboration and Practice views competency in cross-cultural functioning as "learning new patterns of behavior and effectively applying them in the appropriate settings" (King, Simms, & Osher, 2000). **Cultural competency** emphasizes the idea of effectively operating in different cultural contexts using your knowledge, sensitivity, and awareness. "This is beyond awareness or sensitivity," says Marva Benjamin of the Georgetown Technical Assistance Center for Children's Mental Health.

Social workers and other social service professionals have a responsibility to improve their own capability, but they also need to foster competence in the organizations that they develop or for which they work (Barnoff, 2001). Just as we reflect on our own practice, we must take leadership in assisting organizations to examine how their policies and practices affect diverse groups (Parada, Barnoff, & Coleman, 2007; Barnoff, 2001). Unfortunately, delivering culturally appropriate services is more rare than common (Fong & Gibbs, 1995). It requires an honest commitment. Given that there are often so many different cultural groups seeking services at the same agency, and given the diversity that exists within every culture, the achievement of consistently delivering "culturally appropriate services" is a complex goal (George, Coleman, & Baroff, 2007). A few training workshops will not be enough. Cultural competence is, in fact, a lifetime goal toward which we must strive throughout our working lives (Lee, 1999).

An excellent example of multicultural social work can be seen in the Kitchener-Waterloo Multicultural Centre, in Kitchener, Ontario. The Kitchener Multicultural Centre seeks to celebrate multiculturalism with the community, promote racial harmony, meet the needs of specific ethnic populations within the community, assist all new Canadians, and support the community at large. Some of the ways the multicultural centre accomplishes these goals are by providing interpreters, employment workshops, and English as a second language programs. The main goal of the Kitchener Multicultural Centre is to promote diversity within the community, along with promoting the full participation of all residents within the Kitchener-Waterloo community (KWMC, 2009).

## Fairness and the Diverse Society

Galabuzi's (2006) work tells us that the numbers of racialized people in Canada are growing and that this group represents a sizeable proportion of the population, particularly in the major cities. Galabuzi (2009) uses the term *racialized people* to highlight the fact that categorizing people based on race is a social construction (in other words, it is a social process) that is imposed on certain groups of people on the basis of superficial attributes such as skin colour. This categorization process—also known as the racialization process—brings subsequent differential treatment that is endured by these identified groups. An example of this was discussed in Chapter 1, where we talked about "racial profiling" (Galabuzi, 2009, p. 266). In Toronto, 43 percent of the population is racialized; in Vancouver it is 49 percent; it is 22 percent in Montreal and 21 percent in Calgary (p. 6). According to the Department of Human Resources and Skills Development, 70 percent of people entering the labour force are immigrants—of which 75 percent are racialized (HRDC 2001, as cited in Galabuzi, 2006).

Hum and Simpson's (2007) review of labour practices in Canada among racialized populations found that racialized people as a group suffer close to a 16 percent disadvantage when compared with non-visible minorities measured by income. Hum and Simpson's work shows that Canadian employers discriminate on the basis of colour (p. 90). Among racialized people, black men's wage disadvantage is approximately 22 percent, Indo-Pakistani 13.7 percent, Arab 13.7 percent, and Latin American male immigrants 17.7 percent. Native-born Latin American men experience a disadvantage of 38.8 percent. It is clear that this group has a profound disadvantage (p. 97). Recent population shifts (in other words, the increase in the numbers of racialized people in Canada) point to the need for people to learn more about one another and more about cultural diversity itself. We can no longer pretend that these complex cultural realities are not important, nor can we deny the fact that racialized people experience discrimination in Canada. Figure 2.1 describes the average income of some racialized groups. The figure also shows how race intersects with gender in relation to disparities of income.

A complex variety of social situations and social systems marginalizes many communities due to their identity (Church, Bacia, & Shragge, 2008; Dominelli, 2007; Gutiérrez & Lewis, 1995; Iglehart & Becerra, 1996; Rivera & Erlich, 1998).

Respect for cultural diversity requires that you confront the fact of racism. Cultures are not just "different," they are also differentially positioned with regard to the power relations of society. Some cultures are "dominant" (their behaviours, customs, and ideas become the "norm") while others are marginalized. In Canadian society, the dominant culture is white (and it is also heterosexual, middle class, able bodied, Christian, and male). As a result, members of this group walk in the world with certain privileges, most of which are largely invisible to them (Yee & Dumbrill, 2003).

One of the privileges of dominant cultural status is the luxury to see oneself as an individual (i.e., not as a member of a cultural group). Non-dominant groups, however, can rarely escape being defined by their cultural membership. For example, the ability to view one's achievements as solely a product of individual merit, rather than as having something to do with one's dominant group membership, is a privilege awarded to those

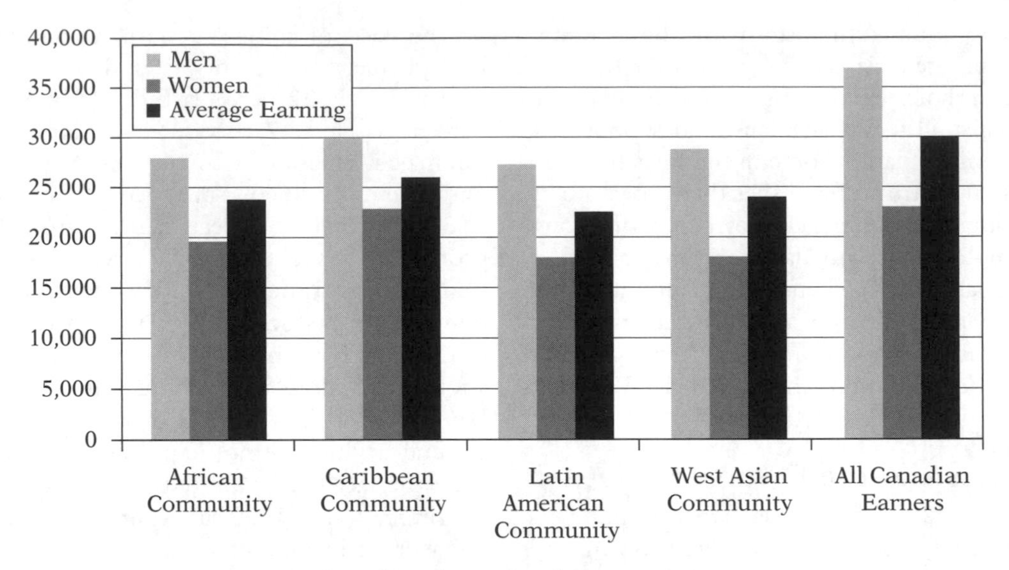


**FIGURE 2.1** Average Income by Selected Racialized Communities, 2001

Source: Statistics Canada. (2003). *The Changing Profile of Canada's Labour Force*. Catalogue # 96F0030XIE2001009, Ottawa.

## • CHANGE AGENT TIP

Here are a few more ideas that can increase your cultural competence:

- Find resource people, particularly from the community, who can help you to understand the group with whom you will be working.
- Recognize that you are coming to the community not to do things for them but with them.
- Recognize that you are learning from the community.
- Avoid romantically stereotyping any group. It is dishonest.
- Refuse to define any group solely in terms of its oppression. That is a demeaning and limiting view.
- At the same time, respect community members' understanding of how their community has been oppressed.
- Give back to the community so that you teach what you are learning.
- Share your biases openly when you are confused, so that community members can correct you if need be.
- Do not support by your silence those words and behaviours that diminish members of other groups.
- Encourage others to speak, and listen to them.
- Acknowledge that your life experiences influence your perceptions and that other people's life experiences shape their perceptions as well. Acknowledge that these can be very different.
- Listen to oral histories about the community and about community members; there are many hints as to how the community became organized in these stories.

who are members of the dominant cultural group. It is clear that racial power relations shape the lives of white people as much as they shape the lives of people of colour (Frankenberg, 1993).

Working for social justice is clearly linked to working against practices that are supported by and contributing to cultural ignorance and racial intolerance. Your ability to effectively promote change requires that you continually learn how to make your own work meaningful and effective with diverse populations. Furthermore, you have a responsibility to reflect on how your own cultural beliefs and practices affect your relationships with various communities.

As an agent of change, you cannot ignore the fact that power relations based on race and other forms of diversity affect you, the people with whom you work, and your relationships. Does this mean it is hopeless to try to work across our differences? No, of course not. But we should all live in acknowledgment of this reality and reflect upon whether our actions are maintaining or challenging disabling conditions like racism. At the same time, we should be excited, not dispirited about this challenge. These conditions are an aspect of our relationships, but they can be worked upon and people can build stronger relations of trust and communication by working together to address them.

When we are focused on the need for change, we can build on our common interests and employ our unique strengths in order to break down barriers. We can all learn with and from each other. If we begin from a place that acknowledges the existence of power relations such as racism and if we are willing to explore how those power relations continue to play out in our everyday interactions as we work together toward community change, we will be successful.

## ● ANTI-OPPRESSIVE APPROACH

A contemporary framework called anti-oppression theory addresses the prejudicial and inequitable relations that communities experience. In this theory, many actions are understood to be part of the processes of exclusion and marginalization. This idea is vital for you as a community change agent to understand because almost all communities you will work with have been marginalized and excluded from full participation in Canadian life. Even your actions as a community worker can contribute to these processes despite your best intentions. From an anti-oppression perspective, every analysis must include an analysis of power. An anti-oppression perspective notes that certain groups and communities are marginalized within systems of power (based on race, class, gender, and other factors) due to the ways those systems operate in the wider society.

How marginalization occurs differs from community to community based on a variety of factors, such as institutional relationships in the community, the mistreatment of community members due to their identity, and the historical experience of the community. Anti-oppression theory tells us that the individual experience of a community member is not separate from the broader social relations that affect her or his wider community. A complex web of interactions links individual to community to society, and all of these interactions affect the experience of community members (Barnoff, George, & Coleman, 2006; George et al., 2007).

### Context

An anti-oppression model is part of a critical tradition in social work that concerns itself with transforming a society seen to be characterized by exploitation, inequality, and oppression into one of equality and freedom from domination (Hick, Fook, & Pozzuto, 2005). Critical social work has a lengthy historical tradition, extending back to the advent of the social work profession, such as, the legacy of some social justice practices of the Settlement House Movement (Bisman, 2004; Moffatt, 2001). Anti-oppression encompasses and builds on earlier critical traditions in social work but is distinct because it focuses on the multiple and intersecting natures of power and oppression.

Those who adhere to an anti-oppression approach seek fundamental change in the structures of society that perpetuate marginalization and oppression (Hick, Fook, & Pozzuto, 2005; Mullaly, 2002). As an approach informed by an analysis of power relations, anti-oppression strives to assist workers to facilitate the personal and political empowerment of groups that are disadvantaged by intersecting systems of racism, heterosexism, ableism, classism, sexism, and other forms of oppression (Barnoff, 2001; Mullaly, 2002). The anti-oppression approach is based on values such as equity, inclusion, and transformation. A central purpose of anti-oppression is to seek social justice for marginalized or excluded groups or communities This is in keeping with the actions and desires of many community change agents in Canada (McGrath, George, Lee, & Moffatt, 2007). Anti-oppression is focused on stopping oppression in all its forms, thereby ensuring equity for all social groups.

In this framework, problems are not seen as individual or personal, but rather are redefined as political issues, rooted in the ways society is organized and therefore as requiring structural as well as individual solutions. An anti-oppression approach recognizes the complex interconnections between personal and public (social) issues (Barnoff & Moffatt, 2007; Barnoff, 2001).

The primary goals of practice informed by an anti-oppression perspective are two-fold:

1. The provision of assistance to those injured by the oppressive social order; and
2. Efforts aimed toward change that will transform oppressive systems (Dominelli, 1998).

An anti-oppression approach to practice is a framework that is relevant to all levels of social work practice, including clinical work, organizational and community practice, research, policy work, and social action. The anti-oppressive framework has been widely taken up in social work schools in Canada and is a developing field of research, practice, and education. As with any good theory, scholars and practitioners differ regarding what this framework is all about, and the topic is widely discussed and debated. At the same time, some clear themes emerge in the anti-oppression literature and are commonly agreed upon as unique aspects of this model.

Currently, many social work academics and community practitioners are engaged in the complex task of integrating an anti-oppressive approach into their work. All levels of practice, including theory, practice, research, and education, are being reconsidered from an anti-oppression perspective (Wilson & Beresford, 2000). The growing literature on anti-oppressive practice provides an alternative view of the social problems faced by many of the people who come into contact with social workers (Barnoff, 2001; Barnoff et al., 2006; Barnoff & Moffatt, 2007; Brown, 2007; Campbell, 2003; Freeman, 2007; Jeffery, 2007). The question of how to successfully integrate an anti-oppressive approach within social work practices is one of the critical questions of importance currently facing the profession as a whole. Barnoff and Moffatt (2007, p. 68) have indicated that anti-oppressive practices of social work are "still very much a work in progress" with "many challenges to be worked out both theoretically and [practically]." It is in the nature of the work of anti-oppression that processes and theory be viewed as open-ended and open to change.

Communication is crucial if we are to improve relations with communities affected by the system's abuse of power (Parada et al., 2007). Anti-oppression theory sees as questionable the fact that based on the operations of power in the wider society, certain groups of people are advantaged while others are disadvantaged. This situation must be challenged, and ultimately changed. "The driving force of anti-oppressive practice is the act of challenging inequalities" (Burke & Harrison, 2002).

Massaquoi (2007) argues that in order to transform community work, we need to focus on three major levels, namely (a) theory/knowledge, (b) education, and (c) practice (p. 176). She further argues that the relations among the different components of these levels require that we value the uncertainties of everyday living and that anti-oppressive theory may need to adapt

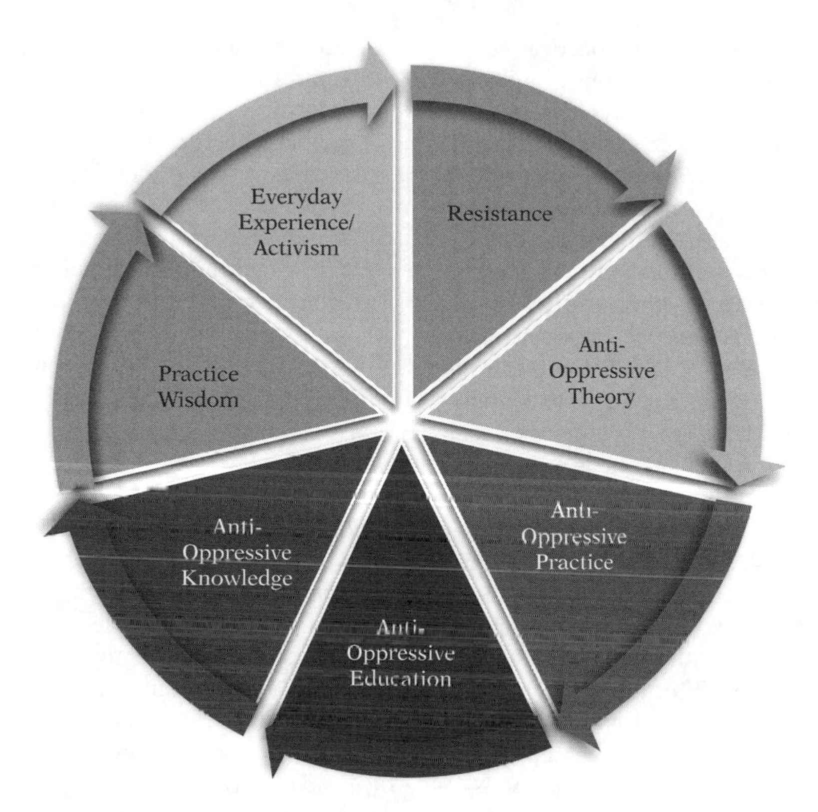


**FIGURE 2.2** The Circle of Anti-Oppressive Practice and Theory

Source: N. Massaquoi in *Doing Anti-Oppressive Practice: Building Transformative, Politicized Social Work* by Donna Baines (editor), Fernwood Publishing Co., Ltd. 2007.

and transform itself. At the same time, when we engage in putting anti-oppressive theory out into the world of everyday practice, we may find that some practices are problematic and need to be challenged and resisted too (p. 176–177). See Figure 2.2.

### Common Themes in the Anti-oppression Literature

1. **Anti-oppression perspective as an approach to practice:** Anti-oppression is a value-based perspective with a particular vision of society. It is a perspective that understands society as being structured by multiple intersecting forms of power that shape everyone's lives based on their membership in particular social groups. Anti-oppressive social work practices include all practices that aim to challenge and change oppressive power relations—in other words, practices that are rooted in a desire to eradicate inequality and to promote social transformation and social justice.
2. **Anti-oppression as a multi-layered, holistic model:** An anti-oppression approach always sees the interconnections between micro (individual, family, groups), meso (organizations, communities), and macro (societal) levels, refusing to separate these into distinct unconnected areas. An anti-oppression approach always explores these interconnections. From a practice perspective, individuals, families, groups, organizations, and communities are all understood as being intimately interconnected within a host of social institutions

and social systems. This perspective sees the way in which social systems influence individuals as well as the ways in which individuals can influence social systems. As a result, anti-oppression social work practices focus on change at every level.

3. **Anti-oppression as a link between the personal and the political:** From an anti-oppressive perspective, when we try to understand so-called individual or personal problems, we always seek to link these problems to their social causes. We view them not as "private problems" that belong to difficult individuals, but rather as "public problems" that belong to, and are rooted in, an oppressive society. From this perspective, we always focus on the link between personal situations and larger social relations of power (such as racism, sexism, and classism). In this way, individuals are not pathologized
4. **Focus on process:** From an anti-oppression perspective, how things are done becomes just as important as what things are done. Anti-oppression practitioners are not concerned just with the "outcome" of a social work intervention, but are also concerned with the "process" that unfolds within that social work intervention. Processes that promote inclusion are particularly valued from this perspective. For example, with regard to decision making, it is important to explore whether and how everyone is involved (or not).
5. **Promotion of collective action:** From an anti-oppression perspective, collective action is critical because it is believed that only through collective action will social change occur. Anti-oppression practitioners, therefore, are often those who focus on community development, alliance building, coalition development, and social action.
6. **Promotion of social justice at the global/international level:** An anti-oppression framework not only sees the local micro, meso, and macro contexts as interconnected, it also highlights the links between the local and the global. Therefore, anti-oppression practitioners would argue that it is important to always acknowledge the global aspects of local social problems as well as to seek to develop knowledge about how the local and the global are interconnected. For example, practitioners might engage with international organizations that are concerned with promoting equity and social justice and enforcing human rights (Alphonse et al., 2008; Dominelli, 1998; Parada, 2007; Wehbi, 2008).

### Community Work and Anti-oppression

*Lesbian, gay, bisexual, transgendered, and transsexual (LGBTT) communities*: Community practice that takes an anti-oppression perspective is found in many communities, including Canada's lesbian, gay, bisexual, transgendered, and transsexual (LGBTT) communities. Change agents who are members of and work within LGBTT communities have learned that constant prejudice and subtle forms of marginalization make it important to work to empower and encourage community members (Kinsmen, 1996; Lepischak & Moffatt, 2007; O'Brien, 1999).

Lepischak and Moffatt (2007) document an elaborate community endeavour that has drawn community members together to support vulnerable queer youth. In the mentoring and housing program Supporting Our Youth, empowerment principles are drawn on so adult members can support youth in the face of prejudicial structures of society. See the Capturing Concepts box.

In these cases of community organizing, the organizers challenge both members of the LGBTT community and people outside that community to rethink the nature of social and community relations. In addition, LGBTT communities have worked at the level of human rights promotion as well as policy to bring about changes to laws to protect community members (Kinsmen, 1996; Warner, 2002). As a change agent, you can learn from the LGBTT community about how the personal and political are interconnected.

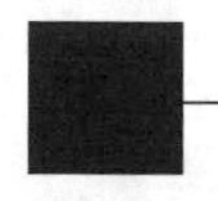

## CAPTURING CONCEPTS

### Supporting Our Youth: Development of a Community-Based Response to Risk and Marginalization

**Bev Lepischak and Ken Moffatt**

A growing number of lesbian, gay, bisexual, transsexual, and transgendered (LGBTT) youth, ranging from 16 to 26 years of age, live on the street in downtown Toronto. Some grew up in Toronto, while others have migrated from smaller Canadian cities and rural settings. Among these youth are also LGBTT newcomers and immigrants who have come to Canada either with their families or on their own. Some of those who originally immigrated with their families have been forced to leave their families.

Many of these youth have no permanent place to live and find it difficult to acquire the resources necessary to maintain stable and secure housing. As a result, their options are limited to rotating through the youth shelter system, living temporarily with friends and acquaintances or living on the street. Most of the young people living on the street are not in school and few have employment income. Instead, they acquire whatever meagre income they can through panhandling, squeegeeing (offering to wash motorists' windows for "tips"), dealing drugs, or working in the sex trade.

During the early 90s in Toronto, the development of new subsidized housing was halted, and reductions in social assistance rates and the tightening of eligibility requirements made it impossible for single persons to maintain adequate housing within the urban private market. Many students were disqualified from collecting social assistance while they attended school, and there was significant pressure for youth to return to their families. This pressure to return to often-hostile families and communities put LGBTT youth's health and safety at perilous risk.

The key player in developing the Supporting Our Youth (SOY) program was the Coalition for Services for Lesbian and Gay Youth. The coalition's mandate was to advocate for the needs of lesbian, gay, and bisexual youth. The coalition functioned as a loose network with voluntary membership based on self-defined commitment to the cause. Membership in the coalition was fluid according to people's ability to commit at a particular time.

The Coalition for Services for Lesbian and Gay Youth had been operating for about five years when it began work on the Supporting Our Youth program. Prior to that, it had sponsored two large and very successful province-wide conferences focused on the needs and issues of LGBTT youth. The consensus among member organizations and individuals participating in the conferences was that government cutbacks had already seriously compromised the lives of youth, particularly LGBTT and street involved youth, and that prospects for developing and funding programs in the immediate future were dim. The conferences and Supporting Our Youth had become the major focus of the coalition's work. Coalition members met as part of the "Toronto caucus" during the second province-wide conference held in 1996. There was an air of hopelessness and resignation about the possibility of finding funding for services and other resources for LGBTT youth. Caucus members came up with the idea of a community-based approach. The next day at the caucus, they proposed a profound change in the approach to supporting LGBTT youth: rather than relying on unstable and shrinking government funding for professional services, efforts should focus on involving the adult LGBTT community in the development of supports for youth within the community.

One of the barriers to making change was the concern that a community-driven response would leave the community vulnerable to the prevailing stereotypes of gay men and lesbians as predators and dangerous to young people. Some participants worried that lesbians and gay men would not become involved due to their fear of the social consequences of this stereotype. There were concerns that the

*Continued*

media and mainstream service providers would be critical and unsupportive of the project. Finally, there were also concerns that predators (straight or LGBTT) might be attracted to a youth-oriented project.

Despite significant gains in human rights and social protections for lesbians and gay men in Canada (protections not normally afforded to transgendered and transsexual persons), youth struggling with issues of sexual orientation and gender identity are victims of Canadian cultural attitudes that continue to be homophobic and transphobic. LGBTT youth are stigmatized and marginalized by peers, community members, families, and educational authorities. They experience isolation, as well as emotional, verbal, and physical abuse, and some are forced to leave their homes. Their social marginalization leads to anxiety, depression, and low self-esteem, which are significant problems within the LGBTT youth population. Rates of suicide, suicide attempts, and substance abuse are disproportionately high for LGBTT youth. One method of coping with these oppressive circumstances is to flee to large urban centres in search of community and safety. There are very few institutions or meeting places where they can meet adults who have successfully dealt with prejudice. LGBTT youth who are newcomers or immigrants or who identify as persons of colour face additional challenges in integrating into a new culture or dealing with the racism that exists in LGBTT communities and in the broader Canadian society.

Although some concerns were voiced, there was unanimous support for the approach envisioned for Supporting Our Youth. Adults would work together with youth to develop supports not currently available and unlikely to be funded through the traditional social service system. Key areas for activities were identified: age-appropriate arts, culture, and recreation; training and employment opportunities; adult mentors; and access to safe supportive housing.

Armed with information from this needs assessment/feasibility study, the coalition applied to the Trillium Foundation, a foundation that supports social projects, for funding of $210,000 over a four-year period. In the end, Trillium responded with a $180,000 grant for a three-year project to commence in April 1998. This was remarkable since no LGBTT-focused project had ever received Trillium funding. We felt a significant sense of accomplishment at this point.

Central to the services developed within the Supporting Our Youth is the mentoring and housing program, aimed at youth 26 years of age and under. It is designed to provide lesbian, gay, bisexual, transgendered, and transsexual youth with access to positive role models who share the realities of their lives with regard to sexual orientation and gender identity, and to safe, affordable, supportive housing.

Hundreds of youth, service providers, and mentors have participated in the program since it was launched in November 1999. More than 100 individuals, representing a remarkable diversity in age, race, ethnic identity, sexual orientation, and gender identity, applied to be mentors during the first three years of the program. Some mentors state that they are motivated by their personal experiences of struggling with sexual orientation or gender identity without the support of positive adults and recognize the value of adult support to youth.

Mentors also claim benefits from the mentoring and housing program. It provides them with opportunities to form positive relationships with young people, to express their care and concern for the youth of the LGBTT community, and to participate in youth culture. Mentors are also able to "give back" to a community in which they themselves have been supported and have achieved a sense of belonging, and to contribute to the effort of building a more inclusive, diverse LGBTT community. Young people involved in the program are also a remarkably diverse group, and increasing numbers identify as newcomers or immigrants or as people of colour. Many are, or are at risk of being, homeless, and few have sufficient income to meet their basic needs. A significant number are former wards of the state, and at least half of the youth participants have histories of mental health problems, substance abuse problems, or involvement in criminal activity or all three.

Many youth living on the streets want to be matched with adult mentors, but because of the huge challenges the young people face in meeting their basic needs while living on the street, it is extremely difficult for most to be matched in a regular one-to-one mentoring relationship. To address this problem, a weekly supper club/drop-in program was developed. It provides street-involved youth with a nutritious meal, age-appropriate activities, opportunities to socialize with peers, and a chance for positive contact with caring adult mentors. It also provides these youth, most of whom have no contact with their families, with a place to celebrate special occasions. More than one thousand young people have participated in over one hundred supper clubs since the program began.

During the three years the program has been in existence, mentors have contributed over 10,000 hours of volunteer time to the project. Adult members of the LGBTT community have also contributed countless volunteer hours in planning, managing, and delivering the program, and acquiring the financial resources to keep it operating.

Adapted from Bev Lepischak and Ken Moffatt, "Supporting Our Youth: Development of a Community-Based Response to Risk and Marginalization" in Bill Lee and Sarah Todd (2005), *A Casebook of Community Practice: Problems and Strategies,* CommonActPress, Toronto, Canada.

## CHANGE AGENT TIP

Anti-oppression community work....

- Is geared toward the eradication of inequality in all of its forms (Lundy, 2004).
- Focuses on power relations that exist between change agents and community members (including individuals, families, groups, organizations, and communities) along with a focus on power relations within the wider society (Parada 2005).
- Redefines professionalism, "with expertise being rooted in more power-sharing egalitarian directions and making explicit the value system to which the professional subscribes" (Dominelli, 2007). Practitioners act in ways that will lessen the "expert status" of the worker and promote power-sharing within change agent-community members relationships. Workers and service users learn from and with each other (Healy, 2005).
- Ensures change agents always value people's lived realities—that is, what they themselves know about their own lives (Baskin, 2003).
- Knows that people experiencing marginalization are the experts on their own lives.
- Knows that there is no such thing as a "value-free" or "neutral" approach to community work. We all have our biases, ideas, and understandings based in our own experience that we bring these to our practice (Moffatt et al. 2005).
- Recognizes that in the context of diversity, community workers are often themselves members of the communities within which they are working (Lee, McGrath, Moffatt, & George, 2002). This can be confusing and difficult for a change agent but it can also with careful reflection on your membership an role be as strength and is often tied to a deep commitment to these communities (Lee et al., 2002; Lee, McGrath, Moffatt, & George, 2006).
- Takes an approach that always positions community members as capable, as having strengths, and resilience. This theory argues that it is important to focus on the positives, the strengths, and the skills that community members bring to the situation. Anti-oppressive practitioners explore the positive aspects of people's behaviours, seeing them as survival skills or strategies of resistance rather than as solely troublesome.
- Takes community members as the starting point (Dominelli, 1998). Community workers respect people's rights to make their own decisions and to chart their own courses. Community change agents value difference and diversity. Change agents do not try to shape the lives of others so that they become more like the workers themselves. Instead, we try to facilitate the attainment of whatever it is that the community members want to become (Lee, 2008).

## ABORIGINAL WORLD VIEWS

Aboriginals were the first people to inhabit the landmass now known as Canada. There are and have always been many different Aboriginal nations and thus multiple Aboriginal world views. Nonetheless, there are common themes in community work that are relevant with respect to Aboriginal world views (Morrissette, McKenzie, & Morrissette, 1993; Smylie, 2009).

All community change agents can learn much from Aboriginal world views since these beliefs are tied to concepts of community and the central importance of the environment to good living. Michael Hart (2002) outlines the foundations of an Aboriginal approach to helping in his book *Seeking Mino-Pimatisiwin*. An Aboriginal approach, according to Hart, is based on the framework of the "medicine wheel." The medicine wheel has many variations, but in general it is a symbol of the universe that is used to help people understand the world and their place in it. It reflects a way of understanding the world, and it integrates a set of important teachings.

Foundational concepts of an Aboriginal perspective, according to Hart, include the following:

- Wholeness
- Balance
- Connection
- Harmony
- Growth
- Healing

*Wholeness* directs us to always try to understand how everything is connected to everything else. The concept of wholeness incorporates all aspects of life and gives attention to every aspect and how each is interconnected. *Balance* tells us that all aspects of a phenomenon require our attention, but always in a way that ensures one part is not focused on to the detriment or exclusion of all other parts. Balance is said to be achieved when a person is at peace with themselves as well as with everything else. It is important for each person to develop each aspect of themselves (mental, physical, emotional, and spiritual). This must be done in a way that does not limit the wellness or potential of others, including family, community, and nation. When we are involved in community change, we must always seek to establish balance. Since communities are constantly changing, we need to be careful how we seek to adjust the balance within the community.

*Connection* encourages us to focus on different types of connections—those within individuals (e.g., the relations between a person's emotional and physical health) and those between an individual and the world around them (e.g., family members, community, and nation). In other words, the concept of connection encourages a focus on relationships.

*Harmony* includes the idea of respect—respect for oneself and for one's relationships with others. It directs us to focus on the goal of achieving peace with oneself and with the larger world around us.

*Growth* focuses on the development of a person (e.g., their body, heart, mind, and spirit) but must be done in a harmonious manner. An Aboriginal perspective believes that all of life is about growth and that growth is a lifelong process.

*Healing* is also viewed as a lifelong journey–one that every one of us engages in daily throughout our lives. In other words, it is seen as a normal state. Healing is the process that restores individuals, families, communities, and nations to wholeness, connectedness, and balance. Because of the belief in connectedness and wholeness, healing is not seen as just an individual journey, but rather as a process that involves individuals, families, communities, and entire nations.

Through healing, one can reach "the good life" for oneself, one's family, and the community. Cooperation, harmony, interdependence—all core concepts and beliefs of the Aboriginal world view—are tied closely to community approaches. From this perspective, problems are conceptualized as dis-connections, imbalances, disharmony, or a lack of wholeness. Healing is the process of rectifying these situations.

Aboriginal scholars in Canada argue that strategies to work with Aboriginal communities must build on Aboriginal culture and traditions and must be based on an Aboriginal world view (Baskin, 2003; Freeman & Lee, 2007; Morrissette et al., 1993).

The reality of Aboriginal oppression within Canada can be seen in the justice system. New policies on crime focus on incarcerating youth who are considered to be "high risk." Since more often than not Aboriginal youth are seen as a group with a disproportionate number of high-risk offenders, they are more likely to be incarcerated. This is true especially within the Prairie provinces. Approximately 60 percent of Aboriginal youth and adults are incarcerated across Canada. This suggests that discrimination is present within the Canadian justice system. The current justice system rarely gives Aboriginal youth the opportunity for alternative punitive measures, such as rehabilitation, which are more frequently applied to non-Aboriginals, suggesting another form of racial oppression. This institutionalized oppression is rarely spoken of and is a serious issue that we cannot ignore (Conrad, 2008).

Across Canada many Aboriginal communities have experienced problems concerning land claims. As one example, in Caledonia, Ontario, the Canadian government has withheld land-claim talks, effectively ignoring the problem. The conflict has escalated into violence, as local Aboriginals set up roadblocks to protest government inaction. The problem is not unique to Ontario. In Alberta, the provincial government has sold land previously promised to Aboriginals to oil companies. This grave injustice happens all too frequently in Canada (McGrory, 2006).

Despite many efforts to end injustice and the oppression of Aboriginal peoples in Canada, we still have a long way to go. On a positive note, in 2008, the Canadian government issued an apology for the legacy of residential schools in Canada. The Truth and Reconciliation Commission is leading the process to reconnect Aboriginal and non-Aboriginal communities. This process has made clear the lack of knowledge that many non-Aboriginals in Canada have when it comes to the history of Canadian Aboriginal peoples. For example, a great many Canadians were unaware of the residential school policy as well as its goals. Lack of awareness is a form of oppression that Aboriginal people continue to battle; hopefully, the Truth and Reconciliation Commission can assist in this regard (Laboucane, 2009).

Jason Cheever / Shutterstock

**It is important to value the world views of groups that are marginalized, such as Aboriginal people.**

When we begin to define an Aboriginal approach to community practice, we must discuss the history of colonization of Aboriginal peoples in Canada (Baskin, 2003; Freeman & Lee, 2007; Lee et al., 2006; Morrissette et al., 1993). Colonization has taken on many forms, including the removal of lands from Aboriginal people and the wide-scale removal of Aboriginal children from their families, both with the establishment of the residential school system and with the wide-scale adoptions of Aboriginal children into white families. These actions have disrupted communities, families, and the spiritual well-being of Aboriginal persons (Carniol, 2005). Colonization is tied to Eurocentricism, which assumes that European approaches, beliefs, and thinking are superior. Aboriginal children have been and still continue to be removed from their communities (Wharf, 2002). In Canada, the imposition of cultural practices and beliefs has destroyed the Aboriginal sense of community (Saulis, 2006; Antone, Miller, & Myers, 1986).

## CRITICAL REFLECTION: A KEY FOUNDATION FOR EFFECTIVE COMMUNITY PRACTICE

At its most basic level, reflective practice is exactly what it sounds like it would be about—that is, reflecting upon your practice, or even more simply, thinking about your practice. The importance of reflective practice has been elaborated by philosophers, economists, and educators, including Martin Buber, Paolo Friere, Karel Kosik, Karl Marx, and Ludvig von Mises. Schon has been an important author in the works that discuss how professionals, including social workers, can learn through reflection (Schon, 1983, 1987). A number of other authors are interested in community and social welfare and discuss the central importance of reflective learning and practise when it comes to the matter of social change (Fook, 2002; Kondrat, 1999; Moffatt, 1996; Miehls & Moffatt, 2000; Moffatt et al., 2005; Todd, 2005).

Reflective practice is practice that values constant critical questioning of every aspect of our work. It directs us to always think about what we are doing, why we are doing it in the ways we are doing it, and how might we do it differently. One of the main features of the process of critical reflection is to link the practice situation with larger systems of power. In other words, critical reflection involves thinking about how the power relations that operate in the wider society (e.g., racism, sexism, classism, ableism, or heterosexism) might also be operating within our everyday practices as community workers. The goal of this reflection would be to make visible how power is created and maintained and how it plays out within the practice situation. Once we have information about this, we can then use it to create change—that is, we

### DID YOU KNOW?

You cannot promote change in a community without learning about the community's history. You will accomplish this through active engagement with community members.

It is impossible to know how to work with Aboriginal communities without knowing about the history of first contact, colonialism, and oppressive processes such as the "1960s scoop" and the history of residential schools (Freeman & Lee, 2007).

Do you know the significance of these events in the relationship between Canada and the Aboriginal peoples?

- The disregard for Métis land claims
- Relocation of Inuit communities
- Residential schools
- The 60s scoop
- The effects of colonization

This is part of the history of important communities of people who have been marginalized in Canada, but unfortunately many non-Aboriginals are ignorant of this history (Smylie, 2009).

can change our practice and stop reproducing power relations that are harmful to the communities with which we are working. We cannot change questionable patterns unless and until we become aware of them.

Critical reflection is important because it can help us become conscious of and correct against our own biases (Fook, 2002; Moffatt, 1996). As we have talked about earlier in this chapter, even if it is unintentional, we can maintain and create patterns of exclusion through our actions as community workers. This is especially true when we practise without critically reflecting on what we are doing (Kondrat, 1999; Moffatt et al., 2005). Reflection also allows us to avoid purely technical or "textbook" approaches to practice that block out the experiences and voices of our community members (Franklin, 1992; Isin & Wood, 1999). Critical reflection forces us to ask if there might be alternative (and possibly better) ways to engage with people and to intervene in communities. It helps us see that what works in one context with one community might not be the best way of working in another. Critical reflection "keeps us on our toes," so to speak, and ensures we are always evaluating ourselves and our practice as community workers.

Change is most likely to occur only after an interactive process of reflection and action. Our actions are determined by a number of factors, including our perception and experience of the world, what we want from it, what we think we are capable of doing, what social relations might limit us from doing, and what we expect will happen as a result of our actions. These perceptions merge into a "theory in action" (even if we are not necessarily aware of this) at the moment of acting (Schon, 1983). We develop our thoughts while we are acting and we develop our actions from our thoughts. We are both using our knowledge and increasing our knowledge while we are acting.

By acting in the world and reflecting on our actions, we create knowledge. In other words, many of our ideas about the world are formed as a result of our behaviours and our thinking about our behaviours. This process of learning is often not conscious. We do not often stop to think about where our ideas come from or how we learned that a particular way of thinking or acting was the best way. Reflective practice helps us to become more aware of our thoughts and actions, where they come from, and what purposes they serve. Reflective practice helps us understand how we develop knowledge based on our thinking and our actions, and how we choose to act in the world based on this knowledge (Fook, 2002). It allows us to work a step at a time—that is, try something, consider its

## ● CHANGE AGENT TIP

You can use reflective practice to become more aware of your own role as a change agent and how you might be affecting or influencing your social work practice. For example, in a situation where you experience a strong emotion, ask yourself questions such as "Why do I feel so emotional?" "Can I use this emotion to work toward social change?" When you are thinking about your work as a change agent, you can ask questions such as "How am I influencing the prospects and opportunities of community members?" "How might I be limiting community members by the way that I think and talk about them?" "Is this the kindest action in this moment?" "Do my actions support a greater understanding of the group?" "What did I learn in this moment?" "How might my learning change if I and the rest of the group try another tactic?" "How are my assumptions, biases, and knowledge being challenged by differences within this particular intervention?"

effect, observe any negative or unintended consequences, and consider a change in direction. This is a more sensitive approach than imposing a fully developed plan on a community, especially one that has been marginalized and has not had a say in its well-being. Good community work requires many thoughtful changes in direction.

This process provides an important perspective for change agents. Reflective practice says that people not only learn about the world from acting in it, but by acting in it, they also change that world. When we recognize this, we will come to see the community members with whom we are working as active co-creators of the world (i.e., as leaders), not just as passive objects that are to be manipulated (i.e., as followers). This is an important shift in thinking (Moffatt et al., 2005).

Guided by this philosophy, we promote the notion of people believing in themselves, their own learning, and the value of their own ideas. We challenge the belief that only the ideas of so-called experts have merit—a belief that reinforces dependency and compliance rather than shared values, creativity, and mutual, cooperative leadership. Locally generated knowledge has tremendous value: people are not only more committed to their actions when knowledge is connected to their own experiences, thoughts, and desires, but the actions themselves will become more relevant.

From this perspective, mutual learning is emphasized. Community workers are not positioned as "experts" but instead as partners in learning and acting. They help to create the process that leads to collective understanding and they participate along with others in using the products of that shared understanding. Though community workers and others with specialized knowledge and important lived experience do contribute their perspectives, a basic and necessary assumption is that every one of us has useful knowledge and insights (Lee & Todd, 2007).

One of the ways of doing this work is to develop "conscientiatization" a powerful, transformative, critical consciousness of the way the world works and of one's relationship to this world. Through this process, people, including community workers, come to see that the way things are is not necessarily the way things need to be. They are challenged to go beyond what they might have thought possible, creating a new awareness of what might be possible and what we might want to work toward (Freire 1973).

## HELPFUL WEBSITES

**Canadian Council for Refugees**

www.ccrweb.ca/documents/aopolicy.htm

The Canadian Council for Refugees is an umbrella organization focused on the protections of refugees and immigrants in Canada and around the world. Through he use of anti-oppressive perspectives they pay particular attention to issues of discrimination and systemic oppression affecting refugees and immigrants.

**National Anti-racism Council of Canada**

www.narcc.ca

The National Anti-racism Council of Canada is an organization working toward the elimination of discrimination based on racism and racialization. It works in partnership with other organizations across Canada. It strives to build networks that advocate for those affected by racialized social practices.

**Assembly of First Nations**

www.afn.ca

The Assembly of First Nations is an organization that defends the interest of Aboriginal people. The AFN represents all citizens regardless of age, gender, or place of residence.

CHAPTER THREE

# Understanding Community Change

**This chapter will help you better understand the following questions:**

- Why are guiding principles important for community practice?
- What is required for a community to be healthy?
- What are the different forms of capital that are important for communities?
- What are some of the common organizing models for community change?
- What are some of the key principles of community development as a model of practice?
- How does community change occur? What are some of the enabling factors for community change? What are some of the barriers to community change?

Theoretical frameworks provide guidance to help you understand what is going on when you engage in community work. In order to link broad theoretical frameworks with our everyday practice, we need principles that help us understand what practice looks like on the ground. Practice principles can direct our action for change, but they are like so many puzzle pieces scattered over the kitchen table. To begin to make some sense out of the emerging picture, it is often helpful to find those pieces with a straight side—the frame that holds the picture together. Practice frameworks for change provide guidance for understanding how you can promote action to change conditions that affect people. These practices do not reveal the whole picture, just its outlines and maybe a few central ideas that you can build around.

Practice principles help us to transfer our learning from one situation to another so we are not always making it up as we go along. Frankly, most of us do act in accordance with some theoretical approach and guiding principles. We just sometimes do not recognize this. This chapter invites you to bring your theoretical principles into the light so you are clearly aware of the ideas that guide your actions. This will make your actions more purposeful, and probably more effective. A solid awareness of your theoretical approach will help you to know what to expect and what you can do about it. A dynamic theory and practice relationship will encourage you to think about your practice so that you are always learning from your experiences. This, in turn, will strengthen your theory, which, in turn, will lead to better action. Theory devoid of action may be irrelevant. Action devoid of theory may be irrelevant as well.

## COMMUNITY PRACTICE AS POLITICAL PRACTICE FOR CHANGE

Community practice in social work in both anglophone and francophone Canada is as old as the notion of social welfare itself. Earlier forms of community practice included women's philanthropic work, the Settlement House Movement, and charity organization societies (Chen, 2005; McGrath, Moffatt, George, & Lee, 1999; Moffatt, 2001). Canadian community practice is rooted in, but not restricted to, Christian philanthropy, social mobilization theories, Marxism, utopianism, communitarianism, social science, popular education, conscientization, social gospel and liberation theology (Campfens, 1997; Moffatt, 2001). Canadian community practice is based on deeply felt beliefs and philosophical principles. The practice of community work is based on a tradition that is concerned with social justice and is driven by principles such as democratization and equality.

Community practice must be situated in the historical and social contexts that define the lived experience of the community—for example, Aboriginal communities' long history of colonialism and "cultural cleansing" has affected the numerous social problems that will require healing practices for a long time. As pointed out in the previous chapter, we must be careful that models of practice and theories of community change take into consideration the history of the community, especially when communities have experienced inequality due to gender, race, ability, class, or sexuality (McGrath et al., 1999). In fact, many communities within Canada have experienced some form of marginalization. The marginalization might result in limits on the social participation of the community and economic deprivation (Lee, 1999; Wharf, 2002; McGrath et al., 1999).

Shragge (2003) points out that some community development practices deal with change without also dealing with power relationships that affect the well-being and health of the community and that this makes the practices ineffective. Marginalized communities constantly have to resist the influence of external factors and social relations that limit the possibilities for full economic and cultural development. Community development as political practice should focus on challenging the status quo, since community is about shared helping, shared support, and shared resources in the face of inequitable relations (Shragge, 2003).

### Developing Inclusive Healthy Communities

Political action can involve community members and create a sense of belonging that in turn allows them to be included as decision makers. Change agents purposefully seek methods for including members in community benefits and community decision making. Communities must accept the challenge of accepting all of their members. This type of work for inclusion requires political processes within the community to work to change their biases and their sense of responsibility, and also to rethink their ideas about who is a rightful member of the community (and who is not). Inclusive communities provide mechanisms for affiliation, shared problem-solving, and mutual growth. They appreciate and celebrate differences. They recognize diversity as a resource, a richness, and a benefit. This means that as a community becomes more accepting, so too can the actual definition of the community change so that new people are welcomed within the community. This ability to welcome is an important marker of a healthy community.

Communities that turn to exclusivity as a response to difficulties are unhealthy. They find formal and informal ways to exclude those whose behaviours, appearances, or identities are different. They knowingly or unknowingly attempt to exclude members according to race, sexuality, gender, class, religion, or ability. Children with developmental disabilities are excluded from schools, racialized persons are discouraged from buying homes, and the encampments of "homeless" people are bulldozed. The rationalizations of exclusivity seek to protect privilege and keep the community from facing the very real challenges of inclusivity and power-sharing.

When community members consider only the limitations imposed by their problems, they are operating from a deficit model—a model that concentrate on things that are not working within the community, blaming those who are different for the social problems. This model is political in that it serves to reinforce outsiders' beliefs in the "sickness" or deficiencies of members of the community. At the same time, however, to be hopeful without having a good critical analysis of limitations can hurt members by having their hopes dashed. Community members can work to a politic of hope and possibility, without being naïve. Community members need to be aware of structural limitations, such as chronic unemployment, poor housing, and poor access to health services, that make it difficult for community members to improve their circumstances, so that they do not blame themselves when something seems impossible to accomplish.

A community that sustains positive connections among its members as well as with other sources of strength within the community, such as safe housing, natural resources, and social institutions like schools, is a healthy community. It also maintains connections outside of itself to access what the community needs: capital for economic development or new forms of art to engage the human spirit. Sustainable community development requires attention to the needs of the system as well as the interaction of the elements within the system to meet those needs (Scherch, 2000).

Faulty connections can weaken the community. Anything that restricts access to a needed resource represents a faulty connection. For example, inadequate public transportation systems can block members' access to employment, and forms of oppression like racism or heterosexism can interfere with relationships among people in a community (Berkman & Zinberg, 1997; DiAngelo, 1997; Dubois & Krogsrud-Miley, 2000). Policing that is not tied to the community needs and is biased in how certain community members are treated is a faulty connection. Connections to unsafe substances also weaken a community. A tainted water supply or an inadequate sewage system are two examples of these types of faulty connections. The ability of the community to meet its needs and manage its relationships with other communities and broader systems will affect the health and development of its individual members, which, in turn, will affect the overall health of the community (Netting, Kettner, & McMurtry, 1998).

## Take a Moment to Discover

As you drive around, ride the bus, or walk through your neighbourhood today, notice the people who are more or less pushed to the fringes of the community, those people who certainly are not the ones invited into the central life of the community. Who are they? How about that woman who is cursing at the cars, the trees, and the street signs as she pushes the shopping cart crammed with her life's possessions? How about the teenager hanging out at the mall? How about the thin sickly man who seems to be wandering? How about the person who asks you for change or a cigarette? What do you think about these people? How do you invite them in? How do you help to keep them away from the rest of us? What is all the security in some neighbourhoods, rental buildings, and condominiums all about? Are these people really a danger? Are there people in your workplace or where you go to school that you wish we could get rid of? Can you justify your feelings? Think about how you might sometimes justify excluding people based on how you think about them and how you characterize them—for example as dirty, unsafe, or rude.

## Different Forms of Capital

If community members are to fully participate in the decisions that affect and influence their well-being and to be involved in municipal, provincial, and federal democratic institutions, local mechanisms need to be developed. When community members can share their living circumstances and then share their discoveries with people within and outside of the community, the community is healthier (Bourdieu, 1986; McGrath et al., 1999). Through sharing among community members, broader issues of social and political importance can be analyzed, criticized, and better understood (Bishop, 1994, 2002; Lee, 1999).

Each community relies on different forms of capital to maintain itself and grow stronger. Daniels (2002) defines capital as "the stock of capacity to do something." A healthy community needs a sufficient supply of various forms of capital. Pretty (2000) has identified a number of sources of capital, including natural or environmental, physical, financial or economic, human, and social. Daniels (2002) adds political capital. The development and exchange of information adds another source of capital.

*Environmental capital* includes the natural features and resources of the area. *Physical capital* refers to things that have been added to the natural environment by human hands. This includes roads, buildings, and other forms of infrastructure. *Economic capital* comes in the form of financial wealth, as well as mechanisms for producing and exchanging things of monetary value. *Human capital* involves the storing of and access to the skills, talents, and health of the members of the community. *Political capital* involves access to the system of policy setting and enforcing in the community. *Information capital* is the generation, accumulation, storage, retrieval, and exchange of data, information, and knowledge. Research and educational activities help to provide information capital. *Social capital* is the system of community norms and interrelationships that produce trust, collaborative action, and community consciousness (Loxley, 2007).

Communities not only need all these forms of capital, but, just as importantly, they need community attitudes and practices that promote the *interaction* of these forms of capital. With its role in increasing connections among community members, social capital may be the key element in promoting the necessary interaction of community capital. A community rich in social capital will likely undertake efforts to develop other forms of capital that may be in short supply in the community. Because of its fundamental value to a community, this form of community wealth receives special attention.

*Social capital* refers to community resources derived from the active engagement of individuals with other members of the community and with what might be called "community life." These engagements provide opportunities for members to relate to each other, and these opportunities lead to benefits to the community as a whole. According to Putnam (1995), social capital "refers to the features of social organization such as networks, norms, and social trust that facilitate coordination and cooperation for mutual benefit" (p. 66). These features include civic enterprises such as street festivals, fall fairs, Meals on Wheels, and food and cultural events, as well as neighbourhood organizations, political party membership at the local level, and advocacy groups. Social capital could also include membership in groups like Parent-Teacher Associations, outdoor recreations groups, biking clubs, labour unions, or even choral societies (Putnam, 1993, 1995, 1996). In other words, we create social capital whenever we become involved with the affairs of our community and with one another in routine, often organized, ways.

High levels of social capital produce tremendous benefits in the form of increased trust, networks of coordination and communication, social participation, civic engagement, and resolution of common problems. It also discourages exploitive opportunism as the members' sense of self expands from "I" to "we." Successes from civic engagement provide encouragement for shared efforts and models for future collaboration.

In communities that have strong social bonding and are rich in social capital, members pitch in to solve common problems (Herbert, 1996). Governance structures and other social institutions function better. Life is simply easier (Putnam, 1995). In contrast, communities in which the stock of social capital is low may cope by believing that community affairs are somebody else's problem. People feel powerless and exploited, and even representative government works less well (Putnam, 1993).

Social capital is a source of fundamental strength for the community. It is a resource that actually grows as it is used and becomes depleted if not used. Rossiter, Blocki-Radeke, Daley, and Eisenstat's (2006) discussion of "wraparound services" points out that the creation of strong social ties at the community level in a marginalized urban neighbourhood, Toronto's Jane-Finch neighbourhood, has been a tremendous aid to youths who have been removed from the school system. The social capital often provided in a school setting can be replaced by carefully considered social structures and constructed relations promoted by community change agents. These new structures of relating are also a form of social capital.

The presence of social capital can help to sustain a community's norms. Unfortunately, these norms may include intolerance, oppression, and authoritarian rigidity (Coleman, 1993; Portes & Landolt, 1996; Putnam, 1996). In a closed community, these attitudes are difficult to change. Communities open up to new information and ideas, and intolerance is challenged. No community is homogeneous, so members need to challenge when social bonding excludes and oppresses certain members of the community.

Communities marked by a lack of social connectedness fail to meet the needs of their members, who can end up living in fear and pessimism. Putnam (1993) cautions, "Social capital is not a substitute for effective public policy but rather a prerequisite for it and, in part, a consequence of it" (p. 42). Agents of community change must be willing to use social capital to promote a synergy among local nonprofit organizations, social structures, and government (Fosler, 2002).

The discussion of social capital has spawned vigorous debate regarding its form, function, measurement, and even its very existence (Portes, 1998). Putnam (2000) continues to explore questions to further our understanding. What kinds of civic involvement are most helpful? What other forms of civic engagement are developing? Is social capital created and destroyed, or does it just change form? How can we build (or rebuild) more? Is social capital similar to other forms of wealth that can be concentrated in fewer hands to promote inequality (McClenaghan, 2000)? The answers to these questions will guide policymakers, professionals, and private citizens to recognize opportunities for promoting interactions that enhance the healthy functioning of communities.

### Take a Moment to Discover

Most of us are engaged in our communities in a manner that is different from the way our parents were. Yet some of us are beginning to value a life more connected to a community of people outside our work. What do you notice about your own contributions to social capital? How many organizations do you participate in? Are some of those organizations organized around identity rather than the local neighbourhood? When was the last time you went to a community meeting that was not required by your work? How often do you vote? Do you shop at stores that are locally owned or do you spend your time and dollars at one of those huge merchandise warehouses owned by a national chain? Are public affairs somebody else's business, maybe the politicians'?

## Community Capacity and Asset Building

McKnight and Kretzman (1988) have introduced a concept of "community intervention" that builds on the concept of social capital. In their attempt to challenge a tendency to focus only on community problems, they propose that we focus on what they call "capacities" in communities. Rather than perceiving community members as people in need, they are seen as resources who have assets, skills, and the capacity to resolve their own difficulties. In this case, the success of community development is tied to the local community initiatives and investments. Faced with the withdrawal of resources from the community, the community must develop its own resources.

Community intervention is based on something called "asset-mapping," which outlines the capacities within the community that are also controlled by community members. Assets can be considered to be the individual qualities and traits of persons, such as skills and experience, or organizational assets, such as voluntary associations, citizen groups, and religious and cultural groups. In addition, McKnight and Kretzman (1988) consider assets within the community that are controlled by outsiders, such as private businesses, nonprofit organizations, and public institutions, such as schools and hospitals. Finally, the community practitioner needs to consider resources originating outside of the community that are controlled by outsiders and that influence the community. To begin the process of community building, an organization focused on asset development needs to be located within the community itself. The individuals associated with the asset development organization engage the community in planned change. The process is akin to building communities "from the inside out." Beginning with community assets and capacities, the organizers also consider those persons and entities that influence the community even if they are not part of the community. In Canada, we have critiqued the assets model because it is too easy to assume that communities work on their own and are healthy simply if they develop their own assets. An important principle of community practice in Canada has been to ensure the responsibility of the state to local communities and differing regions of Canada. So, if one focuses only on the assets of the community, the change agent might forget to also make accountable those outside the community who influence its well-being. Assets building is effective only if those with power outside the community who influence the community, such as municipal, provincial, and national governments, provide adequate resources to the community and when those outside the community take its needs seriously (McGrath et al., 1999).

## Organizing Models for Community Change

Rothman's (1968) model of community practice is considered to be a classic model and is often cited for its simplicity. A number of authors still agree that this model is a good starting point for understanding community practice (Hardcastle & Powers, 2004; Shragge, 2003). Rothman defines three forms of community practice: locality development, social action, and social planning.

*Locality development* happens at the neighbourhood level, where people work together cooperatively to solve local problems. This local action is taken in cooperation with those in power who can influence the well-being of the community. Rothman (1968) explains that locality development involves "broad participation of a wide spectrum of people at the local community level in goal determination and action" (p. 23). This process emphasizes economic and social progress. It is intended that a "wide range of community people [are] involved in determining their 'felt' needs and solving their own problems" (p. 30).

*Social action* is based on the assumption that individuals and groups are oppressed by structural inequalities. In this case, community members engage in active protests and demonstrations to promote change. Social action methods seek more fundamental changes to social structures, organizations, and economic systems. They presuppose "a disadvantaged segment of the population that needs to be organized ... [in order] to make adequate demands on the larger community ... making basic changes in major institutions or community practices" (p. 24). The types of changes sought through social action are a redistribution of power and the reallocation of resources.

The third type of practice, *social planning*, is based on a rational approach to practice. Bureaucrats, technocrats, and experts—usually external to the community—base community solutions on facts pursued through research and logical evaluation. Rothman (1968) tells us that the social planning approach "emphasizes a technical process of problem-solving with regard to substantive social problems, such as delinquency, housing, and mental health" (p. 24). This model envisions that change occurring in a complex world calls for deliberate steps that are clearly defined and laid out. Such efforts require expert planners to guide changes through a maze of bureaucratic barriers with the intention of "establishing, arranging, and delivering goods and services to people who need them" (p. 24).

Expanding on these models for community organization practice, Rothman and Tropman (1987) suggest policy practice and administrative practice as additional approaches for enacting or managing change at the broad level. Further, they suggest that we often need to blend models when acting in the real world.

*Policy practice* involves identifying, analyzing, refining or developing, and implementing policies that guide the operations of government and nongovernment organizations that have an impact on individuals, groups, and communities.

*Administrative practice* involves organizational development and manipulation, including some of the following abilities and activities: assessing community needs, designing programs, maintaining community relationships, and facilitating consensus among organizational constituencies. The administrator guides the processes by which service organizations order and arrange their activities and resources to accomplish their missions.

Kramer and Specht (1983) describe two basic approaches to community organization that they term "community development" and "social planning." *Community development* methods work directly with the people who are feeling the problem to mobilize them to take action. Social action activities are included under community development in this model. Kramer and Specht note that "a typical feature of such efforts is their concern with building new organizations among people who have not been previously organized to take social action on a problem" (pp. 15–16).

Kramer and Specht further explain that "a major feature of this model is that the action system is composed of people who are legally and structurally tied to community agencies and organizations, and their behaviour is regulated and guided by these commitments" (p. 16).

The problem with such broad models as those discussed above is that in reality communities vary by culture, interest, geography, and a host of other factors. It is difficult, therefore, to capture the best way to promote change in simple models when in fact a multitude of variables affect communities.

Rothman's model has been criticized for oversimplifying processes of social change. Canadian authors and community workers have also been keenly aware that it is difficult to separate elements of practice when such elements are blended or work in conjunction with each other (Lee, 1999; Wharf & Clague, 1997). In fact, Canadian approaches to practice are more apt to consider organizing based on social location and identity central to community practice (Lee, 1999; Wharf & Clague, 1997). A group

| Rothman and Tropman | Locality Development | Social Planning | Social Action | Policy Practice | Administrative Practice |
|---|---|---|---|---|---|
| | • Self-help<br>• Emphasizes economic and social progress<br>• Orientation to power structure: partners | • Rational, technical problem-solving<br>• Social problem focus<br>• Orientation to power structure: sponsors | • Redistribution of power and resources<br>• Deals with justice issues<br>• Orientation to power structure: target/oppressors | • Management of policy process<br>• Development or change of policies<br>• Orientation to power structure: varies | • Improve functions of organization<br>• Organizational goals, strategies, and program concerns<br>• Orientation to power structure: varies |

| Kramer and Specht | Community Development | Social Planning |
|---|---|---|
| | • Mobilizing "victims" of community conditions<br>• Building new organizations<br>• Action oriented | • Coordinates efforts of agencies<br>• Changes in agency attitudes, structure, and so on<br>• Workers tied to agencies |

| Rubin and Rubin | Self-Help | Partnership | Coproduction | Pressure | Protest |
|---|---|---|---|---|---|
| Issue-based or Area-based | • Deal with internal problems<br>• Service to community<br>• Little outside help | • Community-defined problems<br>• Receive outside help | • Community takes over<br>• Government functions<br>• Some community decision making | • Community-defined issues<br>• Use conventional approaches<br>• Government policy<br>• Change concerns | • Economic and political change<br>• Wide range of tactics<br>• Force opponents to agree |

**Problem Focus, Power Focus, or Development Focus**

**FIGURE 3.1** Models for Community Change

of Canadian researchers—George et al. (2009), Lee (2008), and Shragge (2003)—who looked at practices in marginalized communities in Canada have come up with additional principles of practice. They argue for the addition of the practice concepts of negotiation, representation, education, and resistance. See Figure 3.1 for the traditional models of Community change. These practice principles acknowledge that usually the communities we work with have to deal with difficult relations with people outside the community. Since the processes of marginalization are ongoing and pervasive, so too the practice is always based on an awareness of these processes and acts to work to counter them.

*Negotiation.* Community change agents are constantly negotiating with respect to money, relationships, and services. Practitioners also negotiate within and outside the community in trying to access information, assistance, support, and resources for the people with whom they work. Negotiation involves complex activities aimed at the various groups and agencies within the community as well as at outside agencies such as government.

*Representation.* Community change agents represent or are the face of their members to the larger community. Participants describe multiple functions of representation, including it being a vehicle for accountability, education, networking, advocacy, and ensuring the voices of community members are heard.

*Education.* Education is as an integral component of the work of community change agents. While representing their organizations and needs of the community members within the larger communities and while dealing with community members, the change agents educate people about the special conditions, including the history, of their community and the processes of community marginalization.

*Resistance.* Resistance involves those activities that are defined by a sense of a strong commitment to struggle and a refusal by community change agents to give in to the forces that they see positioned against the community they work with. A big element of resistance is to insist that the community is working to better itself and give the message to those who have prejudicial feelings about the community that the community continues to work and to thrive and is not going to disappear or go away.

George et al. (2009) agree with the above findings, especially the practice principle of resistance. They discovered that resistance was so important among community change agents in India, where globalization has a tremendous effect on local communities, that it could be described as an overriding principle of practice. Within this principle, important practices include the dual focus on capacity building and the consciousness of globalization; work across various sectors to address needs of community members; political strategies of building broad-based opposition movements; and working with global networks. Since the battle against globalization that hurts impoverished communities is going to be long, the forms of resistance are creative and include performance, entertainment, and philosophical discussion. Resistance is tied to education from the perspective of educating community members that the fight may be long and that they should not blame themselves for global forces.

Minkler and Wallerstein (1997) note that the reliance on locality development and social planning does not reflect community organizing in diverse and marginalized groups. These communities often organize in a manner that is not tied to a local neighbourhood. At the same time, they cannot always trust external experts, who at times have given bad advice to the community by not being sensitive to the many distinct experiences of the community.

Shragge (2003) reconceptualized practices for community change so that community practice can be imagined as a range of practices—sometimes overlapping—from community development to community action. Practice ranges from approaches that encourage integration to those that are conflict oriented.

Rubin and Rubin (1986) focus on diversity in community practice by describing five types of community organizations: self help, partnership, co-production, pressure, and protest organizations.

- *Self-help organizations* identify a problem, recruit members, and provide a service with minimal help from, or interaction with, outside agencies.
- *Partnership organizations* are developed by community members who themselves define which problems to address. These organizations often rely on outside financial assistance.
- *A co-production* indicates that community organizations undertake, with governments, activities that in the past were carried out only by government agencies.
- *Pressure organizations* choose their own issues but try to work within the

conventional rules of government in order to persuade politicians and bureaucrats to change their policies.
- *Protest organizations* usually want to bring about a change in the economic or political system and often work outside conventional rules.

Rubin and Rubin distinguish between issue-based and area-based organizations. "Issue-based organizations focus on a particular issue of concern to a number of people, regardless of where they live and work. An area-based organization focuses on a particular area, such as a neighbourhood, dealing with a variety of problems that affect that particular area" (p. 9).

Bill Lee's (2008) conceptualization of community practice and community research is most useful to understanding community practice from a Canadian perspective. He focuses on community practice that considers diversity, he is concerned with power relations, and he focuses on practices not only within the community but outside of it as well. Figure 3.2 presents Lee's model, in which he captures some of the roles and responsibilities of community practice without imagining them as totally separate. Lee also cautions against practice that occurs too much outside of the interests and culture of community. The advantage of his frame is that the practitioners' role is not solely imagined as working with a neighbourhood or geographically bound area. Although it can apply to geography, it can also be applied to communities of identity in a sensitive manner.

Communities can benefit from any method that addresses community issues in a way that recognizes the capabilities and rights of its members. So there is no one "best" approach for all circumstances. Having said that, we would like to advance the idea that strategies that draw from community development philosophy and practices generally hold a greater likelihood of promoting the health of communities.

## Key Principles of Community Development as a Model of Practice

Community development promotes the recognition, acquisition, maturation, and connection of community assets to benefit the whole. The belief that members of the community itself have the primary responsibility for decision making and action is a fundamental principle of this approach to practice. Community development produces self-reliant, self-sustaining communities that mobilize resources for the benefit of all their members.

One of the notions of community development is the building of community capacity: its ability to store and make use of forms of power or wealth—particularly knowledge and skill (Delgado, 2000). A community (or an individual) with increased capacity knows more things, can do more things, can do them better, and is able to retain all of this for easy access while expanding its potential for continued growth. Increased capacity leads to increased efficacy, which is the ability to produce a desired result or accomplish what you intend to accomplish. It also increases the motivation to set and achieve goals.

Communities that have increased capacity and efficacy are under less stress and are less likely to act or in ways that harm relationships. Their abilities to discover, create, and mobilize resources—both internal and external—to meet their needs prevents or reduces the likelihood that they will engage in harmful or destructive activities. If communities can get what they need through healthy methods, they are less likely to get them in unhealthy ways. And if they continue to increase their abilities, they get even more of their needs met and increase their confidence that they can, in fact, do so. This encourages the community to continue to work to meet its needs and further develop its capacities.

A community functions around certain activities in order to meet its needs. Among

| Informing Elements | Practice on Communities | Practice for Communities | Practice with Communities |
|---|---|---|---|
| Practice relation | Subject/object<br>Power over<br>Exclusionary | Collaborative (with power mostly with practitioner) | Collaborative<br>Dialogical<br>Reciprocal |
| Purpose | Produce new knowledge<br>Determine the truth about the community | Action for community benefit | Community action<br>Skill development<br>Develop and share community's knowledge<br>Sustainable empowerment |
| Community practice role | Academic<br>Expert technicism | Facilitator<br>Advocate | Popular educator<br>Organizer<br>Co-learner |
| Role within the community | Information provider | Collaborator<br>Client | Popular educator<br>Collaborator<br>Co-learner |
| Locus of decision-making power | Community worker | Community worker<br>Advocate/solidarity group | Shared with community members |
| Ethical issues | Informed consent<br>Minimal social change | Informed consent<br>Accurate representation<br>Appropriation of voice | Broad communication with community<br>Informed consent |
| Dilemmas/dangers | Misrepresentation of voice<br>Perpetuation of oppressive relations<br>Reproduction and legitimization of existing social order | Lack of awareness of other point of view<br>Appropriation of voice<br>Limited interaction between decision maker and community<br>Reproduction and legitimization of existing social order | Lack of awareness of points of view<br>Manipulation of the agenda of marginalized persons<br>Fully equal partnership is impossible<br>New and unexpected risks to community in the light of change |
| Benefits | Based on time and monetary constraints<br>Knowledge creation | Knowledge transfer<br>Increased resources and funding | Knowledge transfer<br>Community empowerment<br>Anti-oppression |

**FIGURE 3.2** Concepts of Community Research and Practice

Source: Adapted from Bill Lee, "Will the Real Community Research Please Stand Up? Some critical issues", *Canadian Social Work Review,* Volume 25, Number 1 (2008), Table 1, p. 16. Used by permission.

these basic needs are environmental needs, physical needs, economic needs, political needs, education and information needs, and social and emotional needs. Although each of these aspects of community functioning can be the focus of development efforts, community development usually takes one of three broad forms: economic development, physical development, or social development.

*Economic development* is concerned with the production of goods and services for generating and distributing financial wealth. This includes increasing the diversity and number of jobs or other income-producing activities. *Physical development* addresses the quality and number of the more tangible elements of a community, such as its roads, housing, sewers, sidewalks, or even landscape features. *Social development* strengthens what might be called the community's social infrastructure. This involves expanding its network of relationships, improving interaction among its members, bringing people together to prevent or solve community problems, enlarging the pool of talent and knowledge, and promoting member contributions to the common good. Taken together, they all advance the health of the community by promoting its capacity to provide for its members and create conditions that enhance the quality of life.

## Elements of Community Development Practice

We should take a closer look at the elements of community development. Some of these elements can be found in the work of Brueggemann (2002), Burkey (1993), Ghorayshi, Graydon, and Kliewer (2007), Kretzman and McKnight (1993), McKnight (1995), and Ronnby (1995, 1996, 1998).

*Build on Community Assets.* Resources are what a community has going for itself. Problems or unmet needs can be springboards to action, but action occurs through the use of resources. The simple act of recognizing assets energizes a community and gives it a sense of confidence and a willingness to take action. When the community believes that assets exist, it finds them and uses them. This principle affects the entire manner in which you, as a change agent, look at a community and decide what to do.

*Increase Skills of Individuals.* Change agents purposefully teach media-relations skills, fundraising skills, group meeting skills, computer skills, and a host of other important skills in order to increase the confidence of the community in addressing future situations with competence. Potency and competency are related concepts. Also important is the members' belief in their ability to teach new skills to other community members.

*Connect People with One Another.* The community development process builds relationships and shares talents, information, work, and energy—everything happens through relationships. Connecting people with one another in a purposeful manner produces clear, intended benefits. However, unintended, serendipitous benefits can also be most intriguing. A fundamental question for practice is "Which people should we be talking to?" Once this question becomes a habit, members will expect to build new relationships and will look forward to doing so.

In the early stages of organization, community members tend to funnel communication through the person who has initiated the organizing action or through a few other visible leaders. This is natural and understandable. These individuals are common points of contact, and they generally convey some degree of confidence. It is easy to reinforce this process in many subtle ways. It is also very limiting to the organization if this pattern persists. Patterns that promote less hierarchical or centralizing relationships increase strength over time.

*Connect Existing Resources.* Any project requires the assembly of resources, and it is rare to find them all in one place. Yet the notion that "we can't do it because we don't have..." commonly stalls the development of good ideas. Assume two things. One, the group attempting to bring something to life does not have everything it needs. Two, most of what is needed can be found in the community. Any enterprise in your community, public or private, profit or volunteer, is a resource. Special interests or hobbies are resources, and so are trees and water or a parcel of land.

Whenever you connect resources, you create investors. You extend ownership and participation in the project, broadening its base of support. By connecting resources, you get the things that you need, but perhaps more importantly, you connect more people to what you are doing and why.

*Create or Increase Community Resources.* Community development adds to the community's stock of routinely available assets. Look beyond solving an immediate problem with an eye to bringing something new into existence that will continue to benefit the community. A child care cooperative, a water well, a basketball court, a social club, an art class, a choir, a new business, a tree-lined street—all enrich the community.

*Community Assumes Ownership of Direction, Action, and Resources.* Community members do not just approve plans, they create them. Community members do not just provide input, they make decisions. The community decides what to do and how to do it. What they produce is theirs.

*Promote the Expectation That Community Members Will Do Work Too.* We more fully value the things that we create, and we learn much better the things we do for ourselves. Here is an example from very basic community development to illustrate this point.

Too often, we train people for dependency, helplessness, and hopelessness. We train them to believe that they cannot do things themselves. We usually do this in unthinking kindness—in the name of helping. But always be careful when expecting community members to work that there are structural relationships that make it difficult for members to do the work. Do not add to the oppression by telling them to it themselves in this case!

*Create Beneficial External Relationships.* Each community has a tremendous amount of undiscovered assets, but it is likely that it will still need to draw in more resources from outside its boundaries. It may need to ally with other communities in order to increase power. It may need to draw support from public sources. It may need to create economic enterprises that attract new dollars into its economy. Some specialized talents or particular materials may need to be imported.

Constructive relationships help to promote an exchange of resources between the community and others, and they provide for collaborative partnerships among different communities for mutual benefit. Maintaining wider relationships

Photos.com

**Although community work can be demanding, there are rewards and opportunities for celebration.**

also creates opportunities to influence external forces that affect the community.

*Foster Community Confidence.* All these actions help a community to believe in itself and its abilities. It forgets how to back down and back away. When confronted with a challenge, members of the community assume they can figure out what to do and do it. Also, they believe they will be able to meet other challenges that come their way.

*Build Self-Sustaining Organizations.* For a community to continue to grow in strength, a mechanism for community decision making and action must be maintained. A community must continue to develop new leadership, extend connections to new members, and maintain existing ones. It is more likely to do this by remaining active, by taking on new challenges from time to time. The organization takes care of itself as it takes care of community issues.

*Enhance the Quality of Life.* Community development strives to move past problems, to believe that better is possible—it is even likely, it is certainly deserved, and it can be expected.

## Social Action and Community Development

Development activities enable a community to move forward on community-building activities. Yet on some occasions, community groups need to first secure rights or opportunities that are being denied to them. Groups frequently need to go through a period of social action to assert the case for communities whose members have been exploited or ignored by powerful interests from outside the immediate community. In these situations, the conflict-oriented strategies typical of social action may be needed to initiate a change in the wider

### • CHANGE AGENT TIP

Promoting community change goes beyond simply solving a problem or changing a circumstance. It extends to developing the capacity of the community to recognize conditions that need to be changed as well as the willingness and the ability to act. As change agents and community members, consider how the answers to these questions can inform your decisions and actions as you move toward change.

1. Is there an identified community? If so, who has defined it? How is it defined? If not, is one identifiable?
2. Does the project build the skills of community members? Can these be identified?
3. Does the project produce new leaders and new teachers? What processes are intended to produce new leaders and new teachers? That is, what intentional steps will be taken?
4. Who owns the project? How is this seen? Who holds decision-making authority? If ownership is external, what processes are in place to transfer ownership to the members of the community? Which members?
5. Does the project produce new community resources that can exist apart from the project or after the intended life of the project? How will this occur?
6. Do the benefits or resources created by the project in turn create new benefits or resources?
7. Which community capacities or assets will the project build on? How will these be expanded by the project?
8. Which community conditions does the project intend to change?
9. How does the project promote inclusivity?
10. How does the project build social capital?
11. How does the project acknowledge and meet system needs?

community that recognizes and responds to the rights of the close community. In fact, a community group may need to engage in an extended period of social action before it can direct significant attention to development efforts. The conflict period can be followed by transition stages during which the group moves into more collaborative or developmental approaches.

Social action can bring issues to light and an organization to life, but the community may become stuck there—developing its conflict skills, but little else. To become truly empowered, a community must move beyond reaction to assert its own agenda, cultivating the internal assets that can provide its members with a high quality of life. It needs to become self-directing, self-evaluating, and self-renewing. Some aspect of community development work must take place very early in the organization's life for three reasons. First, many members of the community will shy away from a conflict agenda. However, these individuals still care about the community and want to contribute in some way. Development activities provide an opportunity to help. Second, development activities provide visible signs that the community intends to thrive and is doing so. These indicators become sources of encouragement and pride. Third, development activities create new resources and promote investment. These solidify the community's foundation and strengthen its ability to engage in conflict while discouraging the opposition.

Even though a community may move from confrontation to development, it may need to invoke conflict strategies from time to time to prevent exploitation, to gain access to resources to which it has a rightful claim, or to bring a sense of drama to boost interest. The more a community is developed, the stronger it becomes and the less vulnerable it is to external threats. Well-organized neighbourhoods that have constructively developed their internal assets often find it easier to get their fair share of resources and therefore are rarely targeted as dumping grounds.

Conflict may be necessary because you cannot pursue opportunities if you cannot exercise your rights. Being concerned with people's rights is the starting point, but we must also pay attention to people's abilities and responsibilities. Many advocates—often those from outside the community—miss this point. Treating people as needy rather than as able and responsible is demeaning, disrespectful, and patronizing.

### Action

Community change occurs only through action, and actions can occur only when a certain number of preconditions exist. Actions that promote community change are intended to provoke a response from other people. It is the response that actually sets in motion the process of change.

There must be a tension between discomfort with the current situation and attraction to a new situation. People will act for change only if they are uncomfortable enough with the current circumstances or excited enough by a new possibility. Otherwise, they will maintain the status quo—even if they spend a lot of time complaining about it. Over time, a community can grow accustomed to its discomfort, even growing to tolerate incrementally increasing levels of frustration. A change agent may well act to stoke irritations so that members can break out of their passive acceptance of harmful circumstances.

Taking action requires a belief in the possibility that action will produce a successful outcome. Only in extreme circumstances of duress will people act with little hope that they can be successful. More commonly, we do things only if we think we have some chance of accomplishing what we intend. Whether we are giving up smoking, learning to use a new technology, or fighting city hall, we will choose to do nothing if we think we will not succeed. There has to be some reasonable chance for success.

Recognition of a course of action must be present before action can take place. People may be prepared to act, and be willing to act, but not know how to act. One of the most frustrating experiences is wanting to do something but not knowing what to do. In an emergency situation, people can feel helpless even though they are highly motivated to act. For an action to occur, it has to exist in the awareness of the people who must act. Unless you can see what to do, you cannot do it. Further, appropriate strategies and tactics for acting must be available and recognized.

The credibility of the organizers of the effort, the validity of the issue, and the sustainability of the organization must be strong for action to continue. People commit to and respond only to things they believe are real. A sufficient degree of credibility will always be a precursor to the next level of action. The organization must continually meet spoken and unspoken tests of credibility prior to any action being taken.

Action requires a sufficient degree of emotion. Intellectual understanding is insufficient for action. There has to be some level of feeling—joy, anger, excitement, frustration. A change agent must do more than provide information. He or she must arouse feelings, particularly an enthusiasm for action. Negative residue will be a disincentive for action. If a history of failed attempts precedes the current change effort, the organizers will have an added, invisible barrier to overcome. Perception of a threat is a strong motivator for action. Such perception constitutes a particular form of discomfort with the current situation. The belief that a loss will occur if no action is taken will provoke action. The more imminent the threat, the more readily people will be moved to act.

Each new level of an organization's action requires renewed commitment and conviction. Though past success can bring confidence, each new level presents not only a new condition but also uncertainty and other forms of resistance that new conditions bring. Successful action can motivate for new action—or it can lead to complacency.

## How Oppression Affects Change

Actions involved in promoting community change must take into account the perceptions, experiences, values, and norms of the people affected by the change. Cultural values determine what is of importance, what has meaning, and what has worth. Cultural norms describe which behaviours are permissible and which are not permissible.

The perception of reality is culturally bound and is socially constructed by experiences, interactions, and the meanings attached to those experiences. The stronger one's identity with a group, the more powerful that group will be in moulding perception. The way we perceive our world affects how we relate to it and how we interpret the responses that we get from our actions, influencing the future actions that we will take. People's experiences are constructed by social experiences of oppression based on race, gender, sexual orientation, class, and how they are tied to full citizenship. Too often, individuals are excluded from full participation in the social benefits of being a Canadian based on their social location (revisit Chapter 2 for the definition of social location). It is key to community practice to understand that much daily and structural exclusion happens socially.

Any person participates within a number of different communities—ethnic, religious, professional, geographic, and so on—and each of these groups will influence the person to varying degrees. People often do not think about the fact that they are using their own cultural frameworks as the starting point for analysis and action—organizers included. Interpretation of events is a product of group influence, including the group's historical interpretations. As a community organizer, it is important for you to remember that dominant discourses of whiteness, heterosexism, classism, and racism make invisible dominant norms that we consider to be general and accepted by everybody, making us act in oppressive ways. More continued and intense exposure to a group's belief system will more firmly shape the individual's perception, as will exposure to the rituals that support the belief system and reinforce group membership and identity.

## Change

Change is inevitable and ongoing. Change occurs when a sufficient number of forces heading in a similar direction coalesce. This not only provides energy for change, but it attracts and develops new energy as well. Skillful and purposeful action can accelerate the pace of change and influence its nature and direction.

Change requires a sufficiently receptive environment. Almost any system will accept minor, incremental change, as long as adaptations to the change do not require a troubling expense, including allocation of time or money, or new behaviours. These changes occur almost without notice. Over time, these adaptations will lead to a changed system. However, if the desired change attracts or requires more attention from the system, it must receive active support from enough of the system for change to occur. This means that a sufficient number of system elements care enough to support the change in order to overcome the opposition or the inertia of the status quo. The entire system need not be supportive. If the system is hostile, the change will not take root. Trying to force the change will provoke insurmountable resistance. The conditions must first be altered in order to make change more palatable.

There will always be resistance to change. Resistance comes from many sources. These can be internal, such as doubt, ingrained habits, rationalization of the benefit of the status quo, or even a lack of belief in one's own rights. They can also be external when the change requires that others behave differently. External actors also are plagued with doubts, habits, rationalizations, and lack of belief in the rights of those seeking the change. External resistance is heightened when these others feel that a change transgresses prior agreements or results in a loss of power, control, or access to other valued resources. The degree of resistance relates to the number of adaptations that need to be made and who needs to make them. These adaptations can require building new relationships, acquiring new competencies, assuming new attitudes and beliefs, or rejecting conditions that the actor has helped to create.

Temporary change is more readily accepted. Over time, change that continues to make demands on the system may come to be resisted. Change requires agreement to new structures and allocation of new resources or reallocation of existing ones. Until these agreements are in place and routine, the reality of change is not necessarily secure.

Close communities are collections of people, larger than our family and immediate circle of friends, to whom we generally relate and from whom we draw identity and meaning. The problems and benefits of these communities most noticeably affect us, and we and our immediate associates can have at least some degree of influence in regard to these factors. These communities are close to us, hence the term, and may be our small town or the part of a large city in which we live. We all belong to several close communities—they include our place of work, the school we attend, our local professional association, or our faith community. Close communities provide the most likely arena for community change activities.

Two benefits accrue from a focus on close communities. First, it is easier to mobilize for action. Precisely because we can have an impact on these communities, we are more likely to engage in purposeful action to improve conditions there. We already have relationships with a number of other community members; action

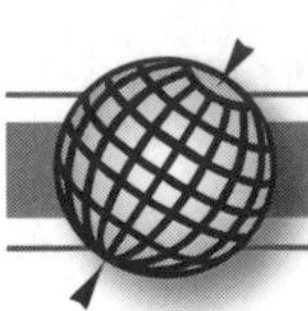

## GLOBAL PERSPECTIVES

NEW ZEALAND—[The European concept of social capital separates family from community.] In contrast, the Maori concept of family (*whanau*) moves seamlessly from the immediate family to the wider family network (*hapu*) and the tribe (*iwi*), where the (extended) family becomes the community and the community is made up of the (extended) family. Social capital is created through networks and relationships that are within all of these expressions of "family" (or community). Thus, in the Maori context, the distinction between cultural and social capital disappears. Cultural capital is an important aspect of social capital, and social capital is an expression of cultural capital in practice. Social capital is based on and grows from the norms, values, networks and ways of operating that are the core of cultural capital.

Membership in customary Maori associations is based on an exchange of obligations and acceptance by the group. The concept of obligation-driven membership includes obligations based on a common ancestry and the cultural dimension that obliges one to act in certain ways. This sense of obligation underpins a Maori concept of voluntary activity. Key concepts of Maori society that relate to social capital include *manaaki* (cultural obligation to welcome and care for visitors), *hapai* (the requirement to apply the concept of uplifting/enhancement), and *tautoko* (providing support within the community) (Robinson & Williams, 2001, pp. 55–56).

INDIA—[Narender Bedi of the Young India Project states that] the way we grow stronger is by spreading our ideology so that potential members really understand what we are about. We need more ideological members because they will fight for the organization and stay with us over the long term. Benefit members, who join only for concrete benefits like new homes, will leave soon after they get what they want (as cited in Mediratta & Smith, 2002, p. 34).

SERBIA—Women at Work['s] aim is to facilitate women strengthening and defining their own economic networks. They do this by

- Creating a directory listing the many skills and businesses by women in a specific area,
- Broadening the income-generating capacities and funding base of local women's groups,
- Coordinating the means of communicating women's economic initiatives in a newsletter,
- Increasing information exchange by organizing the first comprehensive mailing list for women's initiatives,
- Organizing non-traditional skills training: the first home repair workshops for women. (Women at Work, 2002, p. 1)

within this community close at hand is simply more relevant. Second, transforming our close communities holds the promise for transforming the society of which they are a part. The whole is benefited when people are encouraged to strengthen its parts. Two significant dangers exist with this focus on close communities. First, we may divorce ourselves from the struggles and the hopes of other communities or fail to recognize that a number of issues cross community lines. Second, while working to strengthen the close community, we may engage in a perceived gain that is only temporary if we do not link our work to larger forces that shape the conditions within which we are acting (Forrest & Kearns, 2001; Wiborg, 1998). Combining our work with other local change agents can create a collective awareness and fashion the underpinnings for broader action. As examples, capital punishment, air quality, or welfare reform transcend distinct communities.

Addressing these issues requires an alliance of communities. Even though the focus of our action on broader issues may more effectively take place in the context of our close community, the power of our action increases when we ally our efforts with those of other communities.

For smaller local communities such as neighbourhoods to assist one another, governing structures that promote a healthy interconnectedness among communities are necessary. Change agents must overcome attitudes that local communities can ignore one another without consequence or that local benefits result only from a competition of local interests. These attitudes are ultimately destructive, reducing the flow of resources and increasing the possibility of surrender of local control through manipulation. The notion of community change may seem so big and intimidating that potential change agents do not consider its value or its possibility. However, by initiating community change in our close communities, we begin to see its benefits.

## Issues Affecting Change

In addition to the broad previous discussion, through experience, you will discover numerous supporting notions that will inform your understanding of how things work. Three of these deal with conflict, crisis, and relationships—matters which all change agents encounter. Take a closer look.

*Conflict Affects Commitment to Organizing for Change.* Before a group can begin to work together, it must be able to work together. Standing disagreements, jealousies, and rivalries cannot coexist with a commitment to work for change. How many times have you seen this in a family, a group working on a class assignment, or an office staff?

The presence of conflict will erode commitment and eat away at the foundation for building a better future. This is less a problem when the competing groups face a common enemy. That shared interest in an opponent will move antagonisms to the background, but they will still be there. Though the parties may temporarily set differences aside, they remain, lurking beneath the surface. The fear and mistrust are never too far from the work. Resources are warily shared, and the awareness of a temporary truce weakens the relationships on which success depends. If the common enemy appears to be getting the upper hand, competing groups may turn on each other in frustration and blame, becoming unwitting accomplices with their opponent. Although development activities can help to bring people together, if conflict levels are too high, the development or community change work can exacerbate conflicts. If development activities are to be a form of conflict reduction, even resolution, the parties involved must recognize and agree to this strategy. Otherwise, they will undermine the effort to confirm their perceptions and positions. That initial agreement itself requires some reduction in conflict.

But, at the same time, because we know that communities are so complex, we must know that a certain level of disagreement or conflict may persist within a community. This may be a good quality because it may mean that your community is diverse in its social location and opinion. In this case, you do not want conflict to go away; rather, as a change agent, you will negotiate the tensions to allow the group to move ahead.

*Crisis Can Contribute to Community Action.* A crisis, a sudden and overwhelming onset of threats, can often be a catalyst for change. The world has suddenly changed, and the community must change as well. Old patterns and perceptions seem irrelevant or inadequate. Something different must be put in place. Crises wrench a community from its inattention and ignorance. The violent death of a popular high school student. The discovery of e. coli bacteria in the town's water supply. The world as we believed it to be or pretended it to be no longer exists. Crisis can stir us to action.

Crisis can produce retreat as well as engagement, as if running away from the threat can make it go away. If crisis conditions upset but do not overwhelm the community, engagement is the more likely response. If the crisis passes quickly, old patterns may well re-assert themselves.

*Working Relationships Require Communication and Trust.* In community change, everything happens through relationships. As people act with and react to one another, they create a new organism called a relationship. Among other things, this relationship gives meaning to words and actions, defines roles, and sets boundaries of anticipated or acceptable behaviour.

Each person comes to the relationship with ideas, information, energy, talents, money, power, or other resources. Not only does each person bring these, but each also brings a network of other relationships as well as all the resources and networks available there. The matter of influence, acting and reacting, requires the participation of another.

An exchange of resources flows more easily through healthy relationships than through those blocked by hurt or fear. Relationships depend on two necessary ingredients: communication and trust. Relationships take time to mature into full openness, and they need frequent maintenance and attention to keep harmful elements from blocking easy access. An effort characterized by the ability to develop and maintain healthy relationships will have more available resources, an increased ability to weather unexpected storms and challenge setbacks, and an ability to use more of its energy for focused action. It will be more powerful as a result.

**Take a Moment to Discover**

Take a closer look at your community—be it one of your close communities or the wider community. What do you see? What resources can you name that might be underutilized? What treasures might be hidden from view? See if today you can identify something of value that you did not really recognize before.

## CONCLUSION

Effective action is grounded in good theory and practice principles. Several different theoretical perspectives inform the work of community change. Commitment to building a base strong in theory involves consideration of the clarifying ideas of scholars, activists, and especially partners in the community who are working to promote change. A practitioner's use of theory guides action, and reflection on that action strengthens theory.

A change agent must be able to recognize and build on the resources available in the community. This requires both a belief in the presence of resources and an ability to note opportunities for their use. A change agent who sees only threats and weaknesses will invite the community to stay stuck in the belief of dependency and powerlessness. One significant set of resources can be found in the people themselves. Believing in these resources means that you believe in the ability of the people to define their own issues and to rely on themselves to make their own decisions.

Look for signs of strength whenever you can, and draw attention to them. Act on belief in power, abilities, and rights, not victimhood. People, as individuals or as a community, move forward only through the use of their abilities. Perhaps the most important contributor to a community's success is a belief in its abilities rather than a belief in its problems. Help foster that belief.

You will become a more effective change agent as you deepen your understanding of theoretical principles that give guidance to action. As you put theories to the test and refine them, you will discover principles of your own. Understanding these concepts is important, but understanding is demonstrated and becomes meaningful only through action. Change comes by acting. Learn to apply these principles in practical ways that encourage community action.

## HELPFUL WEBSITES

**Paulo Freire Institute**

http://paulofreireinstitute.org

Paulo Freire Institute UCLA brings together scholars and critics who intend to show how his ideas can work in the real world. In addition to links to other Freireian resources, you will find an online journal with contributions from academics and activists alike.

**Center for Community Change**

www.communitychange.org

The Center for Community Change works with low-income people to build power and reshape their communities. Along with news and project updates, you will find practical information here on a host of topics, including advocacy, community development tools, community organization, leadership training, coalition building, and economic development.

**World Bank**

www.worldbank.org/poverty/scapital

The World Bank Group's Social Capital for Development site provides a rich background on the concept of social capital and its sources. In addition, this site has an extensive bibliography on this issue.

**Communication Initiative**

www.comminit.com/en/section5/36/36%2C25

The Communication Initiative offers descriptions of many theories of change and has an international perspective. It is a rich site with access to publications, development news, planning and evaluation methods, and much more.

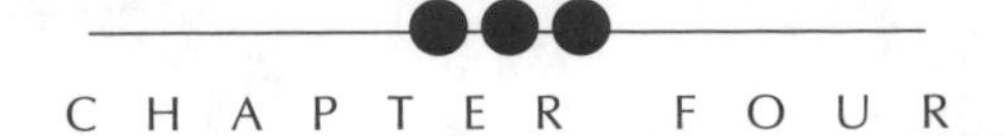

CHAPTER FOUR

# Relating Community Change to Agency Work and Professional Practice

**This chapter will help you better understand the following questions:**

- Why is community change relevant for all social workers?
- What are the main purposes of community work?
- What are the practices that characterize community work?
- What is the relationship between change efforts and professional values?
- What are the skills required for community change?

In this chapter, we will take a closer look at how community change activities fit with professional social work. As you work to alleviate human distress, how can you respond to conditions that directly confront the profession itself? For example, workers within child protection agencies often labour under unreasonable demands that hamper their effectiveness. This is unfair to the children served by the worker, it is unfair to the worker, and it is unfair to the profession as a whole. All workers bear the criticism of a skeptical public that is all too willing to see the profession as the culprit in a situation in which meagre resources produce meagre results.

You may want to respond to these conditions in your work, but can you really do this as a professional? We must hope that private citizens take action on these issues, but we must also hope that actions to shape our communities and our public policies are well informed by professional social work and community leadership. If not us, whom do we expect to do this work? Is this a professional responsibility? We think you can guess our answer. What is yours? On what do you base your answer?

You may have questions regarding the relationship of community and policy change to your professional practice. Many students and practitioners in social work, social services, recreation work, or other disciplines envision a very limited role for themselves in relation to community change, yet they have a rich body of knowledge, powerful values, and a variety of skills to contribute to these kinds of change efforts. Dinitto and McNeece (1989) point out that social work's multilevel perspective makes the profession particularly well equipped to develop social welfare policies. Schmolling and colleagues (1997) emphasize the importance of social policy development for social service workers. They believe that "[social] workers can be, and often are, instrumental in determining unmet needs and in influencing policy" (pp. 283–284).

We believe that community change efforts clearly relate to professional social work practice. We need to see this as part of our job. This is something we should do within our professional role, not outside it. Here is why:

1. Taking action on problems at the community level responds to the basic purposes of social welfare.
2. It is one of the principal methods of social work practice.
3. It is consistent with social work ethics and values.
4. Social work training provides a strong theoretical base that aids our analysis of the need and provides the direction for action.
5. Social work training provides us with a base of skills that enables us to be effective in this endeavour.

This chapter will take a close look at each of these points.

## BASIC PURPOSE OF SOCIAL WELFARE

Canadian authors working in the area of social policy and social welfare concentrate on the well-being of Canadians through the public administration and management of social services and programs at federal, provincial, and municipal levels. Some of those programs are in education, health, income maintenance, and welfare services (Hick, 2002; Raphael, 2007; Westhues, 2006). To provide for the welfare of both the individual and the society, social welfare institutions act to prevent social problems; treat or resolve social problems; educate ourselves, our service users, our policymakers, and our communities about rights, responsibilities, problems, and possibilities; explore how to use what we have to create what we want; enhance the quality of people's lives; and (though we are sometimes reluctant to acknowledge this) enforce measures of social control to preserve social stability. To an important degree, each of these ends depends on community change efforts for its accomplishment.

We cannot prevent high school students from dropping out unless we are willing to make changes in our schools. We cannot expect a community to be well informed about child abuse if we do not speak out to the people who most need to know. We cannot help people to reach their full potential if the best we can offer is support for their labour to survive the daily struggle of their lives. We cannot promote social stability if we fragment social problems into individualized sorrows. Clearly, we are called to go beyond the routine if we intend to meet social welfare goals. And we are called to do this with skill and purpose.

### Three Views of Social Welfare

Three approaches to the purpose and delivery of social welfare are the residual, institutional, and developmental approaches. Community and institutional change figure prominently in two of them. We should take a closer look.

The *residual approach* characterizes much of the social welfare system in Canada. This approach assumes that the family and the market economy are the proper sources for meeting people's needs. Social welfare provides a safety net of supplementary services to catch those individuals who fall through the cracks. Of course, they must fall first. The state should intervene only when everything else fails and only for a short period of time until the person is ready to work and be productive again (Hick, 2002; Callahan & Swift, 2006).

Certain basic assumptions go hand in hand with the residual approach. Individuals and families receive the main attention of residual efforts. The problems confronted are seen as being caused by those being helped rather than by the structural ineffectiveness of the systems in which these people participate. For example, families need help because they fail to work hard enough, not because the prevailing wage rates are too low to feed a family. The first order of business is to encourage the recipient to change, to become more adequate. Services are provided on a temporary basis to get the recipient back in the game. The game itself is not much changed. Often, individuals must prove that they need the assistance and that they are worthy of it. Because individuals are seen as inadequate, there is usually some stigma attached to receiving services, and a dependency relationship is likely to develop. Typical residual programs include counselling and job-training programs (Hick, 2002).

Ontario Works is an example of a residual social program implemented in the 1990s by the Conservative government of Mike Harris. Ontario Works is a residual social program because it emphasizes that people must work to receive assistance. People must either participate in job-training programs or be actively seeking employment. Ontario Work's main initiative is to reintegrate people into the workforce as quickly as possible. However, Ontario Works ignores the many structural factors that stop people from working, such as language barriers, and blames job loss on personal characteristics, such as poor work habits (Mitchell, Lightman, & Herd, 2007; Snyder, 2006).

The *institutional approach* is based on a different set of assumptions (Delaney, 2005). This approach sees welfare efforts as responses to shared social problems. These problems affect a large number of people in common, not one at a time. Services are the right of the service users, regardless of the degree of the problem. There is no requirement to prove need or worthiness; that is assumed. Institutional programs are routinely available and accessible, and those using them are not expected to undergo changes themselves because there is no assumption that something is wrong with them in the first place. Institutional programs are seen as appropriate primary sources for meeting needs, and there is little or no stigma attached to participation (Hick, 2002; Lessa, 2006).

Change efforts are directed at our societal institutions, improving the availability as well as the appropriateness of services rather than improving the person receiving them. Here, the emphasis is on narrowing the cracks in the system, not catching the people who fall through them. The key to solving social problems is developing the power to change conditions or to improve societal responses to them.

Our public education system is an example of an institutional response to a common problem—literacy. Students do not need to prove that they are illiterate before being admitted to Grade 1, nor that they have failed in learning sufficiently at home. Other examples include social insurance programs such as retirement benefits under the Old Age Security Program, a full national health insurance program, or even public parks without parking or user fees.

A third major view of social welfare is the *developmental approach* (Dolgoff, Feldstein, & Skolnik, 1997; Lofquist, 1996). Using this approach, delivery of services moves beyond a problem orientation. According to this view, "it is possible for society to set up a social welfare institution simply to make living better and to fulfill human development, not necessarily to solve a problem" (Dolgoff, Feldstein, & Skolnik, 1997, p. 139).

Community parks or recreation departments, for example, offer a variety of courses. When they do so simply to expand human potential or add to the quality of life, rather than to correct a problem or overcome a deficiency, they are following a developmental approach to the provision of services. Developmental approaches can have an individual focus, like those parks and recreation courses, or a community level approach, like those that work to create housing, or jobs, or that park in the first place.

Figure 4.1 compares problem-solving approaches with development approaches.

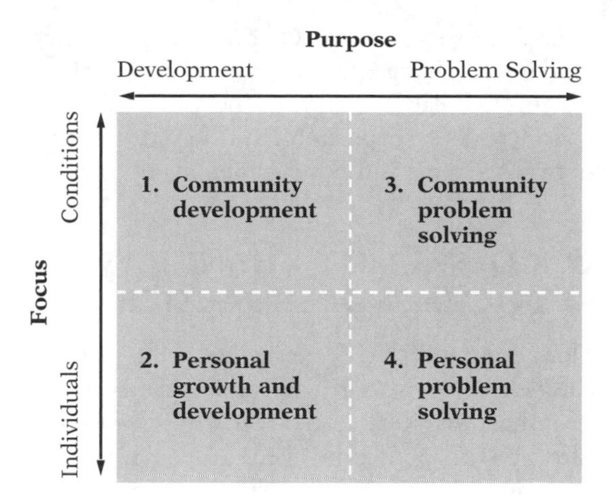


*Development* is an active process of creating conditions and fostering personal attributes that promote the well-being of people.

*Problem solving* is a reactive, corrective effort to bring about change where there is a recognized problem.

**FIGURE 4.1** The Arenas of Action

Source: Lofquist, 1996.

Instead of correcting one individual problem after another and another, community development can prevent problems by improving conditions that affect people.

## Differing Approaches to Professional Practice: Service and Developmental

In this section we discuss how some of the values and practices of community change agents can work within larger social service agencies. We have named the approach most like community work the developmental approach.

A developmental approach to professional practice is very different from the service approach that more commonly typifies professional activity. Developmental approaches build on strengths, identifying resources within the individual, the group, or the community that can be more fully cultivated and utilized. The emphasis is on potential, not problems. The Strengths Perspective in working with families incorporates many development features (Early & GlenMaye, 2000). If we understand community development within the anti-oppressive framework, we also need to pay close attention to the prejudicial and inequitable power relations that communities and individuals experience, even those relations with community change agents and professionals. We need to remember that many actions are understood to be part of the processes of exclusion and marginalization. Even your actions as a community worker can contribute to these processes despite your best intentions.

A developmental approach looks for things or potential to cultivate or resources with which to build. Because services rarely change conditions, but rather, supply accommodations to them, they tend to perpetuate need. Developmental actions help to improve a condition by augmenting the strengths to create something new. Development should strive to assist workers to facilitate the personal and political empowerment of marginalized groups who are disadvantaged. As we have discussed previously, marginalization can be the result of intersecting systems of racism, heterosexism, ableism, classism, sexism, and other forms of oppression (Mullaly, 2002).

How you as a change agent look at a situation and think about what to do will affect the nature of the professional relationship you develop. Problems are not seen only as personal, but rather are redefined as political issues, rooted in the ways society is organized and therefore as requiring structural (rather than simply individual) solutions. Taking a developmental approach to professional practice will help you recognize the interconnections between personal and public (social) issues (Barnoff & Moffatt, 2007). This approach is more characterized by equality in power between the professional workers and those who benefit from the improved conditions by partnering with the workers to improve conditions. In effect, the two are partners.

A service orientation, which often shapes professional activity, starts with the identification of a problem or an unmet need. This approach looks at what is missing. It then delivers services to provide what is missing or to take care of people who are missing what they need. Service is more characterized by a differential in power between the professional worker, who is a more powerful expert, and the recipient, who is dependent on what the worker can deliver. Here, it is easy to fall into roles of giver and receiver or of expert authority and needy complier. Intervention is often given with an attitude of caring, with a desire to alleviate pain or discomfort. Sometimes, it is provided with the intent of social control to manage the behaviour of individuals or whole classes of people through the periodic distribution of a needed resource.

Think about how you see your job and the people who benefit from your work. Do you intend to help them feel better by giving them something they do not have? Or do you intend to find out what they have and then see how they want to use these things to enhance their lives? Do you spend time assisting those injured by the oppressive social order? Or do you spend time working on change that will transform oppressive systems (Mullaly, 2002; Dominelli, 1998)?

Here is a snapshot of the key differences between service and developmental approaches.

| Service | Developmental |
|---|---|
| Focuses on problems | Focuses on assets and capacities |
| Is episodic | Is ongoing |
| Reinforces power relations | Equalizes power relationships |
| Promotes passivity | Promotes capability and initiative |
| Relies on experts | Relies on partnerships |
| Recipient owns the problem | Mutual ownership of possibilities |
| Recipient is isolated and dependent | Links people with shared interests |
| Gives gifts to meet needs | Focuses on what is available |
| Wants to give | Wants to build |
| Believes "This is the best we can do" | Asks "What can we do better?" |
| Maintain conditions | Changes conditions |
| People are serviced | People acquire new skills |

## COMMUNITY CHANGE AS SOCIAL WORK PRACTICE

Does community change really have a place in the delivery of social work and social services? Are most workers not already busy working directly with people in need? And, frankly, are there any jobs out there for change agents? Good questions. The answer to all of them is yes.

### Modes of Social Work Practice

Let us begin with the first question: Is promotion of community change really a fundamental professional activity for social workers and other social service professionals? These professionals have historically been involved in activities to reform community policies and practices, particularly ones that affected low-income and working-class people (Caragata, 2006; Lessa, 2006; Waterfall, 2006). We acted not only to serve the disenfranchised, but to enfranchise as well. It has been part of our very identity. Is that still true today? Yes.

Some observers believe that social work is losing its mission of helping the most marginalized. Some social workers have gone into private practice, and others are engaged in activities that have little to do with altering harmful community forces. The fact that there is a discussion in the profession about the concern that social work is losing its mission underscores its very importance.

Social workers in social service agencies are change agents—at least the good ones are. True, too many end up being problem-processors rather than problem-solvers, sometimes because the agency they work for demands it of them. Sometimes workers lose sleep wondering where or to whom they can pass problems along. Service users are shifted from one person, department, agency, and, if possible, province, to the next until they and their problems get lost—also known as people processing. Of course, the real problem is that at times the work or agency is not aware of broader issues. To provide social services requires a willingness to take part in changing a condition. If that only means helping someone qualify for a public assistance program, rest assured that this is a pretty significant "only" in the life of the service user. Because of the nature of their work or perhaps because of the depth of their commitment, many social workers go beyond making these minimal but very real changes. Some assist service users in changing how they respond emotionally and behaviourally to their circumstances. Others assist in making changes in those circumstances. The differences are really only in scope, focus, and intensity. All social workers must accept the simple fact that improvement means something has to change—and they will play a part in promoting that change. Movement toward community change occurs when social workers can link private anguish with public conditions and act on that understanding. Action is critical because it is believed that through collective action social change will occur. Skills such as community development, alliance building, coalition development, and social action become important.

Alberta has recently seen a group of communities determined to promote healthy living by making it easier to m ake healthy choices and thus reduce chronic disease. Healthy Alberta Communities (HAC) includes the three communities of Norwood/North Central Edmonton, St. Paul, Bonnyville, and the Medicine Hat area. Agencies taking action in these communities include grassroots community groups, private business, and non-governmental organizations, to name a few.

The BC Coalition of People with Disabilities (BCCPD) is an organization that seeks to raise awareness about people with disabilities and create change within communities. Their goals include working at all levels of government to change policies that negatively affect people with disabilities. Also when necessary the BCCPD provides individual advocacy for those who have personally faced discrimination because of their disability. Finally, the BCCPD seeks to develop educational publications on disabilities to help raise awareness across the province. A recent campaign involves advocating for people who have become disabled through car accidents and trying to change a law regarding accident benefits. It is asking for improved benefits during the rehabilitation process of those injured in accidents, to reflect the economic realities of today's world.

All jobs in social services require skill in changing conditions, but many workers are not full-time community change agents. However, *all* social workers will be confronted by the challenge to seek changes in the way things are. Although few individuals are hired specifically by social service agencies for their ability to promote community change, most workers are expected not only to provide services but also to improve delivery of those services and, at times, are expected to sit on task forces about community issues; to be involved in relations to the community of service users; to be involved in community activities in a union or service organization; to develop outreach programs; or to consider how to change the agency to better serve marginalized communities—all these are community change agent tasks. In addition, many positions in community organization and development can be found throughout the country. You will see them if you cast your eye in that direction. The following chapters will introduce you not only to some of the possible roles in community change but to some organizations involved in the work as well. Your ability to take an active part in community leadership will be a definite asset, especially for positions requiring more professional respons ibility. The jobs out there—the ones that mean anything—require you to do more than just fill out forms.

## Direct Work with Individuals

Most social workers work directly with people; unfortunately, we are not short of service users. A worker who is too busy to assist a service user in learning how to contend more powerfully with the situations causing discomfort is much like a teacher who insists that students passively receive information and ask no questions because there is so much material to cover. Perhaps the worker will not play a major role in changing the conditions for the service user, but he or she certainly can do three specific things to help:

1. Assist the service user to understand the forces in the environment that are causing distress, and help them develop skills to confront these forces. In other words, always include an analysis of power. An anti-oppression perspective pays attention to the ways that certain groups and communities are marginalized within systems of power (based on race, class, gender, and other factors) due to the ways those systems operate in the wider society and helps people to find ways to negotiate these systems.
2. Identify those who can play a major role in fostering change, which could include bringing similarly affected service users together or referring service users to other programs or other professionals. Build alliances and advocate together for change (Bishop, 2002).
3. Bring the existence of harmful conditions to the attention of those who are in a position to act on that awareness.

These steps do not require mastering difficult new skills; they simply require that you adopt an attitude that these activities are a necessary consideration in the delivery of effective service.

## Five Stages of Partnership Development

Partnership is one of the ways to work with communities even if it is not the central focus of your job as a social worker even if you work in a big agency.

The notion of partnership is central to working with service users to promote community change. Five levels characterize the establishment of a partnership relationship between professionals and service users in the community.

- At the *first level*, by far the most predominant, professionals talk to professionals about service users and the problems they experience.
- In some instances, things go a little further—to the *second level*. Here, professionals talk to service users. This is usually one-way communication directed "downward" from those with more power to those with less power.
- At the *third level*, service users begin talking with other service users about common concerns.
- And at *level four*, organized groups of service users talk to professionals. Here, it is the service users who initiate conversation, and the professionals are expected to respond. This level is rarely reached.
- The *fifth level* of partnership (the most developed) is characterized by organized service users and professionals working together. They do not just talk to each other; they use their respective resources to collaborate on issues of common concern—concerns selected by the service users.

As an agent of change, at what level do you think your relationship with service users has "gone far enough"?

## A Place for Community Change

Let us examine how community change fits into the methods that professionals providing social services use. Imagine you are looking at a five-pointed star (Figure 4.2). At each tip is one of the five basic activities or methods:

*Individual counselling*, which involves face-to-face contact with individuals and families to help them resolve problems

**FIGURE 4.2** Basic Methods

*Group work,* which uses the resources and support available among members of a group to assist the members in achieving individual or shared goals

*Community organization and development,* which brings people together to get, maintain, and use power to improve the conditions they face

*Research and education,* which involves developing and testing theories, discovering information, and communicating theories and information to people who can put them to use

*Administration,* which involves managing or operating social welfare programs or agencies

Each tip of the star indicates a valid approach to social services. In the middle of the star is the problem or opportunity faced by the service user. Solving a problem or a set of problems may involve using one approach or several sequential approaches to intervention. But we are learning that really one approach is not separate from the other—this is only a way to think about your work. An integrated approach to practice is a more common approach these days. That is, we assume that to be an effective worker you are involved in all these activities during your job. For example, you cannot promote change in a community without dealing with emotions such as hope or fear, so the idea of emotions being solely within the purview of therapists is a false notion.

Another way you can look at community change is through the approach Bloom (1990) describes (Figure 4.3). Individuals operate in different milieus such as family, job, culture, and the physical environment, and each "interacts with the others, influencing and being influenced by them" (p. 6). Sometimes these interactions go well, and sometimes they do not. If these interactions are routinely troublesome, something needs to change, but what? Should efforts be made to change the individual, or should efforts be made to make external changes? Should energy be focused on making the kinds of changes that would bring about equity and promote social justice in the wider society? Should efforts be made to explore the links between personal situations and larger social relations of power (such as racism, sexism, and classism) so that individuals are not pathologized? An analysis of these interactions can focus the worker's interventions and guide the choice of methods you use. You need some beginning awareness of a therapist, case worker, community worker, administrator, and so on to think about how to intervene.

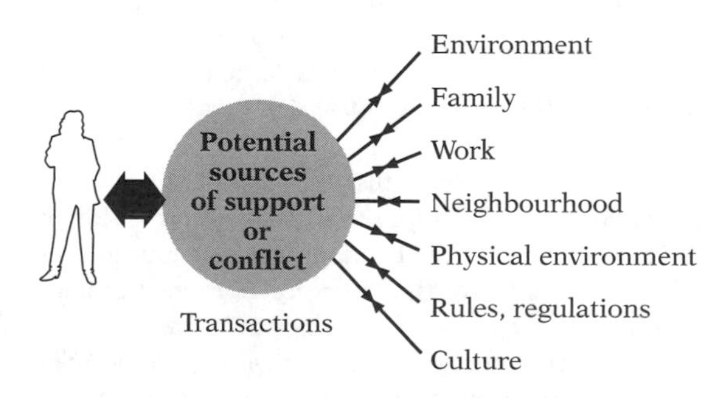


**FIGURE 4.3** Structural Relationships

As a worker in the social service field, you can be involved in many fields, including caseworker or counsellor; group worker or group therapist; community organizer, developer, or planner; educator or researcher; or administrator. However, rarely will you function exclusively in your primary role. At each level of practice, you will come face to face with problems that call out for action to improve conditions faced by a group of people. And at times you will get involved in organizing groups or communities of service users to help them address needs not dealt with in the system of institutions and social service agencies.

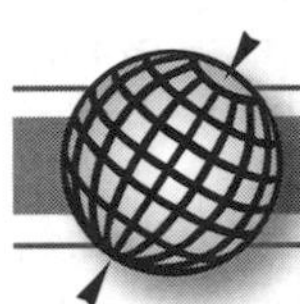

## GLOBAL PERSPECTIVES

BARBADOS—Most experts on development agree that economic growth does not, in itself, ensure a better distribution of income and services, but that social development, which incorporates principles such as cooperation, social justice, and the transformation of social and economic structures, is necessary.

[Detractors warn that] most social service workers have difficulty making the connection between the broad definitions of social development and their day-to-day activities.

The social work curriculum is heavily influenced by the casework approach. Barbados has been undergoing a process of economic development supported mainly by tourism, resulting in cultural penetration, the breaking down of traditional values, erosion of the extended family, pockets of poverty, and a host of attendant problems. To date, the profession's response has been reactive, with minimal impact.

[There is arguably an expanded role for field education to] act as a force for organizational change and as a catalyst for social development. There is also room for further collaboration between field education and the profession to help it develop a voice in social policymaking which it lacks to date (Tucker Rambally, 1999, pp. 486–494).

ZIMBABWE—Since the 1970s, a clarion call has continuously sounded for the social work profession in Africa to shed its remedial outlook and to assume greater relevance in order for the profession to more meaningfully address the needs of the continent's masses.

For social work on the continent to become relevant, the profession must assume a developmental orientation, and this has to start at the level of education.

The developmental approach has been recommended to the social work profession in Africa for a variety of reasons. Most compelling of these is the fact that because of a general lack of resources, the continent of Africa can hardly afford the luxury of continuing to employ the remedial strategy, an approach which, over the years, has proved particularly costly. It is clear that the developmental strategy is simply not suitable for social work institutions in Africa alone; the approach can also be effectively utilized in other regions of the world, particularly the third world, where resources are scarce (Mupedziswa, 2001, pp. 285–297).

EL SALVADOR—El Salvador endured a violent civil war from 1979 to 1992 that took the lives of some 70,000 to 75,000 people—most of them poor. The country was devastated twice in one month by earthquakes that took the lives of about 1,250 people, injured another 8,000, and left many more homeless. Most of the country's wealth continues to be concentrated in the hands of a few families and right-wing forces which are still prominent politically. Poor communities continue to struggle to overcome these hardships and to cope with the failure of the peace accords to measurably improve their lives.

As the primary caretakers of their families, women carry additional burdens. They experience discrimination in the labour market, and are sometimes the victims of family violence fuelled by both the frustrations of poverty and a deep-seated tradition of machismo. AMUSAMECO has designed a project of ongoing weekly meetings with groups of women in several poor and marginalized communities around San Salvador. Trained mental health workers will facilitate the meetings where women will learn relaxation techniques and discuss their experiences of loss. Meetings also address their basic rights to health care, education, employment, and housing, and women's issues such as gender equality, self-esteem, and the right to protection against violence. The program aims to empower participants to become protagonists acting to improve their lives (Allen et al., 2002, p. 63).

SOUTH AFRICA—In the past, social work training was skewed towards the maintenance of the status quo of colonial apartheid and did not provide practitioners with the relevant skills to deal with the problems of the majority African population which was mainly disempowered and disenfranchised. In the pursuit of relevant social work practice in the new order, social work education must therefore be transformed. Indeed, we should like to see the reorientation of all social service practitioners to the demands of a new democratic environment.

Social work is a Western concept, and, at times, has found itself conflicting with the social terrain of Africa. Rather, in clinging to the traditional model, the profession appears to avoid issues inherent to development such as productivity, changing gender roles, people's participation, resource sufficiency, and rural development.

In order for the educators to become relevant in the new socio-economic and political environment, they first and foremost must unlearn past teaching methods and be conversant with developmental trends. Academics are not grounded in theories of development and are also very averse to developmental social work or social development because they have never practised nor bothered to become acquainted with them (Mamphiswana & Noyoo, 2000, pp. 21–29).

## COMMUNITY WORK AND SOCIAL WORK VALUES

Using categories established by the Canadian Association of Social Workers and drawing on the work of a number of other authors, we can highlight many of the critical values that should direct professional social work practice and are a good guide for the work of community change agents:

Postfestum / Shutterstock

**Working in partnership with community members is fundamental to community practice.**

- *Values as preferred conceptions of people.* This orientation focuses on people and their connection to the environment. Five key statements characterize this category. First, professional social workers believe in the inherent worth and dignity of all people and uphold human rights (CASW, 2005). Second, each person has an inherent capacity and drive toward change that provides him or her with the potential for development throughout a lifetime (CASW, 2005). Third, people have responsibility for themselves as individuals and for their fellow human beings, including society. Fourth, people need to belong. Fifth, although people have needs in common, each person is unique and different from all others (CASW, 2005). Social workers practising in Canada uphold the human rights of individuals and groups as expressed in the Canadian Charter of Rights and Freedoms (1982) and the United Nations' Universal Declaration of Human Rights (1948) (CASW, 2005).

- *Values as preferred outcomes for people.* This orientation focuses on the way that society should be organized so that people can achieve fulfillment. "Social workers have the obligation to ensure that resources, services, and opportunities for the overall benefit of humanity" (CASW, 2005, p. 5) are provided to all people. This is done by promoting social development in the interest of all people, particularly those who are marginalized (CASW, 2005; Mullaly, 2002).

  Social workers believe that Canadian society must provide opportunities for growth and development that enable each person to realize his or her fullest potential; must provide resources and services to help people meet their needs and to avoid such problems as hunger, inadequate education, discrimination, illness without care, and inadequate housing; must have equal opportunity to participate in moulding society (CASW, 2005).
- *Values as preferred instruments for dealing with people.* This orientation focuses on how people should be treated. The Canadian Association of Social Workers argues that social workers should "analyze the nature of social needs and problems, and encourage innovative, effective strategies and techniques to meet both new and existing [people's] needs and, where possible, contribute to the knowledge base of the profession"(8).

The call to action echoes throughout these statements of professional values. The actions that you take as a professional are an acknowledgment of your commitment to these fundamental beliefs. Many authors writing about social work identify advocacy focused on both the individual cases and overall causes at the same time as a necessary professional skill (Andreae, 2002; Banks, 2002; Ezell, 2001; Johnson & Yanca, 2001; Kumsa, 2007; Pincus & Minahan, 1973; Schmolling et al., 1997; Zastrow, 1999). You will probably struggle to live up to these ideals throughout your career (Piccard, 1988). Still, it is not enough to simply agree to the importance of these values. You must act on them.

## The Painful Limits of Action

What level of response is needed to effectively confront the suffering that brings people to the attention of social service professionals? If we respond to the presence of disturbing social conditions within our midst by working primarily to soften the pain they cause, does this imply a tolerance for their existence? We appear to be so caring in our efforts to respond to service users' problems, scurrying about helping this service user and that one, never confronting the causes that compelled service users to need our aid. We are so busy with all this caring that we have little time or inclination to do anything else. Does the shallowness of our attention and our action guarantee that there will be many service users in need? What is the real effect of all our busyness? Suppose a Grade 3 teacher calls the child protection agency and provides the following information about a student of hers called Mary.

Her family calls its station wagon home. She is dirty, her hair a haven for lice, the soles on her only pair of shoes threaten to abandon her at any time. She is not doing well in school, can barely read even the simplest of words, and seems unable to get along with other members of the class. What do you think is needed here?

- A new pair of shoes?
- A bath?
- A trip to the nurse's office to deal with the lice?
- A note sent home to the parents of all the other kids warning them of the possible lice infestation at the school?
- A call to Child Protective Services alerting them to the possibility of neglect?
- A visit to the classroom to see how her classmates treat her?

- Temporary shelter facilities for her, her siblings, and her mother, with the hope that her father can find space in the men's shelter program?
- The establishment of a shelter care program for families?
- The establishment of a transitional housing program that would help families like Mary's get back on their feet again?
- The establishment of a homeless people's organization to advocate for decent housing and the provision of support services for people who are homeless?
- Action taken against the very forces within your community that lead to homelessness?

There is a lot you can do. How much will you actually do? Where will you stop? Who carries on from there? What determines your answers to these questions?

You are mulling all this over. There is a knock at the door. The Grade 4 teacher wants to talk with you about Sam. He has a black eye. His dad got drunk last night and hit him. One more child, one more set of problems. And now what is really going to happen to change Mary's life?

Perhaps all you think you can do is help Mary in her struggle with the problems brought about because she has no real home. Are you actually going to go one step beyond responding to the immediate situation? Are you really going to do anything to reduce homelessness?

Make no mistake about it, the actions we take do lessen the discomfort and bring some relief to those who are affected. However, we may be insensitive to the fact that our limited actions indicate an endorsement of, or at least acquiescence to, these conditions that call for all this hurry and scramble of ours. Under the guise of caring, we have reached a point of acceptance of conditions that produce the pain we try to ease.

Imagine you are a worker for the Child and Family Service, a provincial protection agency, with a caseload of 29 service users. Yet, for ongoing cases like yours, child welfare provincial authorities recommend a maximum caseload of no more than 17. Your supervisor walks into your office with another case. You can handle 20 cases competently and professionally. You can handle 25 with some degree of effectiveness. How much real, constructive service do you provide to a caseload of 30?

You cannot say no to number 30. Why did you say yes? Are you truly caring for having done so? Would you have been reprimanded for refusing? How did you and your colleagues end up in such a situation? Does your acceptance of this unreasonable burden demonstrate your dedication and service to those who need you? How much benefit do they really receive? Under the guise of caring, you simply cannot say no. You stay busy doing your best to keep patching things up. You feel so overwhelmed. Do you really have no other choice?

If you believe that your efforts matter, that they do, in fact, improve people's lives, should you accept limitations on your effectiveness and the consequent reduction in the benefit people will experience? Will you just be thankful for whatever kind of support you get? How will you participate in making decisions on how effectively you can provide service? Or is that none of your business? To whom do you want to leave these decisions?

You have learned how to juggle; in fact, you are pretty good at it. You are able to juggle five balls at once. All of them are safe as you toss them into the air—but five is the limit. What happens if someone tosses you number six? What is the effect on the first five? What happens to all your other cases when you say yes to number 30?

Social work and social services are hemmed in by suspicion and lack of community support. We do not practise in a vacuum. Jansson (1997) reminds us that social workers are "more subject to social policies that control, restrict, and regulate their practice" than are most other professions (p. 8). Parada (2004) and Swift and

Callahan (2009) recognize that our careers are continually shaped by changes in the social welfare institution. They point out that it simultaneously helps, limits, and shapes the ways in which we deal with people in trouble. Should we as social workers and social service professionals attempt to shape this institution that shapes our practice?

We believe you do have options for challenging the circumstances that lead to the problems you confront. And we believe you have options for creating conditions that permit you to work effectively. In our experience, workers who have acted thoughtfully and purposefully to confront and resolve systemic problems have produced many positive results. It is not simple. Nor is it impossible. Like any worthwhile professional activity, it is challenging, engaging, periodically frustrating, yet often satisfying, and potentially exhilarating. Simply putting up with problems is hardly ever gratifying, and although it seems safer, it is not easy. You will receive a fuller measure of professional satisfaction by promoting changes that both you and your service users deserve.

### Picking the Battles You Are Going to Fight

No matter what your primary area of service may be, you will encounter situations that will challenge you to extend your change efforts beyond the immediate problem situation to produce fundamental change. The examples just discussed illustrate two types of challenges you are likely to face. The first involves pursuing a problem to broader levels in order to address factors that are external to service users but that contribute to the discomfort service users are experiencing. The second example calls for you to challenge the limitations placed on your ability to perform at the optimum level. If the demands of your job far outweigh the resources you have to do your job (including such intangible things as time and authority), there is little hope of success. The ongoing frustrations of this situation will eat away at whatever effectiveness you may have—and at you as well.

With every single service user you encounter, and in any practice environment in which you work, you will face problems that need to be addressed through organized action for systemic change. This is a sobering and somewhat intimidating thought. Once you recognize the effects that larger forces have on service users and the effectiveness of your practice, you will discover many opportunities to participate in meaningful change activities. But at many times, you need to decide which battle you are going to fight. So, how do you choose? Here are some guidelines.

- Choose an issue in which you are genuinely interested (both intellectually and emotionally).
- Choose a situation that you commonly confront.
- Evaluate whether you can make a meaningful contribution of time, talent, or wisdom.
- Structure your effort so that it has some likelihood of success.
- Address the problem in an effective way.

Remember that changing one regulation or one agency policy can have far-reaching consequences. You are not responsible for solving all of the world's problems, but you can contribute to the resolution of a few. There are a lot of battles out there. Pick yours.

## YOU HAVE THE THEORETICAL BASE

As social workers, you need to be comfortable with the theories available for you to use in your practice. Although you need to pick a theory that you are most comfortable with to promote progressive change that challenges systems, we outline again here some of the theoretical assumptions of anti-oppression theory. For a more extensive discussion of these theories, see Chapter 2.

As mentioned earlier in Chapter 2, a major theoretical base for community work and community change is anti-oppression. Anti-oppressive approaches to social work practice seek fundamental change in the structures of society that perpetuate oppression (Hick et al., 2005; Mullaly, 2002). Personal problems are redefined as political issues that require structural solutions through an approach that not only provides immediate care to those who experience systemic injury but also advances larger change toward social justice (Mullaly, 2002). As an approach informed by an analysis of power relations, anti-oppressive social work strives to facilitate the personal and political empowerment of groups who are disadvantaged by intersecting systems of racism, heterosexism, ableism, classism, sexism, and other forms of oppression (Mullaly, 2002). Anti-oppressive practice values equity, inclusion, and transformation, and it also aims to further the cause of social justice. Anti-oppressive practice is focused on eradicating the ways in which oppressions are manifested within social work practice so as to ensure equity for all social groups. Anti-oppression sees as questionable the fact that, based on the operations of power in the wider society, certain groups of people are advantaged while others are disadvantaged. This situation must be challenged and ultimately changed. "The driving force of anti-oppressive practice is the act of challenging inequalities" (Burke & Harrison, 2002).

Strega (2007) argues for an anti-oppressive way in which to engage service users in the child welfare system. We believe her approach can be used for social workers in social welfare systems in general to engage with communities to

- Understand how the welfare system historically and in the present recreates domination and subordination;
- Moves away from service users' blame and notions of individual dysfunctions;
- Ground our practice in critical theory and the wisdom of current and former service users;
- Understand how our own and our service users' social locations are played out at macro and micro levels (Strega, 2007, p. 70).

When you understand the forces at play, you will uncover many opportunities for beneficial change, including assisting service users to change conditions around them. Your awareness will guide you in selecting the proper context for your action or the points at which you may intervene to help resolve the situation in a way that best meets your service users' interests. This may call for you to work toward community or policy change.

## YOU HAVE THE SKILLS YOU NEED

The notion of promoting community change may sound pretty intimidating, even if you do understand the need for it and its place in professional practice. This may be particularly true if you see yourself as primarily working with individuals or families and you are more comfortable doing that type of work. You may not be confident that you can pull off change in a larger system. You may think you need to develop a whole new set of skills, quite different from those you use in working with individual problems. This is a legitimate concern. Which skills, if any, do social service workers commonly have that can be useful in promoting community change? A review of basic skills drawn from a number of social work and social services texts should shed some light on this question. While reading through these lists, consider how each skill could be useful to you as you work for community change.

Some but not all of the skills of an effective helper may be useful in your developmental focus in your practice in an agency. Here are a few skills from Schmolling, Youkeles, and Burger (1997, pp. 214–219) that may help you be a change agent:

*Empathy and social empathy*—the ability to see things from another's point of view

*Genuineness*—the expression of true feelings

*Self-awareness and critical self-reflection*—the quality of knowing oneself, including the knowledge of one's values, feelings, attitudes and beliefs, fears and desires, and strengths and weaknesses

*Acceptance*—the ability to view the service user's feelings, attitudes, and opinions as worthy of consideration without necessarily approving of the service user's behaviour

*Patience*—the ability to wait and be steadfast, understanding that different people do things at different times, in different ways, and for different reasons, according to individual capacities.

Shebib (2007, pp. 8–14) also discusses "skill clusters" in the process of intervention with service users. Here are a couple that may help you in your developmental approach to social service work:

*Relationship-building skills:* These are basic tools for engaging service users, developing trust, and defining the purpose of intervention. Active listening and defining the relationship are some of the skills in this cluster.

*Empowering skills:* These are skills that help in the process of helping service users to develop confidence and take control of their lives.

Similarly, Lee (1999, pp. 61–64) talks about core skill requirements within the pragmatic model of community organizing. He proposes all the following as core skills of importance for all social workers: listening, information gathering, analysis, facilitation, negotiation, and reflection.

These skills and competencies define your talents as a social worker or social service professional, but they do not define the context of your work. They do not imply limitations on what you can do—just the opposite.

The way in which you use your capabilities may vary according to the change effort you are pursuing, but the same fundamental competencies will guide you in your work. Just like any area of practice, your increased experience will help you discover more and more about what you are doing. You will accumulate your own bundle of tricks, and you will borrow some from other change agents. As you enter the arena of community change, you will find that the fundamental skills you possess as a social worker will help you get the job done. You just need to make the decision to enter that arena, even if only every now and then.

Carniol (forthcoming) developed a practice skill tool where he points out the skills necessary to use in the process of engaging with others, which includes engaging with communities and people in organizations (see Table 4.1). Carniol separates out the skills required to assess, to practise empathy, to reframe, to communicate, to involve yourself in spiritual sensitivity, and to advocate based on various perspectives.

**TABLE 4.1** A Practice Tool

**Social Workers**

| Applying : | Assessment Skills | Empathy Skills | Reframing Skills | Communication Skills (e.g., listening, exploring, focusing, clarifying, encouraging) | Spiritual Sensitivity Skills | Advocacy Skills |
|---|---|---|---|---|---|---|
| ECOLOGICAL and SYSTEMS PERSPECTIVES | Use systems theory and ecological narratives: (1) to explain dysfunctional interactions among different systems (e.g., individual, familial, communal, and formal systems); (2) to explore imbalances between individuals and their environments; (3) to identify areas for reciprocal adaptation by individuals and other systems, to optimize human well-being. | Communicate an understanding and appreciation of the client's feelings and subjective experience (as part of developing trust within a professional relationship). Use this skill in working directly with individuals, as well as with individuals in families, groups, and communities. Develop anticipatory empathy by tuning in, as part of preparing to work with specific client systems. | Aim to reduce clients' sense of hopelessness by suggesting new, more hopeful ways of viewing the situation. Congratulate clients for achievements that are ignored or devalued by others. Invite clients to identify unrecognized strengths within themselves and in their interactions with other systems, to help empower alternative, positive, and more hopeful client responses. | Listen. Explore ways that clients and their environments can better adapt to each other. Focus on services and resources, while affirming client strengths. Explore stress reduction among clients, families, and other systems. Respect and support client self-determination. Mediate or guide client systems in their problem-solving and solutions-finding. | Validate religious and spiritual pluralism. Support spirituality by clients as a strength to cope with stress (e.g., life transitions, crises caused by painful losses). Honour or appeal to spiritual and religious values of compassion and charity within and across diverse communities to encourage more generous help for people in need. | Work at convincing formal and informal systems to better meet client needs, by mediating between clients and their environments. Be active with others in lobbying larger systems for better policies, co-ordination, integration, and delivery of social services. Seek support from private, public, and charitable sectors, for additional resources to alleviate social problems. |

*Continued*

**TABLE 4.1** A Practice Tool (continued)

**Social Workers**

| Applying : | Assessment Skills | Empathy Skills | Reframing Skills | Communication Skills (e.g., listening, exploring, focusing, clarifying, encouraging) | Spiritual Sensitivity Skills | Advocacy Skills |
|---|---|---|---|---|---|---|
| STRUCTURAL and ANTI-OPPRESSIVE and CRITICAL PERSPECTIVES | Use structural theory and liberation narratives: (1) to learn how experiences of systemic oppression (e.g., colonialism, patriarchal capitalism, racism, heterosexism, ableism, ageism) are harming the service user's well-being; (2) to identify immediate survival needs; (3) to explore short-term and long-term goals for emancipation. | Communicate efforts to learn about and appreciate the service user's feelings and meanings (as part of trust evolving within a non-elitist professional relationship). Widen focus to include emancipatory empathy: i.e., dialogue about subjective and systemic barriers faced by others similarly oppressed, and about the courage to name and to overcome such barriers. | Aim to reduce self-blame by co-investigating with service users: (1) external and internalized oppression and (2) external and internalized illegitimate privilege, due to unjustified power over others. Explore new, more hopeful ways of understanding and acting, in light of social justice inspirations and initiatives and solidarities. | Listen. Explore ways that clients may be victims and survivors of oppression. Focus on services and resources, while affirming people's strengths. Model power-sharing with service users. Unmask illegitimate privilege. Support personal and political change to dismantle multiple oppressive practices, while constructing equitable alternatives. | Validate religious and spiritual pluralism. Oppose those religious practices that are oppressive. Learn about and honour spirituality rooted in diverse cultures, including its role in indigenous people's helping and healing. Find spiritual and religious support for progressive personal and social change within and across diverse communities. | Be active with others, including service users, to defend human rights (e.g., to decent incomes, jobs, social services) by organizing grassroots power upward to deconstruct harmful policies, decisions, processes, and structures. Become allies with social movements, locally and globally, for personal, familial, political, economic, and spiritual emancipation. |

Source: Ben Carniol, *Case Critical: Social Services and Social Justice in Canada*, 6th edition. Toronto: Between the Lines Publishers.

## CONCLUSION

As a professional, you will assist people in their efforts to lead full and satisfying lives. You will encounter many obstacles that interfere with that purpose. But if you take the time to look, you will discover many opportunities that can aid you as well. Efforts directed to community or policy change can remove obstacles; you can use those opportunities to make a difference. You may use a development approach, moving past the provision of services to the mobilization of resources to change conditions. These efforts help to further important social welfare goals.

Engaging in change efforts is consistent with basic professional practice methods. Your professional values not only support such activity, they call for it. You have the theoretical knowledge to make sense of the situations you face and to determine effective avenues for intervention. Your training provides you with the skills to initiate and even to pursue action.

You will be challenged to take action. That much is certain. You may not know how you will respond to those challenges, or even if you will allow yourself to recognize them. But if you do respond with a sense of purpose and an intent to be effective, you, in turn, will offer a challenge to conditions that limit human potential.

## HELPFUL WEBSITES

**Community Development Society**

www.comm-dev.org

Community Development Society is an organization of professional practitioners and community leaders. Among the offerings are abstracts from the society's journal, recent newsletters, a handful of "What's New" links, and contact information for local chapters.

**The Caledon Institute of Social Policy**

www.caledoninst.org

The Caledon Institute of Social Policy publishes a series of alternative publications about poverty and ways to improve the conditions of some of those living in communities where poverty is prevalent.

**The Centre for Social Justice**

www.socialjustice.org

The focus of the Centre for Social Justice is the production of research material that helps professionals to advocate for the reduction of the gap between the rich and the poor in Canada.

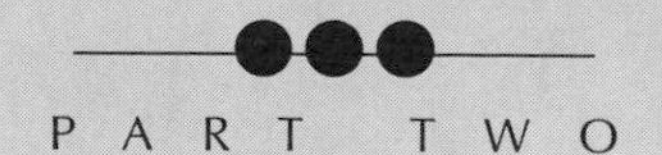

PART TWO

# *Putting the Pieces Together*

Part 2 provides you with a strong foundation to build on. As a worker involved in promoting community change, you will learn quite a lot by experience. However, having a foundation to build on will make learning easier and success more likely.

Chapter 5, Power, describes the concept of power and its use in promoting community change. You will learn how to recognize how power is exercised (or not) in a community, and you will be introduced to techniques for using power. Why you need power to work with communities and how you can work in partnership with communities to empower their members will be highlighted.

Chapter 6, Knowing Your Community, contains a number of perspectives on communities and key community characteristics. This chapter will help you increase your awareness of how communities function to meet their needs. Methods for discovering unmet community needs and unrecognized resources will be offered, and you will understand the importance of recognizing a community's capacity to change.

Chapter 7, Powerful Planning, explores the importance of planning and shows you how to ensure your planning efforts will be successful. Each step in the planning process is described with an emphasis on making planning activities useful in the real world. You will learn to identify and deal with potential pitfalls to effective planning.

Chapter 8, People—The Most Valuable Resource, examines ways to attract people to a change effort and how to maintain their participation. Because most people involved in community change efforts volunteer their time, working with volunteers will be discussed. All communities are diverse, and understanding the importance of recognizing and valuing diversity while also acknowledging similarities among all people is vital to your success. You will be presented with some reflections on how people respond to various challenges inherent in working for change, which will help you anticipate problems and strengthen commitment.

Chapter 9, Raising Other Resources, looks at how you can obtain needed resources for little or no money and how you can raise the money you need to do the work. You will increase your understanding of methods for generating support from individuals and organizations. A multiplicity of specific fundraising techniques will be explained, including writing and submitting grant proposals.

Chapter 10, Getting the Word Out, details various methods for communicating with the members of your own organization and with the public at large. It will help you to figure out which approaches you should take with various groups. You will learn how to use low-cost publicity techniques, and you will be provided with guidelines for working with both print and electronic media.

Chapter 11, Building the Organized Effort, takes you through the steps of developing an organization. You will learn how to use issues to provoke and maintain action. You will understand how much structure an organization needs and how you and others can modify or replace unproductive procedures.

Much of the work of organizations is really the work of small groups, so significant attention is given to matters of group process. As a change agent you will conduct many meetings, so guidelines for running effective meetings are offered. You will examine different types of organizations and their purposes and learn the process for formally incorporating an organization.

Chapter 12, Taking Action—Strategies and Tactics, is the final chapter in Part 2. Basic strategies and tactics for implementing action are described along with a discussion of the strengths and limitations of various approaches. You will consider some fundamental ethical issues involved in your decisions to take action or to refrain from action. You will gain some insights into the strategies and tactics that may be used against you by an opponent.

In actual practice many things occur simultaneously to build and strengthen an organized change effort. Involving people, acquiring other resources, and developing groups are all part of the process of putting together an organization that can make its presence known and take action. You will not actually be working on one aspect of the effort in isolation from another. All these elements relate to one another. Artificially separating these elements provides us with a chance to give each element closer inspection. This tends to be how things work in textbooks. Understand that this is not how things work in the world in which you practise.

CHAPTER FIVE

# Power

**This chapter will help you better understand the following questions:**

- Why is power fundamental to change?
- What are the bases of power in a community?
- What are the strategies for building power?
- How can you act powerfully?
- What are the rights, responsibilities, and consequences of exercising power?

Power—the word itself provokes reaction. We need it. We use it. It often slips unsolicited into our daydreams, at times with pleasure, at other times with vexation. Whether or not we are willing to acknowledge the role power plays in our actions, it will affect what we are doing at any given moment. In this chapter, we will speak frankly of power, for nothing is more central to promoting change than your ability to exercise power. You cannot promote change without exercising power. You cannot simultaneously want things to be different and not want to exercise power in an attempt to bring about the desired change. It is as simple and as difficult as that.

You will be introduced to the importance of knowing your community, and you will be given some steps to help you in that endeavour. You need to understand the circumstances in which you work with power. An understanding of these circumstances is essential to have focus and be effective when working with power.

What is power? Why do you need it? Who exercise it? How can you exercise it? And how can you empower others? In the following pages, we provide some basic answers to these questions and examine other issues pertaining to power—issues that merit your attention.

There are many notions of power, as varied as abstract formulations of power as a force that produces change, practical notions of power by institutions or groups, and personal notions of power over one's self. Of all these various types of power, we will be concerned primarily with two types: political power, which is used to make or shape policies that have an impact on people, and relationship power, which is the power to influence how people relate to one another. Different authors discuss different aspects of power. Bishop (2002) talks about the differences between "power over" and "power with," while other authors talk about how power is "exercised, can be productive, and come from the bottom up" (Foucault, 1978; Fook, 2002; Healy, 2000).

You must be conscious of how power is understood and used in the groups you are working with. Even the word *power* may conjure up notions of exploitation or abuse. Under these circumstances, it is natural for people to want to distance themselves from notions of power. Since strengthening communities requires the use of power, your awareness of different cultural interpretations and applications of power is an essential capability to successfully build the necessary power to change conditions.

## WHAT IS POWER?

In the field of community change, power is the capacity to help move people in a desired direction in order to accomplish an end. Robinson and Hannah (1994) describe power as "the ability to realize one's values in the world" (p. 77). Rubin and Rubin (1986) suggest that power is "the ability to accomplish one's will with or without opposition" (p. 13). Building on Bertrand Russell's perception of power, Dennis Wrong (1995) adds a social dimension by implying that power necessarily involves relationships between people. He defines power as "the capacity of some persons to produce intended and foreseen effects on others" (p. 2). Kirst-Ashman and Hull (2001) add that power also includes the "ability to prevent someone from doing something they want to do" (p. 280). These definitions all suggest that power is something that a person or organization possesses and is willing to use. Power involves some sense of purpose or intention. We expect to meet some need or receive some benefit through the use of power.

Collaboration is the way in which a number of people who have power work together to accomplish their objectives. You can powerfully participate with other parties to create mutually acceptable solutions, even parties whose interests are different from or in apparent conflict with yours. You may combine your power with that of another group in order to bring something new to life. You can use your power to force an opponent to end exploitive or destructive practices or to challenge dominance. Dominance has to do with the manner in which some people and institutions exercise power over others. You can use your power to work with others to improve a condition. You can use your power to create.

The use of power does not have to be manipulative (power over), but it can be. It is not always good (power with), but it can be. If you notice the use of power and like what was accomplished, you will probably think that that use of power is fine. If you disagree with the purpose and the application, not only will you be upset about the use of power, but you will probably notice it more as well (Bishop, 2002; Strega, 2007).

Power does sometimes imply resistance. Sometimes it requires a struggle or a fight. Too often though this is the only way we understand power: people being forced to do something that they do not want to do by someone who can make them do it. These images continue to haunt our understanding of this basic concept. The more we exercise "power over," the greater the opposition. Also the more the use of power will be seen simply because there is a clash of power. Here, it is both the clash and the manner chosen to resolve the differences that call attention to power and shape our reactions. It is not simply the presence of power (Bishop, 2002; Strega, 2007).

Power can be used in a spirit of cooperation as easily as it can occur in a climate of conflict. When someone helps a group of people move in a desired direction in cooperation with a group or a community, they have exercised "power with." The fact there was no difficult conflict does not mean there was no power used. In and of itself, power is neither good nor bad. It is simply, and importantly, the necessary element that provides the impetus during the process of making things different. Elizabeth Power (2001) notes, "In the face of change, power counts" (p. 176). That it may be used to dignify (power with) or demean (power over) depends on the user and the tool.

This brings us to the notion that power is exercised. Healy (2000) argues that power can be understood as something that is "exercised rather than possessed" (p. 43). This interpretation means that power can be found everywhere and that it runs through all forms of interactions, including the personal realm, institutions, groups, and communities. She further argues that what is important is to understand the practices through which power is exercised and how those practices are allowed to continue (pp. 43–44). Mullaly (2002) reminds us that although power may be dispersed through society, we should be aware it is not dispersed equally among all groups or communities.

Power, like many other things in life, depends on the situation, although particular people can have power in many different situations. The relative degree and location of power in a situation is determined by the interplay among the individuals and groups involved. By changing who the respondents are, what they are supposed to do, or the context in which the behaviour is supposed to occur, the power of a particular individual will necessarily increase or decrease.

A classroom teacher may tell students to complete a number of math problems in the next half-hour. The students are expected to comply or face some sort of sanction. An hour later, the same teacher is in the middle of a faculty meeting on budget cuts and makes the same request of fellow faculty members. The teacher's colleagues might not respond so readily. In fact, they might think this teacher needs a little time off and a little help—and not with math problems. The same request produced different results in different situations. In the first instance, the teacher is considered powerful. In the second, the teacher is considered unrealistic.

One view of power involves interactions in relationships between people. For example, if someone were to influence you, the power flows from your perception that someone has control over resources (such as time, money, information, freedom, affection) that are important to you. Therefore, that individual is willing to exercise control to your benefit or detriment. Thus, you behave in a certain way to achieve the gain or avoid the loss you believe will be caused by being provided or denied these resources. The more you are dependent on an individual for these resources, and the more important the consequences of their use or withholding are to you, the more that individual is likely to influence you. It is also possible for people to exercise power based on their institutional and personal locations. When you are exploring how power works in a particular context, you need to pay attention to how some people might have access to power based on their privileged social location (for example, as related to their race, gender, sexual orientation, class, ability, or other social categories).

Strega (2007) argues that social workers in a child protection agency can demonstrate the use of power over a client if they use their knowledge of procedures against clients. She describes this form of power as coercion. These types of actions force clients to respond in one of two ways. They will either be confrontational or they will feign cooperation (p. 78). Neither option is a good one.

If a service user needs something that only a worker can provide, they might choose to do things they might not want to do, or might not otherwise choose to do if they did not desire this particular resource. For example, if a person needs to use a food bank, they might have to do whatever the workers at that food bank ask of them, even if they do not want to do so. They might have to answer questions about their private circumstance or to gather documentation that proves their need. They "choose" to do these things so they can access the food bank and not have to go hungry.

What occurs in relationships between individuals also holds true in relationships between groups. An individual or group who desires influence must somehow communicate the potential for controlling resources. Further, to be effective, this must be done in a way that provides an opportunity for those being influenced to perform the desired behaviour. These pathways to power are shown in Figure 5.1.

For another example of how this works, imagine the plight of an agency director, Earl

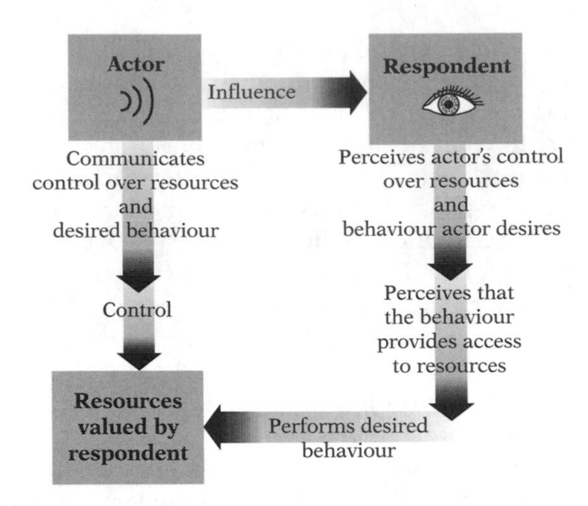


**FIGURE 5.1** Pathways of Intentional Influence Attempt

Blern. Earl is being urged by members of the community to change certain agency procedures that community members believe restrict access to services. A program designed to benefit women who work outside of the home operates from 9:00 a.m. to 4:00 p.m., Monday through Friday. These hours are convenient for the agency but make it impossible for most women who are to benefit from the program to participate. After all, many are at work during those hours.

Earl is fearful that this well-organized community group will go directly to his board of directors and pressure them to fire him if he does not make the changes they want. So Earl complies with the group's demands and changes the hours. Earl perceived that through their contacts with the board and the pressure they could potentially bring, the community could control a resource that is very important to him: namely, the board's favour, and ultimately, his job. The group has power. It was able to accomplish its purpose by changing Earl's behaviour from refusal to a modification of the program's hours of operation to acceptance.

What if this group was not really organized? What if they did not know anyone on Earl's board or did not even think about talking to the board at all? It does not matter. Earl's perception of the situation governed his response.

What if the situation were completely different? What if Earl perceived the group as being poorly organized with no plans to talk to his board or he assumed that no one would listen if they did? He would probably continue to resist. Even if Earl's perceptions were way off base, the group would have no power to influence him until he got a different message, one that changed his perception.

Finally, what if the group immediately put pressure on the board, and Earl was fired? The group would have been powerful over Earl, but they would not have accomplished their goal. By denying Earl the opportunity to change his behaviour in the desired direction and by giving him the message too late, the group would have been ineffective in swaying Earl. Maybe the next director will comply, but it is too late for Earl to remedy the situation.

## DO YOU NEED POWER?

You will learn over and over again that whether an idea "makes sense" has little bearing on what happens. You have probably learned this already. Do you ever have trouble getting around to paying your bills, or doing your studying, or engaging in more exercise? Have you sometimes found that the discovery or introduction of good ideas, ones that were reasonable and "made sense," was simply not enough to change what was happening? It is not that we lack good ideas. It is not that we do not know how to do things more effectively. It is that we do not move past talking about ideas to acting on ideas and further to implementing ideas. Old habits, old beliefs, and old fears often get in the way. These must be overcome to bring something new into existence.

The purpose you intend to achieve will require people to do things differently from the way they do them now. Some of these people will not mind—in fact, they may want to change—but other people will resist. Power

Photos.com

**Community work enables diverse groups to come together and exercise their power.**

must be utilized to awaken support, to get supporters to act in concert, or to overcome opponents.

Understand that somebody's interests are being met by the way things are at the moment. The bigger your issue, the more "somebodies" we are talking about. They are accustomed to things the way they are. They may not want them to be different. Furthermore, some of these people are much more accustomed to getting their way than to giving way. They are used to telling other people what to do. They do not like to be told. These people are not going to like what you are doing. They may not even like you. They are going to try to stop you. This should not come as big surprise to you. These people will exercise power to protect and to further what they see as their interests. How do you intend to deal with that challenge?

## FEAR OF POWER

When we are not accustomed to something, especially if that something makes demands on us, we tend to fear it—where will it lead me? What if I get it all wrong?—so we get our defences up. When was the last time you had a serious conversation about power? Have you ever? Is it any wonder then that many of us feel so uncomfortable when it comes to dealing with power?

Whoever instructed you on how to use power? Is there anything else so fundamental about which we receive so little training? Yet we are expected to use power daily. Teachers are instructed on classroom management. Supervisors are trained to get the most from their staff. In any of these scenarios, is there an honest discussion of power? Yet issues of power are central to all these situations.

Power makes many demands on those who exercise it (Bermant & Warwick, 1985). Using power in an appropriate manner must be done with respect for the rights and legitimate interests of others. This requires that you be aware of others and pay attention to their rights. It means that you must wrestle with the perplexities of what constitutes "legitimate interests." When using power, you have to accept the risk that you will make mistakes and that these mistakes will have consequences. You must be responsible for your actions and accept accountability for them.

Significant change is often accompanied by significant conflict. In fact, there will always be some degree of conflict in a situation of community change, even those largely cooperative in nature. Some of this conflict can be handled creatively and amicably. Some of it will bring anger and the vexations that accompany hostility. At times, people may not only resent what you are doing but resent *you* personally. People may not like you, and you may not like them. Using power will expose the conflict and bring it more clearly into focus.

If you intend to exercise power, you must let go of convenient old excuses that explain away the presence of intolerable conditions. You must cast off the rhetoric and habits of powerlessness. You must recognize your own privilege with regard to race, gender, sexual orientation, ability, or class when interacting with others within a particular community. When you act powerfully, you must learn not to horde power but to invest it in others as a means of producing more. In this way, you exercise "power with." If you fear power, you may actually wish to avoid the responsibility, work, conflict, or other demands it brings. However, if you deal realistically and honestly with power, if you continue to learn more about it, you will become more at ease with its use. Whether your efforts involve an office, a classroom, a city, or beyond, you will feel more alive and you will discover a profound sense of personal fulfillment simply from knowing that you are willing to take part in making a difference.

## WHO EXERCISES POWER?

In a community, a fundamental source of power involves control over resources that are considered important to the members of the community. Getting a fix on how power is rooted in your community can give you a sense of how and why things happen. Your actions will cause repercussions that may help some and frustrate others. Understanding the bases of power that may be affected by your actions will help you to spot potential opponents and allies. Finally, your awareness of sources of community power will help you to figure out where you and your associates may lay claim to some.

Several bases of power exist within a community. If you are promoting change in a community, keep its characteristics in mind, and you will see how the bases of power apply within the community. The more bases of power you have access to, the more you are perceived as being willing to exercise power, the greater your personal credibility, the more likely it is that you will be powerful. Don't forget that "you" can refer to your group or an organization such as a social service agency, not just to you as an individual.

### Common Bases of Power in a Community

There are a dozen bases of power common to most communities. At times power may be more fragmented and shifting as competition within the dynamic complexities of the community results in an ongoing ascendancy and descendancy of various individuals and groups. With so much going on at the same time, one particular individual's power in a particular sphere of community activity may be great, but relative to other individuals and other spheres, it may be much less overall. Remember that all communities are always in some state of change.

Some power relationships are based on perception and dependency. De Jouvenel (1958) describes power as having three dimensions: it is extensive if the respondents are many, it is comprehensive if the actor can move the respondents to a variety of actions, and it is intensive if the actor's bidding can be pushed far without the loss of compliance (p. 160).

In your consideration of power, keep in mind that a person must be willing (or be perceived as willing) to use power for the power base to be meaningful. Bases provide the opportunity for power; they don't guarantee it. Take a closer look at some of these bases of power.

1. *Information.* Possession of knowledge and the ability to control what other people know gives tremendous advantages. Information is the currency of tactical action. People who have a lot more information than others certainly have a clearer perception of what they need to do. In an information age, those who control the symbols of information and the interpretation of those symbols are likely to be among the most influential (Luke, 1989). Power is rooted in perception, so this is a very strong base.

Examples of people with this base of power include newspaper editors, talk show hosts, educators, gatekeepers (those who control the

## CAPTURING CONCEPTS

### Bases of Power in a Community

**Information.** Those who control the symbols of information and the interpretation of those symbols are likely to be among the most influential individuals.

**Money.** People with money can get their way in exchange for their money.

**Laws.** Determining and applying the rules can determine who wins the game.

**Constituencies.** Power over people in a group as well as the power to mobilize a large group can have a significant influence on the community.

**Energy and natural resources.** The more concentrated the energy source or the more limited and locally valued the natural resource, the more powerful those who control these resources will be.

**Goods and services.** The more important that products or services are to the local economy, the more powerful those who control these products will be.

**Network participation.** Having a lot of connections in the community provides access to resources and an increased ability to mobilize people.

**Family.** Special favours and inside information are often offered to family members, and the community may defer to members of well-known families.

**History.** Knowing a community's history, how it has approached similar issues, and where the skeletons are buried can be used to powerful advantage.

**Status occupations.** Occupations that draw prominence and deference give power to the individual or group of individuals currently holding that position.

**Illegal actions.** Illegal activity expands the scope of the game, giving power to those who go beyond the accepted limits or rules of play.

**Personality.** A personable or intimidating style can extend an individual's power by charging the atmosphere.

**Social Location.** All the above aspects are affected by the location socially assigned to people. Structural social workers argue that wider social-economic structures produce personal troubles, a situation compounded by the intersectionality of oppressions (see Chapter 2) that affect how each person, based on race, gender, sexual orientation, or abilities, experiences power and structural inequalities.

flow of information to decision makers), religious leaders, computer wizards, and political confidants.

2. *Money.* If it is not true that anything and anyone has a price, then it is close to being true in a capitalist system. Money provides the single easiest access to other things. Those with a lot of money can buy much of what they want, or they can tie things up so that other people cannot use them. Moneyed people can buy land or products, contribute to political candidates or the United Way, hire lawyers or public relations consultants, and still have enough left over for everything else they need and want.

To get money, they have to go to the people who have it. This creates quite a dependency on those who have money or can provide access to it (recall that dependency is the other basic component of power relationships). In a culture obsessed with money, it is worthwhile to acknowledge that people are fascinated by the rich, seeing them as some kind of cultural superstars. They defer to the affluent simply because of the status that wealth confers.

Examples of people with this base of power include rich people, bankers, investment coordinators and dealmakers, employers, and community foundations.

3. *Laws.* The ability to make, interpret, and enforce the policies governing a community confers a great measure of authority. Determining and applying the rules can decide who wins the game. Rule-making within a community includes formal law and agency or business regulation, as well as company policy. More often than not, laws are designed to maintain the prevailing orthodoxy rather than to challenge beliefs or redistribute power or other resources. To the extent that redistribution is done willingly by those in power, it is often a strategy to raise the stakes against more radical protest. The ability to exercise a degree of influence over who fills rule-making positions is a formidable function. Of course, those who influence the rule makers themselves have power. To a large extent, this is what community power is all about.

Examples of people with access to this base of power include key players in legislative bodies (mayors, city council members, members of the provincial and federal legislatures), campaign strategists, workers, contributors, members of selection committees, chiefs of police, lawyers, judges, members of regulatory bodies, lobbyists, and community executives (city managers, school principals, or chief executive officers of companies).

4. *Constituencies.* The ability to influence the lives or behaviour of large groups of people provides significant power in a community. This includes power over people in the group as well as the power over the group. It can also refer to the power that occurs because the interests of many people in an identifiable group are involved. If the people in the group are dependent on someone for something (for example, a job or a degree), that individual has influence over those people. The power of the group is demonstrated when others are dependent on the approval of the group itself for something (for example, votes or purchases). Community members may act on behalf of the interests of a large group if there is a perception that harming the group's interests harms the community as a whole.

Examples of people and groups with this base of power include major employers, labour leaders, community organizations, business and professional associations, community activists, religious leaders, local political party leaders, and college and university presidents.

5. *Energy and natural resources.* This refers to the ability to control the use of or regulate access to energy produced by means such as natural gas, coal, nuclear sources, water, oil, and maybe, someday, the sun and the wind. This may include the power company or the gas station (particularly if it is the only one in town). Control over specific natural resources, such as land, water, timber, and the like, are included

in this category as well. The more concentrated the energy source or the more limited and locally valued the natural resource, the more powerful this base will be.

Examples of people with this base of power include utility company executives, environmental activists, real estate developers, members of resource regulatory bodies, gasoline distributors, and farmers.

6. *Goods and services.* The more important the product or service is to the local economy, the more noteworthy this base of power will be. Also, those dealing with high-priced yet common products (cars and houses) tend to be more powerful. Again, the more limited the access to the goods or services, the more powerful those who control them are likely to be.

Examples of people with this base of power include department store owners and executives, new car dealers, grain elevator owners, construction company owners, hospital executives, mental health executives, cable television executives, and economic developers.

7. *Network participation.* The good ol' boys network does exist, and the good ol' girls network is emerging. Both networks are also based on the privilege of gender, race, sexual orientation, class, and ability. Having a lot of connections in the community provides ready access to resources and the ability to mobilize select groups of people quickly. In addition, each member of a particular network participates in other networks. Through this process, a person's name, reputation, and influence can begin to grow. There is an assumption that if everybody knows so-and-so or hears the name pop up frequently, this must be an important person (or group). Networks include formal organizations such as the Chamber of Commerce as well as informal affiliations such as business associates. Members of certain groups with select admission criteria are often accorded more influence within the community. Their members may look out for one another a little more in order to affirm group identity.

Examples of people with this base of power include those who have taken part in numerous community activities; members of civic and service organizations (for example, Rotary, Lions); active members of churches, synagogues, or mosques; members of agency/organization boards of directors; owners of businesses; members of country clubs and other private clubs; and members of local leadership groups.

8. *Family.* Family members are part of a fundamental network. The more long-standing, the larger, and the more influential a family is, the more opportunities it provides. This includes deference by others in the community to those who are simply members of important families as well as the relationships that prominent families often develop among themselves.

Examples of those with this base of power include members of influential families. The Thompsons, Westons, Aspers, Bronfmans, Richardsons, Irvings, and Pattersons are some of the moneyed families with influence in this country.

9. *History.* Knowing the traditions of a place, what has occurred before, and where the skeletons are buried can provide an insightful advantage for understanding current philosophies and actions. Though history does not exactly repeat itself, certain trends do cycle. A clear understanding of a community's history can increase credibility. By directly or indirectly relating proposed actions to past patterns, common spoken and unspoken beliefs and fears can be used to great advantage.

Examples of people with this base of power include reporters, local historians, and long-time active community residents (especially school, religious, business, and political leaders).

10. *Status occupations.* Certain occupations draw prominence and deference. Some provide a kind of community celebrity that attracts interest and even fawning attention. More weight is attached to the words and actions

of these people either because their occupation endows them with a degree of expertise or morality believed to be the province of a select few or because the recipient feels favoured by the attention.

Examples of people with this base of power include rabbis, bishops, physicians, head coaches, lawyers, and professional athletes.

11. *Illegal actions.* Some people just do not play by the rules, or perhaps they play by a different set of rules. The standard limits on action just do not apply to the game they are playing. If the consequences of resisting are acceptable to the resister, resistance is likely to continue. However, assessing the likely consequences usually involves a circumscribed set of possibilities based on assumptions of legitimate behaviour. When those assumptions no longer apply, the consequences become difficult to determine or are unmanageable. Resistance begins to break down. The whole idea of overcoming resistance is to make the consequences for resisting less attractive than accepting the proposed action. Removing the limitations of legality or morality can provide an individual with a vast array of options to develop strategies to overcome resistance.

If someone says, "Do this, or we'll see you in court," that can be a difficult but understandable dilemma for which you can prepare. However, if you are told, "Do this, or we'll have someone break your legs"—and you believe them—that gives a different feel to the situation entirely. Illegal activity provides an expanded game. The potential use of violence is just one form that it may take. If one person is willing to use rational argument, whereas another is willing to use argument, bribery, and threats of violence, the latter simply has more weapons. Dealing with this situation is not always as easy as going to the police. Sometimes the illegal participants are the police.

Examples of people with this base of power include gang members, members of traditional organized crime families, drug dealers, neighbourhood bullies, and backroom dealmakers.

12. *Personality.* Some people have developed a personal manner that attracts enthusiasm, support, and respect like a magnet. They project a sense of purpose and confidence in their own and others' ability to accomplish goals. They spark in others a belief that problems can and will be addressed. Other personalities have developed an intimidating presence. They act like they should be taken seriously and use confrontational techniques to discourage opposition. Still others are just so likable and persistent that it is hard to say no to them.

Regardless of the particular approach used, individuals with this base accomplish what they want through dint of their personality and a single-minded belief in what they are doing. They have an air of assurance and are not intimidated by others. The best of these can use a variety of styles and match them to the situation. They have made getting their own way into a kind of performance art.

Though this base of power is different from the preceding ones in that the only resource is one's self, it is nonetheless an important one. Ultimately, it is the atmosphere that is created that determines success. Personality can be an instrumental force in establishing the right atmosphere.

## Common Bases of Power in a Group

Much of the real action of community change occurs within small groups. It is here that most of the work and most of the decisions take place. The basic aspects of power—perception of dependency within relationships—certainly applies to small groups, especially since it is the relationship among members that is the essence of a group. Johnson and Johnson (2003, pp. 244–246) discuss six useful categories of power within groups that apply to communities as well:

*Reward power* occurs when an individual responds to the behaviour of other community members by dispensing valued positive consequences or by removing negative ones. The result is that group members want to gain his or her favour and strengthen the relationship between them.

*Coercive power* is just the reverse. This exists when an individual can respond by punishing other members. Members feel forced to go along to avoid discomfort.

*Legitimate power* is based on the community members' belief that the individual has influence over them due to that member's position. Thus, the treasurer may have some authority over dispensing group funds, or the chairperson may manage group discussion.

*Referent power* is established when others want to identify with or be like a particular individual—or even want to be liked by him or her. Sometimes group members comply out of respect; sometimes they do so to seek approval from a popular person. Remember how people sought the approval of the most popular person in high school? That is one example of referent power.

*Expert power* flows from those who have unique knowledge or abilities that are honestly offered to the community for its benefit. However, if people begin to feel inadequate around such an individual, her or his power can diminish.

*Informational power* is similar to expert power. In this case, the community is influenced by the individual's particular access to information and her or his ability to think and communicate clearly.

These bases of power address the dynamics of what is occurring within a group and how its members relate not only to one another but also as members of a group. They also apply to how the members relate to the objectives of the group.

Remember what we discussed at the beginning of this chapter regarding our understanding of power; we want to move away from a binary notion of power—that is, those who have it and those who do not have it, assuming that those groups are mutually exclusively (Fook, 2002). We use Foucault's understanding of power. Foucault indicated that power can be either positive or negative, it has the potential to oppress or subjugate others (repressive power), but at the same time has the potential to transform (productive power). Power is something that is exercised and not simply possessed through the use of "technologies of power" such as unfair laws and unequal distribution of resources. Maybe the most important aspect of power is that it can be exercised from the top down (repressive) but also from the bottom up (productive power) (Fook, 2002; Healy, 2000)

Foucault also indicated that there is a close relationship between power and resistance. He said that "as soon as there is a power relation, there is the possibility of resistance.... We can always modify [power] grip in determinate conditions and according to a precise strategy" (Foucault, 1988, p. 123). Resistance is not necessarily the same as violence; resistance is a form of response to ways power is exercised (either repressively or productively). Communities of women have resisted different forms of labour discrimination, by using the courts, marching on the street, and claiming their space. Other communities (racialized communities, queer communities) have also use form of resistance that suit their struggles and contexts.

## Determining Who Exercises Power

Power fluctuates within a community as new actors and new issues present themselves for consideration. This occurs even in fairly small communities. New problems, new opportunities, and new personnel create shifts in power.

A good way to determine who is exercising power is by talking to people, especially the more active members of your community. Ask these people who influences them. To whom do they respond, and why? Then ask them who their most difficult opponents and most effective (not just nice, but effective) supporters are. Get some idea of what makes someone difficult or effective. Next, get a picture of the person or people they see influencing other people and how this influence occurs. Finally, ask who they think others would say is powerful and why, and then find out who would be on their list and why. This process will lead to many an interesting conversation, a number of good insights on community power, and a burgeoning assessment of the power present in your arena of action.

Get lists of every group, organization, or event that involves community power. See whose names appear frequently and where. If you can, note who seems to associate with whom or how tentacles of power reach out into the community and come together again (Male, 1993). Obviously you can put a lot of time into this, but once you have a base of information, you will pick up lists as a matter of habit. Be sure to review them to keep them up to date. While you are gathering lists, make up a few of your own with your perception of who is well-stationed in the various power bases in your community.

Remember that local newspapers and magazines commonly prepare not only community power analyses but also feature stories on prominent community leaders as well as rising stars. Special reports on sectors of the community (for example, a review of major employers) can come in handy. Keep on the lookout for these.

### GLOBAL PERSPECTIVES

ETHIOPIA—When the spider webs unite, they can tie up a lion. (Ethiopian proverb)

SRI LANKA—Using life-centred power is not the same as power-sharing. The concept of sharing power is a familiar one. However, we do not always recognize the reality that power-sharing also contains elements of arrogance and dominance. Who is it that decides how the "cake" of power is to be cut and how it is to be shared? Or when it is to cut or not cut? Inequalities can be incorporated into power-sharing. But when we are able to experience power with each other, we become interdependent, and the transformation of one leads to the transformation of all. Similarly, the oppression of one leads to the oppression of all. In experiencing power *with each other* we are interconnected. We are drawn to work together while respecting each individual's identity and affirming our mutual need for each other. Life-centred power is the pivot for instituting life-giving change. It becomes the catalyst for the kind of change that makes transformation of the personal, the organizational, the communal, and the global achievable. (Wickramaratne-Rebera, 1998)

ASIA—I appeal to you—do not do anything, even with the best of intentions, that will destroy the little power and strength that we possess. If you want to empower the poor, please first trust the poor. Have confidence in people's knowledge and wisdom. People can teach you—and not the other way round. Do not come to teach the poor and impose your values and strategies because of false notions that the poor are ignorant, lethargic, and need to be shaken up. (Menike, qtd. in Liamzon, 1997, p. 3)

TAIWAN—Women in Taiwan have not passively accepted their position, but rather they have tried with their limited resources to resist their subordination. Women chairs [of community development associations] have sought to change traditional relationships in the community through competing for leadership positions which take them out of the domestic realm. These women's efforts can convince residents that women should get actively involved in community politics when they want to carry out their ideas. The female chairs have also challenged the definition of mothering as constructed by the government in its Community Development Project. They have actively claimed what is necessary for a definition of good mothering, and have redefined it through their own actions. (Huang, 2001, pp. 369–371)

ITALY—Empowerment is a word that conjures varying connotations, reactions, and images. On the one hand, examples come to mind of massive demonstrations of people power in the streets clamouring for change. On the other hand, there is widespread outgrowth of awakening individuals actively taking on decisions and actions. These awakened individuals take on responsibilities and take control of their live, moving from resignation and subservience to active involvement.

LATIN AMERICA—There are numerous examples of the ongoing social and political upheavals throughout Latin America against neo-liberalism and globalization. Mass mobilizations in Peru, Argentina, Bolivia, Ecuador, and Mexico have made it clear that the Washington Consensus has been received with resistance (Ellner, 2006; Gindin, 2006; Mendoza, 2005; Saad-Filho, 2005a, 2005b). The indigenous peoples, particularly from Bolivia, Ecuador, Mexico, and Peru have also challenged neo-liberalism. Indigenous identity is closely related to oppression, poverty, and marginalization (Nash, 2006, p. 126). Accordingly, indigenous people have presented a strong front against neo-liberalism, arguing that its accompanying structural reforms have furthered their marginalization. (Parada, 2007)

People's organizations [POs] or grassroots organizations define empowerment with a sharp political focus. Empowerment for POs often means social transformation, changing structures that are barriers to change. Even when people's organizations work for economic empowerment, they seek to transform, rather than merely accept, the structures and systems which act as barriers to their obtaining economic and political power. (Liamzon, 1997, pp. 3–4)

---

Those with power are often more comfortable when directing the action from behind the scenes than with being on centre stage. Watch what is going on in your community in general, and with regard to your issue in particular. Is more attention than normal being given to a particular area of town, a particular industry, a particular ethnic group, or a particular issue? Why? Has the normally outspoken critic of this or that grown uncharacteristically quiet? Is there a new road being built through a vacant piece of land?

Pay attention to where and how limited resources are allocated. Which schools get additional space? Which programs get expanded? Notice how undesirable issues are handled. Whose budget gets cut? Where does the hazardous waste get dumped?

Look also to see who responds to whom. Who is asking the questions? To whom do people turn for answers? Who seems to take direction; who seems to give it? Who asks permission? Who provides it? Who can call people to a meeting for tomorrow at 10:00 a.m. and be sure that everyone will show up?

Finally, analyze all this good information. What tentative conclusions can you reach about who is benefiting by plans, decisions, and actions? Who is losing? Who is gaining? Who is paying? People may tell you that they are afraid to do things "because of the risks involved." What is seen as a risk? Who controls the negative consequences if things do not work out? What are these consequences? Asking questions such as these will help you determine who controls the limits of the action and who establishes new boundaries. By gathering information, keeping your eyes and ears open, and calculating who seems to be getting their way and under what circumstances, you will have a good gauge for which actors hold the power in your community.

## ASSESSING AND BUILDING YOUR OWN ABILITY TO EXERCISE POWER

Action itself implies the use of power. How will you respond to the opportunities before you? You may not have access to every form of power you need, but you want to accomplish something. You may recognize that you do have some tools to begin. What could they be? Take a look.

One thing you probably have is a good perspective on the problem situation. You know people are unhappy or hurting and that the condition is unacceptable. A certain power comes from being on the right side of an issue. It may not be enough in itself to win, but it can get you and others going and help sustain you through tough times. Having the advantage of perspective puts your opponents on the defensive. Knowing all that you can about a problem, especially its harmful consequences and the moral issues involved, can be a real asset.

Review the bases of power within your community. Which of these are available to you at least to some degree? Do you have any expertise or information not commonly held in your community? Can you speak with professional authority? Or can you speak with a sound grasp of the particular subject you are dealing with? Do you hold any position of authority or leadership? Here is a tough one: Does anybody like or respect you?

Take a look at the resources at your disposal. Can you mobilize a constituency, or at least begin to do so? Can you talk to a community group to help shape their thinking, or can you get a favourable story on the six o'clock news? Does anyone from whom you need a response depend on you for anything, or perhaps depend on you to not do something? Can you deliver votes? Are laws or regulations in place that can serve your interests? Can you embarrass any important person or group? See Kahn (1970, 1994) and Amidei (1987) for more on these topics. One of the fundamental resources at your disposal is cooperation or compliance. To go along or to "do what you are told" involves a series of actions you can take or withhold. The possibility of many people acting together in organized non-compliance offers a potentially potent advantage (Sharp, 1973).

You probably have some claim on at least one, if not more, base of community power. Take a good look at the possible power capital you possess. Be sure to include your own personal assets. You probably routinely overlook or undervalue a few of the things you have going for you. Now look at those who are or will be working with you as you build an organized effort to promote change in your community. What emerges when each person takes stock of his or her own power inventory? This evaluation should provide you with a more encouraging picture of the means you and your group can use to gain the upper hand.

Establishing your own ability to influence the flow of events involves three basic strategies: making use of existing power, building power through organization, and developing personal power.

### Making Use of Existing Power

The purpose of this strategy is to provide you with well-positioned allies. Two avenues are available for using existing power. First, you can purposefully recruit powerful community members who may be willing to support your aims (we will refer to those individuals who hold power as influential community members or ICMs). Second, you can form alliances with existing power blocs, particularly organizations sympathetic to your cause or those that share a common enemy with you.

The first step in involving those who already have power in the community is to take stock of the connections you and your supporters already have. Next, get in touch with those ICMs whose help you will need. Obviously,

### Take a Moment to Discover

When you are faced with a situation that really bothers you, one you would like to change, what are some of the first things that go through your mind? How do these thoughts lead you toward or away from purposeful action? How do they help or hinder your effectiveness?

this is easier if a relationship already exists. You may need to spend some time reaffirming your relationship, even while you are asking for assistance. Do not hesitate to approach ICMs you do not know, especially if you believe they may be interested in your cause. Working together could be the start of a valuable relationship.

When recruiting the support of ICMs, invite them to understand your problems, and once they have a good grasp of the situation, ask them how, not if, they would be able to help. Be prepared to ask for a specific type of involvement. Generally, ICMs can serve your effort in one of three ways:

1. Influential community members can serve as the public face, providing a certain credibility to your endeavour by signing a letter supporting your position, by appearing with you in public, or by allowing their names to appear on your letterhead. In this case, ICMs do little more than lend their names and stature to your cause.
2. ICMs may go to bat for you on specific problems, using their personal relationships or their position in the community to intervene on your behalf. This may provide immediate benefit while helping you to be taken more seriously in the future.
3. You may recruit ICMs as ongoing participants in your work. You benefit from their direct involvement and get plugged into the current of community power.

While considering which powerful individuals to call on for support, you must also see which groups or organizations can lend you some of their strength. You may feel overwhelmed as a single neighbourhood contending with an insensitive city hall, but if the powerful neighbourhood coalition from across town endorses your operation, the scope of the conflict becomes much different. Look to groups outside your immediate conflict, especially those who will regard your struggle as a reflection of their own. Figure out which organizations have issues, interests, or people similar to yours. Are any of your members also members of one of these groups? Forming alliances with other organizations is an important, ongoing component of the development of power. Supportive organizations can provide you with the same type of help that you can get from individuals, although, because of policies and internal issues, they usually cannot respond as quickly.

Whether your added support comes from powerful individuals or organizations, receiving the backing of those who already have power can get you right into the game. However, a caution should be sounded. Using the power of ICMs and other organizations may not help you to build your organization. The more you rely on them for success, the less you rely on yourselves.

## Building Power Through Organizing Efforts

The most significant and enduring strategy for effective community change is to create a base of power for yourselves. By mobilizing the interest, action, and power of others, you can develop an organized constituency that becomes an authentic base of power. Organizing is a fundamental approach open to any community change agent. When individuals concentrate their power by acting together in planned, purposeful ways, much can be achieved. Chapter 11

## CHANGE AGENT TIP

Give each member of your action group an index card. Ask each person to list the three most powerful members of the community that they would be willing to ask for a favour. Though few of the names you get may be among the most powerful, you will begin to discover your organization's access to higher levels of community clout. These connections will help you establish a bank of power from which you may draw, and it may also provide you with names of potential members of your action group.

contains a detailed examination of the process of developing an organization.

In most situations, you will quickly confront the limitations of your own power and the limits of your own time and energy. You simply need other people, and they need you. This is not only a matter of effectiveness but also one of ethics. It is unlikely that you alone have such a command of the issues that you can speak for all concerned. It is hard to know what really is best for everyone. If you are doing all the talking and all the work, you leave no room for anyone else. You deny them the prerogative and responsibility to act on their own behalf. Frankly, what gives you the right?

## DEVELOPING PERSONAL POWER IN THE BROAD COMMUNITY

Each person in your action community has the potential for exercising more power. Personal power flows from three sources of credibility:

*Credibility as a person:* Do you do what you say you are going to do? Can people rely on you? Do you take control of your actions? Can you be trusted?

*Credibility of your information:* Is your information accurate? Is it timely? Does it consider a different point of view? Is it comprehensive, or is something left out, perhaps purposefully?

*Credibility of your power base:* Will others actively support you? Do you have any resources to withhold or deliver?

Increasing your power requires strengthening these various sources. How do you do this? Consider these issues in reverse order.

### Putting Yourself in the Community

Insinuating yourself in the community involves placing yourself in a position to be known positively, not just by people with community influence but with as many community members as possible. Remember, those who are powerful in a community may also exercise power over others in the community and power can shift. Once involved, you may affect community decisions and use the new relationships you develop to assist your continued efforts to improve the community. You do this by building your credibility in a situation where people relate to you as a person who is capable and at least equal to others whom they value in a serious situation. We do not want to give the impression that you can become fully accepted into any group (marginalized groups usually are not quick to accept, nor that there are not some very exclusive groups that may never include

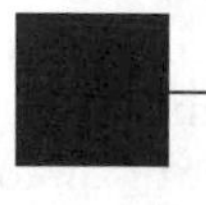

## CAPTURING CONCEPTS

### Working in Partnership with Others: Becoming an Ally

Anne Bishop's (2002) book about becoming an ally with people from marginalized communities encourages you to become aware of your own sources of privilege. This book can motivate you to continue to work on not only your own awareness of different forms of oppression but also how they affect you and those with whom you are going to work. Bishop suggests it is important to encourage others within your own group (your own race—including whiteness—your own gender, sexual orientation, class, ability) to pay attention to how their membership in this group allows them access to power. When working across groups, Bishop tells us it is important to develop the ability to listen actively to others. It is important to acknowledge that everyone in an oppressor group is involved in supporting a form of oppression. Men, for example, must accept that they are the beneficiaries of gender privilege (whether they intend for this to be true or not). Similarly, those who have access to privileges available to those with white skin must acknowledge the advantages of having been born with white skin. If you belong to a privileged group and you want to work effectively in partnership with others, you must move past your guilt, your sense of embarrassment, and your defence mechanisms and instead get to work in partnership with others to end oppression. You do not have to deny your privilege; in fact, quite the opposite. You can use your privilege to help accomplish this goal. At the same time, you must recognize that members of oppressor groups will never be able to see oppression in the same ways as the members of oppressed group do. Bishop pushes people to concentrate on breaking the invisibility of their privilege; she recommends that you not tolerate any form of oppressive statements, jokes, or actions. Be patient, but refuse to accept any form of mistreatment. Do not assume you know what is good for the oppressed group and do not take credit for a particular oppressed group's struggle against their own oppression. Unlearn your form of oppressive behaviours, ideas, and attitudes; be yourself but do not try to appropriate the history of oppressed groups (pp. 96–101).

you as a member. Still, you can be integrated into some pretty vital groups without too much difficulty. Here are some groups you might approach:

• *Local agency boards of directors* generally include a number of ICMs. Because you are not joining a board just to meet people, focus on those agencies whose mission reflects your own interests. From the work that you have done so far, you may have established contacts in the community or in the agency itself with people who can recommend you as a candidate for the board. If so, you have already started the process of becoming included in community decision making. If you know no one who could "sponsor" you, contact the agency director, board chair, or head of the board's nominating committee and let them know of your interest. Spots on agency boards come up routinely, and you stand a decent chance of being selected if you show a genuine interest and can communicate what you can offer to the organization.

• *Community action, problem-solving, or issue groups* often attract community members and provide opportunities for "unknowns" to shine. The major requirements are to show up, start talking, and start working.

• *Political campaigns* are always looking for responsible workers. With your willingness to take on tasks and your competence in performing them well, you will find a steady increase in responsibility and recognition. The more campaigns you work, the more campaign expertise you will develop, and the more your assistance and input will be sought. The relationships you develop with the candidates can be beneficial when they take office. Working closely with the candidate's staff, advisers, and active supporters is also helpful, as they themselves may be or may become important community figures.

• *Public boards and commissions* can provide you with a position of influence. Some local and provincial governments are fairly littered with such bodies. The clerk of each governmental jurisdiction (such as province, county, city, or town) should be able to provide you with a list of the various boards and commissions and their vacancies, along with information on the appointment process.

Other possibilities could include groups that plan and coordinate special events, like an annual parade or fair or various task forces on topics of immediate community interest. Do not be shy about inviting yourself into something that attracts your interest and the interest of other key members of the community.

Because much of the work in these situations takes place in face-to-face group activities, you have a good chance to make a favourable impression. This is especially true when working in newly formed groups where relationship boundaries have yet to be established. Prepare yourself to perform capably, speak up, and take the time to get to know people. You will soon find that you will have accomplished something important simply by demystifying your perception of people who hold power. Those with measurable clout are not markedly different from anyone else. Some are friendly, some obnoxious; some are dynamic, some dull; some are easily open to new relationships, and some are reticent.

Unknown commodities are a little suspect. You are too, if you are an unknown. So become known. You do not need to be accompanied by a brass band. If you are noticeably competent, and even likable, you will be recognized, and you will find yourself included in more discussions of greater importance.

## Some Strategies of Power

Having solid information will ensure that you have a measure of credibility. People give more weight to the words of someone who knows what he or she is talking about. Don't you? Doing your homework involves not only collecting pertinent information but also organizing it in a way that speaks to what is on the mind of your listener. Of course, this means that you had better get a good idea of what actually is on that listener's mind.

Know your topic well enough that you can cite a few specific references or note specific facts. Then check to see what is missing. See if you are uncomfortable discussing any particular aspect. This might indicate that you do not really know something that you think you should know. Or look at your argument from the opposite point of view. Can you identify where it is vulnerable, where you cannot really use data to justify what you believe to be true? Once you have done this honestly, you will have a good grasp of the subject and be able to communicate it clearly.

You can undermine your credibility by misrepresenting the particulars of the matter. If certain details fail to support your position, you are better off acknowledging them and comparing them against the prevailing strength of the information that does support your claims.

Having a good feel for your topic and for the situation in which you are discussing it will give you confidence. You will also give confidence to those who need to determine a course of action by supplying them with a good foundation of information on which they can support a decision. When people depend on you because of the reliability of your information, you have a lot of influence.

One of the best ways to gain trust is through admitting what you do not know about an issue or community. Do not be afraid to admit in a respectful manner what you do not yet know and genuinely engage community members to help you find out what is necessary. Oddly, sometimes when you admit your limitations you gain more influence because community members know you are not acting in a way that makes no sense to their community. When you gain trust and influence, you are more powerful in the community.

Do not get locked into one pattern of behaviour. Be willing to change your approach while holding firm to your goal. You limit your effectiveness by becoming caught in your own need for success if it does not make sense to the people you work with.

Consider your short and long-term gains and losses. The way you handle the situation today will have consequences tomorrow. Remain attentive, and be honest about what you are doing. You can easily rationalize compliant behaviour. When you think you are making things easier to handle at some indiscernible point in the future, it may be that you really just want to avoid a fight. Of course, the reverse could also be true. You may just want to fight now and ignore the consequences. There is no simple answer here. Consider how you can produce an immediate gain in such a way that long-term gains become more likely.

Be on the lookout for areas of agreement. If the emphasis is on disagreement, that will be the only result. The whole point is to forge an agreement, one that serves your interests. Be aware of common interpretations, beliefs, and values. Observe when the other party is willing to move in a direction that is acceptable to you. Though the agreement may not be so much a formal declaration as a change in behaviour, you had better be able to detect signs that can guide you to a satisfactory outcome.

Acknowledge others' need for influence. Each person needs to feel some measure of influence in a relationship. Know that this exists. If you do not intend to allow an opponent any influence, realize that this attitude will increase resistance. Providing room for another party's influence in a way that does not detract from your interests increases the chances for a satisfactory conclusion.

Remember that all behaviour is purposeful. What is the other party telling you by its response? How do you use this information? How are you responding?

How often have you seen people give up their own authority to act by first asking for someone else's approval? You may have done this yourself. Refuse to lightly give away your authority to act. If you determine that something needs to be done, do it. Understand that there may be some consequences you will have to deal with later. Frankly, most of the time this involves an apology for not consenting to someone else's control. Accept your responsibility for others' oppression and your own privilege. Make visible your own privilege and do not deny it or justify it, particularly to those who belong to marginalized and oppressed communities.

Do not "other" those with whom you will work in a community. Exclusion and marginalization have their roots in the process of "othering," which means talking about "them vs. us."

## Take a Moment to Discover

Think back to a time when someone was able to silence you, someone who acted like you did not have the right to raise an issue or voice disagreement. How did this happen? How did you feel about your response? How could you now handle a situation like this differently?

## USE YOUR POWER

Does pursuing your interests faithfully mean that you have to stop being friendly? Of course not. You can be friendly while firmly holding people to their agreements. You can be thoughtful of others while not being dissuaded from what your organization needs to accomplish. Acting powerfully does not imply that you become a less pleasant person, just a more intentional one.

Every change effort involves a "statement about why particular people at a particular time may be ready to challenge power, how they can, and why they should" (Cox, 1987a, p. 241). When you exercise power, you are respecting your rights and the legitimate rights of others. Many of the opponents you will encounter want to maintain policies and continue behaviours that are demeaning to whole classes of citizens. They do not have a right to do this. Although you must acknowledge their interests, you need not accept them as legitimate. It is too bad that change may be painful for those who have grown accustomed to having things their way at the expense of others—those who benefit from the status quo are often those who have privileges based on their race, gender, sexual orientation, class, or ability. Most frequently, those communities and groups that have been marginalized and excluded include Aboriginal peoples, racialized communities, gay and lesbian people, and people with disabilities, just to name a few.

It is not your responsibility to ease the discomfort of those who benefit from the status quo by pursuing your goals with a diminished sense of purpose. You are not called on to protect the non-legitimate interests and privileges of others, no matter how entrenched or long-held they are. The interests of those who struggle with you on your side deserve far more respect.

When you battle *powerful ignorance*, you are likely to meet resistance from those who want to hold onto their practised ways of understanding things or from those who do not have enough concern to listen to what you have to say. This can be frustrating. It is almost like you are trying to get people who are standing still to start moving, and moving in the right direction. When you take on *powerful interests*, your struggle is more difficult. In this case, you are trying to turn or move past people who are pushing you backward.

Whenever your pursuits challenge the advantages of those who benefit from the status quo and the routines that support those advantages, your own legitimacy to act will be criticized. Whether parents, teachers, bosses, or mayors, people with power often believe they have a right to do exactly what they are doing. When you come along to challenge this notion to improve the position of the most marginalized in the community, you are almost automatically seen as acting improperly. A common tactic is for them to attack your very right to question (Staples, 1984).

Somewhere along the line, someone may well call you naïve or misguided, or oftentimes just angry. Maybe you will be called a troublemaker or a rebel, or even a radical. Some of you are not accustomed to being treated in this way and may find these charges upsetting. That is understandable. As long as the picture of yourself comes from you and from the people working alongside you, this will not be much of a problem. However, if your perception of yourself and your organization's legitimacy comes from those you are confronting, you may begin to second-guess yourself. And remember these are strategies of power that are meant to put you off base so it is harder to proceed. Sometimes also you may feel beaten down, put off, or confused. It does not mean it is all over. It simply means you may need to develop a new strategy, take a brief rest, rethink what is going on so you feel good about yourself and your community, or in some cases even push harder.

In fact, the community at large may assume that those who traditionally control the direction of the community simply have the right to do so (Rubin & Rubin, 2001). Challenging this notion not only requires effective organization, but ultimately a change in community attitudes regarding who has the right to exercise power. In a community conflict, you often need to promote your group's right to challenge accepted practices. You may have to inoculate the community (and your supporters as well) against the tactic used to discredit your efforts not only by predicting that it will occur but also by clearly articulating your message.

When you exercise power to get a response from those who do not share your goals, information, or values, you are likely to meet some opposition. This is a predictable part of the process, one that you must address with a clear sense of purpose and a secure belief in the validity of your interests. Your use of personal power to influence elements in a situation should be directed toward advancing the interests of your group. Effective use of personal power is a tremendous tool in the development of the power of your organization.

## EMPOWERING OTHERS

A fundamental task in promoting community change is fostering conditions and beliefs that help others exercise their power. The success of your efforts requires it. More than anything else, your limits are defined by a lack of power. The more people your organization has who are capable of acting powerfully, the more you are able to erase limitations. An organized effort with many people acting powerfully and confidently in concert is far more effective than one with a strong leader and a lot of hopeful followers.

Empowerment involves overcoming sets of beliefs, oppressive structures, and stifling practices that keep people and their concerns isolated from one another (Friere, 1973; Gutiérrez, 1995). Recognizing interests that are held in common with others in similar circumstances and having the ability to connect with one another in purposeful action builds a foundation for strength (Crowfoot, Chesler, & Boulet, 1983; Parsons, 1989). Intentionally promoting the development of knowledge and skills through reflective action builds on that foundation (Parsons, Gutiérrez, & Cox, 1998). In fact, Wenocur (1992) argues that an emphasis on helping marginalized people gain sufficient knowledge and skill to make systems respond to their needs is the highest priority in fields such as social work, as it is essentially related to the fundamental value of self-determination. Gutiérrez and Lewis (1994) emphasize the importance of helping people to make the "connection between personal problems and political issues" (p. 31).

You might be thinking, "How am I supposed to enable others to empower themselves?" Rest easy. It is your job to encourage the process. It begins with the idea that people will work together to overcome obstacles, and it is first expressed in the way you work with others. Empowerment also means overcoming relationships where the provider of help holds the power and the receiver of the help does not. We need to examine the nature of our relationships with those with whom we partner to promote change. Rose (2000) challenges us "to create relationships in which meaning [is] being produced not received, where participants [are] equally valid contributors to defining and shaping the process, product, and purpose of their interaction" (p. 411). This does not require a lot of effort, and it will save you some.

Empowering others requires you to look for guidance in the discussion of the basic notions of power. Recall that power involves possessing resources, influencing others, and determining direction. Many opportunities exist for those involved in your effort to discover and use resources they have as well as to develop new ones. Members can influence one another as well as those outside the organization. Each member will determine what steps he or she will take to further the cause, and each will have an occasion to shape the direction of the overall effort. All these opportunities exist. You just have to recognize them and take advantage of them while promoting the notion that others do the same. The catch is that you have to value these opportunities to even see them in the first place.

You reverse the process of empowerment when you deny opportunities to other participants or when you accept or even encourage them to give opportunities away. We can assure you this will happen. As soon as you get into the habit of thinking "I can do it better myself," you are closing off chances for others to do as well as you, or to learn to do as well (by the way, just because things are done differently from the way that you would do them does not mean they are not done as well). And yes, people do routinely give away the power they have. How many times have you heard "Oh, I'm not really good at anything" or "I don't know, it's up to you"?

Once people begin to believe in their own power, they value and make available their contributions. The result is a richer and stronger organization. Clearly, you alone are not responsible for increasing the power of other participants, although the greater the role you play in the change effort, the more attention you need to give to this concern. Take a look at a number of simple steps that can help you create and take advantage of openings for others to step forward:

- *Ask questions and ask for input.* By seeking information you do not have and by valuing another's ideas, you reinforce something very fundamental. You counteract a common powerful fear people have of being thought of as stupid. You can always acknowledge what someone says, if only by restating the comment to demonstrate that you have clearly heard it. Accepting every part of every viewpoint is phony, though you can generally find something of value in a response. Learn to disagree without putting down an idea or the person who offered it. Recognize good ideas and their originators, and allow other people to have better ideas than yours.
- *Re-route questions.* Feel free to pass on questions asked of you to other people. An occasional "I don't know, what do you think, Hank?" can draw in more people.
- *Promote access to decision making.* Decisions reflect the will of those who have power. If decisions rest on the ideas of a few, only a few will be powerful. If they rest on the input of many, many will be powerful (Brown, 1991).
- *Give recognition and credit whenever you can.* A simple "Good idea, Gladys" or "Thanks for helping out at the meeting yesterday, Zach" can be valuable. Commenting on contributions in the presence of others provides a nice acknowledgment. Formal recognition, such as including names in a newsletter story or awarding certificates and even humorous awards, can be useful too. Let people take credit for the work they have done, but have no tolerance for members fighting over credit. If this occurs, it can be devastating. Such squabbling is usually a symptom of too little credit being given out, not too much.
- *Help people think about statements of inability.* "I can't" or "I don't know" will probably be declared more often than you care to hear. Be willing to ask questions like "If you can't do this, what can you do instead?" or "Can you think of just one thing?" When you stop believing in people's inabilities, you will learn a number of techniques to encourage their abilities.
- *Promote the distribution of responsibility and authority.* There is plenty to do in a change effort. Help spread the tasks around. Ask for help yourself. If someone takes on a project, let that person handle it without you hovering, and certainly do not redo it all after they think they are finished. Although coordination of effort is important, there are many things people can be in charge of, especially if they have a clear understanding of expectations and a chance to shape them.
- *Promote the acceptance of mistakes and acknowledge your own.* Few things are as debilitating as the fear of making a mistake that is going to be made into a big deal. People learn from their mistakes. Sometimes they learn not

to try again. They can also learn how to improve by building on what they have done. Look first to compliment, and question the need to criticize before you do. Include yourself in this too. Acknowledge and learn from your own mistakes without making a big deal out of them.

- *Encourage the development and awareness of resources.* Recalling the relationship of resource use to power, your group needs to do more than increase members' sense of their own personal competence as they shape the nature and direction of the change effort. The organization must cultivate resources that may be used to increase its power. As part owners of these resources, members of the organization experience an expansion of power.
- *Promote the relevance of actions.* Actions that members are expected to take in the name of the organization, especially those that challenge authority, must fit their picture of how the world works. These actions must make sense to them (Cox, 1987a).
- *Promote the recognition of success.* Your organization will win victories, some minor, some major. Pay attention to them. Empowerment occurs through success and the confirmation of effectiveness that success implies. This is true for the successes that individuals achieve on their own as well as those they achieve as members of a group. Just by pulling together you are all going to feel and be more powerful. Yet you will have done even more if the process you use in bringing people together helps them discover and believe in their own personal potency. The most powerful organizations are made up of powerful people. When people feel empowered, they see themselves differently, as more capable, more responsible, and more willing to shape forces rather than be shaped by them. This has consequences far beyond the immediate events.

## CONCLUSION

Every relationship embraces power. It is at the very root of all our relationships. Every relationship involves people responding to one another. With no response there is no relating, no relationship. Relationships between students and teachers, between competing interests in the community, are all marked by the interchange of expectation and response. To be in a relationship is to influence and to be influenced.

Power affects everything we do. It is not only a useful thing, it is essential. Power can be used to enhance the parties in a relationship or to exploit them. If one or more of the parties are dissatisfied with what they are receiving from the relationship, they must use their power to change things for the better. But they can do this only if they believe they have the ability and the right to do so.

If you are going to promote change, you need to exercise power. If you are going to be powerful, you need to decide if you are going to be purposefully powerful or accidentally powerful. If you are going to use power, you must do so knowing that others may not like it. If you intend to be successful, not merely self-important, you will cultivate the power of your partners. Both power and impotence impose choices and consequences. When you make the choice to act with power, you help to set the direction. No longer will you just be told where to go.

## HELPFUL WEBSITES

**EmpowermentResources.com**

www.empowermentresources.com

EmpowermentResources.com has links to many organizations concerned with political empowerment. It also provides information on other resources such as books and networking. The site covers a number of empowerment topics and sources, from the odd to the practical.

**Green Empowerment**

www.greenempowerment.org

Green Empowerment is committed to promoting renewable energy and sustainable development around the world. It supports community-based, renewable energy projects that are economically and environmentally viable with a development goal of fostering self-sufficiency.

**The Citizen's Handbook**

www.vcn.bc.ca/citizens-handbook/welcome.html

The *Vancouver Community Network's Citizen's Handbook* touts itself as the most complete grassroots organizing guide available on the Internet. It has a pretty impressive set of organizing principles and activities, along with a citizen's library.

CHAPTER SIX

# Knowing Your Community

**This chapter will help you better understand the following questions:**

- What are most commonly accepted perspectives on "community"?
- What are the basic community characteristics?
- What are the real and imagined constraints to change?
- What are the five stages of community life?

How you approach your community will be based on what you want to know about it. The community is a contributor of resources and allies and a provider of pitfalls and opponents. You want to know where these are—where to go to get what you need and whom or what to avoid. The community is, after all, where the need for change, the effort to make that change, and the resistance to change coexist. In fact, it is itself slightly or significantly changed by your efforts.

## PERSPECTIVES ON COMMUNITY

Just how much you need to know will depend on the nature of the problem and the size or extent of the change being pursued. Three ways of looking at your community are important to your understanding. The first involves perceiving your community as a community. The second examines the component parts of the community, acknowledging that it is made up of several smaller "sub-communities." The third focuses on those individuals and groups drawn into your arena of action.

### Your Community as a Community

There are a number of ways to think about what a community is. The first, most obvious way is to think about it as a geographic area, a place with defined physical boundaries. If you were flying over the area in a small plane, you could actually see these boundaries. Certain streets mark a neighbourhood's borders. The limits of a development of townhouses or an apartment complex can be clearly determined. The most fundamental characteristic of these geographic communities is that they are places of residence. People are familiar with them because they live there.

Some communities are defined by individuals' shared interests, activities, and affection. These characteristics differentiate them from others. Some communities are primarily based on identity, such as  a feminist community, a community of gay fathers, a Salvadoran community, a community of mental health survivors, or a deaf community. In some cases, these people may choose to live near each other for safety or to take advantage of businesses and services sensitive to their community, but geographic location is not the only determinant of their membership in the community. Meenaghan and Gibbons (2000) describe solidarity and ontological communities of people who have a common heritage, such as religion, language, ethnicity, or culture. These communities can still be complex even if they share one or more of the heritages listed above. At the same time, these communities may assert their own community based in identity within the context of larger, more complex communities. You can see how communities are incredibly complex.

How each person claims community membership may also be complex. For example, people are usually members of geographic as well as interest communities. Perhaps you live in an apartment complex in a certain city and you attend college. You have some common interests with people who live in the same place that you do. But you also share some things in common with other students at your college. At lunch, after the exam has been rehashed, you and some other students may talk about good or not-so-good landlords or apartment managers. Some of your classmates also rent. So here you are. You reside in a particular city. You live in a particular apartment complex. You are a renter. You are a student. Already you are a member of four distinct communities, two geographic and one based in interest and one based in identity. Then again you may also identify with still more communities based on your race, age, or sexuality. And your geographic community may be influenced by your community of identity—you may be a gay or lesbian student who chooses to attend university in the central neighbourhood of a large city for safety and resources sensitive to your needs.

Some observers describe community as a state of being that provides the community and its members with a context for empowered development. In this sense, community is both a process and a desired outcome. Palmer (1993) suggests that community is found at the intersection of the inward and outward life: "Community is a place where the connections felt in our hearts make themselves known in the bonds between people, and where the tuggings and pullings of those bonds keep opening our hearts" (p. 88).

Peck (1987) tells us of the difficulty of establishing a community, but makes it clear that the attempt is well worth the effort:

> Community [is] a group of individuals who have learned how to communicate honestly with each other, whose relationships go deeper than their masks of composure, and who have developed some significant commitment to "rejoice together, mourn together," and to "delight in each other, make others' conditions our own." . . . Genuine community is not easily achieved or easily maintained; its avowed goal is to seek ways in which to live with ourselves and others in love and peace . . . . Once a group has achieved community, the single most common things members express is, "I feel safe here" (pp. 59, 163, 670).

Safety and security are other factors that affect your sense of belonging to a particular community. The World Health Organization uses the ecological model showing the relationship among different level of risks that may affect the security of individuals, communities, and society. See Figure 6.1 for the risk factors affecting communities safety (Whitzman, 2008).

Lloyd-Jones (1989) points out the benefits that accrue from coming together to form a community:

> Individuals both enlarge and restrict their own freedoms by joining such a community. But whatever restriction results is far surpassed by the individual's and the group's ability to achieve established goals while at the same time creating mutual support and pride. (pp. 2–3)

And Brueggemann (2002) calls attention to community as a necessary condition for human development:

> Communities are natural human associations based on ties of relationship and shared experiences in which we mutually provide meaning in our lives, meet needs, and accomplish interpersonal goals. Our predisposition to community insures that we become the persons we

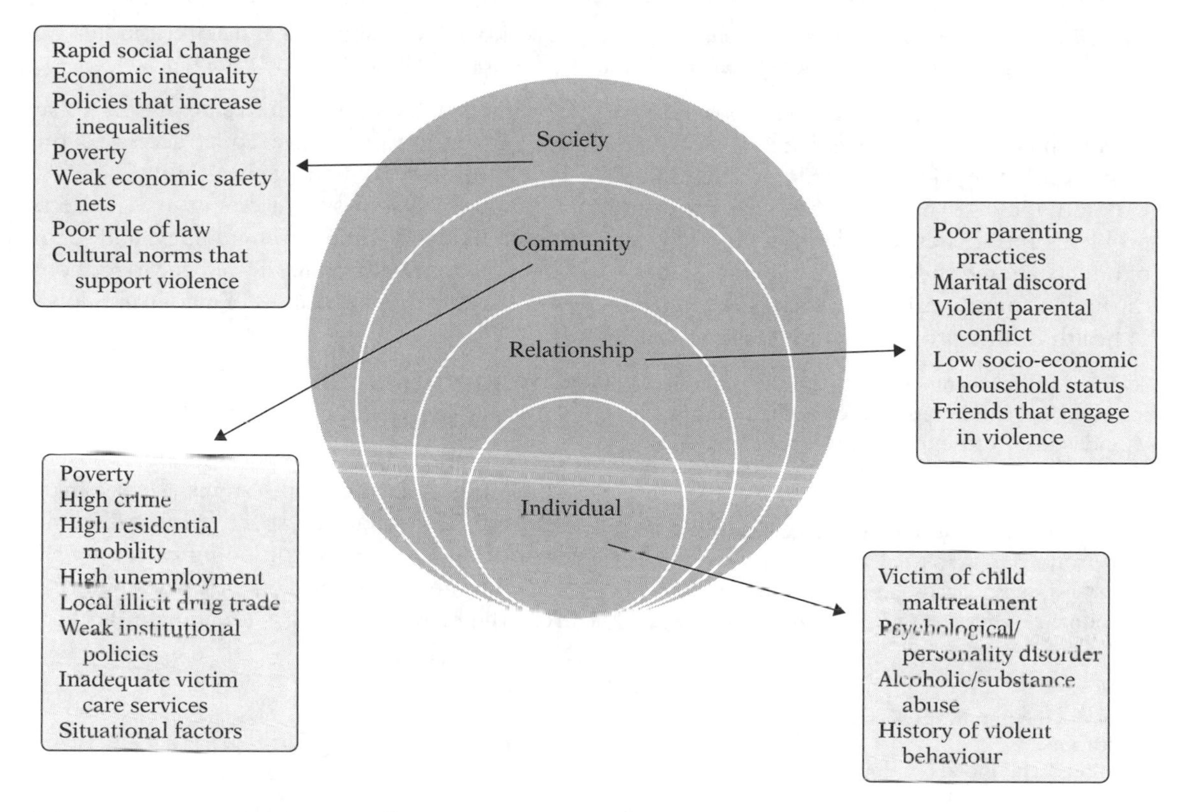


**FIGURE 6.1** Risk Factors Affecting Community and Individual Safety. Whitzman, 2008, p. 56.
*Preventing Violence: A Guide to Implementing the Recommendations of The World Report on Violence and Health* World Health Organization, Geneva, 2004, p. 4, http://whqlibdoc.who.int/publications/2004/9241592079.pdf

> were meant to become, discover meaning, generate ethical values, and develop a culture which would be impossible for single, isolated individuals to accomplish alone. (p. 114)

Lee (1999) mentions three types of communities:

> Geographic—people living in the same geographic areas, such as urban neighbourhood or rural areas; Function or Attribute—people who share or possess common attributes such as gender, religion, unions; Interests—this is a subtype of community function, a strong common interest. (pp. 15–18)

You may view community through a variety of lenses. It may be considered a place, a set of interests, an identity, a purposeful grouping of individuals into a common whole, a fundamental capacity of our humanness, a state of being, a manner of people relating to one another, or a provider of benefits that result from effective interaction. To work with a community, it is important to picture it in terms of distinctness—the clear common characteristics that connect its members. These connections provide the potential for a variety of benefits—particularly if members can recognize them and act on them.

For our purposes then:

> *A community is a number of people who share a distinct social location, belief, identity, or other characteristic that clearly identifies their commonality and differentiates them from those not sharing it. This common distinction is sufficiently evident that members of the community are able to recognize it. Effectively acting on*

> *their recognition may lead members to more complete personal and mutual development.*

A concern regarding the definitions of community mentioned above is what some cynics would call "nice, clean and orderly definitions." Communities as dynamic entities have their own problems and desires for solutions. Another way of understanding the dynamics in communities is through a concept called the social determinants of health, whose proponents would argue that

> social determinants of health are the economic and social conditions that shape the health of individuals, communities and jurisdictions as a whole. Social determinants of health also determine the extent to which a person [or community] possesses the physical, social, and personal resources to identify and achieve aspirations, satisfy needs, and cope with the environment. They are a variety of resources that a society makes available to its members [including communities]. (Raphael, 2009, p. 2)

The implicit assumption in this definition is that not all communities have equal access to the conditions necessary to live healthfully.

Figure 6.2 shows the access issue as it affects communities. Identity communities and geographical communities are affected due to relations of power and other processes of marginalization.

## Communities and Sub-communities

Communities operate on a variety of levels. Recall the discussion of systems theory from Chapter 2. A systems perspective can be helpful in understanding how communities are always made up of various component parts and levels, from the broad to the very immediate. Using a

Access to the important social determinant of health such as

- Early childhood development
- Employment and working conditions, income and its equitable distribution
- Food security, health care service
- Housing, education
- Social exclusion and social safety nets

will be affected by intersectional factors such as

- Gender, race
- Ethnicity, culture
- Age
- (Dis)ability
- Social class
- Sexual orientation

and geographical factors such as

- Rural, remote, northern fly-in
- Segregation and ghettoization
- Unfair geographic access to multidisciplinary and specialist services
- Lack of public transportation/funds
- Environmental patterns: weather, pollution, dispersion

**FIGURE 6.2** Access to Social Determinants to Health.

Adapted from Figure 21.1 Health care and access and intersectionality lens. McGibbon Elizabeth, (2009) "Health and Health Care: A Human Right Perspective." in Raphael, Dennis, *Social Determinants of Health*, 2nd edition, Canadian Scholars' Press Inc., Toronto. Reprinted by permission of Canadian Scholars' Press Inc. and/or Women's Press.

Monkey Business Images / Shutterstock

**Learning all you can about the communities with which you are working will help you become an effective community worker.**

geographic community as an example, the broad community has a name like Halifax, Montreal, or Vancouver. If you look on a map, you see the name printed next to a circle of maybe just a small dot. You may live near the town, but not really in it. Perhaps your kids go to school in Waterloo, but you actually live on a farm several kilometres away. Still, you see yourself residing in the Waterloo area.

A second level of your community consists of smaller divisions that describe sets of people within the broad community. Neighbourhoods, the business community, and the farming community are all types of second-level communities that may exist within this broader community. Some of these smaller communities are clearly defined. Their members frequently associate with one another, and they clearly understand their affiliation with other community members.

Various rituals, boundary lines, or other cues remind people of their membership. If you go to school in Vancouver, you know that you are a member of the university community because you go to the University of British Columbia campus several times a week. You see other students or other faculty and talk to them as part of your day-to-day life. You easily identify yourself with the university community.

Other community memberships are not so readily identifiable. Perhaps you are a single parent. There may be quite a few single parents in Vancouver, but you do not know who they are. You do not routinely get together as single parents. Yet you most certainly do share many things in common with other single parents in Vancouver. This community is real, but the relationships among its members are much less clearly defined. The more that members of a community relate to one another or to an identified place, institution, or activity, the more likely they will be to recognize their membership in the community. The relationship among members is likely to be more patterned as well.

These communities can be divided into even more specific levels. In Vancouver (first level), you have the religious community (second level); within that community, you have various subcommunities, including the Sikh community, the Catholic community, the Muslim community, the Baptist community, and the Jewish community to name a few. If you need to, you can break these communities down even further—for example, into specific wards, parishes, and congregations. The more you break things down, the more likely you are to come to affiliations that are directly meaningful to individuals. People usually find their immediate group to be significant in influencing what they do and how they think about what they do. Think about yourself as a student. Your university and the particular department with which you are affiliated in that university influence how you spend your time. However, the particular class that you take really influences how you spend your time. Your class is a much more immediate group than your university.

You will probably want to work at some particular level of community with which you identify, whose functioning affects your interests enough that you notice it, and where you believe that your actions can have some degree of impact. This set of people and institutions close at hand is called your *close community*.

You do need to understand that these various communities and identifications exist. Close communities can be interlocking (working together so that action is coordinated), overlapping (sharing some common feature), or independent from one another. Each of these configurations has some degree of power and is a potential source of support or opposition. Knowing how your community breaks down and what sets of relationships exist within it gives you some insight regarding whom you may want to involve and how. It will also alert you to potential forces of resistance and guide you in ways to reduce that resistance.

## Communities in Your Arena of Action

Many changes you work on will be of interest to only a small segment of the broad community. Some changes will be of interest to a broad coalition of communities and people. The more important a group or segment of the community is to your effort, the more you should know about it. The immediate community or communities you need to know about are those involved in your particular arena of action (Kettner et al., 1985): the need or benefit community, the action community, and the target or response community.

The *need or benefit community* includes those people who currently experience the problem or could benefit from its resolution. Their endorsement of the change effort is a precondition for action. There are few exceptions to this general rule. Only in emergency situations or in cases involving members of a benefit community who are simply unable to give their consent—infants, for example—would this rule not apply.

The *action community* consists of those who recognize or could easily recognize that a problem exists and are willing to work to resolve it. This includes the principal change agents as well as others who could contribute to making the change.

The *target or response community* encompasses those whose policies, actions, or inactions somehow perpetuate the problem. This community controls the resources that the benefit community needs. For worthwhile change to occur, members of this community must change their practices. Sometimes they are very willing to do so; sometimes they are not. The more carefully you pinpoint this group, the more effectively you can focus your strategy.

You may not find three distinct community groups in your arena of action. For example, if you are working with a neighbourhood to develop a program to visit elderly residents who live alone, the neighbourhood itself is the community that is mobilized, that benefits, and that must respond for change. If you are working with that same neighbourhood to pressure the banks to provide more loans to residents, your efforts must target the banks. The neighbourhood is both the action community that you mobilize as well as the benefit community. If you mobilize schoolteachers on behalf of homeless teens to put pressure on the city government to provide shelter facilities, three distinct need, action, and target communities can be identified.

Although your main focus is on your arena of action, information on *peripheral communities*—communities whose interests your actions may affect but do not now affect directly—is also important. Peripheral communities are standing around on the sidelines, some watching what is going on, some not paying the slightest attention. Even if you cannot take time to learn much about them, you should identify who they are so that you can stimulate support or counter opposition. In the example of teachers working on behalf of homeless teens, peripheral communities could include social service providers, neighbourhoods adjacent to the proposed shelter facilities, and the police department.

The complexity of the issue, its size, its potential for controversy, and the range of communities it will probably affect will tell you how much community knowledge you need to have. As you come to know more about your community, you will become more confident about what you can do to make it better.

## WHAT TO LOOK FOR IN YOUR COMMUNITY

Let us stress that you can and should get moving on your change effort before you have each and every piece of information available about your community. You can spend a lifetime studying and still not know everything you would like to know. You have to balance your need for action with your need for information.

Do not use lack of information as an excuse for inaction. On the other hand, do not dive in headfirst without checking to see how deep the water is. In actual practice, you gather some information (you need to determine how much), and then act. And you keep gathering information while you are taking action.

### Take a Moment to Discover

Walk around and through your house. See it through the eyes of someone who does not know you. What clues are there to help you understand the residents of this little community a bit better? What do you notice that could help you answer some of these questions about these people?

- What inconveniences do they take for granted or have they adjusted to?
- What do they or do they not enjoy doing?
- What values do they hold?
- How do they communicate information?
- Who does what work?
- What work is not done?
- What do the residents do together?
- How do they generate income?
- How many residents are there?
- What else could you find out about these people?

The better informed you are, the more effectively you can use your time. This increases your chances for success. But you are not primarily a researcher; you are a change agent, maybe even an activist. Just be an informed one. The information you need about your community can be organized into five categories:

- Basic community characteristics
- How the community functions to meet its needs
- Unmet needs
- Community resources
- Capacity for and disposition toward purposeful change

As you take a closer look at each category, remember that your community could be your school, the agency for which you work, the congregation of your synagogue or church, or your city. Although these are distinct categories, they sometimes overlap. Think of them as lenses through which you look at your community. These categories represent general things to look for; you will have to determine the specific information you need based on the problem you are confronting.

### Basic Community Characteristics

The information in this category is chiefly objective; that is, it consists of facts. You could get much of this information in a variety of ways. A sampling of questions is provided to give you some guidance in understanding your community's characteristics and the way in which it functions.

One of the first things you will want to know about are the physical features of your community.

- How big is it? What are the dimensions of this community?
- Where do people gather? Are there common places where people meet, either coincidentally or on purpose? This could be the train station, the mosque, or the community centre.

- Are there key landmarks or points of reference? In Toronto, everyone knows the CN Tower. In Vancouver, English Bay is hard to miss, and in Montreal, everyone can find their way to Mount Royal.
- What does this community look like? Is it dirty or clean, old or new, well maintained or in need of repair?
- What are the natural features of the community? Perhaps there is a flood every spring. Maybe there is an abundance of water, trees, and mosquitoes. Water might be a scarce resource, and snow may dot the landscape. The fact that your community is hot or cold, rainy, dry, or mountainous could have an effect on what people do.

Of course, a community is not a community without people. What do you know about these folks?

- What is the population of this community? Does this number fluctuate? In some communities like Whistler, British Columbia, there may be 10,000 people in the summer and 40,000 in the winter. There may be 100 people during the day and none at night. Perhaps the members of the community (for example, most students at a college) stay for only a certain period of time and then move on.
- What is the demographic breakdown? You may want to know how old or young the people are. Whether or not they are married may be important. Income, educational background, ethnic diversity, race, sexual orientation, gender, and cultural traditions could be significant.
- How long have these people been a part of this community? Someone who arrived a month ago will have a different perspective than someone who has been around for 23 years.
- What do the families look like? A community can have many differing family configurations: two-parent heterosexual families, two-parent same-sex families, single parent, extended families, clans, and blended families are all examples. The tolerance of family type and the mixture of family types can affect access to the resources for well-being in a community.
- What is the population density? Are there a lot of people in a small space, or do you see a lot of space with few people?

Looking at the characteristics of a community gives you a picture of the significant aspects or component parts of the community. This is like a snapshot. You see the parts, but you do not see them doing anything. If you were capturing the community with a video camera, you would be gathering information in the second category—you would see how the community functions.

## How the Community Functions

How a community functions is, in a way, its very essence. One way to look at functioning is to examine how the community endeavours to meet its needs. There is a difference between needs, wants, and problems, and for our purposes, needs are those things that a community requires in order to meet its goals and to sustain itself. These are routine, ongoing challenges that the community must address. They are different from problems, which are needs that have not been properly addressed.

As the community functions to meet its needs, it draws on and further develops the domains of capital that contribute to its health. As you recall from previous chapters, those domains of community capital are environmental, physical, economic, human, political, informational, and social (Daniels, 2002; Pretty, 2000). Just like anything you may pay attention to and recognize as important, communities tend to generate needed capital the more they recognize its importance and purposefully attend to its growth. These seven domains become focal points for community development. As you examine how current needs are being met, and capital generated, ask yourself, "How did things get to be this way?" Understanding history can be an important key to deciphering the present.

### Environmental Needs and Capital

The natural environment provides us with a place to be as well as with the elements we need for our very survival. A community needs to protect and maintain this foundation of life.

- Is the air clean to breathe and the water pure to drink?
- Are open spaces available for recreation and visual appreciation?
- How much garbage litters the community?
- Is there an adequate number and variety of healthy plant and animal life?
- Which parcels of land can be used for a different purpose?
- Which landscape features can be resource attractors? Do community members recognize natural elements as defining characteristics? How do environmental conditions affect human interaction?

### Physical Needs and Capital

This set of needs includes those that help us take care of our bodies as well as those that deal with the things we make or build.

- Do people have consistent access to adequate food, shelter, and clothing?
- Is adequate medical care available on a timely and affordable basis?
- Are roads and other transportation systems adequate for getting people to and from their destinations in a timely and safe manner?
- Are there community projects built by volunteers whose completion symbolizes concrete achievements? Murals, gardens, playgrounds, and sculptures are good examples of these (Delgado, 2000).
- Are the waste and drainage systems adequate to protect health and maintain visual attractiveness?
- What is the condition of the buildings?
- Are all the systems routinely maintained in order to prevent problems?

### Economic Needs and Capital

The community's economic system provides a way for its members to develop the means to acquire things that are important to them. Usually, this means money. Each community has some economic needs.

- How do you get access to goods and services?
- What are the income and occupation levels of specialized populations; for example, women, racialized people, and so on? What barriers to equal opportunity exist for these groups?
- Are opportunities plentiful or limited?
- What untapped economic resources exist?
- How is money earned and produced in this community? What are its major industries and services? Is it in growth or decline?
- Do members make their money outside or within the community?
- What forces that are outside of the community influence its economic health?
- Do they have access to financial institutions such as banks and credit unions?
- Are some members exploited economically through devalued labour or sexual exploitation?

### Human Development Needs and Capital

The community relies on the abilities of its members to produce goods and services, solve problems, affirm identity, and manage relationships. Where do they get these abilities and how do they enhance them? Which are seen as important?

- How are talents recognized and skills developed?
- Do members willingly offer their abilities for community efforts?
- How does the skill and knowledge of members affect economic conditions?
- How are non-market talents valued?

- Which new capabilities do current conditions require?
- Which older gifts preserve community traditions and identity and keep members connected to their culture? How are they passed on to younger or newer community members?

### Political Needs and Capital

Community life requires a continuous series of decisions on matters that affect its members. This process involves forming policies that manage resources and relationships. Each community faces a set of political needs, and it will develop a governance or decision-making structure if it intends to respond to those needs. Governance structures usually have clearly defined procedures for gathering information, making decisions, developing rules or laws, describing those rules or laws, and enforcing them. These procedures describe who is allowed to participate in the process and how (Fellin, 2001).

- What connections do members have to sources of political power both within and outside of the community?
- Do members believe they have a right to participate in policymaking?
- What is the formal process for making community decisions? What are the limits and the extent of this process? That is, over what matters is it empowered to decide, and what matters are none of its business? Which services or functions does local government see as its responsibility?
- What are the formal governmental structures? What are the formal positions of leadership and decision making, and who holds them? These are the people authorized or acknowledged by the community to provide direction. What are the informal processes for making community decisions? Each formal process has an informal one that operates within it or outside of it. The formal process often relies on this informal process or is made irrelevant by it. A description of the informal process is the answer to the question "How do things really work?" You will need to dig a little deeper to discover this process. Be on your guard against cynical paranoia as you dig. Informal processes usually depend on relationships of convenience and inconvenience.
- What are the informal positions of leadership and decision making, and who holds them? These positions usually do not have titles, or the power is greater than the title. The people to whom formal leaders commonly look in fear or for support and ideas are likely candidates.
- How do people recognize problems? Some communities rely on official reports. Others acknowledge problems when a group of people engages in advocacy. Some communities have structures for discovering problems, whereas others have patterned ways to avoid looking.
- Who is expected to be quiet, and who is allowed to speak up?
- What are the likely bases of power? In each community, some things give people a better chance at getting what they want. Find out what these are (see Chapter 5 for a detailed discussion of power).
- How are community decisions carried out in practice?
- Do the government and private-sector institutions support or even recognize the existence of the community?

### Information and Communication Needs and Capital

A community needs to know about itself and the world in which it operates. The community has to have information and methods for developing, transmitting, and receiving that information. This set of needs can be called the community's information and communication needs.

- How do members of the community learn what is going on in the community? In the world?

- What values support or limit the use of information technology? Where do members have access to information technology?
- How do people decide what is true?
- To whom do people listen (rabbi, radio talk show host, shop steward)? Who has acknowledged credibility?
- What mechanisms exist for communities to exchange ideas and information? How does the presence or absence of mechanisms affect their ability to even identify as a community?
- What schools and training programs exist for community members? How good are they? What is the degree of community control over these? How is access to them determined? How much financial support do they receive?
- How is new knowledge generated, tested, and communicated?
- What is the philosophical and editorial bias of the major formal providers of news? This could include newspapers, radio, television, employee newsletters, staff meetings, and other mechanisms set up to provide news. How reliable are they?
- What are the informal methods of providing news? What philosophical and editorial biases exist there? These could include the grapevine or rumour mill, the underground or alternative press, unofficial memoranda, and other methods that people use to communicate their perceptions of "what is really going on." How reliable are they?
- What important information does not get communicated to community members? How do you know this?
- How interested are community members in communicating with one another?
- How do institutions and social systems outside the community make it invisible?
- Remember communities are complex and some members within a bigger community may be marginalized. How do the most marginalized community members communicate with each other? Do they have access to information? Are their channels of communication disrupted by others?

### Social and Emotional Needs and Capital

Just like individuals, communities have social and emotional needs. Forming and maintaining relationships is an integral function of the community. People like to get together to feel they are part of something, or they need to get together to accomplish something. A myriad of associations, clubs, and organizations exist within your community. A feeling of well-being and confidence in the future are necessary if a community is to achieve its potential.

- Do members of the community have the desire and the ability to work together?
- Do members of the community feel safe and secure?
- Do members trust one another?
- Do members take pride in the community and their membership in it?
- What are the sources of pride, embarrassment, fear, joy, and other feelings?
- Are members confident of their own and others' abilities, including the ability to recognize and resolve problems?
- Do members feel as if they are part of the community and cared for by other members?
- How do people attend to their spiritual or religious needs?
- Do members feel free to contribute to the community and to achieve personal goals?
- What groupings occur within the community? Many of these have names and rules of membership. Knowing about these groups can help you understand how your community works and can provide you with better access to people.
- How and where do people have fun?
- How do members spend their time and money? Looking at what people do and how they commit their resources will tell you what people value.

The more interested you become in your community, the more you will want to understand it and what it requires. This is not a major project. You will simply begin to look at and think about your community in a different way.

Start thinking about which forms of community capital require more development. As you proceed, you will ask more questions, and you will gain a deeper understanding of the community's assets and needs, and the extent to which these assets are recognized and the needs are or are not being met.

## Assessing the Community's Needs and Resources

Ideally, a community meets the needs of all its members. Of course, this ideal functioning hardly ever occurs. Needs are often undiscovered, undeclared, or considered unimportant by those who could do something about them. Part of your job as a change agent is to reverse that situation. You will work to help a community not only effectively declare its needs so that they will be considered important enough to be met but also discover its resources so that it can act to strengthen itself.

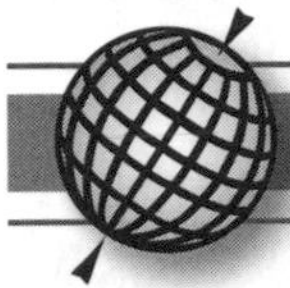

### GLOBAL PERSPECTIVES

UNITED KINGDOM—Given a substantial chance to prove itself, ABCD [Asset-Based Community Development] thinking will contribute to British community work and, more importantly, will lead many communities away from underachievement and dependency. However, it seems obvious to me that ABCD must be adapted to our context, both for reasons of substance and sensitivities about such imports. An alternative for promotion of ABCD principles in the UK might be L.A.D.—Local Asset Development. (Oliver, 2002, p. 1)

INDONESIA—YLK Sulsel [the South Sulawesi Consumer Organization] has been mapping its assets in two ways, as tangible and intangible assets. Tangible assets are real assets that can be accounted for. It is technology or equipment that applies in empowering groups. Intangible assets could be a skill, expertise, and knowledge. The life cycle of an organization is determined by the manner in which both of these assets are managed. Logically, each kind of asset, both tangible and intangible, can be maximized. The use of communications media in a democratic political system, for example, can reform the awareness of a community about its political rights. The use of knowledge of political democracy can create inspiration and provide moral support to the community to keep it struggling to build an egalitarian community, just, and equitable. Good management and maintenance of assets will extend the life of a community. If, for example, good asset management can maintain highways, phones, water supplies, hospitals, and other health services, then the life cycle of city communities will be longer. These are the things to which YLK Sulsel aspires. (Baso, 2000, pp. 1–4)

SWEDEN—If we agree that the development of communities should have its point of departure in the local community, then we must have knowledge of and insight into the essence of social life there: traditions, culture, social harmony and antagonism, etc.

It is essential to include the areas' interaction and value systems in the analysis and the strategy discussion. A comprehensive perspective is required for an understanding of how human beings develop both life and survival strategies.

[These become relevant in the development of social economy, which] is concerned with people's conditions of living and how they make use of resources: human, cultural, social, material, economic (in its narrowest sense) and ecological resources. These are all used to keep and increase the quality of life for the members and for the local community. Social economy has to do with having the central point based on human capability and human resources. (Ronnby, 1998, pp. 67–72)

All communities have resources, starting with the information, abilities, and relationships among the community members. However, few communities have all the resources they need to flourish. If the community has many of the resources it needs but does not use them effectively, it may flounder as well.

To learn more about your community's resources and unmet needs, it is helpful to conduct a community assessment. As with any other aspect of community change, it is important that members of the community play a significant role in researching the community. The generation of information heightens awareness and can provide an impetus to change. If members of the community are not involved in the discovery process, you may miss an important opportunity to develop the necessary investment of community members in the change process.

Participatory action research (PAR) is one approach for involving members. The notion is that those who most experience the events and rhythms of the community are the most qualified to investigate it and direct its use (DePoy, Hartman, & Haslett, 1999). The process is intended to yield discoveries that promote action, refine understanding for future action, and continue to develop members' capacities. Community members are active in all phases of the research process, from designing research questions and developing the methodology, to collecting and analyzing the data and disseminating the findings. PAR needs to be conducted in as purposeful a manner as any other research, and group training sessions for the various phases of the process, during which all participants teach and learn from each other, are important (Alvarez & Gutiérrez, 2001).

For participant research to work effectively, it must fit the style of all the stakeholders, and a core group from the community must maintain consistent involvement. This means that the purposes for the research as well as the various roles and duties must be clear and meaningful for all participants. There are many ways to go about the collection of community information. As you gain a better understanding of the community, its issues, assets, and actors, ask yourself, "Who owns this information, and why?"

The Ontario Women's Health Network, in collaboration with a number of community partners, has developed a methodology of research called "inclusion research" as a way to ensure the voices of marginalized community members are central to the process of developing health policies, programs, and research. In their words,

> The objective of Inclusion Research is to unite researchers from the populations "under study" with professionals in order to collectively define research questions, facilitate focus groups, collect and analyze date and advocate for social change. A strong working principle of Inclusion Research is to move research to action in order to transform the conditions that are at the root of poverty and exclusion. With this type of research, the line between the person doing the research and the people being researched is blurred. Rather than having one expert studying relatively passive objects everyone is an active participant and an expert. (OWHN, 2009, p. 14)

Inclusion research ensures that the voices of marginalized groups are central to the process because a key aspect of its methodology is the use of "inclusion researchers." In this methodology, individual women who are themselves members of marginalized groups are trained to conduct all aspects of the research and are paid to do this work. As the Ontario Women's Health Network notes,

> Inclusion Research is a meaningful way of engaging with women who have experienced marginalization in community-based research. It has proven to be effective at actively involving visible minorities, immigrants, youth, low-income women, women with disabilities, women who have experienced male violence, women with mental health issues, and other marginalized groups whose voices often go unheard. Research creates partnerships within

> the local community particularly with other community-based organizations and provides a way of listening to the voices of women who have experienced marginalization. (OWHN, 2009, p. 14)

For more information about inclusion research, visit the Ontario Women's Health Network on the web and download its Inclusion Research Handbook at www.owhn.on.ca/inclusionhandbook.htm.

### Needs Assessments

Do not define the community according to its unmet needs or its problems. Conducting a needs assessment is tricky business. The danger is that it will do little more than produce a catalogue of maladies that everyone knows about anyway. This simply reduces the community to a repository of problems and confirms desperation. Hopelessness, apathy, and dependency thrive under such conditions.

So, should you bother to conduct a needs assessment? If all you intend to do is to count the community's problems, then, no. Do not do one. If your intent is to discover issues for action, using and developing the community's capabilities, then your assessment may lead to valuable information about community issues. A needs assessment measures unmet needs. Some look at service needs or unprovided services. By the way, this does not always mean social services. "Services" can be either formal or informal forms of assistance. In most cases, a needs assessment looks at community needs that are not being met or necessary resources or activities that are not being provided in the community (New Brunswick Health and Wellness, 2002; Shmyr, 2003).

At the beginning, your main concern is to clarify your focus. You want to start off on the right track. You also want to know that what you are doing matters. A needs or issue assessment will tell you this. It helps to identify barriers to community health, uncover possible issues, and raise community consciousness and commitment to action.

When a community cannot meet its goals or sustain itself, the community has unmet needs or problems. However, goals do not have to be clearly written down. They can be commonly understood. For example, teen parents do not get together to write down the goal "to have healthy children." Common sense will tell you that such a goal exists. If medical care is required to meet this goal, and if members of the community do not receive medical care, then adequate medical care becomes an unmet need, a community issue. You will be attempting to discover such unmet needs: those sources of frustration and barriers to a community's ability to flourish.

Simply saying that a community has this problem or that problem does not do much for understanding unmet needs. You may ask questions like "What is not here that should be

#### Take a Moment to Discover

The overall benefits of the inclusion research are these:

1. It serves to build relationships and foster dialogue that may lead to practical solutions the community supports.
2. It offers a cost-effective tool for gathering input, consulting with, and involving marginalized groups in the planning process.
3. It enables marginalized groups to name their issues and priorities, while participating in effecting change.
4. It can be used with diverse communities with diverse needs and concerns, and can be adapted to a variety of planning needs.
5. Communities are more apt to support the solutions and act on the findings of the research because the research reflects the principles of community engagement such as inclusion, transparency, suitability, accessibility, and accountability.

Source: Ontario Women's Health Network. (2009). *Inclusion Research Handbook,* pp. 14–18.

here?" or "What is not happening that should be happening?" This is language that implies things can change. That is quite different from the use of language that asks for "all the bad things here in our community" Unmet needs may have something to do with recreation, adult involvement, jobs, or the availability of medical care.

A needs assessment is a process for identifying the range of a community's needs or for more clearly understanding a particular need. In addition to an examination of the extent and intensity of a need, the assessment should examine how often the need is felt and for how long. Finally, you also want to know who actually feels this need.

The assessment can include a large population group: for example, a city or even a province. Or it can look at the unmet needs of a smaller population: for example, a neighbourhood, a group of youths in a particular neighbourhood, or workers in an agency. Further, it can be designed to uncover any unmet needs or only those in a certain area, say, health or recreation (Lewis, Lewis, Packard, & Souflée, 2001; New Brunswick Health and Wellness, 2002; Shmyr, 2003). Needs assessments are generally performed for one of three reasons:

- To see if there is any need for action
- To help design or direct some already contemplated action
- To confirm what we already know and to justify an already decided action

The first case forces us to look at a situation we might have been ignoring or simply are oblivious to. In the second case, problems have come to our attention, but we do not have a solid grip on their dimensions. Because we want to increase the odds that our actions will be effective, we take some time to consider what actions are most required. In the third case, we do not really intend to learn anything, so, usually, we do not. The purpose is to show the correctness of a course of action, so we pay attention only to information that supports that claim. This approach is geared more to public relations than to discovery.

To design your assessment, you need to determine six things:

- The community whose unmet needs you intend to clarify
- The range of needs you intend to examine
- The process for getting the information you need
- The method you will use to interpret the information
- The time and money you have to do this
- How this information will be used

A general caution is to avoid overdoing things. You can get so bogged down in hairsplitting details that you end up hating the process and want nothing to do with the findings once you are done. It is possible to design a process that is creative and stimulating, one that you look forward to conducting. Taking a close look at something that has not received its due attention can excite people.

Gathering information about your community and its issues is an essential step in community change, and much has been written about the various methods for accomplishing that task. The following approaches to obtaining information about your community's needs are drawn from the work of Kahn (1994); Lewis et al. (2001); Lotspeich and Kleymeyer (1976); Martí-Costa and Serrano-Garciá (1995); Neuber, Atkins, Jacobson, and Reuterman (1980); Warren and Warren (1984); Warheit, Bell, and Schwab (1984); Berkowitz (1982); McKillip (1987); and Zastrow (1999).

We will also use, as an example of needs assessment, the New Brunswick Community Health Needs Assessment. According to this model, a community health needs assessment (CHNA) is a way of measuring a community's overall health, as well as the health-related priorities of community members. The steps involved include all of the following:

"(1) gathering information about health (fact and opinions);
(2) gathering information about health resources available in the community (assets);
(3) determining what issues are most important for the community (priorities);
(4) building commitment and support to work on addressing community health (partnership)."
(New Brunswick Health and Wellness, October 2002, p. 1)

The reasons for conducting a CHNA include these:

- "to identify the degree to which the health issues exist;
- to identify the prevalence of the health issues i.e. 'how much' they exist;
- to determine how these health issues affect the people in the community;
- to identify assets in the community." (p. 6)

There are five phases of the CHNA process: the orientation phase, the designing phase, the collecting phase, the analyzing phase, and the prioritizing phase. Table 6.1 provides a more detailed description of these five phases.

Moving from the specific of the above example, a beginning step in the process of any needs assessments is to look at information that already exists. Existent or extant data are contained in statistics that have already been collected and analyzed and in reports that have been written. At the beginning, you may be unsure about just what information you need. That is all right. Most projects start out that way. Get some of the information you think you need, and then review it. This will help you focus your future inquiry.

To augment these data, get the views of members of the community. Your issue or needs assessment will have little value if the voices of community members do not shape the results. This step involves deciding how many members you need to hear from and who those members are. Thinking this through will help you determine how to approach them. Do you talk with people individually or in a group? Do you extend an open invitation to anyone who is interested (for example, hold a public hearing), or do you select participants? Do you mail out a questionnaire or meet with people face to face? These are some of the questions you need to answer.

A couple of additional points should be made regarding this aspect of your data-collection process. First, get the perspectives of people who feel the need as well as those who could potentially feel the need. Second, have an eye to the future. Gather information from people whose support you will need down the road as you respond to the needs you identify. Collect the information in a way that strengthens the likelihood of their future involvement. Two sets of people are important for future contacts. One set is the people who will decide on the course of action in response to the recognition of unmet needs, including those who have influence on these decision makers. The second set is made up of those people who will implement the action.

Assessing a community's unmet needs opens the possibility for discovery and declaration. You may help it to become more acutely aware of conditions that block its healthy growth. Your investigation may help the community to realize that its unmet needs are a result of its not using its resources effectively. Or you may help it to demand its fair allocation of resources from the broader community within which it is located. In either case, your assessment should yield issues on which you can mobilize for action.

A key question is "Whose assets do you intend to mobilize to meet the need?" If you do not first look to the community that is the focus of your attention, you are likely to create a response that is out of context with the experience of the community members. A related question you face is "Whom do you intend to mobilize to meet the unmet needs you uncover?" If you use the issues you discover to energize the community to recognize and use

**TABLE 6.1** The Five Phases of the CHNA Process with Identifying Steps

| Phase | Type | Steps |
|---|---|---|
| 1 | Orientation Phase | —Establishing your Organizing Team |
| | | —Discuss their understanding of CHNA |
| | | —Discuss their vision and mission |
| | | —Build relationships |
| | | —Build leaderships |
| | | —Define their roles and responsibilities |
| 2 | Designing Phase | —Define the community profile |
| | | —Identify source local data |
| | | —Identify tools to be used to collect data |
| | | —Recruit volunteers for sub-committees |
| | | —Identify strategies for public education |
| | | —Identify tasks to be done |
| 3 | Collecting Phase | —Organize sub-committees |
| | | —Provide leadership and support |
| | | —Collect qualitative and quantitative data |
| | | —Complete demographic profile |
| | | —Collect community assets and community issues |
| | | —Assign tasks |
| | | —Identify deadlines |
| | | —Keep people involved and informed |
| 4 | Analyzing Phase | —Inventory of all issues identified by community |
| | | —Inventory of all community's assets |
| | | Analyze all data collected |
| | | —Analyze behavior risk factors |
| | | —Provide support and leadership |
| | | —Share outcome with community for feedback |
| 5 | Priorizing Phase | —Identify a priority list of issues with the community |
| | | —Identify a list of appropriate assets with each priority issue identified by the community |
| | | —Keep all stakeholders and community members informed of the outcome |
| | | —Very important to allow the community members to identify the priority and assets |
| | | —Ask the community members, "What's next?" |

Source: New Brunswick Health and Wellness, *The New Brunswick Community Health Needs Assessment*. October 2002. Reprinted by permission of the New Brunswick Department of Health.

its strengths for self-improvement, or if issues call members to action leading to the reallocation of power and resources within the broader community, you have used the information well. If, however, you first look to work with those outside the community as the source of its improvement, you have reinforced the notion that community members are not able or not needed to work within their own community. You have advanced the notion that the community must rely on others who will service them in their time of need.

### Resource Assessments

As you answer questions about community needs, recognize that the community has many resources available to meet these needs. The fact that needs are not adequately met does not necessarily mean that resources do not exist to do the job. Part of the problem has to do with decisions on how resources are allocated. Another part of the problem involves our ability to recognize and develop resources. Though some additional help from outside the community may be required, you will discover that a community often has a lot more going for it than you might have originally thought.

Each community has unmet needs. That is true. It is also true that no matter how poor, each community has resources to meet many of these needs—including the most important resource, people. In fact, a crucial element for success is your ability to recognize and build on actual and potential capabilities that already exist in your community. This will be the foundation of your work. An overemphasis on liabilities is a serious error that colours problem-solving in shades of inadequacy and dependence, undermining any attempt at empowerment.

An assessment of needs or issues provides valuable information but yields only a limited view of the community. To complete your work you need to pinpoint the location of your community's sometimes hidden wealth (Brueggemann, 2002; Delgado, 2000; Kretzman & McKnight, 1997; Lewis et al., 2001). A needs assessment can help to give you an issue focus; a review of resources gives you the energy. In fact, resources that already exist can give you a focus as well. Instead of asking "What blockage do we need to get rid of?" or "What access do we need to open?" you can ask, "What can we do or create with all the things we have?"

You are able to use the same approaches for discovering resources as you do for revealing needs: gather existing data, get information directly from community members, and make and record observations about the community. The methods for community data gathering described later in this chapter can be applied to discovering resources.

Almost anything is a potential resource. Part of the trick is to start seeing things as potential resources. In one sense, resources can be classified according to the needs they meet. For example, if people need to eat, food is the corresponding resource. If people need access to community decisions, the courts could be a corresponding resource. But confining resources to distinct need categories is a tricky and mistaken business. Most things can be used in many ways. The last thing you want to do is to limit the use of a resource or limit your thinking about it.

To discover your community resources, ask members of the community some of these questions:

- What natural resources exist in your community? Examples are land, water, and trees.
- What tangible human-made things exist in your community? Examples are cars, bridges, and libraries.
- What forms of currency are available in your community? Examples include money, barter, and favours.
- What skills and talents exist in your community? Examples include artistic talents, carpentry skills, and computer programming abilities.

- What human qualities and values exist in your community? Examples are honesty, determination, and passion.
- What are the major institutions in your community? Faith communities, schools, and government centres are examples of important institutions.
- What information and knowledge is available in your community? Examples include scientific knowledge, historical knowledge, and inside information.
- What relationships have members of this community developed? Examples include family, friends, natural helping networks, or business associates.
- What resource, asset, or potential contribution do you possess?
- What resources could serve more purposes? For example, a house can also be a meeting place; a mosque can also be a shelter; an office softball team can also be a mutual support group.
- With what resources do you have a personal connection?
- What resources can be combined to produce new resources? For example, what could be produced with a storage room and a dozen employees who each own 100 books?

Susan Blood (2001) notes cultural knowledge as an important component to resources in a community. Cultural knowledge includes the knowledge held by indigenous people, whose ancestors have long inhabited a region, or people who are new to a region, who bring their own traditions to a new community. Other forms of community strength might be found in its stores of resistance—the ability of individuals to struggle against oppressive circumstances—and resilience—the positive, adaptive abilities of people in the face of adversity (Longres, 2000; Mullaly, 2002; Shmyr, 2003).

Many resources go unacknowledged because people fail to consider them to be important. When you begin to see the potential value of things, you will discover resources that you never knew existed. Over time, instead of wondering "What can we do about [some problem]?" you may find yourself asking "What can we do with all these things we have?" This is a very different question.

### Take a Moment to Discover

See if you can find someone in your workplace, class, or neighbourhood who can provide, for free or below normal cost, one of these skills or resources, either themselves or through someone they know:

Computer skills
Grant-writing expertise
Political lobbying
Fundraising experience
Musician
Juggler
Plumber
News reporter
Mechanic

## Capacity for Change and Disposition to Change

All communities have some capacity to change, though some have more constraints than others. Some of the constraints are real. For example, the law may limit the political involvement of certain public employees. Some are practical; for example, single parents may spend most of their time and energy taking care of day-to-day job and family challenges. Many are attitudinal; people believe that nobody else cares or that things simply cannot be changed. They may have little experience or understanding of organizing, or maybe even the mood of the community does not ready it for struggle (Olney, 2001). Even though communities may want things to change, it may be hard for them to confront pervasive values that sustain the status quo. Change requires that we give up a set of beliefs and practices. This is a hard thing for many people to do (Nelson, 2000).

Each community also differs in its disposition to change. Some communities are happy with things just the way they are. Others have grown accustomed to things, tolerating what they dislike. Still others are ready to do something—anything—that might make a difference, now. The desire for change often involves correcting injustices and different forms of oppression, but it is not limited to this. It can also involve providing new opportunities or challenges, escaping the boredom of the routine, or just doing something fun.

Understanding your community's ability to challenge constraints that are real, practical, or imagined, and its desire to do something different, are crucial in directing your activities as a change agent. Capacity and desire for change can be evaluated by asking these questions:

- Are there legal limits on activities that apply specifically to your community?
- How much discretionary time do people really have?
- What really rankles people in your community?
- Do people complain about things? Do they complain in public or in private?
- Do people talk about how they wish things would be? To whom do they talk?

## CAPTURING CONCEPTS

### Five Stages of Community Life

In the first stage, named the **Waiting Place,** people in the community hold a deep sense that things are not working correctly, but they cannot quite put their finger on exactly what it is or what to do about it: it is a kind of "felt unknown." They may be locked into old patterns, such as finger-pointing and looking to place blame.

In the **Impasse** stage, a community hits rock bottom. You hear people saying such things as "Enough is enough!" There is a noticeable sense of urgency in people's voices. Though people may feel isolated from others and though mistrust may run deep, things have crystallized enough that the need for action is clear. Often, people are afraid that they are losing their future; they are tired of "waiting."

During the **Catalytic** stage, a small group of people and organizations emerges to take risks and experiment in ways that challenge existing norms of how the community works. People begin to discover that they share common aspirations for their community and that they can, in small ways, start to make a difference.

Over the course of the **Growth** stage, groups of catalysts expand, networks grow and expand, and a sense of common purpose and direction takes root. People see clear signs that the community is moving forward and can feel and experience much greater leadership. People's confidence in themselves and their community grows. As this stage is moving toward its end, people will start to tire, and networks may begin to fray a bit. New groups asserting a particular view may arise, possibly leading to fragmentation.

A community in the **Sustain and Renew** stage must find ways to bring along new leaders and a new set of spark plugs. Without them, the community will stagnate and possibly begin to decline. To make a successful transformation to Sustain and Renew, the community will take on especially deeply rooted issues that were beyond the community's ability in the first four stages. Purposeful attention is required to reach out and include those who may still have been left behind. The community shares gains with all its members, and not just the economic gains. Here, the community is tending to its soul.

Source: Harwood Group (1999).

- Are people who voice a desire for change criticized and put down or encouraged and supported?
- Are people intimidated by those in positions of authority?
- Do people recognize when they are not doing what they want to do or when they are doing what they do not want to do?
- Have change attempts failed or succeeded in the past?
- Do people go outside of official channels to solve problems?
- Is anyone exploring change in any way right now?
- Does change make some community members simply too vulnerable to further prejudice, exposure, exploitation, or marginalization?
- Will certain changes mean that certain community members will be totally excluded from the involvement within the community or become invisible?

As you answer the questions posed here, and the ones that you will surely add, you will build a storehouse of information that will make things a lot smoother for you now and help your change efforts.

## HOW TO FIND OUT WHAT YOU NEED TO KNOW

You should now have a better idea of what you need to know about your community. In this section, a number of specific sources of information are described together with some ideas on how you can use those sources. Remember, "you" includes all those with whom you are working. Involving other people in all aspects of the discovery process will increase the likelihood that you are gathering helpful information and will elevate its value to the group.

### Valuing the Library

Take a break from whatever you are doing and spend an afternoon at the library. Your public library has a treasure trove of information about your community, and so does your college or university library.

Prepare some questions in advance. This will give the librarian a better idea of how to help you. It will also help you to focus your inquiry. Most librarians are very helpful. Not only do they know books and where to find them, but they enjoy helping people uncover information and discover the other wonders of their library, such as audiovisual resources, computer data banks, and much more. Your local public library can be a storehouse of information on your local community, and university and college libraries may be good resources as well.

You should be able to accomplish several things during your visit to the library, especially if you come prepared with questions. Certainly, you want some specific information about your community. Particular facts, figures, names, and background information will help you answer some of your questions. It is also important to become familiar with the sources themselves. You will never be able to write down or remember everything that is potentially valuable. This is why we have libraries—so you can go back when you need the information.

A typical library will have many publications describing aspects of your community. Some of these will be national publications, some provincial, and some local. Some will be put together by the government -including special reports, such as a report by a special task force on homelessness. Others are put together by private groups, perhaps banks or non-governmental organizations. Most libraries can borrow from other libraries. They also purchase or accept material from organizations if there appears to be sufficient demand for it. Check to see if one of your local libraries is a depository for the federal or provincial government's official documents or for Statistics Canada. If not, see if you can find out where one is. If you cannot find something, do not be shy about asking the librarian for help. Here is a sampler of material that could well be in your library.

*Statistics Canada data.* The best place to find Statistics Canada data is on the Web. By going to www.statscan.gc.ca you can find all kinds of interesting information about your community and others: ethnic diversity, average household income, family size, and many other pieces of demographic data are contained in these publications. Although these data have some limitations, they provide a comprehensive statistical breakdown of the place in which you live.

*City directory.* This gives you the names and phone numbers of the people who reside in your area. Though the information is not much more than what appears in the phone book, the organization of the directory makes it valuable. Names are usually cross-listed by address and phone number. In a neighbourhood campaign, this can be a valuable asset.

*Community profile publications.* Generally published by an agency such as a commerce or tourism department, these profiles give a one- or two-page glimpse of most cities and towns in the province. In many communities, the local United Way also has a comprehensive community profile.

*Newspaper file.* The library should have current subscriptions and files of major local newspapers. This file includes recent back issues of the paper itself as well as older editions on microfilm or microfiche. From time to time, newspapers publish special reports that provide extremely valuable background information. Typically, these reports treat some aspect of the community in depth; for example, profiling the most influential people and community groups or discussing major economic forces affecting the community. Community overview reports are also common and describe the history and key characteristics of the community. From time to time, the newspaper issues special topic reports, providing an in-depth look at a particular social concern such as education, teen pregnancy, crime, or child abuse. Included in these accounts will be the range of the problem, efforts being made to solve it, and the people active in these efforts. In larger cities, numerous minor newspapers serve specialized populations. These are usually published weekly or monthly for specific areas of the city or for special groups such as members of a specific racial or ethnic group, downtown businesspeople, or retirees. Many newspapers are online, and the library may subscribe to the online version of the local paper. Some libraries will have a portal that allows you to gain access to the archives of a number of newspapers with the use of your library card.

*Local magazines.* Most larger cities have a magazine named after them that caters to upper-income readers. There are also publications for local businesspeople and supporters of the arts that carry features on local people or on politics. Many libraries have a large database of local and other magazines, and they will e-mail articles to you in response to reference questions.

*Human resource directories.* These publications are extremely helpful in getting to know what services are provided in your community and the names of the organizations, agencies, and people providing them.

One comprehensive directory may be published by the local information and referral agency, but directories that address specific topics may exist as well (for example, resources for divorced persons or for teens).

*Blue Book of community services.* This wonderful book lists by topic hundreds of organizations in the major cities in Canada. It also provides a paragraph or two about each of the organizations, including addresses and phone numbers. It may be helpful to know not only about the organizations in your province but also ones in other provinces that are working on the same issues you are. Not every city or municipality has such books, but start your search online for your area. Local "community information centres" usually publish "blue books" for their area. For example, in Ottawa, the e-blue book can be found at http://ottawa.cioc.ca/start.asp?UseCICVw=13. In Toronto, the "blue book" has turned into 211.toronto.ca.

*Lists of local clubs and organizations.* Many communities publish a comprehensive list of all local groups, including the phone numbers and names of officers. If your library does not have this resource, check with your local Chamber of Commerce or visitors' bureau.

*Travel or tourism books.* You will be surprised by how much you can find out about your community in these books. Larger cities usually have their own book. Smaller communities may be listed in a provincial guidebook. Remember that these are written for outsiders and tourists, so they are likely to contain "points of interest" information with a little exaggerated local history and colour.

*Economic profiles.* Put together by banks, local development organizations, or the business or economics department of the local university, economic profiles describe the economic sectors of the community and their health. Indicators of economic activity are frequently provided. Again, if this is not in your library, check with a major bank or other likely source.

*Community trends profiles.* Focusing on how people in the community appear to be spending their time and money, established and emerging community trends profiles cover major categories (for example, leisure time). Check with the marketing department of a college or university in your area if your library does not have this material.

*Nonprofit sector reports.* Many cities in Canada have a social planning or similar organization that researches and publishes reports on social issues such as community integration and poverty. These research reports help keep us aware of and accountable for the many people who have been excluded in communities or through community membership.

## Special Libraries

Special libraries may exist in your community. Not all areas have them, so check with your local public library to discover if there are special libraries in your area.

*Law libraries.* These special libraries exist for the purposes of legal research and are usually part of a university law school.

*Specialized government libraries.* Local and provincial planning departments often have their own libraries. Various community plans can be found here, along

> with valuable background data on community makeup and growth patterns. Most provinces' legislatures have provincial government libraries and archives that provide library services to provincial legislators and other government decision makers. They routinely provide background information on issues to provincial politicians and agency people. Although you can go in person, it is usually helpful to go through your provincial or federal legislator with a request for information. Local governments often have their own reference libraries serving city staff and elected officials.

Check to see how accessible these library services are to the general public. You can usually have someone, a staff member or public official, make the request for you (especially if they know you) if you cannot make it easily on your own. Their wide access to information and electronic mail makes these libraries a potentially valuable resource.

## Leaving the Library and Looking for More

You probably have a sneaking suspicion that there is more to finding out about your community than sitting in the library. Suspicion confirmed. You will need multiple sources of information to increase the reliability of your information.

So, where else? Your next stop would include various agencies, organizations, and interest groups that know something about your community. These include government agencies and private groups, both for-profit and nonprofit. Some of these (for example, government agencies) might not be physically in your community.

Once you have established a good general understanding of your community, you will probably want more specific information on some particular aspect of it. Perhaps you want to know more about sub-communities within your broad community. Or maybe you want to know more about specific conditions within your community (for example, childhood illness). In fact, you will probably move very rapidly to this level of inquiry.

Unless you intend to mobilize your entire broad community about something, you will study the broad level only to understand the setting or context in which your close community operates. Though you continue to improve your understanding of the broad community, you will acquire more information about your close community and the situation it faces. Review the sets of organizations that have some particular knowledge about the broad community, and select those most likely to have the kind of specific information you need.

What are you likely to get from these sources? First, personal perspectives—talk to people. Most people are happy to tell you just what they think. Ask them. These added viewpoints of people who work in an area that is of interest to you can fill in the blanks that you find in written material. A further advantage is that this gives you the chance to start building a personal relationship with this source, which could be helpful in the future.

It is generally relatively easy to get information from government, educational, and social service agencies. Information from those who sell the community and from public interest groups is also generally available. Private for-profit firms are less willing to offer what they know, especially if information is something they sell or if it is accumulated to give them a competitive advantage. Because it is so easy to get information from available sources, you may not want to waste your time trying to get something from a reluctant source.

### Take a Moment to Discover

Identify an issue or topic in which you are interested. See how many public or private community groups and organizations exist that might deal with this issue.

You have spent some time in the library and you have received information from organizations, but you are still not satisfied. What now? "What about regular people?" you ask. "Shouldn't I get some information directly from individuals?" Yes, you should, but which ones? Whether you are talking about your broad community or your close community, there are three groups of people whose ideas you can solicit.

People from the *leadership group* could provide you with important insights. These are opinion leaders (people whose points of view help shape other people's points of view), action leaders (people who can get other people to follow or do things), and representative leaders (people who represent the community to people outside of the community), people who offer informal support to community members or even social service workers from the community who serve the community. It is a good idea to ask leaders whose help you may need down the road.

The next group is the *knowledgeable group*, people who are likely to have either general or specific knowledge about the community. These people have a particular area of expertise (for example, child protection social workers, women's shelter workers), are particularly involved in the community (for example, community activists), hold a particular belief about the community (for example, a political columnist), or hold a position that gives them a somewhat unique perspective (for example, a police officer).

The final group is the *at large group*. This consists of members of the community in general, and membership is not particularly based on who they are, what they do, or what they may know.

You have a range of folks from which to choose. Here are some basic ways to get the information, ideas, and opinions that people have to offer.

## Guided Personal Discussions

Ideally, this is a face-to-face discussion. Although it can take place over the phone, it is important to understand the community by being present in it and seeing the places people work, play, and live. These conversations are generally relatively easy to set up if you know the person, and still quite possible even if you do not. Simply call and ask if you can arrange a time to discuss the topic. You will be surprised how committed people are to their communities and their willingness to talk with interest and passion. You need to illustrate a genuine interest in them and their community to get access. Most people will end up giving you much more time than you have asked for. Prepare six basic questions you would like to cover. You can allow the discussion to flow; just make sure that your points get covered. But don't be too controlling. A great deal of information comes from the side conversations you engage in—building a community has to do with wide-ranging dialogue and trust building through discussion.

Active participation in the life of your community is valuable because this involvement puts you in a position to know and to be known. Two benefits flow from this: you learn more about the things with which you come in contact, and you increase your network of personal contacts. Each person you meet also has a network of personal contacts. This provides you with much easier access to information and resources. People are more willing to go out of their way to help a friend, or the friend of a friend, than they are to help a stranger.

## Focus Groups

This creative atmosphere for gathering information and building interest in a topic is made up of people who bring particular perspectives to the discussion of an issue. The group explores the topic with guidance from a moderator. It is usually a good idea to get a mix of people from all three groups previously mentioned—leadership, knowledge, and at large. You do not necessarily want only people who already agree with each other.

A focus group provides a lively exchange of ideas and opinions. Although the group may arrive at a generally agreed-upon point of view,

**● CHANGE AGENT TIP**

A simple guide for discovering the real leader of a community is to ask members of the community two simple questions: number one, "Who would people, in general, say the leader of the community is?" and number two, "Personally, who do you think the real leader of this community is?" If the same person's name pops up frequently in answer to question number two, you have a better idea (not a definite answer) of who the real leader is.

this is not required. Key questions on a certain topic (focus) are prepared in advance. The questions are structured to allow the conversation to flow yet remain on track. Some questions are simple and straightforward; others require more thoughtful consideration.

A moderator or facilitator asks the questions and directs the discussion, making sure that all participants have an opportunity to add their two cents' worth. Acting as facilitator for a focus group can be a good role for a nonprofessional community member (Krueger & King, 1997). The facilitator will see to it that an atmosphere of open discussion prevails. For example, although disagreement is appropriate, intimidation is not. A policy of non-attribution is sometimes followed to encourage frankness. This policy means that although the overall results of the discussion may be used, no particular remark or opinion will be attributed to any participant.

### Surveys and Questionnaires

Surveys can be administered in person, over the phone, or through the mail. The more personal the approach is, the more success you will have in getting the survey completed. This is a good way to get detailed, specific, and consistent information.

A survey can be used to collect information, such as a catalogue of the skills of individuals or the nature of the contributions they would like to make. You can also use a survey to identify interests or concerns or to gather opinions. These types of surveys require a little more care. You can design a scientific survey process that is highly reliable (it can be repeated over and over with the same degree of accuracy) and valid (the information you receive is a correct and meaningful reflection of the group represented in the survey). You are the judge of how scientific you need to be, but six important factors should be considered.

1. *Population to be surveyed.* Are you asking the right people? If you want to know which school activities high school students like best, do not ask the teachers, ask the students.

2. *Sampling.* How many from the general population do you intend to ask, and how will they be selected? If you know the people you want to talk to and their number is small enough, you can ask each one. However, you may want to know what a lot of people think. In this case, your survey group should accurately reflect the general population. If you ask only three high school students about their favourite activity, you might hear things that most other students are not at all interested in. So sample size is important. You also need a good cross-section of the population. If you surveyed 100 students, but all of them were male first-year social work students, you might have a good sample size, but their opinions might not accurately reflect those of the entire student body. Some method of picking people at random is needed. This means that selection of a person to be surveyed is left entirely to chance.

3. *Design the survey instrument.* Figure out what you really need to know, and devise questions that will give you that information. Most often, you are better off if you can ask closed-ended instead of open-ended questions. Closed-ended questions are those in which respondents pick from choices you already offer.

All they have to do is circle a letter or a number, or write down a letter, number, or single word. They are not required to write down their own ideas. They merely react to the choices offered. At times, it is a good idea to ask one or two open-ended questions to give respondents a chance to add their own ideas.

A more personal method of administration gives greater opportunities for open-ended questions. Generally, though, the fewer questions of this type the better. Open-ended questions often put people off. They may not want to take the time and energy to respond. Further, the more you ask people to write, the more time you will spend trying to read the handwriting and guessing what the respondents really mean. Be careful not to let bias creep into your questions. For example, asking "Do you encourage keeping our children ignorant and unprepared for the future?" may not yield accurate information on how a person will vote on a school trustee election. The length of the survey is also an important matter. A survey that is too long will turn people off. If people do not complete the survey, it does you no good.

During your pre test (described next), time people to see how long it takes for them to complete the survey. You can then let future respondents know how long it will take them to complete it. On the top of the survey itself you can write, "This survey takes only five minutes to complete."

4. *Accuracy and clarity.* One of the great fallacies in communication is that people know what we mean. So after you have written it, conduct a pre-test—administer your survey to a handful of people who are not in your survey sample. See if they clearly understand what you are asking. Did these questions, even if clearly understood, provide you with the information you wanted? You will find that, most of the time, you have to revise some survey questions.

5. *Administering the instrument.* The way you conduct the survey is important. Several problems can sneak in. For example, a survey administered by an interviewer, someone who verbally asks the prepared questions, is open to bias. Interviewers should practise beforehand and be critiqued to make sure that none of their mannerisms, including tone of voice, tend to promote certain responses. Surveys conducted by mail have problems as well. Respondents to a mailed survey are likely to be those most interested in the topic. Their ideas may not represent the entire population. You have put a lot of work into preparation of the survey, and you have to make sure it is conducted properly. Try to anticipate problems and prevent them. Finally, respondents need to feel safe to answer honestly. You may need to explain how the results will and will not be used. You may also need to guarantee that the survey will be answered anonymously.

6. *Compiling and analyzing the results.* How you look at the pieces of information and how they relate to each other will help you to get a more complete picture. Ask questions that give you clear data so you do not have to guess what the respondent means.

In summary, for your survey to be helpful, you need to ask enough of the right people the right questions in a way that makes it likely that they will accurately respond to the survey, giving you information you can interpret and use.

## Informal Methods

All sorts of tidbits of information on your community are out there all the time. Anything, whether it's the way streets are named, the number of locks people have on their doors, or good and bad gossip, will tell you something. Once you have decided to notice things, you will. Here are a few ways of keeping your eyes and ears open that will be particularly helpful to you.

### Newspapers Provide More than the News

News is, of course, important. Read the local news section of the paper to keep abreast of what is going on in your community. You can track the progress of particular issues or particular groups in this way. In addition to the general news, pay attention to other sections as well. The editorial point of view of the leading paper

## Take a Moment to Discover

If you work at a social service agency or another type of organization that sees itself as serving the community, are you able to name the leaders of the neighbourhood where your agency sits? That is, who are the people who actually live there? How many people working at the agency can name these leaders? How many actually know them? What do your answers tell you about whom the agency sees as its valuable partners? If you do not work at an organization of this type, interview someone who does, and see what they have to say.

is important to know as it will often reflect the dominant prevailing political philosophy of the community. Pay attention to the editorial position on issues as well as the paper's selection of syndicated columnists.

The section related to business or money often features articles or brief announcements on current or up-and-coming community business leaders. Stories on the community's economic health or particular sectors of the economy are found here too. The community events calendar can introduce you to various groups within the community. The society pages may help you learn about people who are seen to be the key movers and shakers in the community (Kahn, 1994).

Letters to the editor can cue you to issues ready to boil, as well as to what people think about them. And the classified section provides clues about the types and number of jobs available, as well as wage rates. You can also get a good indication of the cost and availability of certain goods and services, such as housing and child care.

When you look at the newspaper, read more than the news. Clip and save those articles you find valuable. Your files will serve as good future references. Make sure you read all the existing newspapers in a community, as each one will have its own particular take on the issues presented. It is important to uncover all the prevailing ideas in a community, not just the dominant ones.

### Strike Up Conversations

Be willing to ask people about their perspectives on the community. Do it even when you are hanging out in the community. Talk to as many people as you can, wherever you are. People waiting around for something, like a bus or for the machine to finish the rinse cycle at the Laundromat, are often willing to pass the time in conversation. People who hear other people talk, such as barbers and hairdressers, and bartenders, often do not mind sharing a perception or two. These are not interviews, just conversations, but they can provide you with extremely important information. Striking up conversations with people whose ideas and opinions are not likely to be reflected in what you might be able to learn from newspapers or other community reports is especially important. Pay attention to the diversity that exists in the community and make sure you are talking to as many people as you can.

### Social Networking Sites and Blogging

A great deal of information can be drawn from information networks. You can learn about key issues, about networks of relationships, and about the activities or meetings that are important to people. These networks have become a very important method for people to organize or make a point, especially from a grassroots point of view.

### Be Present in the Community

You should as much as possible be present in the community to understand what it feels like to be a member. You can learn a great deal from all your senses—sight, sound, touch—to understand completely what the community is about. Much information will come to you in surprising ways, when you least expect it. You may be in a conversation about something as simple as where you got your morning coffee and suddenly a community member decides to tell you how some leaders in the community have been mistreated or how she and others have begun to meet informally in her apartment. You cannot know the community if you do not experience it. This is the most important principle of gaining a knowledge of communities.

## CONCLUSION

As you move from "I" to "we," you will involve people in a way that results in all of you working together to accomplish the goals you share. Depending on the situation you face and how you intend to approach it, you may be working with a handful of people or thousands. These people may come together to work on a specific issue, having little sense that they are a community, or they may already be involved in a well-established community, strengthened with traditions and recognized by a name. Whoever these people are, you should know about them.

Your community extends from broad to specific groups. It includes geographic and interest groups, some of which are highly structured, whereas others may never actually get together as a community. Based on your general understanding of your community's dynamics, and directed by the issue at hand, you need a better awareness of the communities you will mobilize for action, those that will benefit from that action, and those from which you will demand a response.

Get to know the basic characteristics of the people in your community. Grasp how the community functions to meet its needs. Identify unmet community needs, and understand what improvements may be needed as you go about making a difference in your community. Most important, evaluate the resources that your community has on hand as well as ones it could develop. This information will help you to better gauge its capacity to work toward change.

Rely on a variety of sources and techniques to increase your understanding—but do not get stuck in the information-gathering phase and forget about taking action. By discovering the wealth of information in the library, gathering reports from community groups, or just talking to people, you will see your community as alive and fascinating.

The best way to understand your community is to participate in it—take part in its life.

## HELPFUL WEBSITES

**Statistics Canada**

www.statcan.gc.ca/

This is Statistics Canada's web page, which provides information about census and other quantitative information. Many libraries subscribe to this service, which requires a username and password.

**Human Resources and Skill Development Canada**

http://www.hrsdc.gc.ca/eng/corporate/about_us/index.shtml

Human Resources and Skill Development Canada is a federal department in charge of providing support to Canadians to ensure their ability to engage in productive activities. There are two programs that may be of interest to you: Income Security and Social Development (this program provide support to those families and communities that may be facing challenges to their well-being and their active participation in their communities); Skills Employment (this program help those individuals facing difficulties due to labour market changes).

**City of Toronto**

**City of Vancouver**

http://www.toronto.ca/demographics/neighourhoods.htm

http://vancouver.ca/community_profiles/communitylist.htm

These two sites provide neighbourhood news, photos, even local weather. You can get to your neighbourhood in a number of ways: through your city, your postal code, the name of a neighbourhood school, and so forth. It is particularly helpful for those who are new to the Toronto and Vancouver areas.

CHAPTER SEVEN

# Powerful Planning

**This chapter will help you better understand the following questions:**

- What is planning?
- Why is planning important for community workers?
- What are the basic elements of the planning process?
- What are some obstacles to effective planning?

Let's start by recognizing that planning is a necessary and useful activity if done with care. To understand planning as a useful activity and to use it to increase the effectiveness of your change effort, you need the answers to a few questions. First of all, just what is a plan, and what, for that matter, is planning? Next, why should you plan at all? What benefit does it provide? Assuming you have got sufficiently good answers to encourage your further inquiry, you will probably want to know how much planning you need or do not need to do. You will then need to know exactly how to plan. What are some useful planning models? What are some basic obstacles to planning, and how do you confront them? And, finally, what else do you need to know or at least think about when you are getting set to plan? Let us take a look at each of these.

## WHAT IS A PLAN? WHAT IS PLANNING?

The community is the context of your action, and planning provides the approach and direction for your actions. The approach to planning described in this chapter refers to the steps you take to initiate and implement a community change. The procedures used in planning for the continued development of an existing social service agency may need to address other factors beyond the scope of this text, although certain perspectives offered here may have some benefit in those situations as well.

A plan is a set of decisions made with regard to actions to be taken in order to reach a goal. It is the product of the process of planning, an active process that is the opposite of simply allowing events to unfold. A plan can be said to exist when a point in the process has been reached where a coherent set of operations designed to meet a given goal has been determined with sufficient clarity that it may be acted upon (Mayer, 1985; Perlman & Gurin, 1972; Weinbach, 1990).

Determining a coherent set of operations in order to reach a given goal means that you have made decisions on a number of things to do (and not to do) and that these actions are related to one another and are directed to whatever it is you want to accomplish. These actions need to be sufficiently clear so that you know just what to do. Therefore, you have a plan when you have proceeded far enough in your consideration of possible courses of action that you know not only what it is that you need to do to accomplish your purpose but also that you are ready to act.

A plan can be a formal document, or it can simply be the clear understanding of the actions you are to undertake. Where possible, it is helpful to write down your plan. Berkowitz (1982) points out that the act of getting something down in black and white can clarify your thoughts. Seeing your ideas on paper can also make them seem more real to you, thus strengthening your own motivation.

Planning is the process, the series of steps that you take to gather information and make decisions to determine your plan. Here are the steps in this process:

- Decide what you want to achieve.
- Select actions to be taken within a given period of time to overcome obstacles and move you in the desired direction.
- Determine specific tasks.
- Assign responsibility.
- Analyze the outcome of your intentions and actions.

We should probably clear up an important point about planning right now—you never stop planning. Of course, you are not going to spend

## CAPTURING CONCEPTS

### Logic Models

Logic models are useful tools in program planning. They describe the relationship between various aspects of the program and the results they are intended to achieve. Ask yourself, "What do we think we need to put together in order to produce change?" "What does that change look like?" and "Why do we think this approach will work?" A clearer theory of change will emerge when an open analysis of assumptions and expectations occurs. Logic models clarify the ideas and assumptions that go into developing the program and provide a road map linking one part of the journey with the next (Canadian International Development Agency [CIDA], 2000; Kagan, 1999; Osten, 2001; W. K. Kellogg Foundation, 2001). These connections are often presented in a visual display or "map." The specific component parts usually include these elements:

**Inputs** are resources dedicated to the program or used by the program, such as staff time, equipment, money, supplies, and so forth.

**Activities** are what the program does with the resources, such as particular events, actions, processes, or technology.

**Outputs** are the direct products of activities, such as the measurable amount of work accomplished, or tangible things that are actually produced.

**Outcomes** are the changes that result because of all this work, such as changes in the skills or behaviour of the community participants, new policy, or the presence of some new identifiable element in the environment.

**Impacts** are the fundamental, long-range changes that occur in the organization or community as a result of the program.

Going from inputs to impacts implies a series of if-then statements. For example, if you have access to these resources, then you can use them to accomplish your activities. If you accomplish your activities, then you will deliver the outcomes you intended. If you produce these things, then your participants will benefit in these certain ways. If these benefits to participants are achieved, then these significant changes in organizations, communities, or systems can be expected.

| | | | |
|---|---|---|---|
| **Impact** | Improved health among people living in region Y of country X. | | |
| **Intermediate outcomes** | Increased use of clean drinking water by people living in region Y. | | Increased use of health services by people living in region Y. |
| **Immediate outcomes** | Increased access to clean drinking water for people living in region Y. | Increased ability to maintain wells among people living in region Y. | Increased access to health services for people living in region Y. |
| **Outputs** | Wells built in region Y. | Training on well maintenance developed and delivered to people living in region Y. | Regional health centres in region Y rehabilitated and staffed. |
| **Activities** | Build wells in region Y. | Develop and deliver training on well maintenance to people living in region Y. | Rehabilitate and staff regional health centres in region Y. |

**FIGURE 7.1** Example of International Project Related to Water

Source: Canadian International Development Agency-Result Based Management Tools at CIDA: How-to Guide, http://www.acdi-cida.gc.ca/acdi-cida/ACDI-CIDA.nsf/eng/NAT-92213444-N2H#al1. By permission of the Canadian International Development Agency.

all your time planning, as this will not be very productive. You are, however, going to continue to spend part of your time making plans. Planning is an ongoing process. The only way to get a plan "done" is to get all the information about your situation and then keep the world from changing at all. Of course, this is impossible. You have a plan as soon as you have decided what to do about the situation you are facing. You will always be tinkering with your plan, modifying it to meet changing conditions and additional information. Your plan is a living document. See Figure 7.1 as example of project planning guide. You cannot plan for everything, so do not try. Plans also have to be changed constantly to address new information or changing conditions.

If you try to make planning one stage, and action the next stage (in other words, if you try to keep these two activities completely separate), you will encounter several serious problems. First, group members want and actually need to do something to maintain and develop their interest. You can easily choke off the excitement by overemphasizing the need for a detailed problem analysis and a methodically detailed blueprint. You can sell planning as action only for so long. A second problem involves the fact that you are always working with incomplete information. Once you think you are "done" with planning, it is much more difficult to incorporate new information into your plan. And third, the ever-changing nature of situations means that the world in which the plan was originally developed is different from the world in which it is implemented. If you try to base all your actions on a plan that is somewhat out of date, you will be frustrated in your efforts to force the real world into the one envisioned by your plan. Once established, your plan will be shaped and reshaped by new forces and new information that you discover as you proceed with your action. Planning involves vision, discovery, decision making, and action. It is a purposeful way of looking at the future with the intent to shape it.

## ● SOME BASIC REASONS FOR PLANNING

Why plan? Well, for one thing, it is almost impossible not to. Almost everything we do relates to some sort of plan, either implicit or explicit. If you want to achieve your goals of community change, you need to plan. A plan will help you to use yourself and your resources in the most intentional manner. You simply will

## Take a Moment to Discover

Think of a time when a group you were involved with decided just what needed to be done, and then let it go at that. No one actually agreed to perform any specific task. Perhaps this occurred in your family, or where you work, or at school, or with a community action group. What was the result? Was the goal accomplished in a timely manner, or at all? How were the relationships among the members affected?

not accomplish your goals through a random series of actions. The actions you take must be those necessary and sufficient to accomplish the identified purpose, they must relate to the goals as well as to one another, and they must be performed in the proper sequence. You do not have unlimited time and unlimited resources; therefore, you need to use them in the most effective way possible. You need to plan.

Effective planning creates both a sense of urgency and confidence in moving toward your goals. Simply by removing confusion, participants feel more capable. Having shared in consulting to create a plan helps them feel more empowered. This feeling is further strengthened by the knowledge that they have made purposeful decisions from a range of alternative choices. Making necessary tasks clear and relating them to the accomplishment of important goals creates a tension that calls out for action. People feel the need to move, to get on with it. As you move forward, things are going to get in your way. Your plan will help you to see many of those twists, turns, and occasional roadblocks ahead, and to prepare for them. Your plan will help you to identify and marshal resources. Planning will guide your actions to be effective (productive in accomplishing your purpose) efficient (done with the least time and effort) in achieving your goals and, if done properly, will be an engaging process of participation (involved in activities and goals that are meaningful to participants).

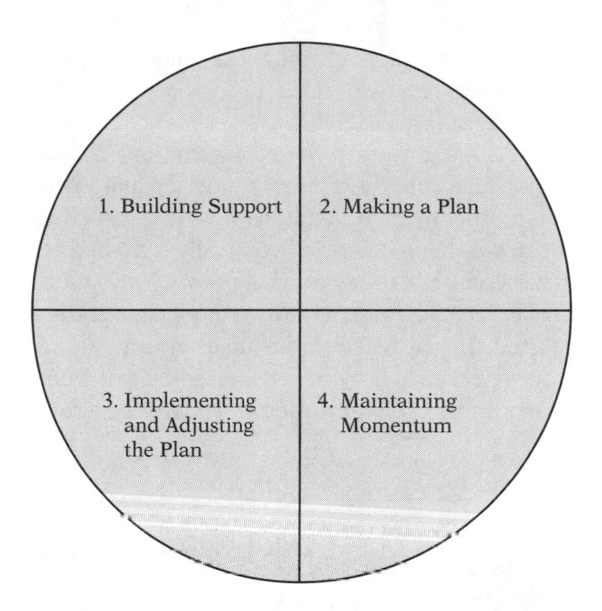


**FIGURE 7.2** Community Development Process

Source: Frank and Smith, 1999, Service Canada website (www.servicecanada.gc.ca). Reproduced with the permission of the Minister of Public Works and Government Services, 2010.

Did you ever notice that in trying to solve one problem, you end up creating another perhaps even larger one? Bad but unintended consequences are often the legacy of good intentions coupled with little forethought. A good plan produces thoughtful action and minimizes the likelihood that your efforts will simply generate new problems. Good planning involves identifying both the promise and the difficulties that exist in any situation. Good planning goes beyond problems; good planning enables you to create opportunities. See Figure 7.2.

## HOW MUCH PLANNING IS NEEDED?

Basically, you need to know where you want to end up and how to begin moving in that direction. The two most difficult problems that most change efforts face are knowing what success looks like and actually taking the first step to get there. The less routine the challenge or goal, the more you will need purposeful planning (CIDA, 2000; Dale, 2004).

Planning to implement community change is similar to the process of writing a paper. Most often, the most difficult words of a paper to write are the first ones. If you really have no idea what you want to say or what points you want to make, you are going to have a tough time getting started. If you make things up as you go along, your paper may not cover the essential issues and may ramble on without focus. Having a picture, before you begin, of what the paper should look like when it is finished, together with an outline to guide you, will help you a lot.

The time you put into your initial planning effort is important, but it should not be exhaustive. You do need to start with some planning. In fact, start with about as much as the participants in your effort can stand. No matter what stage of development your change effort is in, at the very least you need enough planning to know where you want to end up, where you are going next, and what you need to do to get there.

## CAPTURING CONCEPTS

### Vision, Mission, and Values

Most planning processes for formal agencies, other organizations, and even whole communities begin with an examination of three foundation elements. Although the planning described in this chapter may at times be a program of action that may remain less formal, an understanding of these planning components is helpful.

A **Vision Statement** is an energizing, positive view of a future condition that is made more possible because of the presence and work of the group or organization. It can describe either a result of the group's work or the condition of the organization itself. This vision should be compelling, energizing, challenging, attainable, and clear. It is developed by active members of the community. Broad ownership of the vision is essential. This is not just a statement jotted down by a couple of leaders. In a few words, it captures the essence of what the group or organization intends to be and to do. All community organizations in particular, regardless of their degree of formality, should have a vision statement.

A **Mission Statement** essentially answers the question "What is our purpose?" It underscores a community group's or organization's basic priorities and what it will emphasize in order to achieve its objectives. It should differentiate the group or organization, illustrating its uniqueness and particular niche in the community.

The **Values Statement** is a set of statements that respond to the questions "At our core, what do we hold dear?" and "What do we believe is so important that it causes us to do what we do?" These values inform the work of the group and the relationship that it has to community members and to external interests in the community. It also describes the importance of those relationships and how members relate to the work for change and to one another. The behaviour of the work group and its members will manifest these values if they truly shape the culture of work. If not, another set of perhaps undeclared values may be more powerfully operating. The values statements become the standard against which the most fundamental actions and decisions of the organization are measured. It is also a way to ensure the change agent and community members have shared values that help them remember their purpose and help get them through rough times.

These foundations are helpful in all community work and can be a basis for consultations and beginning process. If community work ends up with the creation of a more formal community organization then vision, mission and values need to be addressed to sustain the organization over time, and to effectively pursue an agenda of change. it

At some point, you will notice that your planning efforts have become tedious. People may become bored with this process. When this happens, they may agree to anything just to get the job over with. Planning, then, no longer serves its purpose and may become counterproductive.

Participant interest is a critical driving or limiting force for your planning efforts. You may need to do a little educating on the importance of planning before you actually begin. If people are not actively engaged in planning, it will be hard to get them involved with any enthusiasm. People often confuse "planning" with "inaction." If this is the case, do not use the word "planning." Call it something else, like "figuring out what we've got to do." Some people may be willing to engage in planning as long as you call it something else. No one really wants to participate in a planning process if it does not make sense to them. It is your job as community change agent to help the group discover what a meaningful plan is.

You may also discover that some of your group's members value the contribution of planning: outlining strategies; identifying enemies or other obstacles; looking for friends, alliances, and other resources; and figuring out how all these things fit together. Group members who enjoy the process can be strong allies who can be very helpful in keeping your group looking ahead.

## LEVELS OF PLANNING

You cannot make a detailed plan for everything, and you cannot be so vague that you do not really know what to do. Is there some sort of happy medium? Can you be a little detailed and a little vague? Yes, there is a way around this dilemma, but it is not by striking a balance between being detailed and being vague. The trick is to plan in levels—four levels, to be exact (see Figure 7.3).

Your plan will proceed from the broad to the specific. You begin your plan with your goal, where you want to end up, out there somewhere in the future, and then you move closer and closer to the present, becoming more and more specific about what you need to do. When you have completed the four stages of the plan, you know not only where you are ultimately headed but exactly what you need to do tomorrow to start getting there.

Planning should be a creative activity, yet sometimes we get stuck trying to go from point A to point B in a linear fashion. We may narrow the road by doing so, but we may narrow our thinking as well. One way to open up your thinking is to engage in Mind Mapping (Quick & New, 2000). This is a simple, fun process that uses circles rather than straight lines. Start with a circle in the middle of the page, and work out from the middle in all directions. Allow your ideas to jump all around, filling in circles extending from the core and creating new ones. You begin to see the various pieces of the project or action. Once you have all the circles splattered around, you can begin to see how sets of relationships emerge. You can then fit them together and align them for action. This will open up your thinking and seeing. And it is much more fun and comprehensive than a top-down-only look at things.

No matter how you arrive at these basic components, your plan needs to include these elements:

- A sense of the ultimate desired condition
- A specific target that represents significant movement toward that condition
- The major activities you need to accomplish
- The specific steps to get you going

The first step is to establish the overall intent of your effort (Mayer, 1985). Here, you identify your vision for the future, the end result of what all your work is intended to achieve. For example, if you are concerned about prenatal care, your vision might be "Every pregnant woman in Halifax receives adequate prenatal care."

The next stage is to select an action-oriented target or goal that will help to fulfill that vision.

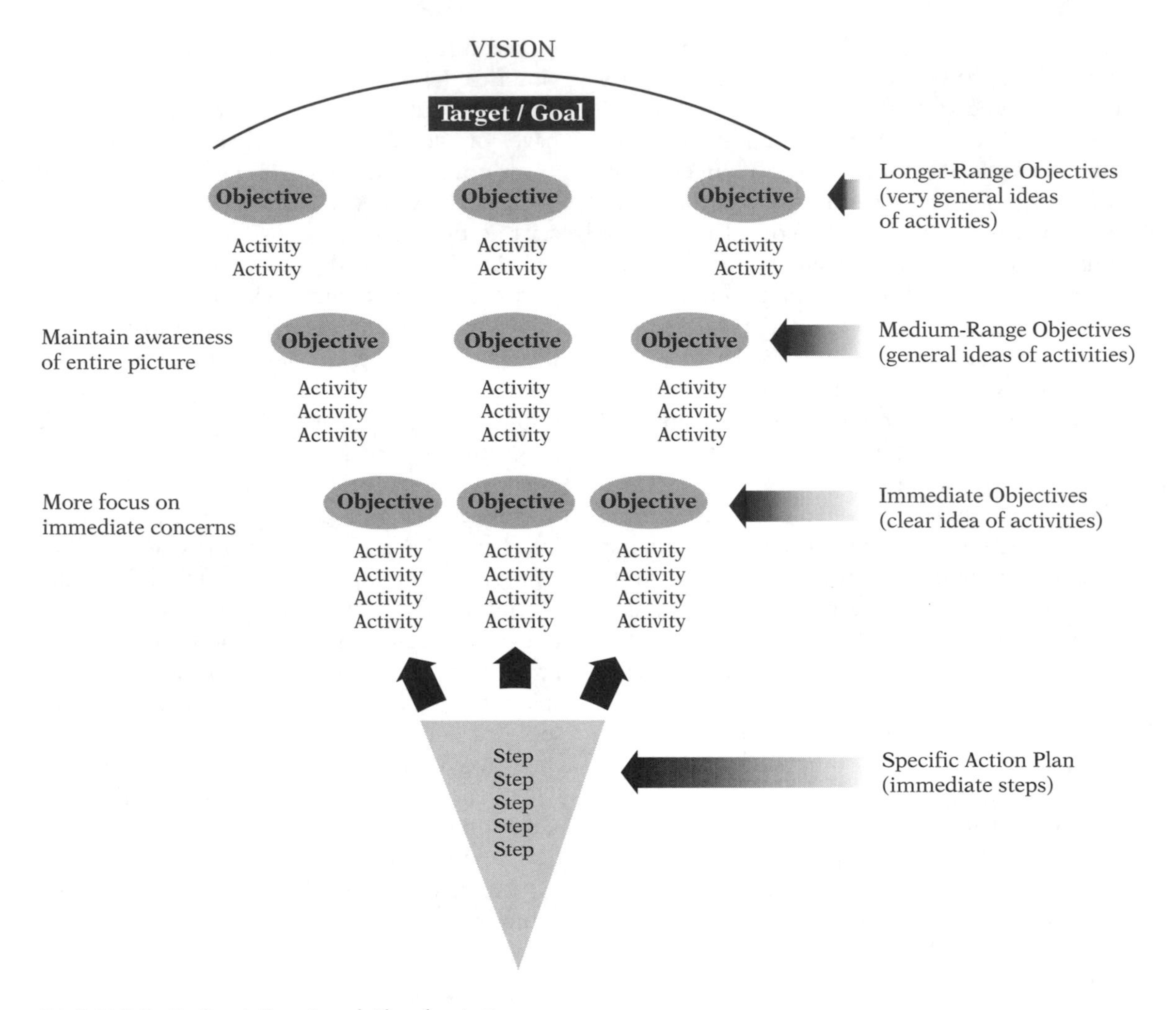


**FIGURE 7.3** A Four-Level Plan for Action

Using prenatal care again, your goal might be "To establish a multi-service prenatal care clinic by [a specific date]."

At the third level, you establish the framework for your effort, identifying the major components of your plan. These components describe the various sets of activities that must be undertaken to accomplish your purpose. Although you do not identify all the activities themselves, note what each set of activities is supposed to produce. These will be your principal objectives. At this level, you also want to get some idea of the order in which you need to achieve these objectives. This tier represents your best thinking of where in general you want to be headed and might include the selection of the clinic site, determination of the range of services, securing funding, or establishing community support.

In the final level, you are identifying which sets of activities you need to be initiating and what needs to occur within each set of activities. You are also figuring out a sequence for these activities and their relationships to each other. These specific action plans clarify what you are going to do over the next one to three months. For example, you may decide that you first need to build community support and that this will lead to involvement of people who can help you determine the range of services, which will set the stage for your fundraising activities. Later on, you can begin to identify possible sites.

Start by identifying steps you will take to gain community support, your most immediate concern. These steps could include contacting the provincial Ministry of Health and Health Canada for statistics you can use to describe the problem, identifying other individuals and organizations who have an interest in the issue, contacting a particular news reporter to do a story on the issue, and other specific actions.

Plans at this level should look no further than three months ahead. In fact, the shorter the time frames the better. This level of planning represents actual, concrete decisions and specific steps. As a practical matter, these immediate plans can usually be determined in daily, weekly, or monthly meetings. Keeping in mind the activity sets you have already selected, at each meeting, ask these questions: "Are there new or different objectives we need to accomplish?" and "What do we have to do next?"

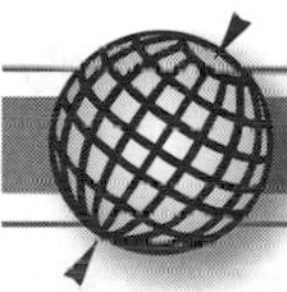

## GLOBAL PERSPECTIVES

COSTA RICA—Unity, commitment, and energy grow strikingly in a group where there is a clear goal which all believe in (Maria, community worker, as qtd. in Kindervatter, 1983, p. 25).

GUINEA-BISSAU—Any group committed to working for development and social justice needs to build supportive structures and patterns. Every new thing begins as a *dream* or vision. It is based on *values*. To make the vision a reality, the group must *set goals* and *find resources*. Committed and trained people are among the most important resources. Setting definite *objectives* will help the group decide what to do to reach the goal, and a *planned program* will detail how to meet the objectives. There will need to be a *budget* reflecting the priorities of the group, and *organization* of roles and responsibilities for *implementation*. Finally, the members of the group must be willing to engage in self-criticism in a spirit of comradeship (Cabral, 1982, p. 107).

GERMANY—Resistance to the steady dehumanization of our lives is growing. It may slow things down here and there, but it is not, by itself, enough to turn the tide. Now is the time for those of us who, at present, allow this tide to sweep us along to generate our own visions of the future, to set against the schemes and projections of the powers that be. . . . The future belongs to everybody. But where are the opportunities, for those wishing to articulate their feelings and aspirations, to express them so loudly and clearly that, although they started out feeling alienated and off guard, they come to see themselves as effective fellow-architects of a world in which they and their children would wish to live?

. . . [A "future workshop" can help people] criticize the existing state of things and determine how to reshape it. . . . The workshop itself begins with the critique phase, during which all the grievances and negative experiences relating to the chosen topic are brought into the open. All the points made are duly recorded and then amalgamated into a few main discussion areas. There then follows the fantasy phase, in which the participants come up with ideas in response to the problems, incorporating their desires, fantasies, and alternative views. A selection is made of the most interesting notions and small working groups develop these into solutions and outline projects (often still of a rather utopian nature). The workshop concludes with the implementation phase, coming back down into the present with its power structures and constraints. It is at this stage that participants critically assess the chances of getting their projects implemented, identifying the obstacles and imaginatively seeking ways around them so as to draw up a plan of action (Jungk & Mullert, 1996, pp. 8–12).

Planning for a relatively short but defined period of time enables you to be very specific and to keep the tasks close enough at hand so that they have some sense of urgency or real purpose. When you plan too far down the road, you can trick yourself into thinking things are so far away you need not worry about them. So usually you do not, and then nothing gets done. At this final, specific level, the series of actions extends sufficiently into the future so that you have a sense of direction and progress, yet the series is close enough at hand that you actually pay attention to it. As you execute your immediate plans, you develop new information to incorporate into your next planning cycle.

As you begin acting, continue planning; keep looking ahead. This routine requires that you keep your focus on exactly what you are going to do over the next month (or so) and on making sure that those actions relate to the sets of purpose-focused activities (objectives) that you need to be working on at the time. Continue to make sure that you have very clear steps to take and that each of these steps relates to movement toward the goal. With this ongoing, action-oriented approach to planning, you are constantly re-examining the relative importance and timeliness of each set of major activities, perhaps modifying them, perhaps eliminating some and adding new ones. Your plan stays fresh, relevant, and clear.

## • CHANGE AGENT TIP

Regardless of how detailed your planning process, you must keep a number of critical factors in mind. Failure to incorporate any one of these matters can undermine all your hard work:

*Clarity of your goal.* All the active members of your group need to agree on and understand the goal and use it to guide decisions and actions. If each of these people were given a piece of paper and a pencil and asked to write down your group's goal, would each piece of paper say the same thing?

*Inclusion.* Do you know all the necessary stakeholders? Are they involved to their degree of interest and ability? Are you leaving any of them out? If so, are there valid reasons for excluding them? (For example, you may not want to include an opponent in your planning.) What do you anticipate will be the consequences of this exclusion?

*Availability of resources.* Be on a constant lookout for people and things you can use. Your ability to marshal resources is one of the most basic sources of strength.

*Clear assignment of tasks.* If people are not sure what to do or how, they probably will not do it. Make sure people know what they are expected to do, how to do it, and by when these things should be done. Doing so moves you toward your goal and builds member and group confidence and capacity. Organization occurs when the variety of required tasks is done in a way that enhances the value of each.

*Reward for work.* Seeing progress is a good reward, but develop and use other forms of reward that are meaningful to the participants. By the way, make sure that people can recognize the progress that is being made. How will that happen?

*Flexibility.* Things will change, and unanticipated events will occur. Will you be able to make the adjustments necessary to keep your plans consistent with the goal that you want to accomplish? Will you be able to make changes without getting flustered? Are you directing your action, or are you just aimlessly responding to events?

*Monitoring, evaluating, learning, and refining.* Routinely check to see if you are doing what you planned to do, and see if it is working. Use your reviews and your actions to keep learning. Use your learning to strengthen and refine your plan.

## BASIC PLANNING ELEMENTS

The following basic planning elements are present to one degree or another in all planning considerations. Sometimes, either because of other demands or the inattention of those doing the planning, they may be only briefly noted. However, each of these elements should be given some considered thought.

### Identify Current Discomfort or Opportunity

Something brought you to this situation of change. Just what is it that people are upset about or dissatisfied with? What better is possible? By uncovering instances of unmet needs or newly recognized opportunities, you give yourself a picture of the current situation that requires some changing. This helps you identify your starting place or your focus.

Remember, you want to distinguish between needs that are going unmet, the causes of the problem, the symptoms of the problem, and the solutions to the problem. These are four different things. All of these are important, and you will eventually make some determination on each. But as you do, maintain an awareness of how your own values and perspectives can colour your perception of these various factors (Ellsworth, Hooyman, Ruff, Stam, & Tucker, 1982). Do not forget your social location and how it affects the way in which you perceive the world (Mullaly, 2002). Looking at causes (forces that interfere with people getting what they need) and effects (those things that indicate people do not have what they need) is valuable in helping you to understand the unmet need as you move toward a solution (Kettner, Moroney, & Martin, 1999). Initially, though, zero in on whatever it is that people need but do not have or that they have but are not using to feel happy or good or at least satisfied. Now that you know what dissatisfaction looks like, it is time to get a view of what better looks like.

### Identify Your Vision for the Future

What do you want to accomplish? What does "equal access" or "gender equity" look like? Your vision is your picture of what should be happening instead of what is now happening. It is the complete realization of your efforts stated in positive terms and clear, simple language. It is a strong declaration of your intent.

### Identify Your Target Goals

What are you actually hoping for? Without a clear vision of what your actions attempt to achieve, it is difficult to define results (CIDA, 2000). As the saying goes, "If you don't know where you are going, you will end up somewhere else."

A problem is simply the difference between where you are and where you want to be. Closing that gap is the intention of planning (Nutt, 1985). This method helps you see clearly just where you want to be. Project yourself into the future and visualize what things will look like once you have responded to the unmet needs. Here is how it works.

- Pick a date in the future, far enough away to give you sufficient time to work to accomplish your goals but not so far that the sense of urgency to act on the issue is lost. For some of the changes you seek, two months into the future would be appropriate. For others, a year or two would be fitting. Still others may require you to look five years down the road.
- Now, pretend that this future date is the present. So "today" is that date; you are there now. Visualize the situation. Go ahead; look around. What do you see?
- Describe everything you see, now that the problem is solved and you have accomplished everything you had set out to do those months or years ago when you started. Identify clear, visual images. For example, you cannot really see "people getting along better," but you can see

"people playing softball in the park." It is hard to know just what "things look better" means, but "all the walls have a fresh coat of paint" gives you a good picture (Schindler-Rainman, 1977).

If your group is just getting started, it should concentrate on turning only one or, at most, two images into reality. Trying to do more than that can fragment your group and stretch your resources past their limits. Or you can end up with the same bunch of people trying to do too much and getting burned out in the process. The goals you select should present you with a moderate challenge. Having a clear idea of where you want to be is a powerful way to make your goals for the future more real. When goals come alive, it is easier for people to commit to moving from where they are to where they want to be.

The goal you select should be one about which people are enthusiastic enough that they are willing to work to make it happen. That is, people pick the thing they really want to accomplish. This may or may not be the "most important" item on your list of images. A common mistake groups make is to select the item that everybody agrees is the most important. Often, this is something people really do not feel capable of dealing with, or, even if the matter is important, it is not really very interesting. To start with, it is much better to pick interesting over important. Make sure everybody knows this from the start. Of course, sometimes the most important, the most far-reaching goal is also the most interesting. Judge if you can accomplish it, and go for it if there is the energy to do it!

The criteria for a good goal should be kept in mind. First, it should be feasible; that is, the resources required to accomplish the goal must be available. Second, it should generate some excitement. Third, it should be clear enough that it gets you all headed in the same direction and you can easily tell when you have reached it. Fourth, the goal should be something your community group will make happen. Finally, the goal should be consistent with the reason that brought you all together in the first place (Dale & Mitiguy, 1978).

## Identify Factors in the Future Environment

You are planning today to institute something that will be in place some distant, or not-too-distant, tomorrow. You have an idea of what today looks like, but how about tomorrow? Consider how your efforts today relate to the future. Recall that any specific plan you prepare is somewhat out of date the moment it is "done." New developments will occur, and you will need to respond to some of these. Which forces might help or hinder your efforts at the time they are actually taking place, not today when you are thinking about doing them? What will occur in that future environment that might make it more receptive or more resistant to what you want to do? What new opportunities does the future hold for your organization? It is in this world, a month, a year, or five years from now, that you will be working. Do you know much about it?

Give yourself a glimpse of the future with an exercise called "creating the future." Select a specific date in the future, and act as if that future date were the present. Then ask participants to consider the following question: "What is going on today that can in some way influence our success in [whatever change you are attempting to implement]?" Some of these factors will be economic, some political, and some technological.

It is helpful to develop this picture of the future over two separate occasions. On the first occasion, create the future for the broadest arenas likely to influence your success. Then, about a week later, do the same for your more immediate spheres of action. Familiarize yourself with publications that forecast future developments. Proceedings from community conferences that attempt to gauge future developments, information from various government planning bodies, and community trends publications should prove helpful.

## CHANGE AGENT TIP

Brainstorming techniques help to generate ideas. Here are a few simple rules for brainstorming sessions:

- Write everything down.
- Everyone offers an idea.
- No criticism of any idea.
- No discussion of ideas during brainstorming.
- Both specific and broad ideas are welcome.
- Stress the quantity not the quality of ideas.
- It is acceptable to repeat an idea.
- Build on one another's ideas.

You can build on people's enthusiasm as they create the world they will eventually work to make real. While you are brainstorming, though, some people will catch on to the idea of clear images much better than others. In the spirit of brainstorming, you do not want to tell people that their ideas are not good enough, yet you do want sharp images. To get around this obstacle, create two columns: one headed IMAGES and the other headed IDEAS.

Encourage everyone to offer their ideas, even if they are not yet sharpened into images. People will soon get the hang of things, and some good ideas that otherwise might be silenced will find their way into the IMAGES column. Planning that is purely rational is limited. Let your intuitive side emerge and allow it to influence your actions.

### Identify Current Obstacles and Current Resources

You have dealt with the future; now you need a picture of the current environment—the arena of action in which you are going to promote change. These are the forces that have an impact on what occurs in the system in which you want to make changes. This requires your attention to its interaction with other systems that affect it.

Kurt Lewin (1951) describes a technique known as force field analysis, which can help you to visualize these interactions. Figure 7.4 diagrams a simple force field. A number of contending forces operate in your arena of action. Some of these forces drive you toward your goal; others drive you away from your goal. A state of tension exists, producing a dynamic situation as forces act on one another. At any given moment, these forces are in relative balance; this balance represents the current state of affairs (for an excellent discussion of force field analysis, see Brager & Holloway, 1978; Bishop, 2002).

Using this method of viewing the current situation can help you determine which forces you can mobilize and which forces you must counter. To get this snapshot, brainstorm all the forces now present that may help or hinder your success. These forces may be tangible items, such as people, meeting rooms, or backhoes, or intangibles, such as apathy, personal connections, or skills.

First, list all those things that might get in your way. Remember, you are listing currently operating forces, not those that may develop. Some common restraining forces include inhibiting policies or procedures, history of failed effort, lack of information, intimidating opponents, ingrained attitudes, and a lack of money. There are, of course, many more, some of which are unique to your circumstances. Generating this list will give you a good idea of the obstacles you face.

Next, list all those things that are going for you. Some common helping forces include the interest of a number of people, talents of the people you know, community or political connections, information, and tangible resources such as a plot of land. Many groups think only of the obstacles they must face or the difficulties they will encounter and fail to regard equally the forces operating

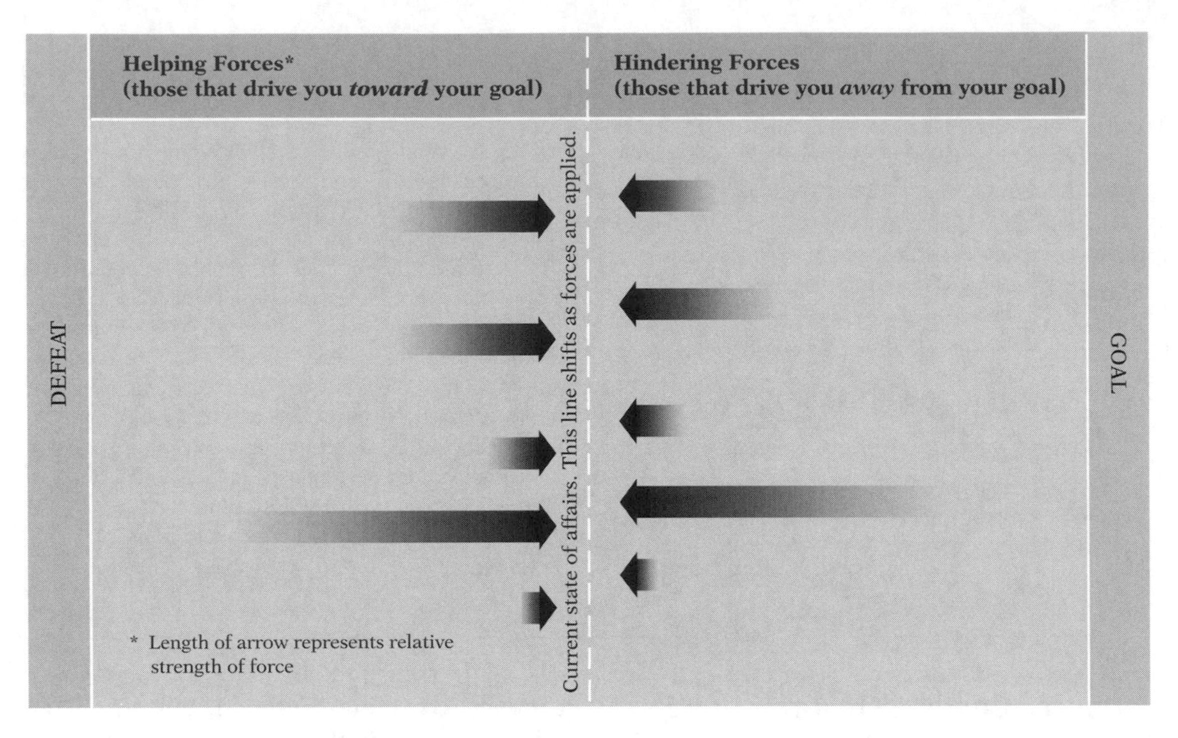


**FIGURE 7.4** Simple Force Field Based on Lewin's (1951) Technique

to benefit them. This leads to discouragement and lost opportunities as well. By examining your helping forces after you have considered your hindering forces, you generate confidence and build on the discovery of resources by beginning to look for them much more actively.

Force field analysis holds that driving and restraining forces are in relative balance. You do have a lot going for you. Unless the situation is rapidly deteriorating, some things present in the environment are keeping the situation from getting much worse much more quickly. What are these things? The most obvious asset that any community has is its people. This is so evident that it is frequently overlooked. Other common forces include dissatisfaction or anger, helpful laws and policies, leadership, money, talents, personal networks, and physical resources. What else is there? What is holding the opposing forces in check? These are some of your helping forces.

After the forces present in your arena of action have been identified, it is a good idea to get some notion of their relative power. You may, for example, assign numerical values to designate how much influence each force may have. This does not have to be a precise measurement, but it will give you an indication of the more important forces you need to think about. As you begin to move to action, remember that you can combine a number of smaller forces to make a more potent one. For example, a lot of people, a small room, and a couple of television cameras can add up to quite a powerful force.

Using force field analysis, you can discover a lot about your current situation in a very short amount of time. It is a good idea to repeat this exercise from time to time to keep your picture of the present, its dangers and its opportunities, up to date.

## Identify Stakeholders

Stakeholders are people who have a stake in what you do. In the broadest sense, stakeholders are those whose interests your actions could benefit or threaten. Their influence is so powerful that they deserve their own category. Mason and Mitroff (1985) identified stakeholders as having purposes and strategies that support or resist your efforts. Those who are supportive have goals generally compatible with your goals and are moving (or would like to move) in the same general direction as you. Resisters, whom they characterize as non-supportive and resistant, or actually oppositional, provide barriers to your success or move in the opposite direction. Take an extra minute or two to think beyond the obvious resisters to identify all of those who have a stake in or can benefit from the current situation. You cannot ignore them, for they will surely make life difficult for you as you pursue a change that threatens their interests.

Some people who benefit from the current situation may seem to have interests similar to yours, but they are currently getting something (for example, funding or good press) as they pursue their activities. Your presence can threaten their piece of the action, their turf. Remember that as soon as you enter the arena of action, the scene changes. You may not be welcomed with open arms. This can be a surprise for you if you are not prepared.

Now, think about those people with interests similar to yours but those who would not be threatened by your success. Think for that extra minute or so about those who would be genuinely happy or who would breathe a little more easily if you succeeded. You may be able to uncover some unanticipated backing. It is essential to involve supportive stakeholders in planning in a meaningful way (Lewis et al., 2001). It is necessary that they develop ownership of the goal. When individuals have a strong attachment to the goal, their personal need to accomplish the goal leads to a strong commitment to the success of the entire group. Playing a role in the development of the goal is probably the best way to promote this strong acceptance. Key stakeholders cannot be limited to information-giving roles. They need to participate in strategy determination, task accomplishment, and decision-making capacities.

## Identify Actions that Use Existing Advantages to Overcome Obstacles

Now that you have a picture of what needs to be changed, what the desired conditions look like, what future forces will influence your efforts, and what forces are now present that will affect your success, it is time to identify what you can do to get to where you want to go.

Decide which obstacle you want to overcome first. Look over your list of helping forces or resources and decide which of these can be used to counteract whatever is working against

### ● CHANGE AGENT TIP

Asking some basic questions can shed light on stakeholders who may have a powerful influence on your change effort. The answers to these questions will help you to discover the stakeholders that your change effort must take into account.

- Who currently feels the problem? How?
- Who benefits from the current condition? How?
- Who could benefit from a changed condition? How?
- Who currently makes decisions on this issue? What is the nature of these decisions?
- Who needs to behave in a different way? How?
- Who is likely to oppose you? Why?
- Who is likely to support you? Why?

you. Generally, pick assets that are easiest to use, although other criteria, such as developing broader participation and keeping yourself from becoming too predictable, should be considered. A clear picture of actions that you can take will emerge from reviewing your assets. If there is time, test a number of alternative actions as you decide what to do. Sometimes, less than the best is better. As you select actions that hold the best chance to get you to where you want to go, make sure these are actions you can actually see yourself doing.

Next, identify the particular steps that need to be taken (such as making phone calls, distributing fliers) in order to activate the resource.

## Identify the Sequence and Time Frame of Actions

Which of these things do you do first? The best way to answer that is to consider what comes last. By working backward, you can better determine how the steps you plan to take relate to each other and to what it is you want to accomplish. You can also figure out how specific actions can bolster or interfere with one another. Make your time frames clear.

One thing you will probably notice is that everything apparently needs to be done by tomorrow, if not the day before. Unless you are dealing with a scheduled event whose timing is beyond your control, it is likely you can pursue a less frenzied schedule. If a frenzied schedule is not really required, it will not be sustained anyway. People will normally do things in about the time they think they need to be done. So there is no need to worry about getting everything done well in advance, and at once. If you jam up the first few months with most of your activities without rest or pacing, participants may feel worn out as soon as the first steps are completed. You will probably discover that many tasks are not completed on schedule thereafter. This can lead to discouragement and to unnecessary conflict. Give yourself some leeway for things running over schedule.

## Identify People Who Will Handle Necessary Tasks

Tasks do not get done by themselves. Designate who is responsible for seeing that each task is completed. There is a key phrase here—"seeing that a task is completed." Individuals taking on the responsibility do not necessarily need to do the job themselves. They just need to make sure it gets done. Sometimes no one in your group has the necessary time, talent, or interest to perform the task, but one of you can usually find another individual, perhaps from outside the immediate group, who does. This may result in bringing a new member into the fold. However you go about this, see that the individual has a sense of investment in the task and a sense of personal responsibility. Tasks will not be completed when no one commits to them.

Sometimes, no one is willing to volunteer to take responsibility for getting a certain job done, although everyone agrees it is necessary. There follows an uncomfortable silence in response to the question "Okay, who's going to take care of this?" Please catch yourself before you volunteer to take on another job that nobody else wants to do. Otherwise, you and

### • CHANGE AGENT TIP

Homan's Rule of 33 states that things will be 33 percent different from what you think they will be, generally on the downside. For example, if twelve people tell you they are coming to your get-together, expect eight. One of the most common "surprises" is that tasks will take 33 percent longer to do than you thought they would take, even if you are generous in your estimate.

the two or three other people who cannot stand silence for an answer will come to be seen as the "main people" in the group—the ones who really are going to worry about getting things done. The other people are then allowed to become less "main" and understand that they have an acceptable role of being less committed. They can then come to expect less of themselves as they come to expect more of you "main people." Unfortunately, you will soon come to share these expectations.

So what do you do? The thing still needs to get done. If you have noticed a pattern developing, talk to the other "main" people beforehand. You can agree to take on your fair share of duties, but none of you will jump to rescue the group by doing whatever no one else seems willing to do. The first thing you can try is to just sit there and accept the silence. It should be long enough that there is some noticeable discomfort. Eventually someone will speak up . . . maybe. If that has not worked, something a little more direct may be in order. You might approach someone directly to see if they will do the task. You might also revisit the task to see if there is something wrong with the way it is thought through and whether people believe it is worthwhile. You may need to risk squandering a few opportunities before people get the idea that the work really is going to be spread around, or it is not going to get done.

An alternative approach is to ask "What will happen if we do not get this done?" Then you ask, "Is that okay with everyone?" These questions usually encourage some members of the group to agree to take charge of the task.

## Identify Indicators that Show Planned Tasks Were Completed

It is sometimes difficult to determine whether a task is completed because we do not really know what "completed" looks like. By selecting indicators of job completion, you can more clearly determine whether you are doing what you said you were going to do. These also help to clarify or make more specific just what the task involves. Indicators are simply your response to the question "How do I tell that it's done?" Dale (2004) suggests that indicators have three important purposes: to evaluate whether something has been done or changes have taken place; to assess future states; to guide decisions that must be made (Dale, 2004, pp. 121–124).

If your task involves holding a meeting, one indicator could be the minutes of the meeting, and another could be a sign-in sheet. If your task involves developing media attention, an indicator could be a record of news stories aired. If

### • CHANGE AGENT TIP

The Next Steps Action Chart is a simple form to keep track of the immediate next steps your group will take. Divide a piece of paper into four columns, and label columns across the top as follows:

Column 1: *Task*. Clear, simple description of the task to be accomplished.

Column 2: *HDYTIGD*. This is the "How do you tell it got done?" column. Identify some simple, objective method to determine that the task was completed (for example, to determine that a meeting occurred, use minutes from the meeting. To determine that an article appeared in the newspaper, use a copy of the article).

Column 3: *Date*. This is the date by which the task is completed.

Column 4: *Person Responsible*. This identifies the person who will make sure that the task is completed. This person may or may not actually perform the task, but she or he will make sure that the task is completed.

Refer to this chart often, and be sure to acknowledge your successes. This is an easy way to keep tabs on your progress toward your goal.

fliers are to be distributed, the fact that you have a flier and a list of the distribution points and numbers distributed could be indicators. These indicators help you to monitor your efforts. You will be able to determine what you did and when. Not only will this help to keep you on track, it will also help you to determine your effectiveness. Evaluating your efforts is important, but before you can determine whether your effort is working, you need to determine just what work you have done.

## Identify Measures of Effectiveness and Indicators of Trouble

To evaluate your endeavour means you must check to see if it is producing the desired results. When you evaluate, ask yourself, "Are we accomplishing what we want to accomplish? Why or why not?" This is different from monitoring, which asks the question "Are we doing what we said we were going to do?" Monitoring asks what is being done; evaluating asks whether it is working (Kettner et al., 1985).

Just as you have indicators of task completion, you should have indicators of task effectiveness. These are your responses to the question "How do we tell if this task produced what we wanted it to produce?" If you hoped that a meeting would lead to increased money from a particular source, your indicator would be more money from that source. If your intent with the news media was to influence the vote of the city council, your indicator would be the council's actual vote.

These are pretty simple indicators, but they give you a sense of how you are doing. Some occasions demand a more sophisticated approach to evaluation. For example, you may need to clearly identify the relationship between actions and their consequences. You may need to determine not only if this particular action directly produced this particular consequence, but maybe also how or why. No matter how superficial or thorough your evaluation procedures may be, you still need to know what your indicators of success are—that is, what outcomes you expect to produce.

In any effort, there are signs of your accomplishments, your growing success. By knowing what some of these are, you can recognize and celebrate their attainment. Maintaining an awareness of your victories, great and small, can keep you driving forward.

## Perform Identified Tasks

Although performing tasks may not technically be part of the planning process, we must not forget that action is what this whole business is about. Consider, too, that action and planning are occurring at the same time. You cannot just stop everything you are doing in order to plan, and you cannot wait until you are finished planning before you act.

## Monitor, Evaluate, and Refine

You need to keep an eye on your plans to keep them fresh, up to date, and relevant to your situation. Whenever plans no longer effectively relate to current conditions, they become deadweight. They also convince people that planning is a waste of time. To keep your planning useful for meeting current demands and giving direction to the future, you must continue to be informed about current and likely future conditions and the effectiveness of your plan.

You set your plan in motion by acting on it. As you act, you change conditions and gather information. Your group changes, and so does the rest of the world in which you are acting. You regularly need to acquire and use three sets of information. One set of information you must gather involves what you are learning from reviewing the indicators regarding task completion. This is your monitoring function. What are you learning from this review? Are people doing what they said they would be doing? Are they not? Can you find out why things are or are not happening? What are you learning how to do better? What is taking more time than you thought?

The second set of information involves your learning from the indicators of effectiveness or trouble. This is your evaluation function. Are you advancing toward your goal? Are you seeing signs of trouble? Are the things you are doing having the intended effect or not? Evaluation can be formative; that is, it is an ongoing assessment, throughout the process, intended to improve your design and implementation. Or it can be summative; that is, it takes place at some particular end point to look at the impact or change that has been produced by the effort (Burke & Prater, 2000). The clearer your goals and indicators, the more

## ● CHANGE AGENT TIP

When examining the impact of a particular change episode, you may miss some valuable information. Because your view is focused only on the planned change, you may not see the other reactions to your efforts that are taking place. Looking only at the planned change gives a limited view and an incomplete understanding of what you are producing. Two evaluation tools can help you to get a broader view. The first is called Measurement of Planned Change, which looks at the degree to which your concrete goals were reached. Use this tool to chart your progress.

The second is called the Catalogue of Progress, which lists the reactions you see that can be attributed to your work. This chart lists the signs that your efforts are making a difference. At the beginning of every regular meeting, the facilitator should ask for a report on any Catalogue of Progress entries. This helps members to refine their ability to recognize the responses their work is producing. It also builds confidence and motivation as awareness that the group is making a difference continues to grow. Project leaders should track both sets of indicators to get a truer picture of gains that are taking place.

**Measurement of Planned Change**

| **Target area** | **Measurement:** ***The degree of change*** | **Measurement method:** ***How we know that change has happened*** | **Measurement date:** ***When we will check to see if change has happened*** | **How to use information to effect action, or** ***what action needs to be taken as a result of this information*** |
|---|---|---|---|---|
| | | | | |

**Catalogue of Progress**

| **Date** | **Event or Reaction** | **Target Area** |
|---|---|---|
| | | |

able you will be to assess progress and measure results.

The third set of information involves the new knowledge and information you come upon while you are engaged in the action. What are you seeing now that you did not see before? What is new in the environment? New obstacles? New opportunities? What new information strengthens your cause? What adjustments do you need to make as a result of what you are discovering? This is your refinement function. What structures are in place for incorporating this new learning into a fresh version of your plan?

From time to time, get together with the people who helped to develop the plan to review and modify it. If you are in a fast-paced situation in which important conditions really do change daily, your plan will require constant attention and fine-tuning. The less rapidly changing your conditions are, the less frequently your plans need to be reviewed, and the lower the likelihood that a review will be conducted. However, the less frequently you review a plan, the more thorough your review needs to be. Do not wait too long between reviews, however. If you find that each review involves a rediscovery of your plans, you have waited too long, and your plans have probably become documents that no longer inform your actions.

Review dates should be built into your planning process. Depending on your situation, this could be every afternoon, every three months, or every October. As we mentioned at the beginning of this chapter, you never stop planning. As long as you intend to learn and to act efficiently and effectively, you will continue to focus your plans.

## OBSTACLES

Toward the end of your planning, take a little time to talk about the pitfalls in the road before you and how important it is to try to identify them. Think now of how you will recognize the signs that a pitfall might be occurring or might be about to occur and determine what you will do when you recognize those signs. Of course, you do not have to develop a strategy for dealing with each possible pitfall, but you do have to learn to recognize them as warnings. Have some fun with the process. Take the lists out every now and then and look at them. If you are aware of possible pitfalls, they will be much more easily avoided, and you will be more confident because you realize what could have happened if you were not paying attention.

You can employ a technique called 20/20 hindsight. Here is how it works. Take an imaginary leap forward to the date that you have targeted for reaching your goal. Then ask the group to look back from there on your effort "today". . . because you failed. Then ask, "From this vantage point, what did we miss in our planning?" "What happened that caused us to fail?" "What faulty assumptions did we make?" "What did we do that we shouldn't have done?" Let's look at some of the things that can get in the way—and maybe even consider a thing or two that you can do to face these obstacles.

### An Unpredictable Future

One of the simple facts about the future is that you really have no idea what is going to happen. By planning, you increase the odds that you can predict and influence the future, but you cannot fully know it or control it. Accept that simple fact, and be willing to be surprised. A misplaced belief that you are able to control all forces will leave you unnerved and unprepared when you discover that you cannot. Anticipate the fact that some unanticipated things will occur. You can and should develop some contingency or backup plans. What is most important, though, is that you roll with the punches if you get hit by something you did not plan for, and that you be ready to take advantage of some unexpected opportunity.

### Misperception about Skill Levels

Most planning situations in community change do not call for sophisticated skills. If you feel hampered by the idea that your planning process cannot move forward because your data collection, data analysis, and consequent decision-making methods are not sufficiently complex, you might be overdoing things a bit. Hagebak (1982) calls this problem the "bog of sophistication." Check also to see that this lack of skill is not simply a justification for not getting started. Large, highly complex change efforts require some sophisticated planning, but most changes are really not all that complex and the elements of the planning process can be rethought to fully involve community members.

Every day, each of us answers the basic questions involved in planning—"What do you want to have happen?" "What do you have going for you?" "What is getting in your way?" "Knowing this, what do you need to do?" We do this so often and so easily, whether it involves driving to the store or figuring out dinner, that we do not even notice we are planning, but indeed we are. You need to recognize that you not only have the fundamental skills but that you use them all the time. All you have to do is to apply them in a different arena. What you already know is probably enough to get you started. Sometimes you might get stuck. If you need to know more, ask a planning expert for some direction or some time. Universities, public agencies, and some social service organizations have planners. You can generally find someone pretty good who can give you a hand.

## Lack of Interest

Most of us are not interested in doing things that are boring and have little value, especially if we do not think we are good at them. Planning is no different. If you want to involve people in planning, you have to confront these three obstacles. To promote interest in planning, first of all you

Photos.com

**Achieving community goals begins with thorough and careful planning.**

have to make it interesting. There is a natural excitement for doing or creating something new; capitalize on this. Do not wear people down with the mechanics of planning. Build on their enthusiasm. Also, give attention to the setting. Consider doing this over pizza or at a cottage on a weekend retreat, or do something else that makes things a little different, a little unusual, a little fun.

Second, you may have to confront people's previous experiences of fruitless planning. Allow them to point out how they will make sure that that does not happen this time. You will not convince the reluctant by talking about the importance of planning. You have to approach the process as if it is important and clearly directed to improving the problem situation. Avoid making planning appear too grand. This often generates skepticism. When planning takes on a life of its own, it becomes irrelevant and cannot live up to its lofty promises. People realize this right away. They will go through the motions of planning, but they will not make an investment in it.

Third, the way you present the concept of planning will give people the message this is something they can do. Calling planning "figuring out what we need to do," for example, will go a long way toward bringing things down to earth. Take your planning process one step at a time. Providing a rough overview of the process can be helpful. However, if you go through an exhaustive list of everything that needs to be done and all the things not to do, you will end up confusing people. Guiding people through the steps one at a time keeps them on track and gives them something specific to do. From time to time, show how a particular step relates to what you want to accomplish so that participants know why they are doing what they are doing.

## Thirst for Immediate Action

When emotions are running high, people want to act. They do not want to mess around with this planning business. They certainly do not want to hear the learned voice of reason telling them to calm down and think this through thoroughly. This is all right. Plan a little bit. The energy that they now have for action is probably more valuable anyway. (The exception to this is if what people want to do is clearly so short-sighted that they will cause more problems than they will solve. Then you might have to get them to stand back for a minute in order to take a broader look before acting.) If you can, get some agreement on where you want to end up, and then just worry about what you can do right now, and how you can do it. After a period of initial fervour, the group is usually ready to determine some longer-range strategy.

You do have a delicate balance to strike here. You do not want to get into the habit of not planning, but by the same token, you do not want to dampen enthusiasm and cut off spontaneity. Over time, certain roles will emerge with some people acknowledged as providing strategic leadership whereas others can be counted on for taking needed action. As long as both aspects are valued, the group stands a good chance of achieving some success.

It is important to have activists who promote action and those who want a planned response in your group. Do not discourage one over the other but rather, as a change agent, encourage a mix of direct action and step-by-step planning. Either type of person can slow matters down by getting invested in their role as expert planner or as activist, especially if they lose focus and do not reflect on the consequences their actions will have on the group. It is vital to keep a sense of purpose. The value of planning is to provide action with a sense of purpose.

A group of participants who shy away from planning may do so because they already have a preferred course of action and do not want to reconsider its effectiveness. They just want to do what they want to do because it is exciting or comfortable or serves their personal needs. Taking a good look at the most effective approach may require a change in preferred tactics. If the tactics themselves are really more important than the outcome, planning will be seen as an irritant and irrelevant.

## Planning to Avoid Action

A concern about planning is that it plays into the hands of *risk avoiders,* who are hesitant to take action and so plan the thing to death. Risk avoiders want to make sure that all risks are identified and minimized before any action is taken. Some want actions to come with guarantees. Sometimes, the effort to plan is easier than the work involved in implementing the plan. After all, you can control the plan, but you cannot control everything that happens when you put things in motion. Testing your great ideas is a lot harder than declaring them. All contingencies must be accounted for, and every detail considered. As the situation changes and new information becomes available, risk avoiders keep retooling their plans. They could do this forever, and probably would if something did not come along to give them a push (something usually does). The sad thing is that despite all their planning, they are not really prepared for action because they do not really want to act.

If you suspect that this is going on, you must confront it. Some of the following questions might be helpful for bringing this concern out in the open: "When will we have enough information to act?" "When will we be ready to act?" "Are we really afraid of action?" "Are we more afraid of failure than we are willing to take a shot at changing things?" "Are we afraid of the work we will have to do if we actually start acting on our plans, or are we afraid our plans will not work?" This questioning can lead to some productive discussion, and it can lead to action as you realize what you have been doing. Be careful not to demean or ridicule people for their fears. That approach will just lead to denial and divisiveness. It really is all right to feel uncertain. If that is what is going on, accept the fact that you feel that way, and accept, also, the fact that you still need to get going.

## Belief That Plans Will Not Have an Impact on Decision Making

There is a game that goes like this: person in authority asks subordinates for their ideas; gives them the impression they are really being listened to; makes them feel part of this shared process; and then goes ahead and does what he or she wanted to do all along.

Has this ever happened to you? Probably. You likely felt tricked or used. It has probably happened to others in your group as well, so do not be surprised when you encounter this sort of skepticism. And do not encourage it by playing the same game yourself. Sometimes, an idea that someone else offers may be less perfect than your own, but it may still be acceptable. Accepting this "less perfect" idea may be the wiser course, especially if it is workable and others have a strong investment in the proposal. Broad ownership of the plan is usually more important than perfection.

Encouraging people to take some responsibility for implementing their ideas (if the group agrees they are worth doing) is one way to show that you take the suggestion seriously. With this approach, the person can make sure that the action will be handled in the way he or she wanted. If you ask people for information for planning, let them know how the information will be used and what purpose it will serve. Also, let participants know how the information will benefit them and the change effort.

## Forgetting to Include People in Planning

Leaving people out of the planning process can be deadly. Some may passively or aggressively attempt to sabotage the direction you decide to take. Others may simply have little interest in pursuing a course they did not help to establish and may not fully understand. In fact, if you do not include people in the process, you have not been an effective change agent who works within the means, purposes, values, and talents of the community. It is from the community itself that the most effective and creative ideas for goals, objectives, and tasks to address the needs and problems of the community are developed.

Take stock of who should be, and who would want to be, included, or at least invited, to help determine your future goals and actions. Look at those people who operate in the relevant systems that your change effort engages, particularly those stakeholders in the need, action, and target communities. Try to figure out roles for those who want to be involved. It may be appropriate to exclude someone from developing your plans. However, if you do, make sure that you honestly examine your reasons for doing so, and also make sure that you have considered the possible ramifications resulting from their exclusion.

## Defining the Problem in Terms of the Solution

Defining the outcome that you want to achieve and defining the means for achieving that outcome are two different things. For example, children in your are threatened by cars speeding down a busy street that they must cross on their way to school. This is something about which the neighbourhood wants to take action. Someone mentions, "The problem here is that we don't have a streetlight at the intersection." The room positively flutters with the simultaneous bobbing of many heads. Be careful here, because you are in danger of defining the problem as a solution. Your problem is not the lack of a streetlight. The problem is that your kids may get hurt. The streetlight may or may not be a good solution, but if that is all you think about, you will close yourself off from thinking about any other approach to achieving your goal. If you put in the streetlight and your kids still get hurt, you have not accomplished your purpose. However, if your kids are safe without a streetlight (maybe you put in speed bumps or a crossing bridge instead), you have solved your problem. Which is more important, your children's safety or a streetlight? Now, which do you want to work on? When you are defining the outcome you want to achieve, ask yourself, "If the situation were different only in this way, would we be satisfied?"

### Take a Moment to Discover

Can you remember a situation in which people making plans about something important to you could have involved you but left you out of the discussion? How did you feel about it? How did that affect your commitment to the plan or your trust in those making the plans?

## Groupthink

Many groups establish norms that prevent the free expression of ideas. In these groups, there is pressure to maintain an agreeable atmosphere free of dissension. The primary goal becomes promoting a shared perception of reality rather than discovering and shaping that reality. Conformity is stressed and accomplished more often by subtle than by direct pressure. Gentle reminders are given to members that the group has things under control and that expressions of doubt are expressions of lack of faith in the group and its leaders. The group conspires to ignore signs of trouble. Open disagreement is seen as an attack on the group and its prevailing wisdom. To suggest that there is a better way or that the group is overlooking something important is just not done.

Participants are not willing to be seen as deviants or troublemakers who upset the group's illusion of unanimity and control over events. To protect themselves and the group from this discomfort, participants censor their own thoughts. People keep their misgivings about a proposed course of action to themselves and then later on will criticize a failed course of action. Janis (1982) has labelled this process *groupthink*. You can see how dangerous this process can be to a group. Their unreal view of reality can have some very real consequences. Agreements that are superficial can fall apart when put to the test. Things that have been ignored can rise up to knock down the group's efforts. The sad thing is that groups often are unaware of their use of groupthink, and they are left confused about what went wrong.

Keep on the lookout for signs of groupthink, and bring it up if you think you may be closing off discussion in order to force group agreement. A good, simple question to ask is this: "Is there anything that we do not want to look at?" When you have the time to use them, techniques such as brainstorming, force field analysis, and projected 20/20 hindsight should give you a good rein on groupthink tendencies.

## CONCLUSION

Planning requires that you acknowledge and accept the fact that you will have to change your behaviour. If planning does not help you figure out what you want, determine what to do, prepare you to do it, and keep you on track, then planning is a waste of time. But if planning increases the chances you will do the right thing at the right time in the right way to get what you want, and you put it to use, then it has been time well spent.

Powerful planning not only gives you direction, it also builds commitment, enthusiasm, and confidence. Planning is a vision of a better future made more possible by the determination of purposeful actions. If you grab hold of that vision and make it yours, if you take those actions in the present to shape the future, if you continue to pay attention and keep your plans alive, one day you will look around at what you have accomplished—and it will feel good.

## HELPFUL WEBSITES

**Canadian Council on Social Development**

www.ccsd.ca

The Canadian Council on Social Development is a "non-profit social policy and research organization focusing on issues such as poverty, social inclusion, disability, cultural diversity, child well-being, employment and housing." It engages in planning processes that are focused on social issues. It also has important listings through subsites to local social planning councils that are located in municipalities across Canada. This site provides useful research resources about Canadian social and community issues. It will help you imagine how to plan for them as well. It provides links to issue papers, research publication, and minutes from planning meetings of planners. It also has an important list of policy initiatives and lobbying that the organization itself has undertaken. The site will help you, as a planner, imagine with whom, how, and what organization you might start getting involved at the local and national levels.

**Canadian Community Economic Development Network**

www.ccednet-rcdec.ca

The Canadian Community Economic Development Network (CCEDNet) is a member-driven organization that seeks to increase the scale and effectiveness of community economic development (CED) by helping organizations and individuals strengthen their communities and create solutions to local needs. The membership of CCEDNet is made up of community-based organizations, cooperatives, social enterprises, practitioners, active citizens, researchers, and other organizations from every region of the country. The site has a many resources, including a tool box of resources to help you engage in your own planning initiatives.

**The Canadian Institute of Planners**

www.cip-icu.ca

The Canadian Institute of Planners (CIP) is a professional organization mostly for planners from planning schools. However, its site provides a useful definition of planning in Canada and lists events and conferences and useful publications.

CHAPTER EIGHT

# People—The Most Valuable Resource

**This chapter will help you better understand the following questions:**

- What are the different ways in which people can become involved in a change effort?
- What are the different types of people, talents, and assets that are needed in order to make a change effort successful?
- How do you get people involved and encourage participation?
- What are some important considerations when working with volunteers?
- Why is it important to encourage and value diversity?
- What are some important things for change agents to know about people in general?

Any change that amounts to anything involves other people, often a lot of other people. Although few people will have sustained involvement over the life of the change effort, many people will play a role in its success. These people are not just sitting around offering advice; they are doing things to accomplish a specific purpose or set of purposes.

In previous chapters, you have learned to better understand your community and how power operates within it, and you have been given suggestions on how to plan your actions to produce the desired results. Yet, unless you are capable of being in several places at the same time, nothing significant is going to happen unless other people become involved. This chapter looks at how you involve people, how you develop and maintain commitment, and how people's talents and energies can be best put to work.

Much of the work in a change effort is commonly done by people who are not paid to do it. This requires special attention. The nature of voluntary activity—particularly when complementing the work of paid staff—is an important consideration. Finally, as you work on various change attempts, you will find yourself reflecting on why people do the things they do to help or hinder. Whether you need 2 people or 2,000 people, you need to understand them and understand how they can relate effectively to one another as well as to the challenges that beckon them in the process of change. Community work and organizing means *people working in concert.* It is both a process and an outcome.

## WHAT DO YOU NEED?

Three types of communities will be affected by your attempt to make a difference: the need or benefit community, the action community, and the target or response community. Taken together, these are called your *arena of action*. There are times when these are three different communities, and times when they are one and the same. Ideally, you want to have people from each type of community to aid you. There may well be conflicts among and even within these groups. Gaining a clearer understanding of these differences and how to negotiate among them will, at the very least, require some information from those who will be affected by your decisions and actions (Patton, 1987). Of course, if the need, action, and target communities are all the same, this is a little easier. If they are all different, you face more of a challenge. Do not forget that you are also part of the community when you are working in it even if you do not normally identify with it. Also, many people who are members of a community are motivated to become change agents because they know the community intimately. It may be that you and your community membership are important resources too.

If you have decided to bring people together to work for change, does it matter whom you involve? If you just get a group of people together, will that not be a good start? The answers are yes and yes. Yes, at first you make do with what you have. Enlist the support of anyone who is interested. From that group, you will be able to get a lot of what you need.

And yes, it eventually does matter who participates. Over the long haul, any random group of people probably will not do. Unless your random group is so large that you are bound to find what you need within it, you need to be more intentional in your recruiting. We stressed the importance of involving people who are affected by plans and decisions in the process of making and planning decisions. As you consider the various ways of generating, utilizing, and maintaining the human resources of your change work, understand that those people who are affected by the actions—particularly members of the benefit community—play a critical role in determining actions and in taking them (Fawcett, Seekins, Whang, Muir, & Balcazar, 1982).

In a similar vein, your community work will benefit from the participation of those who have a role in implementing the change you seek. If the change does not make sense to those charged with implementing it, it will likely be greeted by passive resistance at best and outright conflict at worst. Conversely, if this group has an investment in the change, particularly through participation in its design and the actions to bring it about, there can be a substantial payoff. They will want to see the change work, and they may well extend themselves to see that it does. Because these are the people who will actually end up doing what needs to be done, it is their actions that ultimately determine the effectiveness of the change.

Involving people is a purposeful, ongoing process that addresses three essential considerations. First, the number of people and level of their commitment and participation must fit the demands of the situation. Second, talents and assets must be encouraged among the participants. Third, participants who bring needed personality characteristics will be particularly valuable to the effort. Sometimes you will find one person who can offer all these things to community work, but this is rare. So take a closer look at each of these attributes.

## Level of Participation

What does participation or involvement mean? Does everyone have to operate at the same level of intensity? No, involvement can occur in many different ways. Everyone does not have to have the same zeal. Making fervour a requirement of partnership would eliminate a lot of potential help and power.

There are actually six different opportunities for participation available to those who are interested:

- Leadership, the core group participants
- Community agents, ongoing active participants
- Supporters, occasionally active participants
- One-shot participants

- Advisers
- Inactive general supporters

As a matter of practice, people may change their level of involvement from time to time. Be sure to value every level of participation and do not judge those who are less involved—sometimes their occasional involvement may be key to your success. It is also very helpful to have a pool of general supporters in case matters get political. Even if they move from a more active to a less active role, they may still feel a strong affiliation with the effort if communication with others continues to occur. Remember you are always looking for how to enhance the capabilities and resources of all participants and understanding their special roles.

### Leadership

The core group, that handful of people who worry more, plan more, and provide more direction for the project than others, offers the most active level of participation. The changes sought in community practice are often important in the lives of these people. Even when alone, they think about it, trying to understand more of the dynamics of the situation and what should be done to deal with them. These are the people who keep in close contact with one another to talk about what is occurring. They meet more frequently than required by the routine schedule. They expect to participate in meetings, not just attend them. They make many of the decisions about what needs to be done and understand, for the most part, why. These are the people who want to keep things alive and moving. It is they who feel anxious about the group's support and strength and who feel a real sense of loss should the effort dwindle and die.

The core group might consist of six to ten people—rarely more than that. Sometimes, a couple of people who are deeply committed with good communication skills and democratic methods can be effective leaders to a community action. The need for core group members to keep in steady communication with one another tends to limit its size. Members expect to be part of all major decisions and frequently feel a little hurt—or maybe even very angry—if left out. Members may be elected, self-selected, or specifically recruited. Often they are the people who are willing to work hard and naturally end up in leadership roles. They are often the products of the winnowing process that eliminated those only moderately interested. The core group goes by a variety of names, some of which might include the steering committee, the planning committee, the Friday morning group, or the board.

### Community Agents

Although everyone in the process is a change agent, we are using the term *community agent* here to refer to those people who are ongoing, active participants who support the work of the group and its aims but choose not to take part in all the deliberations. They are willing to follow the leadership of core group members. These participants maintain a steady interest and take part in many of the activities. Along with the core group, they do much of the work and may even have particular responsibility for a major set of functions.

The difference between them and the core group is that participants at this level might not have as clear a picture of the overall plan, program, or action. They may not currently attend all the meetings, may not consider and develop strategy, or may not worry about things in general. There are many reasons they might not be as involved in all the activities of the core group. For example, these community agents may trust the members of the core group and the general direction things are taking, lack the self-confidence needed for deeper involvement, be too busy, might be interested in and energized by a particular aspect of the change, or may just not be interested in overall involvement. You may well find potential (as well as previous) leaders among these workers. An effective group will look for opportunities to develop new leadership and make sure that participation in the core group is open to people willing to make that kind of commitment. Also, a strong core group will try to involve as many community agents as possible in key elements of the change process, such as strategizing direction, planning, and collaborative, democratic decision making.

### Supporters

Occasionally active supporters do things when the mood strikes them or when they are specifically asked. Having a moderate interest, they would like the effort to be a success and will lend a hand. Other occasional supporters have periods of high activity interrupted by stretches of seeming indifference. For some supporters, community change matters hold their attention for only so long before their enthusiasm fades. Others will be quietly following the work of the group and appreciate your communication to them. It is important to maintain communication with supporters, especially since they may be needed at the moment of political challenge, such as direct action or policy lobbying, or for simple tasks that require a lot of people, such as delivering flyers. Although their participation is sporadic, it can be extremely useful. It is often available when requested, and, over time, some supporters develop a stronger affiliation with the group once they discover their particular niche or become interested as you teach them more about the issues through your communication.

### One-Time Participants

This category includes those who do something only once or are involved for only a short period of time and then disappear from the scene altogether. Sometimes these are people who soon learn that they have overestimated their interest or underestimated the cost of their participation. Some discover that the change effort is not what they thought it was. Others simply switch from one thing to another, not quite sure what they are seeking, maybe never really finding it. Still others have a "sneeze experience." Drawn by the excitement that a change effort offers, they step out of their ordinary roles to do some things, maybe even a flurry of actions that they consider to be dramatic. Once they get this excitement or drama out of their systems, they return to the safety of their normal routine. They also may be community members whose life circumstances make it difficult to maintain active involvement—these are people such as the elderly or single parents who may already have a full plate doing the work of their daily life.

Even one-timers can be a benefit to the undertaking. They may take part in activities that require a high level of intense energy for a short period of time. Or they may be willing to join in a show of force and stand as part of a crowd. You may need people to do this. Although it would be nice to have more ongoing involvement, even these limited acts can be useful. Just a caution: do not spend a lot of your time trying to re-energize previous participants if it is pretty apparent that their batteries have gone dead. On the other hand, it may be useful at times to explore the circumstances that make it difficult for these people to be involved. By addressing their concern, you may find these individuals become recruits for more active participation. Their participation may help them with feelings of isolation.

### Advisers

Advisers give little sustained attention to the workings of the community, yet they can be valuable. These are people who can provide particular insights, ideas, or technical information. They are the people that you go to when you want to hold a press conference but are not sure how to do so, or they might tell you how to get a particular action started or how to influence a particular official. Maybe they can give you pointers on how to strengthen your change effort. Most often, you seek out advisers because of their experience in similar situations or because they have expertise in an area about which you know little. For example, they might include professionals such as lawyers, accountants, planners, government employees, or facilitators. These supporters are usually more effective if you initiate their involvement by asking for guidance. When you work with many volunteers, it is unrealistic to expect they understand all the legal, policy, and social structures that affect their action—sometimes it is helpful to call in an adviser to learn about these structures and how to work within or against them. True advisers are different from those self-appointed saviours of the cause who just want to tell you what to do but do not want to sweat themselves.

Many of those whom you will tap as advisers may not consider themselves to be members of your community. Other times they want to offer support because they identify with your cause or they identify as a member of the community. Because they are acting as adviser, they may remain somewhat detached. Often, once they have contributed to what you are doing, they will develop an interest in your success—particularly if you report back on how their counsel was used. Due to the natural resistance most of us have to advice, you may need to legitimize the adviser's role within the community group before their advice can be used effectively.

### Inactive General Supporters

You may enlist the support of community members who have a high degree of visibility and credibility but who may not do much actual work. Their assistance comes in the form of an endorsement of your effort. Questions regarding your intentions and legitimacy will be asked—not always out loud—and the support of influential community members can help to calm these uncertainties and, in fact, signal particular groups that you should receive active support. Participation by these individuals usually comes in the form of an agreement that their name may be used in conjunction with your efforts. Other inactive general supporters are people you may never know. They do not show up for any meetings or work assignments. They probably do not even feel that they are part of the change effort. They watch what you are doing and wish you well. As long as you make an effort to let people know what you are doing, you can trust that these supporters will be there.

So what good are they? Even though they do not participate in any specific activity of the group, they may contribute importantly to its success. Through many subtle means, perhaps talking to a friend, maybe writing an unsolicited letter to a public official, or simply by voting a certain way, they help to create a climate of change. Whoever makes decisions with regard to the change has to pick up signals that the change will ultimately meet with general acceptance, if not approval. Though inactive in your effort, these inactive general supporters help to transform the atmosphere in which you operate. Foster this kind of support for your change effort.

With six potential types of participants, how do you know who is going to be what type? Here are some clues that may point you to those who are likely to be more involved. Look for people who have made some *investment* in the effort or who have some *special relationship to the issue* that you are working on or to the *people* working on it. Next, notice the ways in which people *respond to requests* to help out, as well as the extent to which they *initiate actions* or *offer suggestions* on what they can do. These are probably good candidates for active involvement.

Provide potential members with knowledge about your goals, activities, and other members. Be sure to provide clear opportunities for involvement. People who are unsure of your desire to include them or how they can be included may be hesitant to help out. You may mistake this hesitancy for lack of interest. Check to see that opportunities for involvement are real.

The best advice is to pay attention to people: listen, resist snap judgments, and be patient. When opportunities are real and communication is maintained, people will respond to their level of interest and self-confidence. Over time, you will get a good sense of who wants to participate in a meaningful way and who is looking for something else. Those who are really not interested will not do much. Do not waste your time trying to change that. Figure out how their level of interest can benefit the group and make use of it without pretending it is different from what it is. Those who really are interested will keep trying to help out if you give them a chance. Help them discover how they fit in and always keep an eye out for why some people might feel excluded or overwhelmed by being involved and think about actions that can involve them.

## Talents and Assets

At different stages of your community work, you will need people to do different things. When you are getting started, you need people who can inspire and motivate others. Later, when you are trying to overcome resistance from those who oppose you, you would benefit from people who have strategic skill or influence with the opposition. Although your group will more than likely have to meet most of the essentials on the following list, understand that you will not always have to have all these things available at the same time. Recruit what you need when you need it.

### Numbers

The right number of visible participants will depend on the nature of the change toward which you are working. Attempting to make a change within a small change effort may require the visible involvement of only half a dozen workers. Making a change in a large system may involve hundreds or even thousands of people. Numbers give credibility and a sense of confidence to participants and outside observers as well. People may have to see that others are making the decision to join in the action before they feel good about their own decision to become involved. The people you are trying to impress, particularly the opposition, will take you more seriously if they believe you are more than just a handful of idealists or "complainers." Numbers

## DID YOU KNOW?

### The Committed Visionary

Few, if any, people in the community change will be as committed as those who recognize and act on the need for change. Historically, the vision has been an important reason for community involvement in Canada whether it is a vision based on belief systems, religious or spiritual ideas, utopian concepts, or personal desire for social engagement in a better world. Even in situations that might seem minor, the visionary, the originator of an idea and its required action, will be more dedicated than anyone else. The visionary sufficiently and personally felt the need to act before anyone else. That attachment to the reason for acting is not easily forgotten or dulled. It allows the visionary to weather the storms of doubt, confusion, and temporary setbacks better and longer than anyone else.

Moved unaided to action, the visionary has a greater fullness of involvement and often a greater need for success. Lack of success or abandonment of the effort is much harder for such a person. Abandonment seems to repudiate or at least devalue those initial beliefs that were sufficient to risk rejecting complacency. Only success justifies the initial urge, the risk of taking action. You need to understand this fundamental principle. Few will share, in quite the same way, your belief in the importance of what you are setting out to do. To ignore this invites misunderstanding and disappointment.

also give you access to other resources that your group will require. More people means more access to skills and talents and community connections that can benefit your effort.

### Doers

The people in your group will have to do things, not just talk about them. Some of these things are tedious and time-consuming. You need people who are responsible about making commitments and about following through with them. This includes those willing to take their share of the load without having to be pressured into it. Just as important, however, is the fact that they have to let others take a share as well.

### Opinion Leaders

People, especially when unsure, frequently look to a select few to help inform and shape their perceptions. You know who these people are in your arena of action. Get them involved or, at the very least, work to get them on your side. They give you credibility and an avenue of communication to others who may be uncertain about joining in.

### Potential Leaders

Leaders provide your group with energy, confidence, and direction, along with a host of other things. Without leadership, it is difficult to get things accomplished. Leadership is an essential requirement for any change effort.

Different types of leadership are needed at different stages of the change process, and not all leaders will sustain their interest over time. Further, leaders who were helpful in early stages may be more difficult to work with later. As a result, you may experience a turnover of leadership. This change may not be due to failings of the group but occurs because the action requires new leaders with differing interests. Do not be surprised if it happens. Creating a pool of potential leaders and supporting new leadership is absolutely essential to a long-term effort. It is that basic. One of your primary challenges as a change agent is to identify people who can perform leadership functions. Involve them and help them to develop and practise their leadership abilities. Remember, all current leaders were once potential leaders. Check to see who, among those currently involved, perhaps in a minor way, has some interest in and potential for leadership.

A brief note here about leaders and leadership. Leaders are not necessarily those people who are always in the spotlight. There are many different leadership functions. Some of these valuable roles include strategists, coordinators, public speakers, problem-solvers, and those who help to improve communication and understanding among the members. Trying to find one person who can perform all these actions will be difficult; find several people who can each perform a few of them.

### Motivators

At times things will drag. Sometimes progress will seem slow or nonexistent. People will lose sight of what they are trying to accomplish and why. People will become discouraged. After an initial burst of enthusiasm, the newness and excitement will probably fade. Other demands will be made on people's time and attention. Members will get distracted. You need someone to fan the spark of interest—to help participants see the chance for success and its importance, and to encourage them not only to stay involved and working but to want to do so. Motivators know how to keep the energy going. They know how to have fun. Deadly serious groups generally die. Motivators keep things lively.

### Influence Connections

You need people who have some influence in the benefit, action, and target communities. In community work, it is essential to involve members of the community to be influenced; of course, through involving community members your effectiveness will be enhanced. Those with influence may act as translators. That is, they can explain your group's goals to others—possibly more resistant others—in a way that produces a positive response. They know the right code words and the right concerns and can better communicate within that frame of reference. Understand that this type of communication can require special knowledge or skill. Some individuals with influence will be able to get people to want to go along. Others will make people go along, even if this is not what they want to do. Determine what kind of influence you need, and try to get people who have it.

### Specialized Skills or Talents

Any organized effort requires skills in certain areas, such as writing, planning, negotiating, and running meetings. Chances are that these basic skills will be present in any group of a dozen people, so check first within your current membership to see who has these skills to contribute or who can more fully develop them. If your group is large (or you intend for it to be) or the issue it is tackling is complex, you will probably need some additional skills.

This does not mean that one person always gets stuck doing the same thing. Some skills are shared by more than one member, they can easily be taught to others, or new members with particularly needed skills can be recruited. Generally, the most effective recruiters of new talent are current members who possess the same skill to some degree. They know what to look for, and they are often motivated by a desire to get some help. Perhaps one of the single most critical skills, and one that is often overlooked, is the ability to run a meeting effectively. Take pains to find someone who has this skill and let that person run your meetings.

### Access to Other Resources

In addition to people, you may need a variety of other resources (meeting rooms, printers, and computers) to get the job done. Look for people who are well-connected to a particular resource that you need, to the community in general, or to funds. These individuals may be willing to use their contacts or their own resources to help your group get what it needs.

## The Right Stuff

Your change effort cannot be divorced from the personal characteristics of its more influential members. They will affect relationships among the participants and shape the personality of the change effort itself. Look for these important attributes in the people you want to have actively participating in your group. Hardly anyone will have them all.

- *Capacity to roll with the punches.* This ability is one of the most important qualities to look for in people who are going to play an important role in your group. Every member of your core group should possess this trait. It may not surprise you—now—to know that not everything is going to go perfectly as you proceed to implement the change, but it may surprise you when it happens. Even if people are not purposefully trying to sabotage your change efforts, your plans will likely get knocked off course at times. That is one of the few things about the change process we can guarantee. You want to have people working with you who know this and can handle it when the time comes. Annoying little things will happen: equipment will break down at a crucial moment; someone will forget to follow through on a simple yet important task; it will snow on your Canada Day rally. Big things may well happen too. When setbacks occur, many people get flustered. You need people who can hang in there. People who roll with the punches have a sense of optimism. They believe that things will eventually work out, and because they do, they will help to make that success happen. They are able to keep things in perspective and not get rattled by the unexpected. If you have a few of these folks involved, you will be able to make things happen.
- *A good sense of humour.* A lot of what happens will be funny. People who can

recognize this and help others to do so as well are extremely valuable. Humour energizes, releases tension, and gives us a clearer perspective on the situations that we encounter. Along with this, you want to have people who are playful. You need to introduce some play into your work. Just because what you do is important does not mean it has to be gloomy.

- *Tenacity.* Tenacious people will not let go of a project until it is finished. Change very often requires that you keep the pressure on those who are improperly using their power (Alinsky, 1972). Tenacious people will not back off at a few (possibly empty) conciliatory gestures, nor will they let confusion or uncertainty defeat them. No one will be able to talk these people into quitting when things get tough.
- *Risk-taking ability.* Change means going from the known to the unknown. Risk takers are able to try something new, give unconventional ideas serious thought, and do things beyond what is ordinarily expected. Effective change often demands that this be done. An effective risk taker is neither ignorant of nor overly worried about possible consequences. She or he is personally willing to accept the same risks that are asked of others. This type of person usually has a healthy quality of irreverence. Some people are intimidated by the contrived trappings of power, but risk takers are not. They know that people are people, and they are not afraid of them. Risk takers are willing to stand up for themselves because they know that not doing so may involve an even greater risk.
- *Regard for others.* As people work on the issue, they will be working with each other. Careful attention to both the task at hand and the people working on it are requirements for success (Johnson & Johnson, 2003; Napier & Gershenfeld, 1999). People who can recognize and respond to what is important for other people are a must. They understand that some people will see things differently from the way they see them. This allows them to handle, even encourage, disagreement effectively. They can assert their own point of view without attacking people who think differently. In addition, they will understand that differing social locations create differing possibilities, opportunities, and struggles for others, and therefore they will think and act in a world that reflects this social reality. Regard for others includes the ability to think and act carefully, sensitively, and respectfully about differences.
- *Desire to learn.* The process of change is the process of discovery. Learning is not only a prerequisite for action; it is the result of it. Action puts ideas to the test and produces new ideas. A true learner knows you cannot wait until you know everything before you do anything. You will be learning by doing. A learner delights in challenges, seeing challenges as opportunities for discovery. People who know everything cannot evaluate or easily redirect their actions. They need to limit or ignore contradictory information; they need to make others wrong. The approach of being an expert who knows everything rather than a learner along the path of change can work against innovative and effective change. Learners know they do not know everything, so they do not have to limit themselves by pretending to know. Quite the opposite. Learners do not place artificial limits on themselves. By admitting they do not know, change agents and community members are open to effective change (Moffatt et al., 2005).
- *Responsibility.* Responsible people understand and accept the requirements of their participation. They get things done. They expect they will take care of the commitments they have made. They do not expect other people to do it for them, nor do they expect other people to be

incapable of following through on commitments. They make mistakes, but rarely make excuses. Responsible people take initiative and accept authority, knowing that both are requirements of responsibility. They make and receive suggestions because they value what they do.

- *Decision-making ability.* Progress depends on a series of decisions. Indecisiveness leads to stagnation. The change effort needs to have people who know how to make decisions, who are aware of different styles of decision making, and who know when to use each appropriately. Some situations call for consensus, others are best served by a vote, and yet others may require an individual with authority to make the choice. In making decisions, these people recognize the requirements of the situation, including the importance of maintaining relationships among people in the group and the members' willingness to support and implement the decisions that are made. Sometimes it is important to make a judgment about when to make a decision; to force a decision too quickly can work contrary to your goals. It is okay to allow members to take time to reflect. It is natural to be ambivalent when you are still exploring the issue by looking at variables such as the reaction of other group members to a decision, additional information about the issue or the community concern, and more detailed information on how change will affect them personally. A forced decision can be an act of dominance by the leaders so decision making needs to be done sensitively with a consciousness of the diversity in your group.

Participants will contribute other qualities to the group, but the ones we have mentioned here are basic. Without them, or with too many people who act in the opposite manner, your attempts at change may stagnate or risk falling apart. No matter what else participants provide to the group, they all give a bit (or a lot) of themselves. Who they are and the qualities and characteristics they share will shape the character of the change effort itself.

## GETTING PEOPLE INVOLVED

Maybe you are thinking, "All right, so there are a variety of roles people can fill, and a variety of types of people we are going to need to help with this change effort, but how do we get them involved in the first place?" The answer is simple. Ask them. Although people may be expected to join something, the simple fact of the matter is that not many are clearly asked to do so. You may be surprised with the responses you get when you take the time to ask.

According to the 2004 Canada Survey of Giving, Volunteering, and Participating, almost 12 million Canadians, or 45 percent of the population 15 years of age or older, volunteered during the previous 12 months for a total of almost 2 billion hours. Volunteers contributed an average of 168 hours over the course of the year. Making a contribution to their community was the main motivator for those who participated in volunteering. The most common types of organizations in which volunteers participated were sport and recreation, professional associations, unions, religious organizations, and cultural and educational organizations (Statistics Canada, 2006). Over a quarter of the volunteers indicated they did not volunteer more because nobody had asked them to do so.

To increase the likelihood that your approach will yield helpful, reliable members, follow this four-step process:

- Contact people.
- Give them a reason to join.
- Ask them to join.
- Maintain their involvement.

### Contact People

For people to respond at all, you need to bring your change effort to their attention. They need

Courtesy of Free the Children

**Events like Free the Children's "Me to We Day" mobilize people to work together to bring about change.**

to know that you exist and that you want their involvement. If they do not know about you, they cannot do anything with you. All active members, particularly the leaders, need to understand the importance of developing the membership. This is fundamental. One of the most important aspects of the leader's job is to continue to be on the lookout for people who could be invited into the effort. Initiators of the change effort, in particular, need to fight the very real tendency to keep things to themselves.

Where do you find all these people? First, look around you. Your current contacts with individuals, particularly those with whom you work or who are involved in other community activities with you, will provide you with the best possibilities. When others working with you in the change effort also use their affiliations, the list of potential members can grow dramatically. This is commonly referred to as a snowball technique, and it is a respectable way to recruit in community work because it is sensitive to social networks. It also recognizes that the strength of relations in the network is as important as the individuals themselves (Moffatt et al., 2005).This only works, though, if you are consciously looking to recruit new participants. We cannot overstress that point. Regularly assess what you need, and stay on the lookout for those who can help so you can invite them to join your effort.

Second, understand that you may need to make repeated attempts to contact people. You have to become part of their consciousness. People have many things to think about other than the change effort in which you are involved. More than one attempt will probably be necessary, particularly if your contact is not face to face.

Third, use more than one method to contact potential members. Again, the more indirect

**DID YOU KNOW?**

**LADDER OF COMMUNICATION EFFECTIVENESS**

There is a variety of ways to reach people; the more direct ways will bring you a greater likelihood of success.

One-to-one conversation
Small group discussion
Large group discussion
Telephone conversation
Mass-produced letter
Newsletter
Brochure
News item
Advertisement handout
Electronic social networks

Source: Adapted from Howe, 1985.

your methods, the more likely that frequent as well as varied approaches will be necessary.

Fourth, when making contact with an individual, listen to their concerns as well. See if you can identify some problems or other circumstances you both have experienced (Max, 1980).

Finally, the more personal and direct your contact is, the more likely you will be to receive a favourable response.

## Give People a Reason to Join

In addition to believing in the importance of the group's goals, people join groups for a variety of reasons: they like the task or the activity of the group; they like the people in the group; or the group, though not directly satisfying the person's needs, can be a means to satisfying his or her needs elsewhere (Napier & Gershenfeld, 1999). People who believe in what you are doing, enjoy the activities that you do, like some of the people involved, and see that participation can benefit them are the strongest candidates for membership. Understand that any one of these reasons could be sufficient to encourage a person to join. Both what you represent and the manner in which you represent it are important. You have to establish credibility with people before they will join your effort.

## Ask for Participation

None of us like rejection. Whenever you ask someone to do something or participate in something, you risk rejection. This is why some people do not ask at all. This is an effective strategy for avoiding rejection. Unfortunately, it also might result in low participation rates in your effort.

Some people are reluctant to take part in something that may cause them to alter their routines or their perception of "the way things are." They may have conceded to the burdensome conditions they currently face, and working to change conditions requires trying to imagine new ways to adapt. They may feel they cannot measure up to the demands that involvement may make of them, perhaps exaggerating, in their own minds, just what those demands might be (Mondross &

Berman-Rossi, 1992). Other people simply have other interests. They may genuinely be unable to give time now, and they may say yes later. Accept the fact that no matter how important the issue or how effectively phrased the request, some people will say no to you. This does not devalue you or your concerns. Other members, ideally all members, need to be involved in recruiting. Depending on the size of your group, you may want to have a group of members whose major responsibility is recruitment of new members.

Here are some suggestions that should improve the likelihood that people will decide to work with you.

1. When you make a request of someone, make sure you provide an easy way for the person to respond to you. This is particularly important when the request is indirect, such as through a newsletter, because the response is not immediate. Ask yourself, "If people decide to say yes, how do they let me know, and how do they know that I got their message?" Further, if they do communicate an interest in participating, ask yourself how they know what their next step is. Remember that involvement means action. If you merely say "Thanks for your interest," you have not really promoted their involvement. You need to be certain that they have received your response to their intent to take part and now know what to do.
2. Your request or "message package" should communicate the following elements: the purpose (aims or goals) of your group; its importance; what it does; that it needs people; the types of things they can do; and the way they can let you know their decision to participate. Include in your list of activities that they can do things that are fun (for example, social activities), things that are simple (for example, making phone calls, typing, or giving money), and things that are "important" (for example, meeting with legislators or appearing as a guest on a talk show). Based on your relationship and the nature of your contact (face to face versus a letter), you can modify these elements to best suit the situation.
3. Phrase your request (unapologetically) in the way that is likely to promote the best response. For instance, people may not want to join, but they may be willing to help. Joining may be perceived as becoming involved in endless meetings wrangling over subtle nuances in the bylaws. Helping may be perceived as doing some specific things to benefit the effort. Others may be willing to join by paying a few dollars to be a member, but may not be willing to help, which may imply doing a lot of work.
4. Ask specifically for what you need or for what you would like people to do. Make a clear request for a specific action or set of actions. Include clear options for participation. You may run across potentially valuable individuals who are only mildly interested in participating at the present time but may well develop a stronger interest in the future. Ask them to do a few little things at first, and over time, ask for more as their interest and feelings of competence develop. Even these initial simple requests should represent a level of participation slightly higher than what these individuals would otherwise have considered for themselves. This will make their affiliation with the effort more real.
5. Make your request meaningful and worthwhile. Do not assume that new members are interested in only the most menial tasks. Help them to feel engaged in the vision and democratic nature of your action.

A person's degree of participation relates to their interest and level of confidence, with confidence often being just as important as interest. Confidence is related to three things: their comfort with the tasks or expected activities and obligations; their comfort with the people in the group and their relationship with a sufficient number of people; and their comfort with the culture of the group.

There is an important caution here. Do not mislead people by saying, "The only thing I want you to do is . . ." or "All you have to do is . . ." if you have more that you intend for people to do. Stating one level of expectation while intending another will eventually create resentment. Though subtle, this is significantly different from increasing affiliation by making more important requests when there is more interest. Asking people for more participation should be based on developing interest. In this case, you are making a direct request for a new level of involvement. Do not ask people to do what they really are not interested in doing. Expectations should be mutually clear and moderately challenging.

When you start out, there will be people aware of what you are doing who are not yet willing to make a commitment to join you. They may be waiting for you to prove yourself before they agree to work with you. These can be some of your most valuable members in the future. They are discerning people. They are only going to participate in something that means something (Von Hoffman, n.d.). Then there will be others whose participation you would dearly love to have but who do not have any real intention of making a commitment. They may even lead you on a bit about helping. If you have honestly made requests and created opportunities for participation that remain open, and your desired recruits are aware of your action, then you probably have done enough. You do not need the people who are just not interested.

A number of people will simply seem to find their way to you and pitch in. That is encouraging, and you will experience it. Remember, though, that some people never help simply because no one ever asked them.

## Maintain Involvement

Once people have expressed an interest and they are ready to go, you want to keep them going. You can talk someone into joining, and you can talk them into staying one time, maybe twice. After that, there needs to be more to it because they will walk away before you can do any more talking.

Several ways to promote continued affiliation revolve around some very basic human needs—needs for inclusion, control, affection, recognition, accomplishment, and altruism (Johnson & Johnson, 1997). Maintaining involvement is a matter of responding to these needs, recognizing that their importance varies with each individual and perhaps even with each cultural group (Latting, 1990). Further, personal contact to encourage continued involvement is critical, particularly for those whose personal networks may discourage participation (Rubin & Rubin, 2001). Involvement may also be due to the fact that often we as community change groups work with marginalized communities who have been restricted from participation in mainstream decision making and actions. These people also have the experience of being devalued in larger efforts. The need to be involved is tied to the need to feel empowered, to have influence, and to feel good about participation in your own community (George, Moffatt, Lee, & McGrath, 2003; Lee et al., 2002). Here are some suggestions for keeping valuable members involved in the effort.

Make a special effort to help newcomers feel welcome. Everyone who participates in the

### Take a Moment to Discover

Over the past year, if you stop and think about it, you have probably had the chance to join several groups or participate in some group activity. These may have been social groups or perhaps they involved more formal organizations. Maybe you were personally invited; possibly you just received a form letter or heard an ad on the radio. Which of these, if any, did you decide to take part in? What, in particular, attracted your interest or encouraged or discouraged your involvement? How did the way you were asked affect your decision?

change process you are undertaking has something to offer, be it a skill, particular knowledge, personal connections, or other qualities that can benefit the group. Keep an eye out in order to discover what each person can do, and be willing to ask her or him to do it when the time comes. Few things are as important for building your group as your belief that every person has something to contribute. With this belief, you will find ways to increase the investment of individual members and, in doing so, will increase the cohesion and power of the group. Without it, you will use only the evident gifts of a few while you dull the commitment of many, who may well become members in name only.

Most people feel uncertain in new situations involving strangers, so anxiety is the prevailing and dominant emotion at the start of any group setting (Napier & Gershenfeld, 1999). Change agents need to be aware of the stages of group development, particularly the uncertainty and wariness that accompanies group beginnings (Mondross & Berman-Rossi, 1992).

Give people something to do—the sooner the better. When people respond favourably, give them things to do that they can see as being both meaningful to the undertaking and meaningful to themselves because a sense of personal investment is generated. You will, or should anyway, have a good idea of the types of things that need to be done. Negotiate what you would like them to do and what they are interested in doing but do not force your choice. It is usually a good idea to let them know about other things that need to be done that you would want their help on. You may be surprised—one of those things may be exactly what they would hope to do.

Some people may be new to participating in a change effort so they simply do not know what they have to contribute. Even veterans of other change struggles often do not see how their skills in other areas fit with what the group is trying to accomplish. And some are too shy, modest, or otherwise reluctant to let their talents be known.

Your aim here is to offer participants a range of tasks that, to some degree, match both your and their perception of their level of skill, interest, and time. In some cases, they will know what to do and exactly how to do it. In other cases, people's interest and time grow as their confidence grows. Self-assurance centres on three areas: confidence in knowledge of the issue, confidence in their relationships within the group, and confidence in task performance. Tasks that are short-term and specific are usually better in the initial stages of involvement. Let members make the choice of what they want to do. They are more likely to do a better job on things that they choose to do. Job satisfaction and involvement are important elements that enhance commitment (Dailey, 1986).

Even if you are working with people you already know pretty well, this change effort may be a different experience. It is new. By giving people the necessary background on the task they are to perform (for example, why these phone calls are important, the history of the group, or a brief review of what the issues are) you will enhance people's ability to do the job. They should also know whom to contact if they do have questions. This gives people permission to ask for added clarification if they need it.

Assume your community agents and group members enjoy responsibility and thrive on the success of their participation. Increased responsibility generally leads to an increased sense of ownership in the undertaking. It also increases the person's sense of value to the group. Some people will undervalue their abilities, especially if they have experienced constant prejudice and doubt about their abilities through their daily experiences. As a change agent, one of your most important challenges is to encourage people to unlearn those crippling messages and, instead, to acknowledge their competence, trust in it, and act on it. This means that you have to believe in the fundamental ability of people to do some things well—this includes you, too.

If you are one of the initiators of the change effort, you have established a sense of ownership in the process. The mere fact (actually it is quite a significant fact) that you have got the ball rolling required a special investment on your part. You began your participation in the group with a significant attachment to the change effort and its purpose. People who engage later in the effort may have a differing attachment from yours, so you need to give theirs room to grow. People want to feel that what they do has a purpose. Tell people both why a certain task needs to be done and why it is important. Or give them space so that they might figure this out for themselves.

Give participants a chance to say no to some things without feeling guilty. This is important, especially if someone has been doing a lot for the effort. Acknowledge the contributions the individual has made, and let the person know that someone else can do the job if he or she says no. This will strengthen the "yeses" you receive.

Have people work together. Affiliation with others involved in the effort is important (Floro, 1989). Working together helps people get to know one another better. By relating to other people as well as to the task at hand, members strengthen their bond to the organization. On short-term projects, like addressing envelopes, it is often good to have people get together in groups. On long-term tasks, like doing background research, it frequently helps to have people work together as well. Doing work with others increases motivation and accountability. Members are conscious about meeting the expectations of other participants, so they may do a little more than if they were doing things alone. Work does not have to be the sole focus. The social aspects involved in doing things with other people make the tasks more enjoyable and more attractive. Isolation diminishes enthusiasm and contributes to people feeling lost. Try to avoid this. Also, the working together is really a central goal of community work; it is essentially about building connection, strengthening networks and interpersonal relations, and working in diverse social settings. Thus working together is a central purpose of the change effort.

A number of steps can be taken to strengthen the sense of group affiliation and identity among the members. If your group grows large, it may become less personal. Make a special effort to remember people's names and know how to spell them correctly. Invite participants to activities such as social get-togethers, parties, picnics, or going out for pizza. Members who are new or perhaps unsure of their status in the group (and you will know who these people are) should receive a personal invitation in addition to any general announcement made. You may also put together an electronic newsletter, post e-mail updates to a membership distribution list, or do any number of things that promote a sense of alliance.

Get to know people on a personal level. Personal relationships are the glue that holds the group together. People are able to see that they themselves, not just their interest in the

## • CHANGE AGENT TIP

Try different methods of asking people to do things. Asking people at a regular meeting hits the same group over and over. That might not be desirable. Making a general request to the group itself tends to get the hand-raisers to respond, the same people who always seem to volunteer or get stuck with the work. The sit-backers lose opportunity and responsibility (they may want this, you understand). You may lose them.

Try passing around a sign-up list with check-off columns for most-needed actions. Next to their names, people simply check which one of three or four tasks they will help to accomplish. Another approach is simply to ask specific people to do specific things. Do not ask for volunteers. The point is to purposefully spread the tasks around to increase the number of participants and decrease the number of burnouts.

particular issue, are important. In turn, they communicate this to others.

Ask for ideas and opinions. This brings members into the creative process, deepening their commitment to the change effort. People highly value the things they create and shared processes with concrete results that are created through struggle and good will. A couple of cautions are worthy of mention here. First, it is not a good idea to ask people for ideas about what other people should do. Most of us are quite happy to tell other people a lot of things that would seem sensible and easy to do—as long as we do not have to do them. When you invite suggestions about the direction to take, let members know you are looking for them to take part in putting the ideas into action.

Maintain contact. As they say, out of sight, out of mind—and out of action. The change effort you are working on is not necessarily the single most important thing in the lives of other people involved in the group. Other concerns will demand or distract their attention. You want to increase the chances the effort is something they continue to pay attention to, so stay in touch. Information technology makes this pretty easy, but do not forget to use direct, personal contact as well. True, people have a personal responsibility to maintain contact on their own, but sometimes life gets busy or people have many responsibilities with family, neighbours, and friends that they need to attend to. If you communicate continually with participants, this increases the chances that the effort is one of the many things they will consider.

Acknowledge people and their contributions. Recognize and thank people publicly for their interest and their work on behalf of the group. This does not demand an annual awards banquet (although that is also a good idea). In fact, informal methods can often be more significant. During a meeting, for example, or in a newsletter, it is nice to mention an individual and the work that he or she has done. Look for simple, sincere ways to draw attention to people and the value of their participation. In addition to public recognition, a private acknowledgment can be very powerful. This makes the message more personally offered and more personally received.

### Take a Moment to Discover

Sometimes it is difficult to notice small gains as you labour to implement a change. Nothing is so discouraging as to put forth some energy with little to show for it—especially if this involves taking a risk. Why keep trying? If you have ever tried to master a new skill, you know what we are talking about. Remember when you were trying to learn how to play the guitar or learn to skate? From time to time you had to take notice of how you were improving. This probably helped you deal with some of the frustration. Some of us could not see the progress quickly enough, so we still cannot play the guitar. How can you use these experiences to provide encouragement to others?

Routinely let members know the progress being made. Change usually results from a series of minor shifts rather than a sudden dramatic turn of events, although dramatic changes will occur and they are exciting. However, these are not so much events in and of themselves as they are the culmination of the many actions.

Every so often, step back and note the progress being made. This accomplishment needs to be communicated clearly to those involved. Identify specific achievements, whether there will be meetings held, decisions reached, money raised, conditions improved, or whatever. Develop your ability to see these gains. You may have to specifically look for them. Be able to compare how things were three months ago with where they are today. There will always be things not yet done. Give yourself and your group a periodic break from those concerns. Learn to value and communicate to one another how far you have already come. They will feel good about themselves and seek closer identification with the source of this good feeling.

Progress involves a sense of direction. It is easier to go boldly if you have a good idea of where you are going. As you report on the

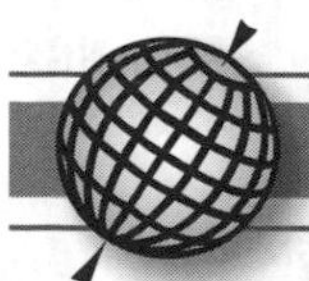

## GLOBAL PERSPECTIVES

SOUTH AFRICA—Building the leadership capacity of individuals and groups who can help systems, institutions, and communities to undertake and sustain long-term change is an essential step in meaningful reform. The leadership skills required include the ability to plan strategically; to manage people, resources, and institutions through the change processes; and to communicate persuasively with a variety of audiences on urgent advocacy issues (Kanyoro, 2000, p. 1).

THAILAND—The task of the change agent is to help people reach their own conclusions and not necessarily always the conclusions of the change agent. By working and struggling together, the consciousness of the change agents and the people should change and reach higher levels. A change agent helps in starting a process of thinking, reflection, and action (Bhasin, qtd. in Burkey, 1993, p. 134).

distance you have travelled, be sure to remind participants that they also know where all of you are going. Above all, promote not only the importance of the things that people are doing but also their value to one another.

## ● WORKING WITH VOLUNTEERS

Most change efforts depend primarily on people who are voluntarily spending their time on the project (Statistics Canada, 2006). People are bound to the effort through their interest in the issue and the commitment that follows from this. They are not specifically paid to bring about this change.

Even if you are working with others in your agency or profession to promote some specific agency change or response to a community problem, you will probably be doing a number of things on your own time. Some activities will take place during non-working hours. Most of what has been said so far in this chapter relates to this typical situation. However, paid staff members are sometimes involved in the process of promoting change. Here are four situations in which this scenario commonly occurs:

- A paid staff person (perhaps you) works in an agency and incorporates change activities into her or his job routine.
- An agency staff person has designated responsibilities for developing various projects aimed at community improvement.
- Paid staff members are specifically hired to help coordinate and direct the change effort.
- The change effort may involve the creation of a formal, ongoing organization or even a new agency, and, in the process of institutionalizing the change, staff are hired to continue a change begun by volunteers.

In all likelihood, even these situations will call for extensive use of volunteers. When volunteers work alongside existing program staff, you need to be sensitive to a set of concerns particular to this situation.

It is easy for relationships between paid staff and volunteers to turn sour even when both parties are initially eager to work together. Volunteers sometimes begin to resent the fact that they are working hard to further the cause yet they do not get paid for their time. Paid staff may get frustrated with the sporadic involvement of volunteers. Or maybe they are relegated to jobs that are nothing but leftovers or seem too simple or are even demeaning. Since so many people in a change effort are unpaid, some may come to feel exploited either by the group but more likely by the entire system that does not value their hard work enough to offer financial reward.

Paid staff sometimes feel threatened by volunteers. They may fear that their jobs will be given over to volunteers. Or, if volunteers are performing similar tasks, they may come to believe that the value of their work will be undermined. It is not surprising that an uneasy tension can develop if these concerns go unrecognized and unaddressed. Having volunteers effectively complement paid staff requires thoughtful consideration.

If routine, predictable work needs to be done by volunteers, specific people need to be scheduled for specific times to do the work. Do not just hope that people will show up. That will not work. Also, expect that about one-third of the people scheduled to help out will find themselves preparing excuses for why they "couldn't make it" when you expected them. Do make sure to overbook.

If a group of people is scheduled for a particular activity, be sure things are prepared so they can get started right away. Waiting until people show up before you figure out what to do can waste time and make you appear unorganized. Take a few minutes to prepare your directions and any necessary materials. Doing so conveys a sense of respect for the volunteers and the task they are to perform. It also gives them a feeling of confidence in knowing what they are to do.

Newcomers generally spend some anxious time guessing at things that veterans take for granted. The level of a person's intended involvement in the change effort and the complexity of their tasks will suggest how much orientation and training is required. Take care to see that people know what is going on and how they fit in. Sometimes, screening volunteers is called for. If this is the case, develop a clear set of screening criteria truly appropriate to the matters at hand. Then develop an effective method to determine whether the criteria are met.

You want to bring together the talents and energy people have and direct these to the purpose of change. When you are working with people, recognize true good effort. If people make a good effort, this is usually a sign they care that things turn out well. If you make people feel that their contribution is weak, it serves to discredit their intent. It is a waste of energy, because you will have to go back and rekindle, reassure, and reestablish confidence in the relationship—not always easy to do when people are giving their time for free. By acknowledging good intent and good effort, you are in a better position to discover what needs to be different next time. Respected people can more easily tackle tough problems, including their own mistakes. If you act toward people as if what they do matters to them, it probably will. Most of the people with whom you will be working, perhaps all the people with whom you will be working, are giving their time to something in which they believe. Not everyone has the same amount of time; not everyone has the same strength of belief. Still, the relationship that all these people have to the group is a voluntary one. Nurturing this relationship requires careful attention.

## Bring Your Anti-Oppressive Practices

One way a change effort becomes limited is by not dealing with social differences between participants in an open and respectful manner; the discomfort people have when encountering someone who is different than themselves sometimes leads them to avoid the tension altogether. Of course, in our complex social environments, community groups that represent the diversity of the community have a better chance of being effective. Sometimes a group of people, even when working from a position of altruism or with a goal of social inclusion, will restrict full membership by working most closely only with the people they can relate to because of similar social background. This limits your change effort since you will not be able to develop the full potential of community engagement; you are also restricting the number of ideas and actions that may be taken by your group. Even

## ● CHANGE AGENT TIP

Here is a trick that can be useful in figuring out the best time to arrange a meeting. Using a simple method developed by Richard Fridena, mark a sheet of paper with seven vertical columns, one for each day of the week. Next, draw horizontal lines across the columns for half-hour blocks of time, starting at 7:00 a.m. and ending at 10:00 p.m. Give each meeting participant a copy, asking them to darken the blocks of time when they cannot meet. Emphasize that this does not mean "don't really want to meet" or "would find it a little inconvenient"—it means "*can't* meet."

After you have collected them, put them all together in a stack. Now, hold them up to the light. Wherever the light shines through, this is a time when you can meet. This usually saves about 19 hours of trying to find the right combination by the "how about Tuesday at 4:00 p.m.?" method. You can modify this little trick to fit a variety of situations.

among progressive change agents, especially when the struggle is tough, it is too easy to slip into an "us versus them" mentality.

Perhaps a more insidious problem is not even regarding others as potential allies or rendering some members of the community invisible—mostly marginalized groups such as racialized members, LGBTT members, and people with disabilities (Mullaly, 2002). If we look only to those we know or to those we consider to be "like us" or to those we are already most comfortable with, we greatly restrict our change efforts. So what will you do? Will you stick to your own group, leaving members of other groups as undiscovered allies? Will you label them as "uninterested" or "uncaring" for not responding to an invitation not extended, or, worse, view them as enemies because they are not working on your side? Of course not, you say. However, in a confusing situation, one in which we are uncertain of our control, it is common to feel a need to affirm our particular construction of reality, and we often look to people who look like us or think like us to find that confirmation (Napier & Gershenfeld, 1989).

Certainly you should be aware of any rationalizations that you or members of your group use to justify not involving a diverse group of people, including those from racialized groups, LGBTT members, or people with disabilities. That is pretty obvious. But how about people who occupy different economic positions in the community, different positions in the hierarchy of the place where you may work, or whose associations are distinct from yours?

Do you treat some people with more respect than others because of the jobs they hold or their particular social location? Do you know how dominant ideas about race or gender might be affecting your community practice? Do you think that because a person is a member of an identifiable group, that he or she holds exactly the same views as every other member of that group? Napier and Gershenfeld (1999) call such mistaken notions attribution errors: "People committing an attribution error assume that the actions of the group reflect the particular attitudes of individual members and that knowing something about how a group behaves tells us something significant about subgroups or individuals within it" (p. 13). What do you know about the traditions, leadership, helping practices, and experiences of various groups that give life to your community? How will your knowledge, relationships, and ability to link networks enliven your change effort and bring to it diverse forms of power?

It is common to grow accustomed to being with a certain set of people, to stay with the familiar. It is sometimes easier to spend time with people who have similar interests, similar routines, and similar methods of communication.

Some of us feel inadequate dealing with people with whom we are not familiar. Yet the need for change probably touches people who are not part of your familiar set.

When you begin to take action on things that need to be corrected, you will start with the people you know pretty well. For many of us, the "people we know pretty well" is often a pretty homogeneous group. The questions are "Will you extend beyond this? Are you willing to challenge your own notions, level of understanding, and anxieties about people of different groups, or will you remain comfortable staying only with people of your own group, whatever group that might be?"

Competence in anti-oppressive practices requires that we value difference and diversity and that we expand our knowledge, communication, and collaboration skills to be able to work well in the context of diversity. We learn about other people, but we also learn about ourselves and how to interact in ways that promote effectiveness and affirm mutual dignity (Cross et al., 1989; CASW, 2005). Our ability to work with diverse groups is not an added benefit but a fundamental requirement. You may have to make a

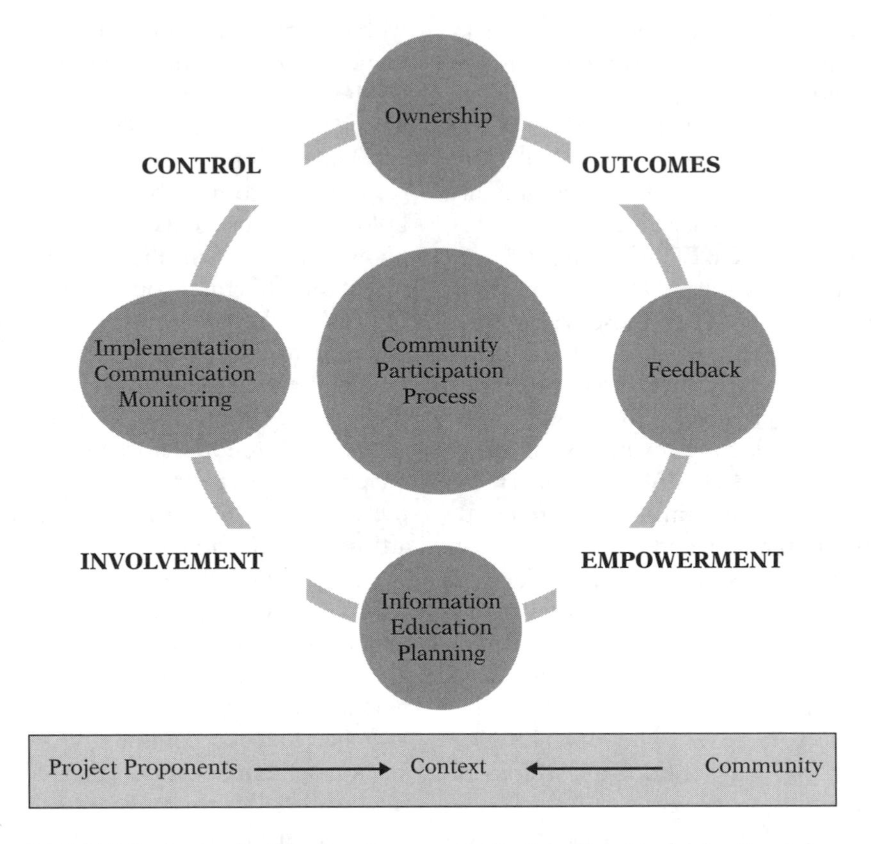


**FIGURE 8.1** An Effective Community Participation Model for Coastal Development Projects

Source: An Effective Community Participation Model for Coastal Development Projects, p. 95, Mathbor, Golam. (2008) *Effective Community Participation in Coastal Development*, Lyceum Books, Chicago, IL, reprinted by permission of the publisher (Taylor & Francis Group, http://www.informaworld.com).

special effort to get to know members of your community with whom you do not commonly associate, learn with other members, and partner with them. Move from "them" to "us." The time to begin doing that is now, not because some special situation calls for your attention and their help but because you believe this is a matter of basic importance.

Mathbor (2008) suggests a model for community participation that has been used internationally and can be helpful in engaging people to participate (see Figure 8.1).

## SOME REFLECTIONS ON PEOPLE

We often do not spend enough time considering people—the raw material of the organized effort. What are they like? Why do they do what they do? What do we need to know about them? These are questions that libraries of sociology and psychology texts attempt to answer, so we do not presume any definitive conclusion here. Still, there are some things that would be helpful for you to consider. This list of observations includes some points that are plainly obvious, but do not be fooled. It is usually the obvious things that we ignore or want to dispense with, and it is usually just such things that are at play.

Here are some things to get you started. The statements offered here are about people in general. They refer to most people much of the time. Of course there are always ample exceptions to these generalizations, but they are accurate often enough to be worth your consideration. See what you can add to this list.

- People are basically good and want to do good things. If given half a chance, they will.
- People are willing to provide help, given the right circumstances.
- People want to be accepted and liked.
- People fear being seen as incompetent, foolish, or stupid.
- People need to feel worthy and able, confident and competent.
- People need acknowledgment more than they need agreement.
- It is not easy for people to break out of routines.
- Lots of people will not ask for help. Consider the barriers to seeking help that are faced by a person who is generally competent, who wants to appear competent, yet who needs help with something that he or she thinks that others think he or she should know.
- People tend to take things more seriously when they are accountable to other people.
- You cannot hold people accountable for things that they do not know.
- People need to feel connected with others yet prized for their uniqueness.
- People need a sense of hope. To act, people need to believe that something beneficial will result from their actions.
- People can only see what their vantage point allows them to see. Vantage points are shaped by values, social location, and experiences.
- People are spurred to action by enthusiasm and anger. They are immobilized by fear and confusion.
- People need to know their role and the importance of their actions in the scheme of things.
- People do not like to think that their time is being wasted.
- People relate far better to a problem or an issue with which they have had a direct, personal experience.
- Under stress, people will often vent their frustrations on the nearest available object, which might be a person, even a friend.

What motivates you? Excites you? Induces fear in you? Anger? Action? What do you try to hide or show? How are other people the same as you, how are they be different? Are you ever truly unique? Watch other people. What

## DID YOU KNOW?

### Everybody, Somebody, Anybody, and Nobody

This is a story about four people named Everybody, Somebody, Anybody, and Nobody. There was an important job to be done, and Everybody was sure that Somebody would do it. Anybody could have done it, but Nobody did it. Somebody got angry about that, because it was Everybody's job. Everybody thought Anybody could do it, but Nobody realized that Everybody wouldn't do it. It ended up that Everybody blamed Somebody when Nobody did what Anybody could have done!

Source: From a cartoon titled *The Facts of Life.*

do you see? What does that make you think about? What conclusions do you reach? Which should you challenge? Develop this practice. Think often about what you can learn from your own behaviour, attitudes, and emotions.

Watch others and think about what you can learn from their behaviour and what you guess their emotions could be. This is an imperfect process, but as you continue to do it, you will find that you learn quite a lot about people and what makes them tick. You will learn a lot about yourself too. Fundamentally, this is what change is all about—your ability to work with or against other people to get something done. If you know yourself and other people better, you will get a lot more done.

## CONCLUSION

Working with people to produce a needed change is a satisfying and sometimes exciting proposition. It will have its trying times too. To get through periods of frustration, notice the progress you all are making toward your goal. The work you are doing to improve conditions will by itself attract people and the skills they possess. Most of the time, though, you need to go beyond this natural attraction and actively seek out the people you need. Learn how to involve people and how to keep them involved. Acknowledge and further develop the interest that people demonstrate, thoughtfully strengthening their relationships to one another and their connection to the work that must be done. You need people to take action; you need action to get people.

If you have more understanding about people, you will be a better change agent. Do not be intimidated by differences and diversity. Seeing the value of people and what they can offer, you will reap the benefit of working with people from a variety of economic, social, or racial groups. Understanding that most people are giving their time, show respect for them and their contributions. In addition, continue to learn more about people; reflect on what frightens them, emboldens them, and moves them to action. Recognize that the human capital of an enterprise is its most valuable resource. With this understanding, you will promote change in a way that gives others a stake in the outcome and the efforts to achieve it.

The change effort requires the involvement of a number of people. Pay attention to the people who make up your change effort, and value them. As much as you value the work that must be done, as much as you value the goals it seeks to achieve, you know it is the people from the community who will accomplish the purposes of change. Without the people, there would be no change, no success. With them, so much is possible.

## HELPFUL WEBSITES

**World Volunteer Web**

www.worldvolunteerweb.org

World Volunteer Web is a global volunteer information portal. There, you can find descriptions of experiences and programs for working with volunteers from around the globe. The site includes a list of research initiatives and studies on various aspects of volunteerism worldwide along with toolkits for working with volunteers.

**Community Foundations of Canada**

www.cfc-fcc.ca/socialjustice/index.cfm

Community Foundations of Canada (CFC) is working toward creating communities in which all citizens have economic opportunity, equal access to high-quality education and health care, cultural voices, safety, and the respect of their fellow citizens. They are working toward ensuring that communities are environmentally healthy and treat their citizens fairly and equitably.

**Aboriginal Rights Coalition of BC**

http://arcbc.tripod.com

The Aboriginal Rights Coalition of BC, or ARC (BC), is a coalition of Aboriginal organizations, the major churches of Canada, and local community groups. ARC (BC) has a vision of a Canadian society in which First Nations are free to exercise the legal and political powers necessary to take control of their own lives, territories, and resources. ARC seeks to achieve this vision through peaceful change, working to build understanding and reconciliation between native and non-native communities, and supporting fair and equitable treaties.

**Egale Canada**

http://www.egale.ca

Egale Canada is a national education and advocacy organization that works to promote equality and justice for lesbian, gay, bisexual, and trans-identified people and their families. Egale Canada engages in numerous diverse activities to promote change including but not limited to research, public education, and lobbying.

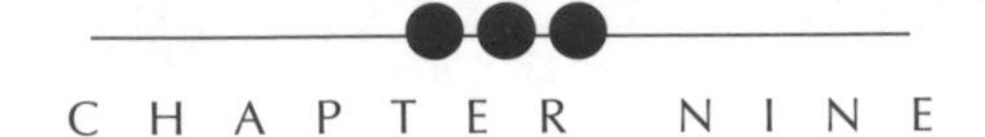

CHAPTER NINE

# Raising Other Resources

**This chapter will help you better understand the following questions:**

- How do we work with people to generate needed resources for our change efforts?
- How do we ask for the resources we need?
- Why do we need to raise money?
- How do we generate funds from individuals? From groups? From organizations? From government sources?
- What are kinds of events are likely to generate resources? How do we implement these?
- What is planned giving?
- How do we use the Internet to generate needed resources?
- What are some important aspects of grant writing?

In the previous chapter, the focus was on people as a resource, the most important resource available to the organization. In fact, the organization is people. It can get by without some other things, but it cannot exist without people. But the members of the organization usually need other resources to aid them in their effort. In this chapter, we discuss what some of those other resources could be and how you can get them.

Most of the time people think that the first thing they must do is go out and get money. Some of the time this is true. But most of the time with some creativity and a lot of hard work, you can get a lot of what you need without spending a cent. A good change agent will know how to get things for free and how to get money for things that are not.

Before you can begin to do either, though, you have to figure out what it is you really need. Determining just what resources you have to have is usually called building a budget.

## BUILDING YOUR BUDGET

The English word "budget" comes from the French *bougette*, a term that essentially means small leather bag (Quick & New, 2001). So you can think of building your budget as filling your bag with the things you will need for your journey on the road to change. It is an ongoing process. You need some things to get the change effort under way. Next, you may need to find more resources to implement the change. Finally, you may need ongoing (and perhaps even greater) resources to institutionalize the change, to make sure that what you started continues. A budget is a view of the organization's future (Hicks, 2001).

For example, a group of you may identify a need to develop a support system for students at risk of dropping out of school. You may need some resources to create an interest in the effort and select the best approach (getting under way). Next, you may need resources to establish such a system in a particular school (implementing the change). Finally, you may need to identify resources that will allow the support system to stay in place for years to come (institutionalizing the change).

In practice you will always be finding out that you need this or that to keep you going. Your budget needs will be somewhat different in each phase of your change process. Something that may be important very early in the game may not be needed at all later, and vice versa. Also, you may find that you only need some item or service for a particular occasion.

In the very early stages of your change effort, your focus is on generating enthusiasm and building support for your idea. You do not want to get bogged down in a lengthy analysis of the resource requirements of the change effort. You may not really even know enough at this point to determine all of what you might need. At the beginning it is common to discover as many needs through your actions as through your planning. However, as time goes on, you will want to give more advance consideration to your organization's resource needs.

Here are eight basic categories of things you may need now or that you will likely need in the future:

*People:* time, skills, talents

*Communication:* printing, postage, telephones, copying

*Equipment:* computers, video cameras, furniture

*Supplies:* pencils, paper, coffee cups, refreshments

*Space:* meeting places, office, storage

*Transportation:* air travel, use of buses, rides to and from out-of-town meetings

*Outside professional services:* training or facilitation, accountants, lawyers, consultants

*Special or miscellaneous needs:* day care, raffle prizes, security, or a band for a fund-raiser

Spend some time talking about each category. You will probably want to skip some categories and concentrate on others. You may readily see needs in one area and not in another, or you may see ways of getting some things and not getting others. Go ahead and start with whatever categories you want. But do not stop there. You will need something, fairly early on, from each category. So, start where you want, but make sure to spend some time on each category.

Take a look at what you need now or will need soon. Brainstorm the possibilities. You do not necessarily need to own anything or have exclusive access to it. You just need to be able to use what you need when you need it.

## WORKING TO GET WHAT YOU NEED

Working to get what you need involves thinking ahead. In the broad sense, this means always looking for opportunities or ways to create them, being quick to make use of a change, thinking a few steps ahead, taking those steps while others sit back, and remaining ready for action. Rather than looking at the limits of your situation, see the possibilities. In regard to resources, make sure you get what you need free or at very little cost. If you work at it, you will get many things from places most people do not, generally because they do not even try. You will get people to give you things, often things that other people have to pay for.

When people, businesses, or organizations give you things or services you need instead of money, this is called an *in-kind contribution.* Soliciting in-kind contributions is an important part of the process. Receiving contributions in forms other than cash might help you in your efforts to attract grant funding because in-kind contributions demonstrate community support (Robinson, 1996). Further, it helps establish a partnership between you and the contributing partner, one that may provide direct financial support later (Picker, 1997).

Businesses are encouraged to participate for their own benefit. In fact, many businesses, particularly larger businesses, already have some sort of public or community involvement program.

In-kind gifts, like any gifts, are good for both the giver and the receiver. Companies may donate employee time and special expertise like tax preparation, boosting morale. Or they may be able to save warehouse expenses by contributing unneeded or depreciated items from their inventory (Picker, 2001). More corporations are providing in-kind support; see how your needs and the resources of businesses and corporations in your area match up (Sinnock, 1995).

There are organizations that act as a bridge between corporations looking to donate goods and services, and charities needing these goods and services. One such organization is "In Kind Canada." If you are looking for donated goods and services, learn more about this organization by visiting its website at www.inkindcanada.ca. Another useful place to look for donated goods and services is Charity Village (www.charityvillage.com).

If you think you do not have the skills or the energy or the personality to ask for the things you need, you are mistaken. The fact is, everybody asks for things, and everybody gives things away. You simply need to learn how to ask for things that your change effort needs, from people who have some reason to give them to you. Though practices may vary from one region to another, in general your organization will benefit from products and services you can obtain for little or no cost.

In time you will enjoy being inventive and discovering new creative ways to get needed resources. Most of the time you will find plenty of resources readily at hand, generally wherever you spend a good deal of your time—at work, home, school, places of play, and places of worship. This means not only you, but everyone else working on your change effort as well.

You can turn your need for certain items into an opportunity to develop support for your undertaking and an investment in your success. By making it easy for people to find ways to give to the effort, you increase your supply of contributors. Whenever someone gives something, you get not only the particular resource they contribute but a little bit of them as well. They become a little bit more a part of the effort, a little bit more interested in its success.

When you and your partners in action have got to the point where you are looking for a particular service or item, ask yourselves whom you know who has it or has ready access to it. If you don't have the resources you need at your disposal, you or the people joining with you in this effort probably know someone who does. In fact, if a group of you spend no more than 10 minutes talking out loud about this, you will almost always come up with at least two or three ideas.

Those resources that are not immediately around you, ready to use, tend to be services, special knowledge or skills, or expensive equipment. Usually, even these are not too far off, although you may have to ask someone outside the membership of your organization.

To help you think about this further, consider some likely sources. First and foremost, consider who among the community you want to organize has ready access to the resource you need. Need a flier done? Is there a printing company in the neighbourhood? Need some artwork? Is there an art department in your school? Need legal services? Are any of your colleagues lawyers or married to one? Start within your own community. This strengthens the ties to the community, gives people a specific way to help out, increases the number of people who have a stake in success, and sets in motion a way for the community to begin thinking of and relating to itself. Believe it or not, a lot of people will be upset if you *do not* ask them. They may be even harder to involve down the road if you overlook them now.

Consider whose self-interest is or could be involved; this is the second group you look to.

## CHANGE AGENT TIP

There is a salesman in Vancouver who sells cars. He sells a lot of them. In fact, a few years ago he sold more cars than anybody else in the country. He didn't even work too hard to do it. He just knew that people knew people, who knew people.

If you buy a car from Ol' Van, he tells you to send your friends to him. If you do, and your friend buys a car, Van will give you a very substantial finder's fee, cold cash. If you encourage a few friends to buy from Van, you can make a tidy sum. Van makes an even tidier one. Pretty soon everybody is buying cars, making tidy sums.

Van operates on the principle that everyone knows 200 people. Somebody among those 200 people wants to buy a car. You and Van are a lot alike. Van needs customers; you need something else, say, the use of a backhoe for a weekend to help plant trees or a band that can supply a little music for your fund-raiser Friday night. Somebody from among the thousands of people the members of your group know is likely to be able to help you out.

Each person who is active in your organization should fill out a personal resources card. This activity is best done in a group, especially after some discussion. You should provide opportunities at a later date to update these cards, because people will always think of more to add and they are also developing access to more resources. (Remember to put all this good information into your membership database.)

What goes on this card? Names and resources (see Figure 9.1); that is, names of people who can do something, and what they can do for your change effort. On the front of the card have the person write her or his name, phone number, and address. Then in each of four columns (two on the front and two on the back), provide space to respond to one of these four requests.

- Name the three most important people from whom you would be willing to ask a favour, especially a political favour, or the use of his or her influence.
- Name three people who have access to the most of whatever kinds of resources your change effort might need and people you'd be willing to ask money from to help this effort.
- Name three people you'd be willing to ask to give something other than influence or money. (Write what you'd ask for.)
- Name three skills or talents you'd be willing to contribute to this effort.

That's it. You now have an immediate resource bank.

You will have to offer some guidance on filling out this card. The immediate reaction of a few might be "But I don't know any important people." Calmly explain that you just need the three most important or richest or beneficial people they do know. That may be a kid brother, a neighbour, or a local paint dealer. Any of these can contribute one dollar, one letter to an MP, or help in painting the office. We all know people we can ask to do a little something for the cause. Take no more than 10 minutes to fill out the card. Any more time than that will make the process too tedious.

To give you an idea of how powerful this little resource bank can be, consider this: If you have only 10 people involved in your effort, and the average contribution they get from each of the "richest" people on their list is $10, you have immediate access to $300. Most attempts to get something accomplished start with less than that.

*Continued*

## CHANGE AGENT TIP

**Side One**

Name ______________________ Phone (home) ____________ (work) ____________

E-mail Address ______________________________________________

| Three most important people from whom I would ask a favour, particularly a political one. | Three richest people I would be willing to ask for money to help this effort. |
| --- | --- |
| Name ______________________ | Name ______________________ |
| Position or Significance ______________________ | |
| ______________________ | Name ______________________ |
| Name ______________________ | |
| Position or Significance ______________________ | Name ______________________ |
| ______________________ | Any additional names? |
| Name ______________________ | Name ______________________ |
| Position or Significance ______________________ | |
| ______________________ | Name ______________________ |

**Side Two**

Name ______________________

| Three people I would be willing to ask for something other than influence or money. | Three skills or talents I would be willing to contribute to this effort. |
| --- | --- |
| Name ______________________ | Talent/skill ______________________ |
| Ask for ______________________ | ______________________ |
| Name ______________________ | Talent/skill ______________________ |
| Ask for ______________________ | ______________________ |
| Name ______________________ | Talent/skill ______________________ |
| Ask for ______________________ | ______________________ |

**FIGURE 9.1** Personal Resources Card

Two powerful motivators are economic self-interest and prestige.

Many times people will give you things free or at a reduced cost in hope of receiving some other returns later. These returns could include better access to a new group of customers, your continued business, or referrals for business.

People's sense of personal prestige can be used to your advantage as well. Does helping you out make someone look good? Does turning you down make someone look like a lout? Does anyone's stature increase or diminish according to whether or not he or she responds to your request? People who see themselves (and are seen by others) as "doers" love to be able to deliver; they also hate thinking that other people think they cannot get something done.

Other likely sources have some degree of self-interest but may have other motivations as well. People and organizations who are philosophically disposed toward you have resources of their own that they may be willing to share. In almost every community, at least one or two groups share your general concerns, even though their specific emphases may be different from yours. Consider how your success benefits the things they are working on. By now you have done your homework on your community, and you know who these people are.

For example, if you are involved in developing a neighbourhood tree planting program, consider the number of environmental, conservation, and beautification organizations that exist in your area. If you are undertaking an effort to keep teen parents in school, think about the various organizations working on education, child abuse, economic development, mental health, or a host of other issues related to teen parenting. Nongovernmental citizens' groups are the most likely sources of help, but do not rule out public and private agencies in your quest for the things you need.

Places where you spend your time and where you spend your money are places where you have built a relationship. They probably want to see you again. They may have something you can use. Ask for it. Among these are organizations to which you belong or that hold events you attend. These can be religious, civic, or social, whether your synagogue or your yoga class.

Also on your target list should be businesses or dealerships you regularly patronize or have recently patronized. Where do you buy your insurance, where do you do your banking, where do you get your tomatoes? Any or all of these might be willing to help you meet some specific need. Your presence or your hard-earned dollars are an investment in the success of these enterprises. You can certainly ask them to invest in yours.

Finally, there are relatives, friends, and acquaintances. Even if no one in this personal network of yours can offer what you are looking for, they might be willing to help find someone else who can.

## Ask for What You Need

Now that you have determined what you need and considered who might have it, it's time to figure out who will be doing the asking and how. Then, you need to ask.

The simplest direction is that whoever has the best connection to the most likely source should do the asking. Most of the time this practice will work. However, sometimes you will need to spread the asking around a bit. Otherwise, you may find that you have the same two or three people doing all the asking. Having a number of people involved in acquiring needed resources helps create an attitude that we are all looking for ways to add to the effort. Further, success in this endeavour will solidify the person's attachment to the change effort. This last point is particularly important. A person will usually take some particular pride in this accomplishment and feel closer to the organization that has benefited from it.

Exactly how you ask does depend on the situation. Regardless of the situation, though, there are a few things to keep in mind to improve your chances. First, the more personal the request, the better. Talking with someone face to face will usually get you a lot more than writing a letter.

Second, show how the giving helps the giver. Everyone has some personal interest involved, even if it's not economic self-interest. Be able to identify and show how giving meets the giver's interest. Third, show how the giving benefits the recipient. Each of us likes to know that when we do something it matters. Be able to describe clearly what a particular gift will do for the change effort. Finally, close the deal. You are not asking someone to think about helping you. You are asking them to actually do it. Get a yes or a no when you ask. At the very least, get a time when you will hear the yes or no. Then follow up.

Do not be afraid to ask. The issues you are working on are worth it. The worst thing that can happen is that someone will say no.

After a while you will develop a positive and hopeful way of thinking that believes that what you are doing is good and that there are lots of people out there who are able and willing to do something to keep things moving ahead. You will not think twice about asking for things you need. It will be routine. It will begin to affect the way you go about things in general. And, if you have got a good group of people to think and act this way, you will be very hard to stop.

## Get to Know Your Community's Resources

Many of the items and services your change effort will need can be found for free. The local bar association will help you find lawyers who

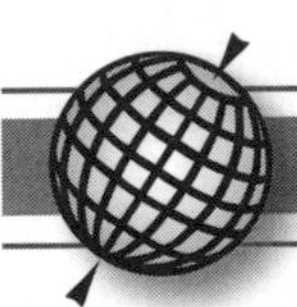

### GLOBAL PERSPECTIVES

SCOTLAND—[I]t did not take long for development officer Sian Langdon to realise that the Kickstart Programme is not about getting instant results. . . . Sian is one of a network of officers throughout Scotland helping voluntary and community groups develop the skills to make the most of funding opportunities. . . .

Sian and the Inverclyde Voluntary Sector Forum organised an awareness-raising day aimed at people living in Inverclyde. "We brought in outside funders to tell people about what opportunities are out there. . . .

"People were delighted with the information on offer and lots said it had given them ideas. . . . I also work one-to-one with groups to help them find out about funding and go through the application process. . . . Sometimes you sit down with people and discover that their group hasn't yet got a constitution or a bank account, and you need both of these if you're applying for funding.". . .

In Glasgow, Kickstart officers . . . have put together a comprehensive funders' timetable—a regularly-updated, electronic list of funding opportunities for voluntary and community groups in Glasgow. (Communities Scotland, 2002, p. 2)

FRANCE—Here are a few tips for organizing. Beg or borrow the best equipment you can get your hands on—and if you are lucky enough to have some, share it with other groups. Unless you want to give a feeling of togetherness to people who are already convinced of your point of view, you have to remember that few people will trouble to read sloppily presented information, even if it is true. Good souls exist in every profession—advertising, journalism, and printing among them. Try to take advantage of their professional skills to make the information you want to get across really speak. Try also to recruit people with technical skills so your material can be well conceived, well presented and imaginative. It costs no more. . . . When people come to your meeting, don't let them get away without giving their names, contact information, and special skills and whether they would participate in future planning or action. Never waste a chance to find out who supports you. . . . Never be well-bred when it comes to talking about money. Working for change is usually volunteer, but it is never free. People should contribute (and be told specifically why they are being asked to do so) every time you get them together. (Susan George, 1986, pp. 255–256) will work on certain cases for free. Schools, hospitals, and faith communities can offer meeting space. People who sell, rent, or use the equipment you need will be a big help as well. Some, like auto dealers, may donate used cars. A construction company may donate the use of a front-end loader and an operator for a day. Some real estate offices may let you use their phones for a couple of evenings. And many companies will contribute computers that are outdated for their use but perfectly adequate for yours. Your success in finding these and other resources will depend in large part on how well you know your community, how many people you know, and how many people know you.

You can often find such resources on the Internet, by searching sites like Charity Village, or, as mentioned earlier, using organization such as In Kind Canada that match charities with corporate donors looking to make in-kind donations of goods and services.

## GETTING AND SPENDING MONEY

In your efforts to promote change, you will not only have to get needed resources and money, you will have to spend money as well. Some things you can get for free or cheap look that way. Sometimes that is okay, sometimes it is not. Your effort has a certain image it wants to project. Some of the things you may be able to get for free might not fit the image you are trying to project or just will not do the job, so you may have to pay for them. For example, maybe for one special all-day get-together you need a stylish conference room and all you can get free is the church basement. Or perhaps you have reams of donated low-quality paper, but you believe it is important for your letterhead to be very high quality. Some things are worth paying for.

### Staff, an Expensive Item

One of the most important things you may have to pay for is people. Certainly people are the most valuable resource. They are also the most costly if you need to pay for them, and there are times when you definitely should.

This is an expense you normally do not incur until you are in the implementation or institutionalization phase of the change process, if at all. Paying for staff is the single most expensive item for almost any organization. Unless the organization is engaged in raising funds for things it gives away (for example, a food bank buying and then giving away food), most of the money it raises will be spent on people who work for the organization. All the other expenses taken together will rarely outweigh the expense of staff.

If we do not have to pay anyone to do the work, we will save a lot of money, right? Absolutely. Given this, sometimes the best approach is to get someone or even several someones to donate their time and work for free. However, this is not always the best way to proceed.

If all four of the following factors are present, the use of nonpaid staff for ongoing support makes good sense. However, all four factors must be in place.

1. The work does not need to be done according to a tight schedule. Certainly, a specific amount of work does not need to be turned out every day.
2. The work does not place a high number of unusual, unpredictable, or inconvenient demands on the worker. People will not commonly be asked to go out of their way to do something.
3. You do not have to worry about the worker's ability to do the job properly. The work does not require a set of sophisticated skills, and there will not be much confusion about whether the job is being done right.
4. The worker is fairly easy to replace if he or she should lose interest or needs to drop out for one reason or another.

If any of these things are not true, there will probably need to be paid staff somewhere on the scene.

Although it may mean that you need to raise more money, hiring staff can make very good sense. Paid staff usually has a stronger sense of obligation. They expect to be and can be held accountable. There is an agreement that provides mutual benefits. A paycheque not only provides benefits to the worker but also affirms the agreement he or she has made.

One of the key duties of the paid staff is to generate more support for the organization, including more funding. Generally, the position should be able to pay for itself and generate additional revenues. This certainly does not rule out the continued use of volunteer help. The use of donated time will always be important. Paid staff should be able to enhance the effectiveness of this kind of contribution.

Other personnel costs come in the form of specialized services you are not able to obtain for free. These will frequently be in the area of legal or financial services; for example, bookkeeping and filing financial reports and documents. The more ongoing or pressing your needs for specialized services are, the more likely you will have to pay for them. Also, if the activity involves a significant use of one person's time (for example, a lawyer pursuing a lawsuit or an accountant conducting an audit), you can expect to incur some costs.

### Keep Some Money in Reserve

In addition to whatever personnel costs you have and the necessity to purchase items you cannot obtain for free, you will need money to cover a variety of unanticipated expenses. It is a good idea to have an adequate contingency fund available. You cannot be certain when you will need to have some extra dollars on hand, just be certain that you do. It is a good practice to have enough money in the bank to provide operating costs for six months over and above any anticipated income. The size and the nature of your particular organization may dictate a smaller or larger backup fund. Still, you should plan to have something in reserve.

## FILLING THE COFFERS

Getting money to promote the cause is an essential matter for agents of change. It is not the root of all evil. We need to treat money like any other resource that is critical to our success, valuing it appropriately and developing skills to acquire and use it wisely. Kim Klein (2000) provides a good perspective. "Nonprofits that work for social change must themselves be agents of change. The ways we think about money, raise it, spend it, save it, invest it, and plan for it are some of the most basic elements for modeling a world we want to create" (p. 155).

Remember also that when you ask for money you are not taking anything away. You are giving someone a chance to do something meaningful and important. You honour a potential contributor with your request. Knowing just how important your cause and the issue you are working on is, why would you hesitate to invite someone to take part? When you think of yourself as the giver rather than the taker, it changes how you approach this opportunity.

If you are so self-absorbed that asking for money is all about you and your insecurities, you will not be able to build the relationships that are needed for change to occur (Klein, 2000). Greenfield (2002) makes the point clearly: "Fundraising is not about money—it's about relationships" (p. 4). Your fundraising approach must be geared to the abilities of the members of your group who will be involved. Though all members should have a role, a few will take on greater responsibility. The design for dollars that you all come up with has to meet what people are willing to do. As their experience and confidence grow, people may be willing to do more and more risky things, like directly asking someone for a cash donation (Klein, 2002).

If, after all, you do need some money, how do you go about getting it? To answer this question you first have to answer a couple of others. The first critical question is how much do you need. A variety of techniques will yield you hundreds of dollars. These are great if you need hundreds of dollars; they are a waste of time if you need

## DID YOU KNOW?

### The CARE Test

Techniques for raising money must pass the CARE test:

Comfort for the donor in the cause, the solicitation method used, and how the approach is made.

Anticipation of the request and preparedness with adequate information that encourages a decision to give.

Readiness to give because of a conviction that the money will be well used for charitable purposes that serve the public good.

Enjoyment in the act of giving, and a welcome to the invitation to give again.

Source: Greenfield, 2002, pp. 473–474.

tens of thousands of dollars. Next, you have to consider whether you need a steady income or an occasional infusion of funds. Generally, the larger your budget, say over $10,000, the more predictable your income base needs to be. These are the two basic questions. They will set your general direction. As you begin to select various options, you will need to ask more specific questions.

One more proviso is worth mentioning. Getting money will cost you something. Whether that is postage, printing, refreshments, or your time, it will cost something. Think this through. You want to be sure that what you are likely to get is worth what you had to spend to get it.

Further, no matter how you approach the business of getting money, you will have to invest your own thoughts, time, and energy. You need to plan and to take action on your plan. You have to monitor activities to make sure that you are doing what you intended to do. Finally, you need to evaluate your approach to see that you accomplished your goals and that whatever investments you made in the process were worth it.

Figuring out how to get money can often be a fun, creative, even exciting process.

Two basic paths will get you to the rainbow's end. The first involves asking individuals to give you their own money. The second involves asking individuals to give you other people's money. In the first instance, people make decisions on behalf of their own interests. In the second, people make decisions on behalf

## Take A Moment To Discover

Here are some common, ineffective relationships organizations have with their money.

- The organization insists on a level of financial security that few individuals could ever aspire to. It is afraid to use its money, keeping dollars locked away in various savings funds. It confuses fundraising with fund hoarding.
- The organization keeps expenses very low, sacrificing quality of work and morale. It confuses fundraising with fund squeezing.
- The organization drifts into financial security by changing the course of its work to attract funding for projects (and, as we might add, it limits or changes its work to appease a funding source). It confuses fundraising with fund chasing.

Have you seen any of these?

Source: Kim Klein, 2000.

of the interests of a group, organization, corporation, foundation, or government agency (Breiteneicher & Hohler, 1993).

Each change effort will use a different approach based on the amount of money it needs, the types of activity in which it is involved, the current level of community acceptance, its need for short- or long-term support, its level of skill and interest in pursuing different approaches, and the time and money it can spend to raise more money. If you seek money from individuals, you will soon see that there is an almost endless assortment of ways to get individuals to give you money.

Although getting money from corporations, foundations, and the like has its own twists and turns, these organizations usually share one thing in common: a written proposal or grant application will likely be required. The length and nature of these will vary, but you can expect to be doing some proposal writing for all sources other than individuals. Developing excellent grant-writing skills is essential.

## CONTRIBUTIONS FROM INDIVIDUALS

Decisions made by individuals will determine whether you will get money from any source and if so, how much. However, this particular category involves getting money directly from people with no intervening structure. In other words, we are talking about people giving you their own money, not somebody else's.

Imagine Canada's analysis of data from the 2004 Canada Survey of Giving, Volunteering and Participating (Hall, Lasby, Gumulka, & Tryon, 2006), notes that 85 percent of the Canadian population 15 years of age and older (a total of over 22 million Canadians) made a financial contribution to a nonprofit organization in 2004. Together, this group of Canadians donated a total of $8.9 billion. The mean value of each individual donation was $400, and the median was $120 (this means that half of the people contributed less than $120 and half contributed more). As well, 86 percent of Canadians aged 15 and over (that is almost nine in ten Canadians) reported making an in-kind donation to a nonprofit organization in 2004. These in-kind donations consisted of clothing, toys, or household goods (79 percent) and food (63 percent). The report notes that "taken together, almost all Canadians (94 percent) made either a financial or an in-kind gift over the course of the year." (Hall et al., 2006, p. 14). Religious organizations are the most well supported by Canadians, but 43 percent of Canadians made a financial donation to a social service organization in 2004, with 10 percent of the $8.9 billion donated going to support social services (Hall et al., 2006).

Imagine Canada's analysis reveals that while many Canadians do donate to nonprofits, it is actually a small group of people who are contributing the bulk of the dollars. "The 50% of donors who gave $119 or less in 2004 accounted for 6% of the total value of all donations. In contrast, the 15% of donors who gave between $325 and $869 contributed 20% of all donated dollars. Even more striking is the contribution of the 10% of donors who gave $870 or more and accounted for 62% of the dollars given. Taken together, the top 25% of donors accounted for 82% of the value of donations" (Hall et al., 2006, p. 14). What does this mean to you?

Although a small group of people are contributing the bulk of the money, it is important to remember that 85 percent of Canadians did make a donation in 2004 and therefore, while middle- and upper-income individuals may give more total dollars, all members of your community are potential contributors to your effort.

### Inclusive Fundraising

If you think of fundraising only as getting money from rich white guys, you are really missing the boat—or the bank. Some fundraisers overlook certain groups such as women and racialized communities because they assume there will not be a good return on their investment of time or energy trying to obtain money from these groups. They are wrong.

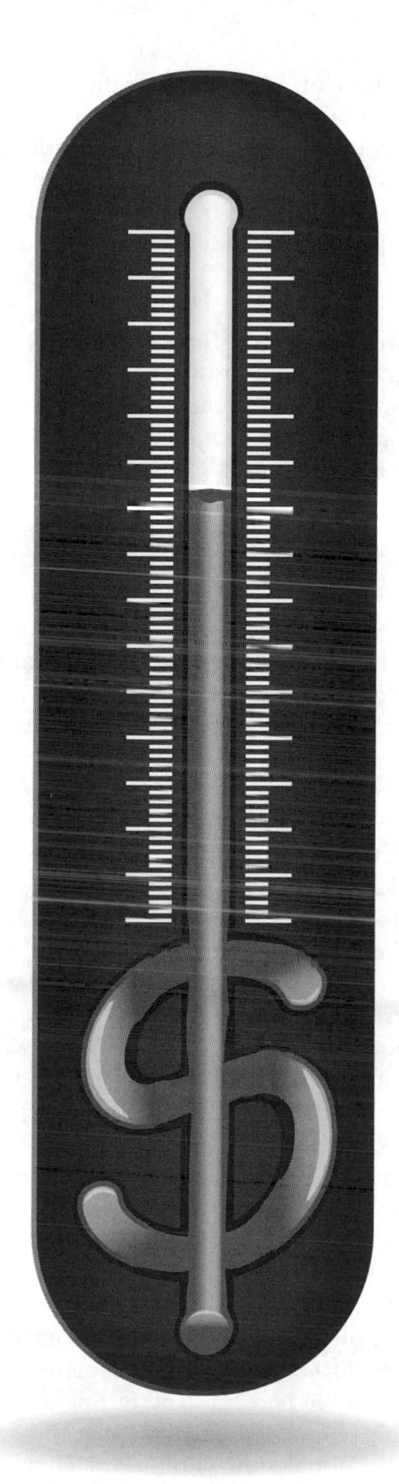

VECTORACER/Shutterstock

**Raising needed resources will enable communities to achieve their goals.**

### Recognizing Women as Philanthropists

In Canada, in 2004, women were more likely to donate to nonprofit organizations than men. Eighty-eight percent of women (as compared to 82 percent of men) made financial donations. Using the mean as the average, men give larger average donations ($430 from men, and only $374 for women), but the median donation for men and women is almost identical, with women giving a slightly higher amount ($120 from women as compared to $117 from men). In spite of these data, women are often overlooked as a target group for fundraising (Marx, 2000; Nichols, 2001).

Kaminski (2001) points out that women and men have similar motivations for contributing, but "women respond to different 'triggers'" (p. 364). Shaw and Taylor (1995) classify these as the six C's of women's giving:

*Create:* Women often give to create something.

*Change:* Women give to bring about social change.

*Connect:* Women seek a sense of personal connection to the project.

*Collaborate:* Women like to work together as a group and do not respond well to competitive fundraising appeals.

*Committed:* Women are committed to the causes they support and are more willing to volunteer time to these causes.

*Celebrate:* Women like to celebrate their accomplishments and have fun.

Although the opposite is not necessarily true about men, these six C's are particularly important for you to think about when you focus on contributions from women. Women, particularly those who have participated in volunteer work, are often quite ready to give (Sun, 2001). Kaminski (2001) further points out that women do not believe they are asked to give at the same levels as men. Two prominent vehicles for women in fundraising are women's funds and women's circles. Women's funds focus their grant making on issues that affect women and girls through organizations that are predominantly governed and managed by women. In the United States, the Global Fund for Women, for example, which was started with a $500 donation by each of three women in 1987, gave more than 400 grants totalling $4.5 million in 2003 (Brotman, 2002).

In Canada, the Canadian Women's Foundation is an important resource. It is Canada's only national public foundation that has as its express purpose improving the lives of girls and women. You can visit them on the web at www.cdnwomen.org. According to its website, it has granted more than $17 million since 1991 and has distributed these grants to more than 800 programs in every province and territory in Canada.

> Women's giving circles offer another opportunity for women's collective contributions to have a significant effect. Typically, members of a giving circle contribute a set amount each year—for example, $1,000. The pooled funds give the group the ability to make sizable grants. While many individuals find the $1,000 entry beyond their reach, the membership can be split among sisters, partners, or friends. One of the important aspects of giving circles is that the members are actively involved in the grant-making process. So not only do members have control over the use of their funds, but they become more attuned to community conditions and further opportunities to provide leadership. (Kaminski, 2001)

One example of an innovative approach can be found in the Women's Fund Giving Circle established by The Winnipeg Foundation. According to an article on the website of Charity Village, this is a "pilot project to support the development of giving circles by providing matching dollars in the early years of development so the capital could grow and participants could get involved in grantmaking right from the start" (Luchuk, 2008). Donors involved in this giving circle are able to choose varying degrees of participation. Women who make a minimum contribution of $1,500 over a five-year period are able to be involved in decision making about which projects will receive funding. Various kinds of projects have been funded from this giving circle, including summer camps for children with cancer, projects promoting literacy, and transitional housing projects (Luchuk, 2008).

### Fundraising and Philanthropy among Immigrants in Canada

Immigrants in Canada made financial donations to nonprofit organizations at almost exactly the same rate as those born in Canada, with 85 percent of immigrants compared to 86 percent of Canadian-born people making donations in 2004 (Hall et al., 2006). The financial donations from immigrants to Canada amounted to 20 percent of the total of all donations in 2004. The 2004 Canadian survey found that length of time in Canada was related to the amount of money donated: "Among immigrants, those who have resided in Canada for longer periods of time tend to give more than others . . .. Immigrants who arrived in Canada in 1995 or later are less likely than others to give (77% donate) and give lower average amounts ($278). In contrast, those who arrived in 1994 or earlier gave larger donations, on average, than native born Canadians. In particular, those who arrived in Canada before 1967 are noticeably more likely to make donations (94%) than either other immigrants or native-born Canadians (86%) and made substantially higher average annual donations ($644 compared to $394)" (Hall et al., 2006, p. 24). Immigrants and nonimmigrants are equally likely to donate to social service organizations (Hall et al., 2006).

### Fundraising across the Country

The national rate of financial contributions by individuals to nonprofit organizations in Canada is 85 percent. Interestingly, Imagine Canada's report demonstrates that the percentage of the population who make such donations varies according to location. Newfoundland and Labrador, as well as Prince Edward Island, had the highest rates of financial giving (93 percent of the population), while Nunavut had the lowest rate (63 percent). In rank order, the rate of giving in all the provinces and territories is as follows:

| | |
|---|---|
| Newfoundland and Labrador | 93% |
| Prince Edward Island | 93% |
| Nova Scotia | 90% |
| Ontario | 90% |
| New Brunswick | 88% |
| NATIONAL RATE | 85% |
| Manitoba | 84% |
| Quebec | 83% |
| Saskatchewan | 82% |
| Northwest Territories | 79% |
| Alberta | 79% |
| British Columbia | 77% |
| Yukon | 76% |
| Nunavut | 63% |

The Imagine Canada report cautions us to be careful before making any broad conclusions about what these geographical differences might mean. "Charitable giving is affected by a variety of factors including differences in economic conditions, social and cultural values, and the personal characteristics of the citizens who make up provincial and territorial populations. Furthermore, financial contributions are but one of several ways in which individuals can choose to support one another and their communities. Drawing conclusions about regional variations in generosity without a full understanding of these factors, may, as a result, lead to inappropriate comparisons" (Hall et al., 2006, p. 25).

## Six Basic Steps

Getting money from individuals involves six basic steps, no matter what approach you use. By breaking it down into steps, we run the risk of making the process seem overly complicated. In actual practice, you will be able to mentally check off each step (and you should do this) once you have repeated the procedure a few times. The more experience you gain in asking for money, the simpler and more routine this process will be for you.

First, it is helpful to know whom you are asking. *Identifying your prospects* is a fundamental step. "Who" comes before "how" (Breiteneicher & Hohler, 1993). Understanding how much you need and when as well as whether you are looking

### DID YOU KNOW?

#### Ten Questions, Plus One

If you want money, you need to answer ten questions, plus one.

1. Who has it?
2. Who is likely to give it to you?
3. Where do you have a connection with these people?
4. When are they in a giving or spending mood?
5. What message do they need to hear?
6. How do you send that message?
7. Who sends that message?
8. How do you make it as easy as possible for people to respond?
9. How do you acknowledge and nurture people for the future before and after they give?
10. What resources do you have to direct this effort?

Plus one:

- What other questions do you need to ask?

for a nonrenewable gift or building a substantial base of income will guide you in your selection.

Second, you need *to nurture these prospective givers.* Once you have identified the prospects, establish some type of relationship with them. This includes developing their awareness and interest in your efforts (Baird, 1997; Brakeley, 1997; Flanagan, 2000; White, 2001).

Third, think about and *prepare a message* that will be most effective in producing a favourable response. You need to take into account what this particular individual needs to know and feel to decide to contribute money. You need to put together a message that will provide that information and stir those emotions.

Fourth, you need to *deliver that message.* Think of how and in what circumstances you can most effectively communicate your message to the people who need to hear it. The more direct your communication and the clearer your request, the more effective you will be. Recalling the "ladder of communication effectiveness" should give you some ideas on techniques you can use (Breiteneicher & Hohler, 1993; Freyd & Carlson, 1997; Klein, 2000; Reinhart, 1990; Seltzer, 2001).

Fifth, after you have sent your message, *follow up* to see that your message has been received and that any pledges made were kept (Baird, 1997; Mutz & Murray, 2000).

Finally, *say thank you.* In many situations, particularly when you have made a direct personal request, a personally written thank you is an important step, even if you did not receive a contribution at this time. Remember, there is always tomorrow (Baird, 1997, Flanagan, 2000; Klein, 2000).

## Direct Requests

The most effective way to ask someone for money is to do it directly, face to face. The more money you are asking for and the less experience the prospect has in giving to a cause like yours, the more you need to be prepared when making your request. Even if you are making a minor request from a friend, do not assume that preparation is unnecessary (Klein, 2000). Here are a few things to know and do that might help you.

### Know Your Prospect

- Gauge how much the prospect is capable of giving.
- Determine the prospect's likely motivators and to what facts and emotions he or she is likely to respond.

### Prepare Yourself for the Contact

- Know in advance what you will say. Be able to clearly and simply describe what you need and why. Practise out loud so it does not sound awkward.
- Describe why you think the undertaking is important to the prospect and what his or her contribution will mean.
- Be willing and able to answer questions.
- Determine if anyone else needs to be involved in making the request.
- Arrange the right time, place, and people to ask the prospect.

### Make Contact

- Make your request.
- Get the money then and there, or at the very least arrange a time when you can pick it up.
- Thank the prospect.

## TIPS

- People give to people. The asker's relationship to the giver is important (Breiteneicher & Hohler, 1993). We respond best to an appeal from someone who is trusted for some reason other than his or her link to the organization asking for the money. A request or recommendation from a friend tops the list (Roper, 1999). Many studies and surveys have explored why people give to charity. Tax advantages are almost never near the top of the list. The donor's relationship to the organization or its mission is far more important as is a recognition of the organization's needs and a belief that the money will be spent wisely (White, 2001).

• Promote personal involvement. Some ways to do this include inviting prospects to take part in lectures or public meetings, personal issue discussions, presentations to other groups, and to volunteer. Nonprofit agencies particularly want to make sure they are grooming a new generation of investors (donors) and that their fundraising techniques increase civic engagement rather than keep donors distant (Hall, 1996; Reinhart,1990).

• People are more likely to respond when asked to give an immediate contribution than when a delay between the request and the receipt of the donation exists (Reeves, Macolini, & Martin, 1987).

• People are more willing to help out someone who has done them a favour or who has given them something (Regan, 1971). Consider buying your prospect dinner, lunch, or a coffee. Have you done anyone a favour recently?

• Discuss common opinions and values at some point in your conversation. This provides a shared frame of reference and a recognition of affiliation that makes the request easier to state and easier to meet.

• Ask for a specific dollar amount (Flanagan, 2000; Mutz & Murray, 2000). You might ask: "Is this an amount you are comfortable with?"

• Smile. Lawyers teach witnesses to smile at the jury because research shows juries believe a witness who smiles more than a witness who does not (Flanagan, 2000).

• Major donors will often contribute to exciting programs with their hearts more than their heads. Exciting means bold or visionary more than controversial (Panas, 1989).

• You never offend a person by politely asking for too large a gift. Most are flattered that you think they could give that much (Reinhart, 1990).

• Reward or in some way recognize contributors, paying careful attention to provide special rewards to major givers (Baird, 1997).

• Using emotion can help. Pride, outrage, guilt, affection, and fear are common emotions that promote a response.

• You may get a "no," but a "no" in fundraising may be a "not yet." To deal with a "no," you might ask: "Is there something that concerns you about whether this would be a good use of your money?" This allows you to continue relationship building and to explore other options while creating an opportunity to answer unspoken questions (Mutz & Murray, 2000). If you receive a "no" to a specific dollar request, you can also ask: "How much might you be able to give at this time?" You want to create an option between your requested amount and zero.

• Keep in contact with donors, especially major donors. Maintaining attention shows donors that you take their interest, not just their money, seriously (Klein, 2000).

## Take A Moment To Discover

Many of us are uncomfortable when asking people for money, so we tend to put a lot of distance between the asker and the giver. We are often more concerned with taking care of our discomfort than with getting what we are asking for. We usually end up with good protection from discomfort when we do this but with not many more dollars than we started with.

Think about how often we ask people, friends, relatives, co-workers, and the like for money for routine requests. We might commonly ask for money for stamps, gas, snacks, and pop—or at least we expect people to chip in. Sometimes we also ask people to spend money to go out on a Saturday night to attend a hockey game or a movie.

Reflect on the last week or last month. How many times have you asked or expected someone to spend money for something, regardless of what it might have been? How many times have you been asked?

Think about the circumstances surrounding the request for money. What can you learn from thinking about the times you ask people to give you money, or to spend money to be with you, or when they ask you to give money? How would you ask any of these people for money to support your change effort? Today, ask one person to give you money for something, ideally for some worthy cause you support.

Your ethics will guide you in all of this. Obviously, you are not going to ask someone to do what he or she cannot do. You are not going to play on people's emotions simply because you can do so. You are responding to feelings that are legitimately present in the situation. You are not making your relationship dependent on a contribution. You will understand that increasing your effectiveness within ethical bounds may itself be ethically required, or you would not be doing this in the first place.

## Pitching to Groups

If you can not directly ask an individual to give you money, your next best bet is to ask them in a group, the smaller the better. Groups can achieve a shared or group view of a situation and exert peer pressure on their members to respond appropriately. Groups can be addressed as a unit to solicit funds from the group itself as a single contribution, or contributions can be requested from individual members of the group.

When preparing to make your pitch to a group, consider many of the same things about the group as you did with individual donors—estimate their ability to give, their giving history, and get some background information on the organization itself. Understand, also, that most groups are worried about your legitimacy, especially if you are newly established. Your approach to them must take this into account.

Receiving money from the group itself, rather than from the members of the group, requires a different process. Many groups and organizations, especially those that routinely make donations of over $1,000, have a formal process established for handling requests. The larger and more formal an organization is, the more extensive the process is likely to be. The more you know about the process, the greater your chances of receiving funds. This process generally requires a written proposal together with a short verbal presentation in support of the proposal. Follow the guidelines described later in this chapter on funding from organizations.

## Memberships

Requesting an annual membership fee from participants in your organization is a simple, effective way to raise money and increase commitment (Greenfield, 2002). This approach tends to make your organization a more formal one, bringing more expectations and responsibilities. If you want to keep the relationship among members purely informal, you may want to skip this method.

In your effort to "recruit" members, start with individuals who by word or action have already expressed an interest in the organization or its goals. Each of these people should receive a personal request that they become members.

It is easier to ask for a membership than for an outright donation. You are acknowledging interest and inviting participation as well as asking for money. Potential members have the opportunity to gain a sense of affiliation. They have a choice to belong. As members, they are not considered nor do they consider themselves outsiders who are asked to give to "you." Instead, they become part of "us" and to some extent become recipients of the contribution as well as makers of it. By asking every person who has expressed an interest in your effort to become a member, you can quickly add to your coffers. Even though the amount you raise from this group is likely to be relatively small, it's worth the effort.

After asking everyone who has shown some support for the effort, the next step is to contact those who are potential beneficiaries or supporters of the organization's work. Again, a personal, face-to-face request is far more effective than any other method. A simple plan should be worked out to reach as many people in this group as possible. At the very least, when anyone from the organization has contact with another person who could gain from what the organization is doing, or is likely to support what the organization is doing, that person should be asked to be a member. This is a habit that should be consciously developed among the members of your core group. If only a handful of members routinely recruit and you have no other plan for approaching these potential contributors, you will still steadily build the organization and provide new income.

### TIPS

- Keep membership dues low, below what people are able to give. Membership dues simply get people involved in the organization; you can ask them for other help later.
- Consider having several levels of membership with different privileges and benefits for each level (for example, voting and nonvoting). The higher the level, the higher the fees.
- Your membership form should be simple to fill out and return. If you can collect it on the spot, you will get a much higher rate of return.
- Keep an accurate database of your membership, including key information that allows you to contact members for education, mobilization, or fundraising. Once a year print it out, and with a small team of you who have been around for a while, go through it line by line to make sure everything is accurate.
- Include the line "make your cheque payable to" on the form. If the donation is tax deductible, say so.
- You can also ask for other information such as special knowledge, skills, community contacts, or interests. Do not require this information, otherwise the form may become irritating to fill out.
- If you are asking for members during a speech or presentation, do so toward the end of your talk. Forms should be passed out right after you make the request during, not after, your presentation. Get it into the hands of your listeners; do not make them come up and get it. Take a moment before you conclude your remarks to allow people to fill out the membership form.
- Have a modified form, used for presentations, that requires only essential information. Also have a box that says, "I cannot pay you now, but I will later."

The third step in developing a member base is to invite people to join whenever your organization contacts the general public. This, too, should become a habit, and it is an easy one to acquire. Membership forms should appear in all newsletters and be available at all public events. Each public speaking opportunity should be accompanied by a call for people to become members. Members should receive something in return for their contribution (Hicks, 2001). Membership cards are easy and inexpensive to produce. They should look good. Attractive, plastic laminated cards that fit easily into a wallet or billfold are the best.

Newsletters are important in reaffirming participation. Each membership organization should have one. It is important to remind people that they are members and why. If it is easy to provide other benefits, do so. Special event invitations, discounts, or other rewards available to members only are helpful. However, do only what is easy to do. If you make the process too complicated, you turn a simple technique into a time-consuming one. Newsletters do not have to be costly to create and distribute. If you have access to the e-mail addresses of your members, you can send newsletters electronically.

Members become the source of future funds and friends. Each year you ask members to ante up. Although not all continue, most will, providing the organization with a reliable source of income.

Periodically you should make a special appeal to members for additional donations. This should be tied to a special situation or challenge to the organization. Although you do not want to barrage members with these requests, you will periodically be able to draw money as well as goods and services from members in addition to their membership fees.

## Indirect Requests

Indirect requests to individuals include all techniques other than a face-to-face request for a contribution. These tend to be requests over the phone or by mail or e-mail..

Indirect methods produce a much lower response rate but have the advantage of reaching many more people. Even if individuals do not respond to one particular indirect request, their awareness of the organization is increased, and they may respond at another time.

Further, those who do respond become part of your donor base. You will resolicit these people from time to time for additional contributions. Most people who give once will give again, usually at least two more times. As long as you cover the initial costs of your solicitation campaign, you will eventually make money if you have a planned resolicitation campaign. An exception to this would be large mailings of tens or hundreds of thousands that may actually lose money on the first round. Campaigns of that sort understand that initial costs are an investment in a high future return. Ideally, you want to do more than just cover your costs. You want to make money the first time. Understand, though, that *resolicitation of identified donors is where the real money is.* Your rate of return on resolicitation is a great deal higher than that on your initial request.

Some groups do what is called prospecting. This means that their initial contact is done mainly for the purpose of discovering prospects to add to their base of donors for future contacts and additional dollars.

Keep accurate and thorough records on all donors. Building your donor base is a basic concern. You do not want to start from the beginning each time you go out to ask for money.

## Direct Mail

Direct mail is effective for prospecting and resolicitation. The most common way in which a financial donation was made to a nonprofit organization in Canada in 2004 was in response to a direct mail request, with 15 percent of the total number of donations being made in this fashion (Hall et al., 2006). However, it is important to know that unless you have either a fantastic mailing list (one that is likely to provide a high percentage of contributors), or a huge mailing, you will probably not make a lot of money on your first general request. In fact, you may well lose money on the first go-round; a return of 1 percent or more from a decent list is considered acceptable (Klein, 1992). However, continued resolicitation of the contributors who do respond can bring you future profit in the long run (Lautman, 2001). So, do not give up on your donor list too quickly.

Direct mail is best used as part of a long-term process for building a constituency base (Klein, 1992; Lautman, 1997). The quality of your list is the most important ingredient in this type of fundraising (Barnes, 1989; Lautman, 2001). In addition to costing you money, direct mail requires considerable time and energy. You need to gather lists, design your mailing piece, stuff and address all the envelopes, and gauge the best time for sending all this out. For these and other reasons, most smaller or new organizations do not use direct mail. Larger, well-established organizations do find this method profitable. They have the resources to put into it.

This method exists because if you have the resources and you do it right, it can make lots of money. Some companies specialize in direct mail and can run your whole campaign for you. Others specialize in renting lists (for example, the list of all subscribers to a particular magazine who live in a certain postal code area). Direct mail techniques have become increasingly sophisticated. If you believe your organization would benefit from pursuing this method of fundraising, check to see which organizations in your area might be able to help you. See if you have any special connections that could lead to some free or low-cost consultation. Remember, it is important to be sure the organization is reputable before you do business. Do your research.

Direct mail campaigns can be made more successful when you target a particular group of people—perhaps people you already have a relationship with (for example, your members), people who have already supported your organization's fundraising efforts in the past (for example, those who purchased raffle tickets you sold last year), or people who you think might be predisposed to support the work you are doing because of their prior involvement in something similar.

## Telephone Support for Small Mail Campaigns

On its own, telephone solicitation—calling people at home and asking them for money to support your work—does not tend to produce excellent results. For example, in 2004, only 3 percent of all donations being made in Canada were as a response to a telephone solicitation (Hall et al., 2006). This type of solicitation was made even more complex with the introduction of the National Do Not Call List, which prohibits organizations from soliciting people who have registered their numbers on the list, unless the organization meets certain criteria. (For more information on the National Do Not Call List, visit the website at www.lnnte-dncl.gc.ca.) However, the telephone can be a useful tool to increase the impact of a letter sent to a select group of potential donors. A mailing of 500 can easily be followed by three nights of follow-up calling. This will measurably increase the number of contributions the letter could generate on its own.

The initial letter should be signed by an individual who has some favourable status in the eyes of those receiving the letter. Ideally, he or she should be a member of the group receiving the letter, known personally by members of that target group, and be identified with the issue. For example, a successful homebuilder who has spoken publicly on the issue of homelessness could be a good letter signer for other homebuilders asking them to contribute to an effort that works with homeless people.

Sometimes an individual who is outside the immediate target group but held in high regard by those in the group will make an effective letter signer. The highly popular coach of the university football team, writing to those same homebuilders, or a nationally respected environmentalist, writing to a local environmental group, may produce a good response.

On some occasions, particularly if your organization is not well known, you may want to have several people sign the same letter. Having several signatures on the same letter gives the impression of broader support and increases the chances that those receiving the mailing will respond to the name of a person they trust.

### TIPS

- Write the letter for the signer. Most signers do not want to take on the job of composing a letter. Provide an opportunity for the signer to review and modify the contents to reflect his or her personality.
- Use facts and emotions in your letter to which the target group is likely to respond. Frame the message in a way that makes the most sense to them.
- Mention that this mailing is going to only a select few people.
- Include a P.S. on the letter saying that someone will be calling in a few days.
- Include a self-addressed return envelope with the letter.
- Ask the signer if he or she would be willing to make a few follow-up calls. If so, you can indicate this in the P.S.
- Personalize your outside envelope. Handwrite or type the address. Save mailing labels for some other time (Brentlinger & Weiss, 1987).
- Send your letters with first-class postage. Use stamps, not metered mail.
- Handwrite a code number or the person's name on the return envelope you have inserted. This reminds people that you are paying attention to who is responding and who is not.
- Have the letter signer actually sign each letter and write a personal note on as many letters as possible. Something like "Don, I hope to hear from you" would be sufficient.
- Using another name, include your own address and phone number on the list so you can see how the process is working.

It is particularly important to get good lists when using this technique. The names you select should be those who are much more likely than the general public to respond to both the issue at hand and the person or persons signing the letter with the amount of money you need. "Getting good lists" involves doing a lot of research. One possible way to begin is by finding organizations that are doing similar work to the work you are doing and looking at their lists of supporters, by checking their promotional materials and newsletters, and by going to their fundraising events and seeing who is listed as a sponsor in their program. This way you begin building a list of people and organizations who you know are already predisposed to support community work.

## Events

Special events can be a lot of work to organize and, if not done well, do not always generate a good return.

Event fundraising usually means that you are introducing an activity into the community calendar that is interesting enough that people will want to give you money to join in the fun. Events can attract attention and energize your members and supporters, affirm your connection to the community, and showcase your organization's leaders (Greenfield, 2002; Hicks, 2001). They can offer a clear focus for activity and help members and others in the community learn how to work together.

Your awareness of the community calendar is important. You want to make sure that you have taken into account religious holidays, sports events, cultural festivities, long holiday weekends, and other potential conflicts. Less risky than creating your own event is to capitalize on an existing community activity. The work and worry is much less in this case, though the money may be as well. Though you can just sit back and collect the profits, your early involvement in planning will give you the chance to see that the event is handled in a way that supports the image of your organization. Also, you want to make sure up front just how much you will receive from the revenue generated by the event. Generally about 10 percent of the gross revenues is a fair amount (Allen, 2001).

There are five basic types of events: those requiring attendance and ticket sales, those requiring participation and registration fees, those that other groups do on your behalf with a select community of potential contributors, those that are small select gatherings, and those that serve as a promotion of your organization as well as some other product or service.

Some events can be considered as much people-raising events as fundraising events. In this case, you try to get as many people to take part in the activity as possible while making just a little bit more money than you need to cover your costs. Here, the cost to the participant is very low because you are more concerned with bringing out a lot of people than bringing in a lot of money. Once you bring people in, you introduce them to your organization and you collect their contact information so you can resolicit them for future campaigns or events.

Many groups are disappointed when they have a great turnout and little money to show for all the work. If you only make a $2 profit on every person who shows up, you will need 500 people to attend to make just $1,000. Making $1,000 after many, many hours of work can be deflating. On the other hand, getting a crowd of 500 people to support your organization can be a tremendous boost and may very well pay off well into the future.

You have to have a number of things going for you to hold a big event that raises a lot of money. First, you have to have a lot of resources to put into planning and organizing and promoting the event. This usually means people (and their contacts) and money. Second, you need to have plenty of time in advance of the scheduled date to work on the project. Six months or more lead time is a good standard for larger affairs (Allen, 1997; Greenfield, 2002; Ulin, 2001). Third, your event should be sufficiently unique or attractive to a large group of probable respondents. This requires that you have access to a lot of people who would truly consider taking part. Finally, your organization, or the issue on which you are working, must have strong credibility in the community. The members of the community have to know about you and your issue and care about your success.

Smaller events are obviously much easier to organize. However, even small events have the same four demands, just on a reduced scale.

Make sure to check any legal requirements, such as permits, and consider what insurance, if any, you may need (Allen, 2001; Greenfield, 2002).

Remember to collect names, addresses, and phone numbers of those attending each event. These names can be added to your contributor or support list, which you will resolicit for future income (Klein, 1992).

The event is not really over when it's over. There are a number of things to take care of after the big day has come and gone. For one, you will want to make sure that all necessary expressions of thanks are sent. You also want to do an assessment of the event to see what worked well and what needed more attention. If you plan to repeat the activity, make sure all your records are in order: guest lists, budgets, expenses, actual revenues, printed material, assessment notes, and other artifacts you can use to guide your next affair (Ulin, 2001). Establishing an event as an ongoing activity can be beneficial. Repetition allows you to continue to improve its quality while introducing a fairly predictable source of funds into the cycle of your fundraising activities.

### Ticket Events

Paying, usually in advance, to attend something a little bit out of the ordinary is the essence of this approach. Contributors do not have to do anything but show up. Food and entertainment are the common features of these fundraising events. Dinners, plays, concerts, famous and semi-famous speakers—all are used as ticket events.

There are two important elements for success. First, select a drawing card that is sufficiently interesting to prospective contributors. This may include the other people in attendance. People may not want to miss an important social occasion that all the "right" people attend. It's fair to say that socializing is the main event at a major benefit (Brentlinger & Weiss, 1987). The more out of the ordinary your request, the more special it should be. For example, coming up with something to lure people out on a Tuesday night is more challenging than getting people to eat a midweek lunch.

The second necessary component involves selling all those tickets. Your success will be ensured by setting the right price for the event, getting those tickets into the hands of contributors, and getting the money out of their pockets. Although tickets are frequently sold at the door, it is the advance ticket sales that normally determine your success.

---

## TIPS

- Don't count on your drawing card or invitation to sell most of the tickets. Ticket sellers usually sell far more tickets than the event itself would. Ideally 80 percent of your tickets will be sold before the first invitation is sent (Greenfield, 2002).
- Get a very detail-oriented event manager to coordinate the work (Allen, 2001; Ulin, 1997).
- Consider getting corporate sponsorship to underwrite the event, but recognize that sponsors need benefits such as visibility or high-end clients attending the event (Freedman, 1996; Ulin, 1997).
- Promote your event to groups and individuals most likely to attend. A good invitation list is essential. Any advance publicity about the event is helpful. Figure out how your drawing card is newsworthy. Fliers, mailings, telephoning, and newspaper notices should be used. The strategy here is to keep the event in the public eye and build a sense of anticipation (Brentlinger & Weiss, 1987; Ulin, 1997). This is particularly important for major events.
- Make it easy for contributors to buy a ticket even if no one asks them to purchase a ticket. Have a phone number they can call, an order blank they can fill out, or an online system.
- Ticket sellers should be grouped into teams of five, with team leaders. Team leaders check weekly on team members' progress. This need not and should not be heavy-handed. Each member should expect to be contacted about progress. Team leaders need to follow through.
- Team competitions motivate ticket sellers, and especially team leaders. You will be surprised to learn how important it is for some sellers to get "credit" for a sale. Winning teams should get a prize or some form of recognition.

• Provide other incentives for ticket sellers. One free ticket for every 10 sold is often a good idea, especially since not all ticket purchasers will show up anyway.

• People often buy tickets mainly to please the ticket seller. The nature of the event and the cause are important, but the ticket buyer's relationship with the ticket seller or the organization the seller represents is usually more important.

• Encourage some people to buy a block of tickets, not just one. For example, businesspeople sometimes buy an entire table of tickets for a dinner event, giving seats to employees or clients, or donating the table back to the organization to fill the seats with people who otherwise would not be able to afford to attend the event.

• Send "save the date cards," a notice mailed as much as six months in advance, to prospective patrons. Their purpose is as much to stake a claim to the community's attention as it is to reserve a spot on the calendar (Brentlinger & Weiss, 1987).

• Whenever possible, get news coverage of your event. You will have to determine some newsworthy angle that will attract coverage. Remember, your event can give more than money. It is a tool for public relations as well.

• Get meaningful donated items to be used as door prizes, and include a mention of these on printed tickets and in your promotions.

• Publicly, formally, and clearly recognize all volunteers who made the event a success. This includes acknowledgments in the event program, a personal letter, and mention to the audience on the day of the event.

• Make sure members of the media get special attention and that they know whether they are to be treated as regular guests. If not, provide a media room with plenty of food and beverages, a media kit, and someone to show them around and introduce them to key attendees. Help them get the story you want (Allen, 2000).

• Prepare and follow a checklist of things to be done. This requires advance planning. Have a checklist for things you need to do in the months, weeks, and days leading up to the event. The length of your checklist will be determined by the size and complexity of your event (Allen, 1997; Brentlinger & Weiss, 1987; Greenfield, 2002, Ulin, 2001).

• Do what you can to keep your expenses down. The lower your costs, the higher your return. Know what all your expenses are, and find ways to reduce them. Shopping around will lead you to bargains.

• Using celebrities may be a good idea for your event. Many celebrities will waive their appearance fee if they believe strongly in the issue. They will also attract immediate attention to your organization and issue.

### Registration Events

These events are similar to ticket events, except that the contributor is asked to do more than just attend. The contributor pays to become a participant, not just an attendee. Such events usually provide some benefit that lasts beyond the event or the opportunity to engage in an enjoyable activity. Workshops, conferences, and seminars are examples of the first type. Bicycle tours, fun runs, and golf tournaments are examples of the second.

Registration events are commonly targeted to a specific group such as counsellors, day-care operators, golfers, and other everyday people. This makes it somewhat easier to select an attractive activity. The challenge is to design the activity in such a way that it stirs interest and effectively meets expectations.

#### TIPS

• Most registrations will come in during the week prior to the event. Do not sit back and wait for this to happen, but do not get panicky too early and call off the event.

• Figure out in advance how to make the event look and feel successful even if you only get half the registrations you expect. How you arrange seating in a room and how you design where people congregate at the beginning of the event are two ways to do this.

• Make sure you have direct access to your target group, and involve them in planning the event.

• For conferences, you can make money by renting space to vendors who hope to sell products or services to those who attend.

• If your event involves something measurable, ask participants to "sell" pledges or sponsorships. Participants ask their friends, neighbours, and innocent passers-by to contribute a certain amount, say 50 cents or $5, for every goal scored, every kilometre run, or every basket made. Sponsors can also contribute a flat dollar amount. This can be as high or low as they please. Participants who bring in a certain amount in pledges above the entrance fee may have the fee reduced or eliminated.

• Send a letter to prospective participants. Enclose sponsor sheets for the participant to fill out.

• Understand that you will need to devise a simple money-collecting mechanism and that not all those who have pledged will make good on their promises.

• Send a thank-you letter acknowledging your receipt of the registration fee.

• Provide participants with some mementos of their involvement. Baseball caps, T-shirts, and pens printed with the name of the event are good souvenirs. These can serve as enticements as well.

• Get high-profile people to take part in your event. Featured speakers, local elected officials, or local athletes can serve this purpose.

---

Registration events have a further benefit in that they capitalize on what people do anyway. Professionals attend conferences as part of their work routine, golfers golf, and runners run. Registration events do not ask people to do much out of the ordinary or to add much to a busy schedule.

You will not have to go through all the bother of selling tickets, but you will have to promote registrations. Except for the ticket-selling process, registration events require about the same things as ticket events. You need to promote the event, do advance planning, make a checklist, and keep your costs down. Because registration events deal with a narrower potential contributor group, they are often a little more manageable.

### Events Coordinated by Other Groups

Many groups hold activities for their members that serve as fundraisers for community service activities. This often involves something like an athletic tournament, a barbecue, or some modest entertainment. The sponsoring organization will usually split the proceeds with you. They do most of the work, and the event is directed to their members. The community service orientation of the organization is fulfilled in a way that gives their members something enjoyable to do.

---

## TIPS

• Get out your list of local clubs and organizations, and send a letter to each group on the list whose assistance you would want. The letter should include examples of things the group could do to benefit your organization and how the two of you would work together. Follow up the letter with phone calls to the organizations most likely to respond.

• Have clear, written agreements about what each of you will do and how money is to be collected and divided. Keep this simple; after all, they are doing you a favour.

• Unless the sponsoring group has a well-established community activity they do as a community service fundraiser, you should shy away from events that go beyond the membership of the sponsoring group. These are usually pretty small-scale events and are best kept that way by having the sponsoring group work with the people and the activity they know best.

---

## Sales

Selling a service or a product is a pretty standard way of raising relatively small amounts of cash. Bake sales, car washes, and yard sales are the most frequently seen examples of this approach.

A newly emerging source of funding is through a much more comprehensive earned income program. These are ongoing entrepreneurial enterprises that make use of sophisticated business practices to provide a steady source of funds for the organization. Some examples of social entrepreneurship include auto repair, restored bicycles, plant nurseries, thrift stores, creating and selling posters, educational tours, self-defence classes, and gift baskets. You get the idea.

Fundraiser Andy Robinson (2002) has captured a number of sound ideas for developing an earned income program, and he presents numerous examples in *Selling Social Change: Without Selling Out*. He offers a number of cautions for organizations considering entry into the world of social entrepreneurship. First, stop and think whether you may already have enough work to do. Is this something you really want to take on? How will this affect your attention to your fundamental mission? What are the potential tax liability issues? Do you really have the up-front capital that is required? Have you thought about the fact that these enterprises sometimes lose money? Still, if you think you have good answers to these questions, you may want to forge ahead and see if you can craft your niche within the marketplace. Some organizations that take the plunge bring in not a hundred dollars but a hundred thousand.

Here are some tips from Robinson (2002):

- What assets—goods, services, intellectual property—do you have that someone might buy? This could include training and publishing.
- Get some outside help from your local college or university business program, nonprofit resource centre, local or regional community loan fund, local businesspeople, or local economic development agency.
- Have passion for your idea.
- Develop a sound business plan and a marketing plan based on market research.
- Keep your expectations modest.
- Most commerce is conducted business-to-business, not business-to-customer. How can you best serve area businesses, including government and nonprofits?
- Seek funds from social lenders like some credit unions or community loan funds.
- Lead with your mission, but do not forget your customers.

Let's say you are a small, volunteer organization with more modest means and goals. What might you do? Whether it is a cupcake or a full product line, the basic notion is to put as good a product or service in front of as many people who are likely to spend money on it as possible.

So, if you are holding a yard sale, begin collecting items early from as many sources as possible to make sure you have a lot of good things to sell. If it's a bake sale you are holding, make sure you have a variety of goodies at a range of prices. Then select a spot where people who have the munchies are likely to pass by. Outside the college cafeteria or right outside the church after services are good bets. If it's cars you wish to clean, try to corner the busiest intersection in town.

Selling products made especially for you (for example, T-shirts or baseball caps) is a little trickier. You usually have some initial investment to make, or you get a small percentage of the overall price of the object. If you think you can sell a lot of these, it may be worth doing. Your best bet is to sell items on a variety of occasions to a captive audience of potential supporters. Rallies, conferences, and other special events provide captive audiences.

Sales of candy and nuts and other dentists' delights also require a high volume to make a profit. Items that sell for a dollar or less make it easy for someone to "contribute" to the organization and get something in return.

Because success requires a lot of people selling a lot, a lot of organization is required as well. Sales teams with team captains and clear accounting methods to keep track of the product and the money are essential. The companies that provide the products can usually instruct you on how to set up your promotion and keep track of your sales.

Holding an auction is another method of sales. You have to spend time and energy locating quality donated items for sale, promote the auction effectively to attract a good number of buyers, and then conduct the actual auction so it runs smoothly and gets you as much per item as possible. This includes selecting the best order for auctioning the items, holding an auction preview, and preparing a program. A professional auctioneer is generally well worth the money for the directions he or she can provide as well as his or her skill in working the buyers. Some auctioneers will volunteer their services for non-profit organizations. Many professional auctioneers are members of the National Auctioneers Association of Canada. Some provinces—for example, Saskatchewan and Manitoba—have their own associations as well. Check out their websites at www.saskauctioneers.com and www.manitobaauctioneers.com.

Online auctions are another option. According to an article posted at Charity Village by Trebesch and Robinson (2007), online auctions are one of the most effective online fund-raising tools that exist. They note that two main advantages of an online auction are an increased number of potential bidders and, because they can last for weeks, improved visibility of the auction and thus the organization. Trebesch and Robinson recommend MissionFish as a useful online auction tool that is affiliated with eBay.

What you choose to sell and how you choose to sell it are limited only by your creativity, the resources you have to put into the effort, and, of course, the legal restrictions you may face.

## Planned Giving

The concept of planned giving means a gift that is of sufficient magnitude that making it is integrated with the donor's personal financial plan or estate plan. The way the gift is made is designed to benefit both the giver and the receiver. Obviously, gifts of this type usually come from the more well-to-do. This method of developing an organization's resources is on the rise and can provide tremendous financial stability for formal organizations. Much of the information on planned giving provided here is drawn from the Nonprofit Counsel (1986) and from Moerschbaecher and Dryburgh (2001), as well as Clodman and Pearce (2006).

Clodman and Pearce (2006) define planned giving as follows:

> Planned Giving is a philanthropic program by which a donor can arrange a substantial gift for the future. As a planned gift is often made from accumulated assets that have taken a lifetime to build, the emphasis is on "planning" and is focused on the donor's needs and objectives. These include the retention of capital, tax planning, estate planning, continued support of the charity and financial security. Planned gifts are designed so that the donor realizes philanthropic objectives while maximizing tax and other financial benefits. (p. 1)

Probably the most common planned gift is a bequest in a will. However, the gift can take on many forms, such as trusts, pooled income funds, or other mechanisms designed to increase both the ease of making contributions and their value. Some of these methods will provide income to your organization soon, whereas others will have an impact many years down the road. According to Clodman and Pearce (2006), some such possibilities include gifts such as these.

- Cash, cheque or credit card
- Securities
- Bonds
- Real estate
- Interest-free loans
- Retirement savings and Life Income Funds

Does this all sounds pretty technical? Well, it is. That is why you should seek the assistance of a lawyer, a bank trust officer, an accountant, or another professional knowledgeable about planned giving if you intend to pursue this approach.

Generally, planned giving has been seen as an avenue only for older and larger organizations. Experts are now saying that every formal organization, no matter how small or how new, should have a planned giving program. Planned giving, through endowments, for example, is not limited to the elderly and the wealthy. Many people of modest means, as well as younger donors, are creating endowments (Leher, 2000).

## Looking in Nooks and Crannies

You must always be willing to explore a broad range of options for raising money. Did you know that placing coin collection canisters by the cash registers of 100 restaurants can bring you

$20,000 a year? Or that you can easily make $75 just by having 20 members of your organization save returnable cans or bottles for about a month?

How about pennies? There are untold creative ways for collecting pennies. A local bank or credit union branch might sponsor a "bring us your pennies" week on behalf of your organization (Goldstein, 1993), or a radio station could promote a penny week. You can dream up all sorts of ideas. In addition to all the pennies you get (which, of course, do turn into dollars), you can get tremendous publicity, lots of dimes and quarters, and, yes, even loonies and toonies from people who want to support your creative cause (Lynn & Lynn, 1992).

How about a donation of commercial property, a huge untapped resource for nonprofits? Millions of dollars of commercial real estate may be available for donations. Is there a sports franchise in your area? Many have foundations, and some plan to expand their contributions to help their communities (Join Together Online, 2000).

Look for every chance you can to raise money. If pursuing a particular opportunity does not distract you from your main purpose, take advantage of it. Some things should become routine, second nature. Every one of your newsletters should include a way for people to give you money. Many a community presentation will provide you with an opening to ask for financial help. Make use of every opportunity.

## USING THE INTERNET AS A FUNDRAISING TOOL

The Internet is essentially a communications tool. It allows you to reach more donors more quickly in more ways.

Donors are way out ahead of fundraisers when it comes to use of the Internet (Greenfield, 2002). With millions more people every month connecting to the Internet, this medium has now become a routine aspect of daily life. While you are reading this, potential donors are online gathering information and transacting business. Though organizations have not done much asking through the Internet, this is how a growing number of donors want to be asked (Flanagan, 2000).

Two essentials for Internet fundraising are a good and secure website and a usable database. Your website not only helps to establish your credibility and the importance of your issue, but it can offer your viewers many opportunities for affiliation. Be sure to provide a link for contributions on every page. Make sure members can easily provide you with updated addresses and other contact information (Fox-McIntyre, 2001). Keep your friends and donors close at hand. Collect e-mail addresses. Not just once in a while. Always. Your database of supporters is your most fertile ground for growing stronger commitment and harvesting continuing financial support. Everyone on your list is a potential contributor. Think of them that way. Treat them that way.

You may want to work with an application service provider (ASP) to add sophisticated features to your website such as donation forms, shopping carts, event registration, and many other useful highlights. Though there is usually a set-up fee, this can be a simple solution to a complex problem.

There are many ways to keep in contact and encourage more active involvement through your use of e-mail. First, however, a gentle reminder about courtesy. Let people both "opt in" and "opt out" of your list (Flanagan, 2000; Greenfield, 2002). Though you will find different ways of asking for addresses, send solicitation or invitation mailings only to the addresses that have been given to you by the person who holds the address. At the end of any mass mailing, provide the receiver with an opportunity to unsubscribe or be removed from the list. Do develop a privacy policy, and post it on your website (Poley, 2001). Do make sure that you check with a lawyer to see which laws governing fundraising on the Internet apply to you. For example, some auctions or raffles may be considered gambling. Your Internet message reaches far and wide, so laws beyond your geographical location might become relevant as well.

You can also make use of online services to help you with your Internet-based fundraising. One excellent service is CanadaHelps (see its website at www.canadahelps.org). CanadaHelps launched in 2000, and today it facilitates over $10 million in donations to charities in Canada every year. The advantage of using a service such as CanadaHelps is that it takes care of all the administrative work related to collecting and processing donations (including issuing the tax receipts). Your organization does not have to set up its own online donation facilities. CanadaHelps does not charge any administrative fees but does take 3 percent of all the donated money. This charge is often well worth paying in exchange for not having to do the administrative work. This work is never free; if you do it yourself, someone still has to be paid for their time. According to its website, CanadaHelps is "Canada's only donation portal that provides access to all of Canada's 80,000 charities, from national organizations like national cancer charities to smaller groups like local animal shelters and soup kitchens." It also can provide security and thus peace of mind for your organization and your donors: "On any pages where you share personal information or perform financial transactions, CanadaHelps.org encrypts your data using Secure Socket Layers (SSL), allowing you to send and receive information without the worry of having it intercepted." When donors go to the site, they can select as many charities as they want. With the click of a mouse, they make their donation and receive a tax receipt right away. Charities are notified immediately when a donation is received.

? DID YOU KNOW?

### Making the Most of the Internet

Most mid-sized and large cities have a professional fundraising group such as a chapter of the Association of Fundraising Professionals that meets monthly. Attending these get-togethers can give you some good ideas and some profitable contacts. The Canadian national office of the Association of Fundraising Professionals is located in Ottawa. There are many, many ways of using the Internet to reach potential contributors (Fox-McIntyre, 2001; Greenfield, 2002; Hodiak, 2001; Johnson, 2001; Stein, 2001). Here are a few ideas.

*Some uses for your website:*

- Calendar of events
- Event registration
- Membership renewal
- Secure means of giving with a credit card
- Online pledge form
- Opportunity to provide an "In Memory" or "In Honour" gift (called commemorative or tribute giving)
- Sales of items
- Promotion of your organization's income-producing enterprises
- Online auctions

*Some uses for your e-mail:*

- Bring content to your audience, keeping them informed of issue developments and your group's successes with periodic brief messages
- Distribute your online newsletter with organization news, issue information, key contributors and recognition of outstanding work, specific needs, and ways to contribute
- Send personalized updates, thank-yous, and special invitations
- Send direct requests for contributions at a critical point in an issue campaign
- Send general solicitation letter
- Direct readers to visit your website

## SECURING FUNDS FROM PUBLIC AND PRIVATE ORGANIZATIONS

You now have some good ideas of how you can get money from individuals. Getting money from other groups and organizations, including the government and private foundations, is another potentially valuable approach. This involves negotiating an intervening process, which serves as a kind of barrier or filter between you and the people who make the decisions. Almost every potential funding organization has some process you must follow.

This means at least two things to you. First, understand the procedures for each particular funding source and follow them well. Second, understand that, even with this approach, it is people, acting as individuals or as a group, who make the final decisions. Their decisions will be based on objective reasoning as well as a variety of other influences. Get to know the funding procedures and get to know the people as well as you can.

The process for approaching funding organizations for money has many similarities to the way you approach individuals. First, identify prospective sources of funds, and then target those that are most likely. Second, establish contact and nurture prospective sources. Third, prepare and submit a written proposal to the funding source, and follow up on that submission. Fourth, prepare and offer a verbal presentation to the funding source, and follow up on that presentation. (Though this step is not always required, it is helpful to be prepared). Fifth, say thank you and nurture future relationships.

### Identifying Prospective Sources

Increasing your awareness of all the possible sources of funds is an ongoing process. First of all, look at groups whose interests or goals are compatible with yours. Next, consider professional groups that may be interested in your concerns. Third, find out all you can about community service groups and their funding priorities. Following this, think about the businesses and corporations that serve your area. Funding programs, such as the United Way, would be the fifth set of potential contributors. Foundations are another possible source to consider. Finally, get to know how the various levels of government can be involved in funding your operation. Whether your organization is a registered charity will make a difference in which funds you can access. Many sources of funding are available only to registered charities. Registering as a charity, however, is a complicated process and can take a long time. The Canada Revenue Agency is responsible for registering charities. You can find out everything you need to know about charitable registration at www.cra-arc.gc.ca/tx/chrts/menu-eng.html.

It is helpful to know a little more about each type of funding source, from those whose processes are likely to be informal to those whose procedures are increasingly formalized. The more formal and large the funding source is, the more formal and complex their process is likely to be; also, the more likely they will be to fund formal, incorporated organizations. Smaller, local funding sources tend to be more flexible.

#### Like-Minded Groups

These are groups that share values similar to yours. They may well be promoting an issue that is similar to yours. Groups that see themselves as working on the same issue, trying to mobilize or influence the same constituency, will also see themselves in competition with you. If this is the case, they will probably be more interested in protecting their turf than in giving you money. However, groups that have a related political or issues agenda may welcome another group into the playing field by making a contribution to get you going or to help with a special need.

The process is likely to be informal, usually involving your making a direct request to the group during one of their meetings. Ask for a specific amount for a clearly identified purpose, and show how their contribution promotes your mutual concerns. Do your homework before the meeting by getting to know a member or members of this group. Find out how much the group would be willing to give. Ask for an amount in that range when you make your pitch.

Though the contribution is likely to be modest, this can be an important step in fostering alliances that will be helpful in the future. Be willing to return the favour to other groups when your ability to help out is developed.

**Professional Groups and Associations**

Some organizations promote the interests and issues relevant to a particular profession. Dentists, nurses, accountants, social workers, and turkey farmers all have professional organizations. Many of these will have local chapters in your area. Some of the things you are working on will be a natural for two or three of these groups to support. If your request can reinforce the group's issues, its image, or the self-interest of its members (ideally all three), you can reinforce your chance for a favourable response. If

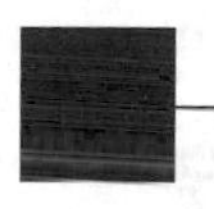

## CAPTURING CONCEPTS

### Understanding the Terminology of Funding

Knowing the common language of the funding process is important. Here is a brief overview of the terms you are likely to hear.

An **RFP** is a request for a proposal. If a funding source, often some branch of government, is sending out an RFP, it is seeking proposals from community groups to provide a particular service. Often, your proposal will be in response to an RFP.

**Matching funds** are dollars given to an organization if it can come up with some additional dollars elsewhere. Often, the match is expressed in terms of a ratio. For example, a 3:1 match means that for every dollar you raise elsewhere, the funding source will give you $3. If you raise $250, the source would give you $750, for a total of $1,000. There are frequently minimum and maximum limits on matching funds.

**Pilot programs** and **demonstration projects** are somewhat experimental. Usually, a funding source will give you money for just a couple of years to get the program up and running. The premise is that other funding sources will pick up the tab after the initial funding has run out if the program has merit. It may also be intended that the program be used as a model for others to follow. **Seed money** is given to start up a new project, usually covering initial expenses and salaries. **Start-up funds** do about the same thing.

The **funding cycle** is the time during which a funding source accepts new proposals and awards grants. Different funding sources have different funding cycles. A **fiscal year** is a budget year. It describes a 12-month period during which money is spent on an organization's program. Different funding sources use different fiscal years. Some follow the normal calendar year, beginning January 1 and ending December 31. Another common fiscal year, one often used by government funders, begins April 1 and ends on March 31.

When a government source awards a **grant** to another organization to provide funds to enable the receiving organization to perform a specified set of functions for an agreed-upon dollar amount, it begins to refer to that organization as a **TPA** or **transfer payment agency**. Relationships with transfer payment agencies are normally formalized through a purchase of **service agreement** or **contract** or a **memorandum of understanding.** This contract sets forth the terms of the relationship, including the nature and extent of the services the receiving agency will perform, the amount of funding the purchase agency will provide, and a schedule of payments.

you are developing a program to assist people with AIDS and their families, for example, check to see if any of these groups has expressed a particular interest in this topic. These would be the first groups to approach.

Professional associations normally want you to put your request in writing. Most often this works to justify to their membership any support given to you. The decision to give you money will probably be based more on your initial discussions and verbal presentation than on your written proposal. The organization's local board or steering committee will hear your request. Try to get a commitment from them at that time. A delayed decision or one routed through their committee structure may mean that enthusiasm for your request is lacking. This may be a signal for you to develop more support.

The amount of money you receive will probably be minimal. Even associations of the wealthier professions often do not give large amounts. There are exceptions to this. Some organizations see their support of community efforts as a routine function. Where this is the case, you may receive more money. However, the process is likely to be more complex, with your written request carrying more weight.

### Community Service Clubs and Organizations

Clubs and organizations such as the Lions or Rotary Clubs are formed to give their members status, opportunities for socialization, a mechanism for providing service to the community, and recognition for that service. Take these factors into account when approaching service organizations.

Most of these groups have a well-defined area of interest, and the recipients of their help must be seen as worthy of support. Therefore, children, the physically challenged, or those struggling to overcome serious obstacles may be favoured. Getting the support of the organization's leadership beforehand will smooth the way. A well-prepared, factual, and emotional presentation will play an important part. It is sometimes helpful to make a purely informational presentation to the general membership that spurs interest several months before you make any request for money.

These groups will give by taking on something as a project, making a modest one-time contribution, or by "passing the hat" at a meeting, usually a breakfast or luncheon. The more your request falls within the group's special project interests, the more money you will be able to receive.

A particular set of community service groups have raising and dispensing money as one of their main purposes, if not their primary purpose. These organizations follow a fairly structured funding process. Their grants can range into the tens of thousands of dollars. You can find a detailed listing of service clubs in Canada on the Charity Village website (www.charityvillage.com).

### Businesses and Corporations

Larger corporations that are major employers in your community will almost always contribute to the community in the form of donations. Smaller businesses frequently will as well. Corporate giving is big business. Imagine Canada, using data collected by Statistics Canada, engaged in an analysis of the charitable giving patterns of corporations in Canada and found some interesting patterns. Their analysis, published in an Imagine Canada Research Bulletin (Easwaramoorthy, Barr, Gumulka, & Hartford, 2006) shows that in 2003, 3 percent of businesses claimed approximately $1 billion in charitable donations (according to their tax returns). The authors note that although this amounts to a large sum, for these companies, it is less than 1 percent of their total pre-tax profits. Almost half of these corporate donations came from just two industries, finance and insurance (32 percent) and manufacturing (19 percent). The sector that gave the largest percentage of their pre-tax profits was accommodation and food services (2.6 percent). Only 1.7 percent of businesses with annual revenues of less than $1 million claimed a taxable donation in Canada in 2003. In contrast, businesses with annual revenues of over $25 million contributed at a rate of 40.3 percent. Interestingly though, these companies, while donating at a higher rate, are not the most generous givers—they donated only 0.6 percent of their pre-tax profits to charities and nonprofits.

Corporations in Canada could also do much better at designating their donations to social service organizations. Together, social services, environment and development, and housing organizations accounted for only 9 percent of all corporate donations in 2003 (Easwaramoorthy et al., 2006, p. 3). While the total amount might be less than it should be, corporations remain an important avenue of support to nonprofit organizations in Canada.

*Strategic philanthropy,* a term coined more than 20 years ago by Nina Kaiden Wright, describes an approach corporations use to evaluate the most effective way to spend their donations (McKay, 1988). The intent is to publicize the corporation that promotes the community project. Some observers characterize corporate giving as enlightened self-interest, a belief that contributions benefit the businesses in the long run by promoting a healthier community and business climate (Picker, 2001; Zippay, 1992). Further, customers are more likely to purchase from companies that supported a cause (Burlingame, 2001; Riley, 2000). John L. Mason (1988), former president of the Monsanto Fund, uses the phrase "investing for results." Those responsible for fund investments must be able to demonstrate that the fund supports the objectives of the corporation.

Contributions are often tied to corporate marketing strategies, with many donation dollars coming from marketing budgets (Hunt, 1986; Picker, 2001). The term has now become common. Generally this involves contributing a certain amount to an organization for every product sold. This type of business support of a community cause not only brings in more money for the community organization but attracts greater public awareness and involvement as well (Burlingame, 2001).

Many corporations are going beyond giving away dollars to actually making a conscious investment in strengthening the community. Increasingly, corporations are becoming involved in "venture philanthropy" and "social entrepreneurship." A useful resource for learning about venture philanthropy can be found at www.venturephilanthropyguide.org. Organizations such as Social Capital Partners, which is located in Toronto (www.socialcapitalpartners.ca), work with corporations to help them strengthen their contribution to community.

Corporations usually have special priority areas (for example, hunger or education), and they tend to target their contributions to projects that address these interests. Often, the chief executive officers or members of corporate allocations committees determine funding priorities based on their personal interests and social contacts (Sheldon, 2000; Zippay, 1992).

Another important concern is geographic (Morth & Collins, 1996; Picker, 2001). Corporations with large numbers of employees in regional offices or plant locations throughout the country tend to target their giving in local areas (Webb, 1982). Remember to mention any volunteer support your organization receives from the company's employees (Breiteneicher & Hohler, 1993).

The larger the business and the more distant the ownership from the community, the more complex the sequence of activities to secure funding is likely to be. The reverse of this is true as well. The smaller the business or closer to the community the ownership, the simpler your request can be. This includes, believe it or not, just walking in and asking.

### Labour Unions

In many parts of the world labour unions are involved in serving their communities. Labour unions provide a variety of resources to support community efforts. Not surprisingly, unions frequently contribute labour—particularly skilled labour. Plumbers, electricians, carpenters, and other workers donate valuable skills that you may not be able to afford to purchase.

Not only do union members and their organizations donate time, but they give money as well. Just as you would with any other prospect, it is important that you do some research to see how your project links with the interests and giving ability of a particular labour organization you might approach for a contribution. A good starting point would be the Canadian Labour Congress. Including labour unions in your resource development plans establishes a connection with a group of workers already organized for action and with a history of giving. This can be a potent way to extend your resources.

### Federated Funding Programs

Federated financing refers to campaigns conducted by one agency for others. Usually, the fundraising group is itself a nonprofit agency or an arm of another body such as a corporation (Mirkin, 1978). Federated campaign organizations commonly have four functions. First, they develop membership from participating agencies. This involves screening new applicants as well as monitoring current members to assess the appropriateness of their continued involvement. Second, they raise money for their members through a combined appeal. Third, they assess a range of community needs. Fourth, they allocate funds to their members based ostensibly on the determination of community needs and the members' ability to meet them.

The largest and perhaps best-known federated campaign is the United Way of Canada—Centraide Canada, the national parent organization of local United Way branches. It has been in existence since 1887 and operates in many communities throughout the country. According to the website of the United Way of Canada (www.unitedway.ca), there are 122 United Ways across Canada, based in ten provinces and two territories. The website states, "Next to governments, the UW-C Movement is the largest funder of the voluntary sector and social services in Canada. Each year, UWs-Cs raise upwards of $440 million, the vast majority of which is reinvested in local communities to support programs and services directed at improving the social conditions of Canadians."

Because of the tremendous amount of money and publicity it generates, the United Way demands your attention, but it may be difficult for new members to break into the United Way club. The United Way sets its priorities based on identified community needs. Receiving United Way dollars usually means accepting some limitations. Pursuing other sources of funding (for example, approaching corporations) may be restricted, especially at the time of year when the United Way operates its annual campaign. An agency's appeal in the community and its consequent ability to help the United Way attract funds may be an important reason for its inclusion in United Way membership.

The United Way has a very formal process, including submission of a written proposal, a verbal presentation, and normally a site visit. Get as many members of your agency's board as you can to attend these presentations. Those individuals who make funding decisions like to see clear demonstrations of board involvement and support.

Begin building social relationships between members of your organization and volunteer members of the United Way funding committees. Though you should properly stay within the prescribed process when making a request for funds, it does not hurt to have people who like you make the decisions.

### Foundations

Foundations exist to give away money and promote certain interests. In Canada, the foundation sector is strong and represents a diverse group of individual foundations with multiple funding interests. According to the website of Philanthropic Foundations Canada, over 8,400 foundations are registered in Canada, with about 2,300 of them currently active. The vast majority (almost 84 percent) are private family foundations. The total assets of these foundations are approximately $13.9 billion, and in 2004, they distributed over $ 1.2 billion in support. The distribution of these foundations across the country reflects the population, with 64.9 percent being in Central Canada (Ontario and Quebec), 31.6 percent being in the western provinces (British Columbia, Alberta, Saskatchewan, and Manitoba), and 3.5 percent in the Atlantic provinces and the territories (Newfoundland, Prince Edward Island, Nova Scotia, New Brunswick, Yukon, Nunavut, and the Northwest Territories.)

Some foundations are publicly funded and can be national (for example, the Aboriginal Healing Foundation) or provincial (for example, Ontario Trillium Foundation and the Wild Rose Foundation in Alberta). Others are privately funded and can operate as part of a corporation (for example,, Royal Le Page Shelter Foundation, Nissan Canada Foundation), as a family foundation (for example, Zukerman Family Foundation, or J.W. McConnell Family Foundation), or as a community foundation (for example, The Lesbian and Gay Community Appeal Foundation, the Community Foundation of Newfoundland and Labrador, the Jewish Community Foundation of Montreal). Some sports franchises even have foundations (for example, Raptors Foundation).

Foundations generally give to organizations with some sort of track record. Rarely do they give to start-up organizations, though they may give to an unincorporated group that links with one that is incorporated. They like to fund specific projects rather than provide general funding for ongoing programs (Geever, 2001).

A lot of homework on your part is essential prior to approaching any foundation. This point cannot be overstated. By visiting Charity Village on the web (www.charityvillage.com) you can gain access to a long list of foundations in Canada. Perhaps the most significant document you will need to research foundations is the Canadian Directory to Foundations and Corporations, which is published by Imagine Canada and is available online (www.imaginecanada.ca). This is the largest database in Canada with information on more than 3,000 foundations, 150 corporations, and 90,000 indexed grants. The directory is updated every week, and organizations can purchase a subscription to use the directory for one or two years at a time. This directory can be vital in helping you narrow your search.

Foundations can be divided into six categories (Allen & Regional Youth Project, 1981; Lewis, 2002; Pendleton, 1981):

*General-purpose foundations.* These are the particularly large and well-known foundations. They have a wide range of projects and operate with relatively few restrictions. Generally, they are interested in very large projects.

*Special-purpose foundations.* These foundations restrict their funds to a geographic area or a specific field of interest.

*Corporate or company foundations.* These foundations are established by corporations or companies to handle most of the funds donated by the company. Some corporations donate funds through the corporation in addition to their corporate foundation. Also, many corporations will match an individual employee's contribution to a charity of the employee's choosing, but only if the employee brings it to the attention of the corporation by filing the proper forms.

*Family foundations.* These are usually smaller foundations under the control of the family that set them up. Their grants fall within their areas of personal interest. Many of the smaller family foundations are not included in published listings.

*Operating foundations.* These organizations use their resources to conduct research or provide a direct service.

*Community foundations.* This type of foundation operates with many small funds centralized under community management. Grants are usually restricted to a particular geographic area. However, many of these local community foundations do have large assets and a broad range of interests. This makes them a good potential source for your community change effort.

Your approach to foundations starts by sending a letter of inquiry to each foundation on your target list. Express your interest and describe your organization, including a list of other groups that support you. Ask for more information on the foundation, including award procedures. After about two weeks, follow up your letter with a personal phone call. Always make personal contact unless you are explicitly told not to. You should quickly acknowledge receipt of any information from the foundation with a personal response.

The decision to make an award to you will generally be based on the strength of your proposal. Verbal presentations are not often required. Gifts range from hundreds to hundreds of thousands of dollars. Many foundations provide matching grants as well, giving you money to match what you have raised elsewhere. Not only does this often make your proposal more attractive, but it may provide more incentive for members of your organization to raise more money (Klein, 2000).

## Public Funding

Government funding provides a high percentage of the budget of most social service agencies. Though government agencies rarely give money to organizations that are not incorporated, small agencies and new programs in existing agencies do receive government funding. Similar to foundations, public funding can go to a small organization operating under the umbrella of an established, incorporated nonprofit.

"Government" really means governments. Your organization may work in an area that cuts across various municipal, provincial, city, and county government lines. Each is a potential source of funds. So when we use the term *government,* it does not refer to just one government body. Different layers or levels of government exist, each with its own organizational structure and procedures.

How do you get money from the government? Good question. The answer is complicated by all those various levels of government and the various programs each government operates. Here are a few guidelines that point the way.

• *Get information.* Find out what funds various levels of government have to deal with social concerns such as yours. Discover through which mechanisms, departments, and programs they give this money. You can get a detailed list of government funding programs by visiting Charity Village on the web (www.charityvillage.com). You can also visit government websites directly—for example, www.canada.ca for the federal government's website. Make sure you check every level of government you might be interested in (for example, provincial and municipal). Once you are at the website, use the search function to search for "funding" or "grants" or "RFPs" and other related keywords.

Establish contact with people in government funding agencies. Call them. These individuals know what is going on and can alert you to upcoming opportunities. Also, agency policymakers can help you discover money stashed in various bureaucratic hiding places and find ways to make this available to you. Discover and make use of notification procedures used by government agencies. Get on a list to receive requests for proposals. Then start building those contacts.

Develop a rudimentary understanding of the budget, particularly the budgets of local governments. The more you know the better. You do not have to drive yourself crazy, but do understand where and on what the money is intended to be spent. Review the most likely budget categories. This will give you some indication of how much money is available in your interest area. Also, you can use your agency contacts to find out if and how some of this money can be directed to support your organization's endeavours.

• *Get help.* Develop a relationship with politicians and their staffs (for example, your city councillor, member of Parliament, member of provincial parliament). They are helpful in identifying possibilities and supporting your requests. Politicians who can get credit for delivering the goods to their constituencies have additional motivation. Supportive administrative staff in government agencies can give you information and direction.

• *Get public attention directed to your issue.* This will be helpful in making requests to provincial and municipal governments. One of the functions of government funding is to keep people quiet. Attracting community awareness and concern to your issue can attract government money as well. Another role of government is to promote and support helpful private efforts. If your group becomes recognized as a valued community resource, government funding sources may be happy to show their investment in your mutual success.

• *Get involved in the budget-building process.* Find out how the various departments of your provincial and municipal government participate in development of the budget, and work with them to include funding in the new budget to deal with your area of concern. It is easier to get money if it is there in the budget in the first place. The submission of a formal proposal is usually part of the funding process. Get a well-written proposal describing an effective approach to addressing a recognized problem into the right hands on time. Do not be afraid to ask for guidance as you are preparing your proposal.

### Get to Know the People Involved

Regardless of the type of organization from which you are seeking funds, be it the federal government or the local PTA, you will be dealing with people. You cannot overlook this. The personal relationship that develops might be the most important factor affecting funding (Webb, 1982). Establish a good, friendly, and appropriately personal rapport with the individual or individuals who serve as your contact within the funding sources you court (Geever, 2001; Golden, 2001; Schumacher, 1992; Sheldon, 2000). Follow his or her advice and direction. Ask questions. This gives the contact a stake in your success.

Yes, politics is involved. The process is not pure. Yes, it is often whom you know. Yes, people do help one another with favours. Most people would rather work with someone they know, in whom they have confidence and trust. Grantors are no different. Inside advocacy is a big part of the game. Make use of opportunities to meet grant makers, and cultivate those relationships.

## GRANT WRITING

Skill in proposal writing is a valuable asset in your organization's efforts to acquire money. Whether your intended funding source is a corporation, a foundation, or a unit of government, some sort of proposal will probably be required. When we say "grant writing," what we really mean is ***proposal writing***. Your proposal is your record of what you want to do and how.

A critical aspect of any grant-seeking process is making sure you have done an adequate amount of research on possible funding sources. Narrow your list to only those whose interests, resources, and requirements match your organization's goals, abilities, and characteristics. Some funders place lots of restrictions on the use of their dollars; others require that you do extra work for which no funding is provided. Make sure the conditions of the grant are something you can live with (Burke & Prater, 2000; Geever, 2001; Quick & New, 2000).

Once you have identified a possible funding source, then, to the extent possible, prepare that funding source to receive your proposal favourably. The quality of your relationship may be as important as the quality of your proposal (Golden, 2001). Next, clearly think through just what the program or activity you are describing in your proposal is intended to accomplish. After this, figure out just what you actually have to do to meet that goal; that is, effectively plan your activity or program, including its likely costs and evaluation procedures. These steps warrant a significant investment of time and creativity. What you write in your proposal is the product of this effort. Consequently, it is well worth your time to take this preparation phase seriously.

Given the complex nature of some proposals, you may well want to assemble a team to guide both the planning and the proposal preparation. If you do not do this work up front, you are much less likely to be awarded a grant. If you do somehow get lucky and get a grant, though, your project may well fall apart because you have not built a proper foundation. Future funding is affected by how well you handle this project (Browning, 2000; Golden, 2001; New, 2001; Quick & New, 2000).

When you have clarified your purpose and approach, sit down and write your proposal following the guidelines provided by the funding source and organized in the way most meaningful to the funding source. After the proposal is written, packaged in an attractive, easy-to-read manner, and submitted (on time!), you need to muster the appropriate support to reinforce its positive reception.

Written proposals vary in length according to the requirements of each funding source. In some cases, a written proposal of one page will suffice. In others, you may need more than 100 pages to provide all the information requested. Although each funding source will have its own preferred format and areas of emphasis, there are some pretty standard components to a proposal. Your written proposal essentially responds to four questions.

- What problem are you trying to resolve?
- How do you intend to solve this problem?
- How much will this cost?
- How can you tell if your program works?

These four questions can be broken down into as many as 15 distinct proposal categories. These categories and many of the tips that follow have been drawn from our own experience and the guidance of numerous authors who describe the grant-seeking process (Browning, 2000; Burke & Prater, 2000; Coley & Scheinberg, 2000; Flanagan, 2000; Geever, 2001; Geever & McNeill, 1997; Golden, 2001; Mitiguy, 1978; Morth & Collins, 1996; New, 2001; Picker, 2001; Quick & New, 2000; Robinson, 1996).

The complexity of your proposal will be governed by your particular funding source. Most funding sources provide a clear set of guidelines for you to follow in preparing your proposal. Do follow these precisely (Smith, 1989). One of the major reasons proposals are rejected is simply their failure to follow prescribed guidelines (New, 2001). There is no need to make your proposal more complicated than required, and doing so may work against you. Your proposal may include some or all of these pieces.

- *Cover letter.* Keep this brief, rarely beyond one page. In this letter you tell the funding source who you are, what you intend to do, why, and how this relates to the funder's interests. This should be on your official letterhead, addressed to a specific person, and be signed by an officer of your organization.
- *Title page.* This states the title of the project, to whom it is being submitted, the date of submission, the name and address of the organization submitting the proposal, along with the name of a contact person (or proposal author) from the submitting organization.
- *Abstract or proposal summary.* This brief summary is one of the key elements of your proposal. In it you clearly and concisely describe your response to the four basic questions mentioned previously. In

addition, tell the funding source a little bit more about your organization. To some extent, this is an expansion of your cover letter. Still, this should be kept short, no more than two pages, generally much shorter than that.

- *Introduction.* In this section describe your organization in more detail. The purpose here is to demonstrate your credibility as an organization capable of pursuing a project. You may also include particularly interesting aspects about your organization as they relate to the project you are proposing.
- *Problem statement.* In this section provide some background information on the issue you intend to address. You may describe how long the issue has persisted in your area, how this issue is manifested (what does it look like?), and other efforts that have been undertaken to solve it. Describe the range and depth of the issue, both through your use of statistics and in narrative discussion. You want to communicate to the funding source that this is an important issue that demands attention.
- *Goals or proposed response.* Here you describe what needs to be done to address the situation or what long-range goals you seek. Do not describe your specific activities in this section; instead, clarify the broad accomplishments expected by your effort. You may also phrase this section in terms of solutions; that is, what broad solutions does this issue require?
- *Statement of objectives.* A program objective is a statement of a concrete, measurable result of your program within a specific length of time (Cavanaugh, 1980). These objectives relate to your goals. You cannot be vague here; clarity is important.
- *Implementation or methodology and management.* In this category tell the funding source exactly what you will do, and when, to accomplish your objectives. Tell the funding source how you will use your resources, including facilities, equipment, and personnel, to achieve your desired results. You will also describe how you will oversee the effective use of these resources, how you might disseminate information about the project, and your work to make ongoing improvements.
- *Personnel involved.* The people who will be working on your project are important. Provide a brief background description (one paragraph will usually suffice) on each person who will have an active role in the project.
- *Budget.* The funding source needs to know on what you intend to spend the money you receive. Prepare a line-item budget reflecting the various expenses required to undertake this project. Often, the budget section lists other sources of revenue and indicates which expense or portion of expenses will be covered by the source from which you are seeking funds.
- *Budget narrative.* In this section, briefly describe the expenses listed in the line-item budget. You may also provide a brief explanation or justification of the importance of these expenditures. Point out the amount and type of support the project will receive from your organization.
- *Future funding.* If your project involves more than a one-time activity, the funding source will probably want to know how you intend to continue the project after this particular grant runs out. Commonly, funding sources provide money for a limited period of time. If they intend to make an investment, they will want to know that you are currently preparing to keep the program (and their investment) alive.
- *Monitoring.* It's important that you keep track of your activities to see that you are doing what you said you were going to do. In this section, clarify how you intend to keep tabs on your proposed activities.
- *Evaluation.* The funding source will want to know how you will go about determining

whether you have met the stated goals, and why or why not.

- *Appendixes or addenda.* Put any information in this section that does not fit into any other category but is still important for the funding source to know. This could include endorsement letters from other organizations or noteworthy individuals, the names and titles of members of your board of directors or other active community supporters, clippings regarding your organization, affiliations with other organizations or other funding sources, and additional statistics or other supporting data.

## TIPS

- Do your homework on prospective funding sources. This can never be said enough. At the very least know who the key players are, what the source is looking for, and how they want you to relate to them.
- Keep your writing short and to the point. If you are not sure if something belongs in your proposal, it probably does not. Proposals to corporate givers and small foundations are typically short.
- Write in a straightforward, person-to-person style. Remember, these are people reading your proposals, not computers. Use active voice.
- Send your letter directly to the proper person, and double-check the correct spelling of names. Do not send "To Whom It May Concern" or "Dear Sirs."
- Avoid jargon, bureaucratic language, and acronyms. Funding sources are more impressed with what you can do than with how you can sling the lingo.
- Humanize the proposal. Let the voices of those who will benefit come through.
- The cover letter and proposal summary are the first things most reviewers look at. These are your keys. Make them work.
- The title of your proposal should be clear and grab interest.
- Ask questions. If any part of the guidelines is unclear, no matter how small, be sure to ask for clarification so you know exactly what to do.
- Throughout your proposal, make sure you clearly demonstrate how your project effectively furthers the goals of the funding source. Your goals are important, but so are theirs.
- Avoid the common problems that lead to proposal rejection: not clearly identifying and substantiating a significant problem, and lack of clarity about how monies will be used for project activities. Other common problems include methods not suited to the scope of the problem, no clear evaluation plan, objectives not clearly measurable, and an unreasonable time schedule (Coley & Scheinberg, 2000).
- The proposal will be reviewed by several people, so do not make them tear apart some fancy binding to make copies. Most prefer that the pages of your proposal be clipped together. Some do not even like staples.
- Make sure your proposal is easy to read, with lots of white space and type not smaller than 12 point.
- Have at least two other people read and comment on your proposal. These should be people who are not familiar with your work. It must be simple and easily make sense to them.
- Follow up. Do not sit around for weeks or months waiting for a reply. Unless you are instructed to do otherwise, contact the funding source about two weeks after you have delivered your proposal. Then ask when would be a good time to re-contact. You want the funding source to know that you are taking the proposal seriously, but you do not want to be seen to be bothering them. Also, this provides you with an opportunity to offer additional information that would be helpful in securing the grant or to clarify any misunderstanding. Further, this strengthens the personal relationship between you and your contact person at the granting organization. Strong personal relationships are often as important as strong proposals.
- If you do not get the grant, find out why. This communicates purposefulness on your part. Do not complain or criticize. You may have another opportunity. How you handle your learning and relationships now may affect the next opportunity.
- Say thank you. Even if you do not get the grant, it is important to express your appreciation for having been considered. You do hope that you will have an opportunity to work together in the future. Your "thank you" helps foster future opportunities regardless of the outcome of this particular proposal.
- Stay in touch once you have received the grant. From time to time send project updates, news clippings, letters from people who have benefited from the project, and other indications of your project's success. Pick up the phone for conversation on occasion too.

## Take A Moment To Discover

A proposal can have a number of elements. The complexity of a proposal is related to the complexity of the project for which funding is sought and the requirements of the funding source. The following list reviews seven different elements for a standard proposal. Put yourself in the place of a proposal evaluator. Critically look at each element of your proposal. Score each element from 1 (very poor) to 6 (superb). What would your total score be? What weaknesses did you discover? As it stands, would your proposal be funded?

*Summary* Clearly and concisely summarizes the request.

| | |
|---|---|
| I. Introduction | Describes the agency's qualifications or "credibility". |
| II. Problem Statement or Need Assessment | Documents the needs to be met or problems to be solved by the proposed funding. |
| III. Objectives | Establishes the benefits of the funding in measurable terms. |
| IV. Methods | Describes the activities to be employed to achieve the desired results. |
| V. Evaluation | Presents a plan for determining the degree to which objectives are met and methods are followed. |
| VI. Future or Other Necessary Funding | Describes a plan for continuation beyond the grant period and/or the availability of other resources necessary to implement the grant. |
| VII. Budget | Clearly delineates costs to be met by the funding source and those to be provided by the applicant or other parties. |

Source: The Grantsmanship Center.

## VERBAL PRESENTATIONS

Occasionally a verbal presentation may be required.

Some presentations will occur before the proposal submission. These may provide you with an opportunity to receive an invitation to submit a proposal. Others follow upon delivery of your proposal. These presentations allow the grantors to meet with you and discuss the merits of your project.

Some groups have turned a probable no into a yes with a well-handled presentation but the reverse can also happen as a result of a poor presentation.

### TIPS

- Anticipate objections, even draw them out. This gives you a chance to openly discuss whatever reservations may exist in the grantor's mind.
- Know your program, what you intend to accomplish, and how.
- Be straightforward. If the grantor feels you are being deceptive or beating around the bush, he or she may think you really do not know what you are talking about, or worse.
- Be well organized. Your presentation should flow logically from one subject to the next. Rambling around may cause the grantor's interest to wander away.
- Bring audio or visual enhancers to your presentation. These would include films, computer-generated presentations, charts, or photographs. Use these to support your presentation, not substitute for it.
- Put materials into the hands of the people who are hearing your presentation. Again, this could include charts and graphs or photographs. You may want to do this toward the conclusion of your presentation so that during your presentation the audience is looking at you, not the materials in their hands.

## COLLABORATION

When organizations work with one another rather than against one another to get funding it may be beneficial to all. Your organization can benefit from forming partnerships with other organizations, using your combined resources to seek out and secure funding. By dividing the work, both in getting funding and in completing the project, a lot more can get done. Many donors, whether individuals or foundations and government agencies, look favourably on collaborative efforts (Klein, 2000; Quick & New, 2000). Demonstrating community leadership on issues as sensitive as funding enhances the image of your organization to funders, constituents, and other key community players. More important, it may help stimulate a new way for organizations in your community to relate to each other, allowing you to accomplish much more (Fallon, 1993).

## ● STRINGS ATTACHED

Each source of funds comes with strings attached. Some are threads, some steel cables. If you depend on contributions from the general public, you must keep the trust of that public and continue to demonstrate your worthiness. If you receive money from the federal government, you may find the regulations governing the use of those funds make sense in Winnipeg, for example, but seem a little crazy in Quebec City. If United Way dollars support what you are doing, you may be expected to avoid controversial activities, especially those aimed at one of their large contributors.

Acknowledge that the strings are there and that you will have to keep on good terms with the puppeteer, or be willing to run the risk that some of what you want may be left dangling.

## ● CONCLUSION

No matter how big or small, old or new your effort is, you will need to generate additional resources. Many times you will be able to directly receive needed goods or services. Sometimes you will need to raise money to acquire them. Regardless of the approach you use, you will be asking other people, either as individuals or as representatives of organizations, to provide the resource support you need. Target your efforts to those most likely to respond favourably. Develop and nurture relationships with those who may be able to invest in your success and ask them to do so. Your request may take any number of forms: a direct person-to-person request, a letter, an organized presentation, or even a formal written proposal. Thoughtfully and purposefully prepare and deliver your request to increase the chances of a rewarding response. Acknowledge and thank the people who have considered contributing to the realization of your goals.

The various techniques described in this chapter should give you some direction toward your pot, or at least your cup, of gold. More than that, however, they should spark your own thinking, your own ingenuity. In your own unique fashion, refine the methods described here and come up with some creative ones of your own.

## HELPFUL WEBSITES

**Association of Fundraising Professionals**

www.afpnet.org

The Association of Fundraising Professionals (AFP) represents nearly 28,000 members in more than 190 chapters throughout the world, working to advance philanthropy through advocacy, research, education, and certification programs. The association fosters development and growth of fundraising professionals and promotes high ethical standards in the fundraising profession.

**Association of Professional Researchers for Advancement (APRA)**

www.apracanada.ca

A professional association open to Canadian researchers, front-line fundraisers, and others with an interest in the field of advancement research. The site includes extensive guidelines regarding privacy, ethics, and donor rights. Membership benefits include networking, access to a membership directory, a quarterly newsletter, and mentorship opportunities.

**Big OnLine**

www.bigdatabase.ca

This organization provides a comprehensive searchable database with detailed information and profiles on over 25,000 foundations, corporate donors, matching gift programs, in-kind donations and government grant makers. They also provide various writing tools (such as step-by-step guides as well as templates for the writing of funding proposals) and can offer fundraising consulting services.

**Canada Revenue Agency Charities Division**

http://www.cra-arc.gc.ca/chrts-gvng/menu-eng.html

The government site of the Canada Revenue Agency (CRA) registers qualifying organizations as charities, gives technical advice on operating a charity, and handles audit and compliance activities. The site includes listings of all registered charities in Canada, information for donors, and checklists for charities to review the responsibilities of operating a registered charity in Canada.

**Canadian Association of Gift Planners**

www.cagp-acpdp.org

This professional association of over 1,300 members brings together charitable representatives with donor advisers. Experts in charitable gift planning, members work with donors to achieve their highest philanthropic goals through thoughtful, tax-wise, well-planned giving.

**Canadian Council on Social Development**

www.ccsd.ca/pubs/2003/fm/fm.html#_blank

The council provides information resources and tools for organizations and communities on issues related to financing and capacity, both at the community and national levels.

**Canadian Fundraiser**

www.canadianfundraiser.com

This site provides information for the not-for-profit sector management on profit sector management information service includes a monthly newsletter from The Hillborn Group Ltd. (owner of Charity Village). They also offers a library of books on fundraising and nonprofit management as well as workshops in communities across Canada.

**The Centre for Non Profit Management**

www.cnpm.ca

The Centre for Non Profit Management at the University of Victoria "builds leadership and management capacity in the non-profit sector." It offers innovative education programs, conducts research, and prepares reference materials and resources for nonprofit organizations.

**Centre for Sustainability**

www.centreforsustainability.ca

The Centre for Sustainability (CFS), which serves British Columbia's not-for-profit sector, provides

*Continued*

a gateway to information and reference materials on organizational change and renewal, communications, marketing, fundraising planning, and working with consultants. It also publishes an e-newsletter and operates the Partners in Organizational Development Technical Assistance Program.

**Charity Village**

www.charityvillage.com

This is a major source of information, including news, jobs, services, and resources for Canadian nonprofits. The site has more than 3,000 pages of information and is accessed by over 25,000 people each day. It contains a wealth of vital information about funding sources, fundraising ideas, and fundraising resources.

The library on the website has many helpful articles and newsletters covering fundraising strategies, board development, and human resource management, as well as marketing, communications, and technology. Visit it at www.charityvillage.com/cv/charityvillage/lib.asp.

**Imagine Canada**

www.imaginecanada.ca

This organization serves charities in Canada. For a fee, it makes available its print or online directory of foundations. It contains information about topics such as trends in philanthropy and provides resources relevant to charities in Canada.

**Philanthropic Foundations Canada**

www.pfc.ca

This is the national membership organization for Canada's independent, grantmaking foundations. It is a registered charity, whose stated mission is to promote the growth and development of effective and responsible foundations and to foster a social and regulatory environment that encourages philanthropic contribution. On its website you can find information about philanthropy, grantmaking, and its network of members.

**Voluntary Sector Knowledge Network**

www.vskn.ca

This excellent website is part of the Centre for Non Profit Management. It includes information on fundraising with detailed descriptions on a wide range of topics, including leadership and governance; community and government relations; fundraising; financial management; accountability and evaluation; managing people and information and communications technology. Its "Ask a Mentor" service lets staff and board members from nonprofit organizations ask questions of specific interest to them. For books and periodicals on fundraising planning, sponsorships and donations visit its annotated collection: www.vskn.ca/fund/fund_booksr.htm.

CHAPTER TEN

# Getting the Word Out

**This chapter will help you better understand the following questions:**

- How can we spread the word about our community change efforts and get people to know about and be interested in what we are doing?
- How do we identify the people we need to reach?
- How do we communicate our message to the public?
- How do we gain the attention of the media?

Some things are too important to be kept secret. The need for the community change you are seeking and the attempts taken to bring about change fit nicely into this category. Getting information to people and getting information from them are crucial activities in your efforts to promote change.

As a change agent you will need to go beyond your professional circle of supporters and begin to foster a wider spread of community awareness and dialogue. To build needed community support, you will also need to reach out and inform people who do not know much about the issue and may never even have thought about it.

Earlier, we looked at ways to get information from and about your community. In this chapter we look at reasons to get information out as well as some of the ways you can reach people who can use the information to aid the cause you are working on.

Regardless of the size or type of your community—a social service agency, a neighbourhood, or even an entire city—your ability to effectively inform others is a great asset. Some methods described in this chapter (press conferences, for example) are more appropriate for informing larger audiences. Yet you can apply the basic concepts for reaching people with your message to all the different communities you focus on in your change efforts.

## IMPORTANCE OF MAKING YOUR EFFORTS KNOWN

Drawing attention to your actions and the need for them serves several purposes. Why you are communicating to people will affect how you choose to do it. Let's look at several major reasons you might want to get the word out.

### Let People Know You Exist

Your organizing effort is a new force in the environment. It will move people in new directions, sometimes in directions they do not want to go. This movement occurs when people react to what you and other members of your group or organization are doing. But you will have no reaction—you probably will have no members—if no one knows you even exist. This is the starting point and the first reason to publicize your intent and your action. People have to know there is an interest in changing things before they can decide what to do about it. Spreading the word will give some people hope and enthusiasm and other people worry.

## Stir Interest

People hear that old ways are going to be challenged. People start talking. People start thinking. In some cases, people even start acting. Provoke people. You do not have to get people mad, but you do have to get them thinking differently and thinking about behaving differently so they will begin to believe in the possibilities.

You have to overcome the inertia of inaction or acquiescence. The rumblings of interest begin to alter the circumstances in which you are operating. With your help, interest will build on itself, setting things in motion.

## Expose the Issue and Educate for Action

It is easy, and fairly common, to take refuge in ignorance. The security that comes with not knowing is a powerful force in keeping things as they are. Bringing the issue into focus shakes people out of their complacency.

It is sometimes safer to pretend a problem does not exist, especially if you feel powerless to do anything about it. When people begin to see what is really going on (at least from your perspective), they begin to understand the various aspects of the issue and, most important, how it affects them. Awareness makes it harder to tuck things away out of consciousness.

Ignorance is not always a purposeful choice. Sometimes people simply do not know. So many things compete for our attention that we scarcely notice some things, but we might be willing to do something about them if we did.

Those who are responsible for maintaining the problem would just as soon keep other people unaware. They especially do not want their own roles and their responsibilities for the problem or issue noticed, nor do they want to be held accountable for their actions, or lack of them. By exposing the ramifications of the problem and who is involved, you can agitate people and counter the very powerful process of ignorance.

Education, however, is not sufficient for action. Too many groups make the mistake of assuming that if people know about a problem they will act on it. They even have "education" as the major goal. Education may be a precondition for action, but in and of itself it is not necessarily action. Merely knowing about something does not guarantee action on it.

Once people have a clearer picture of a situation, you can introduce them to ways of putting their awareness into action. Help people see that they can act, and probably should. Show them how and what steps they can take. This is a necessary part of the process of educating to promote change. People who are aroused want to know what they can do. Do not leave them hanging. Take advantage of the opportunity you have created.

Education will help create a climate for change. Not everyone will be so concerned about an issue that they will want to spend their time working on it. Still, they may be supportive of those who do. You need this kind of support. A hostile or insensitive environment will make things harder for you and aid those resisting change. A more knowledgeable, supportive atmosphere affects the tone of the contest. Potential resisters may see the handwriting on the wall and make a less than concerted effort to maintain the status quo.

## Attract New Support

Building your effort involves building membership in it. The message you send out regarding the need for action will bring people into your group. People who care enough to move ahead will be glad to know that others are involved in the issue. Your organizing effort gives them a way to express their interest.

### Strengthen Affiliation

The notoriety or the positive image your effort receives increases the attachment of those who have already become involved. It contributes to a feeling that they are part of an alliance to be reckoned with. As members of such a group, they feel more important or more powerful. As other people come to regard the change effort more seriously, its participants are reinforced for their commitment. This bolsters resolve and enhances motivation to press forward with the work of the organization.

### Credibility

We will frequently mention credibility or allude to its importance. It is a central element necessary to your efforts to promote change. Are you real? Do you have the power you say you have? Is your information accurate? Your credibility will be challenged both directly and indirectly by supporters and opponents alike throughout the life of the change effort.

You are asking people to believe in what does not yet exist. This is not easily done. Whether for members, those you hope to influ ence, or the public in general, uncertainty is hard to act on. For people to commit to something, they need to let go of some fairly tendencies to stick with what they already know even if that is problematic. They require at least some evidence that letting go is a good idea. The less credible or believable something is, the more reluctant they will be to affiliate with it. The more they are able to believe that something is for real, the more willing they will be to respond to it.

If handled correctly, your efforts to communicate your presence, your purpose, and your progress will provide you with this most powerful benefit. Credibility establishes the foundation for all the other benefits. It makes them possible.

## IDENTIFYING THE PEOPLE YOU NEED TO REACH

You will be communicating different types of information to four different groups:

- Your supporters, whether active or general
- The target or response community
- The general public
- Members of the general public who might be especially touched by your organizing

It is most important that your membership be kept informed. Your participants should be apprised of the progress of and particular challenges to your operation. Tell them what is going on. Be sure your direct supporters are well informed about the issue or problem you are trying to rectify. Keep the issue before them to keep them in touch with the purpose you share and to deepen their understanding and commitment. From time to time provide a motivational piece. These are intended to maintain, and periodically heighten, enthusiasm. Finally, let participants know about specific organizational needs they may be able to meet.

Continue to educate other constituents of the action and benefit communities regarding the problem, the goals, the activities of the organization, and the sources of resistance. Keep them aware of roles they can fill.

Positive change results when people who have a good idea also have the power to implement it. Two fundamental things you need to communicate to the target community are the strength of your ideas and the strength of your support. Regardless of whether the target community actively opposes the changes, you will have to overcome some forms of resistance, even if that just happens to be old habits.

The target group should know what it is you expect them to do; that is, what and how they are to change. Extend opportunities to them to participate in solving the problem. Finally, they should be aware of the important activities of your organizing effort, including large and small victories that enhance its position in the eyes of other community members.

On some issues it is important to have the general public take notice. See Figure 10.1 for those who participate in the communication process. There are times when even relatively small changes would benefit from broader community awareness. When you communicate with the general public, you usually do so either to gain broad approval and sanction for your activities and concerns or to rouse it to action. Inform the public of the validity of your concerns and the unreasonableness of your opposition. You want the public to understand how your success will benefit them and that your failure will be their loss. Finally, you want the general public to know that you are alive and kicking. Let them know some of the things you are doing, and periodically remind them of your issues. Also, sometimes it is important to educate people about the ethical, philosophical, and practical concerns of the social and community issues that are the reason for your organizing efforts.

In some types of organizing, you will be empowering individuals who might not be involved and whom you might not even know. For example, if you are organizing on issues associated with identity by sexual orientation or gender with a specific group, others in the general public who share that identity might be especially touched and influenced by your actions. Your communications will show sensitivity to their special needs and the positive influence your local action may have more generally on people or communities who feel marginalized.

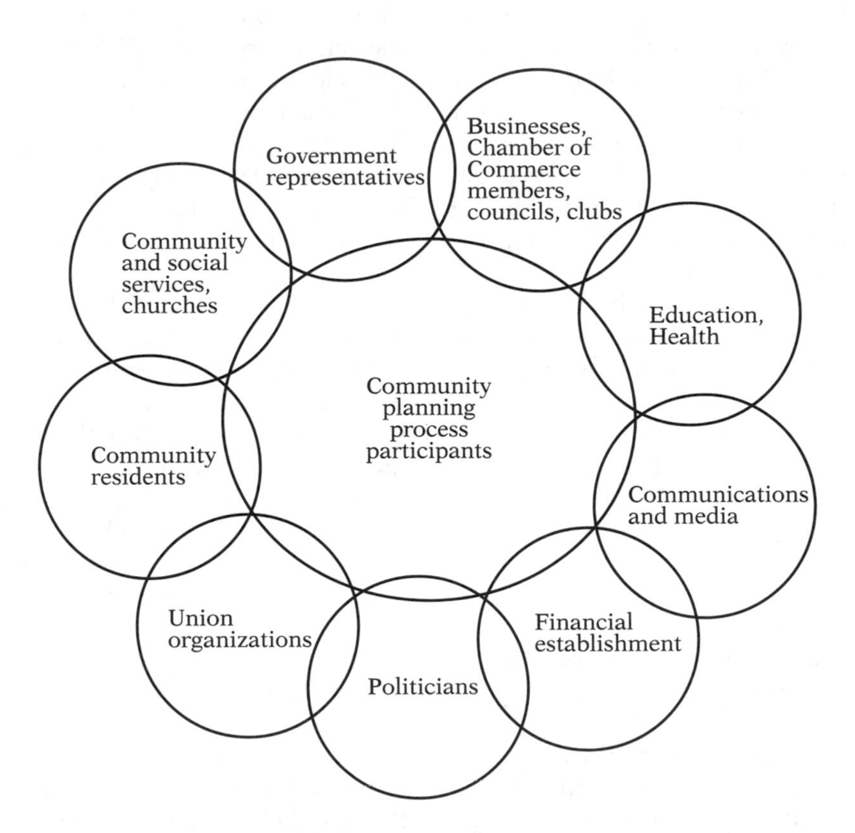


**FIGURE 10.1** Who Participates in the Process

Source: Service Canada website (www.servicecanada.gc.ca). Reproduced with the permission of the Minister of Public Works and Government Services, 2010.

## THREE IMPORTANT ISSUES IN COMMUNICATION

The basic reason you communicate with people is to get a reaction from them. You want them to think or to know something, do or not do something. Therefore, you take care (or at least you should) to prepare the proper message. The disappointment of many change efforts can be traced to a lack of attention in preparing and sending an effective message. To prepare an effective message, pay homage to the three Important Issues in Communication (see Figure 10.2):

- *The market:* the recipients of your message, the people from whom you want to get a reaction
- *The medium:* the technique or device you use to get the message to your audience
- *The message:* what your audience needs to hear to respond

When we fail, it is often because we start by saying what we want to say without giving adequate consideration to who is going to hear it and how. We get things backward. The message is the last thing we should consider. The audience is the first. The medium fits in between.

The entire process of getting the word out is driven by the reactions you want to get from the differing people. It is as simple and as complex as that. Paying attention to how the message, the medium, and the people you are trying to reach relate to each other will strengthen the impact of your communication. Just who are these people you want to influence? What response do you want from them? What do they need to hear to trigger that response? Will they respond best to facts, emotion, or intellectual argument? In what ways do they receive information? Which methods do they trust? Which of these can best carry the message you want to send? Which methods would your audience

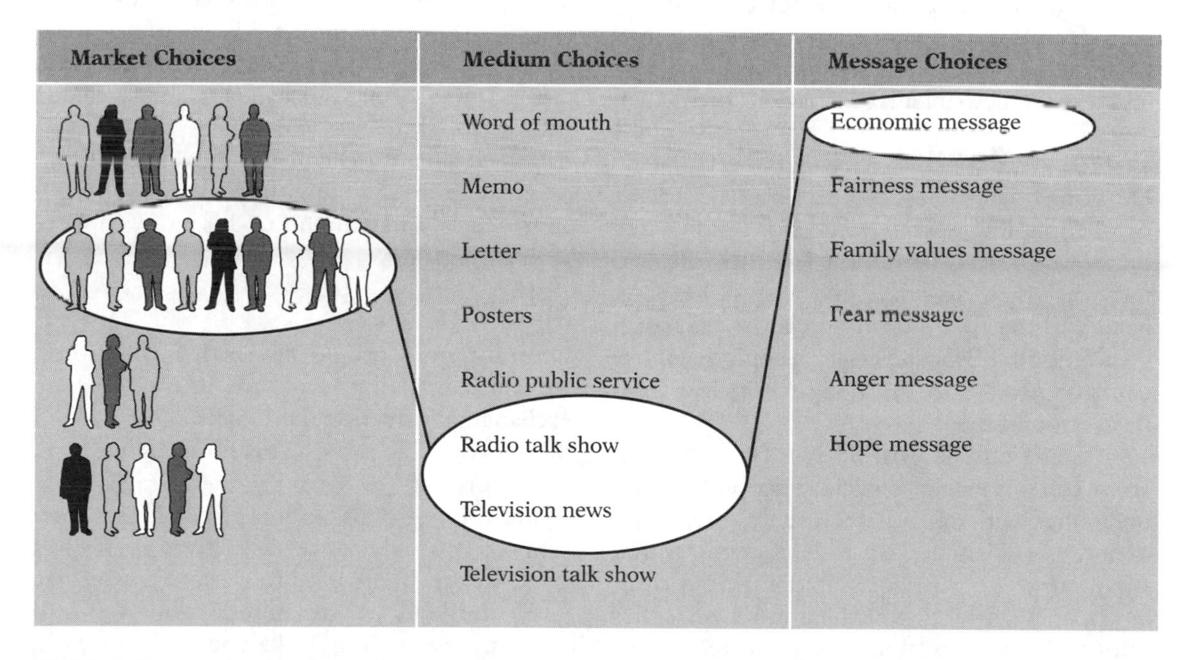


**FIGURE 10.2** The Three Important Issues in Communication

Example of relationship between the Three Important Issues in Communication: pick the right market, select the right medium, and send the right message.

consider to be appropriate for your message? You will probably want to consider other things as well, but this is enough to get you started.

The audience—the people you intend to influence, and therefore the messages you send—will no doubt vary from one change project to the next; so too will the vehicles you use for delivering the message to the market. Nonetheless, you will more than likely use some standard methods. You will be more effective if you understand how to use these methods to your advantage. Of course, in really effective community organizing, the audience also becomes change agents alongside of you.

## TECHNIQUES FOR SENDING THE MESSAGE THAT YOU CONTROL

Some methods for getting the word out are under your control or largely under your control. That is, your group is responsible for preparing and sending the message rather than having to convince or rely on someone else (such as the news media) to do that for you.

### Word of Mouth

Do not underestimate word of mouth! Talk it up! People involved in your effort should tell everyone they know (and a few they do not) just what they are doing and why. It has long been said that word of mouth is the best form of promotion. This is because people regard as truth or near truth the things they hear from those around them.

When you talk with people about the situation you are facing, especially people who are unfamiliar with it, be sensitive to their level of interest. Plant seeds; do not give lectures. Build curiosity; do not assume it. Avoid turning people off by giving them more than they want to know. It is usually better to tell people a little less than they need to know rather than a little more. The type and number of questions they ask will let you know how interested they are. On the other hand, do not hold back information that is important for them to know about their well-being. That could come across as condescending or patriarchal. Disclosure of information is a bit of a dance.

One effective technique involves asking questions and then listening. Set people to thinking about how they feel about the issue, and see if they can relate it to themselves in some way. Try to pick up on that feeling. Guide people to reach their own conclusions on the matter. But also be willing to change how you think about the issue based on their feedback. They become more attached if these judgments are their own beliefs, not just yours. You should have a few standard points you want to make. Some people will make a judgment on your effectiveness based on how well they think you listen.

Consider a more formal campaign in addition to spur-of-the-moment conversation. This may include a planned strategy with specific individuals "assigned" to those you particularly want to influence. This communication can still be done in informal ways, such as telephone conversations or e-mail exchanges—it is just that people in your campaign are assigned people to talk to. Or you may assign teams to directly contact individuals in certain groups or areas in your community. A door-to-door approach in a neighbourhood is an example of such a campaign.

### Meetings

Obviously, the people involved in your project will be meeting from time to time to plan, exchange information, and make decisions, but other people meet too. This provides you with an opportunity to spread your message. Concentrate on groups and organizations whose support you would like to cultivate. This is a good way to build allies too. Most groups will give you the five or ten minutes you ask for to make a presentation. Make your points clearly, using examples and facts to back them up. That is, be prepared. Using a little emotion often helps but be careful not to overdo it.

Let the members of the group know what you want from them. Ask for it, clearly. Then be quiet. Wait for the response. Be present in any of the group's discussions on the issues that are important for you and for the group. You may be able to inject some insight, and it will be a lot harder for them to turn you down when they are looking at you. Hang around if you can at the end of meetings to have chats with people. It is often an effective means of getting your message across—and it is friendly!

Always leave some written material behind. A one-page summary of your points or a brochure and your request are usually all that is necessary. Make sure that whatever you leave has your group's name, if you have one, and a way for people to contact a specific person in your group.

## Newsletters

A regular means of communicating to your members is necessary to keep everyone linked to the effort. If your group has more than a handful of members and these members do not see each other regularly, you might want to develop a newsletter. Newsletters enhance the feeling of legitimacy and permanence of an organized group. They help supporters keep in touch with your group and its agenda. But newsletters take time to produce, and if you need to pay for printing and mailing, they can cost money. Of course, today many of the newsletters are sent by e-mail but they still require writing, design, and layout so they require resources.

A few simple suggestions will help your newsletter accomplish its purpose of communicating to supporters and strengthening their sense of affiliation: Keep it simple and personal, keep it regular, and put one person in charge.

First and foremost, someone needs to take on preparation of the newsletter as his or her major contribution to the group. If nobody really wants this job, do not try to put out a newsletter. You would only get a couple of issues out before it would fizzle and that might give the false impression your organizing effort is failing.

Next, make sure it is published on a regular basis, preferably monthly. Sporadic or hit-and-miss publications give the impression that other efforts by the organization are sporadic or halfhearted.

Finally, remember that you want people to actually read the newsletter. Rarely should it exceed four sides in length. (There are, of course, exceptions to this, particularly for newsletters whose purpose is to examine a range of community issues.) A basic line-up of articles would include these regular columns: news, editorials, featured personality, and upcoming activities or events. That's all you need.

Do not forget that your change effort is made up of people, not just issues. Look for ways to spread credit around when describing gains the effort has made. When featuring an individual, profile the personal side, not just the professional side, and always mention some reason the individual is supporting the cause. Use humour, cartoons, pictures, or simple graphics, and keep the articles short. Solicit articles from supporters to distribute the workload and promote a sense of ownership.

Newsletters are good for reaching outside your group as well. Include people on your distribution list who are not active in your effort but who should be kept informed about your organizing effort, particularly members of the news media. Features in your newsletter can become the basis of news stories. It also is a way of keeping your effort alive and keeping an ongoing awareness of it to outsiders.

### Take a Moment to Discover

Today you will probably pass by quite a few signs that beckon your attention to a community event or to an item of information someone thinks you should know. Will you read any of these? Maybe a few, but not most. What do you think determines this? What can you learn from your answer?

### ● CHANGE AGENT TIP

Places where people are bored are wonderful places to post or leave materials you want people to read. Elevators, grocery store checkouts, laundromats, doctors' offices, food banks, and buses are some favourites. Of course, nothing beats the back of the door in the stall of a public washroom.

## Brochures

There seems to be a natural desire for some people to want to develop brochures. Before you do, stop and ask yourself: Who is supposed to read this brochure, how will they get it, and what are they supposed to do once they have read it? If you cannot come up with good answers that justify the time and possible expense of printing a brochure, you should not produce one. Unless your change effort involves establishing a permanent program or alliance or organizing a significant conference, you probably do not need a brochure.

If you decide you need a brochure, there are some basic things you should know. Most brochures are simply a standard 8 1/2- by 11-inch sheet of paper folded in thirds. This arrangement gives you five panels for graphics and information and a back panel for an address if it is to be mailed.

The purpose of your brochure will be informational, giving your vision for change, answering questions and conveying pertinent details, or invitational, arousing curiosity and encouraging some steps toward participation in something. Decide which emphasis you want, and stick to it. If you want people to read it, keep these tips in mind as you develop your brochure:

- Think space; brochures with too many words are rarely read.
- Keep your sentences short and avoid jargon.
- Use a hook to grab attention and get people to peek inside; bold statements or questions often do the trick.
- Work with an experienced printer; most will provide you with valuable guidance.
- Consider using a union printer; aside from philosophical reasons to do so, some groups will scrutinize your literature wanting to see the union label.
- Think about how it can be presented as a PDF file on the computer so it can be sent electronically.

Using the desktop publishing program on your computer, you can easily play around with a number of options to develop a brochure. You can design and print a brochure quickly for an immediate need, but for wider distribution and ongoing use you will want to have a well-printed piece on high-quality paper.

## Position Papers

If your group has taken an official position on a particular matter, you may want to prepare a clearly written statement that convincingly articulates your position. This is particularly useful in communicating your point of view to government bodies, community task forces, and the news media. A position paper provides an explicit statement of your beliefs and protects you from people who want to misconstrue your position. It also provides you with a good tool to help shape the development of policy, especially if you are trying to influence the decisions of a working group looking into the matter. Other groups will rely on the work you have done, sometimes using your work in place of work they would otherwise have to do for themselves. If you offer your viewpoint only verbally, you have to trust that your comments will be remembered, and remembered accurately. A position paper can serve as a backup to

● CHANGE AGENT TIP

Someone in your group, maybe you, will be talking to other groups of people to inform them about your issues and to draw their support. Here are a few tips that can increase your effectiveness and comfort.

**Two Essential Questions**

- What do you want from this group?
- What do they need to hear or know in order to respond?

**Basic Outline for Presentations**

- Describe what you are going to talk about overall; introduce key topics.
- Describe the specific topic or subject of your presentation; define the topic if necessary.
- Identify who you are to be able to talk about this subject.
- Describe why this subject/issue is important.
- Present information on the issue.
- Give examples of what this subject/issue looks like in everyday life.
- Describe what you would like the group/audience to do; specify the nature of your request.
- Describe who will benefit from the group's action; particularly identify how the group can benefit or how the people they directly care about can benefit.
- Summarize key points.
- Thank the group for the opportunity to present, their attentiveness, and their response.

**Some Tips**

- Build a common connection between you and the audience and relate your message to what is important to them.
- Get the audience involved by asking questions to get them thinking.
- Personalize your message; tell it through the eyes and voices of those most affected.
- Provide concrete data and the views of other experts.
- Provide a simple handout; one page is generally best.
- Show a few slides, pictures, or graphics to enhance your words; this can even be one word or one sentence.
- Make eye contact; even just looking at foreheads works.
- Use humour; do not force it though.
- Have a standard story or phrase you can use.
- Compliment the audience whenever possible.

amplify the points you make when using other forms of communication.

The length of a position paper will vary according to the complexity of the issue you choose to address. It may be as short as a single page, or it may be 25 pages long. The paper should outline why the issue at hand is relevant to your group, why your group has authority to speak to the issue, what your position is, and how you support your position. Your support should demonstrate philosophical, rational, and factual justification.

If you are preparing a paper that exceeds five pages, provide an abstract that summarizes the entire paper in two or three paragraphs. Use headings and subheadings to highlight key sections. Supply a bibliography showing the sources you used to develop your position. For particularly long papers, it is also generally a good idea to include a table of contents. As with any written material, make sure it is well written.

## Community Presentations

Making presentations to other community groups or at a community forum is a useful way to shape the community's perception of your group's concerns and establish the climate for change. This affords you the opportunity for a face-to-face discussion with people who are themselves part of an organized power base or who are interested in community affairs.

You need to identify people associated with your change effort who are interested in making presentations and solicit invitations for them to speak. In some cases, you may need to train them either in public speaking or in the facts associated with the social change your group is associated with. Each of these elements is important.

Not everyone is interested in public speaking, and certainly not everyone is good at it. Ask your group members and supporters to volunteer for this assignment and also ask them to identify people they think would be good speakers. Then make a particular effort to recruit people who have a special interest and ability in public speaking. Sometimes the most effective public speaker can turn out to be someone in your community who has never done it before but is close to the issue and understands it intimately. Public speaking is not something you want to talk people into doing.

Training is an important component of your program. Each speaker should be comfortable with her or his standard presentation, be well versed in the organization's goals and positions, and be practised at handling questions, particularly the tough ones. Each speaker should learn how to relate your group's concerns to the concerns of the audience. It is probably good to attend some of the engagements so you can see what is working. Sometimes you do not need to interfere with the speaker's message when you judge how effectively the audience is receiving it. Be open to creative suggestions from community members for engagement of others.

Seek out opportunities to make presentations. Many groups use guest speakers. This includes college classes, civic and fraternal organizations, community affairs groups, religious groups, and others. Libraries, hospitals, and major employers often sponsor community lecture series. You may want to present to another community group that is involved in change even if they are an informal group. They can turn out to be important allies. Look in the community events calendar in the newspaper to get an idea of the type of speaking possibilities typical of your community. Then send out a letter to appropriate groups announcing your availability and respond quickly to the invitations you receive.

In some cases, your speakers' program should be part of a purposeful campaign. It is more effective if you target particular constituencies you want to influence. Personally arrange opportunities to address specific groups whose members may play a role in any community debate on your concerns.

## Fliers and Posters

Fliers and posters can be inexpensive ways to notify a lot of people or foolish ways to waste a lot of paper. There are many examples of effective posters—often with a striking image or a simple slogan to catch the eye. You probably pass by them every day. With advent of desktop publishing and graphic programs, community groups have been able to create quite sophisticated images and deliver clear messages.

By giving thought to just a few things, you can improve the quality of the ones you produce. The first point to think about is how you are going to distribute your material. If you produce 500 fliers, you want to make sure that 500 end up in public, not neatly stacked on somebody's desk. You cannot hand people a fistful of fliers and expect that they will distribute them for you. The process must be more purposefully managed. This matter should be cleared up before you print your first piece.

The next point concerns where you post your information so people will notice it. Places where people go to look for information are obvious, though not always the best, choices.

Too many bulletin boards are so cluttered with outdated information that nobody really pays attention to them. Most of the time people will not stop to read a poster, so it is a good idea to put them in places people are moving toward or where they are already stopped.

Your message has to capture attention. Striking design and sharply contrasting colours do this. One dramatic word or picture will command more attention than several. Think space. A few easy-to-read words is far better than an essay. Finally, tell people what they need to know. If you can do this in a provocative or clever way, all the better; the reader will remember more.

## Social Networking

Social networks have become a common mechanism for communication. Social networks such as MySpace, Facebook, and others allow users—individual or communities—to interact with one another, particularly with those who have common interests. The number of users has increased dramatically. MySpace claimed to have around 300 million users at the beginning of 2008; Facebook claims to have around 13 million, which includes 85 percent of university students in North America (Kwon & Wen, 2010).

Using traditional interpretations of social network theory, Kwon and Wen (2010) draw on Garton et al.'s definition of social networks:

> [a] set of social entities that includes people and organizations that are connected by a set of socially meaningful relationships and who interact with each other in sharing similar values.

Social networks move people away from face-to-face contact and toward online communities. Web-based services also value relationships of individuals within communities and provide a means to share information and to forge connections. Social networks are a valuable means of connection and communication for change agents.

Community groups have especially become actively involved in social networking sites, which are conducive to quick messages, widespread delivery of messages, and creating an online community of like-minded people. Social networking sites have become a requirement for most community groups to make people aware of their events. Another advantage is the ability they give people to respond quickly and easily to say if they are attending, so you have a sense of how many people are coming and can plan accordingly, and who is attending (if a key person declines the invitation, for example, you may need to follow up with a call and try to convince them). Because of the efficiency of communication and immediacy, social networking has been used effectively to create a ground swell of activism about time-sensitive issues, an issue being considered in Parliament, or an intrusion such as unwanted construction in a neighbourhood.

## Internet and Online Resources

Pretty much every activity discussed above can be done online—even group meetings through chat. Increasingly, people look to the Internet for information and communication, so be conscious to design all your materials so that they can be delivered as PDFs or word-processed files as well. Sometimes it is quite a simple matter to reorganize material. Other times, think of the special qualities and creativity that the Internet makes possible. The Internet offers a host of possibilities for getting your message out to the world—or just to your neighbourhood. Websites, electronic newsletters, listservs, discussion groups, and other options are available to you. But remember, it is a complementary tool— community organizing is all about direct contact between people in the real world.

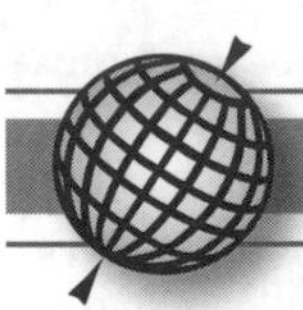

## GLOBAL PERSPECTIVES

PAPUA, NEW GUINEA—Real dialogue (or deep mutual personal speaking and listening) . . . is not just telling, it is listening. It is not just teaching, it is learning *with*. It is not extending knowledge; it is discovering the richness of knowledge already present in the life of the people. . . . As the animator listens and shares in the life of the community, he/she will become aware of the discontents, the worries, the deep and nagging questions of the people, the social, economic, and political affairs. As the animator begins to see and understand, then his/her role becomes more concrete because now the animator can help the people to see. This can be done by re-presenting to the people the life situations they are having difficulty seeing. Their condition is like being inside a box and therefore not being able to see the box. A re-presentation can help the people to get out of the box to see it. (Melanesian Council of Churches, 1977, p. 220)

MEXICO—Information and discussions about sexuality and human rights are necessary precursors to social change. Telemanita uses television and video to advance the progressive organizing work of lesbians in Latin America. This activist-media organization has trained more than 60 women representing 40 groups in the region, sponsored 5 annual screenings of videos made by women, and produced a number of videos . . . about Latin American lesbians, which have all enjoyed both regional and international distribution. Telemanita also co-hosted the first Encuentro Metropolitano de Lesbianas y Lesbianas Feministas in Mexico City, and has co-sponsored various lesbian film festivals in Mexico, Costa Rica, Puerto Rico and Colombia. (Allen et al., 2002, p. 18)

## REVIEW OF METHODS OTHER PEOPLE CONTROL

Some people are in the business of communicating information, and at times you will use them to help get the word out. You can pay public relations and advertising companies to help you with this. Among other services, they will help you design materials and develop and buy advertising. If you have a lot of money, you may want to buy their expertise. Check around to determine what professional assistance and paid advertising can do for you and which agency can best serve your needs. Of course, when you do this you are talking about an even bigger commitment of financial resources, and it may run counter to the notion of community members working together on an issue. There are times it makes sense however.

Most change efforts are not beset by the problem of what to do with all that extra cash. They need to figure out how to do things for little or no money. As we said in other chapters, do not forget that sometimes paid professionals are willing to volunteer for a community change effort because it is close to their heart or they are community members. Some people in the communication business will help you publicize your concerns for little or no cost. There are other ways, as well, to communicate with little cost. These fall into four categories: other groups and organizations, public service advertising, entertainment and public affairs programming, and news media.

When it comes to communicating outside your group to the rest of the community, it is important that multiple people are included. If it is always your face that is in front of the cameras, and if your words are the only ones quoted in the press, people outside (and maybe even inside) your group will begin to think that the group is just you and a bunch of followers. This is not a helpful image to promote. In addition, members of your group may start to feel

Salim October / Shutterstock

Learning how to become media savvy will assist you in promoting your work.

disempowered if the change effort is associated only with you.

Make a special effort to have a number of faces for the public to see and a variety of voices who can speak on the issues you (all) are facing. To establish easy access to your group, identify a particular individual as a contact person for those outside the organization who want to get your group's views and reactions to issues or events. The contact person may then help connect those who have such requests with any one of the organization's members who is prepared to respond. It may be appropriate to have one contact person, but it is most definitely not right to feel that only one person really knows what is going on, that only one person should get the attention. A number of people can represent you well if representation becomes an expectation and a responsibility. Some members will be better than others, yes, but some are definitely better than one.

## Other Groups and Organizations

The main ways other groups can help you are by allowing you to make a presentation to their members and by providing you space or coverage in their publications. Think of all the publications in your community in addition to the regular newspapers: employee newsletters, social service newsletters, and community interest group mailings to name a few. Most of these are potential vehicles to carry your message to a specific constituency. This is particularly true if the group's interests are similar to yours or if a member of another group is involved in your project.

Personally contact the individual in charge of the publication. Be ready to explain how information on your project would be valuable or of interest to their readers. Ask for publication guidelines and deadlines. You will be surprised at how frequently your request for publication is accepted.

Groups who share a similar viewpoint can assist you in other ways. On some occasions, say, at a news conference or a public hearing, other organizations may offer public statements on your behalf to lend emphasis and credibility to your assertions. They can also help by making routine announcements for you to their own constituencies. When you thank assisting organizations for their help, let them know of any reaction or benefit you received as a result of their assistance.

## Public Service Advertising

Many change efforts use this form of communication to enhance their efforts to reach the public. The standard approaches include free billboard space, newspaper community announcement columns, electronic bulletin boards, and radio and television public service announcements.

### Billboards

Outdoor advertising companies might donate billboard space to community groups for special projects or events. Usually, this also includes the cost for putting up the signs. The signs are posted on a space-available basis. This means that some of your signs may stay up for a long time in some very out-of-the way location or for a short time in a prime spot. Customarily all you have to pay for is printing. The billboard company can direct you to printers who handle this type of work, and the outdoor advertising company will show you how to design a billboard, including some tricks that will help you reduce your printing costs. Be aware that your sign should have no more than 10 words on it. Also, the sign company may not be sure just when there will be free space to hang your sign, so make sure you give them plenty of lead time.

### Newspapers

Newspapers run several community announcement columns. Typically, one column provides information on upcoming community events, whereas another describes services or resources available in the community. Each column appears regularly on a certain day, say, every Sunday or every Thursday. Watch for the section in which the columns run, and then contact the editor for that section. The editor will let you know what you have to do to get your information printed. In addition to big city or national newspapers, do not forget the many local community papers that can reach people close to your change effort and in some cases give a more local community feel to your message. Seek out the papers that reach differing communities by identity and think of the many communities your group members belong to. For example, there may be many Spanish-speaking people in your community or the broader community affected by your change. Try to place an article or ad in a Spanish-language paper. Perhaps you want to reach the LGBTT community members and are uncertain whether they feel welcome in your change effort. You may decide to make sure to get the word out through a paper focused on a LGBTT readership.

Many newspapers have an online events column listing more community activities than appear in the paper. You can go to the paper's website and add your event to the list there as well.

### Electronic Bulletin Boards

A number of communities have their own bulletin board and allow groups to post events and other activities. Some larger organizations, such as the United Way, also provide bulletin boards offering a community calendar.

### Radio and Television Public Service Announcements

Some of the following suggestions are drawn from information prepared for the United Way by Ruby and O'Brien (1978) and Smucker (1999). Public service announcements (PSAs) are not the same thing as news stories. They are,

## CAPTURING CONCEPTS

### SOCIAL NETWORKING

Although you have effective control over your message on social networking sites, remember that sites such as Facebook and Myspace are commercial enterprises. They are not constructed solely for the purposes of community betterment, although they can be an effective tool.

**MySpace**

MySpace, the largest of all social networks on the web, is the third most visited site in the United States. Users communicate on blogs and forums, share pictures and videos, and create groups based on common interests. Many nonprofit and philanthropic groups use the website.

**Facebook**

Facebook has become increasingly complex. Users can post text, images, and video. You can choose levels of privacy so that your message is widespread or addressed to a key group of people. You can communicate publicly or privately. It is an effective complementary tool and is used by all ages. Some communities, such as the LGBTT community, have used Facebook effectively to communicate locally as well as globally about local, national, and international issues and events.

**Profiles**

One of the best ways to start having an online presence for your group is to create a profile for it on a social network site and invite people to become online members of the site. You can post video, text, and pictures on your profile. You can also send updates to group members from this profile to keep them informed. In some cases, people may be so committed to your cause or action that they will include a link to your profile on their personal profile page. They may also update their personal status to mention your events or activities.

in effect, commercials for your project. They are handled by different departments at the station and are seen as a service to the community and to the organization featured. They usually describe a service the organization offers, a need the organization has, or an upcoming organization activity.

*Radio PSAs.* Radio PSAs are relatively easy to prepare. It is helpful to contact each station to find out if any particular format is preferred. This serves a number of purposes. First, it establishes contact between you and the station. Second, it helps you provide the station with material that is easy for it to use. Third, it gives you a good reason to do a follow-up contact with the station to ask if your materials were in the proper form and if they have any questions regarding the content. You are really doing a follow-up to remind them of who you are and to reinforce the importance of your announcement. Follow-up contact is important whether or not you made a previous contact. Now, most public service directors will tell you this is not necessary, that they will air whatever they can fit in. In actual practice, though, they do develop certain preferences, whether they know it or not. They tend to air more frequently those announcements that are easy for them to handle, that are well written and well prepared, and that help people they know and like. I have seen significant differences in results between groups who simply send out material and hope it gets played and those who put in a little extra effort to establish contact and prepare their material well.

Make no mistake; this is a very competitive business. Radio stations routinely receive many requests for "free advertising." You need to do something to make yours stand out from the rest. Here are some guidelines to help increase the odds that your message will get on the airwaves.

• Write your message in a way that sounds good when it is read out loud. Most radio PSAs are not prerecorded, though some are. The deejays do not want to read a statement that sounds too awkward or stilted. Read your announcement over a few times and modify it until you get the right sound. Though the deejays will probably change it a bit themselves to suit their own style, the less work they have to do, the better.
• Time your announcement. Standard spots are 10, 15, or 30 seconds in length. Often stations just want their deejays to describe your announcement in a sentence or two. Each station will have its preferred standard. At the end of each announcement, note its length. Remember that professional announcers can read with emphasis faster than you can. A general guideline is two and one-half words per second.
• Type your announcements in large type using capital letters only. If you have proper names, spell them out phonetically as well. Use double or triple spacing and wide margins. Some stations that use shorter PSAs prefer that the announcements be typed on index cards.
• Include some sort of hook to get the listeners' attention. People don't remember boring messages. Probing questions, humour, and dramatic statistics are good devices. Some stations like announcements that have some emotional content (but refrain from being too melodramatic), whereas others prefer those that are purely descriptive or factual. If you have not discovered preferences while doing your "homework" on the stations, then send two versions of the same announcement.
• If you include a phone number in your announcement, it should be the last thing in your announcement. Repeat the number if you can.
• Some stations will let you record your own PSA. This personalizes the message more. Using your own name in the announcement further individualizes it.
• If you have an ongoing need for public service airtime, consider using a three-weeks-on, two-months-off airing schedule. Periodically rewrite your messages. This schedule keeps your messages fresh with both the audience and the station, while it gives the impression that you are always around.
• Enclose a brief cover letter with your material. This should describe who you are, mention the importance of the announcement to the community and your program, and ask the station for their help in informing the public.
• If you can make the time (and you really should try), it will help your cause to hand-deliver your announcements to the station. This is particularly true the first few times you work with a station before you get to know the people at the station and they get to know you.
• Send a follow-up thank-you to stations that aired your message. Note any response you received from the community that could be related to their support.

*Television PSAs.* The process for television public service announcements is similar to that for radio except that television *PSAs* have both the benefit of, and the requirement for, visual support. You can make your production as simple or as complex as your time, skill, and budget will allow. Television stations prefer to air announcements that are well made, so even if your production is simple, avoid looking cheap.

There is a lot of help available to assist you in producing your spot. Community-access cable television stations will train you in the use of video equipment. Students from the media or public relations departments of the local college or university may be able to help you as part of a class project. Advertising companies occasionally donate their services to the right cause if requested to do so by the right person. Even the local network affiliate station may produce your announcement at very little cost if a key person at the station takes a real interest in your project. Here are some suggestions to help you get your message across.
• Get to know the public service director at each station. The person who fills this role will also have other duties at the st ation. She or he will give you helpful directions on how to

work effectively with the station. Because each station may have some unique procedures, ask for directions and follow them.

• The written format of a television PSA uses two columns. The left column provides the directions for the video (for example, if you are using slides, it would show the sequence in which they should appear), and the right column provides the directions for the corresponding audio.

• If you are using slides to convey your point, use clear 35-mm slides with a horizontal presentation. Remember that a television screen has a 3:4 ratio, so any artwork you prepare should conform to that ratio. Your slides will probably be cropped, so take this into account when selecting pictures. Pictures that convey action are usually better than those showing someone's face, unless the face communicates a certain drama or elicits an emotional response. Use one picture for every 8 to 10 seconds of audio. Too many different visuals are distracting.

• Having a local personality as a spokesperson can give you credibility and recognition. It also makes producing the spot a relatively easy matter. (Do not use a media personality or your spot will only run on the station for which the individual works.) Avoid the talking head approach; cut away from the speaker a couple of times to show some other action, or have the speaker involved in the action. Get a signed release from each person seen in your announcement.

• Your visuals will tell your story. Thoughtfully consider what you want your viewer to feel. Then choose images that will produce that response. In fact, turn the sound off when you are reviewing your PSA. If you are getting your point across well by the visuals alone, you have done a good job.

• Prepare an audio script, perhaps including music, that evokes a response from the viewer and complements the video portion of your spot.

• Standard television PSAs are either 10, 20, or 30 seconds in length. Ten-second or even 9-second spots have a better chance of airing. There may be more open time slots for this length and, since many PSAs are 30-second productions, there will probably be fewer spots with which yours will have to compete.

• You may have a better chance getting your spot aired on independent stations. Though their audience may be smaller, this may be offset by the fact that your announcement is shown more often. It is worth it to make a special effort with these stations.

• Many stations are willing to make a dub (a copy) of your PSA and to send the dub to other stations.

• Get to know the traffic manager at each station. This person slots the paid commercials and the PSAs and, in some cases, has discretion in deciding which PSAs get aired and when. If there is some open time that can be filled with PSAs, and they know you and like your project, you are likely to have more success.

## Entertainment and Public Affairs Programming

Essentially this approach involves appearances on talk shows. Community talk shows have long been the staple of local television programming. You will reach some people who have an interest in your community, and you have the opportunity to educate viewers. An additional benefit is that it makes your supporters feel good. There is something about being on TV that makes people feel important. It can be fun to see your group or members of the group on the air. It also hones your skills in representing your project to the public. What you receive from an appearance on one of these programs is certainly worth the small effort they require.

Many opportunities are also possible with radio talk shows, and they can be quite supportive. For example, many university-based radio stations tend to have politically progressive shows and are interested in community issues and actions. Public radio stations and television stations such as CBC often are in need of informative community change agents, especially for phone-ins on their local and regional stations. You can also volunteer with the National Campus and Community Radio Association, an organization with 72 station partners across Canada. This association is open to community activities, student leaders, and members of the community in general (www.ncra.ca).

A number of simple steps can help you take advantage of the potential these television and radio programs offer you.

*Do a little homework on the show itself.* Watching or listening to the show a few times before your appearance will give you a sense of the program's flavour and an understanding of how the host approaches topics and works with the guest. You may pick up on the host's biases, way of asking questions, or a propensity to do most of the talking or to let the guest have a free rein. Most hosts want to set their guests at ease because a comfortable guest is a talkative and engaging guest.

*Get the facts straight.* Your use of statistics or ability to cite a particular study communicates that you are well informed on the subject and deserve some consideration. A simple technique is to prepare an index card that outlines the points you want to address. Next to each, note a statistic or reference to jog your memory. When doing a radio show, you can keep your index cards right in front of you as well as any other material you want to use. If you are doing a call-in show, you are likely to hear from people who disagree with you or who don't fully understand your perspective. This gives you a wonderful opportunity to show the strength of your ideas. While preparing, review your list of points and imagine that you are on "the other side." What would your objections be? Consider how your facts and reasoning could counter those objections. You can add these notes to your index cards as well. This exercise will help you communicate to supporters and opponents alike.

*Provide background material to the show host.* When you schedule your appearance, ask the host how much in advance he or she would like this information from you. Usually a week in advance is sufficient. You can suggest this. Provide the host with a small packet of information regarding your effort that includes a one-page description of your group, what it intends to accomplish, and why. Also, provide a set of sample questions that address points you would like to have emphasized and that can guide the host in developing additional questions. Clearly indicate that these are sample questions; do not imply that the host is incapable of coming up with inquiries of his or her own. (The less

## • CHANGE AGENT TIP

Orchestrate call-in shows. This is a simple way for you to influence the direction of the conversation in a way that puts your efforts in the most favourable light. You have taken some pains to get airtime and to prepare yourself well. Now complete the job. Use the airtime fully to your benefit. It is rare that this is done effectively.

You need just a handful of supporters, each prepared with two questions. Each person has a primary question and a backup question in case an "unscheduled" caller phones in with a question that is close to one of your prepared ones. Use good judgment. Do not overdo things, and do not ask a question that has already been asked by someone else.

When you prepare your questions, include some that appear to be hostile to or in opposition to your point of view, but ones for which you have a good answer. Also, write them in the way that people really talk. Perfectly proper grammar and a two-dollar vocabulary are not commonplace on call-in shows. Establish some kind of order or time schedule for your supporters to call in.

controversial your project, the more comfortable the host will be in using these questions.) Other elements can include newspaper stories on your project, position papers or statements you have produced, a list of your goals and objectives, general project descriptions, or brochures. Do not overwhelm the host. Just pick from whatever you have that would give someone a good understanding of your concerns and your organization, and use a marking pen to highlight key sections.

You want to make things as easy for the host as possible. A well-prepared host invigorates the discussion and helps you emphasize important topics. The easier you make the host's job, the more willing he or she will be to work with you. It is also more likely that you will be invited back.

Be interesting, using stories, examples, and humour to illustrate your points. The simplest direction is to tell your story in human terms. How can your audience see themselves, their family or friends, or the things they value in what your organization cares about or what it is doing? What can they find funny or frustrating or moving? Guests who are engaging, well informed, well prepared, and who make the host's job easy are welcome ones.

Talk shows give you an opportunity to personalize your organization and its concerns. They give recognition to your efforts, are a boost to your supporters, and help you reach people with whom you would not ordinarily have direct contact. They can attract a few new supporters, quite a few opponents, and encourage the climate for change.

## News Media

What is news, and how do you get the people in the news media to report it, preferably in a way that furthers your interests? News is something that has just happened or is about to happen. It is unusual, affects a lot of people, affects someone generally considered to be important, or affects someone the audience can identify with. Thus your group activities or your presentation of issues may be of interest to people who create news items for papers, Internet, or broadcast. Sometimes you will get cold calls and will determine if it is in your group's interest to engage in the report. Sometimes you can suggest that an item is newsworthy and approach writers or producers in person. In some cases, the controversy created by your project makes it newsworthy. In this case, be measure and careful in your response so that your group is not mischaracterized. There are times, though, when you may wish to be provocative to encourage greater coverage.

Some of these items can be news for an organization:

- Election of officers
- Issues and events
- Significant projects
- Actions that attract attention or have consequences for the community
- Significant community meetings
- Important speakers, important visitors
- Release of the results of studies or fact-finding activities
- Special awards won or given
- Member participation in national or world affairs

For news to be reported in a way that furthers your group's interests, you must provide good, accurate, informative facts that put your group's concerns in a good light and respect the professionalism of the people in the news media. Even then be prepared—sometimes your story will be sensationalized or quotes will be taken out of context but it is still worth the effort. Your major local newspaper or journalism society, or perhaps a public interest group, may publish a manual to assist you in working with the media.

Getting in or on the news is essentially a business of form, of information, and of relationships. As is true in so many other areas, good relationships are surely as important as anything else. Let's take a look at how this game is played.

### Building Productive Relationships with News Media

Just who are these news people, and how do you get to know them? Almost anyone who makes decisions on what gets printed or aired as news is a potentially valuable person to know. For the print media, mainly newspapers, the key people are the city editor, the assignments editor, feature and editorial page editors, editorial writers, and reporters, both the beat reporters and the general assignment reporters. The beat reporters will probably be the most important among this group. Of course, it does not hurt to know the managing editor and the publisher either, but they are not as immediately involved with writing and preparing stories and editorials.

For the electronic media (that is, radio and television, online papers, search engine news sites, Internet blogs) the cast is about the same. Most radio stations have lean news operations. In addition to the news director, radio stations also have people who read the news, and some have full-time reporters. The news and talk stations have larger news departments, but even these tend to be small except in major news markets. Local affiliate television stations and some independent stations have standard news departments. You will notice different levels of commitment to the news operation even among stations in the same city. The most important personnel for you to know in television news are the assignments editor and the producer. Also helpful to know, but of lesser importance to getting your story on the air, are the reporters, the news director, and the anchor people. Both radio and television stations have station managers who set the general policies of the station, but they are not typically involved in the day-to-day production of newscasts.

Editors make the basic decisions in news operations. For example, they decide what types of stories they are looking for, which stories will be covered, the amount of attention the story will merit, and which reporter will be assigned to a particular story. Editors have most of the formal power, but they work behind the scenes. The people with whom you will have the most face-to-face contact and with whom you will most likely develop a relationship are the reporters. Reporters can influence editors' decisions, and they do the most critical job on the news team—they report the story. Reporters gather information, decide what is important (the angle), and communicate their impressions through the story they prepare. Television news producers are becoming more influential in deciding what they want to air and the story angles. Though the editors decide which stories get covered, reporters can and do suggest story ideas. Do not forget that your current reporter friend may one day become an editor.

To identify reporters who may be interested in your issues, watch the news and read the paper. Notice which reporters seem to cover which types of stories. Newspapers have some reporters assigned to a particular beat. These reporters look for and report stories on particular subjects; for example, the goings-on at City Hall, crime, health, or economic matters. They also have general assignment reporters who are not tied to a specific area. However, even these reporters do have some areas of interest, though they may not always be free to pursue them. A few television reporters have a specific area on which they concentrate, but most work on general assignment with some particular areas of interest and expertise. By paying close attention to the reporters and the stories they cover, you can begin to get to know them.

Of course it helps to meet them. The basic ways are pretty routine. The most likely way you will meet a reporter is by contacting her or him directly about a story. This may result in an interview, which gives you the opportunity to get to know the individual better. If the work you are doing in your change effort has attracted media attention on its own, you may be contacted for an interview by the reporter. Another opportunity is the talk show. Some reporters also serve as hosts of talk shows. Your appearance on the show gives you an excellent chance to begin building a relationship with the reporter.

Once you meet them, how do you build a relationship? Essentially you do this the same way you would with anyone else you would like to know better. Being friendly is a good start. But there is a bit more you can do.

- Be well prepared for your interview. Assist the reporter in getting a good handle on the story. Have your facts straight and at your fingertips and be able to convey the essential elements of the story. If there is an opposing view, acknowledge it, but show how yours is better by comparison.
- Be straightforward. Evasive people do not gain much favour with reporters. Certainly you will represent the facts in the way that best supports your position, but do not misrepresent them. You want reporters to be able to count on your information.
- Be polite. Even if the reporter seems unfriendly, maintain your courtesy. This does not mean you should be apologetic for your concerns or your actions, nor does it mean you have to act as if you are in any way less important than she or he is.
- Though you may make suggestions about things, like other people to contact or ways to visualize an issue, never tell reporters how to do their job or imply that they do not know how.
- Invite reporters to make a presentation on the news media to a group in which you are involved. This could be a college class, a professional organization, or a church group.
- Get together with reporters for lunch or after work for some refreshment. Get to know them on a more personal level. You may ask for a meeting for the purpose of discussing an issue or a potential story. This allows you to help the reporter more fully understand the complexities behind a situation. It also gives you the chance to get to know one another better. If the invitation was purely social, do not use this time to discuss your particular agenda, except in the broadest of terms. If the reporter wants to bring up a particular question, fine, then you can talk about things more specifically.
- Be seen as a good resource. Let reporters know the things you are involved in, but do not be a name-dropper. If you have expertise in particular areas, let them know. Call reporters from time to time with potential stories they may be interested in. You will find that you will be contacted for assistance with other stories. Often this will involve helping the reporter identify a person with knowledge of a particular subject. Or it may involve some specific information. If you don't have the information they need but you think you might be able to get it, tell them you will work on it for 10 minutes and get back to them. Then you make some quick phone calls. This is much better than giving the reporter more phone calls to make or saying "I don't know."
- Put reporters on your organization's mailing list. This keeps them aware of what you are doing and gives them some story ideas.
- Never, ever ask reporters to do you a favour by running a story, and never tell them that they have to do a particular story.
- Yes, reporters make mistakes. Ask for a correction only on a serious error. When asking for a correction, explain why you believe it is necessary. This is a touchy matter, so be particularly respectful when making your request (Kirst-Ashman & Hull, 2001).
- Once you have got to know a particular reporter, keep in touch.

### Providing Good Information

Good information is, first of all, accurate. The facts you provide are reliable and give a suitable representation of the situation. Assuredly, you want to paint a picture that serves your purposes. Draw attention to factors that support a point you want to make or that distracts notice from a situation you do not want examined. Though you may stress certain details over others to emphasize a circumstance, do not exaggerate your case by overstating specific facts. For example, if 100 people showed up for an event, you can say that you were excited that so many people attended, but do not say that the crowd was more than 250.

Good information is interesting and relevant. Try to draw a connection between yourself and the reporter's audience. The audience should be able to see themselves in what you experience. Stories related to recent news items are easier for the audience to associate with.

Good information is unusual. Show how the condition you are describing is not commonplace or not acceptable.

Good information is important. Demonstrate that what is happening or has happened affects a lot of people or some particular person or thing the audience highly values. An increase in taxes or the destruction of a historic landmark could be considered important information.

Good information is thorough, yet concise. The information you provide touches on the classic "five W's and an H": Who, What, Where, When, Why, and How. Address these fundamental points in as succinct a manner as possible. Clearly stress important factors, but do not lecture on them.

Many times you provide information through an interview. When responding to a reporter's questions, try to give distinct, direct, 10- to 15-second answers, and throw in a few quotable lines. Long responses with no pauses make it harder to hold the reporter's attention and leave you to the mercy of the reporter or the editor who must capture the main points of your message.

This is particularly true of television, where news stories are rarely more than 90 seconds long, and usually less. Before taping your interview, spend a couple of minutes going over the essential aspects of your story with the reporter. This will assist the reporter in asking you the right questions, and it will help you get oriented so you can distill the main ideas you want to communicate.

Remember that anything you say to a reporter can be used in a story unless you clearly state beforehand that what you are saying is "off the record." Even then, some reporters will try to figure out how they can use the information. Do not say it unless you can handle reading it. If the reporter cannot use the information, you have to ask yourself why you are bringing it up in the first place.

### Using the Proper Form and Style

*Initial contact.* Knowing whom to contact for a story is the first step. If you have established a relationship with a reporter or an editor, that is a good starting point. If you have not, it is proper to start by speaking to the appropriate editor. When contacting a television station, ask for the assignments editor. For newspapers, talk to the city editor or the city desk when you have a story involving hard news. If you have a feature story, speak to the proper feature editor or tell the city desk that you have a story intended for the "feature side." They will direct you to the right person.

Selling your story involves thinking about it from the editor's perspective. Why would the audience care about this story? How does this idea relate to recent news? You would also want to know what the caller has available to help get this message out. Dealing with these concerns will help you sell your story. Remember that you have two audiences. You must convince your first audience, the media, that your story has merit to get to your second audience, the general public.

Many reporters have seen it all. The ways that most groups present information is so routine that when reporters or editors see something new they flock to it. Further, if you can convince reporters of the validity of your position on the issue, they will make your point for you.

Objectivity is a rarely achieved condition in news reporting, and it may be rarely intended.

Here are some ideas that will help you get your story noticed:

- Always think visually, especially for television. Find a way to tell or reinforce your story using images.
- Tell the story through the eyes of the person most affected. Let this person's voice be the one to tell the story.
- Jar the media out of their preconceived idea of who you are. Show a side of yourself that they do not know.

Carefully study the newspapers and the TV news for a week or two. You will learn quite a lot. You will see how stories are handled and what gets attention. Most of all, you will see what reporters are looking for. Give it to them.

*News releases.* Communicating with the news media by means of a news release is common practice. So common, in fact, that an editor may have to wade through dozens before getting to yours. It is important to recognize that you are in competition with others who want attention.

Generally, a news release has four essential elements: a title and date, contact information, release date, and text. Figure 10.3 provides an example of a standard news release. When writing your release, put all the important information in the first paragraph, ideally in two sentences. This includes the who, what, when, where, why, and how. This is your "lead." Your lead should entice the reader to want to know more. Since editors cut from the bottom, make sure that your most important information is at the very beginning of your release. Each

**NEWS RELEASE**
*(The words "News Release" should appear in large, bold print at the top of the page.)*

| Name of your organization: *(if you don't have stationery)* | Contact person(s): *(with titles)* |
|---|---|
| Address: | Phone, fax, e-mail: |
| Today's date: | For Immediate Release (*or* For release: *date*) |

**Sample News Release Format**
*(Start almost halfway down the page with a 3- or 4-word slugline that says what the story is about.)*

Begin the text of your story a few spaces below your slugline. Remember to use your five W's and your H in the first paragraph. You should double or triple-space your text and use wide margins. This enables the editor to make changes.

Use standard 8½-x-11-inch white paper.

If you have to go to a second page, write the word "MORE" three times across the bottom of the page.

MORE MORE MORE

Sample News Release Format/Page 2 of 2

Start the new page with a new paragraph. At the top left of the second page write the slugline and "Page 2 of 2." Do not exceed two pages for a news release.

At the conclusion of the release, put the number (30) in parentheses or put a series of pound marks ###### or put the word "END" three times across the bottom.

Because your release goes to the electronic as well as the print media, use the words "news release," not "press release."

(30)

**FIGURE 10.3** Sample News Release

subsequent paragraph should have information that is of decreasing importance. Use short words, short sentences, and short paragraphs, usually no longer than two sentences. News releases are straightforward pieces, so avoid humour and cute phrases. Using direct quotes from individuals can spice up your release, but clear the quote with the person before using it. Try to keep your release to one page.

More and more editors are relying on e-mail. In some newsrooms, editors do not even check the fax machines frequently. Call the news outlet before you send your release to alert them to the fact that it is coming. The advantage of e-mail is that you can also attach some nice visuals, such as photographs, to support your story and make it more interesting. Most reporters include an e-mail in their stories so it is easy to contact them. If the reporter does not include it, often there is information within the paper about how to contact them. Online papers encourage direct public postings by readers to stories. There may be times you choose this option to make a simple point related to your group.

If your group has a website, put your news releases and news stories there in addition to sending your notices by e-mail. Some newsrooms have individuals who comb through local Web pages for stories.

*News conferences.* When your group has a particularly compelling story or announcement to make, a news conference may be in order. This is an effective approach for attracting a lot of attention to your concerns. Since news conferences are for special occasions rather than routine stories, you should use them sparingly. Giving attention to a few special details can help your news conference run successfully.

Send a teaser news release a week in advance. This release announces the news conference and promotes interest in it. All the essential details regarding time and location are included, along with a description of the purpose and the participants. In describing the purpose, state things in a way that will spark the curiosity of the editor receiving it. For example, you might say that information will be provided showing that a major government agency is operating in violation of a law and is in danger of facing millions of dollars of sanctions. Or you might promise to show how more than 100 children died last year because of the inadequacy of prenatal care services and how this problem is costing the government millions of dollars. You want to whet their appetite without giving away your story.

Call the media people you have invited on the day after they received the release. The stated reason for calling is to answer any questions regarding the arrangements for the conference. Do not answer any questions about the substantive issues you plan to discuss at the conference itself. Of course, the real reason you are calling is to heighten their awareness and interest. Call again the morning of the event as a reminder.

There may be times when you want to call a quick news conference to rally attention to an immediate issue. The sense of urgency can promote reporters' interest in the event. These types of conferences may be useful in calling attention to a controversial community development before an opposing side has determined how it is going to handle public discussion on the matter.

Do not answer questions about the subject of the conference before it takes place. You may get a call from a reporter who is trying to pry the story from you. Resist the temptation to give it away. Once the story is out, there is no reason to hold a news conference, and no one would attend anyway.

Generally, the best time to schedule a news conference is Monday morning at 10 o'clock. News builds during the week as stories develop and compete with new stories. Things start more or less fresh on Monday; it is a slower news day, and all the news crews are at full strength. Ten o'clock is the beginning of the workday for many reporters. Scheduling your conference at this hour draws their attention before other stories emerge throughout the day.

Hold the news conference at a familiar or particularly significant and visual location. Reporters and editors don't want to waste time figuring out how to find some out-of-the-way place. They want a location they can get to easily and that underscores the issues being discussed. This adds to their ability to cover the story. A strong visual image captured in a photograph or on videotape can heighten the impact of your words.

Prepare news packets. Include in the news packet the text of your presentation along with a news release describing the conference. Also provide a one-page fact sheet and any supporting information that may help reporters understand the issue more fully or give them an additional angle on the story. Pass these out halfway into the conference. (You do not want to give them the story before the conference starts or have them sit there reading, not paying attention to what you are saying.) Personalize the packet. Make labels with the reporters' names, and stick them on the packets right before you hand them out. It is a small detail, but it is one of those things that show you are well prepared.

In some cases, you may choose to have a prominent speaker. A familiar and important face lends credibility to your cause, attracts attention, and makes your conference more newsworthy. Do not have more than three speakers.

Make the presentation brief, followed by questions and answers. The main prepared remarks should not exceed 15 minutes. Shorter is better than longer. Prepare yourself to anticipate reporters' questions so you have good, pointed, concise responses. If attendance by non-reporters, supporters, or the general public could be considered appropriate (and it usually is), have them sitting or standing where they will be caught by the camera.

Arrange for interviews immediately following the formal presentation. Let the reporters know who is available for interviews. More than one person should be prepared to be interviewed.

Have good visuals. In addition to what the location has to offer, you may have models, displays, large charts, or other visual aids to help with your presentation and to reinforce your comments.

Make sure that your audio system is clear and sufficiently powerful. This is particularly important for news conferences that are conducted outside.

Have refreshments. Coffee and donuts go a long way toward establishing goodwill.

Provide dramatic information. You have a captive audience; send them a strong or provocative message. Have them leave wanting to tell other people what you had to say.

Keep a list of who attended for possible follow-up.

*Event coverage.* Your organization will be involved in other newsworthy events. Protests, important meetings, and community service functions might be good events for calling out the news media. Many of the steps involved with a news conference apply here as well. Send out an advance news release, give thought to the location, have people prepared to be interviewed, and have printed material to distribute to reporters.

Your material and your comments should focus on the purpose of the event, not the event itself, since event activities should be self-evident. Show how the activities relate to the purpose; do not just emphasize the activities themselves. Although reporters may not use the news release you hand out at the event, they may well feel you forgot something important if you do not prepare one. So do have one available, and remember to keep it to one page.

*Editorials.* Editorial support, particularly from the community's major newspaper, is extremely valuable. It says that what you are doing is not only important to know about but also that it merits approval. Contact the editorial page editor or one of the editorial page staff about their writing an editorial in support of your concerns or allowing you to prepare a guest editorial. Arranging a face-to-face meeting is

## CHANGE AGENT TIP

Using a few carefully placed letters to the editor, you can generate plenty of community discussion and turn a small issue into an important one. You can also keep an issue going, preventing it from fading from public view. In addition, you can stimulate the interest of the news media and generate further coverage of the matters you are working on.

Here is how it works. Invite people over for a letter-writing party. You only need about five people. Each person writes a letter addressing the basic subject. This is the first group of letters. These are mailed a couple at a time, with a few days between each mailing.

Make a few of your letters provocative so they will stimulate this additional community response. You will notice that other people in the community will begin writing letters as well.

preferable, though not always necessary. Unless the editorial board is very familiar with the topic, spend some time educating them about the importance of your issue and the strength of your position. Providing documentation of your points is particularly important. It is helpful to understand the editorial slant of the paper and to be able to show how your agenda relates to specific positions they have taken in the past.

*Letters to the editor.* One of the most widely read sections of the paper is the letters to the editor. They offer you a useful vehicle for generating community discussion of your concerns and for influencing community opinion. Not all newspapers print all the letters they receive, and the ones they do print are often edited. A few hints will strengthen the likelihood that yours will receive attention. First, keep your letter under 200 words. Next, recalling that editors cut from the bottom up, put all your essential details in the first few sentences. Refer to some story that has recently appeared in the newspaper or the letters to the editor column. When providing your name, also add any title that can lend credibility to your words. Send your letter or e-mail neatly typed and free from grammatical or spelling errors. Finally, include your phone number.

*Deadlines and other details.* The more you know about how to make the job easier for members of the news media, the more they will want to work with you. You will learn many of these things by doing. You will learn when you have to reach a reporter to make the evening paper. You will learn that two-thirds of the people get their news from television and that television news gets many of its stories from the newspaper. You will learn that it is not really a community issue until it has been in the paper.

You will learn that you enjoy working with the news media. You will learn how good it feels when your message goes out and the community begins paying attention to the importance of the things you are doing.

## CONCLUSION

Take purposeful steps to communicate with your supporters, your targets, and the community at large. The means of communication you choose and the messages you send will be geared toward your understanding of the market, those people you intend to influence.

There are many methods at your disposal. Some, such as word of mouth, newsletters, brochures, and position papers, are largely within your control. Others require assistance from people outside your group. These may include the use of billboards, public service advertising, appearances on talk shows, or getting your efforts and issues described in the news.

When you get the word out about your group effort, you attract much more than just attention. You pave the way to new supporters and the resources they can provide. You establish the credibility of your issue and your efforts to resolve it. You awaken the community's interest and get it to recognize that the need and the possibility to improve the community exists. You start moving the momentum for change in your favour and in so doing make it much harder to try to make your group and its concerns go away.

## HELPFUL WEBSITES

**Spin Project**

www.spinproject.org

Spin Project provides an excellent set of tutorials, publications, and other resources to guide activists on working with the media and bringing issues to public attention. Their *SPIN Works!* is an activist-friendly and extremely useful media guidebook. Spin Project also provides consultation to grassroots groups working for social change.

**Common Cause**

www.commoncause.org

Common Cause is a good example of an organization that assists reporters through its website. Check out its "On Deadline" section that helps reporters find useful information. Its "Press Library" holds a large set of news releases, and its "Pressroom" provides lots of additional resources for reporters and others.

**Xpress Press**

www.xpresspress.com

Xpress Press provides very helpful articles on working with the media as well as a free monthly electronic newsletter about interactive public relations and media relations on the Internet. It also provides numerous other services for a fee to help you get your message out, including contacts with journalists in more than 70 countries.

**Canadian Association of Journalists**

www.caj.ca/

Canadian Association of Journalists (CAJ) offers helpful resources on issues involving access to government records and activities and freedom of information education. This is also a good site for understanding ethics of journalism and other matters pertinent to professional journalists.

**Canadian Broadcasting Corporation**

www.cbc.radio-canada.ca/docs/policies/journalistic/

This is the web page of the Canadian Broadcasting Corporation (CBC). It provides a good review of the accountability policies of the public media corporation.

CHAPTER ELEVEN

# Building Community Action Organizations

**This chapter will help you better understand the following questions:**

- How do you develop a community action organization?
- What are some of the important stages of organizational development?
- What are some of the various stages of group development?
- What are some of the possible pitfalls in developing groups and organizations? How can these be overcome?
- What are the different organization types, characteristics, benefits?
- What is involved in incorporating an organization?

A successful change effort needs more than an initiator. It needs a number of people working together, using their knowledge and talents and time in an organized way, and it needs issues to get and keep things moving. To build your organization you first need to gather some of the parts: people, information, other resources, issues, and some time. Then you put these parts together in a way that allows them to work with each other, using the potential of each to produce a desired result. Making this happen requires organizing, structure, and flexibility.

*Organizing* is the process of obtaining and putting the necessary pieces together to accomplish your purpose. *Structure* refers to the deliberate, agreed-upon methods for handling predictable or routine activities and tasks. *Flexibility* is the ability to change tasks, responsibilities, and structures to better achieve your goals according to the particular demands of your set of circumstances. Together, all these elements make up the organization.

Building an organized effort brings into focus all those matters we have discussed in previous chapters. Information, community, power, people, resources, communications—all of it. Your organization fits all those pieces together and puts them to use.

But how much organizing do you need to do, and how much structure needs to exist? These two questions have the infuriating answer of "It depends." Some of the factors on which these depend are your purposes for organizing in the first place; the number of people involved; the nature of the issues on which you are working; the number, complexity, and relationship of your tasks; and the intended longevity of your organization.

If your intent is to develop an organization that will provide a large number of people with a permanent base of power to contend with a range of fundamental issues, you need to pay a great deal of attention to the organizing process and the development and maintenance of supportive structures. But if your goal is to rectify a specific concern, and you are bringing people together only for as long as it takes to deal with this particular matter, less attention is needed for crafting your process and establishing your structure.

One way of thinking about these differences is by asking yourself the question "Is the organization itself more important than the particular problem we're working on, or is resolving the problem itself more important than putting together an organization?" Or to put it another way: "If we lose on this matter but strengthen the organization, is that good or bad?"

A word of caution about structure—keep looking for the right balance. Too much or too little structure can scuttle your efforts. If you "just let things happen," you may end up spending a lot of time going nowhere until a few more compulsive or impatient souls start telling everyone else what to do or end up doing it themselves. This is not a good prescription for organizational success. However, if you assume you have to create procedures for any eventuality, you are going to bog your work down with a lot of unnecessary rules and regulations that do not fit the situation you are facing, and you will not know how to handle unpredictable or unplanned occurrences.

As your organization develops, you will start feeling a need to make certain matters more routine. For example, you may need to determine who calls meetings, who runs them, and who keeps track of what you are doing. Having people agree to hold certain positions within the organization may be a way to provide some management of these items.

As you grow, more separate tasks need to be done, and you may notice that having everybody doing everything gets confusing at the very least. Maybe it would be better to work in teams, each with certain areas of responsibility. If each

## CHANGE AGENT TIP

To identify issues, you will want to get a sense of what is bugging people. Maybe, though, you or other folks in your group find it a bit hard to just walk up to people, especially if they are strangers, and ask them what's bothering them. How do you start this conversation? How do you get people to open up? There is a simple method to break the ice and get good information.

Construct a simple survey asking people to respond to three specific issues you have selected. (Make sure you leave off a couple of good issues.) You can use a simple ranking system from "extremely upset" to "don't mind at all." The point here is to keep it short. The survey is mainly a tool for getting at other things that are annoying people.

Once you have your survey put together, go knocking on doors, sitting in laundromats, stopping by offices, or wherever you will find the people you need to talk to. When you make contact with people, ask your three questions to get them started. Then ask them to identify two other things that aggravate them and why. Talk about these items, and ask a few follow-up questions. You will find that people like to give their opinions, especially if they do not have to prove they are correct.

This approach will accomplish three basic purposes. First, and most important, it will help you discover what is on people's minds. Second, you can use it to stir them up a little. The discussion will bring some irritants to the surface, prompting people to recognize that everything is not necessarily okay as it is, and getting them a little restless to do something. Third, it will help you and the other participants make contact with people and get to know them better.

decision—from the colour of your stationery to the menu for your community luncheon—must be fully approved by every member, you will not be able to move forward with your work in a timely manner. Perhaps you need to agree on who needs to make what type of decisions, and how they are to go about doing so.

Generally, a good practice is to allow your structure to emerge in accordance with the emerging needs of your organization. This means that you have to be attentive to the needs of your organization. Some of these needs can be easily anticipated; some have to be discovered. When you notice things that require routine attention, clarify responsibilities or develop procedures to take care of them. Be willing to modify and improve those procedures. This may mean getting rid of them altogether.

Becoming more organized helps you build and focus the interest of participants and other resources. However, organizations are not built out of thin air. They must have a reason for being. When enough people are concerned about something to move toward action, there is the beginning of organization. Organizations are brought to life by issues and are built by working on them.

## BRINGING THE ORGANIZATION ALONG

No two change efforts are quite the same, so it is with some hesitance that we suggest a "typical" set of organization-building activities. Yet it is helpful to have guidelines that can provide some sense of how to go about the process. Keep in mind that although an organizing effort typically follows these steps, your particular situation may demand a slightly different order or timetable. Remain flexible, and tune in to the needs of your change effort.

### Identify What's Bugging You

What is it that you seem to keep coming up against? What is it that sets your blood to boiling, makes you shake your head in disgust, or leads you and your associates to complain? Try to put your finger on what it is you wish were different. Recall that identifying the issue is not the same as identifying *the* solution, which refers to how you can make things different.

This step particularly relates to change episodes you initiate as someone who has a personal interest in an issue. If your intent is to organize people rather than to solve a particular problem, you will need to identify what is bugging them.

### Think About It for a While

Now that you have a good idea of what is irritating you, see if you can figure out why. Think about what makes it so annoying to you and maybe to others. Now is a good time to sit down with one or two people who might feel the same way you do.

Based on what you know, try to figure out the problem. What seems to cause it? What seems to keep it going? Who gains from keeping things the way they are? Who would be inconvenienced by a change? Spend some time mulling it over. Try to focus in on the issue you want to address.

### Do a Little Homework

Test your assumptions. Doing some sort of preliminary community assessment is beneficial. If there are facts and figures to be gotten, get them. The more you know about the issue, the better you can communicate your concerns. You will also be more credible to those who must consider whether they will respond to you, and you will feel more confident about what you are doing. (As your organization grows, your command of the issue needs to grow as well.)

Express yourself clearly and succinctly by organizing your thoughts. There is nothing wrong with jotting down a few phrases and saying them out loud to hear how they sound. You do not want to prepare a script, but you do want to be able to make some poignant comments. You will never really stop doing homework, but you should not wait until you know everything before you act.

## Identify Other Interested Individuals

Thinking about the issue and the homework you have done will help you identify groups of people as well as specific individuals who are affected in one way or another by what is going on. Find out not only what they think about the issue but also how they feel it or experience it. Make a prospect list of these candidates, and add to this list as your change effort evolves. Just because someone should care does not mean that they will. Talk to people one or two at a time. First, approach those you feel most comfortable with and who will take the least amount of convincing.

As we have said many times before, much social services work, whether that be individual therapy or community change, occurs through the development of effective relationships. Spend some time getting to know your potential partners a little better if you do not know one another well already. Gaining confidence in each other and firming your understanding of what you each think and feel about the problems you face will help you deal with the uncertainty inherent in working for change. Throughout this process, you need to strengthen the belief that you can actually do something to improve your situation. The less well you know each other, the more time you should put into building these relationships. This is a crucial time in building the organization. Your ability to attract initial encouragement and actual support will probably persuade you to continue your efforts or convince you to forget the whole thing, at least for the time being.

## Identify Those Who Are Willing to Do Something

Most of the time you will start by working with people you already know. You will work with them because you feel comfortable with them and have some confidence in them. They will work with you for the same reasons. Generally, it is better to talk to one or two people at a time; the more natural or more a part of your routine this is the better. You do not have to have a meeting to talk to people. Meetings sometimes imply a degree of formality or commitment that people may not be comfortable with; casual conversations can be more helpful at this point.

Eventually you do need to ask for a commitment. Something like "Let's do something about this, okay?" followed by "What do you think we should do?" is helpful not only to get people to agree that they will somehow be involved but also to get them thinking about what they will do. They must put themselves in the picture of action.

Every conversation should include this question: "Who else should we be talking to?" Remember, you do not just want a small group of friends who tell you how right you are, you want to build some sort of an organization. Go back to your original prospect list. Are there any individuals on that list to whom you should now be talking?

By this time you may have only three or four collaborators. You and your collaborators should each agree to get a commitment from one or two additional people. Letting these new recruits know who else is involved usually provides some reassurance.

You do not need to go from 2 people to 200 overnight. You can get quite a lot done with 6 or 8 people.

## Have a Small Group Meeting

The main purposes of this first meeting are to reinforce your feelings about the issue and to strengthen your commitment to each other and to solving the problem. Other important concerns include shaping and clarifying the issue you will address, providing leadership opportunities for people other than yourself, and figuring out what your next steps should be.

Two potential dangers should be avoided at this initial get-together. The first is just sitting around complaining about the situation and not making any concrete decisions on what to do about it. Your energies are better spent working on getting rid of the problem rather than simply complaining about it. The second is trying to make detailed plans for all the work that needs to be done, with an implication that it all needs to get done right away. This can lead to a beginning burst of creative energy followed by a feeling of being overwhelmed. Members may feel drained just thinking about all the additional work and spend the next few days crafting excuses as to why they cannot be involved after all. The fact is that you survived this week without all the work being done. You will probably survive the next one even if things are not markedly different. There is a lot you can do to improve this situation; you do not need to do it all at once.

Do the simple things right away. Generally, it is more difficult to start doing things than it is to actually do them. So make it as easy as possible for people to start. Simple does not necessarily mean unimportant.

You need to find some balance between confirmation of your beliefs, directions for the future, and specific tasks to complete in an identified period of time. In fact, all meetings should include identification of *specific tasks* to be done by *specific people* by a *specific date.* Keep the number of things to do reasonable and useful. They should yield some clear perception of progress. Further, all meetings should allow you to get to know each other better and to enjoy each other's company.

Finally, two items for consideration at your first meeting will become routine matters for future discussions: Who else should we involve, particularly someone with leadership potential; and what else do we need to know?

## Recruit and Do Your Homework

During the time between your first and second meetings, you should be active in moving the effort forward on your immediate objectives. This might sound obvious but you would be surprised at how many change agents use this time simply to wait for the next meeting. Complete any assignments you agreed to do.

Although you may use interviewing to prospect for new members, it is often better to ask a new recruit to help you with some particular task. Now that things are beginning to roll, this allows you to say "join us" in a clear, simple way. Even though some people may hesitate to "get involved," they may be willing to help out with a specific identifiable job.

Continue doing your homework on the issue and the community, especially the community in your arena of action. Find out how similar communities or groups have dealt with this problem. Obtain a more accurate understanding of who is likely to support or oppose you and why. Begin to discover who benefits from the current situation and how they profit. You also want to uncover the costs involved in maintaining these conditions and who has to pay them. Do they pay in dollars, in anguish, or in lives? This is the time to more fully develop any needs or resource assessments that may be required.

## Hold Your Next Get-Together(s)

In addition to the ongoing purposes of strengthening your resolve and continuing the development of leadership, this meeting should focus on an analysis of the problem situation. Define your issue focus and plan for action. Begin to develop broader strategies and tactics. A lot of the homework you have been doing will be used during this meeting, so information sharing is critical.

The answers to some basic questions should help you understand what you are facing and provide some direction for your action. The first set of questions centres on principal members of the community. Who are the important actors? Who makes decisions on this issue? What are the nature and consequences of these decisions? Who feels the problem? Who else needs to feel the problem; that is, whose behaviours need to be different? Who is likely to oppose you and why? Who is likely to support you and why?

The next set of questions relates to the actions you would consider taking. Knowing who needs to feel the problem, how can they feel it? To what will they respond? What do you need to do to get the right people behaving in the right way? You may not get complete answers to all these questions at this meeting, but you should make substantial headway. Answering these questions will help you develop strategies and tactics.

Your planning efforts should start taking shape, moving forward with the processes outlined in Chapter 7. If your objective is to resolve problems rather than to establish a broad power-based organization, focus most of your planning attention on actions to produce the desired change, not (for now) on building the organization. Look for opportunities for some easily completed mini projects or quick, initial victories.

Depending on the issue you are tackling, all this may be a lot to accomplish at one time. If you notice that members are getting weary of the process, take a break until the next time you get together. This next meeting should not be too far off if you want to sustain the momentum and complete some basic work. In the meantime, make sure there are a few specific things you and your collaborators can do to keep a sense of progress. For example, this may be the time to begin raising other resources or exploring alliances with other groups.

At the completion of this stage, you have clarified your goal and the major areas or sets of activities you need to work on. This will suggest some areas on which members can concentrate their energy. This is a very important development. By breaking the overall enterprise into practical packages, participants can better understand and manage what they have to do. With the emergence of this division of labour, you can help participants make sense of what needs to be done and how their efforts fit into the overall picture. The result is less confusion and more efficiency.

Although it is helpful for members to have a clear set of tasks on which they can focus, allow for the fact that members may want to take on new duties from time to time. The fact that members have particular responsibilities does not mean they should always be stuck doing the same things. Members should always have opportunities to develop their skills and commitment by undertaking new responsibilities.

## Do What Needs to Be Done

It is a good idea to work together in teams, even if the team has only two members. Working in teams allows for a creative exchange of ideas, helps prevent members from being disconnected from the effort or from each other, and provides motivation as individuals usually want to be seen as responsible contributors to team success.

Members and teams need to keep in communication with each other. Make sure the various teams get what they need from one another and that their work fits together. It is usually necessary to have a liaison committee or a steering committee to serve this function. Members of this group regularly communicate with each other to be sure that the work of the teams is coordinated and that necessary information is exchanged in a timely way. Also, they are commonly empowered to make decisions that do not require full discussion by the entire organization or that need to be made within a very short time frame. With each team having an identified liaison, any member of the organization has easy access to other teams. (Notice that a structure is starting to emerge.) It would be a mistake, however, to require that teams communicate to each other only through the liaison. Such arbitrary rules can become a source of unnecessary conflict and can hamper communication.

At this point it is time to appoint a "follow-up coordinator." Finally, you should start thinking about what you want to call yourselves. Understand that most of the work of the organization does not occur at meetings, but between them. Teams should get together as needed.

## Get Together Again

Celebrate your accomplishments and your victories. This is a valuable exercise. If you only look at how far you have to go or the work you still need to do, you will soon feel worn out. By this time in your organization's development, you have come a considerable way. Turn around and look at the ground you have covered. Paying attention to your gains is energizing.

Look for ways to incorporate some easily arranged social activities into your work. Perhaps a "no business" get-together is in order about now, or maybe a combination of social and working sessions.

Although you need to continue refining your action plans, you now begin seriously discussing matters pertaining to the organization itself, not just to the work of the organization. Make decisions on formalizing the organization. Are there any positions that need to be formalized and filled? Do you need a treasurer, a secretary, a chairperson? Do you need a bank account? Do you need routine meeting schedules, agendas, minutes, and other formal procedures? Do you need to establish bylaws that delineate the formal procedures of the organization, particularly who gets to vote on matters affecting the organization? The answers to some of these questions rest with the decision on what kind of organization you want to be. Later in this chapter we describe various types of organizations.

If you anticipate that your organization will grow so big that all the members cannot get together to discuss concerns and make effective decisions in a timely manner, a specific policy-making group will be needed. Usually called a board or a steering committee, this group makes the fundamental decisions that determine the direction of the organization and the way it is to function. It also oversees the activities of any staff hired to carry out these policies on a day-to-day basis and makes decisions regarding significant expenditures of funds.

These are all items you may discuss during this meeting, which is mainly given over to matters of the organization's growth and development. A special team should begin working on those mechanisms critical to enabling the

## CAPTURING CONCEPTS

### The Follow-up Coordinator

Most of us intend to do the things we commit to do, but the distractions of the everyday world often leave our well-intended promises locked in the I'll-get-to-it-when-I-can vault. How can action groups deal with this very normal dilemma? Appoint a follow-up coordinator. This is an extremely valuable position and one that every group should have. The key point is that this role must be understood, formalized, and mutually accepted; that is, the group needs to clarify what the job is and agree to select a particular person to do it. Basically, the follow-up coordinator does three things:

- Records everyone's commitments during the meeting.
- Reads back the commitments (along with completion dates) at the end of the meeting to make sure everyone has the same understanding.
- Calls the responsible person a few days before a task is to be completed to check on his or her progress. Although the follow-up coordinator may help the responsible person figure out how to complete the task, the follow-up coordinator does not assume responsibility for doing the work. This is really a very friendly reminder call; it brings people's commitments back to their attention so they can act on them.

When the role is agreed upon and understood, the follow up coordinator's duties help reinforce the idea that the organization is working and that people are doing what they are supposed to do. This job is so important that the follow up coordinator should rarely take on any other responsibilities for the group.

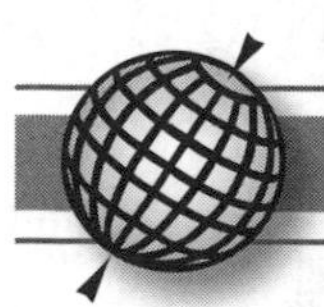

## GLOBAL PERSPECTIVES

AUSTRALIA—We want less talk and more action. But uncoordinated, poorly planned action can get pretty messy. The future is in the hands of the people who are willing to sit through meetings, more meetings, more meetings. The *right* meetings, of course: meetings which lead to action. (Ruth Lechte, 1983, p. 3)

ZIMBABWE—We want to be helpful in groups, to learn to work as a team. There are some animals we don't want to imitate in our group behavior: donkeys, stubbornly refusing to change their opinions; fish, sitting there with a cold, glassy stare; rabbits, running away when there is conflict or tension; peacocks, showing off and competing for attention; ostriches, burying their heads in the sand and refusing to face problems; lions, fighting whenever others disagree; monkeys, fooling around and chattering; snakes, hiding in the grass and striking unexpectedly; chameleons, changing color according to the people they are with, or rhinos, charging around upsetting people unnecessarily. (From *Training for Transformation* by Anne Hope & Sally Timmel, 1992.)

CHINA—Go to the People

Live with them,

Learn from them,

Love them.

Start with what they know.

Build with what they have.

But with the best leaders

When the work is done

The task accomplished

The people will say,

"We have done this Ourselves."

(Lao Tsu, 700 B.C.)

BURKINA FASO—In rural Upper Volta (now Burkina Faso), the village chief and his council decided that they desperately needed a solid and safe footbridge built over a small gully that filled up with raging water about 2 months every year and cut the village off from its fields and access to a nearby market town. The village had managed to construct a rickety log bridge, but every year there was at least one fatality from someone falling into the gully.

Good decision, but there were many challenges. The local government dismissed the village request because a new paved road and bridge were "imminent." The villagers lacked reliable advice on their options for getting a footbridge built—what needed to be done and the resources required. The village itself had great difficulty pooling village resources due to animosities stemming from family feuds that went back several generations.

Sometimes difficult challenges are not enough to stop an idea. The village family heads unanimously expressed a deep-felt need for the bridge. They had all suffered from the current situation. The turning point came when family leaders promised to lay down their differences and cooperate to have a dependable bridge. A spillover benefit was that three other villages downstream would also benefit from the bridge as a dependable access to the nearby market town.

The village was able to draw on the assistance of a Peace Corps volunteer, who found another, who had training in civil engineering. Good to have some help, but you need real materials to build a bridge. The chassis of an old junked truck would be the bridge frame. Wooden boards would need to be bolted to the bridge frame. Small causeways would need to be built up with clay and rocks, and masonry cement walls would need to reinforce the gully walls up- and downstream from the bridge. The boards and cement would cost about $500. The labour would require seven-person crews working over a 3-month period. The women and children carried the rocks, sand, clay, and water to the site. The men built the causeways and mixed the cement. The village also needed a mason to supervise the work. Fortunately, one of the village men had recently learned some masonry skills.

The village found a source of "self-help" funds for the materials, and the local governor agreed to transport the truck chassis to the village. The village council organized the labour by family and by week in such a way that members from feuding families did not have to work together in the same crews!

The bridge was completed 2 weeks ahead of schedule. The Peace Corps volunteers provided some early guidance, and after the initial planning stage, the village took over. When the village volunteer did venture over to the site, he found that he was just in the way.

Fifteen years later the volunteer received a letter from a villager saying that the bridge was still in great condition and had been faithfully kept up by the village. He also indicated that the paved road was still not built. (John Scheuring, 2002)

---

organization to operate smoothly while aggressively pursuing its goals. This team's recommendations should be proposed for adoption at the next general meeting.

## Go Public

Select a name. A name gives you identity and solidifies you as an organization. It signifies to you that you have actually brought something to life. You become more than "a bunch of us who want to do something." Your name should be easy to say and to remember, and it should let people know what you are about.

Go public. Promote the fact of your existence. Announcing yourselves puts your name and purpose into people's awareness. Proceeding quietly can be counterproductive and confusing to potential participants. Are they being encouraged to participate or not? People are often a little suspicious about secretive or unknown groups. Regardless of whether they are supporters or opponents, it is hard to reckon with something they do not know much about, which appears to have little broad support, or which perhaps does not have enough confidence in itself to clearly, publicly state its case. Going public will make an opponent more worried about the attention, interest, and support you will draw. A supporter will be encouraged to see that helpful actions are being taken and that you are real.

There are different levels of going public. Some of these, like purposefully spreading the word, being open about your intentions and your actions, and posting fliers promoting the issue and inviting participation, might be done at an earlier stage. Press conferences, public demonstrations, and other acts can be used as forceful coming-out events. Any activity that seeks recognition of your group as an entity in the community should stress what the issue is and what you have been doing about it. Plans for future actions and invitations for participation should also be announced.

## Hold a Formalizing Meeting

The purpose of this meeting is to adopt recommendations regarding key aspects of structure and procedure, familiarize new members with your purpose and program, and reinforce your collective will to succeed. It is here that you approve the bylaws and elect officers to formally establish yourselves as an organization. Prepare to work on a set of more formal vision, mission, and values statements. Not every organized change effort needs to reach this stage; only those requiring sustained action over a period of time will need this degree of formality.

During this meeting you have to strike a delicate balance between having things well organized and ready for decisions and remaining open to suggestions. Because there are likely to be new members who are not really certain about what is going on, leave some clear opportunity for them to ask questions and contribute ideas and leadership. You cannot simply allow for this, you must encourage it. Otherwise it all looks like a "done deal" cooked up by a few insiders who will reduce everyone else to the role of spectator. Provide background on what has occurred to date, who has been involved, what you intend to achieve at the meeting, and why. Leave some non-pivotal leadership positions open to nominations from the floor, and solicit the participation of newcomers to fill them. By taking steps such as these, you can let both new and old members know how they fit in without having to throw all the work you have done out the window and start over from scratch.

Though this meeting will emphasize matters pertaining to the organization, it must not be devoid of action items. Decide on a number of actions to further your agenda to keep you directed to your business and to sustain your momentum.

### Begin Indirect Recruitment

Up to this point, recruitment efforts have been personal, generally face-to-face. If the issue you are tackling requires a larger organization, you now need to reach out beyond your personal networks to a larger audience, inviting the participation of people none of you know. Although your personal efforts will continue, extend your welcome much further.

### Keep Working, Monitor Progress, and Confirm the Actuality of the Change

Continue to move your agenda forward by identifying and completing tasks, particularly those that institutionalize or make permanent the changes you seek. Understand that once the change has been agreed to you will need to monitor its implementation. You may discover that you will need to keep the pressure on to ensure adherence to agreements that are to result in changes.

Implementation will not be easy. Unanticipated problems and other setbacks will occur. Those who resisted the change may attempt to undermine its genuine realization. It is not uncommon for changes to be temporary. A situation that appears to have been changed may well revert to the previous condition once the pressure to pursue new directions has been removed. Maintain vigilance and an unmistakable willingness to take action until changes are incorporated into the day-to-day life of the community (Kettner et al., 1985).

## DEVELOPING YOUR ORGANIZATION

You cannot separate building an organization from developing leadership. Even if your effort involves only 10 people working together for six months, this subject requires your purposeful attention. The larger you aspire for the organization to grow and the longer you intend for it to be around, the more critical this concern becomes.

### Develop Leadership

Developing leadership entails more than looking for the one leader to replace you. It means looking for several leaders to work alongside you, some of whom may assume aspects of your role when it is appropriate for you to leave the scene. Leaders are those people who routinely demonstrate the ability to influence others in an attempt to move the group forward. Leadership more accurately refers to the behaviours that provide the influence. The reason for making the distinction is that by seeing leadership more in terms of behaviours than as people you open up the possibilities for leadership to be expressed by any number of members in the organization. This keeps the group vital and self-reliant rather than dependent on a few.

Particular types of leadership roles are important to the organization. At least six basic needs for leadership exist in organizations:

- Guiding strategic and tactical decisions
- Inspiring and motivating others to encourage accomplishment of tasks
- Providing direction and coordination of efforts
- Representing the organization to the public
- Negotiating the organization's interests with other individuals, groups, and organizations
- Addressing internal relationship issues

Different people can fill each of these roles; you do not have to worry about finding someone who can play them all.

Potential leaders possess some degree of commitment and capability. Both of these attributes can be strengthened over time. You can start developing leadership by encouraging the people who are currently participating in the organization who demonstrate a willingness to provide some leadership. Some of these individuals will turn out to be effective leaders, and some of them will not. Some potential leaders will hold back, so you may not notice them at first. Perhaps they are a little unsure of themselves, or perhaps they are a little unsure of the organization, its sincerity, or its prospects for success. These potential leaders may take a little while to survey the scene before deciding if making a greater effort would be worth it. There will also be some individuals who are not currently members of the organization, but whom you will deliberately recruit because of your awareness of their leadership capabilities.

One implication of this is that you will probably experience a turnover in leadership. The people who are eager to get something going may not be good at sustaining their own efforts, much less the organization's. The organization has different needs in different circumstances and at different stages of its development. Do not be disappointed if the early leaders drift away from the organization. In fact, it is very likely this will occur. That is one of the reasons you always need to be on the lookout for new leaders.

How do you develop these potential leaders into actual ones? A good beginning is to let other members know that you do not have all the answers, that you are finding your way too. One of the best ways to kill off emerging leadership is to convey that it is not needed or not wanted. To counter that possibility, actively encourage others to take a greater role, see to it that opportunities exist, and then get out of their way.

A beginning means of encouragement is soliciting ideas, especially as they relate to the six basic areas of leadership. Leadership involves some degree of risk taking. The potential leader must feel sufficiently safe before he or she will demonstrate real leadership. Safety levels vary among people. Some establish confidence pretty easily, whereas others take a while. By asking for ideas, you get some gauge of capability while inviting a small leadership commitment in a nonthreatening way.

You may notice that one or two members of your group, perhaps including yourself, are seen as the arbiters of which ideas are good and which are not. If this pattern persists, your efforts to develop new leadership will be phony and remain superficial. You need to demonstrate your trust in the judgment of emerging leaders if your efforts to develop leadership are really going to mean anything. By deferring judgment to others and following their lead, you send a message to everyone that there are more than just a handful of people capable of providing direction.

You may need to do more than provide encouragement and opportunity. You may need to provide some conscious mentoring, working closely with those who seem capable of and interested in assuming a greater leadership role. Pass on what you have learned through your own training and experience, particularly your experience in this effort.

### Take a Moment to Discover

Think back to a time in your experience with someone who was a leader, especially after the leader had been absent for a while. Maybe this was your teacher, a member of your choral group, or your coach, someone in whom you all had confidence. How did you feel and perform when that person was gone? How did you feel when that person returned? All of you in the class, in the group, or on the team had work to do or contributions to make that the leader did not take away from you. Yet in his or her presence you all seemed to perform better. Who could offer that type of leadership in your organization?

## Expect Natural Turnover

After an early period of enthusiasm, a few of your numbers will disappear. Do not be surprised if half of your initial group is gone after six months. Do not be worried either. (Well, do be worried if these individuals have not been replaced by others or if overall interest and participation is steadily dwindling.) Some loss is natural. There are many reasons. It is harder to keep something going than it is to start something. Some people get discouraged by not seeing immediate results. Others may find that they are not really very interested in the issue after all or can find nothing very meaningful to do about it. Some would rather talk a good game than play it. Yet others will move away, get a new job, fall in love, fall out of love, or have some other experience that takes them away from the action.

As long as your issue is sufficiently important and you make an honest effort on some basic fronts, your numbers will be sufficient to do the work. Here are some things you can do to cut down on the loss of membership:

- Help members find specific ways to contribute
- Offer encouragement to the unsure
- Provide opportunities for leadership
- Establish a sense of overall direction
- Strengthen relationships
- Keep in frequent communication, including personal communication between leaders and others in the organization
- Recruit and involve new members

Things to avoid doing are wasting energy worrying about who is no longer active and wasting time chasing after people who really are not going to maintain their involvement. While some absences could have been prevented, and you can learn something by doing some reflecting, most of your turnover can be accepted as natural. You will continue to grow if you focus your energies in a positive direction.

## Get People Doing Something Right Away

All that early energy and enthusiasm needs some focus to keep it from dissipating. An activity that is a stimulating change from the routine can serve important functions of unifying the participants and providing them with an opportunity to enjoy working together. A specific project or event people can undertake quickly works best. This is not an activity that is carefully thought out and then patiently explained to the group. No, these are best born of the spontaneous ideas that just seem to pop out of group discussion. The best ones are tangible, like painting a mural, creating a banner, conducting a food drive, or digging in for a Saturday neighbourhood tree planting. Even something social like a barbecue, a weekend campout, or a fun-filled retreat could work. Anything that will get people going and confirm their identification with the effort will do.

This focal activity becomes an enjoyable experience that attracts the interest of new members, becomes part of the group's history, and, by moving the group forward, introduces it to a range of other possible activities.

## Know that Things Will Take Longer Than They Should

We all know that change takes time, but we tend to throw that understanding out the window when dealing with our own efforts to make change. Though your work should and will accelerate the process of change, maybe even significantly, it will not make it immediate. Sorry. If you can maintain the odd state of eager patience, you will be effective while still being pleasant to be around.

## Decide if an Easily Achieved Gain Is Better Than One Gained from Struggle

You may be able to pick up the phone, call a friend, and easily solve a problem your budding organization is facing. Is this the best thing to do? Not always. Often it is more beneficial for the organization to gain a sense of accomplishment by achieving something through hard work. Your decision is based on what, at the time, the organization needs most.

### Accept the Reality of Unearned Dividends

An improvement in the community will benefit everyone, not just those who helped to bring it about. If a neighbourhood park gets built, people who never worked on the project will swing on the swings or play on the basketball court. This can cause resentment and create divisiveness. Do not presume to know why each nonparticipant does not become involved. Instead, focus on those who are involved, and create honest, ongoing opportunities for people to become involved according to their abilities. Then just accept unearned dividends as a fact of life.

### Move Past Reaction

During the early phases of building your organization, you may be responding primarily to some discomfort experienced by the members of your community that is caused by an outside authority. You may initiate action by trying to stop something from happening or by trying to end a harmful practice. These can be effective motivators.

At some point, if your organization is to grow beyond an immediate issue, you will need to promote your own agenda. Go beyond a series of essentially defensive struggles to assert your own program of action. When this occurs, you are much more in charge of your own destiny. You are provoking reaction rather than acting provoked.

## THEORY OF STRUCTURAL LIMITATIONS

Most community action organizations are developed and run by people who saw or felt a need to act and were unwilling to sit still. Most of these people are volunteers. Their attraction to the organization is rooted in the goals and action agenda of the organization. Participants may join an organization for a number of reasons—for example, liking the people involved with the organization—but most leaders' level of commitment is related to what the organization is about, what it is trying to do.

That's great for providing energy and direction for action, but it may not be all that great for handling the nitty-gritty details that keep the organization running. Organizations, like any other system, require routine maintenance and attention to many little chores that help it survive and grow. This is not too difficult when the organization is fairly small, but taking care of a larger, growing organization is something that many volunteer leaders just do not want to do. As the organization expands, it reaches the limits of the structure that volunteers have put into place to manage organizational activity and development. There's often not enough to hold it together, and the effort more or less collapses from its own weight (Guerra, 1999).

We refer to this as the donut hole theory. Maybe not the most apt term because donuts stay pretty small, and the batter is cooked all at once. Organizations keep getting bigger, and their parts are "cooked" in fits and starts. Still, the picture of a hole in the middle of an expanding mass is the picture we get whenever we see this happening.

To survive its own growth, an organization needs to specifically recruit and develop leaders who will undertake the management of routine organizational tasks, or they must be able to hire staff to perform those activities. This will be essential to sustain your organization. It cannot be overlooked.

## GENERAL STAGES OF ORGANIZATIONAL DEVELOPMENT

It is normal for your organization to go through certain stages in its development. Though these periods of growth are fairly predictable, the length of time it takes to pass from one stage to the next will vary with different organizations.

The seven common stages of organizational development and maturation are introduction; initial action; emergence of leadership and structure; letdown, loss of members, and floundering; recommitment, new tasks, and new members; sustained action; and continued growth, decline, or termination.

## Introduction

This marks the very beginning of your effort. You recognize your (or the community's) frustration with current conditions and begin to talk to each other about it. You begin to understand the issue more clearly, get to know one another better, understand your feelings about the situation, and decide to do something to make a change.

## Initial Action

This stage is characterized by a handful of original members doing an armful of tasks. Common tasks include contacting potential supporters, gathering information, preparing written statements, and holding meetings to figure out what it is that you want to do and how to go about doing it. Enthusiasm, energy, and regard for one another are usually high.

At this stage, groups often make their first presentation (often unsuccessful) to those who are in a formal position to do something about the problems the community faces. They soon realize that more work needs to be done to secure significant change.

## Emergence of Leadership and Structure

As the next steps are being considered, members frequently turn to a few leaders for direction, clarification, and encouragement. A need to make decisions and organize work more efficiently is recognized, and procedures are established. Work proceeds as members gain a clearer picture of what they need to do. A clearer sense of purpose begins to take hold.

A few of the original cast drop out as the early period of inspired activity gives way to more routine work. Another common deterrent to maintaining participation is the tendency for some early leaders to focus on their own agendas, seeing only their own solutions to problems, and generally ordering others around. Even though these "leadership" actions may be done with apparent politeness, they soon wear thin. Leadership struggles may well occur as the group continues feeling its way.

## Letdown, Loss of Members, and Floundering

It is not uncommon for organizations to go through a period of doldrums. The early energy has waned, and nothing seems to be happening. Members may become emotionally fatigued. If no concrete gain can be seen or if no interesting action has taken place, people may lose focus and question whether the effort is going anywhere. The organization will lose some members, and those who stay may vacillate between being angry at the defectors and struggling to keep their own faith.

This is a critical time for the organization. If no visible activity involving a substantial number of members occurs or no identifiable victory can be claimed, the effort is likely to wither. If the organization can make it through this period successfully, it can take future occasions of listlessness in stride more easily.

## Recommitment, New Tasks, and New Members

Leadership asserts itself during this phase to motivate members and assure them of the value of their involvement. Work is broken down into coherent, manageable assignments, and members feel good knowing what they have to do and how their work fits in with the overall scheme of things. New members are recruited, and they bring vitality and new ideas. If members can point to a particular accomplishment, they begin to feel good about themselves again and renew their belief in the organization. A more genuine sense of purpose is realized.

### Sustained Action

The organization's program moves forward, and members can readily acknowledge gains on several fronts. Setbacks are seen as temporary, not terminal, and a sense of confidence, and perhaps even pride, takes hold. Many of the early leaders play less active roles, and new leaders step forward. New projects are considered and undertaken. These new ventures occupy the time and devotion of only some of the members. Everybody does not have to be involved with everything.

As the organization continues to grow, more formal means of communicating among members are developed.

### Continued Growth, Decline, or Termination

*Scenario 1.* The work continues, but nothing new or interesting seems to happen. Leadership remains in the same hands, and the same verses keep getting repeated to the same songs. Those who have the most investment in the effort struggle for a while to put the best face on things while not really doing much to refresh and restock the organization. They may work harder on their own responsibilities and take over other people's jobs. After a while they, like the rest of the members, run out of gas. People stop showing up, work is done sporadically and less well, and for all practical purposes the organization exists in name only, if at all.

*Scenario 2.* The work of the organization is completed, and it is time to go home. Sometimes when this occurs, the members are not quite sure what to do with themselves. There is a little restlessness as members still get together to try to figure out what to do next before it finally dawns on them that they are, in fact, done. This is a good time to deliberately recognize accomplishments. Holding an event that celebrates the group's successes and declares an end to the effort allows members to feel a sense of achievement and completion, enabling them to move on to other things. In the absence of a commonly proclaimed conclusion, members just drift off into other interests with vague feelings of being unfinished.

*Scenario 3.* New projects and new challenges bring more members and continually recharge the interests of participants. Periods of stagnation or confusion are recognized and managed. New leadership urges the organization forward. The authority of the organization's reputation paves the way to further accomplishments. The community and the individual members feel strengthened by their affiliation with the organization.

## • SMALL GROUP PROCESSES

The work of organizations is largely the work of groups. Most of the stuff of organizing for change—discussing, plotting, planning, decision making, and camaraderie—occurs in groups. Building a successful organization demands an understanding of the functioning of groups. Purposefully building around the support and close communication a small group can be a helpful method of organizing (Breton, 1994; Gutiérrez, 1995). The information in this section dealing with small groups has been drawn from Tuckman and Jensen (1977); Tropman, Johnson, and Tropman (1979); Konopka (1983); Brown (1991); Home (1991); Sachs (1991); Mondross and Berman-Rossi (1992); Napier and Gershenfeld (1999); Lumsden and Lumsden (2000); Zastrow (2001); Johnson and Johnson (2003).

### Task and Relationship Dimensions

Two basic levels of group operation require continuing attention. The first of these, the *task* component, is directed toward accomplishing the group's purpose. The group puts energy into determining which steps must be taken to accomplish the goal, taking the necessary steps, and keeping their work moving forward. All those actions that conduct the group toward these achievements are called task actions. If the task component receives little attention, the group will not accomplish very much.

The second principal element of a group's operation is the *relationship* or *maintenance* component—the ability of group members to work well together, to effectively manage their conflicts, to maintain their involvement, and to feel good about themselves as individuals and about the group as a whole. All those actions not directed at the work of the group but directed at enhancing harmony among individuals and between the individual and the group are called relationship or maintenance actions. Maintenance activities are most important for organizations that intend to stay together for a while. Taking care of relationship issues after a sequence of intense task activities is especially vital to the organization's continued health. If the relationship component receives little attention, the group will probably fall apart.

Any action that strengthens the group on either the task or relationship level can be considered a leadership action. Johnson and Johnson (2003) identify a number of specific leadership task actions that can promote group effectiveness:

*Information and opinion giver:* offers facts, opinions, ideas, feelings, and information

*Information and opinion seeker:* asks for facts, opinions, ideas, feelings, and information

*Direction and role definer:* calls attention to tasks that need to be done and assigns responsibilities

*Summarizer:* pulls together related ideas and suggestions and restates them

*Energizer:* encourages group members to work hard to achieve goals

*Comprehension checker:* asks others to summarize discussion to make sure they understand (pp. 196–197)

Relationship or maintenance actions include these jobs:

*Encourager of participation:* lets members know their contributions are valued

*Communication facilitator:* makes sure all group members understand what is said

*Tension releaser:* tells jokes and increases the group fun

*Process observer:* uses observations of how the group is working to help discuss how the group can improve

*Interpersonal problem solver:* helps resolve and mediate conflicts

*Supporter and praiser:* expresses acceptance and liking of group members (pp. 196–197)

## Effective and Ineffective Groups

Johnson and Johnson (2003) have identified characteristics of effective and ineffective groups (see Table 11.1). Ongoing attention to factors present in effective and ineffective groups will help you monitor the functioning of your own group. This will help you identify specific areas where improvements can be made. Johnson and Johnson have developed a simple, valuable model that will help you maintain awareness of essential issues.

Four other critical factors for group effectiveness have been identified by Kaner, Lind, Toldi, Fisk, and Berger (1996):

*Full participation:* All members are encouraged to speak up and say what's on their minds.

*Mutual understanding:* Members need to understand and accept the legitimacy of one another's needs and goals.

*Inclusive solutions:* Members take advantage of the truth held by all members, not just the quick and the powerful but the slow and the shy as well.

*Shared responsibility:* Members recognize that they must be willing and able to implement the proposals they endorse.

**TABLE 11.1 Characteristics of Effective and Ineffective Groups**

| Effective Groups | Ineffective Groups |
|---|---|
| Goals are clarified and modified so that the best possible match between individual goals and the group's goals is achieved; goals are structured cooperatively so that all members are committed to achieving them. | Members accept imposed goals; goals are competitively structured so that each member strives to outperform the others. |
| Communication is two-way, and the open and accurate expression of both ideas and feelings is emphasized. | Communication is one-way, and only ideas are expressed; feelings are suppressed or ignored. |
| Participation and leadership are distributed among all group members; goal accomplishment, internal maintenance, and developmental change are underscored. | Leadership is delegated and based on authority; participation is unequal, with high-power members dominating; only goal accomplishment is emphasized. |
| Ability and information determine influence and power; contracts are built to make sure that individuals' goals and needs are fulfilled; power is equalized and shared. | Position determines power; power is concentrated in the authority system; obedience to authority is the rule. |
| Decision-making procedures are matched with the situation; different methods are used at different times; consensus is sought for important decisions; involvement and group discussions are encouraged. | Decisions are always made by the highest authority; there is little group discussion; members' involvement is minimal. |
| Structured controversy in which members advocate their views and challenge each other's information and reasoning is seen as the key to high-quality, creative decision making and problem-solving. | Disagreement among members is suppressed and avoided; quick compromises are sought to eliminate arguing; groupthink is prevalent. |
| Conflicts of interest are resolved through integrative negotiations and mediation so that agreements are reached that maximize joint outcomes and leave all members satisfied. | Conflicts of interest are resolved through distributive negotiations or avoidance; some members win and some members lose, or else conflict is ignored and everyone is unhappy. |
| Interpersonal, group, and intergroup skills are stressed; cohesion is advanced through high levels of inclusion, affection, acceptance, support, and trust; individuality is endorsed. | The functions of group members are stressed; individuality is deemphasized; cohesion is ignored; rigid conformity is promoted. |

Source: Johnson & Johnson, *Joining Together: Group Theory & Group Skills*, Table 1.2 "Characteristics of Effective and Ineffective Groups", p. 26, © 2003 by Allyn & Bacon. Reproduced by permission of Pearson Education, Inc.

### Take a Moment to Discover

Imagine a situation in which a group of you are trying to accomplish something. This may be planning a party, preparing for a class presentation, or even cleaning the house. Review the lists of task and maintenance leadership actions, and put a check next to those you see yourself routinely providing. Next, put a star beside those you seldom do. Now look at what you have marked. What does this suggest to you about your leadership style and what you think is important?

## Stages of Group Development

Napier and Gershenfeld (1999) describe five stages in the evolution of working groups: the beginning, movement toward confrontation, compromise and harmony, reassessment, and resolution and recycling. These stages are built on the classic work of Tuckman and Jensen (1977), who described the five stages of group development as forming, storming, norming, performing, and adjourning.

Before members ever enter the group, they have some idea about what is going to happen.

These ideas colour their perceptions during the *beginning stage*, which is a time of watching, waiting, and testing out how to act. Gradually, people become more comfortable in the group, drop their polite façades, and begin acting more like themselves. This stage is characterized by *movement toward confrontation*. Questions arise over who makes decisions and how. Concerns over matters of control and freedom are expressed, and leaders are criticized. Members try to firmly establish their place in the group, seeking prestige and influence. This is bound to cause some conflict. After a while, members realize that if this continues the group will disintegrate.

This recognition ushers in a period of *compromise and harmony*, during which the group tries to reverse destructive trends and reopen communication, drawing members together. A period of goodwill ensues with tolerance for different behaviours and more acceptance of individuals. Collaboration increases, and competitiveness is reduced. Though openness and honesty are encouraged, members are careful not to step on one another's toes, and there is a subtle pressure to preserve the spirit of harmony. As a result, resistance goes underground, making it harder to make decisions. Feelings of confidence and relief give way to increased tension. The group realizes that a kind of superficial fellowship needs to be replaced with some other approach.

During the period of *reassessment*, the group may try to impose greater restrictions in an attempt to streamline procedures and increase efficiency. Or it may delve more deeply into its problems. This can lead to the group realizing how vulnerable it is to personal needs, suspicions, and the fears of its members. Members come to see how these issues affect the ability of the group to accomplish its goals. By establishing mechanisms for appraising its operations and making adjustments, the group can build on the foundation established in the previous phase. It legitimizes the expression of feelings that are not always positive or that may produce conflict. The group realizes that its survival depends on increasing shared responsibility as well as personal accountability. This, in turn, increases trust and individual risk taking.

During *resolution and recycling*, the group realizes that periods of conflict and periods of harmony are normal, and conflicts are handled easily and quickly.

The final stage is the *termination* or *adjournment stage*. At this point the group has decided to finish its business and members go their separate ways, though some may retain some level of connection.

Groups can get "stuck" at various points in their journey. Also, they may go back to earlier stages of development from time to time. It is helpful to understand these phases so you can recognize events occurring within the group as signs of normal group development. With this understanding, you can help guide the group as it matures and be patient with events that might otherwise appear worrisome or baffling.

## Common Pitfalls for Groups Promoting Change

Not surprisingly, every organization experiences some problems as it tries to get organized. A number of probable trouble spots can make the road a little rougher than you would like it to be. Keep your eye out for these problems. Each problem is followed by a list of symptoms to watch out for.

### Inflexibility

- Overinvestment by individuals in their ideas, positions, and plans; unwillingness to see how changes to ideas, positions, and plans offered by others can help the group achieve its goals.
- Failure to see early plans as tentative.
- Inability to "roll with the punches" and take setbacks in stride.
- Defining problems in terms of solutions instead of in terms of needs.
- Lack of contingency plans; no "Plan B."

### Intolerance for Confusion

- Belief that things will not or cannot work out all right.
- Premature need to have complete answers to all questions; belief that these answers will never arrive.
- Need to know what everyone else is doing, and why.
- Lack of belief in one's own ability to figure things out.
- Need for guarantees.

### Poor Group Process

- More talkative members not actively withholding comment and inviting or allowing less talkative members to participate.
- No purposeful effort to assist less talkative members to develop confidence in their ability to make verbal contributions.
- Less talkative members not accepting invitations or opportunities to contribute.
- Lack of clear, mutual understanding about what the group intends to accomplish; lack of clear and agreed-upon expectations.
- Members' inability to state what is important or what needs to be done to achieve success.
- Lack of summarization; lack of checking to see that members share an understanding of decisions.
- Development of a "repository of all knowledge"; that is, an individual who is supposed to know everything so other members are relieved of their responsibility to know.
- Over- or under-emphasis on task demands.
- Lack of purposeful attention to group process, or too much attention to matters of group process (including the "heavy duties"; that is, every little problem becomes a "serious issue that I think we need to discuss").
- Expecting someone else to solve something you see as a problem.
- Not taking time to enjoy each other's company.
- Believing that having fun is a waste of time; viewing tasks as work only.

### Inadequate Communication

- Exaggerating or understating the importance of issues, concerns, or problems.
- Inability or unwillingness of members to declare needs in a way that people can act on them.
- Belief that everyone thinks things are as important, as good, or as bad as you do.
- Ignoring diversity and assuming that everyone wants to be treated the same way you want to be treated; not considering how others would want to be treated.
- Inability to listen to what is important to other members; inability to "go past the words." (Hint: Could you write down two things that are clearly important to each person with whom you are working and clearly state how each sees these are being met?)
- Making inexplicit agreements.
- Not understanding how the actions of one team or group within the organization affects the agenda, matters, or concerns of the others.

### Lack of Distributed and Developed Leadership

- Decision making by just agreeing with you.
- Current leadership is too directive.
- Current leadership states opinions as facts.
- Leadership invested in "experts."
- Unwillingness by members to assert leadership.
- Constant complaining by members who are less involved in leadership actions.
- Inability of leaders to promote leadership skills of others; lack of purposeful distribution of leadership tasks.

### Lack of Follow-Through on Tasks

- Lack of honest understanding that "didn't have the time" often really means "didn't take the time."
- Inability to break tasks down into manageable units.
- Too many excuses.
- Frequent statements that things are "in process" or "being worked on."

### Turning Fears into Anger

- Communicating that less involved members are not concerned or not intelligent.
- Intolerance of another's peculiarities or well-intentioned mistakes.
- Your fears are greater than your faith in others.
- Making up problems that do not exist.
- Assuming or imposing arbitrary limitations on what you can do.

### Poor Development Efforts

- Lack of purposeful recruitment efforts.
- Lack of purposeful fund- and other resource-raising efforts.
- Lack of purposeful development of new leadership.

Most of these problems can be resolved early on if members recognize them and decide to handle things differently. A group that routinely assesses how it is working is able to acknowledge and deal with its internal problems. With such an orientation established from the very beginning, periodic general reminders will take care of most of the problems.

Still, some individuals might not get the message. Even after a group discussion of behaviours that can promote or hamper the ability of people to work together, they persist in acting in a counterproductive way. This needs to be brought to the attention of the errant members, ideally in a way that does not cause embarrassment. You can call direct attention to things when they happen without attacking an individual. You can help by saying something like "Hang on for a minute, Malik. You just interrupted Abdul. He may not be finished." Or, if need be, it can be discussed in private. If it is truly a problem, though, it cannot be neglected. Dealing with these situations in a matter-of-fact manner before they get to be persistent problems will minimize the chance that an angry confrontation will be needed to clear the air.

Two final points are worth making here. First, you are not the relationship police who has the job of keeping everyone on the cooperative straight and narrow. Every member should be encouraged to deal with things that are getting in the way. Second, obviously, not every little mistake needs to be pounced on. Many things (as long as they are not part of a pattern) can safely be ignored.

Photos.com

**Effective use of facilitation skills will enhance your ability to engage others in the development of a community organization.**

## Meetings that Keep the Momentum

Meetings that produce nothing but future meetings can be the death of the movement (O. M. Collective, 1971). A seemingly endless series of reports, hit-and-miss conversations that randomly address items of importance, discussions that spend too much time on minor concerns and too little on major ones, matters routinely held over for yet another meeting—you have seen these characteristics in "action," and you have winced at the thought that tonight you have another meeting to attend.

You may well have attended more bad meetings than good ones. This should not and doesn't have to be the case. Too many meetings

### DID YOU KNOW?

#### Twenty Tips for Productive Meetings (Plus One)

1. Know why you are having a meeting, and design your procedures to accomplish your purpose. If your proposed meeting does not clearly and logically relate to action or increased group cohesion, do not have it.
2. Pay attention to matters of scheduling. First, select a date that gives you enough time to implement the decisions you make at the meeting. It does no good to come up with a brilliant idea that you just cannot act on because you have left yourself so little time to do anything. Second, select a date and hour that allow for as many of the key participants to attend as possible. Next, give yourself enough time during the meeting to take care of the needed business. Finally, select a site that is convenient and appropriate for the nature of the meeting and the size of the group.
3. To the extent possible, make sure participants know and understand the purpose and type of meeting beforehand. Send out pertinent information in advance of the meeting so individuals can start off mentally prepared. (Though you should encourage participants to read over the material you send, do not expect that everyone will do so. You had better briefly review the key points of the material before you begin a discussion on it.)
4. Prepare yourself well with material, information, and any supplies needed to conduct the meeting. Review minutes of previous meetings and reports related to the topics under review to get your bearings straight before the meeting begins.
5. Develop an agenda that allows for the major items to be discussed. It is generally better to place important issues at the beginning to make sure they receive their due attention rather than rushing through them in the closing minutes. Know how much time should be spent on each item. If more time is needed as the meeting progresses, negotiate for it, clarifying that other items may get little or no time. Do not have the meeting go longer than advertised unless you have negotiated for the extra time. If more time is needed on an issue that can wait for resolution, ask a few people to work on it and provide a recommendation for action at the next meeting.
6. Decide how long the meeting should last. People can usually meet for about an hour and a half before their minds begin to wander to things more interesting. Marathon meetings that go on for hours can be useful at the beginning stage of the organization when enthusiasm and a sense

of mission are running high or when preparing for some critical event in the life of the organization. They can make the circumstances seem more dramatic and the people involved in them more important.

7. Do not try to do too much at one meeting. Your preparation for the meeting should include a review of the topics for presentation and an assessment of participant interest as well.
8. Establish group sizes appropriate for the degree of discussion necessary. A large group may be broken into smaller groups for discussion with time allotted for reporting back to the entire group.
9. Pay attention to matters of structure and space. Whenever possible, participants should sit in a circle. Leave an extra chair open for a late-arriving member, but otherwise try not to have too many open seats. Too much space between people decreases the energy and the potential for group cohesion.
10. Have fun. A little playfulness can be an important element. For example, asking participants to bring snacks can contribute to a more congenial and relaxing atmosphere and increase involvement.
11. Use the talents and the interests of the participants. Unless you are simply giving information to a passive audience, remember that each participant is a resource.
12. If all members do not know each other well, take time for introductions. "Icebreaker" activities may be helpful in building new relationships. These can be as simple as having each person say a little about themselves and state what they intend to get out of the meeting.
13. Clarify the intended outcomes at the start of the meeting. During the meeting, periodically check with the participants to see how you are progressing toward their accomplishment.
14. As you begin the discussion of items, bring people up to date with recent developments. This can be particularly helpful to new members.
15. Purposefully keep the discussion on track, periodically summarizing the key points and identifying areas of emerging agreement. This can be done gently. You do not need to be heavy-handed.
16. Make explicit, specific decisions that are clearly understood by everyone. Do not let a lot of talk about something that needs to be done substitute for definite decisions and assignments about doing it.
17. Follow the general ground rules for effective discussion: Pay attention to spot those who are trying to speak and encourage them to do so; invite comments from the more quiet members; acknowledge contributions of members; encourage controversy in a climate of respect, recognizing that which is important to one another.
18. Use decision-making methods that are appropriate to the importance of the topic; for example, consensus on important items and majority vote on minor ones.
19. When a matter is settled, move on.
20. Close the meeting. Summarize the main points and decisions made during the meeting, identify the next steps to be taken, and recognize progress being made by the organization toward its goals.

*Plus One.* You've just concluded a successful meeting; give yourself a pat on the back. But are you done yet? Not quite. Write down your understanding of matters immediately after the meeting, including impressions, next steps to take for the direction of the effort, and specific tasks. Make sure you write down your own assignments.

accomplish too little, waste time, or are just plain dull. One of the great ironies is that most of us have frustrating experiences at meetings most of the time, yet the notion that just anyone can run a meeting persists unquestioned. The title of "chair" does not by itself confer magical powers that enable its holder to handle a meeting well. A poor conductor will inhibit the performance of an orchestra; an ineffective chair will hamper the productivity of a meeting (Tropman et al., 1979). Meetings should provide or revive energy, not sap it.

Actually, learning how to run a meeting effectively is much easier than many people make it out to be. By using your time, your participants, and yourself purposefully, you can accomplish quite a lot by bringing people together. Keep your focus on the goals for the meeting, pay attention to both the task and maintenance needs of the group, use a little common sense, and you will have meetings that maintain interest and inspire action.

Running meetings will quickly become routine for you. The danger is that it can become so routine that you become sloppy. Going over a mental checklist before each meeting is a good habit to get into. The more you are primed to get the most out of your meetings, the more you will produce, the more time you will save, and the more momentum you will build.

## TYPES OF ORGANIZATIONS

Not all organizations are the same. Distinctions are based on issues considered, type, design, and purpose. You have a variety of organizational configurations from which to choose to bring people together to work for change. Some common types of organizations include membership organizations, open organizations, coalitions, networks, core groups, and steering committees.

### Membership Organizations

Membership organizations are characterized by having a prescribed method for individuals to establish their affiliation. Normally this consists of paying dues. Organizations may establish other criteria as well. These can include setting minimum qualifications for membership, nomination and selection procedures, written agreements detailing the rights and duties of membership, a code of ethics or conduct, and other policies that more strictly define membership. In addition to codifying requirements for membership, some organizations develop a number of symbols and rituals that serve to further strengthen the members' identification with the organization and their bonds to one another. Examples are a Shriner wearing a fez, the Girl Guide promise sign, and a member of the Lions Club having to pay a fine for not shaking everyone's hand before the start of a meeting. Use of special signs is more commonly the case when group affiliation itself is a particular value.

All organizations develop some set of symbols or norms that convey a sense of uniqueness. Yours will too. You most likely want to cultivate a broad membership in a welcoming atmosphere, so more restrictive admissions practices and elaborate customs are probably both unnecessary and unhelpful.

Dues are perhaps the simplest and the most effective method to distinguish formal membership. One of the main reasons for establishing dues is that in so doing you ask someone to explicitly declare support and affiliation. You literally confirm the member's investment in the organization's goals. Since your intent is to both strengthen and increase participation, it is a good idea to keep the cost of dues low. Though you can raise money through the payment of dues, doing so is usually a minor consideration.

Because they have taken steps to confirm the individual's connection to the group, membership organizations can generally depend on a stronger commitment from their participants than can less formal groups. Defined membership makes it much easier to identify, contact, and mobilize proponents of an organization's point of view. These organizations also have a better gauge on the degree of support they have and, if need be, can point to their roster as evidence of that support. They can unequivocally assert the fact that they are speaking for a genuine constituency.

## Open Organizations

Most membership organizations intend to be permanent, and over time they will pursue an array of interests. In contrast, open groups tend to be more focused on current issues and often do not plan to solidify the organization's development. Those involved are more likely to identify with the issue than with the organization. Building the organization is done primarily to accomplish a specified purpose rather than being a goal in itself. Thus, codifying membership policies is less of a concern. There are few barriers to membership. In organizations of this type, whoever says he or she is a member is a member.

Open organizations readily accept new participants. With concerns related more to the organization's agenda of change than to its procedures, prospective participants find it easy to become involved in the organization and its work. This can be an asset for a group working on a specific concern, especially one that can be resolved in a matter of months.

Since participants have little actual commitment to the organization itself, it is often difficult to sustain allegiance. Members tend to come and go unless the program of change is very specific and time limited. It is common for work to be fragmented and for many projects to be dropped before completion. Of course, this can also be true of membership organizations. It is just more likely to occur when the participants' ties to the organization are loose and when no one is quite sure who is really involved. Open organizations certainly can structure their procedures, though a spirit of informality is more common to these groups.

Some open organizations have a very specific focus and concentrate most of their energies on accomplishing a defined objective. A political campaign or a group working together to change a particular agency policy are examples of such groups. Groups that work to resolve very limited issues are often called *ad hoc groups*. Another type of organization with a narrow focus is a *task force*. This variation describes a temporary collection of people who commonly have some special expertise that is particularly helpful in dealing with the problem at hand.

Not all open organizations have a restricted scope. Some have a broader agenda. The main function of these organizations is to provide an opportunity for people with similar concerns to have access to one another. They are loose confederations of like-minded souls. In these cases, the organization's agenda becomes a part of the community's ongoing register of concerns, and from time to time the members focus on specific projects. A local committee on homelessness or an AIDS awareness council may fit this description.

## Coalitions

Coalitions are organizations of organizations (Figure 11.1). They are created when a group realizes that its power base is too small for it to successfully pursue an important issue, so it joins forces with others who are affected by the same issue. When these various organizations agree to work together, the coalition is born. Collaborative efforts are gaining increased attention from funders and activists alike, and attention to coalition building practices have grown as well (Chavis, 2001; Mizrahi & Rosenthal, 2001; Wolff, 2001).

Many coalitions are of the ad hoc variety, formed to address a particular concern and disbanded once that particular matter is resolved. Others become more permanent organizations, usually with a single broad focus such as health care, hunger, or reproductive rights (Checkoway, 1987; Cox, 1987b; Dale, 1978; Kahn, 1991).

Putting a coalition together provides a number of benefits to the change effort. One particular advantage is that the coalition has ready access to resources that have already been organized. Each member has something already in place that is of value to the coalition. This may be volunteers, money, good relationships

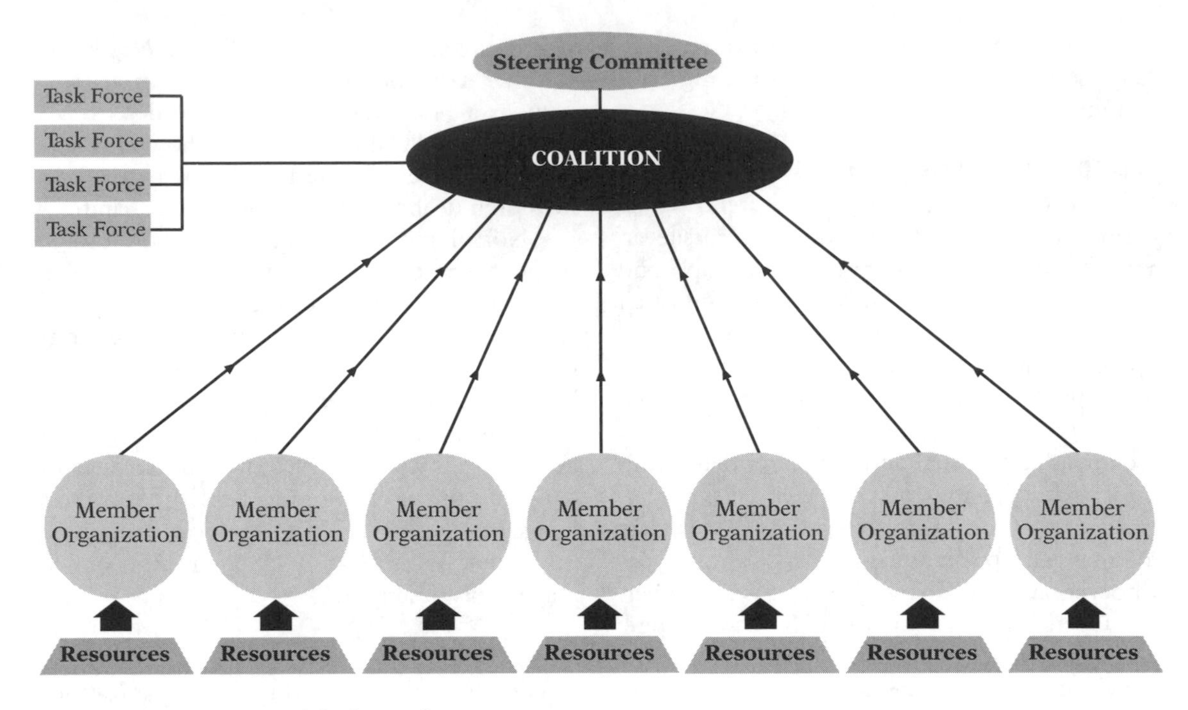


**FIGURE 11.1** Model of a Coalition

with lawmakers, or leadership ability. Also particularly important is the ability to inform and mobilize a large number of people in a fairly short period of time. Each member probably has staff, a board of directors, and a constituency it serves. That could represent quite a horde of troops. Coalitions often have an easier time gaining identity and acceptance in the community. Many of the participating organizations bring established community credibility; their names and their leaders are recognizable to the media and to other members of the community. Finally, involvement by a variety of groups working on the issue gives it an almost immediate degree of legitimacy (Jansson, 1994).

Coalitions, however, have some built-in conflicts. Among them is the protection of turf that often characterizes relationships among groups operating within a generally similar arena. Participation in a coalition requires members to not only divide their time with yet another group but often their loyalties as well. If the coalition is the result of a funder's directive rather than participant initiative, commitment to the new organization may be restrained, and if a lead agency is designated in this arrangement, power and control imbalances can threaten relationships. As the coalition gains strength, one additional concern is that the power and voice of smaller, emerging grassroots organizations may be muted. Dealing effectively with these conflicts promotes the coalition agenda and can markedly increase community capacity as well.

Assembling a coalition involves a series of steps somewhat similar to bringing new members into any organization. The first step is to determine whom you would like to have involved in the coalition. The second is to contact them, emphasizing how the issue affects their self-interest. The third is to secure some commitment to the coalition from each organization. Next, you need to involve the member groups in the work of the coalition. Of course, throughout the life of the coalition, you need to maintain communication with those who are involved.

You will take several things into account in selecting potential members. The best starting place is to enlist the support of organizations with whom you have already established a relationship. After this, a little critical thinking is in order (Kahn, 1991). The first question you should ask is "Who is most likely to join?" Organizations that serve people who are affected by the issue or that have compatible philosophical positions are likely candidates. So, too, might be those whose particular interests, talents, or knowledge relate to your issue. Could the carpenters be interested in your community renovation efforts? Could the insurance brokers help you curb drunk driving? Coalitions working on a legislative agenda may want to present a mainstream face to legislators (Berg, 1999).

The next question is "Who has what we need?" In addition to the more obvious resources of expertise, numbers, and money, make sure you have members in your coalition who can relate to the different publics you intend to influence.

Contacting potential members is best done through a face-to-face discussion. This allows you time to answer questions and clarify how the aims of the coalition fit the interests of the organization whose involvement you seek. Additionally, explain any benefit the organization could receive through participation in the coalition. If possible, bring along an individual who is well regarded by the targeted organization to help you make the pitch.

It is important to get a written agreement from those who are willing to be publicly involved. It is always a good idea to first ask the organization how they may help the effort. You can build on these ideas for further commitments. The easiest way to obtain a record of agreement is to develop a simple commitment form that spells out various general categories of commitment. Another approach is to ask for a letter of support written on the organization's stationery. Whichever way you choose, it is important to at least secure permission to list the organization as a member of the coalition. Although some organizations cannot, for reasons of their own, become official members of the coalition, they can publicly endorse the coalition and its goals. This should be offered as an option to those who decline membership.

From the very beginning, enlist other members to help with the recruitment effort. This increases their commitment as well as the coalition's field of contacts. Once you have a number of organizations signed up, it is time to hold a general meeting. Take this opportunity to build further enthusiasm for the undertaking and strengthen cohesion among members. Also, clarify members' roles and expectations and underscore the value of participation and the potential for significant accomplishment that exists as a result of those now present in the room.

You will find that a relatively small percentage of member organizations will be regular active participants. However, this core can accomplish a lot by using the many resources at the coalition's disposal. This may range from asking one or two members to perform some specific activity to occasionally mobilizing the entire membership. It is important, though, that these resources be used. Making direct requests of member organizations increases their feeling of involvement in the effort. Organizations rarely asked to do anything will lose interest and will most likely not follow through when they are finally asked. One important thing to remember is that each participating organization is concerned about many other things. One of the consequences of this is that requests for action should be made directly if at all possible. General requests of the membership are likely to go unheeded.

Communication among member groups is a crucial concern for the coalition. From simple matters like sending a follow-up note to those who agree to become members to holding coordinating meetings or sending out periodic progress updates, matters of communication must be given a high priority.

## DID YOU KNOW?

### Building a Successful Coalition

Mizrahi and Rosenthal (2001) surveyed more than 40 coalitions in an examination of factors that affect their success. Here are the top 10 internal factors that respondents reported as contributing greatly to their success:

- Commitment to the issue, goal, or cause
- Competent leadership
- Commitment to coalition unity
- Equitable decision-making structure and process
- Mutual trust, respect, and tolerance
- Broad-based constituency of members
- Achievement of interim victories
- Ongoing contributions of resources by members
- Shared responsibility and ownership
- Provision of benefits to coalition members

Coalitions commonly form committees or task forces organized around various functions to which the coalition needs to attend. These may include fundraising, media communications, advocacy, lobbying, and research. A coordinating committee composed of committee leaders and other interested members should be set up to manage the affairs of the coalition. This committee also helps plot overall strategy and direction. Open access to participation in this committee is vital. A general rule is that anyone who wants to be on it can be. Clear and meaningful opportunities to be involved in decision making will check the growth of divisive fear and mistrust.

Coalitions can be very effective and can provide you with credibility and resources very quickly. Keep in mind that with so many varied interests involved, coalitions require a high degree of attention to maintenance matters.

## Networks

Networks are distinct types of organizations that link people through a series of interconnected personal relationships (Figure 11.2). The intent is to establish and nurture these relationships so that each member is connected in some way to all others. Networks are not created to deal with a particular problem; rather, they are established to promote very broad goals. Networks put like-minded people in touch with each other so they can share resources and further common interests. This arrangement dramatically increases the availability of support and practical assistance.

Whereas a coalition is a collection of organizations, a network is fundamentally person-centred. Networks usually involve people who hold leadership positions or are fairly active in the community. Many, if not most, of the participants work in social service agencies. The

## ● CHANGE AGENT TIP

Have some sheets of newsprint hanging on the wall of the meeting room listing separate tasks or areas of responsibility that need to be handled. One should say something like: "Another job I am able to do." When a sense of purpose and enthusiasm has been generated, ask members to wander around the room and sign up for a task they would be willing to work on. Have a few people prepared to be among the first to volunteer. These sheets can be used to develop the coalition's task forces or teams.

assumption is that these individuals are able to activate resources other network members could use. This can be something tangible, like providing space for a meeting; it may be a service, like conducting a presentation on discharge planning; it may be a skill, like helping to set up a computer; or it may simply be help in cutting through the red tape.

A network is built on the idea that people are more willing to be helpful to someone they know and trust than to a stranger. So, a principal aim of a network is to have as many people with similar interests get to know, trust, and commit to help each other as possible. Therefore, an individual is invited into the network not so much to help with a particular problem as to be available to help in general.

Network

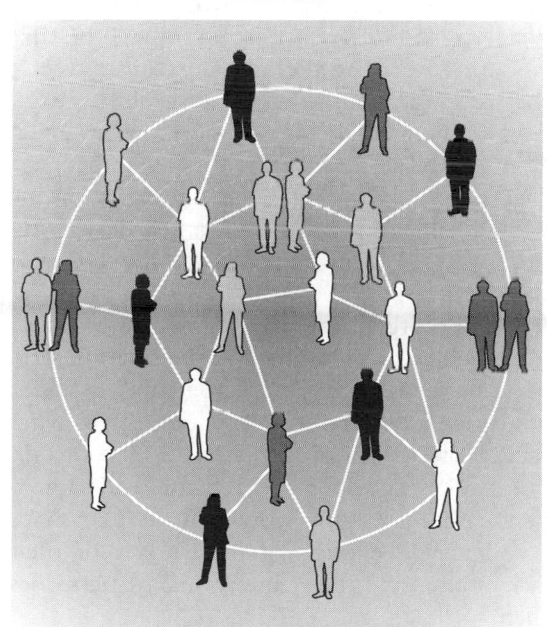

**FIGURE 11.2** Model of a Network

Members of a network are connected to all other members. Each member can contact any other member to make a request. Members bring personal and professional resources to the network.

In addition to the emphasis placed on building personal relationships and sharing resources, networks stress the importance of circulating information. The assumption is that many of the network participants are "in the know." Members help one another keep current on developments within their areas of interest. They also assist in putting the word out when one of the members needs some special help. A particular agency usually serves as a clearinghouse of network information. Regular newsletters and routinely updated membership lists (which identify particular resources members have committed to share) add to the storehouse, as do frequent get-togethers among members.

Dosher (1977a, p. 6) identified four main functions that networks provide:

- Communication linkages and information channels for the exchange of needs and resources
- Participant support systems and resource sharing
- A means for coordination, cooperation, collaboration, person and program actualization, training, and capacity-building
- A means for collective action

Ideally, the network is established at an initial meeting conducted in a workshop-like atmosphere. These key network concerns should be addressed at this first gathering (Dosher 1977b, p. 1):

- The purpose(s) of the network
- Network function or goals
- Recognition of personal values
- Deepening and strengthening interpersonal relationships
- Structure and member roles
- Identification of member resources
- Future plans and responsibilities

A network is a process for bringing people together to advance a particular public policy or practice (advocacy network) or to assist one another and to serve mutual needs (exchange network). Members of a network are committed to sharing information and resources (Langton, 1982).

Some networks are structured simply to facilitate the connection between individuals and serve both advocacy and exchange purposes. Such a network is not formed to take a position on specific community issues, but the process does facilitate network members getting together to take action, though not in the name of the network. Because of the many connections members have made through the network, it is easier for people to join forces to organize an advocacy campaign, a legislative action program, a workshop, or a bake sale. Those who want to be involved in any given project can do so, and those who do not can just sit back if they like.

Every one of us has our own personal network—those people we know and for whom we would do a little extra. An organized network simply brings all these networks together so people can ultimately benefit from one another's particular abilities and "connections."

## Core Group and Steering Committee Organizations

Some organizations have almost no structure at all. Such groups are characterized by a handful of highly motivated participants making most of the decisions and doing most of the work as well (Figure 11.3). These groups tend to be interested in resolving particular problems rather than in developing the power of the members of their community. (The exception to this is when the community is so small that a significant portion of that community are members of the core group. A group of social service professionals working on agency employment conditions might fit this description.) Non-core group participants in the change effort have only a mild sense of affiliation with the organization, and their action is commonly limited to periodic demonstrations of support, such as letter-writing campaigns or rallies.

If the number of active members of the organization stays small, it is likely that those who function as the core group will serve as unelected directors of the effort, probably without declaring that they make up any formal decision-making body of the organization. Core group members usually do not hinder others from becoming involved in the inner circle, but they do not actively encourage it either. If relative outsiders are willing to jump in and work, and at the same time try to figure out what is going on, they can do so. However, core group members are commonly not terribly interested in spending much time preparing new members for more active roles.

As the organization grows, or if it seeks increased legitimacy, active members may establish a steering committee to oversee progress. The steering committee positions may be filled by election, though this does not have to be the case. It could well be that whoever meets as the steering committee is the steering committee. As you might guess, few, if any, formal standing committees exist. "Committees" form when a few members get together to work on a specific task; meanwhile, other small groups are working on other tasks. When the task is completed, so is the committee.

If the organization continues to grow, or if it decides to take on challenges in addition to those prompted by its original formation, it may well develop a greater degree of structure. However, most of these organizations do not stay around long enough for that to happen. Either they stop working when they have accomplished enough of their goals, or their lack of attention to organizational matters does them in.

Core groups can be highly efficient and can successfully address a limited agenda, but it is difficult for them to sustain enthusiasm for long periods. With little effort directed to building for the future, groups like these tend to come and go.

**FIGURE 11.3** Model of a Core Group
A core group is an action-oriented organization with little formal structure. An "inner circle" of highly committed members does most of the work and makes most of the decisions. Membership in the inner circle is open to anyone willing to do the work.

## ● CONCLUSION

There is a lot to complain about. Sometimes it just feels good to let off steam. Sometimes it feels even better to use that steam to accomplish something. You are probably not the only one around who thinks things could be better than they are right now. When you set your mind and energy to finding some of those other people and working together to actually make a difference, change is inevitable. Your very decision to join forces and to act transforms the nature of things. The chances are that you will also accomplish some, maybe even all, of the specific changes you seek. You are moving from hoping things will change to making changes.

Every person in your organization always has some energy, but like batteries on a store shelf it may be just sitting around. Maybe all that energy is going in different directions and is being wasted. Acting together in an organized manner will bring more resources to bear on the situation and make your energy much more efficient, more focused, and more powerful.

Your recognition that problems do not have to be tolerated will move you through a series of actions that will result in coalescing forces directed toward change. Identify others who are willing to work alongside you. Gather more information on the community and the issue that affects it. You and your partners will come together to determine which steps you will need to take, and you will take them. You will experience bursts of enthusiasm when all things seem possible, and you will hit the doldrums and question the probability of your success. And you will keep moving forward.

You may start with just a handful of people, but your organization will grow. It will become more structured to meet the emerging demands it faces, yet it will remain flexible to ensure that procedures make your work easier rather than getting in the way. Some of the people working with you will drop out of the effort, but you will add new members to strengthen your numbers. Recognize that developing leadership and developing the organization are inseparable.

Since most of the planning and work will be done in small groups, pay attention to group dynamics. Particularly, help the group perform the tasks it needs to perform while enhancing relationships among members of the group. Know that conflict and controversy are not only inevitable but hold the potential for strengthening the group and its efforts. Recognize and deal with those pitfalls that predictably face any group working for change.

And you will have meetings, large ones and small ones—many meetings. Make sure all these meetings have a purpose, that you all know what that purpose is, and that you take practical steps to see that the purpose is accomplished.

The type of organization you become will reflect the demands of your situation. It may be a small, temporary alliance of individuals working to achieve a modest improvement in the community, or it may develop into a formal enterprise that becomes legally incorporated, with or without charitable status.

This process of putting the pieces together to build an organized effort will be a challenge. You will be exasperated, and you will be excited. You will be doubtful, and you will be confident. You will get angry, and you will laugh out loud. Perhaps above all, you will take a degree of satisfaction from the fact that you were able to get something done, and that this mattered.

## HELPFUL WEBSITES

**CANADA REVENUE AGENCY**

www.cra.gc.ca

Explore this website to learn more about developing your organization, including information about the benefits and drawbacks of incorporating and/or becoming a registered charity.

**ACORN (Association of Community Organizations for Reform Now)**

http://acorncanada.org

This democratic, multicultural, grassroots organization is committed to the goal of a bottom-up approach to solving problems in local communities. Members elect representatives and decide which issues to campaign on and how best to move these campaigns forward. ACORN is active in 75 cities across North America and has been active in Canada since June 2004.

**Help the Aged (Canada) (HTAC)**

http://helptheaged.ca

A non-denominational, nonprofit international development organization, HTAC has been dedicated exclusively to assisting elderly people living in poverty in Canada and the developing world since 1975.

**Human Development Council**

www.sjhdc.ca

The goal of this nonprofit social planning council is to improve the quality of life of the members of its community, Saint John, New Brunswick.

**Jubilee Fund**

www.jubileefund.ca

Located in Winnipeg, the Jubilee Fund is an organization that works for social justice through ethical investing in projects that contribute to community development. The fund provides flexible financing in the form of loan guarantees for individuals and organizations who do not qualify for traditional financing. The fund has a history of support for projects such as affordable housing, worker co-ops, and nonprofit daycares.

**RESULTS Canada**

www.results-resultats.ca

RESULTS Canada involves citizens lobbying their elected representatives to create the political will to end hunger, eliminate poverty, and create a better world. Established in Canada in 1986, RESULTS is active in eight provinces and is the only national network of grassroots action groups dedicated exclusively to reforming Canada's foreign aid policy.

CHAPTER TWELVE

# Taking Action: Strategies and Tactics

**This chapter will help you better understand the following questions:**

- What are the major strategies and tactics for action that are commonly used by community workers?
- What are the strengths and limitations of each of the major strategies and tactics for action?
- How can each of the major strategies and tactics be best used to promote community change?
- What are some important strategic and tactical considerations for community workers?
- What are some tips and tricks to address common barriers to using these strategies and tactics?
- What are some of the common strategies and tactics that others might use to try to prevent community change?

The frustrations with present conditions or the excitement of creating new ones can run up against the reality of taking action. Too often we can pick up the murmur of a potential difficulty and magnify its volume until we become frozen before taking action. Good intentions wither into half hearted attempts accompanied by strains of "I'll see if I can . . ." or "I'll think about doing . . ." or the death knell: "I'll try to . . ." If you look for reasons not to take action, you will find them. You just have to decide whether these are more important than the reasons to act.

If you intend to act, accept the fact that in community work, uncertainty comes with the territory. Acknowledge the misgivings that influence you to hold back. Be aware of what you might be thinking:

- You cannot act until all the details are covered.
- You cannot act because you might not succeed.
- You cannot act because you do not know exactly what to do.
- You cannot act because no one has done this before.
- You cannot act because there will be repercussions, you may get into trouble, someone may not like you, or you may have to do some real work.

As we have said throughout the book, there are times that uncertainty is good since it makes you open to the ideas of others and makes you more sensitive to what others are saying, especially those from a different social location than yours. If you are uncertain, you may simply need more information. At the same time community change involves action so at some point you need to take the risk and act. It is a balancing act.

Some feelings of insecurity might slow you down, but if you are determined, they will not keep you from moving forward. By your action, you can overcome barriers. You need to think more action oriented thoughts—thoughts like these:

- All the details will never be covered; I can accept that.
- I do expect to accomplish something important.
- Most of what I know I have learned by doing; this is no different from anything else, and I certainly have enough basic skills and knowledge to at least get started.
- Sure, there will be repercussions, including the fact that I can take some pride in what I am doing, I'll get to know some good people even better, and I may even have fun.
- There will be hassles; I can handle them.
- Sometimes there will be failures along the way but that does not mean there will never be successes; some of these successes might even be unexpected.
- If things are not going as I had hoped, I will reconsider my plans for the community project and develop a new direction or strategy for my actions.
- You can always change a plan of action and make endless changes as long as you see some effective result in your actions.
- Sometimes you learn through surprise—you learn things you could never know by the reactions—environmental, social, personal—to your actions.

Understand the best you can the realities of the situation, good and bad, and accept them. Then you can start doing things that lead to changes. It is not lack of money or support or authority or skill or any similar thing that compels people to sit still. These certainly are barriers, but they are ones that can be dealt with. It is feeling immobilized to confront the barriers, real and imagined, that preserves conditions that should be changed. Community practice is all about acting—and continuing to act—based on the belief that things should and can change make the difference. You can start without resources, and you can proceed when they are in short supply and then consider how you have done.

Taking action is an important step (Figure 12.1). Every change effort requires that someone begins to do something differently. Every successful change is the result of action. Distilled to its essence, the process of change involves taking goal-directed action, strengthening your organizing efforts through the effective involvement of others, maintaining communication to keep the reality of the change effort and the relationships among members strong, and continuing to make purposeful decisions. You must always reflect on your actions, and use this

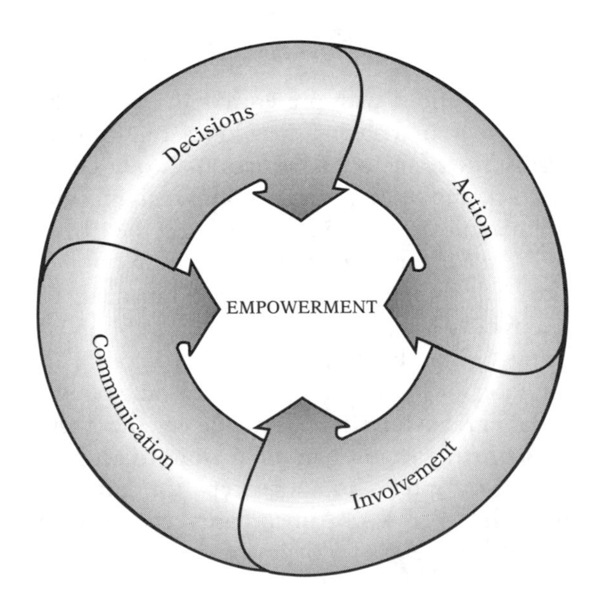


**FIGURE 12.1** The Process of Change and Empowerment

reflection to develop new strategies or reconsider the politics of your practice (Moffatt et al., 2005). Action. Involvement. Communication. Decisions. Reflection. Action. If you remember no more than this and adhere to it, you can look forward to numerous successes.

The decision to act is the precondition to accomplishment. The clearer that decision, the stronger your actions will be. This decision depends on two things: that the chances to gain something meaningful are sufficiently high and that the dissatisfaction with the current state of affairs is sufficiently strong. To sustain action, you, as the change agent, must keep these two factors in focus, at times emphasizing the prospects for success while at others intensifying the bitterness over current conditions. You need to do this both for yourself and for the other participants in your change effort. If one or the other of these ingredients is irretrievably lost, it is time to move on to something else.

It all boils down to this. None of your ideas, desires, or plans will teach you about community practice unless you act on them in some fashion. Once you have decided to act, here are some approaches that can make your actions more effective.

## MAJOR ACTION STRATEGIES AND TACTICS

"Have the situation dictate the strategy" is a component of community change. Each situation that you face will provide you with a set of unique variables that recommend one strategic approach over others. Be sensitive to these cues as you decide on your strategy. The selection of the approach that you take must be based on your group's ability to take the best advantage of your strengths and the openings the situation offers you. The choice is driven first by what exists in the situation, which is then matched to your group's sense of strength, group's vision, an openness negotiate an action across diverse social locations within the group, and available resources (Moffatt, Barnoff, George, & Coleman, 2009). As you proceed all these—strategies, process, and resources—will change so be certain to be adaptable.

Avoid the trap of becoming limited in your choices, which is the result of never allowing yourself to consider different methods. Doing the same thing all the time leads you into yet another trap, that of being predictable. Especially in a conflict situation, if the other side

### ? DID YOU KNOW?

#### A Checklist for Action

The questions on this checklist will frame your perspective of any setting for action. Your need to answer these questions will guide everything you do, and your ability to answer them will powerfully increase the likelihood of your success. Check your checklist often.

- From whom do we want to get a response?
- What response do we want to get?
- What action or series of actions has the best chance of producing that response?
- How do our actions produce immediate gains in a way that helps us achieve our long-term goals?
- Is everything that we are doing related to the outcomes we want to produce?
- Do some of the actions replicate the troubling conditions we seek to change even if such action is unintentional?
- How will we assess the effectiveness of our chosen approach in order to help refine the next steps we should take?
- What are we doing to keep this interesting?

always knows what you are going to do and can predict how you might argue the issue, they can more easily prepare to control how they respond, and you could lose an important advantage. Also be prepared to dream rather than get caught up only in what seems most practical. Be creative. Use your imagination to assist your efforts.

As Alinsky (1972) points out, "The action is in the reaction" (p. 129). The person or persons from whom you seek a reaction are members of the target community. We refer to them as the *target* or the *respondent*. Our use of the word *target* is not meant to imply opposition. They may or may not be in conflict with you, although in most cases there is some degree of hesitancy or resistance. The target is simply the focus of your efforts. Be cautious about your expectations. You can make a mistake by presuming that a target is either hostile or eager to respond favourably.

## TIPS

- The purpose of any strategy or tactic is to provoke the target into a reaction that will be helpful to your cause.

A strategy is the general framework of, or orientation to, the activities you undertake in order to achieve your goal. It is not a particular action, but rather, a series of actions that take into account the anticipated manoeuvres of your organizing effort as well as those of other parties, particularly the target. It is the overall approach to action that sustains your effort by giving it a coherent direction. Erlich and Tropman (1974) refer to strategy as the "orchestration of influence attempts" (p. 175) that brings together and consciously blends a variety of different components of action. They add that a strategy "takes into account the actions and reactions of key allies and adversaries as they bear upon achievement of the proposed goal" (1987, p. 258). Four basic strategic approaches can be pursued. Of course there are many others, but in this case strategies that are tied to your use of power are being outlined:

- Confrontation
- Negotiation
- Collaboration
- Cooptation

*Confrontation* involves bringing the demands of one party to the attention of another and forcing compliance. *Negotiation* is the process of bringing parties with different needs and perspectives to an agreement. *Collaboration* occurs when parties contribute resources to accomplish a common goal. Finally, *cooptation* results when parties share common beliefs about matters and when the success or failure of one party produces corresponding feelings of success or failure in the other.

Two important outcomes of the change process are (1) the institution of new agreements that create a change in the environment and (2) new relationships among various parties. In practice, these basic strategic approaches may represent stages in an overall attempt to forge and maintain agreements between parties. Each succeeding approach envisions the parties in closer relationship. For example, when parties are in confrontation, they are usually far apart regarding the matter at hand; when they are collaborating, they are working together. So you may use one approach to set the stage for activities in the succeeding one if you intend to move the other party into a closer relationship with you. That is, you may use confrontation to get the other party to negotiate, which may lead to collaboration, which in turn may result in coopting your former opponent (Figure 12.2).

Of course, you may neither need nor want a closer relationship. You may confront and force the other side to agree with you with little or no negotiation, and you can negotiate a settlement that does not include a subsequent series of collaborative activities. So the agreement that you reach by employing one or another of these strategies is based on what you are capable of producing given the factors present in the

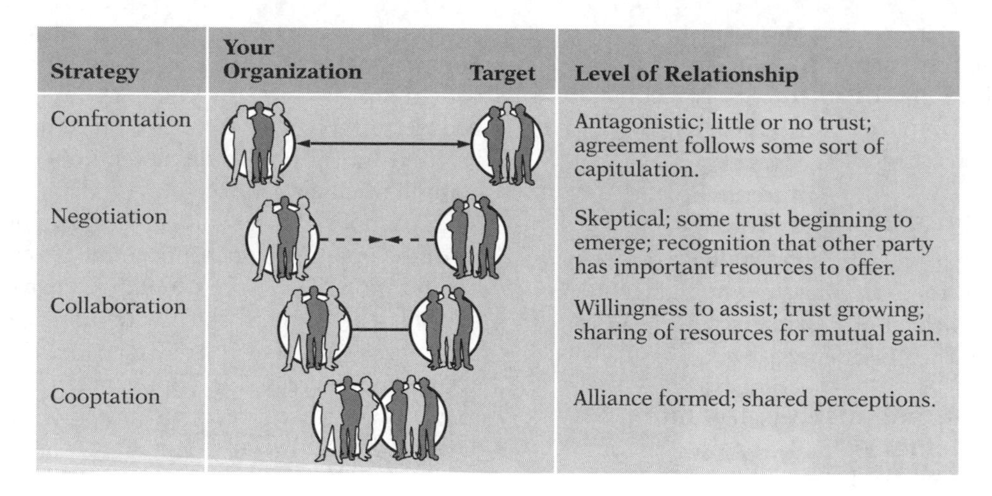


**FIGURE 12.2** Linking Strategy Choices to the Relationship Between Parties

situation at hand, the current nature of the relationships among parties, and the relationships that you ultimately wish to develop.

Tactics are specific activities designed to elicit a particular response from the target within the context of a discernible strategy. They can be further defined as "an action or phase of a strategy implemented to attain a limited objective which is instrumental to the attainment of a desired end state or goal" (Conner & de la Isla, 1984, p. 245n). In selecting tactics, you need to know who the target is, what response you want, what will influence the target to respond in the desired manner, and how that response fits with your overall strategy to accomplish your purposes.

All of this means that you have to do a little homework before you launch into action (Figure 12.3). Here are the major elements that you need to study:

- The issue
- The target

| Elements | Things to Know |
|---|---|
| Issues | Basic facts; causes and effects of problems; solutions applied in other places; rights and obligations of parties |
| Target | Probable reaction to specific tactic; principal decision makers; degree of and rationale for support or opposition; strengths and vulnerabilities; cohesion |
| Your support and alliances | Degree of commitment; numbers; probable reactions to opponent's tactics; cultural norms; strengths and vulnerabilities; cohesion |
| Other resources | Awareness of needed additional resources; availability and location of resources; steps required to gain access to resources |

**FIGURE 12.3** Considerations for Your Selection of Tactics

- Your support and alliances
- The resources at hand
- Diverse needs and diverse reactions of your community members based on their social locations

## Confrontation

Confrontation is the strategy that you use when you need to compel a target to change its position or behaviour. In these cases the target becomes the opponent.

### Situations in Which Confrontation May be Appropriate

- The target refuses to meet with you.
- The target is unresponsive to your call for change.
- The target does not expect a fight from you.
- The target cannot effectively defend itself from a confrontation.
- The target does not want attention.
- You need to show that the target is vulnerable.
- You need to crystallize the issue.
- You want to dramatize the issue.
- You want to draw attention to your group.
- You need to energize your group.
- Your members need to feel a sense of power.
- Your members are especially angry about an injustice.
- You need to show that you are willing to be confrontational.
- You need to attract allies.

As the community change agent, you want to avoid confrontation among community group members. Rather you can use this method as a political tool to force governmental institutions or private organizations that affect the well-being of your community to make a change when they are being intransigent. In confrontation, you exercise the power of your organizing effort and community group to challenge the unresponsive attitudes of others on a particular issue, in a particular context. Define the extent of the conflict and focus your power on a fixed area. For example, you may not be more powerful than the provincial government, but you may be able to force a local welfare office to change its procedures if it is affecting a number of your community members.

To employ this technique, set the vulnerability of the opponent against the strengths of your organization. The more carefully contrived this match is, the better. It starts with understanding what the respondent is likely to be sensitive to. Your tactics increase the opponent's discomfort to the point that it becomes more palatable to agree with you than to maintain resistance. You must be able to devise a plan so that either the degree of disturbance or its duration is something you can sustain much better than the opposition can.

Confrontational methods are usually showy because you must get your opponent and others, including the media, to notice you and to respond in some way. Also, the added attention increases the perception of community pressure and contributes to a climate of controversy that is often bothersome for the opponent.

### Strengths of a Confrontational Strategy

- The presence of an external opponent that is the focus of your organization's attention significantly strengthens cohesion.
- By picking your fights purposefully and beating a formidable foe, you increase the perception of your group's power.
- You can intimidate targets, making them less likely to give you problems on other matters or more likely to be agreeable to your concerns in future situations. The mere threat of confrontational tactics in the future may be sufficient to accomplish your purposes.
- Success may provide your group with a tremendous emotional uplift.
- You may be able to catch the other side off guard, especially if they are not accustomed to being met by planned, organized confrontation from groups such as yours.

- Confrontation may be based in moral suasion and justice. You may simply be so correct in your position as a community group that you feel the need to do whatever is necessary to force change. This comes with a lot of emotional power.

### Limitations of Confrontation

- This strategy requires a strong commitment by your members. Their commitment can be put to the test, exposing possible weak spots in your group's efforts.
- A loss can be discouraging and emotionally draining. It can lead to internal bickering as members look to blame someone, often those close at hand, for failure.
- The other side may become less willing to work with you in the future and may become passive-aggressive in their implementation of agreements (this is much more likely if you do not keep the heat on them).
- You may discover you enjoy this approach so much that you engage in confrontational methods just because you like the show, not because they are effective, and you become more impressed with developing tactics than with producing outcomes.
- You may discover that you so dislike the emotions like anger this strategy requires that you look for ways to avoid its use, even when it is clearly indicated.
- Some groups within your community, especially those who have been marginalized and feel disempowered, may feel more vulnerable through exposure during confrontation.

Confrontation requires a sharply defined opponent. This can result in an oversimplification of the situation in which assigning blame becomes the easy answer. When you blur lines of responsibility to intensify the focus, you run the risk of ignoring other relevant factors that may impinge upon the problem. You may forget that a major reason for confrontation is that changing your target's behaviour disrupts established patterns, allowing you to move aggressively on related aspects of the situation. Your supporters may become disheartened to discover they may be just getting started; they are not done. Further, if you think that changing your target's behaviour solves all your problems, you can lose sight of your own areas of responsibility and capability. This blurred view may reinforce a belief in your own powerlessness. After all, if the target is fully responsible for the situation, you are fully dependent on its actions or lack of actions for your own welfare.

### Tactics and Tips for Confrontation

*Freezing the target.* Keep your focus clearly on the target. Refuse to be distracted by others, often allies or subordinates of the target, who try to get your attention. When using this approach, your concentration is sometimes riveted to a single individual. Keep this one target in your sights and attempt to isolate it from its buffers or bases of support. You may need to engage in a series of actions in order to get and keep the target interacting with you.

This tactic is especially useful when the target is easily identifiable, when the target tries to get you to deal with others who have limited authority to act, or when attempting to respond to a number of allied opponents would diffuse your energy and dilute your efforts.

*Personalizing the issue.* This issue is related to freezing the target, and it essentially involves linking a particular person with the problem you are attempting to rectify. The intent is to make life difficult for someone whose actions or inactions marginalize, disadvantage, or oppress others. Pressure is brought to bear on the individual through a variety of means. Commonly, the target is cast as the cause or the maintainer of the problem as well as the suffering it produces. The target comes to symbolize all that is wrong with the situation. Typical methods can include public ridicule, constant interference with the target's routines, as well as exposing the target's arrogance, ignorance, incompetence, or the difference between the individual's public statements and private actions.

This tactic tends to cause the target's tentative supporters to shy away, for fear of becoming targets themselves or of being painted with the same brush. It will, however, tend to solidify the target's hard-core support. This may strengthen resistance, but it may also result in a small group of particularly nasty opponents becoming cut off from their support and going down together.

Your actions may result in removal of a particularly offensive individual from a position of power. However, simply removing one person from the scene rarely removes the conditions that cause the problem. Personalizing the issue sends a message to the target system regarding the seriousness of your intent and your willingness to hold those who perpetuate the problems accountable for their actions. This tactic is particularly effective when the target has little strong personal allegiance, is arrogant or offensive, and is prone to hasty or imprudent reactions.

*Holding accountability sessions.* Public officials may want to hide from your group's demands. Hold them accountable. This tactic keeps them firmly and publicly on the hook. An accountability session is a large public meeting where elected officials or public administrators are faced with publicly supporting or opposing your group's specific demands. You ask for their response on the spot. Since these sessions rely on political pressure, they are most useful for public officials rather than corporate targets (Midwest Academy, 2001). This is not a public hearing, discussion, or education session. This is a call for support for your positions. The target is literally on stage in front of hundreds of people, subject to a show of the massed power of your group.

Careful and detailed planning must be put into such an event, starting with making sure that your target has (or small number of targets have) some meaningful power to do something about the issues. Matters such as making sure you have a written acceptance of your invitation, inviting the media, arranging the facility, preparing a step-by-step production of the show, and clarifying and rehearsing specific roles for your members are required. Because the target's responses are recorded on a highly visible, large chart and scored as "yes," "no," or "not clear," members need to be prepped as to how to react to what the target is really saying. All this activity suggests that you need to do a good bit of organizing and power-building before you attempt to hold an accountability session (Midwest Academy, 2001).

This is a chance for public officials to shine and receive the dramatic and boisterous support of a large group of organized constituents or to feel the anger of those whose concerns have just been rejected. Because the members of your group get a big boost from the energy and their show of power, it is helpful to have some public officials stand on stage and agree with you.

*Getting outside help.* This procedure involves seeking the assistance of others, particularly organized groups, who are outside your immediate arena of action and who are sympathetic to your cause. Ask potential allies to endorse your concerns and provide you with specific acts of assistance, such as making public statements on your behalf, loaning you volunteers, or arranging meetings with key individuals. Outside allies have access to a greater number of audiences than you do and may well have direct access to some decision makers who will not give attention to your organization. It is particularly helpful to draw the assistance of a group that has broad public approval or credibility. Outside allies may include persons such as lawyers or specialists who can help you to argue your side.

This tactic tends to demonstrate the breadth of your support and the legitimacy of your position. It helps you to keep from becoming isolated yourself, aids in keeping a resistant opponent distracted, and increases the resources at your disposal. If your group is small, new, or relatively unknown, outside help will be beneficial.

*Using disruptive tactics.* These activities generally fall under the rubric of direct action. According to Staples (1984), direct actions occur "when a group of people take collective action to confront a designated target with a set of specific demands. The group action involves people directly with the issue, using their numbers or strategic high-profile acts as a means of pressuring their opponent" (p. 3).

Procedures for handling disputes are the responsibility of those who control the procedures. Standard approaches may give the opponent the upper hand as these procedures are usually designed to protect those in power rather than to accelerate needed change. You may need to change the game so that your opponents have to respond to *your* procedures. This puts them on unfamiliar ground. They are not so sure how to react, and they will probably make some mistakes.

You can take a variety of actions to throw an opponent off balance and out of the comfort zone of predictability. Sit-ins or occupations, picketing, boycotts, and mass demonstrations are among the most common forms of attention-getting activities. Because they are familiar, your opponents may know how to respond, so you may need to add something new. However, even though they may know how to respond, they usually do not want to, and they generally would like to avoid trouble.

Often, the most effective disruptive tactics emerge from the situation itself. A busy office may be frustrated by an endless series of phone calls that tie up the lines and prevent any work from being done. A public agency may be hamstrung by countless requests for different public documents. Rush hour commuters may become angry at a traffic stoppage, become incensed with everyone (this includes you), and demand that something be done to settle this. Convention proceedings may be interrupted by the staging of a guerrilla theatre act. Be creative, and be willing to do the unpredictable. One of the worst things that can happen is that you are ignored. Actions that attract notice at the outset may quickly become part of the landscape. Take pains to make sure this does not happen.

The usual process for engaging in disruptive tactics is to escalate the disruption in accordance with the resistance you meet. This conveys a sense of mounting pressure. However, as Kahn (1970) points out, reversing the practice by directing a major action on a relatively minor issue may prove effective by catching the other side off guard.

*Civil disobedience.* Defined by Rubin and Rubin (1986) as "intentionally and publicly disobeying a law and the passive acceptance of the consequences of disobedience" (p. 261), civil disobedience may take a number of forms. It may involve diverting the water from an irrigation canal, setting off building fire alarms, or refusing a court order to return to work. Perhaps the most common example is unauthorized occupation of a building or a site. If you are going to engage in civil disobedience of any kind, preparation is extremely important.

You should be well aware of the possible and probable consequences of your actions and be prepared to accept them. Participants need to be well rehearsed for the actions they are to take or not take. If those taking part are likely to be harassed or taunted by those opposing the action, they should have experience role-playing this situation prior to the event. Should arrest be likely, or even desired, participants must know how to conduct themselves throughout the arresting and booking process. Arrangements for bail or legal representation must be worked out beforehand. Organizers must have undertaken a reconnaissance of the area to maximize the effect of the operation and avoid problems. It is a good idea to get some special training from those who have experience conducting these actions. If you and your members know what to expect, you will be able to stand firm and make an important statement.

Use this approach when you need to grab attention from an unresponsive or delaying target or when the broad community is tolerating, or refusing to take a hard look at, problematic conditions. If you want to provoke people into taking sides, dramatic actions help. These methods are effective at revealing opponents as oppressors or calling attention to an unjust or absurd law, ordinance, or regulation. They can energize the members of your organization and strengthen their commitment to the cause.

Threats of action may be sufficient to produce the response that you want. Often the image of the event in the opponent's mind is more fearful than the event itself. If you do make a threat, be sure you are ready to back it up with action.

*Diversionary issues.* When using diversionary tactics, you get the respondent worrying over a set of secondary concerns or alarming actions that you might take. In their distraction, they agree to your primary point or allow you to institute a change before they can move to stop you.

One community group attempting to establish a much-needed community agency was being thwarted by established agencies that felt their territory was threatened. The community had just conducted a special drive and raised a large sum of money to deal with the problem. Representatives of the various community agencies and government bodies gathered together to address the problem as a body officially appointed by the mayor. Immediately, the advocacy group demanded that it receive all the money raised. This precipitated an onrush of arguments as each agency vied with the others to lay claim to a share of the pot. In the midst of all the commotion, the advocacy group asked that the decision on divvying up the funds be put on hold for a moment while design of the proposed new agency was approved. So concerned were the participants to get back to the business of dividing the spoils that they unanimously endorsed the proposal in a matter of minutes. This was done in a packed community hall before news crews of three local television stations and both major daily newspapers. The advocates gave interviews describing the new agency and its benefits, and the event received strong media coverage. By the time the opponents realized what had happened, it was too late to go back on their agreement to support the new agency, to which they had even decided to award a token amount of money.

## DID YOU KNOW?

### Five Criteria for Selection of Tactics

1. It is likely to produce the desired response from the selected target: that is, it will probably work.
2. You and your allies feel confident that you are sufficiently capable to pull it off: that is, you really think that you can do it, know how to, and will.
3. You have sufficient resources: that is, you have enough of what you need to make it work.
4. It builds your group: that is, it provides leadership opportunities, skill-building opportunities, cohesion, confidence, and so forth, and it attracts attention and new members.
5. It is consistent with your ethics.
6. It is negotiated among group members so that even those who may not be comfortable in engaging in the tactic at least are supportive of those who carry it out.

This tactic can work when your target is concerned with a number of issues. Exaggerating one issue may increase the target's feelings of vulnerability to that issue and keep it so preoccupied that other matters seem less important. Resistance to other matters then breaks down.

*Developing dependency on a particular project.* This is somewhat like a diversionary issue. In this scenario, your organization undertakes to help the respondent accomplish something of major importance to it but of minor importance to you. Because of the particular assets that your group possesses (for example, credibility within the benefit community), you can assist the respondent a great deal. After the respondent has made an investment and the project is under way, ask the respondent to make a commitment to something important to your organization, usually on an unrelated matter. Knowing that you can withdraw your support and ruin its special project, the respondent may be willing to go along with your request.

For this technique to be successful, the respondent must care more about the particular project than about the matter you want changed. Further, you have to be emotionally and ethically prepared to withdraw your support from the project and allow it to fail. This tactic functions well with a target who has been passively resistant to your efforts or who acts in a paternalistic manner toward your group.

*Partners in collusion.* This gambit is a variation of the good cop/bad cop routine. In that game, the bad cop berates and generally mistreats a suspect. With a threat and a flourish, the bad cop then exits the room, leaving the suspect alone with the good cop, who is sympathetic and kind. The good cop then asks for cooperation so that the suspect will not have to deal with the bad cop. The good cop may suggest a dislike for the bad cop and his or her tactics and may even hint that the suspect's assistance can be a way of getting at the bad cop. The suspect decides to cooperate with the much more reasonable good cop.

The good cop in your case would be an advocacy group that appears to be reasonable and well mannered, especially in contrast to the inflammatory rantings and public displays of a different, apparently more radical community group that fulfills the role of the bad cop. The role of the suspect in this little drama is played by the target of your intentions. Just like the cops, the two groups are acting in accordance with a planned tactic. The "bad" group can be picketing, while the "good" group, with carefully chosen respectable representatives, asks for a meeting. After agreements have been reached, both sides can claim victory while making sure not to discredit one another. After all, you both have constituencies that you need to keep happy and possibilities for future mutual actions to protect.

This tactic can be effective in bringing together two groups with similar interests but different action orientations. The target may be able to rebuff either group's approach, but the purposeful combination of the two changes the situation significantly. This approach may move the target toward cooptation by the "good" group.

*Lawsuits.* Most people would prefer to avoid being sued. Enter the threat of a lawsuit in order to get the target to pay attention to you. Although large companies and government organizations often find themselves the subjects of lawsuits, being sued is no trivial issue to them either.

Many individuals, especially those who have come to tolerate, if not accept, a condition of powerlessness, are unaware of their legal rights and their opportunities to assert them. Participation as plaintiffs in a lawsuit can bring members a sense of strength and power. Legal action allows them to assert their rights in a forum that must take their concerns seriously. Your willingness to seek redress through the courts demonstrates that your group refuses to be pushed around. It shows that you are willing to make your claims and to back them up. It forces the target to reckon with you.

If you do threaten legal action, be sure that you can back it up. Determine that you are on a strong legal footing before you make your threat, and follow through by filing a suit if your issues are not resolved satisfactorily.

Once you are in court, the proceedings can drag on for a long time, especially if your opponent decides to try to tie you up or simply outlast you. Meanwhile your members' enthusiasm can wane if there are few other fronts on which you are working. This can lead to discouragement. So, as you consider this tactic, take care to become well versed in what you can expect. Know the type of resolution that you seek, understand your opponent's options and likely responses, and ascertain the probable costs in both time and money that this commitment will require.

You do not want your members to just sit around during the time it takes to settle the suit, so rarely will pursuit of legal action be the primary focus of your activity. Still, there are ways that members can participate in the process. They may actually serve papers on your opponent, a rather empowering action; they may take part in the deposition process, allowing them to directly confront the target; and they can perform some research and information-gathering tasks (McCreight, 1984).

Using legal tactics requires a close coordination between the group and its lawyer. Decide whether you will include the group in the action, use small suits to focus your case, or file a class action. You may also need to sensitize the lawyer to the developmental needs of your group and their relationship to the lawsuit (McCreight, 1984). Having a lawyer as a member of your group is a definite asset, especially if he or she agrees not to be compensated until you prevail in your litigation. If this is not available to you, there still may be ways for you to receive representation without a great deal of financial strain.

Be prepared for the fact that as soon as you mention the possibility of litigation (or most any conflict tactic, for that matter) the target will accuse you of being disruptive, as if you are the problem, not the target's policies or the actions that you intend to change. If they respond this way or in similar ways, such as acting as if you have harmed the warm relationship between you, take it as a good sign. You have made them uncomfortable. Still, be careful about how you present your legal options. You do not want to make wild threats, nor do you want to prematurely close off exploration of other avenues.

Lawsuits can be effective when the legal rights of your group or its members are being abused. It can also be the tactic of choice to accomplish some other purposes. Lawsuits may be an effective way to attract attention from diverse audiences. Your action may gain the interest of regulators, the media, legislators, and other potential targets (League of Women Voters Education Fund, 1977). Legal action, or the threat of it, can motivate the target to work more seriously with you on the matter at hand. Through the discovery process of litigation, you may be able to acquire some valuable information about your opponent that would normally be unavailable to you. The publicity or attention that your suit attracts can increase your group's credibility (McCreight, 1984).

*Use appropriate channels.* The use of institutionally designed appropriate channels is loathed by some change agents. Generally, they fear that this lets the target control the process and that it threatens to stall their efforts. These fears are well founded *if all you do* is concentrate your efforts on trying to make these channels work.

There are some valid reasons for pursuing officially designed procedures, while not fully relying on them for your success. First, they may work. This may come as a shock to some, but it does happen. Second, by not following procedures, you give the target an out for not dealing with you. The target can easily represent itself as the victim of an ill-informed if not disrespectful group. Such a response may be generally accepted by less involved members of the community, which may be most of the community. You may end up undermining some potential support. Third, by taking the appropriate steps, you can clearly demonstrate that you have acted in good faith but that the procedures just do not work. You can show that the target is insensitive, arrogant, or incompetent in dealing with your legitimate issues. The target is now on the defensive.

It is important to develop a backup plan for what you will do when the prescribed procedures fail. However, do not wait until the breakdown has been proven before you try to figure out what your next steps will be. Have some point in mind at which you can declare the process to be a failure. This allows you to be prepared to emphasize your message about the ineffectiveness of the system and to switch quickly to your backup plan. This quick change in the game is likely to catch the target off guard.

This tactic is particularly appropriate when you are dealing with a bureaucratized organization.

*Cutting off support, particularly financial support.* You may be able to weaken an opponent not only through direct confrontation but also by eroding some of its major assets. Take some time to analyze factors critical to the opponent's operation. It may be more profitable to focus your actions on these critical supports than directly on the opponent itself. A good starting point is money. Generally, reducing the opponent's ability to get and use money will force it to change its behaviours. For example, a bank needs depositors and a store needs customers. If you can influence depositors or customers, especially one or two major ones, to change their practices if the target does not change what it is doing, you can strike a severe blow. Maybe a recalcitrant agency counts on United Way funding, which you can hold up with negative publicity and direct lobbying.

Photos.com

**Community workers need strong skills in negotiation and mediation.**

Find out where the money comes from, and you will usually find a good wellspring of power.

Other important sources of support include people whose endorsement is necessary for the target's success. Drawing these people away from the target or reducing the enthusiasm of their approval can harm an opponent.

This tactic is most appropriate when engaged in confrontation with a powerful opponent. It sends a strong message to other potential targets that you are willing to implement tough measures to achieve your goals. Consider making an example of one particular opponent if you are fighting several similar opponents. Do not forget that the other side can play the same game with your support base too, so be careful about how you decide to proceed and be prepared for what might happen as a result.

Confrontation requires acceptance of risk, clarity of purpose, and a high level of emotional energy. If handled well, it is capable of producing dramatic changes.

## Negotiation

Negotiation is a good strategy to use when the response community is willing to work toward an agreement and your prospects for working out a favourable settlement will not be significantly improved in the practical future. Though all strategies call for an understanding of your target, negotiation, which involves a distinct type of relationship, places a premium on your understanding of the cultural and political frameworks of your negotiating partners.

### Situations for Which Negotiation May Be Appropriate

- You can neither convince nor force the respondent into full compliance with your demands.
- Your group can no longer effectively sustain confrontation.
- Your group needs to see progress toward accomplishing some gain.
- The respondents have indicated an awareness of the legitimacy of your concerns.
- You have identified something that both sides can exchange to meet your interests.
- You can provide the other party with a gain that assists them and serves your interests.
- You want to build a working relationship with the respondent.

Negotiation is a process of reaching an agreement between or among parties through a discussion during which each agrees to use or withhold available resources or to perform or refrain from performing certain acts (for this discussion, we will consider negotiations between two parties, although more parties could be involved. The same principles generally apply in situations involving more than two parties). The decision to enter into negotiations rests with the perception by the parties that there is something to gain from participating or something to lose by not doing so. To negotiate, the parties have to be willing to come to an agreement. Further, there must be an overlapping range of acceptance (Rubin & Rubin, 1986); that is, what is at least a little acceptable to one party is at least a little acceptable to the other. If the ranges do not overlap, if the parties cannot find mutually acceptable items, then negotiation is not possible.

During negotiation, be aware of the interests of both parties as well as the relationship that exists between you. This helps you to identify possible short- and long-term costs and benefits. For example, you may negotiate an agreement beneficial to you that harms the other party and weakens the relationship between you. Or you may be so concerned about maintaining a relationship that you make an agreement that provides you with very little immediate benefit.

The relative power of parties affects the negotiation process. Of the many forms of power involved in the negotiation, two are particularly significant. The first is the extent to which one party depends on the other to accomplish its goals or meet its needs. The second, and related, concept is the extent to which a negotiator has desirable alternatives to the negotiation. The ability to walk away from the negotiation to another attractive alternative will dramatically increase a negotiator's power. Research by Tenbrunsel and Messick (2001) reveals that negotiations among parties of dramatically unequal power tend to be less productive, take longer, and be characterized by more competitive behaviour. Further, these authors point out that differences in power lead to increased uncertainty, which produces more self-focused interpretations of the situation and less shared understanding. If you are in a generally low power position with regard to your target, you will want to be able to focus your power or to develop alternative choices in order to equalize power in a specific situation.

Negotiation takes three basic forms. Negotiation can be *positional,* a process in which parties declare their positions and try to go as far as they can with their position. For example, you think that you and your friend should go out for Thai food, and your friend wants to go out for Indian food. Your position is Thai, your friend's is Indian. You try to convince your friend of the merits of Thai while acting in a way intended to get the decision to go your way. Meanwhile your friend is doing the same about the glories of Indian. You are both locked into your positions, and your bargaining will likely take on a win-lose quality.

The other basic form of negotiation is *outcome oriented,* a process in which you identify the broad outcomes that you want to achieve based on the parties' respective needs, not their positions. Alternative choices are generated based on a clear understanding of the needs of the parties. Neither party has to devalue the other's interests. Each merely needs to value an agreement that meets the needs of both parties. Using this approach, you and your friend determine that what is important is that you eat something soon and that it tastes good, fills you up, and does not cost very much. This opens up the possibilities. Who knows, maybe you decide to go to a restaurant where you can each eat different things.

The third form of negotiation is particularly tied to your *social location* as a practitioner. You need to negotiate your role with community members and community agencies. Your position shifts or is negotiated depending on tensions that exist for you as a community change agent. This is especially true if you are a change agent who is also a member of the community. In addition, the community change agent is often required to negotiate with others outside or peripheral to the community. This is especially true if you share the identity of the community you are working with. Whether you like it or not, sometimes you are treated as if the whole community is like you so you have to carry yourself with this in mind and negotiate relationships carefully, especially those where prejudice occurs. Your practice will include a lot of work on the nature of relationships. This process of negotiation never stops and has no beginning or end. It is not a linear process leading to a negotiated settlement but rather is a daily practice that seeks to keep issues alive and to mobilize people and resources to deal with them (Lee et al., 2002).

### Strengths of a Negotiation Strategy

- You are likely to end up in a more favourable condition, even if you do not get everything you want. Getting only half of what you want is probably an improvement over what you have now.
- You set a precedent that negotiation can occur. Your foot is now firmly in the door. When you were little, did you ever try to talk your parent into letting you stay up an extra half-hour to watch something "really important" on TV? Even though he or she agreed to do this "for this time and this time only," you probably knew this meant you would be able to negotiate again.
- You might get more than you expected.

- The other side's ability to gain something makes them more accepting of your gains.
- The opening discussion allows you to bring issues to the table that have not been formally acknowledged. Even if you do not immediately gain much on some of them, you have put them into the awareness of anyone who observes the negotiation.
- You begin to develop a relationship with the other party that is much more within your control.
- You are constantly aware of your social location and use it as a tool to get things accomplished, to work with others in the community and to challenge prejudice.

### Limitations of Negotiation

- You can negotiate away some non-negotiable items.
- By focusing on the wrong agenda or spending too much time on peripheral issues, you can accept the appearance of gain while gaining nothing of real value. For example, you may find yourself discussing where the road will cut through the neighbourhood rather than whether it should be there at all.
- You can settle for too little and weaken the legitimacy of your call for future concessions from the other party.
- You can look like you were too soft to your own constituents, weakening their support and confidence. You can look like pushovers to the other party, which may lead them to take you and your concerns less seriously.
- You can damage future relationships by selfish or subservient actions.

### Take a Moment to Discover

Have you ever lost sight of the importance of a relationship as you bulldozed ahead to get something that seemed important to you? Or have you ever been so afraid of losing someone's favour that you did something that went against the grain? What did you learn from these experiences? How can you apply what you learned in those instances to your role as a change agent?

### Tactics and Tips for Negotiation

Some minor or simple negotiations require application of only a few of these suggestions. Determine the degree of importance that the outcome of negotiation holds for you as well as the degree of difficulty you are likely to encounter in achieving your goals, then treat the negotiation process accordingly.

- Be prepared. Have an agenda. Know your facts and figures and have them written down. Select an advantageous time and place for conducting negotiation sessions. If the negotiations are particularly important or difficult, clarify the various roles that members of your team will play, and rehearse some of the probable negotiation scenarios.
- Have a clear goal in mind.
- Be willing to renegotiate.
- Find out what the other side wants or needs, and see if you can give it to them. You do not have to, but see if you can. If you do, determine when and how you will do this, and possibly in exchange for particular benefits that you seek.
- Be willing and able to package items or issues in order to provide a wider range of negotiating possibilities.
- Identify how agreements will be monitored and what sanctions, if any, will be applied for nonconformance.
- Get a third party involved if you are in a decidedly less powerful position.
- Confirm agreements in your own words.
- Be fresh, well rested, and eat right (this does matter).
- Be willing to break off negotiations or to take a break.

- Get to know the people on the other side; let them get to know you and your concerns. Be aware that people need to save face and will go to great, often unreasonable, lengths to avoid losing face.
- If you spot a problem with the negotiation process, bring it up for discussion.
- Summarize frequently.

### Methods for Positional Negotiation

If you decide that it is in your best interest to pursue positional negotiations, these suggestions can help you to gain an advantage over the other party.

- Ask for more than you need, but be sensible; do not exaggerate to absurdity.
- Prepare a retreat plan that delineates how you intend to use various items in your negotiation. To do this, you must clearly identify your non-negotiable items, your important items, and your giveaway items.
- Ask more questions than you answer. Generally, let the other side do more of the talking.
- As time goes on, people sometimes become more willing to agree, if only because they want to move on. You can use this to your advantage by dragging on or exaggerating minor issues, moving to more significant ones to a point in time when the other side is worn down.
- Spend detailed time on items you are willing to give away. This draws attention to the item, making it appear more important than it really is. As a result, you may more easily get something important to you because the other side now "owes" you one.

A number of authors provide additional insights into the negotiating process, for the most part reflecting a bargaining perspective. Brager and Holloway (1978, p. 196) have these points to offer:

- Relate your concerns to the other party's frame of reference.
- The more you can demonstrate commitment to a position that is credible to the other party as irrevocable, the more you are likely to win your point in the settlement (many others expound on this point, including Schelling [1963]; Pruitt [1981]; and Rubin and Rubin [2001]).

Rubin and Rubin (2001) make these suggestions and observations:

- Negotiators should remember that they speak for a constituency, not just for themselves.
- Make sure you get specific commitments, expressed in verifiable terms, not "We'll do something about that."
- Before the negotiating session, your team should simulate or role-play the negotiation, including having some of your team play the roles of the opponents.
- The negotiating team must figure out in advance just how and what they are going to concede while still coming out ahead.
- Consider counterproposals carefully. Be willing to call for a break in the action in order to discuss new offers among yourselves.

Splain (1984, pp. 166–170) recommends the following guidelines.

- Insist that your organization is dealt with as the only bargaining agent.
- Formalizing the bargaining committee and thoroughly preparing for the negotiations represents a critical set of tasks. It requires a more serious detailed effort than preparation for any single action or leadership meeting.
- You must lay the ground rules. Five key rules follow: all relevant information necessary to bargain in good faith must be made available; agree on the timetable (dates and times) as well as the location; identify the other side's bargaining team, and clarify any questions of authority and

accountability; agree on whether bargaining is open to observers or closed; and agree whether any non-bargaining activity (for example, using the media) will be allowed during the bargaining period.
- Be capable of demonstrating flexibility in your range of styles. Be able to employ soft (friendly) or hard (aggressive) tactics.
- Avoid getting publicly locked into a position.
- Use informal conversations to break an impasse, or let neutral third parties define a beneficial compromise.

## Methods for Outcome-Based Negotiation

One of the most significant contributions to the art of negotiation is contained in the book *Getting to Yes,* by Roger Fisher and William Ury (1991). The authors call their approach *principled negotiation.* The concept involves starting with a clear understanding of the *legitimate interests* of the parties. It proceeds to the generation of alternative strategies to serve those interests. The selection of the subsequent course of action must meet the tests of fulfillment of the parties' requirements in a way that can be measured by objective criteria.

Fisher and Ury contrast this with traditional negotiation, which starts from a *limited set of positions* designed to meet the interests of only one party, irrespective of the other's interests (Figure 12.4). Such a process is characterized by a test of wills, not merits, and results in invalidating the other's interests (which are tied to its positions) rather than exploring issues to discover possibilities of agreement.

As a general practice, principled negotiation has a number of advantages, especially when you are dealing with a more powerful competitor. This style of negotiation helps to even the playing field and keep you in control of factors in the situation that are more likely to be in your favour. Items irrelevant to the issues and over which you may have little control carry much less weight in this process.

The methods that Fisher and Ury outline enable you to fully commit yourself to necessary actions. As long as you think you have the right and the capability to insist on being treated respectfully—Do you?—you need not have any hesitancy about acting in a manner that is principled, whereas you may be reluctant to fully engage in a process that relies on being devious and clever or undermining the other party. By insisting on dealing only with the facts and merits of a situation, you do not have to accept non-legitimate interests as legitimate.

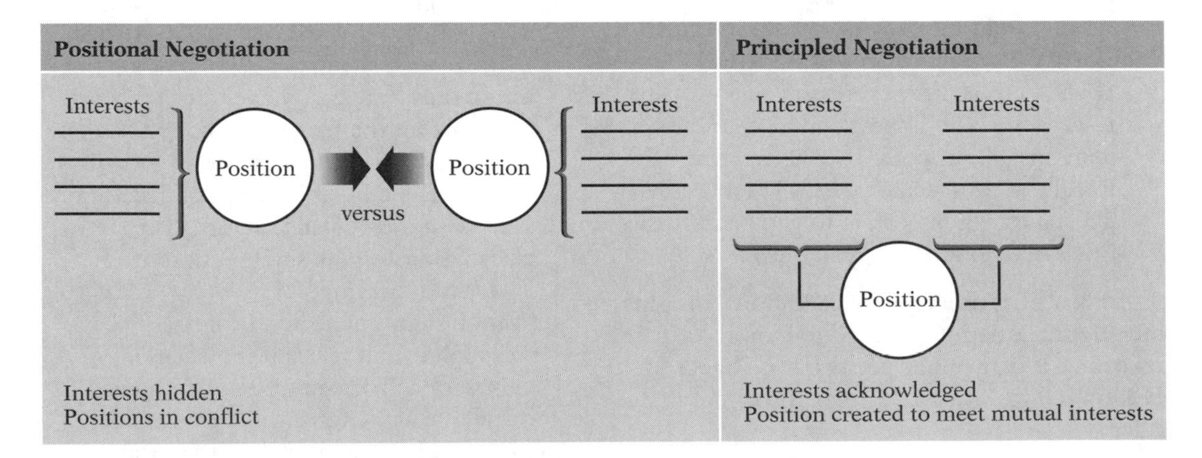


**FIGURE 12.4** Difference Between Positional and Principled Negotiation

Negotiation requires preparation, purposeful attention to detail, and an ongoing awareness of alternative choices. Further, it requires an intentional decision regarding the methods that you will use to reach agreement. When used effectively, negotiation can bring about a solution to current problems in a way that fosters opportunities for future problem solving.

*Social location negotiation* is constant and daily. Sometimes you may choose to use your position as a member of a community or a change agent to deliberately affect negotiations and work through relationships. Other times it will be forced on you, particularly by external agents. In these cases, you need be clear headed about this necessity of your practice. Other times, you might let it pass as you might be too tired to react to prejudicial treatment from outsiders, and that treatment may take up energy to remain focused on the task of change. When you share the identity of your community, you negotiate for them as a face of the community. The negotiation may be multifaceted—for example, you negotiate with target groups about how to speak with respect to your community or how to listen to the ideas of marginalized people. You may have to negotiate respectful, healthy personal and institutional relations in order to progress through change. As a change agent who shares the identity of your community, your negotiation is to think about how to protect yourself and your

## DID YOU KNOW?

### Some Advice on "Getting to Yes"

1. "The most any method of negotiation can do is meet two objectives: first, to protect you against making an agreement you should reject, and second, help you make the most of the assets you do have so any agreement you reach will satisfy your interests as much as possible" (p. 97).
2. The stronger the other side appears "in terms of physical or economic power, the more you benefit by negotiating on the merits. To the extent that they have muscle and you have principle, the larger the role you can establish for principle the better off you are" (p. 106).
3. "Separate the people from the problem" (p. 106). Be hard on the problem, soft on the people.
4. "Negotiators are people first" (p. 18). "People's desire to feel good about themselves, and their concern for what others will think of them, can often make them more sensitive to another negotiator's interests" (p. 19). "On the other hand, people get angry, depressed, fearful, hostile, frustrated, and offended. They have egos that are easily threatened" (p. 19). "To find your way through the jungle of people problems, it is useful to think in terms of three basic catego ries: perception, emotion, and communication. The various people problems all fall into one of these baskets" (p. 22).
5. "Interests define the problem. The basic problem in a negotiation lies not in conflicting positions but in the conflict between each side's needs, desires, concerns, and fears" (p. 40). "Behind opposed positions lie shared and compatible interests as well as conflicting ones" (p. 42). For a wise solution, reconcile interests, not positions. Insist on objective criteria. Don't try to settle differences of interest on the basis of will. "Negotiate on some basis independent of the will of either side, that is, on the basis of objective criteria" (p. 82).

*Continued*

These criteria should be legitimate and practical and should apply to both sides.

6. Hold people personally accountable for their actions and their information.
7. Acknowledge the interests of the other party as important to the negotiation.
8. "Look forward, not back" (p. 52). "You will satisfy your interests better if you talk about where you would like to go rather than about where you have come from. Instead of asking the other party to justify what they did yesterday, ask, 'Who should do what tomorrow?'" (p. 53).
9. "Invent options for mutual gain" (p. 56). "Four major obstacles inhibit inventing an abundance of options: premature judgment; searching for the single answer; the assumption of a fixed pie (the situation is seen as essentially either/or; either I get what is in dispute or you do); thinking that 'solving their problem is their problem'" (p. 57), an orientation that creates reluctance to think up ways to meet the interests of both sides.
10. "Never yield to pressure, only to principle" (p. 88); that is the integrity of the process.
11. "If you have not thought carefully about what you will do if you fail to reach an agreement, you are negotiating with your eyes closed. The reason you negotiate is to produce something better than the results you can obtain without negotiating" (p. 100). Therefore, determine your BATNA (Best Alternative To a Negotiated Agreement). "That is the only standard against which any proposed agreement should be measured. That is also the only standard that can protect you both from accepting terms that are too unfavourable and from rejecting terms that it would be in your best interests to accept" (p. 100).
12. "Apply knowledge, time, money, people, connections, and wits to devise the best solution for you *independent of the other side's assent* [emphasis added]. The more easily and happily you can walk away from a negotiation, the greater your capacity to affect its outcome" (p. 106). This is really all about power. In other words, you will be stronger by the extent to which you do not depend on the negotiation.
13. If the other side refuses to focus on the merits, just don't respond to the game they are playing. "In effect, you change the game simply by starting to play a new one" (p. 107). Still, the other party may attempt to engage in trickery. Three basic tricky ploys that may be used are those intended to deceive, those designed to make you emotionally uncomfortable, and those that lock the other side into their position. "There are three steps in negotiating the rules of the negotiating game where the other side seems to be using a tricky tactic: (publicly) recognize the tactic, raise the issue explicitly, and question the tactic's legitimacy and desirability—negotiate over it" (p. 130).
14. "Don't be a victim. It may be useful at the beginning of the negotiation to say, 'Look, I know this may be unusual, but I want to know the rules of the game we're going to play. Are we both trying to reach a wise agreement as quickly and with as little effort as possible? Or are we going to play "hard bargaining" where the more stubborn side wins?' Whatever you do, be prepared to fight dirty bargaining tactics. You can be just as firm as they can, even firmer. It is easier to defend principle than to defend an illegitimate tactic" (pp. 142–143).

Source: Excerpted from *Getting to Yes*, 2/e by Roger Fisher, William Ury and Bruce Patton. 

community. Our best advice in this situation is to be aware of what is going on in your relationships and determine how people are constructing, responding to, and treating you and those who share your identity. It is important not to ignore these relations since this is the heart of community practice. These relations can negatively influence your sense of vitality as a worker. If you are conscious of them and push back through negotiation, it can help you reach your goals as a community change agent.

## Collaboration

Collaboration occurs when two or more parties share resources to accomplish a goal important to them all. They go beyond the mutual acceptance of a course of action; they "co-labour." That is, they each perform some measure of work in order to accomplish the goal. When the strategy of collaboration is used, the target becomes a *partner* in a common enterprise. The shared goal need not be equally important to all parties, nor do they necessarily pursue it for the same reasons. For one group, the particular, observable end to be accomplished may not be all that important, but the ability to establish a working relationship with their partner may be. Or perhaps collaboration offers relief from accusations of callousness through the appearance of sensitivity that participation in a cooperative venture can bring. In fact, the partners do not even have to like each other to collaborate—although it makes things much easier if they do. Whatever the reason, the common goal unifies their respective motives and provides the impetus to work together.

### Situations for Which Collaboration May Be Appropriate

- The respondent has resources that you need and from which you can benefit.
- You have resources to offer.
- You need to carry forward the results of negotiated agreements.
- You recognize that you can give the respondent a way to meet some of its needs if the respondent helps you meet yours.
- You want to develop a working relationship with the respondent.
- You want to show that you can get the respondent to react to you, and you are looking for ways to make it easy for that to happen.
- You want to increase the respondent's dependence on you.
- You want to educate the respondent through close or ongoing contact.
- You recognize that the respondent is agreeable and wants to work together.
- You want to establish new attitudes and practices in the community.
- You want to work together even though community members have different identities and social locations. No one person can understand them all, but through collaboration, a more thorough understanding can be developed.

We talk a lot about cooperation, but most of us are not really skilled at developing and maintaining collaborative relationships to meet community problems. It is hard enough to work together on a class project or to get five families to go on a camping trip together. Getting groups who are nervous about one another's motives or their dependability to join forces is a formidable task, though it is possible if thoughtfully done.

As one strong advocate of collaboration points out, agencies and organizations do not cooperate, people do. Collaboration is *people deciding to work together* (Hagebak, 1982). Yet these people are tied to organizations each with their own policies, procedures, traditions, and formal and informal goals. These and a host of other barriers interfere with the purposeful attention to matters that collaborative relationships require. Still, as Hagebak (1982) points out, "when it gets right down to basics, the decision to cooperate—or become a barrier—is a *very personal decision*" (p. 33).

Before a group can begin to work together, it really must be able to work together. Standing disagreements and rivalries do coexist with a commitment to work for change at times. As much as possible they need to be openly dealt with in order to reach the point of collaboration (Moffatt, Barnoff, George, & Coleman, 2009). How many times have you seen this in a family, a group working on a class assignment, or a team in a workplace?

If development activities are to be a form of conflict reduction, even resolution, the parties involved must recognize and agree to this strategy. Otherwise, they will undermine the effort in order to confirm their perceptions and positions. That initial agreement itself requires some reduction in conflict.

Some of your partners will be coerced or convinced to collaborate with you. Others, with interests and motives similar to yours, will be eager for the opportunity. For collaboration to be effective, even the most well-intentioned partners must confront a number of matters that threaten to weaken their relationship or scuttle it altogether. Doing so successfully can provide for creative, powerful relationships and a cooperative spirit, which can ultimately extend to other matters.

### Strengths of a Collaborative Strategy

- The resources that can be brought to bear on the situation automatically increase.
- You may be able to move your partner into a greater appreciation of problematic conditions and their ability to have a positive impact on them.
- You can teach your partner more effective ways of serving the benefit community.
- You may increase your partner's dependence on you, thus altering the balance of power.
- If carefully nurtured, collaborative relationships can establish a whole different way of addressing community dilemmas. Collaboration makes future problem-solving much more efficient by taking energy away from maintaining battle lines and putting it toward improving the community.

### Limitations of Collaboration

- Social tension can cause partners to pull back into a posture of self-protection as soon as complications emerge. This undermines cooperative intent, rendering the effort practically ineffective and emotionally unsatisfying.
- You may become less willing to bring a partner to task on other matters for fear of reducing their collaboration on your shared undertaking.
- The partner may take all the credit for success, and blame you for failures.
- You, who may be more committed to the success of the actual project, may end up doing a far greater share of the work.
- Energy, sometimes a great deal, is required simply to maintain the relationship.
- You may lose some autonomy as you provide your partner with a degree of control.
- A breakdown in the collaborative relationship can make it much more difficult for parties to work together in the future.

### Tactics and Tips for Collaboration

A collaborative relationship needs to function on both the task and relationship levels. Each of you should be clear and reasonable about what you expect to get from the venture and what you expect from your partner in order to achieve your goals. You are going to have to tell people your expectations, perhaps more than once, and hold them accountable. Though many aspects are unique to each of these relationships, a number of general topics should be carefully examined. You need to proceed with a steady and mutual recognition of the importance of each of these items.

*Clear agreements.* You can prevent a multitude of problems by explicitly delineating the tasks to be performed and the type and extent of resources to be shared. Clear, mutual understandings also help coordinate efforts and resources. Hagebak (1982) warns that memory is imperfect, perceptions differ, and forces affecting our decisions change. So even when working with partners who are friendly, it is best to put agreements in writing.

*Decision making.* You and your partner need to determine which decisions must be made in a manner that requires joint approval and which decisions each of you can make without the approval of the other. If there are multiple partners, you also need to determine which style of decision making you will use. Consensus usually works best. Essentially, consensus exists when two conditions are met: Each party is able to clearly state what the decision is, and each party agrees to support and implement the decision. Other methods, such as majority vote or decisions by an executive committee, may be appropriate.

*Monitoring and evaluation.* Believe it or not, all good intentions and wonderful ideas do not pan out. Keep track of how partners are living up to their agreements and how well plans are working. Clear agreements and plans will aid in this process. Since you cannot foretell the future, accept the fact that refinements and renegotiations are part of the game.

*Recognition.* Each of you needs to receive some acknowledgment from your constituencies that you are serving their interests. Stories in the local media, personal letters acknowledging your work, or appearances from other partners before your group are likely ways to get this recognition. Quotes from your partner regarding how your contributions help them and how the project helps your constituency can be useful. Be willing to provide the same sort of recognition to your partner.

*Trust.* A sufficient amount of trust in each other or in the strength of some external mechanism that holds parties accountable (like a contract or an oversight body) is a prerequisite for collaboration. Acting in a trustworthy manner yourself is the first step in promoting this quality. In situations in which there is some hostility between partners, the other party might suggest that you refrain from some legitimate activities that that party just does not like. They may be using the relationship to get you to cut back on some of your other activities. You need to assess for yourself whether you are living up to the specifics and the spirit of the agreements you have made on the matter at hand.

*Leadership.* There has to be a force to keep the momentum going—and going in the right direction. An ability to spot potential problems, bring issues and opportunities to the fore, and effectively coordinate activities is necessary. The strength of the agreements themselves is not sufficient to accomplish these requirements. People from your group, and ideally from the other's as well, need to clearly understand the necessity of providing a leadership function within both the work and the relationship realms of the program. Leadership functions can be shared among a number of community members.

Here are some additional points to help make collaboration work.

- Make sure that the timetable for task completion, and especially the pay-off period, is realistic and mutually understood. Make sure that partners know when certain activities need to be done and that they have a sense of progress. Sometimes the more tangible benefits take a while to realize. It may take some time to complete a soccer pitch or turn a profit on a business venture. You do not want partners to get discouraged and give up because they had an unrealistic idea of when they would achieve returns.
- Provide opportunities to create a sense of ownership in the venture. This is especially important for reluctant associates. Involve partners in things such as naming the project or designing a logo. It will be hard for them to undermine a project for which they have been involved at every stage.
- Provide public acknowledgment of the respondent's participation in the combined venture. This lets many people know the expectations your partner is to meet.
- Use vehicles, such as the letter-to-the-editor column, to call attention to your partner's contributions and to encourage future ones.
- Give tangible awards, such as plaques or certificates, at a presentation before your

group as well as your partner's. You can do this while you are working together in a way that suggests a future productive relationship. Do not leave recognition until everything is completed.

- Privately acknowledge good work. You can do this with a comment or in a personal letter. It is better to make reference to something specific than to make general statements.
- Work together on tedious or demanding tasks like letter stuffing or digging holes for a tree planting. You can easily introduce a social component into these activities that strengthens the relationship as you really do work together.
- If your partner is creating a problem, bring it to his or her attention in a direct, matter-of-fact manner. Do a gentle confrontation. Wherever possible, let your partners make corrections to the problems they have created.
- Take note of what is working and the advantages each partner is reaping. It is a bad practice to focus on problems while taking good things for granted, yet it is a common one. When you pay attention to things that are going in the right direction, you emphasize a positive focus and build confidence in the relationship. This also helps you to keep problems in perspective and to deal with them more effectively. Failure to deal constructively with problems is often a sign that there is little confidence that the relationship can handle any conflict.
- Get to know one another personally. The less we know about people, the more we have a tendency to make up things about them, especially if we begin to encounter problems. Though you do not have to become fast friends with your partners, a more personal, informal relationship can help cut through artificial barriers that are common in more reserved relationships. Further, a built-in accountability exists among people who know each other well, as long as one party doesn't use the relationship to take advantage of the other.

Collaboration requires attention to maintaining agreements and relationships. By greatly increasing the resources available, a more comprehensive improvement in a situation can occur more easily, and the experience of collaboration can establish progressive methods for understanding and acting on future challenges.

## Cooptation

People's perception of reality is strongly shaped by their affiliations. You may decide that you can accomplish more by bringing certain actors or groups of actors into the fold than you can by keeping them at a distance. Through continued exposure to your perceptions, even opponents can begin to see things your way. In fact, this strategy is especially geared to opponents. Barker (1999) describes cooptation as a "strategy for minimizing anticipated opposition by absorbing or including an opponent in the group's membership" (p. 105). Kirst-Ashman and Hull (2001) describe it as "eliminating opposition to a cause, plan, or organization by assimilating opponents into the group favouring the cause, plan, or organization" (p. 422). Cooptation occurs when the beliefs and attitudes that others hold about a situation conform to yours.

Cooptation usually begins when a formerly antagonistic party changes its manner in regard to its opponent. This party will often appear to be more accepting of its previous opponent and in some way invite the adversary into a relationship of greater congenial contact. This may even include offering a means of formally joining the inviting party's ranks.

This gambit is frequently used by powerful resisting groups to undermine their more grassroots opposition, but it is available for use by grassroots organizations as well

(Crowfoot et al., 1983). It is not uncommon, for example, for key leaders of the opposition to be offered jobs in the competing organization. Or perhaps appointment to a special committee that appears to carry some status or special privileges is arranged. Such tactics are intended to weaken an opponent's resolve by giving those who make the offer an appearance of being fine folks after all . . . and, in fact, their positions do not seem to be that unreasonable either. Those who have been coopted will begin to soften their opposition or risk losing this newfound acceptance by their former enemy. They may begin to justify this new moderation by finding merit in a previously scorned point of view. When this occurs, a former opponent accepts, usually unwittingly, a position of furthering the interests of the coopting party.

People are susceptible to this ploy for a variety of reasons. They may be so tired of the antagonism that they are eager to pick up on any change in attitude. They may believe that the new, more amiable relationship provides greater opportunities for influence. They may be flattered, or even simply relieved. The strategy of cooptation is usually purposefully manipulative.

### Situations for Which Cooptation May Be Appropriate

- The opposing group is uncooperative and is not a good target for confrontation, perhaps because it is highly regarded by most of the community.
- Maintaining an adversarial stance will result in only isolated gains or a standoff.
- A few key individuals who have some influence within the opposing group are amenable to some sort of affiliation.
- There is a particularly vocal critic that you would like to silence.
- Your group does not have the capability for effective confrontation, nor does it have the resources needed for collaboration.
- You can weaken opponents by bringing them into your organization, where their opinions will be in the minority (Barker, 1999).
- You will probably be in an ongoing relationship with the respondent, and you believe that a productive, working relationship can develop if purely antagonistic positions are changed or not adopted at all.

Some people are uncomfortable with the notion of cooptation. It somehow does not seem quite right. The fact that cooptation is more covertly than overtly influential makes it different from most other strategies. It does not make it better or worse. This strategy is simply another way of bringing an opponent over to your way of seeing things. You are choosing to work more closely with an adversary, and you are providing the adversary with an opportunity to better understand your needs. Ultimately, any strategy is intended to persuade the respondent to accept the legitimacy of your beliefs. Cooptation is a more subtle form of persuasion in which you invite respondents into your perspective rather than directly countering theirs. Others may not like this approach because it does not strike directly at problem-causing policies, nor does it maintain a clear distinction between conflicting camps. Points that can be made through open confrontation may be obscured, and it can appear to blur the lines between good and bad.

There are times when distinctions need to be emphasized and the nature of the conflict dramatized. At these times, cooptation is the wrong strategy to pursue. However, not all opponents must always be seen as evil or kept at arm's length. The notion that opponents can never accept and act on the validity of your interests is a fairly limiting one. The question is, how do you ultimately get them there? Pursuit of this strategy is based on the belief that greater understanding and at least a partial alliance will lead to more change than the more direct use of power.

### Strengths of a Cooptation Strategy

- You can defuse a potentially harmful critic.
- You can maximize a former opponent's commitment as he or she identifies with your self-interests.
- You can gain some insights into the workings of the competition.
- You gain access to a community or organization that has been closed to you. The coopted party can serve as a kind of translator, communicating your interests with an understanding of the codes and perceptions of the other group. This person can also act as an introducer, helping members of your group to gain some degree of acceptance in the other group.
- This strategy requires little investment of energy or resources.
- An obstructing group can become an allied group.

### Limitations of Cooptation

- Those whom you invite in may have no interest in working with you and may use information that they obtain against you.
- You may inappropriately soften your stand and become reluctant to hold your new-found friends and their organizations as accountable as you should (you become a little coopted yourself).
- You can be transparent in your attempts and come off as insincere and manipulative, further damaging relationships.
- You can get caught up in the game of coopting people, thereby diminishing your own personal integrity.

### Tactics and Tips for Cooptation

- Cooptation is a process that works over time. The target of your intentions is eased into a greater appreciation for your point of view. Be aware that respondents are likely to be at least a little cautious, so go gently. Avoid the temptation to put people down for past sins or to prove that they or their organization are wrong, or you will just promote defensiveness and maintain existing frictions.
- It may be helpful to place the target on one of your key committees, even your steering committee or board. Though the degree of responsibility that you give will be based on the nature of the relationship with the group that the target represents, some degree of importance must be attached to the role to ensure the individual's interest and involvement. Also, greater responsibility deepens and accelerates the process of cultivation.
- Each target should get the message that he or she is seen as a team player.
- Once targets have had some time to become acculturated to the needs of your group, invite them to help seek solutions to the problems that you face, particularly as these relate to working with their own constituency.
- Do not attempt to coopt too many people at a time. Two important targets are plenty.
- Whomever you attempt to coopt must have credibility within the opposing community.
- A good person to target is one who has cooperated with you in the past.
- Remember that the purpose is to draw in and build support, not to set someone up as a fool who will suffer some loss because of your actions. Aside from the obvious ethical problems with harming someone, it will probably come back to haunt you.

Cooptation requires patience and a belief in the possibility that someone who has previously interfered with your success can become an advocate for your cause. It can curtail resistance and establish valuable links to key constituencies.

## GLOBAL PERSPECTIVES

NIGERIA—(July 15, 2002) Unarmed village women holding 700 ChevronTexaco workers inside a southeast Nigeria oil terminal let 200 of the men go Sunday but threatened a traditional and powerful shaming gesture if the others tried to leave—removing their own clothes. Most Nigerian tribes consider unwanted displays of nudity by wives, mothers, or grandmothers as an extremely damning protest measure that can inspire a collective source of shame for those at whom the action is directed.

About 600 women from two nearby communities are holding ChevronTexaco's giant Escravos terminal. They range in age from 30 to 90—with the core group being married women 40 or older. The women want the oil giant to hire their sons and use some of the region's oil riches to develop their remote and rundown villages—most of which lack even electricity. The people in the Niger Delta are among the poorest in Nigeria (Associated Press, 2002c).

(July 16, 2002) The unarmed women holding 700 ChevronTexaco workers in a southeast Nigeria oil terminal agreed, Monday, to end their siege after the company offered to hire at least 25 villagers and to build schools and electrical and water systems. . . . "We have to do a much better job of having communities involved in our business. We now have a different philosophy, and that is do more with communities," [ChevronTexaco executive Dick] Filgate told the women (Associated Press, 2002a).

(July 18, 2002) Hundreds of unarmed women seized control of at least four more ChevronTexaco facilities. . .even as the ten-day occupation of an oil terminal by other village women ended. . . .

The women involved in the latest takeovers, all members of the Ijaw tribe, were refusing to leave until they had met with senior company executives to press their demands for jobs and community improvements (Doran, 2002).

(July 26, 2002) Village women chanted jubilantly Thursday after ending their week-long occupation of ChevronTexaco oil pipeline stations in exchange for jobs, business loans, schools, and hospitals (Associated Press, 2002b).

SOUTH PACIFIC—Change rarely takes place when people are "comfortable" or think that they are comfortable. A tension must develop before people or groups can undergo meaningful change. These tensions are often expressed as a felt need, and are finally articulated in one way or another. Community development workers who merely help people to become "comfortable," who do things *for* people—identifying and analyzing their problems for them and "doling out" answers—are part of the problem, not part of the answer (Melanesian Council of Churches, 1977, p. 220).

ISRAEL—We had a group of community workers in the city, in the neighbourhoods, a staff of young street workers, and also the Golden Age Club participants. . . . We organized a committee of aged people and some other volunteers. We started organizing them to fight, to get health coverage for thousands of people in Jerusalem.

First of all, we had a real problem, because the elderly were afraid to confront anyone. So we started working with them. We engaged in role-playing, because when we took them to the Mayor and to the rabbi, they suddenly became passive—they couldn't even talk. So I told them, "I am the Mayor. Oh, you are very nice people . . ." And little by little they became more aggressive. They learned how to be more and more aggressive, and they started going to people in the newspapers. They started learning how to present their problems. That took about five or six months of work.

The municipality ignored the problem of reopening the centers because it would cost a lot of money. . . . So we decided to move on to other tactics. We issued a warning that the funeral of the next man to die would leave from the house of the Mayor . . . and from the home of the Minister of Health. We realized that behind every position, or agency, there is a man with his weakness. You have to find the weakness. We found that such threats were very effective.

*Continued*

Next we came with around eight hundred aged, and we demonstrated in [the Mayor's] office. But [the Mayor] was quite clever. He brought the demonstrators Coca-Cola and other things to drink, and that was not helpful to our conflict. He treated them as guests.

Then we went to the Ministry of Health. They were less clever than [the Mayor], and they closed the doors, so the aged threw stones at the office. . . . Later this same night . . . they came to an agreement to give many, many people their health insurance . . . without paying money, like socialized medicine. That was the result of this fight (Amiel, 2001, pp. 105–106).

## OTHER STRATEGIC AND TACTICAL CONSIDERATIONS

### Ethical Engagement

Consider the ethical dimensions of your action or inaction. If you set up an opponent, may you have unfairly or unnecessarily abused another human being? If you allow a serious problem situation to persist because you will only engage in polite tactics, how does your mannerly approach honour those whose suffering is prolonged?

Your time is much more wisely spent firmly rooting yourself in ethical practice. Review your commitment to ethics and keep it alive. Examine whether you are justifying your unethical behaviour in order to be strategic. Then ask yourself why you would do that when community practice is based on beliefs and principles such as engaged citizenship and hope (Tenbrunsel & Messick, 2001). Your behaviour may very well change from one situation to another, because your ethics inform and drive every important decision that you make. Your steadfast commitment to integral ethical principles will guide you to act differently as you face different challenges to your beliefs.

### Recognize Mutual Benefits

Along with basic concerns regarding selection of a strategy mentioned at the beginning of this chapter, three overriding considerations should be kept in mind. First, you need to think about how a certain approach will help your change action to accomplish its particular goals. Next, you need to consider how the strategy will aid in the continued development of your group. But that's not all. You must also take into account the benefit the target perceives from pursuing a course of action that you desire. If you have given thought only to what you want them to do and not why they will want to do it, you have thought things through only halfway. You need to consider why the target will respond, from their point of view—not yours.

So your deliberations on strategy must include not only what you need but what they need as well. This raises a number of questions. What's in it for them? Or what's important to them? Will the target readily recognize a benefit, or will you have to sell them on it? It is important to remember that, in many cases, the change may require the respondent to move into unknown territory or even accept a loss of power. It is also important to remember the fact that just because a course of action "makes sense" may have little bearing on the response you will get. What makes you think the target will respond in the way you want it to?

The more clearly you can focus your actions on the (rational, normative, and emotional) things that are important to the respondent, the more direct and meaningful the response will be. Although this may very well mean you select a strategy that will cause the respondents discomfort for resisting, you will generally find that the more easily the other party is able to recognize a benefit by pursuing the action you want them to take, the less resistance to change you will encounter. The more convincing you need to do, the more resistance you can expect. By discovering a course that can provide direct benefits to each party, you weaken both the interest in and the legitimacy of opposition.

If you can identify some things that each party is eager to accomplish and select an approach that provides for that accomplishment, the change effort will be fairly smooth. If, however, you are the only party to receive a direct benefit, then the change effort is likely to be a more difficult undertaking.

## Create a Receptive Environment

A host of elements and actors is present in any situation. In most cases, only a few of these will be directly affected by your efforts to bring about change. Those who must respond to your attempts will look for signals in the environment that favour or oppose new directions. Prior to taking action directly related to the change you intend to make, you may take steps to help create a climate supportive of or at least nonresistant to change. This could involve an information campaign, inclusion of specific opinion leaders in your planning efforts, or other approaches.

As Julian (1973) observed, change comes about when a "significant number of people—or a number of significant people" (p. 9) agree that a problem exists. By creating this impression, you not only encourage acceptance of new ideas but you also make it easier for decision makers to respond favourably.

## Understand the Power-Issue Relationship

Your base of power must be larger than the issue on which you are working. A base smaller than the issue is a formula for failure. Yet this is a common construction for most groups, especially when they are first starting out. Essentially, there are two responses to remedy this situation (Figure 12.5) (Bishop, 2002; Healy, 2005).

The first step is to partialize the issue. This approach involves separating the goal into distinct aspects and pursuing each aspect, one at a time (this can also refer to separating a community into component subgroups and organizing one group at a time). Frequently, this is done by breaking the goal down into its sequential steps. You then concentrate on phases of the change, taking the less risky or controversial ones first. For example, you may not be able to make all the changes you want in the operation of the local welfare office. Problems exist in the way the expedite program is operated, the hours of operation do not meet the needs of the community, the application form is too long, and the staff is rude. By partializing the change episode, you may first concentrate on implementing a series of in-service training workshops designed to sensitize the staff to the needs and anxieties of service users. From this may come a greater awareness of the validity of other concerns, and the staff may become allies for agency change rather than opponents of it.

Partializing helps you to set the stage for future efforts. It provides your group with

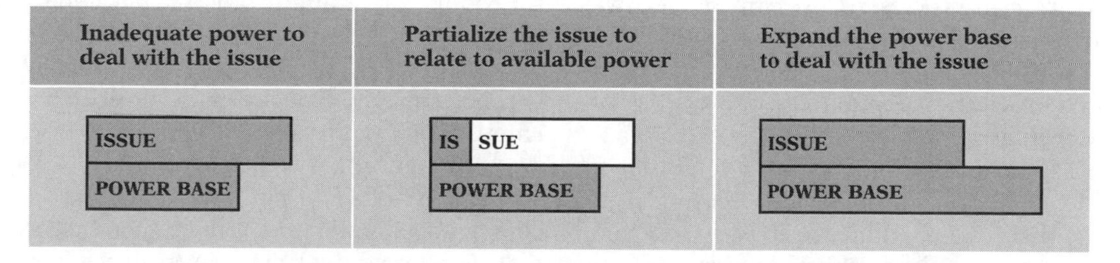


**FIGURE 12.5** Relationship between your issue and your power

You must have an adequate base of power to deal with the issue you confront. If your base is too small, you need to partialize the issue, expand your power base, or do both.

the motivation of a victory while giving you a stepping-stone to additional challenges. The danger is that you may settle for this initial victory and never move on to more meaningful changes. Bear in mind that the target might grant you a small gain as a type of concession to buy you off or distract you from more sweeping changes. It is necessary to keep the goal you have partialized in clear perspective.

The second procedure is to expand your base of power. Generally, you do this by acting on a more limited aspect of the overall goal—the partialized portion. You act not only to accomplish that immediate goal but to intentionally draw in additional resources (greater numbers, community attention, money, expertise, and so on) as you are acting. As your base of power grows, you are able to take on greater and greater parts of the issue, and then you can move further to deal with other issues. With more successes, more power, including strengthened alliances with like-minded groups, you can "move these victories to a larger scale" (Mirazo, Hicks, Taylor, & Ferlazzo, 2001, p. 41).

### Get the Right People in the Right Places

The quality of many decisions is directly related to the quality of the decision maker. If the actions of a particular decision maker are going to be crucial, it may be important not only to attempt to influence that decision maker but to influence who holds the decision-making position in the first place. Your group may decide to actively participate in processes to determine who will hold pivotal decision-making positions. This may mean taking part in political campaigns, search or selection committees, or confirmation proceedings.

The simple fact is that it is a lot easier to influence those whose beliefs are similar to yours than it is to influence those with whom you have some fundamental differences. This is especially true if you contributed to an individual's successful effort to obtain the position. Working to get the right people in the right places could be an efficient investment of your time.

## TRICKS FOR SPECIAL OCCASIONS

A limitless number of special techniques can be used to strengthen the effectiveness of your change effort. Remain aware of the little things that are important to your success, and see if a little twist here or there can give your project or cause a boost. Be inventive and have a little fun while you are at it. Here is a sample of particular tricks you can use to address common hindrances.

### Stacking a Small Room

The conference room where you are to make your presentation is located on the ninth floor. You could use the exercise, but the elevator is faster. Six people get on the elevator with you. At the third floor, two more people step aboard. One more squeezes in at the fifth. "What brought this crowd?" you wonder. By the time you have made it to your ninth-floor destination, you are beginning to feel claustrophobic. All ten of you tumble into the same conference room. It is a very nice, comfortable room with a large table surrounded by plush seats. Additional chairs line the walls. The place can easily hold 50. After their passage on the crowded elevator, the people separate into three little groups seeking their own places in the room apart from the others. They find seats along the walls as you go to the head of the table. No one else enters the room. Finally it is time to begin. You look up, notice all the empty chairs, and think to yourself, "Hardly anybody showed up. What's wrong?"

The use of space can give an impression of community disinterest or create the sense that there is a movement afoot. You may want to convince dubious members of the community that everyone is on board with the project, or you may want to demonstrate overwhelming community support to an opponent. If you expect 30 people to show up, schedule your function in a room that can comfortably seat about 20. Set up only 15 or so chairs to start off. Have a few stacked up in the room and the rest easily accessible in the room next door. As people arrive and chairs are being set up, you can be "amazed" by the tremendous turnout. If people have to stand along the walls, so much the better. Even those who are not in on the ploy will not mind having to stand as long as the show is good.

## Defusing an Opposing Argument

Pre-empt the opponent's argument or plan by releasing it first. Let your audience know just what is coming, and then discredit it. This leaves the opponent offering something that people have heard before and about which they have at least some suspicions. They have been inoculated against its impact. This approach allows a group to be forewarned and thus forearmed. The opponent is put on the defensive and may even be forced to abandon or alter a favoured position. Of course, you may even anticipate and announce this likelihood.

## Keeping the Record Straight

Amnesia seems to strike some targets when it is time to make good on promises made. It seems as though they were "misunderstood," and they did not really mean what you thought they meant. In the course of a discussion, some outrageous statements may be made, ones that especially if made politely may go unnoticed or, if noticed, may be tolerated. These common occurrences can be dealt with by having a member of your group volunteer to serve as a secretary and take minutes at the meeting.

Nobody actually likes to be the minute taker at a meeting, so rarely will anyone compete with your volunteer for the honour. Yet the minute taker is one of the most powerful people at any meeting. During the meeting, this person can record, confirm, and note the confirmation of promises. The minute taker also has the authority to interrupt the proceedings at any point to "ask a question for clarification." This gives them the chance to call attention to a comment or ask a speaker to further explain some objectionable statements. By acting in his or her official capacity, the minute taker can expose points without being argumentative. As long as the individual does not overplay the role, the minute taker can control the meeting.

The minutes should be widely distributed, making sure that key points confirmed during the meeting are underscored. You need to anticipate that some of the targets will object to the record, so be ready to effectively counter these gripes. The "volunteer" should be well prepared to perform the function. Spend a little time discussing and perhaps even role-playing this position.

## Individualized Petitions

A petition provides a simple way for people to voice their opinion. Twenty-five people can sign a paper attesting to their support for an idea or a statement. Still, it is only one piece of paper. It is much better to have 25 pieces of paper, each one asserting the same support for the desired action.

In addition to the printed message and signature, each person could be encouraged to write a one-sentence personal note on the bottom of the page. Most people are willing to do this, especially if you are prepared to suggest some topics about which the individual may want to comment. You can even suggest some comments when it seems appropriate.

If you put a fold in each sheet and then stack the opened sheets on top of each other, it makes for a more impressive pile. You can present two pieces of paper with 50 signatures or a fluffed-up batch of 50 papers, many with personal statements. Which do you think will have the greater impact?

## STRATEGIES AND TACTICS TARGET MAY USE ON YOU

You are not the only group considering the actions it can take to gain an advantage or head off a threat. The target, particularly in a conflict situation, is trying to provoke a response from you that would advance or protect its interests. It is helpful for you to consider a few common schemes you are likely to face.

### Buffer Groups

Beware the formation of a committee established to "explore and seek resolution to shared concerns." Though sometimes a few of these things really work, most of them are set up by those under attack to diffuse energy. They become part of a pseudo problem-solving structure that simply adds another layer between you and the respondent while allowing the respondent to establish some control over the action setting (Crowfoot et al., 1983).

First of all, recognize the process for what it is and, even if you do participate, place your trust in other activities you control. Refuse to accept limitations on your actions as a condition of membership. Be willing to declare the process a sham and walk away from it. The opponent is likely to want to hang on to the appearance of cooperation, so you may be granted some concessions to appease your threats.

### Divide and Conquer

In a conflict situation, the target is likely to try to drive a wedge between you and your partners or among the members of your organization itself. This is usually done by granting some temporary favour to one group over the other, spreading rumours, or promoting an agenda that is likely to bring dispute to your ranks. Discuss this probability among yourselves in advance, and see if you can guess what your opponent will try to do. By making a game out of it, you can strengthen your resolve for unity and belittle your opponent's methods.

### Absence of Decision Makers

As a variation of the buffer group game, the target may serve up a variety of individuals who can "transmit your concerns" to those in authority. You can transmit your own concerns. If people do not have the authority to act, do not waste your time meeting with them.

### Vague Agreements

Any agreement lacking specific outcomes to be produced by specific actions of specific people according to a specific timetable is phoney. Common "agreements" include those to "take action" or to "resolve the problem," or worse, "to look into the matter." There are a number of ways to dress up delays or inaction as agreement. Be careful to make sure that what you are agreeing to is meaningful.

Acknowledge that the "agreement" represents a good starting point, but not a real agreement. Then specify the steps and the time frame acceptable for forging a true agreement.

### Telling You What You Want to Hear

This is one of the most effective tricks in an opponent's arsenal. This ploy is especially effective with those who are uncomfortable challenging authority, do not really want to do any more work, or who yearn to be "right" over being effective. Be prepared to hear a variety of pat responses that by themselves mean nothing: "I agree with you," "Yes, you're right," "You have raised some valid concerns." These are some of the standards. Be mindful not to let these statements reduce your impetus for useful action. Use the apparently favourable response to push for actions to back it up. You may answer by saying something like this: "That's great to hear; now let's focus on exactly what you are going to do."

### Endless Meetings

Much, if not most, of your work will be done during volunteer hours. By calling meeting after meeting after meeting, the target can simply wear you out. The time spent at a meeting is increased by the time spent thinking about and preparing for the meeting. This can add up. Quite often, the people who call these meetings are paid for their time, so they may be happy to meet forever. If you suspect this is happening to your group, first confront the target about it. Then start placing strict requirements on the justification for meeting. Make sure that the intended outcome of the meeting is realistic and logically related to movement on your goals. If there is no real need to have a face-to-face conversation, tell the target you will discuss matters over the phone.

You can play this game too. Have a good supply of "alternates," so that any number of people can attend meetings rather than just a few. If the alternate is not sufficiently versed to make a decision, state that the decisions reached at the meeting must be ratified by the membership. If an alternate needs to be brought up to date with the current state of the proceedings, make sure the target is requested to do so during the meeting. The need for the target to regularly reorient new participants, who may be no more than message transmitters to your organization, can dampen enthusiasm for this ruse.

Do not be shy about scheduling a meeting at a time and in a place that is convenient to you but inconvenient to the target.

## Requests for Volumes of Information

Check to see how the target intends to use the information you produce. If they cannot clearly demonstrate that this information leads to action, tell them you prefer to spend your time in more constructive ways. Another response is for you to request payment for producing certain kinds of information. If they are not willing to pay for a "study," ask them how this information can be so valuable.

## Withholding Information

The target may promise to provide you with necessary information that is rightfully yours. They promise, but do not act. They may continue to delay to drain your momentum and to keep you from being able to move or make decisions. Do not wait. At the time you request information, establish deadlines and methods for ensuring accountability. Be willing to make an issue over the broken promises, invoking the intervention of third parties or other parties who have power over the target. You may be tempted to withhold information or action until the target gives you what you need. This may work on some occasions, but inaction on your part may play into your opponent's hands.

Especially when you are dealing with a public institution, learn how to request information under the Freedom of Information acts, and be willing to exercise that right.

## Overwhelming You with Information

There may be some truly important data provided in the volumes you get, but you will have to wade through mounds of relatively meaningless information to discover it. An opponent may use this tactic to say they were more than forthcoming with their information and they did in fact tell you of their plans, so you should not be surprised by the unfolding of events.

Your tendency will be to set things aside until you have time to read it all. It may gather an inch of dust before that time ever comes. By then, it may be too late. To protect against this, have someone in your group prepared to critically pore over any information you receive. This information could prove invaluable in your future efforts to promote change.

## Providing You with Special Attention or Offerings

Be wary of opponents bearing gifts. Although you want to allow for the fact that people do change their attitudes, it is wise to consider the context in which special favours are offered. If there is an expectation that you will back off on your pursuit of issues or if you are to be seen as more important than other members of your organization, your benefactor may not be operating from the most kindly of intentions. You may decide to accept the gift and pass it along to someone else. Or you can decline altogether.

### Feigning Injury or Hurt Feelings

Avoiding accountability is important business to some opponents. Unable to deal with the facts of their behaviour, they may try to gain some sympathy by acting unjustly accused or unfairly harmed. What they are really trying to do is change the agenda and put you on the defensive. You do not need to explain yourself, nor should you feel apologetic or guilty for adhering to the importance of the facts of the matter. You can defuse the opponent's tactic by giving your opponent a clear, specific way to be a partner in problem resolution. Their refusal to do so can become an enduring symbol of their insincerity.

## SUGGESTIONS FOR CHANGE

As we have reflected on the diverse types of change efforts we have been involved with over the years, we have come to recognize some fundamental ideas. Here are some suggestions for promoting community change. Remember them, and use them to further your own change efforts.

1. Do not forget to hustle.
2. Keep the cycle of empowerment rolling.
3. Do your homework.
4. Hit your opponents in their self-interest.
5. Have those who feel the problem play a significant role in resolving the problem.
6. Have the situation dictate the strategy.
7. Have a quick, initial victory.
8. Prevent unintended consequences.
9. Keep your options open.
10. Do things on purpose.
11. Roll with the punches; be prepared to be flexible.
12. Commit yourself to learning.
13. Be prepared to take risks, and do so often.
14. Be prepared, knowing that your identity is on the line—although this will sometimes be a positive resource for you, other times it might make you a target.

And the final one, should you forget everything else:

15. Laugh and have fun.

## DO YOU HAVE WHAT IT TAKES?

As you get ready to move from talking about doing something to actually doing it, take stock of the assets that your group brings to the scramble. Be sure that the basic factors crucial for action are clearly present in your group. This will help you to detect any weak portions in your foundation that may need some shoring up before you press the issue. Check to see that you are well supplied with the following ingredients.

- *Clarity of purpose.* Your issue is clear and compelling, and your sense of purpose certain and strong. You are able to articulate both your issue and your purpose.
- *Commitment.* You and the other members of your group have made a conscious commitment to do what it takes to achieve success. You are determined not only to take action but to adequately prepare for it as well.
- *Interest.* There is sufficient interest in the issue from a sufficient number of people.
- *Community members.* There are enough people willing to take on whatever time-consuming tasks are necessary so that one person does not get stuck with it all.
- *Leadership.* An appropriate range of leadership has developed so that one person does not try to do the things that other people could and should do.

- *Information*. You know what you need to know to act and prevent unintended consequences.
- *Risk taking*. You and the other participants are willing to take risks.
- *Power*. Your organization has enough power to get a response from those from whom you need a response at this particular stage in your change episode.

## CONCLUSION

You will not put up with things the way they are. You have acknowledged a need to take action. You involve more people, giving you the power and resources you need. You keep talking to each other, and you make decisions. With a clear sense of what you intend to accomplish, you have assessed the situation in order to determine the most effective strategies and their accompanying tactics to advance your goals. You have determined how the ideal selection of actions fits the real capabilities of your group. You have actually gone out and implemented your actions purposefully and evaluated their effectiveness.

You have committed yourself to the success of your venture. You are determined to be persistent. You enjoy the company of your partners. And you do not take yourself so seriously that you cannot recognize and benefit from the humour that comes as a welcome visitor to most any situation. Though maybe you are just starting out, you smile. You have probably already won something important.

## HELPFUL WEBSITES

**Resist! Collective**

http://resist.ca/about

The Resist! Collective is a group of Vancouver-based activists working to provide communications and technical services, information, and education to the greater activist community

**Rabble.ca**

http://rabble.ca

Rabble.ca is a site for progressive writers, activists, and journalists from across Canada. The site was launched April 18, 2001, just before the protests against the Summit of the Americas in Quebec City. It is an is issue-based site and offers stories and points of view you will not often find in the mainstream press. From the many activists that contribute to the site, you will learn of many actions, strategies, and tactics that can help you influence community and social change.

**COMM-ORG: The On-Line Conference on Community Organizing**

http://comm-org.wisc.edu/

The COMM-ORG is a listserv whose mission is to connect people who are interested in the craft of community organizing. The site also provides information for organizers and those who study and teach about community organizing. It was co-created and is edited by a Professor and community organizer from the University of Wisconsin, Randy Stoeker.

PART THREE

# A Closer Look at Some Examples of Change Contexts

Not far from where you are sitting right now, there are people who are frustrated by circumstances that seem beyond their control. Opportunities are hidden or denied. Services do not work. Insensitivity has grown from indifference to erode hope.

Not far from where you are sitting right now, people are deciding to take action to direct their future. Somebody started the process that brought these people together— maybe somebody who, two years or even two months ago, never thought about challenging "the way things are."

How will it turn out for these people? Will they fail? If so, why? What will get in their way? Will they succeed? If so, why? Will they just be lucky, or will they do the right things?

Today, what do they know about producing change? Do they know much about the community that will be affected by their efforts? How will they generate the power they need? Will they waste their time trying to plan for every possibility, or will they fail to plan at all? How will they attract others to their cause, and will they work well together? Will they be able to raise the money and other resources they will need? How will they spread the word about what they are doing and why? Will they be able to define issues in order to produce the reaction they want? What steps will they take to become more organized? Will the strategies and tactics they select fit the situation they face?

You know something about each of the questions they will have to answer. You are probably much more prepared to begin the process of promoting change than most people who actually take the risk to do so. If you were in a meeting today, you would have important contributions to make.

As you engage as a community change agent, you will encounter many systems that have an impact on the people you serve. You will have many chances to initiate changes to remove the barriers that people face or to create new programs or new promise. Different arenas of action were covered in a general way in Chapter One. In the chapters in Part Three, you will be given a closer look at three examples where you may very well have the opportunity to develop and use your skills to promote change. As you already know these are only examples. Community change happens in many communities, in many settings and through many mechanisms.

The *neighbourhood* might be one type of community we focus on for change. What occurs or does not occur in neighbourhoods has a tremendous effect on the quality of life of the residents. Neighbourhood change can take many forms, whether it's more fully developing the helping systems that already exist, establishing neighbourhood self-government and economic vitality, or challenging oppressive and prejudicial relations in a neighbourhood.

In Chapter Thirteen we explore the meaning of neighbourhood and gain an understanding of the importance of neighbourhood functioning. You will see how neighbourhoods change over time, and you will learn about neighbourhood organizations. You will discover various ways to strengthen neighbourhoods, and you will be given some insights into important factors that will affect your chances for success.

*Organizational change* skills are particularly important for professionals working in human services. Our organizations can be vehicles for fostering beneficial change or mazes in which good ideas and good services get lost. The process of improving existing services or developing altogether new approaches involves some change in service organizations. Service organizations are our workplaces. Their degree of effectiveness or ineffectiveness has an impact on our own ability to render quality assistance. The satisfaction we derive from our work is closely related to the functioning of the organization through which we work.

In Chapter Fourteen you will gain a clearer picture of the characteristics that influence the behaviour of organizations. You will consider several different types of changes that organizations can make in the community and that you can make in organizations, and you will learn more about the obstacles and opportunities that affect the change process. You will be introduced to key ingredients of organizational change, and you will be provided with a number of specific tactics that will increase your effectiveness.

*Legislative change* is increasingly recognized as a critical activity for social workers and human services workers. Policies that emerge from legislative bodies can set in motion an array of forces that limit or expand opportunities for the people we serve. The extent and availability of public resources is directly related to legislative decisions. Even the manner in which services can be provided is shaped by the actions of those who set public policy.

A variety of legislative assemblies, from town councils to the Parliament of Canada, pass laws that affect our communities. A number of avenues exist for influencing these legislative decisions. One of the most effective of these is the practice of lobbying. Specific lobbying activities become far more productive when made as part of an organized lobbying effort.

Chapter Fifteen focuses on efforts to influence the actions of provincial legislatures because these bodies are more accessible to the average worker and because the policies they establish have significant consequences. You will learn how to prepare yourself to take part in the work of affecting legislation. You will gain an understanding of the legislative process, and you will see how the essential components of a legislative action campaign work together. Basic lobbying activities and methods are explained, and you will be given a number of tips for increasing your effectiveness.

CHAPTER THIRTEEN

# Enhancing Neighbourhoods

**This chapter will help you better understand the following questions:**

- What are the effects of neighbourhood quality on stress?
- What are the factors affecting neighbourhood health?
- What are the models of neighbourhood change?
- What are the characteristics of successful neighbourhood organizations?
- What are the neighbourhood's revitalization components?

All of us who live in a city live in a neighbourhood. Most of us who live in a town live in a neighbourhood. For most Canadians, the quality of our lives is affected by the conditions that exist in the area captured by the view from our front door. Our neighbourhood may be a densely populated place where row houses snug against each other, a high-rise apartment, or a condominium development. Neighbourhoods might be made up of mixed forms of housing or a tract of suburban single-family dwellings.

## WHAT IS A NEIGHBOURHOOD?

A neighbourhood is made up of the interaction of three things: residents, residences, and land uses that either support these or coexist with them. Though it would be hard to have a neighbourhood without residents and residences, land uses among neighbourhoods vary. Parks, streets, stores, offices, factories, open spaces, and other natural or constructed features help to shape and define the neighbourhood. Although careful planning by municipal governments has attempted to separate noxious uses from residential areas, in many Canadian neighbourhoods industrial or commercial activities may exist, endangering the health and well-being of residents.

Neighbourliness refers to the residents' awareness of one another and their positive interdependence. We are not just bodies in search of a warm, dry place to spend the night. Who are neighbours? Of course, they are the people who call the place home—whether or not that home is rented or owned, temporary or permanent. To some extent, anyone who spends a significant amount of time there is a neighbour. Some of our neighbours have no homes at all—they may sleep in a car or have to sleep on a relative's couch. The degree to which we are aware of our neighbours, especially those who are different from ourselves or who live in vulnerable circumstances, and the sense of affiliation we feel toward each other and the area in which we live affect the quality of our neighbourhood.

When we live as if some of our neighbours do not exist at all or when we judge them or stick only to our own kind or to ourselves, we render the neighbourhood nothing more than a coincidental occupation of a plot of land.

Neighbourhoods come in many shapes and sizes. Wide variations of neighbourhoods exist not only among cities but within the same city. To some, a neighbourhood is home to hundreds of people. To others, the term may describe an area of 75,000 people (Downs, 1981; Hallman, 1984; Kotler, 1969). Schwirian (1983) defines a neighbourhood as "a population residing in an identifiable section of a city whose members are organized into a general interaction network of formal and informal ties" (p. 84).

Our place and how we have arranged it tells us something about who we are. Rubin and Rubin (2001) point out that "control over space permits a definition and expression of culture, especially a culture that stands in opposition to dominant groups" (p. 102). Ahlbrandt and Cunningham (1979) have summarized a neighbourhood as a community, a market possessing purchasing power, a service area, a provider of shelter, a political force, and an actual or potential level of government. Neighbourhoods are complex social organisms. In Canada, we pride ourselves on how diverse some neighbourhoods have become, and we find it hopeful that diverse people can live side by side.

So a neighbourhood is made up of both tangible and intangible elements. Anything that either enhances these or detracts from them affects the quality of the neighbourhood and the lives of the people experiencing it.

As you can see, neighbourhoods resist clear definition. In fact, Downs (1981) states that "no one definition has come into widespread acceptance among neighbourhood residents themselves, neighbourhood organizations, or academic analysts" (p. 13). One of the most meaningful observations is in some ways the simplest and in some ways the most complex. Wireman (1984) says that "a neighborhood is the area named by residents when asked: 'Where do you live?'" (p. 38).

We each have our own personal neighbourhood. Essentially, your neighbourhood is what feels like your neighbourhood. This, however, is a dynamic perception. Your understanding will be affected by your age, how long you have lived in the area, how much time you spend in it, whether and how far you have ventured on your walks, and other factors that influence the type and degree of your interaction with the various elements of your neighbourhood. Think about your own neighbourhood. What pictures do you see?

## Neighbourhood as a Focus of Attention for Community Change Agents

Why should we care about strengthening neighbourhoods? First of all, the people living in them matter. Researchers have linked neighbourhood problems to chronic stress and increased health risks among residents, particularly in lower income neighbourhoods (Steptoe & Feldman, 2001). A neighbourhood stress index called the City Stress Inventory indicates that neighbourhood characteristics can influence depression, anger, and self-esteem (Ewart & Suchday, 2002).

Sometimes geography can be used to separate people by class and to disempower groups of people by not offering enough resources for the neighbourhood. A report written by the United Way of Greater Toronto and the Canadian Council on Social indicated that families in poor neighbourhoods suffer from "poverty by postal code," which reflects the incoherent planning by local governments that does not provide equal services to rich and poor neighbourhoods (United Way, 2004).

> Over two decades, the rate of child and family poverty has gone down slightly, to 9.5% (637,000 children) in 2007 from 11.9% (792,000) in 1989 (LICO after-tax). That small change over twenty years is striking in light of an unprecedented period of growth since 1998 and in bold contrast to the growing gap between Canadian families with the highest income and those with the lowest

> income. The most recent figure does not reflect the impact of the current recession and economic disruption. Nor do the numbers adequately show the shameful situation of First Nations' communities where 1 in every 4 children is growing up in poverty. (Campaign 2000, 2009 Report Card on Child and Family Poverty in Canada: 1989–2009, page 2.)

Martinez-Brawley (2000) notes that "despite modernization, the daily round of life for millions of people is carried out in relatively small, circumscribed, local settings. Modern dwellers draw a manageable radius around their homes, at least as a mental referent" (p. 210). She further elaborates, "Primary ties and local sentiments give real direction, though not always positive, to the daily activities of most people. People live day to day within the intimate confines of a locality. The most universal of all human experiences happen 'at home,' where one's deepest emotions are revealed" (p. 227). In addition in the era of globalization some people can identify and move across neighbourhoods, cities and even nations due to their access to resources. Others are more than ever confined to living in a small geographic area or neighbourhood because they might not even have enough money to take the bus, subway or streetcar outside their neighbourhood.

Wagner (1995) has pointed to the emergence of a community sector, which he says favours maintenance and survival over social impact. This new community sector is defined as "a loose amalgam of existing and yet-to-be created non-profit organizations (self-help groups, neighbourhood and member-based organizations) that develop new approaches and financing mechanisms to address neighbourhood concerns. They link three activities: social service, economic development, and capacity building, and create a local vision and renaissance of activity" (p. 12).

Morrison and colleagues (1997) argue that differentiation among the roles of caseworker, group worker, and community organizer is not functional to a "holistic approach that emphasizes the environment as well as the person in the environment" (p. 533).

Housing and child poverty are examples of issues that can have a neighbourhood focus yet are also important to consider in a broader context. During the Ontario election in 2007, the Hamilton Roundtable for Poverty Reduction called for a provincial poverty strategy and worked closely with the local community in developing recommendations. The goal of the strategy was to reduce the number of children living in poverty in Ontario by 25 percent in five years. This would mean moving 90,000 kids out of poverty during that time (or approximately 6,085 children in Hamilton). In July 2008, the Hamilton Roundtable for Poverty Reduction hosted the province's largest consultation with Hamilton residents on the lack of progress of the Ontario Poverty Strategy. More than 200 residents attended and spoke about their priorities for poverty reduction. Some of the key themes had a neighbourhood focus but needed resources from outside the neighbourhood. They included the following:

- Respect for individual dignity and flexible government policies to decrease barriers that keep people in poverty.
- Access to child care as an investment in children's future.
- Opportunities for children to fully participate in community and school life, whether through affordable school trips or community recreation programs.
- Education and skills development as a bridge to prosperity for children.
- Employment supports and livable incomes for low-income workers in a changing workforce.
- Access to health services in low-income neighbourhoods to enhance community wellness.
- Greater integration of services.
- Flexibility of access to services.
- Affordable, accessible, and safe housing to provide a stable base for moving out of poverty.

- Recognition of the importance of neighbourhoods as innovative and community hubs. (Chamberlain & Weaver, 2008)

## Some Fundamental Challenges to Neighbourhood Health

We cannot assume that neighbourhoods are all the same, we cannot assume that people enjoy home ownership, nor can we assume that residents within a neighbourhood are all the same. Shapcott (2009) provides some examples of the degree to which people were marginalized in Canada during the last two years of the 1990s:

- There was a 97 percent occupancy rate at shelters for the homeless in Edmonton, Alberta.
- Saskatoon reported that 68 percent of the people using its homeless shelters were First Nations peoples even though they represent only 8 percent of the population.
- St. John's, Newfoundland, found a major problem with "hidden" homeless, that is, people living in illegal and substandard housing.
- From 1995 to 1998, the number of people sleeping on the floor in one shelter tripled from 3,887 to 10,758. (Shapcott, 2009)

In some poor neighbourhoods efforts to serve and strengthen the community come and go, making it difficult for residents to trust in and commit to organized groups. A high turnover of community groups leaves a fragile and transient civic infrastructure (De Vita, Manjarrez, & Twombly, 1999). Sometimes the turnover is caused by loss of jobs due to globalization, the lack of affordable housing, or the lack of business commitment to a country, town, or neighbourhood. Dealing with these challenges means we must become skilled at recognizing and using the resources we have around us.

### DID YOU KNOW?

#### What Is Core Housing Need?

A household is said to be in core housing need if its housing falls below at least one of the following standards: adequacy, suitability, or affordability (Prentice, 2009).

- Adequate dwellings are those reported by their residents as not requiring any major repairs.
- Suitable dwellings have enough bedrooms for the size and makeup of the resident households, according to National Occupancy Standard (NOS) requirements (one of the indicators developed by Canada Mortgage and Housing Corporation to determine the space needed to avoid being designated as crowded).
- Affordable dwellings cost less than 30 percent of before-tax household income.

(Lewis, 2009; Prentice, 2009; Canada Mortgage and Housing Corporation (CMHC). Housing In Canada Online - Frequently Asked Questions, 2010. )

As of 2006, 1.494 million Canadian households, or 12.7 percent of these households, were in core housing need. The number of households in core need was essentially unchanged compared to 2001. Since there were fewer households in Canada in 2001, the percentage of households in core need had been higher in 2001, at 13.7 percent (Prentice, 2009; The Cooperative Housing Federation of Canada, *The Dunning Report: Dimensions of Core Housing Need in Canada*; Second Edition, p. 3).

## Neighbourhood Assets and the Saint John Neighbourhood Assistants

"The participation and input of people are vital to the relevance and success of [neighbourhood] initiatives." So begins a report on the Vibrant Communities Saint John (VCSJ) projects (Makhoul, 2009). Sometimes we focus on neighbourhoods because they are in trouble; in other cases, we may choose a neighbourhood focus because the neighbourhood is so vital. Here, we look at one of the many communities that are part of the Vibrant Communities project, an undertaking to reduce poverty in Canada. Makhoul continues,

> Getting people out to community events—especially when they are struggling to meet family and job commitments—can be difficult. However, attending an event can be the first step in building relationships with neighbours and learning about useful community-based programs and activities. It all starts with the right invitation.
>
> In the summer of 2006, Vibrant Communities Saint John (VCSJ), began supporting resident-led development in two neighbourhoods—Crescent Valley and the South End. They offered new programs for building skills, and used resident and partner input to identify neighbourhood goals and priorities. In 2008, VCSJ expanded that effort to the City's five priority neighbourhoods—parts of Saint John where residents and community groups are working to create opportunities for people living in poverty. VCSJ created Neighbourhood Assistant positions as a means of gathering input for local action plans. The decision recognized that residents with lived experience of poverty are the best people to both spread VCSJ news and gather information on community needs and priorities. Says VCSJ Coordinator Wendy MacDermott: "An evaluation of our early neighbourhood work confirmed that one-to-one contact brings people out of their homes and into the community.
>
> "One of our first Neighbourhood Assistants had taken it upon herself to knock on people's doors and personally invite them to events and meetings. We decided to expand on her efforts and build that sense of identity and connectedness in all five priority neighbourhoods. We hired people who were either on fixed or limited incomes as part-time Neighbourhood Assistants for six-month terms."
>
> VCSJ organizers believe that hope is the key ingredient in neighbourhood mobilization. Neighbourhood Assistants build hope by connecting residents with one another and showing that the larger community cares about them. The Assistant position—though short-term—has helped people build the skills and confidence they need to take their own next steps to prosperity and fulfillment. One former assistant, for example, is now the manager of her neighbourhood's provincially funded Community Access Centre.
>
> Neighbourhood Assistants are supported and guided by the neighbourhood Community Developer, a newly created VCSJ staff position.
>
> The Community Developer provides learning opportunities, guidance, and mentorship, and focuses on progress toward neighbourhood plans . . .. Says Wendy MacDermott: "The most important job for both the Neighbourhood Assistants and the Community Developer is to get people coming out to events, and we're already seeing the results of their efforts. People who were previously too busy to participate are now organizing. One group of teens took the idea from the children's book *Stone Soup* to build a collective dinner . . .. Young mothers concerned about a racial assault started a discussion group and have connected with anti-bullying groups. Together they hope to inspire the whole community to focus on what we all can do to make Saint John a safe place to live."
>
> In 2008, Neighbourhood Assistants organized barbecues, connected residents with relevant programs, shared information about activities and events, and represented resident concerns to a variety of VCSJ partners (e.g., community policing, leisure services and community centres, and discussions about the province's forthcoming poverty reduction strategy). Residents and organizers in the five priority

neighbourhoods are now participating in a planning process that will guide much of the work for each Neighbourhood Assistant in 2009. VCSJ anticipates that, as part of their duties, each Assistant will engage 20 new residents. As they gain confidence and meet more people, Assistants will also be in a position to identify good candidates for the positions they vacate. Building resident engagement all starts with a friendly outlook and an enthusiastic invitation. (May 2009, *Saint John Neighbourhood Assistants Inspire Hope*. Anne Makhoul. Copyright 2009 by The Caledon Institute of Social Policy, 1390 Prince of Wales Dr., Suite 401, Ottawa, ON K2C 3N6 Tel: 613-729-3340, fax: 613-729-3896 email: Caledon@caledoninst.org www.caledoninst.org )

As with most forms of community change, meeting the challenges and enhancing the quality of neighbourhoods involves the identification, mobilization, and connection of neighbourhood assets and community capital.

**TABLE 13.1** Organizations Used to Meet Human Needs of a Neighbourhood

| | Service Providers** | | | | | |
|---|---|---|---|---|---|---|
| | | Based Within Neighbourhood | | Based Outside Neighbourhood | | |
| **Human Needs and Services*** | **Private Nonprofit** | **Private Profit** | **Government** | **Private Nonprofit** | **Private Profit** | **Government** |
| Employment | | | | | | |
| Services | | | | | | |
| Jobs | | | | | | |
| Commercial | | | | | | |
| Sale of Goods | | | | | | |
| Services | | | | | | |
| Income Support Programs | | | | | | |
| Credit | | | | | | |
| Housing | | | | | | |
| Utilities | | | | | | |
| Food | | | | | | |
| Clothing | | | | | | |
| Safety | | | | | | |
| Transportation | | | | | | |
| Education | | | | | | |
| Recreation, Arts | | | | | | |
| Health | | | | | | |
| Social Services | | | | | | |
| Governance | | | | | | |
| Civic Participation | | | | | | |
| Communal Events | | | | | | |
| Religion | | | | | | |

*Detailed services and activities should be added under each human need.
**Individuals, families, and informal groups will also be responding to human needs.
Source: Hallman, 1984.

## QUALITY NEIGHBOURHOODS

It is naïve to think that families are completely self-sufficient, particularly in this highly mobile country. Assistance is not as readily available through extended family systems as it once was. Most families meet their needs through their interaction with other systems.

Clearly, the neighbourhood is one of those valuable systems. Neighbours can provide one another with a range of practical and emotional support. These connections provide psychological benefits by strengthening our attachments to a wider human community and by helping us recognize the reality and importance of our interdependence. More effectively functioning neighbourhoods are more likely to offer their members the benefits of "neighbouring" (Keller, 1968).

Of course, not every neighbourhood is blessed with an abundance of developed internal resources. If the needs of their residents are to be met, neighbourhoods must work to develop internal resources and collaborate with external institutions in order to obtain the needed assistance. They should have the flexibility to shape services to best fit the area's particular requirements. These neighbourhoods can be further strengthened by attracting resources that enable them to create and develop their own institutions (Suchman, 1994; Wireman, 1984).

Hallman has developed a chart that is helpful in assessing the presence of needed resources and services in the neighbourhood and the organizations involved in meeting them (see Table 13.1). Reviewing this chart will help you see how, by whom, and where these needs are being met or not met adequately. Observe that neighbourhood needs are met to some degree by a combination of individuals or groups based both inside and outside the neighbourhood. By taking advantage of opportunities to strengthen basic neighbourhood elements, workers in the business of providing human services can significantly benefit the families who reside there.

## POLITICAL PROCESSES OF NEIGHBOURHOODS

Neighbourhoods are always undergoing some degree of change. People move in and out. Some dwellings deteriorate; others benefit from the attention of paintbrush and hammer. Some trees, if there are any, wither and die; others bloom and, perhaps, new ones are planted. Forces outside of the neighbourhood, such as the general economy, attitudes of lending institutions, and changing local ordinances, help or hinder neighbourhood improvements. The rate and direction of change can also be influenced by the presence of a purposeful change agent.

### Political Capacity

Departing from what he sees as an overemphasis on physical and economic factors affecting neighbourhood change, Rick Cohen (1979) has focused on a political analysis and presents his stages from the point of view of development. According to his perspective, a neighbourhood can be economically rich while remaining politically poor. The first of Cohen's stages is a *disorganized neighbourhood*, one in which there is no organization capable of providing leadership. In these neighbourhoods, a change agent could act as a catalyst while nurturing people with leadership potential. In *primary institutional neighbourhoods*, a few basic organizations, such as churches, schools, and fraternal and social clubs, exist. The change agent acts as a mobilizer, strengthening the linkages among families and neighbourhood institutions, changing the orientation of residents from inward to outward, further developing leadership, and developing neighbourhood resources. *Civic neighbourhoods* are beginning to deal with issues of neighbourhood interest. A group claiming civic concerns as its primary purpose is developed. The organizer's role is that of process facilitator, assisting the neighbourhood by helping to get its resources and groups to work in harmony. A *networked neighbourhood* has a civic group with strong support, and nearly every block is represented in the organization. There is a danger that the organization may become too centralized and bureaucratized and that it may engage in nonproductive political tests of wills with municipal officials. The result of these conflicts could be stalemate and inaction. By assisting the organization as a strategist and negotiator, the change agent can help the neighbourhood group to navigate through some stormy waters. In a *mass communal neighbourhood,* everyone is a member and participates in a neighbourhood organization or civic group. The neighbourhood is concerned with a wide range of issues, and it delivers services. High voter turnouts, widespread participation in organizational activities, many different people in leadership roles, and an increasing control of neighbourhood resources are indicators of a mass communal neighbourhood. The change agent acts as a maintenance assister who helps to keep the neighbourhood from slipping into stagnation.

Cohen points out that many neighbourhood organizations are born of controversy and opposition. The group starts off in an underdog role. When its political capabilities significantly increase and successes mount, the organization may be set adrift as it realizes it has outgrown its original identity. It may experience some aimlessness as it searches for a new identity. Mastery of political influence may result in the neighbourhood pursuing its own interests at the expense of other neighbourhoods or other people in the neighbourhood. A lack of awareness of the interdependency among neighbourhoods may lead to the NIMBY (Not In My Back Yard) phenomenon, producing destructive, selfish conflicts ultimately harmful to all.

*Political-economic* explanations of neighbourhood change emphasize forces at play beyond the neighbourhood's boundaries. These include the actions of a variety of monied interests (such as developers, banks, and construction companies) who work together to influence property values and government decisions regarding revitalization efforts. Their manipulation of broader

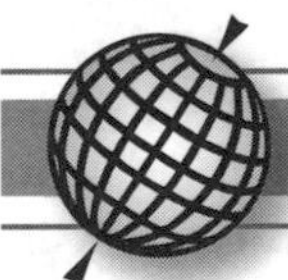

## GLOBAL PERSPECTIVES

UNITED KINGDOM—[I]t is important not to see the neighbourhood as just a territorially bounded entity but as a series of overlapping social networks. We should not underestimate the importance of physical change, physical boundaries and local landmarks in creating a sense of belonging and identity, but the differences between neighbourhoods may perhaps best be understood as the differences between the form and content of social networks. It is these residentially based networks which perform an important function in the routines of everyday life, and these routines are arguably the basic building-blocks of social cohesion—through them we learn tolerance, co-operation and acquire a sense of social order and belonging. Who and what we are surrounded by in a specific locality may also contribute in important ways to both choice and constraint and, less tangibly and more indirectly, to notions of well-being and social worth. (Ray Forrest & Ade Kearns, 2001, p. 2130)

ARGENTINA—The new neighbourhood associations have organized community purchases of food at reduced prices, as well as volunteer brigades of skilled workers who reconnect homes to the public service grids when their electricity, household gas or water supplies are cut off for failure to pay their bills. The assemblies' projects range from a community vegetable garden to a neighbourhood bank in which people can put their savings . . ..

Neighbourhood associations on the west side of Buenos Aires successfully pressured the Edesur power company to consider the possibility of a 180-day suspension of cut-offs due to delay in paying bills. Assemblies in other neighbourhoods are demanding discount electricity rates for the unemployed. (Marcela Valente, 2002) community decision making results in assistance to some areas of the city and inattention to others, with the ultimate beneficiaries being the monied interests themselves. Other forces, such as rising or falling mortgage rates, taxation policies, and availability of land for development, also have relevance for neighbourhood growth or decline.

*Social movement* explanations for neighbourhood change focus on the effects of neighbourhood organizing, including issue identification and development, action to achieve neighbourhood goals, and citizen participation in municipal decision making. The effect of these organized activities (if successful) is certainly change. These changes may make the area more attractive to current residents as well as to a host of newcomers, some of whom may be considered to be "invaders."

## UNDERSTANDING NEIGHBOURHOOD ORGANIZING

Your efforts to improve neighbourhood conditions might involve a single project or the development of a loosely knit community of people or trigger the development of a neighbourhood organization. Your neighbourhood organizing might assist the progress of an existing organization. Sometimes you will bring people together to undertake a particular project, and sometimes you will aid in developing a permanent organization that itself will undertake diverse projects and provide other functions. As you begin to gain a better understanding of what the neighbourhood needs and has, you may come to the conclusion that a concentrated and comprehensive approach to organizing is ultimately needed. If your primary professional responsibilities do not lie in the area of community organization, you may not be able to make the type of investment the thorough approach to organizing would require.

There are at least six choices available to you. One course of action would be to initiate a modest but meaningful change with a definite beginning and end for your involvement. The neighbourhood receives the direct benefit of the change—itself an important accomplishment—and it may awaken the residents' recognition of their capabilities and spur some of them to take some further actions. Even if no subsequent action directly follows the change episode, it may indirectly contribute to efforts further down the road.

An example of the first choice is the guide for the planning process developed by the Winnipeg neighbourhood partnership (see Figure 13.1).

Recognizing that continued resident action may not happen of its own accord, you may decide to take the second option, which involves purposefully using the change to develop leadership and continued interest. If you can further link the nascent neighbourhood organization to other support systems (for example, a successful organization from another neighbourhood that can serve as a mentor), the effect of your particular change episode may be more long lasting. This second approach requires greater involvement than the first.

Your third alternative is to get help. There may be individuals or groups in the community that can sustain a deeper level of involvement in working with the neighbourhood. Your main contribution is to discover the particular resource and help to establish the relationship between the neighbourhood and those who will provide organizing assistance.

Your fourth choice involves convincing an agency to become more actively involved in the life of the neighbourhood.

A fifth option might be to engage with an identity community within your neighbourhood to improve its participation in the neighbourhood. For example, you might want to get involved with a group of LGBTT persons to make neighbours aware of the issue of gay bashing and violence against LGBTT persons in the neighbourhood. The purpose of organizing may be multifold. Strengthening social support among LGBTT community members, increasing safety for LGBTT members, and making the neighbourhood more aware of LGBTT issues are just a few goals you can meet through one undertaking.

|  |
| --- |
| Establish a **Neighbourhood Planning Team** of residents, landlords, business owners, community organizations, local agencies, and other neighbourhood stakeholders. |
| Develop your neighbourhood **Vision** by gathering information about the areas.<br>• Describe the neighbourhood's strength and weaknesses.<br>• Describe its opportunities and assets. |
| Based on your neighbourhood assessment and your community consultation, draft a **vision statement**. |
| **Confirm** the vision with your community. |
| Develop the **Action Plan**.<br>• Goals<br>• Objectives<br>• Actions statements<br>• Measurable indicators<br>• Project descriptions and budgets |
| Distribute the plan and seek **community approval** through open houses, workshops, meetings, questionnaires, etc.—formal plan approval by City's Community Committee. |
| **Implement** the plan.<br>• Develop projects.<br>• Develop budgets.<br>• Solicit funding.<br>• Oversee implementation. |
| **Evaluate** the plan using the measureable indicators identified.<br>• What did we do well?<br>• What have we learned?<br>• Where do we go from here?<br>• Review the plan and adjust, if necessary. |

**FIGURE 13.1** Steps in the Neighbourhood Planning Process

Source: Manitoba Intergovermental Affairs and the City of Winnipeg's Planning, Property and Development Department, *A Guide for Developing Neighbourhood Plans*, page 9, 2002. Permission to reproduce this material is provided by the Queen's Printer of Manitoba. The Queen's Printer does not warrant the accuracy or currency of the reproduction of this information. By permission of the City of Winnipeg.

The sixth choice is a combination of the above approaches. You need not focus on just one, and in fact focusing on a number at once will likely strengthen neighbourhood organizing.

Whether your participation is modest or substantial, an awareness of neighbourhood organizations is useful. In addition to the authors specifically identified, the ideas in this section were also drawn from and shaped by the Aspen Institute (1999); Bratt (1987); Burghardt (1982); Brueggeman (2002); Clay (1979); Dupper and Poertner (1997); Fantini and Gittell (1973); Fellin (2001); the Institute for Community Economics (2002); Kennedy (1996); Kretzman and McKnight (1993); Mayer (1984); the National Center for Economic and Security Alternatives (2002); Rich (1979); Scheie, Williams, Mayer, Kroll, and Dewar (1997a, 1997b); Suchman (1993, 1994); Suchman and Lamb (1991); Thomas (1986); Wagner (1995); Warren and Warren (1977); Williams (1985, 1989); Wireman (1984); and Wolpert, Mumphrey, and Seley (1972); The Social Determinants of Health Group in Canada (Shapcott (2009);

Bryant (2009); Galabuzi, (2009); Social Economy Centre at OISE/UT (Quarter, Mook, & Armstrong [2009]).

## Types of Neighbourhood Organizations

Fisher (1984) describes three approaches to organizing that are based on how neighbourhoods are envisioned:

> *Social services.* The neighbourhood is viewed as an organism. Efforts are made to build a sense of community, particularly by providing social service organizations. This method lobbies for and emphasizes delivery of social services.
>
> *Political activism.* The neighbourhood is viewed as a political entity or power base. Absence of the power that is needed to defend the neighbourhood is seen as the basic problem. Efforts are made to give people more control over their lives. Strategies are rooted in the presumption of a conflict of interest between the neighbourhood and those in power outside of the neighbourhood.
>
> *Neighbourhood maintenance.* The neighbourhood is viewed primarily as a residential area. Efforts are vested in protecting property and its values. Neighbourhoods using this style of organizing are usually free of major problems. (pp. 9–16)

But increasingly there are *issue-based neighbourhood* organizations focused on everything things such as insensitive policing in a multiracial neighbourhood, rampant development by private developers that affects the quality of life in a neighbourhood, or nondemocratic municipal politicians. The issues are too many to list, but there is a strong Canadian tradition of this type of neighbourhood organizing.

And there are *identity-based* neighbourhood organizations in which people with similar identities congregate for support and political action.

Some neighbourhood organizations regularly interact with their local governments. Such a relationship may provide benefits to both the neighbourhood and the government in the form of participatory decision making. Though this may involve only opportunities for an exchange of information between the two groups, more significant collaborative efforts also occur.

Simpson and Gentile (1986) identify three forms of neighbourhood organizations related to governmental processes: advisory councils that are officially established by the municipal government, independent neighbourhood groups that have claimed governmental or political powers, and groups that have been organized by or incorporated into an official government neighbourhood program.

In addition to these general categories, Hallman (1984) describes a number of other neighbourhood organization classifications.

> *Neighbourhood association:* used for two purposes, advocacy or low-budget, self-help activities; has individual members, representatives from other organizations, or a combination; ranges from block clubs to multi-issue neighbourhood organizations.
>
> *Neighbourhood coalition:* an organization of organizations; tends to concentrate on advocacy and neighbourhood organizing but might sponsor a neighbourhood corporation or program operations.
>
> *Neighbourhood advisory committee:* usually set up by a government agency in order to deal with issues related to its mission; has an advisory role in program planning and possibly in program implementation and evaluation; selection of members might be by an administrator, nominees of specific organizations and interests, or a combination.

*Association managed communities* are concerned with rules proscribing or prescribing behaviour or with providing avenues for neighbour interaction. A typical *homeowners' association* concerns itself primarily with the maintenance of neighbourhood facilities (for example, a community pool) or the preservation of the physical attractiveness of the neighbourhood. Participation as a voting member is usually limited to property owners, so renters rarely have any real voice. Homeowners' associations are sometimes more concerned with regulating residents' behaviours than with advocacy on behalf of the neighbourhood. They are often set up and even managed by the corporation that built the housing development. Advocacy issues are commonly related to protection of property values. It is common for the original developer of the tract to establish the association. Condominium associations that run the public areas of a condominium and ensure the ongoing existence of the condominium as a business enterprise also fall into this category.

*Tenants' associations* may be considered to be a type of neighbourhood organization if you consider an apartment complex or similar housing configuration to be a neighbourhood. Certainly these organizations at the very least exist within neighbourhoods. Tenants' organizations are primarily developed to secure and protect the rights of renters and to ensure they receive well-maintained, safe housing.

Social service agencies, both public and private, may develop a *neighbourhood service centre* (if the centre is not developed, established, and operated by the neighbourhood, it would not technically be a neighbourhood organization). Although the operators of the centre usually defer to the authority of the sponsoring agency, centre staff will, from time to time, engage in advocacy or development efforts on behalf of the neighbourhood. These activities complement the provision of direct services such as counselling or job training programs. As a social worker or human services professional, you may have the opportunity to develop such a centre or to refine the nature of the programs that it offers.

As you can see, no one basic type of neighbourhood organization exists. Organizations are shaped not only by the particular needs of the neighbourhood but also by the interests of the organizers. Factors such as the extent of the organizers' interest, awareness of organizing options, and availability of time may well be reflected in the design of the organization.

## Activities of Neighbourhood Organizations

A brief rundown of common activities undertaken by neighbourhood organizations provides some examples of the things you may be able to accomplish by bringing people, not only residents, but also individuals and groups from outside of the neighbourhood—particularly local government, schools, religious institutions, social service agencies, and private foundations—together in the effort to strengthen the vitality of a neighbourhood.

You can accomplish a great deal to enhance the quality of life for neighbourhood residents simply by encouraging and supporting the further development of natural helping networks that exist in the neighbourhood. Here are some ideas you might try:

- *Social interaction:* newsletters providing information on resources, neighbourhood personalities, and neighbourhood and community events affecting the neighbourhood; intergenerational mentoring; exchange of resources or services for mutual assistance; participation in neighbourhood organization decision making, operation, or activities
- *Resource exchanges:* tool banks within or among neighbourhoods; toy libraries; recycling of building materials; co-ops such as babysitting or food purchases; skills banks
- *Community education:* forums; speakers; credit and noncredit classes
- *Involvement of youths and older neighbours:* young people on neighbourhood councils; partnership in service-learning; neighbourhood history project; youth-run training and information programs; home repair projects for older persons; storytelling projects

© Jim West/Alamy

**There are many activities that community members can engage in to improve their neighbourhoods.**

- *Monitoring services of local government:* garbage pickup; fire protection; police protection; street maintenance and repair; sewer maintenance and repair
- *General improvements*: traffic; zoning enforcement; neighbourhood planning
- *Security:* identification of household items for burglary protection; safety and security inspections; foot patrols; neighbourhood watch; community policing in collaboration with neighbourhood prevention efforts; neighbourhood-based public defender and mediation services; a cadre of community youth workers working with service agencies and law enforcement
- *Service delivery:* day care; visitation of elderly; shopping services; provision of emergency food; substance-abuse counselling; services designed for particular groups such as children, young people, older people, or single parents
- *Political empowerment:* voter registration activities; voter turnout activities; candidate forums; public hearings; participation in coalitions; organization of power bases
- *Improvement and redesign of local schools:* family resource centres, providing an array of wellness and human services; schools to function as activity and community learning centres with increased hours of operation; schools serve as resource attractors for community development efforts; schools transformed into community development and education centres; neighbourhood involvement in classroom activities, service-learning, and school decision making

Many of these activities can easily fit into more than one category. As you become more involved in the neighbourhood, you will intentionally develop activities that serve a variety of purposes. The "spillover" effect of programs often produces additional positive benefits, such as

## DID YOU KNOW?

### Organizations and Resources

A number of public and private organizations can direct you to information, technical assistance, or other resources that you might need as you work to strengthen your neighbourhood. You can contact them via the Internet, or pick up the phone and talk with staff (phone numbers are available on their websites). Here's a list to get you started:

- The Canadian Alliance for Community Health Centre Associations
- Canadian Business for Social Responsibility
- Canadian Community Investment Network Cooperative
- Calgary Association of Self-Help
- Canadian Community Economic Development Net
- Childcare Advocacy Associations of Canada
- Consumer Association of Canada

intergenerational contact or contact across diversity and difference, development of leadership, or increased commitment to the neighbourhood.

## Basic Change-Related Tasks

Neighbourhood change is similar to any community change endeavour. For the community to act on the possibility of change, two conditions need to be present: The residents must be sufficiently unhappy with current circumstances, and they must have a sufficient degree of belief that their actions can produce a successful outcome. For the change to be made, the neighbourhood must have sufficient power and resources to introduce the change and to sustain it.

The information in previous chapters provides you with a solid foundation for building and sustaining an organized neighbourhood change effort. A brief review of important elements geared specifically to neighbourhood change, with suggestions from Gatewood (1994); Hallman (1984); Kretzman and McKnight (1993); Schwab and Ringel (1991); Suchman and Lamb (1991); and Suchman (1993, 1994), underscores the key phases.

To get off the ground, neighbourhood organization often needs an initiator, someone to get the ball rolling. This could well be you or the person who brought the interest for improving the neighbourhood to your attention. In addition, a neighbourhood organization needs to do the following:

- *Promote communication.* Neighbours need to talk among themselves to recognize dissatisfaction, stir up interest, and begin to build some level of trust. This may occur through informal conversations with residents, a door-to-door resident contact campaign, informal small group meetings, block-by-block organizing, or by other methods.
- *Do its homework.* A better understanding of neighbourhood characteristics, concerns, resources, leadership figures, needs, institutions, and other elements should begin in the early stages. Continue to develop a good information base. Essential here is the recognition, documentation, and use of the wealth of assets of individuals (including "strangers"; that is, the marginalized members of the community—the young, the old, and the labelled); local associations and organizations from stamp clubs to neighbourhood organizations; local institutions, including parks, libraries, and community colleges; natural attributes such as vacant land,

proximity to downtown, trees, rivers, scenic views, and historic sites; and local community leadership.
• *Develop issues.* The ability to define and articulate concerns will help to build momentum.
• *Hold initial meetings.* You need to introduce the idea of an organization, begin to formalize the organization, identify beginning plans and related actions, and make decisions.
• *Take initial action.* Do something to help confirm the reality of your organization and its capability. Usually these are specific, visible actions such as placing a stop sign. Or they are beginning actions that lead to further actions such as inviting an elected official to meet with your group.
• *Celebrate accomplishments.* Draw attention to the gains you have already made.
• *Recruit members.* Attract new participants to your effort.
• *Further develop plans.* Plans can become more comprehensive. Remember to include not only the people who live in the area but those who work or go to school there as well.
• *Further develop organizational leadership and structures.* Identify potential leaders and provide them with opportunities for demonstrating initiative, influence, and direction. Clarify organizational issues through development of various committees, promulgation of bylaws and, perhaps, preparation of articles of incorporation.
• *Engage in fundraising and the acquisition of needed items.* Obtain the resources needed to operate the organization and to pursue its activities.
• *Take further action.* Engage in actions or tackle projects that have a more significant impact on the neighbourhood.
• *Expand power.* Create linkages with other sources of power, join coalitions, create media attention, or undertake other activities that promote your group's ability to influence decisions affecting the neighbourhood.
• *Work through tensions.* All neighbourhoods are not the same nor are all community members the same so of course there are tensions in organizing. This does not mean organizing is a failure or at fault. It is just that these need to be carefully explained, attended to, and facilitated.

This rough sequence of activities offers an overview of some of the basic tasks you will need to perform. This process is not really a step-by-step guide, since some of these actions will overlap with one another or even occur simultaneously. Also, although some of these activities have a beginning and end point, most will be ongoing throughout the life of the organization.

## Tools for the Neighbourhood Builder

You can put a number of models and programs to use in building a strong neighbourhood. Here are some you may want to learn more about.
• *Community Development Financial Institutions (CDFIs).* These institutions include community development loan funds, community development banks, community development credit unions, and micro-enterprise loan funds. CDFIs provide access to credit in specifically targeted areas for individuals and organizations who are often denied financial services by traditional banks. Funds are often geared to small entrepreneurs. The Canadian Community Investment Network Co-op, established in 2004, is a national cooperative dedicated to bringing together the voices of community investment in Canada. Its mission is to strengthen the capacity of its members to expand access to capital and support services for social economy enterprises and economically and socially excluded individuals and communities across Canada. The goals of the Canadian Community Investment Network Cooperative are to

- promote the alternative community investment sector
- support the sustainability and growth of member organizations and the sector
- work to increase the amount of accessible and affordable capital for use by member organizations

- improve the capacity of practitioners through improved practice and information sharing
- work with all levels of government to improve the regulatory environment for community investment in Canada. (Asimakos, 2009; Canadian Community Investment Network, http://www.communityinvestment.ca/index.html; retrieved January 19, 2009)

• *Canadian Community Reinvestment Coalition (CCRC).* This nonprofit, non-partisan coalition of anti-poverty, consumer, community economic development, labour, and small business groups has campaigned for bank accountability in Canada. CCRC service is non-binding and is available to any individual or small business with a complaint. It specializes in consumer protection. CCRC works with other services that can protect consumers such as the Ombudsman for Banking Services and Investments (OBSI). If you have complaints about financial services you can contact it. For concerns and complaints about life and health products and services issued by life insurance companies, contact the Ombud Service for Life and Health Insurance (OLHI). For problems concerning home, car, and business insurance, contact the General Insurance Ombud Service (GIO).

• *Canada Mortgage and Housing Corporation.* This is a federal government agency in charge of producing information about market data and research, including the Canadian Housing Observer, which reports on Canadian housing needs (Shapcott, 2009 p. 233).

## ADDITIONAL FACTORS RELATED TO SUCCESSFUL NEIGHBOURHOOD CHANGE

Attention to a number of general principles that apply to neighbourhood change and empowerment will give you a better understanding of this arena and also strengthen your effectiveness.

### Sources of Strength

*Membership development is a key matter.* Groups with large memberships are taken much more seriously by actors outside of the neighbourhood and by residents as well. More members means more resources, more clout, more potential leaders, and so on.

*Interaction develops commitment.* Neighbours' interaction with one another and with neighbourhood services, such as the local grocery store, will increase favourable sentiments toward the neighbourhood. Sentimental attachment to the neighbourhood is further increased when residents can participate in networks that not only meet their own needs but that help them to recognize they have important contributions to make to others within the network. This has implications for building a sense of community. Neighbourhood changes that increase these positive sentiments may be accomplished through rather small and low-cost efforts (Kretzman & McKnight, 1993; Morrison et al., 1997; Putnam, 1995; Roach & O'Brien, 1982; Wagner, 1995).

*A shared perception of threat can move people to action.* Mobilization of neighbourhood resources is more likely when the neighbourhood is perceived as threatened (Thomas, 1986). "Neighborhood organizations, regardless of the income of their constituents, share a single overriding goal: defense of their turf" (Williams, 1985, p. 112). In Toronto in the 1970s, neighbourhoods organized successfully against the Spadina expressway, planned to go through the middle of these neighbourhoods. Not only would neighbourhoods have been severed from one another, but the pollution associated with vehicle use would have increased. In 2009–2010, a similar battle was being waged in the same city. Neighbourhoods would be affected by the construction of a diesel train line running from the city centre to the airport. The Clean Train Coalition is arguing for electric trains, which are quieter and cleaner and more relevant to the neighbourhoods on their route if stops in those neighbourhoods are added.

## Economic Considerations

The neighbourhood is an economic system. It has wealth, enterprises, and a flow of money, goods, and services in and out, and circulation within. Its wealth may be seen in buildings and physical facilities, land, equipment, and machines (ownership can be near or distant), as well as in the personal wealth, talents, and skills of its people. It has commercial and industrial enterprises and public and nonprofit organizations. All of these have capital investments and goods. They hire people and give out money through paycheques and public welfare programs.

All neighbourhoods have a cash flow. As an example, a neighbourhood with 2,000 people with a per capita income of $7,000 has an annual income of $14 million. The proportion of income that circulates within the neighbourhood and how much is spent outside of it determines the degree of benefit that the neighbourhood receives from its money input. "A net inflow of dollars adds to prosperity, a net outflow leads to decline" (Hallman, 1984, p. 83). There have been initiatives in Canadian cities to keep the economy more local and avoid the flight of money to large global enterprises. For example, some neighbourhoods have "shop local" campaigns, and others have special dollars that you can exchange for services in a kind of barter program. In addition, many communities have seen a tremendous growth in local markets that sell foods from farmers close to the city and ensure, in some cases, healthy food in the neighbourhood.

## Diverse Perspectives

*Skepticism may be the order of the day.* Many neighbourhood residents will take a "wait and see" attitude toward your new organization. They may have been disappointed by past attempts at neighbourhood change, or they may be mistrustful of claims that "I'm from the government (or social service agency), and I'm here to help you."

In poorer neighbourhoods, residents may have learned that they fall way down on the local government's and the wider community's list of concerns. They may have developed an outlook of impotence, and they certainly have little faith in pursuing matters through "appropriate channels," which more often leads to a runaround than to resolution (Williams, 1985).

*A number of different interests affect the community.* The individual resident wants some things that conditions in the neighbourhood influence. Perhaps he or she wants security, maybe protection of property values, possibly social relationships. The neighbourhood residents in common, as a community, also have things that they want. Many of these will be the same as individuals' wants—good schools, responsible policing, and well-maintained streets. Some may be different.

There is a range of cultural perspectives in most neighbourhoods. Change agents need to recognize that cultural backgrounds and different patterns of interaction among groups can affect what people see, value, or dislike in current situations or proposed actions.

# ENHANCING THE PROSPECTS FOR SUCCESS

Neighbourhood change and empowerment is a process of discovery and action. The suggestions provided here should help to build successes, establish neighbourhood potency, and increase your awareness of this arena of action.

*Tackle issues that are within your capability.* Remember that the specific problems on which you intend to take action cannot be larger than your base of power and resources. If you are not faced with an immediate problem, gain some experience and develop a track record on smaller actions before you deal with bigger ones. If you do not have that luxury, expand your power base by establishing connections with community institutions and other community groups, or attempt to partialize the issue.

Many of the issues confronting neighbourhoods are related to more fundamental community and social problems occurring beyond neighbourhood boundaries. Your organization can ally itself with others as a way of making inroads to more fundamental problems while it takes action in the neighbourhood to counter their effects. For example, you may participate in a movement promoting economic justice while undertaking economic development activities in your neighbourhood.

Understand that as you address larger issues, you are likely to need support, assistance, and actual resources from groups outside of the neighbourhood. These may be governmental units, lending institutions, or community activist groups.

*Realize that not all good ideas are feasible.* Some projects are just too complicated, given the current abilities and clout of the neighbourhood.

*Move from reacting and petitioning to negotiating and mutual problem solving.* From time to time you will interact with local governments in order to head off potentially destructive actions or to secure specific benefits for the community. Your ability to act assertively as a partner rather than as a supplicant is a key distinction in the maturation of your organization.

*Plan for higher-level results.* Link activities to outcomes that change conditions (Kibel & Miner, 1996).

*Develop methods and practices to handle internal disputes.* Internal squabbling and unresolved conflicts drain energy and undermine resolve. Keep clear records regarding money—a common source of conflict. Focus more on action than on arguments over arcane sections of the bylaws.

*Identify neighbourhood leaders.* People who are visible and credible in the neighbourhood, such as the rabbi or the storeowner, may be able to provide leadership, particularly in the early stages. People who are known to hold professional or authority positions, such as a doctor, schoolteacher, architect, or police officer, are often looked to for direction. Get to know the various neighbourhood networks. Each is influenced by an informal leader.

*Understand local government systems and forms of government.* Find out which governmental jurisdiction has authority over specific matters of neighbourhood concern. Typically this would be city or county government. Also, discover the formal structure of authority in the local government. For example, does your city manager or mayor hold more authority? Are your community's representatives elected by ward or by a general election of the entire community?

*Discover "administrative guerrillas."* These are officials in local government who believe that community involvement is desirable, and act that way. They can provide valuable contributions, particularly in giving you inside information and in influencing the perceptions of other officials on neighbourhood matters (Thomas, 1986).

*Get help from those who have more experience.* There is no sense reinventing the wheel. Take advantage of technical assistance.

*Establish mentoring relationships.* Learn to benefit from the experiences of more established neighbourhood organizations. Establish a mutual understanding of the mentoring relationship; otherwise, the older organization may grow impatient with requests for assistance, or the younger organization may feel irritated by unsolicited advice. Establish some mentoring mechanism such as once-a-month breakfasts for the leadership of both groups. You will discover that both groups benefit. Be mindful of the potential for jealousies and the mentor's need to pretend to know it all.

## LIMITS OF NEIGHBOURHOOD ORGANIZING

There has been a tendency in the past to assume a simple conceptualization of community practice as a form of neighbourhood organizing among neighbours with shared interests. This approach to community organizing and neighbourhoods is not sufficient to address the marginalization of communities that is created by intransigent societal forces. In addition, some historical forms of community organizing such as neighbourhood organizing, although useful in some cases, are not adequate methods or approaches to deal with how complex Canadian communities are, the diversity of communities, or the relationship of communities to networks outside the neighbourhood. Perhaps the way forward is to imagine the local always in a dynamic relationship with global forces. Imagine the local, such as the neighbourhood, as a site of new knowledge creation and a place for new resources to be discovered and created without oversimplifying local experience (Alphonse et al., 2008; McGrath et al., 2007).

## SOME FINAL CONSIDERATIONS

Major setbacks in life can knock us down. They can demand much of our energy as we struggle to get back on our feet. Sometimes, though, what really wears at us, tears at us, a little here, a little there, is the accumulation of all those things that tell us we just don't count. Whole groups of people are written off because of where they live. Whole groups of people, even those living in more affluent settings, can grow to accept conditions that numb the spirit. Our neighbourhood, our place, is so much a part of our daily lives that we cannot escape the meaning that its life holds for us.

When we act in a way that says that we matter, that we are to be taken seriously, that we are no longer to be ignored, we rediscover elements of dignity. Neighbourhood action is a way to reclaim and confirm our dignity. Participation in neighbourhood organizations affects the feelings that residents have about their own lives and their environment (Downs, 1981).

You may think, "What can I possibly do? Where can I even start?" Each neighbourhood has something, some resource or capacity that can be a starting point.

Think about how you plan to approach the business of neighbourhood change. Do you intend to develop from within, using local strengths and vision? Do you believe that the most important direction and resources must come from outside of the neighbourhood? The way you answer these questions will direct what you do.

Similar to your work in any change effort, you will do some things very creatively and very well. You will also make mistakes. You may fear that you will not be as good as you need to be. Burghardt (1982) has a valuable commentary on this matter. He says that "holding onto this fear has been the undoing of many organizers, for the simple reality of organizing life is that good organizers are always making mistakes and being a little less effective than they ought to be" (p. 27).

As you recognize the value of learning by doing, you will recognize your increasing capability as you gain experience. Your experience may lead you to help transform a neighbourhood and, in the process, transform the people who live there.

## HELPFUL WEBSITES

**University of Toronto Research Centre**

www.urbancentre.utoronto.ca

The University of Toronto Research Centre publishes research and studies related to housing issues affecting Canadians. They also publish in areas of international housing, but its main area of research is urban topics. It is an excellent source of up-to-date information, education, and training.

**Canada Mortgage and Housing Corporation**

http://cmhc-schl.gc.ca/

Canada Mortgage and Housing Corporation is a federal organization in charge of providing information to both consumer and business in areas related to housing such as buying a new house, insurance, finance, renting. For business they provide information regarding house market, research highlights.

CHAPTER FOURTEEN

# Increasing the Effectiveness of Established, Formal Organizations

**This chapter will help you better understand the following questions:**

- What are the types of changes that might be needed in social service organizations?
- What elements affect the behaviour of organizations?
- What are some of the processes that influence organizational change?
- How can you increase your effectiveness in producing organizational change?

In this chapter the focus of discussion is on formal, well-established organizations; among them are the social welfare agencies that you may work within. These kinds of organizations have some characteristics not necessarily present in the less formal, grassroots organizations preceding chapters have focused on. However, they also have many similarities.

Organizations are creatures of human design, empowered by the strength of human creativity and purpose, and limited by human foibles and ignorance. Organizations can be bungling or competent. They can be shortsighted or forward-looking. They can be defensive or insightful. They can be productive or wasteful. They can neglect or take care of themselves. In short, organizations are collections of people, and they tend to act, not surprisingly, like people.

Most of the work of social service professionals is done through some organization, usually a public or private agency. The usefulness of this work is, to some extent, constrained by the imperfections of those organizations themselves as well as the larger context within which those organizations operate. Improvements in the quality of our organizations translate into improvements in the effectiveness of our work.

Thus organizations themselves become arenas for change. Workers in social services are not the only ones who have noticed the need to improve their organizations. Business corporations, large and small, have been the subject of many a writer's or consultant's attention. There is much to be learned from the examples, good and bad, that the business world provides. Yet despite their many similarities, it would be naïve to think that social service organizations and private, for-profit businesses should operate in the same way. Their purposes are different, and certainly the societal demands they face are not the same.

Many of the thoughts and suggestions we provided in this chapter have been informed by our experience. But they certainly are not our ideas alone. As well, you will find the perspectives of a number of writers in the following pages. We have particularly relied on the observations of Belasco (1990); Bishop (1994, 2002); Brager and Holloway (1977, 1978); Cohen and Austin (1994); Dubois and Krogsrud Miley (2000); Frey (1990); Goldberg (1980); Gottleib (1992); Gummer (1978); Heintze and Bretschneider (2000); Holloway (1987); Hyde (1992); Kettner et al. (1985); Kirst-Ashman and Hull (2001); Litwak, Shiroi, Zimmerman, and Bernstein (1970); Lumsden and Lumsden (2000); Magliocca and Christakis (2001); Martin (1980); Morgan (1997); O'Looney (1993); Patti (1974, 1980); Patti and Resnick (1975); Quarter, Mook and Armstrong (2009); Resnick (1978); Resnick and Menefee (1994); Richan (1992); Roloff and Paulson (2001); Senge et al. (1994); Sherman and Wenocur (1983); Weinbach (1984); and Wernet (1994).

Organizations certainly respond to outside pressure. They need to and do respond to threats, opportunities, and trends in the larger political and economic environment. In fact, if they do not respond, they may cease to exist. But it is not those forces alone that lead to change. Members of the organization, perhaps even you, will work to ward off direct demands for change "outsiders" may make. One likely reason is that members feel threatened by the implication that if they were doing their jobs well, no pressure would need to be brought. Another related reaction is defensiveness. There is often the perception that those outside the organization "just don't understand." They do not understand the organization's mission, its funding constraints, the value of its current methods, the difficulties involved in making the change, and on and on. This increases the value of making changes from within.

All people who make up an organization are capable of initiating some change, although the discussion of organizational change issues is frequently directed to the top leadership of organizations. Executives and administrators are counselled on ways to streamline the organization, develop strategic initiatives, assess the orientation toward change of key players, or manage personnel for greater productivity. Although effective action from those in the highest positions of the organization can produce important changes, the responsibility and opportunity to promote change should hardly rest only there. In the course of your daily activities, each of you will be able to identify barriers to effective client service or opportunities to create even more effective approaches. Regardless of your formal position in the organization, that recognition will spark an interest in organizational change. It is to you that this chapter is addressed.

As a worker, it is likely you will come face to face with some fundamental value conflicts as you work within an organization, especially a large one. You may want to promote the interests of clients, whereas the organization wants to promote its status. Your values of being readily responsive to changing conditions and promoting the value and uniqueness of each individual might be at odds with an organization interested in maintenance and predictability. Organizational values of service may run counter to your beliefs about empowerment. A host of other conflicts may also be in store.

You must recognize that these value conflicts are likely. If you expect them, you are less likely to be thrown off stride when they show up. You need to develop attitudes and skills for dealing with them constructively.

Change efforts initiated by workers who are not in formal leadership positions face a number of obstacles. Rarely does front-line staff have formal authority to initiate change. Doing so requires workers to engage in activities normally seen as outside their areas of responsibility. Further, the strategies and tactics required to promote recognition and response to a given issue may conflict with organizational norms and expectations of "professional" behaviour. This is further complicated by a sort of necessary role reversal. That is, low-authority people are encouraging high-authority people to take the organization in new directions. They have, in effect, become the leaders. That is not a situation many formal leaders take lightly.

The authority embodied in professional ethics may transcend certain arbitrary limits on worker authority. A belief in professional responsibility may drive workers to seek changes that will benefit the people they serve. Social service organizations recognize the value of professional ethics. You should not dismiss this practical asset. In addition, in each organization there is the likely availability of peer support as well as assistance from some who hold higher positions of authority. Together, these dedicated individuals can mobilize for change.

Still, a tension often exists between the worker's responsibility to advance client interests and the worker's loyalty to the agency. You might be faced with this tension throughout your career and will have to respond to it. We would argue that the worker's primary duty is to work on behalf of service users.

## TYPES OF GENERAL CHANGES

As a worker in social services, you may seek changes in the way the organization relates to outside influences (for example, government authority or expectations of funders), to its immediate stakeholders (for example, service users), or to its internal processes (for example, agency policies and procedures). Five basic types of changes are typical.

1. *Mobilize the organization to engage with outside influences for the benefit of service users or staff.* Workers may attempt to involve the agency in public policy discussions relating to changes in laws or in regulations affecting public programs. The agency may be asked to become an advocate on matters involving funding, particularly as they may affect benefit levels of public social welfare programs, compensation for employees, or increases in the number of program staff (resulting in an improvement in service delivery). Encouraging a public social welfare agency to vigorously seek an increase in the number of staff positions in order to substantially reduce caseloads would be an example of this type of activity.

2. *Removal of procedures that inhibit service.* All rules at one time made sense, or at least seemed to. Unfortunately, some rules or procedures take on a life of their own and outlive any usefulness they may have had. Sometimes rules that made sense in one situation are applied to situations that have different demands. Or rules are created apart from the context of day-to-day reality. They are fashioned more out of concern with what might happen than with what actually does happen. The list could go on. The simple fact is that some rules serve neither service users nor the goals of the organization. Workers can gain relief from cumbersome or inappropriate rules and procedures by seeking to establish more helpful or empowering policies.

3. *Program or project development.* Workers may institute entirely new programs or undertake a new project within a program to better reach an underserved population. For example, establishing a creative arts program for youth within a neighbourhood might represent a new direction for an agency traditionally wedded to providing only individual counselling services.

4. *Program or project modification.* Workers may alter the design of existing services to increase benefits to service users or to promote accessibility and utilization of services. This may involve a change in service methods (for example, from individual to group counselling). It may also deal with matters such as program relevance to service user needs, program location, or community awareness of the program.

5. *Involvement of service users in setting agency direction.* Most workers would adhere to the principle of service user decision making

with regard to choices related to individual matters. Yet this same ethic is often conspicuously absent when it comes to the design and delivery of services. Workers may redress circumstances that promote dependence and program irrelevance by investing service users with the skills and authority to influence agency decisions. An example of this would be including service users on agency boards of directors and other agency advisory committees.

## ELEMENTS AFFECTING THE BEHAVIOURS OF ORGANIZATIONS

Why do members of social service organizations or the organizations themselves act the way they do? We will not pretend to provide you with a comprehensive answer to that question, but we can offer a few insights to help you make sense of some of the things you might see.

### Organizations Exist in a Larger Context

Organizations are constantly responding to obvious and subtle pressures from outside (and inside). Your awareness of these pressures will help you develop and direct these forces to accelerate change in a desired direction.

A social service organization is influenced by an array of external forces to which it must respond to justify its very existence. The fact that these forces are often at variance with each other creates a tension within the organization that can produce problems. Particularly, the contradictory values and beliefs of the general society relating to social welfare are often evident in conflicting directives issued to organizations and expressed through the behaviour of social service organizations. Imagine the various constituencies an organization must try to please: diverse political interests, funding sources, professionals, service users, other agencies, referral sources, and the general public. When you consider the number of disparate interests to which it responds, you will begin to understand some of the reasons the organization might not always operate in the ways that you think might be best.

Here, again, you are faced with both a dilemma and an opportunity. By collaborating with interests both inside and outside the organization, you may be able to neutralize some of these forces while marshalling others. When these forces are focused on a particular aspect of the organization's functioning, you can influence both the rate and the direction of change.

The more you understand the organization's relationship to its external environment, the more you will be able to recognize opportunities to strengthen the organization. Even though your agency may be operating in the world of nonprofits, it is still operating in a competitive marketplace. Its ability to make strategic decisions to reach groups that have not been effectively served by other organizations or to better serve those currently using its services can attract resources that help the organization flourish.

#### The Organization as a Political Entity

An organization is a political entity. Those who have the power to set policies usually do so (knowingly or unknowingly) in a way that serves their own interests. Do not make the mistake of ignoring this process or assuming that it confirms the evil lurking in the hearts of policymakers. It is a fairly normal process, one in which you probably engage from time to time in your personal if not professional life. Whoever is involved in decision making tends to make policies reflecting their own norms, values, and beliefs. In the process of involving more people in decision making, you will influence development of new norms as you mix new values and beliefs into the policymaking process.

#### The Organization as an Economic Entity

The organization provides a type of product (a service) to the larger community in exchange for the resources (usually funding) it receives. It must always be cognizant of its relationships with resource providers (funders, donors) for if it does not maintain positive relationships it may not be able to continue its work. Organizations also have internal economic pressures. Decisions are constantly being made with regard to how an organization's funds will be allocated to its various components. For example, which programs will receive more (or less) funding in any given fiscal year? The ability to provide or withhold funding to various programs within the organization can affect relationships within the organization. Certain behaviours produce rewards; others can be costly. An informal exchange system of rewards and favours is also always in operation. Both formal and informal systems have a powerful influence on the nature and direction of change within the organization. You need to take them into account.

### The Organization as an Ideological System

Which fundamental beliefs drive the organization? What convictions about what it should and should not do direct its actions? How does it view its mission? How highly does it value its very approach to providing service? How strong is its adherence to its history and traditions? What doctrines does it hold to be true? By understanding the organization's view of its purpose, its process, and its past, you can introduce change in a way that reduces resistance.

### The Organization as a Social Entity

Social service organizations are different from many other types of communities in the degree of interaction among the members and the degree of meaning members attach to their participation. In few communities do members spend a significant portion of their waking day in direct relationship with one another and with their common purpose. Neighbours may see each other from time to time, social workers meet in professional gatherings a few times a year, and cycling enthusiasts may pedal past one another on occasional Saturdays. Workers in social service agencies see each other almost every day, for hours. They work side by side or together to advance the community's goals. They assist or interfere with each other's professional careers. The time they spend supporting or gossiping about each other is probably greater than the total time most of them spend in general conversation with members of any other community in which they participate.

Since so much of their time is given over to their involvement with this community, what goes on there becomes very important. Many members even derive their personal identity from their participation in the community: "I am a social service worker, a program manager, a counsellor."

These are not trivial matters. They intensify the change experience. On the positive side, it is much easier to contact members and much easier to bring them together. However, it is also much easier for change to be threatening to some members as well

## Structural Characteristics of Organizations

The structure, processes, and philosophy of the organization as well as the perceptions of its members will have an impact on how you proceed to make changes. What is the size of the organization? Is the organization composed of many different programs and functional units or only a few? The more complex an organization, the more forces that can assist or inhibit the change effort that will have to be recognized. Does the organization have a centralized hierarchy of authority? Does your boss have a boss who has a boss who must get yet another boss to approve the change? Your assessment of whether the organization vests decision making in the hands of a few or invites broad participation will suggest the tactics you will use. Does your organization have an elaborate set of rules governing everything from hiring practices to bathroom usage? An abundance of policies usually inhibits change, although you may be able to find some policies that provide justification for change.

In all organizations people know incompletely; that is, each person has limited access to information. Those people who work at the front-line level are more able to comprehend problems encountered by service users. Those who struggle to balance the budget are more likely to know of the potential financial strain various programs impose. Organizations with a high degree of specialization or a rigid hierarchy of authority feel the burden of perceptual differences more severely.

With some people allowed access to information and others denied, or with some people attentive to their narrow concerns while others worry over very separate matters, it is likely that different if not contradictory perspectives will emerge. In these organizations, the ability to have and to hold particular information may define a person's domain. A desire to protect the domain may contribute to a reluctance to share information, thereby further impeding communication. As a change agent, you need to see that other people will often see the situation differently.

## ADDITIONAL PROCESSES INFLUENCING CHANGE

See if the experiences, conditions, and possibilities described here appear in your organization. Each will affect your ability to institute change.

### Overcome Success

Believe it or not, success can get an organization stuck. An organization that is doing very well in a particular area may need to look at the example of other organizations to see how past successes might have led them to dismiss or miss new challenges and opportunities. As long as nothing changes, tried-and-true methods will usually work. When conditions change, however, the same methods may become irrelevant or worse.

### Overcome Failures

Workers may have made attempts to improve the organization with little to show for their efforts but frustration. They may become jaded to new efforts (yours) and seek the protection of cynicism. Your challenge to present conditions may remind other staff of the unpleasant accommodations they have made to put up with day-to-day problems.

Feelings of powerlessness may express themselves in a variety of behaviours. Some workers may bounce from one personal crusade to another. Some may become passive and do whatever they are told. Others may find ways to sabotage the organization. Still others may reduce uncertainty through abdication, withdrawing into their own personal little niche, retreating to the safe service of regulations, or leaving the organization altogether. Of course, many will become martyrs, working hard, but unappreciated, in the selfless cause of others.

Although many of your colleagues may be inspired by the potential for change, you are wise to remain mindful of the reticence or the disabling coping responses past failures may have wrought. Expect that people want to do a good job. However, they may be afraid to get their hopes up.

### Recognize Potential Problems

Throughout the preceding chapters, we have explored a number of problems associated with promoting community change. In fact, the mere thought of the potential for problems is enough to chill to inaction the enthusiasm of many a potential change agent. Although we do not want to belabour the idea of obstacles, your awareness of certain problems due to the unique nature of the organization as a community will help you keep things in perspective.

• *Procrastination.* Members of this community are engaged in other community projects, mainly their day-to-day work. There is enough for them to do to stay busy and distracted with these immediate tasks, so additional work on the change effort gets pushed to the side.

Relax. The problem is mainly a perceptual one. By using the techniques you have read about in previous chapters, you will keep moving forward. It is especially important to keep communicating the vision, keep making decisions, take concrete (even if minor) actions, and involve more people.

• *Critics.* A few people will make light of your enthusiasm or your vision. Some will find fault with your methods, if not your intention. Some will tell you directly; most will not. Because these are people you work with, their criticisms may have more of a sting. Anticipating the likelihood of this response will decrease the irritation you might feel. Responses to the criticism? Directly invite the critics to join with you. Ignore them. Learn from the criticism. Though the content of the criticism may provide some help in improving your effort, the fact of the criticism will be important information. As those of you involved in the undertaking provide encouragement and support to one another, you will deal with this and other obstacles constructively.

• *Unintended consequences.* Because the change you are proposing will be affecting a complex community, it may well produce additional significant impacts you did not anticipate. Some of these will be good, some will not. With an eye toward evaluating actual and likely results of your actions and a willingness to make modifications, you can avoid the most detrimental repercussions.

The more you are able to connect your change effort to the organization's ideology, goals, structure, and member relationships and attitudes, the more likely you will celebrate a successful outcome.

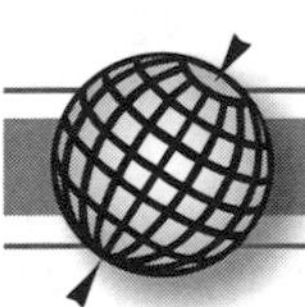

## GLOBAL PERSPECTIVES

PERU—I consider dealing with changes in large bureaucratic organizations to be a dynamic process. The majority of changes usually come from the different decision levels. Changing the procedures and redistributing the shares of power at the interior of these institutions generate immediately major changes. The possibility of generating changes depends on the leadership, the initiative, and the particular structure of the bureaucratic organization. As the more traditional and big an institution is, it will be more difficult to generate changes. Many times changes happen because of external factors or agents that affect the institution as a whole. (Mario Zolezzi, personal communication, September 16, 2002)

AUSTRALIA—Understanding issues of integrity in human services organizations requires not simply examining the vocational ethic and how staff arrive at compromises between their ideals and the realities. It involves examining the significance attached to changes and the manner of determining a moral project which can withstand the rigour of critical analysis and the rigours of changing organizational forms within which commitments are to be enacted. Constructing integrity which sustains hope, then, invokes both personal exploration and socio-political analysis—and places them as mutually reinforcing. (Martyn Jones, 2000, p. 377)

## PRINCIPLES FOR INCREASING YOUR EFFECTIVENESS

Kirst-Ashman and Hull (2001) have developed an easy-to-remember process for initiating and implementing organizational change called IMAGINE.

**I** Start with an *Idea*.

**M** *Muster* support and formulate an action system.

**A** Identify *Assets*.

**G** Specify *Goals* and objectives.

**I** *Implement* a plan.

**N** *Neutralize* opposition.

**E** *Evaluate* progress.

Once you have made the decision to make a change, your effort will be enhanced by paying attention to these basic elements.

### Know Your Issue Well

• Gather the necessary facts and figures regarding the change you propose.

• Find out the history of this issue. Has the change been sought in the organization before? If so, what happened? What lasting effect resulted?

• Has the change you are proposing been tried elsewhere? Has it ever worked? What can be learned from that? How can you use this information to garner support for your ideas?

### Involve Service Users as Partners

• Appreciate the benefits of service user involvement. If service users can easily see how the proposed change affects them, they can be a tremendous asset to the effort. They can help shape the change, increasing the prospect that it is indeed helpful and relevant to their experience. Service users can make demands on the organization that the worker may not be able to make, both in terms of standing and tactics. Further, it is much harder for resisters to rationalize away problems or to justify inaction to service users.

• Promote service user empowerment. When workers assist service users to recognize additional dimensions to their private struggles, when workers communicate their belief in service users' abilities to act on their own behalf, and when workers indicate a willingness to learn from service users as partners, empowerment of service users has benefits far beyond the immediate change.

### Gain the Support of External Advocacy Groups

• Strengthen your effect. The ability to send a message from the outside that is consistent with the message you are sending from the inside increases the credibility of the message and the chances it will be heard. Additionally, close working relationships will decrease the possibility that groups with similar interests but different information and perspectives will operate at cross purposes.

• Assess the organization's perception of external actors. The impact of external support (or opposition) depends on how widespread or strong the organization perceives it to be.

• Understand that public agencies respond to pressures in the political environment more than in the economic environment (Heintze & Bretschneider, 2000).

### Capitalize on External Threats and Opportunities

• Seize the moment. Timing is critical to change efforts. Point out current conditions that will help the organization recognize how the proposed change can provide a public relations or financial benefit or ward off a potential loss.

### Create Support Systems That Sustain Worker Involvement in Change

• Bolster your resolve. Workers often need each other's tactical and emotional support to become comfortable with taking and using power. An active support group can establish an empowering worker subculture within the organization that may replace a fragmented, defeatist orientation.

• Understand the purpose and functions of an empowerment group. A support group of this type is *not* developed as a temporary mechanism to deal with a particular problem. Empowerment groups are *not* mechanisms for complaining and reinforcing values and beliefs of impotence. Members of an empowerment group commit themselves to meeting regularly, sharing problem-solving responsibility, recognizing the resources each member brings, and taking responsibility for their own actions within the organization. These actions provide a constructive way to deal with frustration, reduce worker burnout, and protect against divide-and-conquer tactics.

## Identify Stakeholders, Attract Investors, and Secure Allies

• Realize that the most critical determinant of success or failure is involvement of a significant number of people in shaping the vision.

• Know who the significant actors are. Who is interested in promoting the change? Who will directly benefit? Who has authority to approve or deny the change? Who are the opinion leaders? All members of the organization are potential actors. Though some have more formal power than others, all who are aware of the change effort make decisions to ignore, support, or oppose the change. They all will decide to get involved or refrain from involvement.

• Discover the extent, degree, location, and temperament of support or resistance. What resources will these people use to support or resist?

• Identify the stakeholders in the current situation. Where and how can they find a stake in the new situation?

• Don't ignore the needs of the staff who have to implement the change. The final features of the change will be shaped by their hands.

• Avoid alienating potential allies who may not support you in the early going.

• Recognize the resources every single organizational member can potentially contribute: access to information; control of information; relationships with other actors; credibility, reputation, or standing; personal skills or expertise.

• Maintain the commitment and support of critical actors. Keep people oriented to the need and what's going on to meet it. Keep people up to date with what is going on in the change effort. Remind actors of the value of the roles various people can and are playing. Determine how to use various mechanisms to communicate that the vision is working.

## Understand the Culture of the Organization

• The culture of the organization will be the single most powerful force affecting change. Significant change in the organization requires purposeful, above-board discussion about the silent influence of organizational culture and ultimately a clear agreement to change it. Over time a series of minor alterations will create cultural changes, particularly if these build on cultural traits that already exist. However, these must be steady and vigilantly maintained in order to ultimately transform the organization. Without intentionally changing an organization's culture, it will essentially return to its previous state no matter who is at the helm.

• Some organizations emphasize control and allegiance to authority and procedure, whereas others, on the opposite end of the spectrum, are committed to openness and outcomes. The rhetoric of an organization does not always describe its true character. If you can present your change as being culturally consistent, and if you adhere to cultural norms in the way you present it, your chances for success will be higher than if you ignore cultural conditions. Here, you amplify certain aspects of the culture that support the change.

**Ensuring the organization's board of directors is well informed will assist them in making appropriate decisions.**

- Understand alliances and antagonisms, especially among decision makers. You can gain valuable information by observing meetings, asking questions, and cataloguing complaints. Pay attention to the types of relationships that exist by noting who refers to whom, who defers to whom, and who spends time with whom.
- Determine which supporters can hold which resisters accountable.
- Understand and use informal networks of communication.
- Get to know the official documents and approved statements of the organization. Key information to collect includes policy manuals, authority/organization charts, promotional material the organization sends out, and budgets. These can help you spot entry points for introducing change to the organization. You will be able to identify formal relationships and procedures. You will be able to discern differences between rhetoric and practice, real and phony threats, and other inconsistencies. You may well discover that "policies" that supposedly influence decisions do not really exist at all.
- Recognize that written standards of behaviour may have little influence over decisions and behaviour (Roloff & Paulson, 2001).
- Acknowledge but do not rely too heavily on hearsay.
- Ask yourselves: "Which aspects of the current culture empower us, and which aspects don't?"

## Create a Receptive Environment

- Create an awareness of the need for change. Identify and thoughtfully disseminate symptoms of problems. These may include letters from service users (with their permission), data on important outcomes, positive reports on other providers or other motivating comparisons to your "competitors," and worker observations.

- Consider having a workshop (or periodic workshops) to identify opportunities for improvement. Keep this focused on a particular area of operation. Participants should include staff of different levels of authority.
- Decide where in the organization you need to initiate discussion of the problem.
- Develop your own personal influence with respect to the problem. Take steps to increase your credibility and standing.
- Understand the mission of the organization and relate the change to it.
- Consider proposing the change as being so linked to organizational values and other activities that it represents little real change at all.
- Commit yourself to learning, and promote the idea of a learning organization, one that purposefully uses its experiences to increase effectiveness and inform its actions. All actions of the organization become connected with discovery.
- Begin by focusing on one particular aspect or area of the organization. This is less threatening. Ideas are introduced to other parts of the organization, not forced on them. In a learning organization, changes in one area become models for another.

## Expect, Identify, and Deal with Resistance

- Recognize that resistance is not necessarily a bad thing. The need to test your ideas against resistance will reduce the chances for unintended consequences, and it may lead to new discoveries. Avoid "tuning out" problems that need to be addressed.
- Understand that most people do not look positively on new ideas that they think will turn their world upside down, and adding on lots of reasons why the change must take place rarely makes things better (Denning, 2000).
- Recognize that bringing the change closer to reality can energize supporters and opponents alike.
- Determine the degree of similarity and difference in goals between supporters and resisters.
- Be cautious about expecting too much from your connections. Although your friendly relationship with a formal decision maker will be helpful, do not assume that it is sufficient to ensure approval of the change.
- Understand the sources of resistance. These could include lack of information or differences in information, apathy, fear, psychological investment in current operations, differing interests and commitments, lack of clarity in defining the proposed change, responses required from other components of the organization, or personal animosity among participants. Also, recognize the impact recent history or other current demands have on the organization. For example, an organization that has just recently recovered from major turmoil will be more interested in promoting stability than change. An organization in the midst of budgetary woes will not want to take on additional financial burdens. An organization distracted with other issues will probably give little attention to less significant change requests.
- Seek resister involvement and contributions.
- Avoid responding to hostility with hostility.
- Keep a formal record of events and agreements. Clarify timetables for actions. Your group should determine what consequences will follow if timetables and other agreements are or are not kept.
- Be prepared to confront likely manifestations of resistance. Some of the more likely include high-authority actors claiming little or no authority on the issue, vague statements of support with no concrete actions to indicate support, delays, exaggerating minor or unrelated issues, or divide-and-conquer tactics.

## Reduce Personal Risks

- Sometimes people are reluctant to step outside narrowly defined roles without first getting permission from those in authority to do so. Some individuals believe that working for change goes hand in hand with experiencing some personal loss. Their fears become

## DID YOU KNOW?

### Ten Sources of Resistance or Support for Organizational Change

Frey (1990) has identified ten possible sources of resistance or support for organizational change:

1. *Perceived advantage.* Not all proposals will benefit all groups within the organization. Not adequately assessing the perspectives of particular groups (decision makers, implementers, staff) can lead to resistance.
2. *Effort.* The heavier the investment of time and energy on the part of various organizational actors, the more difficult it is to sustain a high level of interest and commitment.
3. *Risk.* These are the costs incurred if the proposal fails to meet its objectives. There are three types of high-risk proposals: (1) proposals that, once adopted, cannot be terminated or reversed without incurring a substantial cost; (2) proposals that must be implemented in their entirety and cannot be done in stages; and (3) proposals that conflict with the dominant values of the organization.
4. *Sunken costs.* Proposals that challenge the investments the organization has made to support certain institutional practices will be resisted.
5. *Understandability.* An inability to condense complex proposals into simple language that is compatible with the values of the particular audience will interfere with acceptance.
6. *Ability.* The organization has to believe it has the capacity to carry out the proposed change. Assume that any proposal that requires additional funds is likely to be resisted. This does not mean you should give up the effort to promote change. However, you may be required to be more creative in order to help facilitate actions that have resource implications.
7. *Depth and distance.* The more the proposal seeks to change basic goals and objectives, rather than just procedures, the more resistance will increase. Also, the greater the number of administrative levels it must pass through, the greater the chances of resistance.
8. *Idea and ideology.* Innovations that have been tested are less likely to be resisted. Those that fit the ideology of the organization are also more likely to receive support.
9. *Need.* This reflects the organization's sense that something ought to be done to fix a problem. The more that belief is shared, the more responsive the organization will be. However, just because people agree that "something must be done" does not mean there is agreement about just what that should be, how it should be implemented, or who should be responsible for implementation—another source of resistance.
10. *Generality.* This refers to the scope of the proposal. The more aspects of the organization that are affected by the proposal, the more it will be resisted. Proposals that affect only a small part of the organization are more likely to be tolerated.

Keep each of these factors in mind as you assess the feasibility of your proposed change and develop your strategies and tactics.

magnified when conditions or colleagues challenge them to take part in change-promoting activities.

• Appreciate the benefits as well as the hazards. The discussion of risks itself may exaggerate their potential. In many cases, change agents experience not only strong personal fulfillment but significant professional recognition for their actions. Even so, our fears may lead us to pay more attention to instances when working for change leads to trouble. The fact is that there sometimes is a risk involved, and exaggerated or not, it should not be naïvely dismissed.

- Understand that the nature of the change, the breadth of support for the change, the tactics used to promote the change, and the outcome of the change effort are all factors relating to the consequences for change agents. You may have the chance to influence these elements in a way that reduces risk.
- Recognize attempts to intimidate change agents. One of the more common methods used by those in authority who are resisting the change is to encourage general discomfort and focus attention on one or two individuals as the "cause of all this trouble." They attempt to distract attention from the issue and attribute the pursuit of change to some character flaw exhibited by primary advocates of change, reducing matters to a "personality issue." This may frighten off potential allies and those who are hesitant to support, especially those who look to people in authority to tell them what to think. Anticipate the tactic. You who support the effort need to talk openly among yourselves about how you will handle the situation when it arises. Provide support to one another that is visible to everyone who is aware of the conflict.
- Do not have primary advocates of change who can become separated from other core group members. Have several people in visible roles. Develop a strong support base.
- Find yourself a partner who supports your potential and who strengthens you.
- Know your rights. Be prepared to clearly assert them if disciplinary action is brought against you.
- Put yourself in a position within the organization that gives you standing to promote change. This can be a formal position or a quasi-formal position, such as a member of an internal committee.
- Manage the perception of the change effort, particularly as it relates to the motivations of those most highly involved.
- Keep your discussion related to the beneficial impact of the change. Do not engage in personal attack.
- Focus on mutual benefits. Whenever appropriate, endeavour to diminish the fears and discomfort of opponents.
- Maintain an awareness of the message your personal demeanour communicates. If you act outraged or outrageous, do so on purpose.
- Remember, you work in the organization. The way you pursue change will leave an impression on the organization, your work community. In your selection of strategies, see if you can select an approach that helps you achieve your goal in a way that humanizes this community and makes it more respectful of its members.
- Use your head to avoid unnecessary risks. Do not give opponents added reasons to discredit you.

## Implement and Confirm the Change

- Complete the job. The change agent's work is not done when the organization agrees to accept the change. Agreement signals an expansion or shift in attitude, but in practice the change has not yet occurred. Actually putting the change in place is what the whole business is all about. Those changes that alter the inner workings of the organization also need to be woven into the tapestry of its daily life to ensure their permanence.
- Attend to essential tasks. To make sure the change becomes fixed within the organization (to the extent that anything is or should be fixed), you need to accomplish two important objectives. First, establish connections with other parts of the organization so these other parts begin to make use of and ultimately rely on the benefits of the change. Next, quickly move to establish clear, predictable, useful procedures. Although there will be an initial period

of trial and error, it is important that other people, especially those within the organization, soon learn how to relate to the innovation. Confusion will create frustration and impede the desire of others to make use of the change.

- Acknowledge and perform critical roles. The change needs *champions* who will continue to assert its importance and benefits, *interpreters* who help explain what the change is and how it works, and *troubleshooters* who are alert to problems in implementation and can identify appropriate action (Brager & Holloway, 1978).
- Make necessary refinements. When your good ideas hit the reality of implementation, you will discover that a number of adjustments must be made. Some of your assumptions will be proven incorrect, and some things you did not previously think of will demand your attention. Expect that you will need to make modifications and be willing to do so. It may be helpful to publicly advance the idea of a "shakedown cruise," a period of time for working the bugs out. You have then created an expectation that alterations are an anticipated and reasonable part of the process.
- Move quickly to secure additional resources. Certain types of changes require specific resources, such as money, staff time, or space. If you are pursuing a change of this sort, you may find out that it requires more institutional support than you had thought. The time to seek additional resources is early in the implementation stage. At that time, there is likely to be an air of enthusiasm and a desire by most people for the project to succeed. If the project stumbles around for a while, people will lose interest and those in authority may be unwilling to commit new resources to an endeavour when its survival is questionable.
- Evaluate the change to see if it is doing what it is supposed to do and not creating new problems.

## SOME FINAL CONSIDERATIONS

It is unlikely that the problems plaguing your organization happened all at once. Unless the organization is faced with a major crisis, you will probably not "fix" it all at once. In the overall scheme of things, your efforts may represent only minor changes. However, each one of those changes may have major significance to the people who are immediately affected. Further, these things add up. Taken together, those minor changes you initiated will probably make a major difference.

Improving your organization is an ongoing process. Do not be surprised if one change uncovers a need for other changes. You will discover that many of the changes you brought about will fall short of your hopes. We hope this will not discourage you. Though imperfect, your efforts will lead to advancements, ones that would not have occurred if you remained confined within a narrow definition of what it means to be a professional in the field of social services.

CHAPTER FIFTEEN

# Lobbying for Change

**This chapter will help you better understand the following questions:**

- What elements are involved in the process of lobbying?
- How do you influence your elected representatives so that their decisions better reflect your community's interests?
- How can community workers intervene in the lawmaking process?
- What are the basic components of lobbying as a strategy of community change?
- How can community workers ensure their lobbying is effective?

Developing social welfare policies is hardly a simple process. It is influenced by the divergent values, motivations, and beliefs of all who have a role in defining and refining them. Competing viewpoints—from those held by the diverse members of the general public to those of elected and appointed public officials—find their way into laws and regulations that direct and govern our social welfare system. Political conflicts over the nature, causes, and necessary responses to social problems find momentary resolution in the decisions of public officials (DiNitto, 2000).

Policy practice is a compelling and vitally important method of professional intervention (Jansson, 2002). Your ability to shape the framework of policy within which resources are distributed and opportunities are provided or limitations enacted can meaningfully affect thousands and thousands of lives. Involvement in the legislative arena, where many policies are given birth, is a significant form of policy practice.

This dynamic process is always open to revision and redirection. It is open to influence. community change agents decide to participate in this process or to refrain from doing so. Either way, there are consequences for the community and for the people these organizers intend to serve (Ezell, 2001). Even if you do not participate in the development of a lobbying campaign, your first-hand knowledge of the effects of proposed legislation can speed up the refinement of legislation and prevent harmful consequences. It can, that is, if you know how to communicate what you know and if you make sure that you communicate it (Hofford, 2001).

One of the most meaningful ways that you as a citizen and as a professional can have an impact is by lobbying public officials. By *lobbying* we mean purposeful communication with a public official with the intention of influencing a decision the official may make on a specific matter (Hrebenar & Scott, 1982). The Lobby Act of Canada passed in 2008 defines lobbying as

> the development of any legislative proposal by the Federal Government, or lobbying on the passage, defeat or amendment of any bill or resolution, advocating for amendments to any regulation. (Blumberg, 2008, p. 1)

Lobbying may be done on a number of different levels. You may communicate with elected officials, from the local city council to the prime minister, in order to influence actions on public issues. You may provide information and insight to a government official who is writing regulations on a public program with the hope of increasing the effectiveness of that program. Although all three levels of government (municipal, provincial, and federal) can have an influence on your community, in this chapter we concentrate on lobbying for change in legislation at the provincial and federal levels.

Your understanding of the legislature requires an awareness of the way in which participants operate at both formal and informal levels. Certain rules of etiquette and of process should be recognized and commonly observed. The game-like character adds yet another dimension to this environment. For all these reasons, we describe this arena of change with a degree of detail.

The suggestions presented in this chapter were drawn from our experience as well as from the work of Blumberg (2008), Common Cause (1992), Dear and Patti (1984), Ezell (2001), Gotfin and Lombardi (1988), Haynes and

## GLOBAL PERSPECTIVES

ASIA—To empower people through advocacy and lobbying, it is necessary to challenge existing conventional development paradigms and practices, promote development alternatives and influence development policies and systems of government. . . . To undertake this, the following specific steps are recommended:

- Training, research, and documentation on advocacy and lobbying strategies, tools, and techniques.
- Strengthening local/national advocacy and lobbying groups.
- Promoting cooperation among existing networks, initiating a meeting among the principle Asian networks to design working mechanisms for information-sharing, concerted advocacy, and lobbying.

(Colombo Statement of Asian NGOs and People's Organizations on: People's Empowerment in Asia, as cited in Liamzon, 1997, p. 29)

ISRAEL—The connection between social work interventions and national politics is indirect, hidden, and unspoken, and literature about the issue hardly exists. However, there are many situations occurring around the world, where avoiding paying direct attention to national politics damages the implementation of social work activities. As an example, we can point to situations in which a country enters a state of war. Such situations affect the entire population, including social workers and their clients. They create fear and anxiety and increase the level of stress that might affect the behavioural and emotional functioning of both social workers and clients. The source of these threatening issues—that is, the national policy is often not discussed in professional activities, since it is not related to the typical problems addressed in social work. Social workers are usually not perceived as responsible for national political decisions, nor are they perceived as having any influence on them. Therefore, the subject is barely discussed between social workers and clients, among social workers or in social work literature. . . .

The main goal of politically oriented intervention is to open up new alternatives in situations where it seems to severely threaten the existence of specific client populations (Michel Shamai & Amnon Boehm, 2001, p. 343–344, 355).

## DID YOU KNOW?

### The Legislative Process in Canada

Canada is a parliamentary democracy: its system of government holds that the law is the supreme authority. The *Constitution Act, 1867,* which forms the basis of Canada's written constitution, provides that there shall be one parliament for Canada, consisting of three distinct elements: the Crown, the Senate, and the House of Commons. However, as a federal state, responsibility for lawmaking in Canada is shared among one federal, ten provincial, and three territorial governments. The Canadian parliamentary government has the following essential features:

- Parliament consists of the Crown and an upper and lower legislative Chamber;
- Legislative power is vested in "Parliament"; to become law, legislation must be assented to by each of Parliament's three constituent parts (the Crown, the Senate, and the House of Commons);
- Members of the House of Commons are individually elected to represent their constituents within a single electoral district; elections are based on a single member constituency, first-past-the-post or simple-plurality system (i.e., the candidate receiving more votes than any other candidate in that district is elected);
- Most members of Parliament belong to and support a particular political party;
- The leader of the party having the support of the majority of the members of the House of Commons is asked by the governor general to form a government and becomes the prime minister;
- The party, or parties, opposed to the government is called the opposition (the largest of these parties is referred to as the Official Opposition);
- The executive powers of government (the powers to execute or implement government policies and programs) are formally vested in the Crown, but effectively exercised by the prime minister and Cabinet, whose membership is drawn principally from members of the House belonging to the governing party;
- The prime minister and Cabinet are responsible to, or must answer to, the House of Commons as a body for their actions; and
- The prime minister and Cabinet must enjoy the confidence of the House of Commons to remain in office. Confidence, in effect, means the support of a majority of the House.

Adapted from the *Compendium of the House of Commons, Procedure Online: The Legislative Process. http://www.parl.gc.ca/compendium/web-content/c_g_legislativeprocess-e.htm.*

Mickelson (2000), Hofford (2001), Hrebenar and Scott (1982), Lamiell (1984), the League of Women Voters (1976), McLean (1980), Pertschuk (1986), Richan (1992), Siglin (1999), Smith (1979), Smucker (1999), and Speeter (1978). In particular, we draw heavily from a document entitled *House of Commons Procedures and Practice* (2009).

## GETTING STARTED

Your decision to act as a lobbyist should be based on a strong commitment to the issue that is the focus of your attention. Your belief in your purpose will help you overcome many obstacles, and your sincere dedication will make those whom you hope to influence more receptive to your message. The fact that your group may not have a lot of money or may not be able to contribute to political campaigns can be significantly offset by the number of people who can be mobilized. The self-interest of elected officials is, first and foremost, votes. Demonstrating your ability to move voters to awareness and action is a fundamentally important element in the lobbying process.

*Know the regulations governing lobbying in your province.* Each province has its own set of regulations. You can usually find out how these apply to you by contacting the office of your provincial member or review the *Lobbying Act* provided by Office of the Commissioner of Lobbying of Canada. (The members of provincial parliaments are known as MPPs in Ontario, MNAs in Quebec, MHAs in Newfoundland and Labrador, and MLAs in the remaining provinces and territories.)

*Be aware of the impact of your activities on the tax status of the organization you represent.* If you are acting on behalf of a registered charity, check with its accountant or lawyer to be sure you are operating within Canada Revenue Agency guidelines. The *Income Tax Act* does restrict Canadian registered charities in the type and quantity of political activities (Blumberg, 2008).

*Develop a legislative agenda.* Do you intend to support or defeat legislation? Are you going to develop new legislation, influence proposed legislation, or modify legislation in process? Understand that some of the things you do will not have an immediate payoff but will set the stage for later dividends. It is not uncommon for passage of a significant proposal to take several years of effort. As a result, you may want to provide encouragement to your group by including in your agenda some issues for which you can claim victory in one legislative session.

*Be clear about what you intend to accomplish.* Before seeking legislation, make sure that changes in law are really the best way to accomplish your purpose. Changes in administrative policy or administrative rule that do not require a change in the law but a change in government policy, operations, or procedures may accomplish what you want. Many elected representatives are impatient with those who seek legislative change when simpler methods will do.

*Gain an understanding of the legislature both federally and provincially.* Use local sources, particularly public interest groups such PovNet (Poverty Network), which works on community advocacy, the Provincial and Territorial Anti-Poverty Strategies, and Poverty Reduction Campaigns to provide direction. Many advocacy groups have written material that will help you. Check with them to see who publishes political directories. These will be a great aid in helping you understand basic elements of the legislature and identifying its members.

*Accept coaching from veterans.* As you become more and more involved, you will come to know a number of people who have a great deal of experience and expertise.

*Subscribe to publications.* Special publications that deal with legislative matters are commonly available. Read the sections of the daily newspapers that deal with political and legislative topics. Put your name on government mailing lists in order to receive legislative digests (brief summaries of legislation that has been introduced) and other related materials. You may also be able to track legislative information through various computer networks.

*Explore your federal and provincial governments' Web page.* Every province has a website; so does the federal government. It is likely you can get committee agendas, committee rosters, a biography of each legislative body, and a host of other valuable information. Other levels of government also have websites that are similarly useful.

*Find allies.* Successful lobbying employs the energies of many people. Discover who shares your interests and work with them to develop a coordinated approach to the lobbying effort. Throughout the campaign, look for other individuals and groups who can provide assistance. A formal coalition of organizations can have a strong lobbying presence. Using the Internet, you can contact other activists and advocacy organizations throughout the country. They can help you with background information, including sample legislation.

*Organize membership through your lobbying efforts.* Undertaking lobbying activities is an excellent way to build your change action. Members can play a number of roles, and the process itself is exciting. With its connection to political power, there is a good potential for members to become empowered through their participation in events. Active involvement will increase your group's recognition and establish it as a power that deserves attention.

## BASIC COMPONENTS OF AN ORGANIZED LOBBYING EFFORT

A comprehensive approach to promoting change by influencing political decision making should mobilize and direct community support, create positive community perceptions of the issue, and provide direct contact with elected officials. In addition to some of the general aspects of an organization, the following elements will strengthen your hand as you play the lobbying game.

*Legislative team.* People on this team will work directly on the legislation itself. Most of these members will be in direct contact with the elected representatives or leader of the opposition or leader of other parties, although some will be engaged in research and materials preparation. This team is composed of members of your effort and allied organizations and efforts as well as elected representatives and their staff members. Ideally you will create a team of players. It may also include members of the premier's (provincial) or prime minister's (federal) office. Make sure you have team members on the inside gathering information and exerting influence as well as members on the outside who can mobilize the general public. It is important for you to be aware of who is involved in what committee and the purposes of those committees that influence your change agenda.

*Alert networks.* An alert network is designed to mobilize a large number of people in a short period of time. Alert networks can be used to turn people out for rallies and demonstrations, call members to assist in some simple but labour-intensive organizational tasks (like getting out a large mailing on short notice), or to communicate their opinions to selected targets. Your lobbying effort will mainly use the alert network for communication, and it is designed for this purpose. Alert networks are quantity contact systems. Their main purpose is to generate as much constituent contact as possible. The more common components of an alert network are a telephone alert system, mail, e-mail, Facebook, Twitter, and fax alerts.

A telephone alert system is generally a telephone tree or a variation of a boiler room operation (see Figure 15.1). In a simple telephone tree, one person calls two (or more) other people, who in turn call two others, who call two others, and so on. In addition to calling the other members of the tree, the person receiving the call is to call her or his elected representative and communicate a specific message. Each recipient of a phone call is to write down the message to be delivered to the next tree member, as well as to the elected representative, in order to make sure that it is delivered accurately. Therefore, keep the message short and to the point. Most legislatures have a toll-free number for connecting constituents to their representative.

A tree is usually organized into branches with each branch having its own captain. It is best to develop branches according to voting districts. The captain sees to it that the calls are completed without the chain being broken. The last person, on the "bottom" of the branch, is to contact the captain.

If, after a certain period of time, the captain is not called, she or he will initiate action up from the bottom (there are many variations to this system. The intent is to make sure that the message doesn't get stopped or changed somewhere along the line).

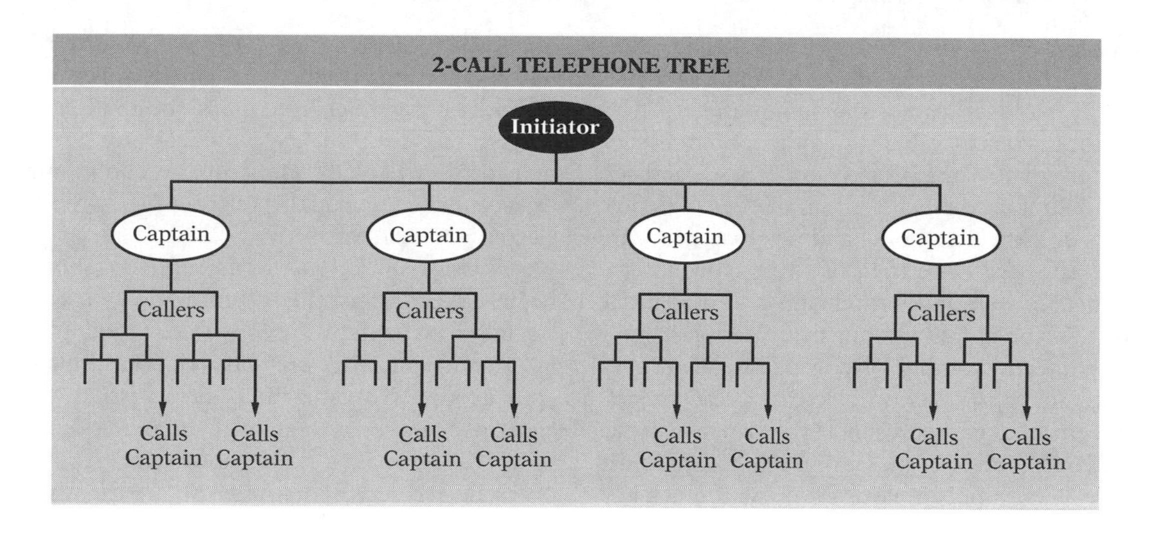


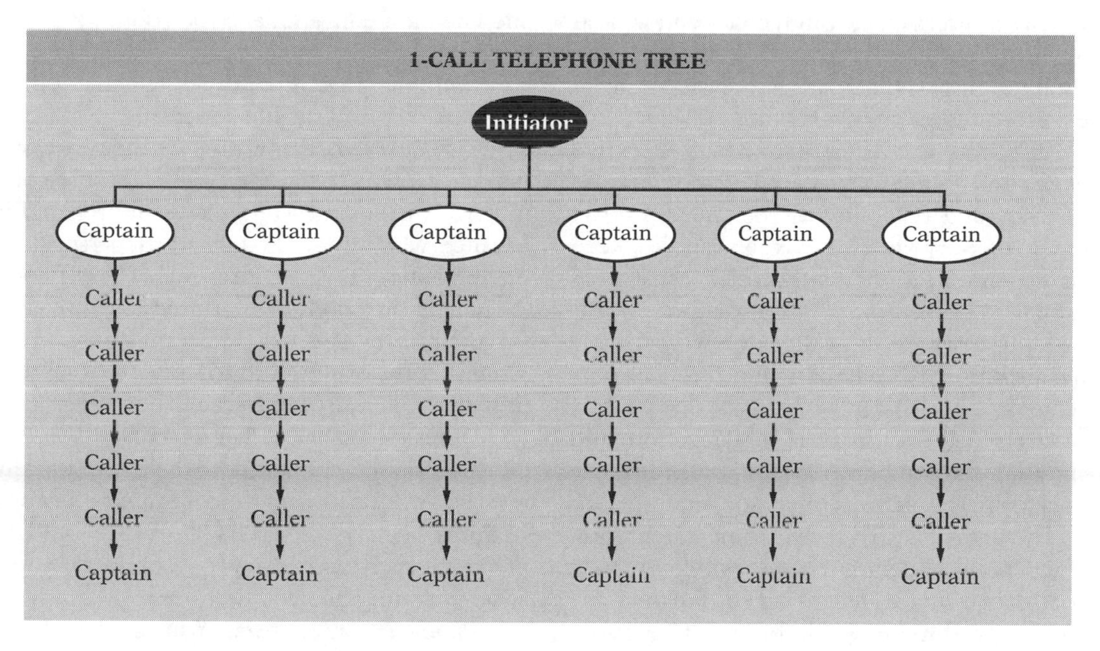


**FIGURE 15.1** A Telephone Tree Gets Your Message Out Quickly

A boiler room approach is designed with the intent of increasing accuracy and making sure that unanswered phones do not stop delivery of the message. Using this method, a small team of callers, usually six or seven, all call from the same location, perhaps from a social service agency. Each caller has a list of about 40 alert members to call. The members receiving the call only need to call their elected representative. In two nights of calling, two different teams can call hundreds of members.

A mail alert is a special request made to the alert members by mail. The letter is sent in a specially designed envelope emphasizing the emergency nature of the request. The letter details the specific request of the member.

E-mail alerts are a simple but effective way to notify your members and other potential supporters of the need for action. These methods can help you to reach a great number of people very quickly. Facebook and Twitter alerts are very effective since they offer immediate communication among participants and are simple to use. The ability of your organization to rally a significant number of constituents can make quite an impression on elected representatives' offices. Elected representatives also use social networks and e-mail, and these technologies provide members of your group with quick and easy access to our democratically elected leaders who set direction through policy and legislations. E-mail addresses are commonly printed in legislative guides. They are also available from the elected representative's office.

Fax alerts can be structured in the same way as a telephone tree. A fax alert can increase the clarity and reliability of your message, but there may be problems if you want to keep your communications confidential. Most professionals have access to a fax machine, so this procedure works well for them. However, many other groups do not have routine access to fax machines.

Alert networks require organization and maintenance. Members need to agree in advance to perform the actions they are requested to do. They must also receive some orientation and written instructions so they will know how to perform when called to do so. Further, the members need to be kept informed of key issues to which they may be asked to respond. This is usually done by means of periodic written updates, typically through e-mail. Finally, the alert system should be used neither too little nor too commonly. There needs to be some frequency of use, especially during the legislative session. Otherwise participants may have to relearn the system each time it is employed. Underused alert systems will fall apart due to a lack of maintenance.

*Quality contact development.* This is a system for getting specific, particularly influential community members to contact specific elected representatives. Quality contacts are those individuals who have clout in the community or who have a particular relationship with the elected representative.

*Member of the House dossier.* You should begin collecting as much information on each elected representative as possible. Good basic information includes previous relationship with your group or organization and its issues; key legislative interests; regional interests; committee assignments; professional background; other elected representatives who are friends or enemies, or who have influence; political allies and enemies; educational background; personal interests; social acquaintances; key campaign contributors (this is easily obtainable public information); and quality contacts.

*Testifier bank.* From time to time you may need to present testimony before a House committee. It is helpful to have a team prepared in advance who can present various perspectives on the issue you are addressing. These people should be purposefully recruited and prepared for their role. You do not want to scramble around at the last minute to find someone who might be able to speak to the issue.

*Speakers' bureau.* A handful of well-versed, effective public speakers can help to communicate your positions to community groups. Members of your speakers' bureau should be prepared to handle likely questions that may arise, including hostile questions.

*Public affairs program.* You can bring your particular message to targeted community groups through presentation of public affairs programs. These are designed to help community groups examine important community problems and governmental responses to them. Such programs are effective in recruiting individual participants or coalition members.

*Media relations.* An organized strategy for getting your message out through the media should be developed. Stories, editorials, and

## DID YOU KNOW?

### How a Bill Becomes a Law in Canada

In the Parliament of Canada, as in all legislative assemblies based on the British model, there is a clearly defined method for enacting legislation. A bill must go through a number of specific stages in the House of Commons and the Senate before it becomes law. When the House of Commons is in session, the following steps are taken. Find out when the Parliament begins its session and how long it is likely to last. Be aware of all legislative deadlines, such as dates for the introduction of legislation and dates for completing bills in a particular chamber.

1. *Notice.* A member or a minister who intends to introduce a bill in the House of Commons must first give notice to the Clerk of the House. The title of the bill to be introduced is then placed on the *Notice Paper* for the next sitting of the House. There are separate requirements that apply to the notice for private bills. Special rules deal with the introduction of bills that involve the expenditure of public funds. At this time the sponsor of the legislation will work with interested parties to work out the actual language of the bill. The sponsor is the MP who will introduce the bill and work for its passage. There are circumstances when the sponsor has little or no interest in the legislation.
2. *First Reading.* The first real stage in the legislative process is the introduction and first reading of the bill in the House of Commons. A member normally provides a brief summary of the bill he or she is introducing.
3. *Second Reading and Referral of a Bill to a Committee.* The second reading stage of the legislative process gives members an opportunity to debate the general scope of the bill. Debate at this stage must focus on the principle of the bill. The bill is then heard in the committee. At this time, committee members may hear testimony on the bill from interested parties and make changes or amendments to it. If the bill needs substantial work, it may be referred to a subcommittee of members of the full committee (even though a bill has been assigned to a committee, it may not be given a hearing. You may need to work to get the bill heard in the first place).
4. *Referral of a Bill to Committee before Second Reading.* A minister may move that a government bill be referred to a committee before second reading. This allows members of a committee to examine the principle of a bill before approval by the House of Commons and to propose amendments to alter its scope.
5. *Committee Stage of Bills.* Most bills are referred for review to the standing committee whose mandate most closely relates to the bill's subject matter.
6. *Report Stage of a Bill.* Following consideration in committee, there is an opportunity for further study of the bill in the House during what is known as report stage. Members, particularly those who were not members of the committee, may, at this stage, propose motions to amend the text of the bill. When deliberations at report stage are concluded, a motion is put forward to approve the bill (with any amendments).
7. *Third Reading and Adoption of Bills.* Third reading is the final stage that a bill must pass in the House of Commons. It is at this point that members must decide whether the bill should be adopted. Debate at this stage of the legislative process focuses on the final form of the bill. The amendments that are admissible at this stage are similar to those at second reading stage. Once the motion for third reading has been adopted, the Clerk of the House certifies that the bill has passed. The bill is then sent to the

*Continued*

Senate with a message requesting that it consider the bill.

8. *Senate Consideration.* The Senate follows a legislative process that is very similar to the one in the House of Commons. In cases where the Senate adopts a Commons bill without amendment, a message is sent to the House of Commons to inform it that the bill has been passed and Royal Assent is normally granted shortly thereafter.
9. *Royal Assent and Coming into Force of the Bill.* The ceremony of Royal Assent is one of the oldest of all parliamentary proceedings and brings all three elements of Parliament together (the Crown, the Senate, and the House of Commons). Royal Assent is the stage that a bill must complete before officially becoming an Act of Parliament.

Adapted from the *Compendium of the House of Commons, Procedure Online: The Legislative Process. http://www.parl.gc.ca/compendium/web-content/c_g_legislativeprocess-e.htm.*

letters to the editor published in local newspapers can have a strong impact on elected representatives. Appearing in the newspaper, particularly, or on television gives your organization and its spokespersons added credibility with elected reperesentatives.

*External coalitions.* It is unlikely that your group alone can mount a significant legislative campaign (although you can have an impact on legislation that has a limited scope). Coordinating your efforts with other organizations and groups will help to draw attention to your efforts and provide the resources you need to accomplish the range of tasks that are necessary.

Lobbying campaigns that intend significant changes and that encounter well-organized and well-funded opposition will develop other elements to complement this basic approach. If your lobbying aims are fairly narrow, you may not need to fully develop each of these components. However, the more attention you give to each aspect, the stronger your foundation will be.

## BASIC LOBBYING ACTIVITIES IN CANADA

If you become involved routinely in legislative action, you will soon discover that it is a year-round endeavour. Periods of intense activity may be followed by periods that are much less hurried. A good portion of the work occurs outside of the legislative session. Be sure that the elements of your campaign are in place and ready to go when the session begins. Even if you are going to work with your member of provincial or federal Parliament on just one piece of legislation, it is important that you get an early start.

The following sequence of activities assumes that you have taken care of some of the initial tasks described earlier, such as registering as a lobbyist (for example, see the Toronto Lobbyist Registry [Blumberg, 2008]), developing your agenda, and gaining an understanding of the legislative process. Now you are ready to put your efforts to work lobbying on behalf of your concerns.

*Gather and prepare information.* Assemble data, personal stories, legislation from other provinces, and other information that helps you understand and communicate your issues. Prepare various background pieces and fact sheets.

*Develop relationship with elected representatives (members of the Parliament) who can possibly sponsor the bill or bills important to your community.* By the time a notice is given to the Clerk (see box above), you will have an internal relationship with key elected representatives and staff members and members of your and other organizations and perhaps some other lobbyists.

Continue to develop relationships with members of the House during the time the House of Commons or provincial Parliament is in session. A solid relationship with elected representatives who share your goals and interests would allow you to keep track of a bill that is important to your community; find an elected representative who can give you the inside scoop, one to whom other members listen, is a good legislative debater, or is in a position of influence (for example, leadership or committee chairs).

Not every member of the legislature will have equal interest. Particularly, some members who share your interests will have limited responsibility (backbenchers or elected representatives who are not members of the cabinet). Identify and work additional members who can help.

*Target/rate.* To determine the degree of support or opposition you will have, it is very helpful to develop a system for ranking each member (remember when we talk about member, we are talking about a member or members of provincial or federal Parliaments), particularly those who serve on committees likely to hear your bill. You can choose a simple scale of one to five to indicate how favourable each member is likely to be to your concerns. You can obtain this information by reading various publications, talking to other political activists, or checking voting records with different groups (for example, Canadian Federation for Sexual Health [formerly Planned Parenthood Federation of Canada], Egale Canada, Sierra Club Canada, or the local Chamber of Commerce). You will probably revise this "score card" from time to time during the actual session.

*Determine your monitoring systems.* Figure out how you will keep alert to rumours regarding bills that are important to you, hear about proposed action on them, and track their progress.

*Establish a relationship* with an elected representative or representatives *who can sponsor and co-sponsor a bill that is important to your community.* Ideally, these will be individuals who have some influence within the legislative procedure and serve on the committees likely to hear the bill. Further, the member who sponsors the bill that is important to you should be committed to it and have time to give it attention.

## ● CHANGE AGENT TIP

Here are ten tips to guide you in making your argument—effectively.

1. Be able to argue the other side's point of view as well as your own. This will enable you to
   - Identify weak points in your position that you may otherwise ignore
   - Better understand the opposing frame of reference so that you can communicate to it
   - Anticipate arguments so that you can pre-empt or counter them
   - Inoculate potential supporters by letting them know what your opposition is likely to tell them
   - Emphasize your strengths relative to the weaknesses of the other position
   - Demonstrate that your position is based on a strong command of the issue
   - Discover possible areas of common ground or common interest
2. Let the listener know your position, your professional expertise, and your experiences.
3. Focus on aspects of the issue where the listener's knowledge and values are similar to yours; relate your argument to an outcome that you both desire.
4. Emphasize your areas of agreement with the listener.
5. Relate the issue to the listener's interests and personal experiences.
6. Relate the issue to consequences for constituents.
7. Use real-life examples, humour, and simple logic.
8. Elicit some emotional response.
9. Avoid jargon.
10. Role-play your discussion. Have a friend play devil's advocate.

*Encourage your* elected representative *or those* elected representatives *who support a bill important to you.* If a bill is important to your community, encourage a supportive elected representative to introduce the bill early in the sitting of the House. This will ensure more time for you to work it through the various hurdles.

*Use media as appropriate throughout the session.*

*Keep in contact with the Prime Minister's or Premier's Office or the minister in charge of introducing a bill as needed during the session.* Obviously, if the prime minister or premier or minister in charge is hostile to your position, or would simply hope to avoid the issue, your contact would probably only be of a general nature.

*Lobby the committee directly.* Begin to meet with members of the committee. Also, begin to organize constituent contact and other indirect methods of influencing members. Do not forget to follow the rules established by the Office of the Commissioner of Lobbying of Canada in the *Lobbying Act* and the *Income Tax Act*, which says that "a registered charity can be involved in non-partisan political activities as long as it devotes substantially all (90%) of it resources to charitable activities" (Blumberg, 2008, p. 8).

*Target committee votes.* Determine which members of the committee should receive most of your attention. You should have a clear understanding of which committee is dealing with a particular issue.

*Prepare testimony to present to committees.* Prepare testifiers and shape the message to be presented to the committee. Your message should be geared to specific elected representatives and to the media. Remember that the House Committees have the power to call experts to explain issues that may bring clarity to particular issues. Standing committees often need the collaboration, expertise, and

Photos.com

**Parliament Buildings, Ottawa.**

knowledge of a variety of individuals to assist them in their studies and investigations. Usually these persons appear willingly before committees when invited to do so (*House of Common Procedures and Practice*, 2009).

*Continue lobbying.* Once your bill passes committee, direct your attention to other elected representatives whom you have targeted for lobbying. Indirect methods such as demonstrations and media stories could be used at this time (you

## ● CHANGE AGENT TIP

Here are some tips for getting the most from face-to-face contacts with your members of the House of Commons (federal) or members of provincial legislatures.

1. Make an appointment by phone.
2. Arrive on time. Dress appropriately. Everything you do should be related to leaving a good impression on the elected representative and her or his staff.
3. Be respectful the time allotted for the appointment.
4. Identify yourself, including your professional position. If you are a constituent, say so.
5. Commend the elected representative for current or previous actions that you admire.
6. Identify the bill you are discussing by name and number. If speaking to a particular point, refer to the page and line.
7. Provide the elected representative with your one-page summary or fact sheet. It is often helpful to have an additional packet of information with a one-page "table of contents" that includes a one- or two-sentence description of each piece in the packet. If you are suggesting new language, have that prepared to hand to the MP.
8. Present your case. (If you believe it is likely you will be given the time to engage in actual discussion, you can save some of your points to address concerns you anticipate the elected representative will bring up. This conveys the notion that you are responsive.) Listen carefully to the elected representative's concerns; don't minimize them. Be clear about your position and just what you want the elected representative to do. Remain courteous. Avoid putting the elected representative in a defensive position. That deepens resistance.
9. Refer to the support of other elected representatives who hold similar views as the elected representative to whom you are now speaking by using their comments.
10. On occasion, arrange to meet with the elected representative in the local district, particularly on your turf or at a site affected by the legislation. Have the elected representative meet with a small group of three or four of you. Provide different "fronts" for the elected representative to see (for example, educator, business leader, religious leader, or other person with a readily identifiable perspective). The members of the group should be carefully selected. They should clearly understand mutual roles, and each should be well prepared. You should have a lead presenter and someone prepared to manage the conversation.
11. Get a commitment if at all possible. The more publicly the commitment is made, the stronger it is likely to be. If you cannot get a commitment at this time, let the elected representative know that her or his decision is important to you. Politely say that you will call after she or he has had time to give the matter more thought.
12. Thank the elected representative, regardless of the outcome.
13. Notify your allies of the outcome.
14. Send a thank-you letter to the elected representative. Provide answers to any questions that were raised, and tactfully reiterate one or two essential points.

need to determine how much and what type of attention you want to draw to this issue). Constituent contact should swing into high gear.

*Repeat the process with the Senate.* Essentially you must do the same things to pass your bill in the Senate as you did in the House of Common. If your relationship with elected representatives who sponsored the bill is stronger in the House of Common, see how they can assist you in your efforts to get internal support from the other house.

*Lobby the Prime Minister's or Premier's Office.* Members of the lobbying team and their constituents should make contact with the prime minister or premier or her or his staff to urge that the bill be passed. Indirect methods and direct constituent contact could be employed as well. The type and degree of indirect methods will depend on the prime minister's or premier's position on the bill. Do not wait until the legislation has passed before making contact with the prime minister or premier to begin conversation on the issue and determining the degree of support or opposition.

*Organize an override effort if need be.* This usually requires lots of direct lobbying by members of your internal and external teams, mobilization of constituent contact, and use of visible indirect methods.

*Celebrate.* It is important to have a victory event involving all key participants soon after the session ends.

*Begin to monitor implementation.* A new set of activities (outside the scope of this chapter) now needs to take place to influence the development of regulations and other procedures that will enable the new law to fulfill its promise.

## Letter Writing

One of the most effective ways for you to get your voice heard is to write to your elected representative. Both e-mail and traditional letters will work. The more undecided an elected representative is and the less controversial the issue, the greater the impact such letters will have. Elected representatives who are more concerned about re-election are especially sensitive to letters from constituents. Here are a few tips that will give your words greater influence.

- Letters should be timed for the greatest effect; for example, early in the session to build momentum or shortly before a vote on the bill.
- Consider having a letter-writing party with members of your group. Have people bring their own stationery. Supply some yourself. Have several different types available. Use different types of stamps. Letter writers should be instructed on how to prepare their letters, but the letters should be written in their own words. Do not use specific phrases.
- Do not send form letters. Use your own words. Avoid jargon and slogans.
- Use personal letterhead or business stationery if possible.
- Because envelopes are usually thrown away, put your return address on the letter.
- Identify the name and number of the bill, and state your reasons for writing; especially relate issues to personal experiences. Show how the bill affects you, your family, your community, your clients, or your livelihood. Clearly identify yourself as a constituent if you are one. Mention the number of people whom you serve or represent.
- Open and close your letter with statements that establish rapport, such as "I know you are concerned about. . . ."
- Ask the elected representative to *do* something in the first or second paragraph. For example, ask the representative to vote a certain way.
- Make sure your facts are accurate.
- Be reasonable. Do not ask for something that is beyond the elected representative's ability to provide.
- Thank the elected representative if she or he has voted the "right" way on another issue.

- Focus on one issue per letter.
- Ask for a response.
- Write a thank-you letter if the elected representative does what you requested.

## Testifying

Your participation in committees' work gives legitimacy to your issue and your organization. It gets you on and in the record. It gives you access to a larger audience through media coverage of the hearing. It demonstrates visible action to your members, and it gives them an event in which they can take part. Your ability to turn out a crowd signals broad support for the measure, which will embolden those elected representatives who are thinking of supporting your position. Your testimony can provide supportive elected representatives with a rationale and justification for their actions.

Although testimony and demonstrations of constituent interest at public hearings may help a very few elected representatives make up their minds, rarely will it be effective in changing anyone's mind. Testifying, therefore, is a complement to more essential lobbying activities. It should not be the centrepiece of your efforts.

Coordinate your presentation with other members of your team and with other groups who support your position. Coordinate testimony with the committee chair if you are on friendly terms. Prime supporters on the committee with questions that will enable you to emphasize specific points.

To the extent possible, coordinate the order in which your testifiers will present. Consider how you want your argument to build. Understand that initial testifiers can stake out the dimensions of the debate, and they are more likely to get media coverage. Those who testify toward the end of the proceedings can counter arguments, re-emphasize key points, and leave the last impressions.

Prepare two papers, one for submission for the committee's written record, and one for your presentation. Make sure there is a one-page summary of key points for the elected representatives.

Prepare your testimony by role-playing with friends or members of your team. Similar to preparing for an argument, someone should play the devil's advocate. Anticipate questions and prepare responses. Avoid seeking last-minute suggestions; they will only confuse you.

Tailor your presentation to the elected representative s whom you most want to influence. Make distinct points using a combination of personal experiences and factual information. Here are some things to touch on:

- Your interest in the bill, and how you arrived at your conclusions
- Who will benefit
- Who will be hurt by inaction
- Cost efficiency of the measure

Tie your message to dominant themes that are emerging in the legislative session (concern over crime, health care, or other topics).

It is normal to be nervous.

When making your presentation, begin with "Mister or Madam Chair." Then state your name, title, your agency or organization, and your position on the bill. Then state your case. Refer to the page and line numbers for specific comments. Keep your presentation between five and seven minutes in length. Do not repeat yourself and do not repeat previous testimony.

When you have completed your presentation, ask for questions. When answering a question, first address the committee chair, then address the member asking the question.

Remain both courteous and direct. Convey the notion that committee members are reasonable individuals. Approach them in a way that emphasizes common interest. Do not argue with committee members, and do not attempt to humiliate any particular elected representative. If an opponent questions your information, honestly try to answer the question and return to your main points.

If your opinion is questioned, restate the question in a manner that allows you to reiterate your basic position. If the questioner persists, it is proper to restate your basic position and state that you respect the fact that you each have different views of the matter and that you hope "we can agree to disagree."

If you do not know the answer to a question, say "That's a good question. I don't have that specific information before me. I will look into it and get you the information right away." *Do not fake an answer!* Be prompt in your follow-up.

Speak to the media as well as to the committee, using a few catch phrases.

After you have answered all the questions, thank the members of the committee for their interest and their attentiveness to your presentation.

If you are clearly in a no-win situation, consider staying away from the hearing altogether in order to make a statement or to render the opposition's show a non-event.

## OTHER THINGS YOU SHOULD KNOW OR DO TO INCREASE YOUR EFFECTIVENESS

Your credibility is your greatest asset. Your credibility is based on three things:

- *You as a person.* Build trust. Never lie, mislead, threaten, or act in an arrogant manner. Do not promise what you cannot deliver. Keep confidential information to yourself. Do not back people into a corner. Do not ever say or write anything you do not want attributed to you. Develop and use a sense of humour. Be courteous. Say thank you.
- *Your information.* Provide compelling specific facts and give them a face, showing how the situation affects real people. Do not exaggerate the truth or the situation. Double-check the accuracy of your information. If you do not know the answer to a question, promise to get the information. Follow up in a timely way to requests for information.
- *Your ability to exercise power.* Be able to mobilize constituents and quality contacts. Demonstrate an ability to use the media. Generate letters in support of your position. Turn people out to legislative hearings. Generate workers for campaigns. If you can, generate dollars for campaigns.

*Get known.* Once elected representatives know you (or in some cases know about you), they will pay more attention to your calls, letters, and opinions. Get involved in political campaigns. Attend legislative receptions. Send letters to newly elected officials introducing yourself and information on your issue. Attend and speak out at meetings with elected representatives. Invite officials to your agency or neighbourhood; serve as a tour guide. Arrange to provide a briefing on issues.

*Observe the body in action.* Attend a few sessions or committee hearings. Keep your eyes open. Listen and learn. This will help you to feel familiar with the environment before you begin to take action.

*Understand the standard approach in deciding whom to lobby. Lobby supporters first*, to alert them, activate them, and inoculate them from opposition arguments. *Lobby "undecideds" next*, preferably with support from their peers. *Do not lobby strong opponents.* You can use your time for more important things. You might not be able to change their minds, and you may excite them into more vigorous opposition.

*Get to know key staff people.* Working with staff is extremely valuable. They may be more accessible than the elected official, and they may let you know how the official really sees things. Staff members often shape elected representatives' perspectives, and they sometimes develop strong interest in the legislation they work on.

*Acknowledge that there are few permanent friends and few permanent enemies.* Do not alienate people, write them off forever, or take them for granted. Elected representatives are engaged in a number of battles. Past disagreements can be forgotten when building new alliances.

*Understand the ways for keeping a bill alive.* A bill can be resurrected as an amendment to another bill. A person who voted against the bill can ask to have it reconsidered (you may use this as a planned tactic). Understand how to use the initiative and referendum procedures for your province.

*Know your strengths and weaknesses.* Avoid the tendency to underestimate your strengths and exaggerate your weaknesses. Be accurate in your assessment.

*Do not grab personal credit.* Allow elected representatives and, whenever possible, your group to get the attention.

*Recognize that* elected representatives *are overwhelmed with information.* Do not assume or act as if your issue is the only one that matters. Assert your point while recognizing that elected representatives have many other issues to think about. Determine how you will make your issue stand out.

*Know your issue.* For your own uses, prepare an issue brief, summarizing the history of the issue, noting the key players, organizing key facts and figures, and outlining arguments on both sides. This will empower you as you realize that you know far more about the topic than most of the people with whom you will be dealing.

*Prepare fact sheets.* Provide elected representatives' media people and others with a one-page summary of your issue. Describe the costs and the impact of responding to or ignoring the issue. Provide opposing points of view and counter them. Include your name, your organization's name, and a phone number, e-mail, and postal address where you can be reached.

*Get to know other lobbyists.* Particularly get to know like-minded lobbyists. Lobbyists, especially those with common interests, do meet regularly. Become part of such a group. Lobbyists help each other out in a variety of ways, not the least of which is with an exchange of information.

*Get to know your opposition.* Find out who is opposed to you and why. Talk to them. This will help you to better understand their frame of reference and information. You may even discover that their opposition is based on misperception or misunderstanding, a situation you can remedy.

*Understand the* elected representatives' *screens.* Elected representatives must contend with a huge number of decisions. In determining how to approach an issue, they see how it fits with their own philosophy and values, their constituents' or region's concerns, their party leadership or caucus positions, and advocacy groups with which they identify. When you are working with elected representatives, see how they define the situation under discussion. On what aspects do they focus? What do they think they know about it? How does it fit with their value system?

*Expect some loss of support.* The more controversial your issue, the more likely a few of your supporters will get a little weak in the knees. You will lose a few votes. Be psychologically prepared for this.

*Anticipate the likelihood of compromises.* Rarely will you get everything you want. You may understand this as you begin the process, but when faced with the need to agree to less than what you want, or to make a trade-off, you may feel real disappointment. Be clear about what you have to have—and what you cannot have. Concessions can help you in the long run or limit the possibility of future negotiation. Once the deal has been struck, are you in a better position to move forward, or will you remain mired at this point? When faced with a problem, see if you can respond by bringing new ideas to the table rather than by retreating on important concerns. At what point is not making a deal a better choice?

The need to make compromises tests the relationships in an organization. Ideological purists may bang heads with dispassionate pragmatists. Deals will serve some interests better than others. Discuss how you will handle compromises before you are faced with them. Clarify who among you is empowered to make agreements with the opposition.

*Do not accept a bad bill just to get "something."* Other interests may be making deals on the bill at the same time you are. Be aware of the fact that your original piece of legislation may end up with so many amendments you hardly recognize it. If this occurs, "your" bill may no longer effectively accomplish its intended purpose. Be prepared to withdraw your support from the legislation or even act to prevent its passage in the event that changes are more harmful than helpful.

*Be persistent.* Know that it may take a few years before a legislative proposal becomes a law. During each session you may develop support that you can build on in subsequent sessions. Your continued attention generates greater understanding and acceptance of the idea, particularly if it is given organized support from key constituencies.

*Create a responsive structure.* Your organization will need to respond quickly to legislative events. Develop mechanisms for rapid decision making. Notify allies immediately of any changes, especially changes in the team's position on any point.

*Monitor your messages, your relationships, and your egos.* Everyone on your team should be communicating identical positions to elected representatives. Be very careful not to undermine yourselves by sending conflicting messages. Pay close attention to group maintenance issues, and never let disagreements among you be known to anyone outside of the team. Internal bickering that becomes public will seriously weaken your effort. Do not make yourself look good at the expense of any team member.

*Learn how to kill bad bills.* Killing bills is easier than passing them. By reviewing the legislative process, you can see that the bill must cross many hurdles before it becomes a law. You can trip it up at many different points.

Use delaying tactics so there won't be enough time left in the session to pass it. Get the bill referred to a subcommittee that has difficulty meeting and agreeing. Have your elected provincial or federal representatives ask for staff to do time-consuming research on the bill. Temporarily remove the bill from the committee agenda (these and other delaying tactics are more likely to be successful if the bill does not have a sufficient number of strong supporters). Get the bill referred to a committee chaired by one of your supporters who can use the prerogatives of the chair to bury the bill. Amend the bill to death. Create confusion by raising doubts about its ultimate costs, its questionable legality, its consequences for a particular group of citizens (elected representatives do not want to be seen advancing a questionable proposition, one that just might do more harm than good). Generate adverse media attention and public displays of constituent opposition. Elected representatives who are in powerful positions (members of the Cabinet) can use their influence to make passage of the bill costly to their colleagues who are supporting it.

## • SOME FINAL CONSIDERATIONS

Perhaps you can understand the accuracy of public interest lobbyist Mike Pertschuk's (1986) description of members of his profession. "Public interest lobbyists," he says, "perform prodigious feats: as coalition builders—builders of mutual trust, confidence, sustained activity—as social psychologists of victory. They are strategists, parliamentary wizards, rag-pickers of intelligence, networkers of knowledge, accurate head counters, deployers of experts, media mavens, modulators of intemperance. . . . They are the physical embodiment of watchful constituencies. . . . To their younger colleagues they are teachers. And they teach not only the needs and the skills, but the joys of political engagement" (p. 24).

Your confidence will grow with your awareness of the process, your preparation, and your experience. In fact, it can grow dramatically. You will quickly pick up on the legislative culture, the game, the methods, and the key players. The activity can be pretty contagious. You might even get hooked.

# REFERENCES


Adams, D. L. (1995). *Health issues for women of color: A cultural diversity perspective.* Thousand Oaks, CA: Sage.

Ahlbrandt, R. S., Jr., & Cunningham, J. V. (1979). *A new public policy for neighborhood preservation.* New York: Praeger.

Alinsky, S. D. (1972). *Rules for radicals: A pragmatic primer for realistic radicals.* New York: Random House.

Allen, C., Diaz, P. A., Duong, T., Gallo, M. M., Moreno, A., & Snee, J. (2002). *Grantmaking docket.* New York: Funding Exchange.

Allen, H., & Regional Youth Project. (1981). *The bread game.* San Francisco, CA: Glide Publications.

Allen, J. (2000). *Event planning: The ultimate guide to successful meetings, corporate events, fundraising galas, conferences, conventions, incentives and other special events.* Toronto: Wiley.

Allen, S. (1997). Benefit event fundamentals. In J. M. Greenfield (Ed.), The *nonprofit handbook: Fund raising* (2nd ed., pp. 278–298). New York: Wiley.

Allen, S. (2001). Benefit event fundamentals. In J. M. Greenfield (Ed.), *The nonprofit handbook: Fund raising* (3rd ed., pp. 480–499). New York: Wiley.

Alphonse, M., George, P., & Moffatt, K. (2008). Redefining social work standards in the context of globalization: Lessons from India. *International Social Work,* 51(2), 145–158.

Alvarez, A. R., & Gutiérrez, L. M. (2001) Choosing to do participatory research: An example and issues of fit to consider. *Journal of Community Practice,* 9(1), 1–20.

Amidei, N. (1987). How to be an advocate in bad times. In F. M. Cox, J. L. Erlich, J. Rothman, & J. E. Tropman (Eds.), *Strategies of community organization: Macro practice* (4th ed., pp. 106–114). Itasca, IL: Peacock.

Amiel, A. (2001). Community organizing and neighborhood planning in Jerusalem: A profile of Avner Amiel. In J. Forester, R. Fischler, & D. Shmueli (Eds.), *Israeli planners and designers: Profiles of community builders.* Albany, NY: State University of New York Press.

Anderson, R. E., Carter, I., & Lowe, G. R. (1999). *Human behavior in the social environment: A social systems approach* (5th ed.). Hawthorne, NY: Aldine de Gruyter.

Andreae, D. (2002). Canadian values and ideologies and social work practice. In F. J. Turner (Ed.), *Social work practice: A Canadian perspective* (pp. 9–19). Toronto: Prentice Hall.

Antone, R., Miller, D., & Meyers, B. (1986). *The power within people.* Deseronto: Peace Trees Technologies Inc.

Asimakos, S. (2009). Building local assets: Community investment in Canada, 2008. Retrieved January 19, 2010, from Canadian Community Investment Network Co-operative: www.communityinvestment.ca/pdf/Building%20Local%20Assets%20-%20Community%20Investment%20in%20Canada,%202008.pdf).

Aspen Institute (1999). Introduction to CCI's [Online]. Available: http://www.commbuild.org/html_pages/introtoccis.htm.

Associated Press. (2002a, July 16). Nigerian women, oil facility reach pact. *Arizona Daily Star,* p. A6.

Associated Press. (2002b, July 26). Protesters win jobs, loans from oil firm. *Arizona Daily Star*, p. A16.

Associated Press. (2002c, July 15). Women threaten shaming gesture. *Arizona Daily Star*, p. A7.

Baird, J. A. (1997, March). The three Rs of fund raising. *Fund Raising Management*, 14–17.

Banks, S. (2002). Professional values and accountabilities. In D. Adams, L. Dominelli, and M. Payne (Eds.), *Critical Practice in social Work* (pp. 28–37). Basingstoke, England: Palgrave.

Barker, R. L. (1999). *The social work dictionary* (4th ed.). Washington, DC: NASW Press.

Barnes, D. (1989). Direct mail trends you need to know about. *National Fund Raiser*, 15(12).

Barnoff, L. (2001). Moving beyond words: Integrating anti-oppression practice into feminist social services. *Canadian Social Work Review*, 18, 67–86.

Barnoff, L., & Coleman, B. (2007). Strategies for integrating anti-oppression principles: Perspective from feminist agencies. In D. Baines (Ed.), *Doing anti-oppression practices: Building transformative politicized social work* (pp. 31–48). Halifax: Fernwood.

Barnoff, L., George, P., & Coleman, B. (2006). Operating in survival mode challenges in implementing anti-oppresive practice in feminist social services agencies in Toronto. *Canadian Social Work Review*, 23(1/2), 41–58.

Barnoff, L., & Moffatt, K. (2007). Contradictory tension in anti-oppression practice in feminist social services. *Affilia: The Journal of Women and Social Work*, 22(1), 56–70.

Baskin, C. (2003). Structural social work as seen from an Aboriginal perspective. In S. Wes (Ed.), *Emerging perspectives on anti-oppressive practice* (pp. 65–79). Toronto: Canadian Scholar Press.

Baso, Z. A. (2000). Managing assets, empowering humans. Global Network Electronic Conference [Online]. Available: http://www.philanthropy.org/GN/KEN/gntext/fullview_economic rights_poverty_empowerment_zohra.htm.

Belasco, J. A. (1990). *Teaching the elephant to dance: Empowering change in your organization*. New York: Crown.

Berg, L. (1999, July). *Organizing to win*. Arizona Education Association leaders' conference, Litchfield, AZ.

Berkman, C. S., & Zinberg, G. (1997). Homophobia and heterosexism in social workers. *Social Work*, 42(4), 332.

Berkowitz, W. R. (1982). Community impact: Creating grassroots change in hard times. Cambridge, MA: Schenkman.

Bermant, G., & Warwick, D. P. (1985). The ethics of social intervention: Power, freedom, and accountability. In W. G. Bennis, K. D. Benne, & R. Chin (Eds.), *The planning of change* (4th ed., pp. 449–470). New York: Holt, Rinehart & Winston.

Bishop, A. (1994). *Becoming an ally: Breaking the cycle of oppression in people*. Halifax: Fernwood.

Bishop, A. (2002). *Becoming an ally: breaking the cycle of oppression in people* (2nd ed.). Halifax: Fernwood.

Bishop, C. H. (2001). *Making change one person at a time: Assessing change capacity within your organization*. New York: AMACOM.

Bisman, C. (2004). Social work values: The moral core of the profession. *British Journal of Social Work*, 34, 109–123.

Blood, S. K. (2001). *Cultural knowledge transforms community* [White paper]. Rogers, MN: Madii Institute.

Bloom, M. (1990). *Introduction to the drama of social work*. Itasca, IL: Peacock.

Blumberg, M. (2008). Lobbying and Canadian charities: To register or not to register. Retrieved January 4, 2009 at www.globalphilanthropy.ca/images/uploads/Lobbying_and_Canadian_Charities_to_register_or_not_to_register.pdf.

Bordieu, P. (1986). The forms of capital. In J. G. Richardson (Ed.), *Handbook of theory and research for the sociology of education* (pp. 241–258). New York: Greenwood Press.

Boushell, M. (2000). What kind of people are we? Anti-racism and social welfare research. *British Journal of Social Work*, 20, 71–89.

Brager, G., & Holloway, S. (1977). A process model for changing organizations from within. *Administration in Social Work*, 1(4), 349–358.

Brager, G., & Holloway, S. (1978). *Changing human service organizations: Politics and practice*. New York: Free Press.

Brakeley, G. A., Jr. (1997). Major gifts from individuals. In J. M. Greenfield (Ed.), *The nonprofit handbook: Fund raising* (2nd ed., pp. 422–441). New York: Wiley.

Bratt, R. G. (1987). Dilemmas of community-based housing. *Policy Studies Journal*, 16(2), 324–334.

Breiteneicher, J., & Hohler, B. (1993). *Quest for funds revisited: A fund-raising starter kit.* Washington, DC: National Trust for Historic Preservation.

Brentlinger, M. E., & Weiss, J. M. (1987). *The ultimate benefit book.* Cleveland, OH: Octavia Press.

Breton, M. (1994). On the meaning of empowerment and empowerment-oriented social work practice. *Social Work with Groups*, 17(3), 23–37.

Brill, N. (1998). *Working with people: The helping process* (6th ed.). New York: Longman.

Brink, S. (2001). *Lack of food security: Focussed literature review and research framework.* Hull, PQ: HRDC Publications Centre.

Brotman, B. (2002, May 1). Granting funds, getting answers. *Chicago Tribune*, p. 8.

Brown, C. (2007). Feminist therapy, violence, problem drinking and re-storying women's lives: Reconceptualizing anti-oppression. In D. Baines (Ed.), *Doing anti-oppressive practice: Building transformative politicized social work* (pp. 128–143). Halifax: Fernwood.

Brown, L. N. (1991). *Groups for growth and change.* New York: Longman.

Browning, B. (2000). *Grantwriting for dummies.* New York: Hungry Minds.

Brueggemann, W. G. (2002). *The practice of macro social work* (2nd ed.). Belmont, CA: Brooks/Cole.

Bryant, T. (2009). Housing and health: More than bricks and mortar. In D. Raphael (Ed.), *Social determinants of health* (pp. 235–251). Toronto: Canadian Scholars' Press Inc.

Burghardt, S. (1982). Organizing for community action. Newbury Park, CA: Sage.

Burke, B., & Harrison, P. (2002). Anti-oppressive practice. In D. Adams, L. Dominelli, M. Payne. (Eds.), *Social work: Themes, issues and critical debates* (2nd ed., pp. 227–236). Basingstoke, England: Palgrave Macmillan.

Burke, J., & Prater, C. A. (2000). *I'll grant you that: A step-by-step guide to finding funds, designing winning projects, writing powerful grant proposals.* Portsmouth, NH: Heinemann.

Burkey, S. (1993). *People first: A guide to self-reliant, participatory rural development.* London: Zed Books, Ltd.

Burlingame, D. F. (2001). Corporate fund raising. In J. M. Greenfield (Ed.), *The Nonprofit Handbook: Fund raising* (3rd ed., pp. 638–647). New York: Wiley.

Cabral, A. (1982). Unity and struggle. In I. M. Wallerstein & A. De Branganca (Eds.), *African liberation reader: Documents of the National Liberation Movements: The anatomy of colonialism* (Vol. 2). London: Zed Books, Ltd.

Callahan, M., & Swift, K. (2006). Back to the present: Rethinking risk assessment. In A. Westhues (Ed.), *Canadian social policy: Issues and perspectives* (pp. 203–223). Waterloo, ON: Wilfrid Laurier University Press.

Campaign 2000. (2009). Report card on child and family poverty in Canada: 1989–2009. doi: http://www.campaign2000.ca/reportCards/national/2009EnglishC2000NationalReportCard.pdf.

Campbell, C. (2003). Anti-oppressive theory and practice as the organizing theme for social work education: The case in favour. *Canadian Social Work Review*, 20.

Campfens, H. (1997). *Community development around the world.* Toronto: University of Toronto Press.

Canadian Association of Food Banks. (2007). Hunger Count 2007. Toronto: CAFB. Retrieved September 9, 2009, at www.cafb-acba.ca/english.main.cfm.

Canadian Association of Social Workers. (2005). *CASW code of ethics and guidelines for ethical practice. doi:http://www.casw-acts.ca.*

Canadian International Development Agency. (2000). Planning and implementation of SWAPs: An overview. Retrieved November 25, 2009, www.ccic.ca/_files/en/archives/aid_2000-10-10_planning_implementation_of_swaps.pdf.

Caragata, L. (2006). Housing and homelessness. In A. Westhues (Ed.), *Canadian social policy: Issues and perspectives* (pp. 267–291). Waterloo, ON: Wilfrid Laurier University Press.

Carniol, B. (2005). *Case critical: The dilemma of social work in Canada.* Toronto: Between the Lines.

Carniol, B. (forthcoming). *Case critical: The dilemma of social work in Canada* (6th ed.). Toronto: Between the Lines.

Cavanaugh, J. (1980). Program and resource development. In R. L. Clifton & A. M. Dahms (Eds.), *Grassroots administration: A handbook for staff and directors of small community-based social-service organizations* (pp. 13–24). Pacific Grove, CA: Brooks/Cole.

Chamberlain, M., & Weaver, L. (2008). Feds must join poverty fight: Despite our innovations, there is so much to do. Retrieved March 29, 2010, www.thespec.com/article/480891.

Chavis, D. M. (2001). The paradoxes and promises of community coalitions. *American Journal of Community Psychology,* 29(2), 309–321.

Checkoway, B. (1987). Political strategy for social planning. In F. M. Cox, J. L. Erlich, J. Rothman, & J. E. Tropman (Eds.), *Strategies of community organization: Macro practice* (4th ed., pp. 326–342). Itasca, IL: Peacock.

Chen, X. (2005). *Tending the garden of citizenship: Child saving in Toronto, 1880–1920.* Toronto: University of Toronto Press.

Church, K., Bacia, N., & Shragge, E. (2008). The turbulence of academic collaboration. In K. Church, N. Bacia, & E. Shragge (Eds.), *Learning through community: Exploring participatory practices* (pp. 1–22). Dordrecht , London: Springer.

Clay, P. L. (1979). *Neighborhood renewal.* Lexington, MA: Lexington Books.

Clodman, S., & Pearce, E. (2006). *Well advise: A planned giving reference source for professional advisors.* Toronto: Civil Sector Press.

Cohen, B. J., & Austin, M. J. (1994). Organizational learning and change in a public child welfare agency. *Administration in Social Work,* 18(1), 1–19.

Cohen, R. (1979). Neighborhood planning and political capacity. *Urban Affairs Quarterly,* 14(3), 337–362.

Coleman, J. S. (1993). The rational reconstruction of society. *American Sociological Review,* 58(1), 1–15.

Coley, S. M., & Scheinberg, C. A. (2000). *Proposal writing* (2nd ed.). Thousand Oaks, CA: Sage.

Common Cause. (1992). *Common cause action manual.* Washington, DC: Common Cause.

Communities Scotland. (2002). *Money advice for groups.* Action for Social Justice in Scotland, 9, 2.

Conner, A. N., & de la Isla, J. (1984). Information: An effective change tool. In F. Cox, J. L. Erlich, J. Rothman, & J. E. Tropman (Eds.), *Tactics and techniques of community practice* (2nd ed., p. 245n). Itasca, IL: Peacock.

Conrad, D. (2008). Aboriginal youth: Crime is a big issue in this election campaign. Retrieved October 20, 2009, from Can Wes Media Works Publications, www.canada.com/edmontonjournal/news/letters/story.html?id=d9f426d6-2b0a-44bc-8806-b9e81a07b2c9.

Corey, M. S., & Corey, G. (1998). *Becoming a helper* (3rd ed.). Pacific Grove, CA: Brooks/Cole.

Cormier, S., & Hackney, H. (1993). *The professional counselor: A process guide to helping* (2nd ed.). Boston: Allyn & Bacon.

Cowan, G., & Egan, M. (1979). *People in systems: A model for development in the human-service professions and education.* Pacific Grove, CA: Brooks/Cole.

Cox, F. M. (1987a). Communities: Alternative conceptions of community: Implications for community organization practice. In F. M. Cox, J. L. Erlich, J. Rothman, & J. E. Tropman (Eds.), *Strategies of community organization: Macro practice* (4th ed., pp. 232–243). Itasca, IL: Peacock.

Cox, F. M. (1987b). Arenas of community practice: Introduction. In F. M. Cox, J. L. Erlich, J. Rothman, & J. E. Tropman (Eds.), *Strategies of community organization: Macro practice* (4th ed., pp. 187–212). Itasca, IL: Peacock.

Cross, T. L., Bazron, B. J., Dennis, K. W., & Isaacs, M. R. (1989). *Towards a culturally competent system of care* (Vol. 1). Washington, DC: Georgetown University Child Development Center.

Croteau, J., Lark, J., & Lance, T. (2005). Our stories will be told: Deconstructing the heterosexist discourse in the counselling professions. In J. Croteau, J. Lark, M. Lidderdale, & B. Chung (Eds.), *Deconstructing heterosexism in the counselling professions: A narrative approach* (pp. 1–16). Thousand Oaks, CA: Sage.

Crowfoot, J., Chesler, M. A., & Boulet, J. (1983). Organizing for social justice. In E. Seidman (Ed.), *Handbook of social intervention* (pp. 253–255). Newbury Park, CA: Sage.

Dailey, R. C. (1986). Understanding organizational commitment for volunteers: Empirical and managerial implications. *Journal of Voluntary Action Research,* 15(1), 19–31.

Dale, D. (1978). *How to make citizen involvement work: Strategies for developing clout.* Amherst, MA: University of Massachusetts, Citizen Involvement Training Project.

Dale, D., & Mitiguy, N. (1978). *Planning for a change: A citizen's guide to creative planning and program development.* Amherst, MA: University of Massachusetts, Citizen Involvement Training Project.

Dale, R. (2004). *Development planning: Concepts and tools for planners, managers and facilitators.* New York: Zed.

Daniels, S. (2002, August 29). Understanding communities as systems. Presentation to University of Arizona Cooperative Extension Annual Conference, Tucson, AZ.

De Jouvenel, B. (1958). Authority: The efficient imperative. In C. J. Freidrich (Ed.), *Authority, nomos, I.* Cambridge, MA: Harvard University Press.

De Vita, C. J., Manjarrez, C, & Twombly, E. (1999). *Organizations and neighborhood networks that strengthen families in the District of Columbia.* Washington, DC: The Urban Institute.

Dear, R. B., & Patti, R. J. (1984). Legislative advocacy: Seven effective tactics. In F. Cox, J. L. Erlich, J. Rothman, & J. E. Tropman (Eds.), *Tactics and techniques of community practice* (2nd ed., pp. 185–197). Itasca, IL: Peacock.

Delaney, R. (2005). The philosophical and value base of Canadian social welfare. In J. Turner & F. Turner (Eds.), *Canadian social welfare* (pp. 13–27). Toronto: Pearson Education Canada.

Delgado, M. (2000). *Community social work practice in an urban context: The potential of a capacity-enhancement perspective.* New York: Oxford University Press.

Denning, S. (2000). The *springboard: How storytelling ignites action in knowledge-era organizations.* Boston: Butterworth-Heinemann.

DePoy, E., Hartman, A., & Haslett, D. (1999). Critical action research: A model for social work knowing. *Social Work,* 44(6), 560–569.

Devore, W., & Schlesinger, E. (2000). *Ethnic sensitive social work practice* (5th ed.). Boston: Allyn & Bacon.

DiAngelo, R. (1997). Heterosexism: Addressing internalized dominance. *Journal of Progressive Human Services,* 8(1), 5–22.

DiNitto, D. M. (2000). *Social welfare: Politics and public policy* (5th ed.). Boston: Allyn & Bacon.

DiNitto, D. M., & McNeece, C. A. (1989). *Social work.* Englewood Cliffs, NJ: Prentice-Hall.

Dolgoff, R., Feldstein, D., & Skolnik, L. (1997). *Understanding social welfare* (4th ed.). White Plains, NY: Longman.

Dominelli, L. (1998). Anti-oppressive practice in context. In R. Adams, L. Dominelli, & M. Payne (Ed.), *Social work: Themes, issues and critical debates* (pp. 3–22). Hampshire: Macmillan.

Dominelli, L. (2007). Challenges to internationalizing social work curricula. In L. Dominelli (Ed.), *Revitilizing communities in a globalized world* (pp. 375–382). Aldershot, UK: Ashgate Publishers.

Dominelli, L., & Campling, J. (2002). *Anti-oppressive social work theory and practice.* New York: Palgrave Macmillan.

Doran, D. (2002, July 18). Women seize at least 4 other Nigerian oil facilities. *Arizona Daily Star,* p. A9.

Dosher, A. (1977a, February 17). Networks: A key to person-community development. Paper presented to Office of Youth Development, Department of Health, Education, and Welfare, Denver Hearings.

Dosher, A. (1977b, November 2). Networking workshop outline. Paper presented to Pima County Children Youth and Families Community Network, Tucson, AZ.

Downs, A. (1981). *Neighborhoods and urban development.* Washington, DC: The Brookings Institution.

Dubois, B., & Krogsrud-Miley, K. (2000). *Social work: An empowering profession* (4th ed.). Boston: Allyn & Bacon.

Dupper, D. R., & Poertner, J. (1997). Public schools and the revitalization of impoverished communities: School linked, family resource centers. *Social Work,* 42(5), 415–422.

Early, T. J., & GlenMaye, L. F. (2000). Valuing families: Social work practice with families from a strengths perspective. *Social Work,* 45(2), 118–130.

Easwaramoorthy, M., Barr, C., Gumulka, G., & Hartford, L. (2006). Business support for charities and nonprofits. *Research Bulletin,* 13(2).

Edwards, E. D., & Edwards, M. E. (1995). Community development with Native Americans. In F. G. Rivera & J. L. Erlich (Eds.), *Community organizing in a diverse society* (2nd ed., pp. 25–42). Boston: Allyn & Bacon.

Ellner, S. (2006). Venezuela: Defying globlalization's logic. In V. Prashad & T. Ballve (Eds.), *Dispatches from Latin America: On the frontlines against neoliberalism* (pp. 93–104). Cambridge, MA: South End Press.

Ellsworth, C., Hooyman, N., Ruff, R. A., Stam, S. B., & Tucker, J. H. (1982). Toward a feminist model of planning for and with women. In A. Weicker & S. T. Vandiver (Eds.), *Women, power, and change* (pp. 146–156). Washington, DC: National Association of Social Workers.

Erlich, J. L., & Tropman, J. E. (1974). Overview of strategy. In F. M. Cox, J. L. Erlich, J. Rothman, & J. E. Tropman (Eds.), *Strategies of community organization: A book of readings* (2nd ed., p. 175). Itasca, IL: Peacock.

Ewart, C. K., & Suchday, S. (2002). Discovering how urban poverty and violence affect health: Development and validation of a neighborhood stress index. *Heath Psychology*, 21(3), 254–262.

Ezell, M. (2001). *Advocacy in the human services.* Belmont, CA: Wadsworth.

Fabricant, M. (1985). The industrialization of social work. *Social Work*, 30(5), 389–395.

Fallon, D. (1993, January). Collaboration: Effective fundraising in the 90's. *Contemporary Issues in Fundraising*, 20–23.

Fantini, M., & Gittell, M. (1973). *Decentralization: Achieving reform.* New York: Praeger.

Fawcett, S., Seekins, T., Whang, P., Muir, C., & Balcazar, Y. (1982). Involving consumers in decision making. *Social Policy*, 2, 36–41.

Fellin, P. (2001). The community and the social worker (3rd ed.). Itasca, IL: Peacock.

Filley, A., House, R., & Kerr, S. (1976). *Managerial process and organizational behavior* (2nd ed.). Glenview, IL: Scott, Foresman.

Fisher, R. (1984, Summer). Neighborhood organizing: Lessons from the past. *Social Policy*, 9–16.

Fisher, R., & Ury, W. (1991). *Getting to yes: Negotiating without giving in* (2nd ed.). Boston: Houghton Mifflin.

Flanagan, J. (2000). *Successful fundraising: A complete handbook for volunteers and professionals* (2nd ed.). Chicago: Contemporary Books.

Floro, G. K. (1989). Innocence and satisfactions for a shared life voluntarism. *Wisconsin Sociologist*, 26(1), 7–14.

Fong, L. G. W., & Gibbs, J. T. (1995). Facilitating services to multicultural communities in a dominant setting: An organizational perspective. *Administration in Social Work*, 19(2), 1–24.

Food And Agriculture Organization of the United Nations (FAO). (2009). Declaration of the World Summit on Food Security. Paper presented at the World Summit on Food Security.

Fook, J. (2002). *Social work: Critical theory and practice.* London: Sage.

Forrest, R., & Kearns, A. (2001). Social cohesion, social capital and the neighbourhood. *Urban Studies*, 38(12), 2125–2143.

Fosler, R. S. (2002). *Working better together.* Washington DC: Independent Sector.

Foucault, M. (1978). *The history of sexuality.* New York: Pantheon.

Foucault, M. (1988). *Madness and civilization: History of insanity in the age of reason.* Toronto: Vintage Book Edition.

Fox-McIntyre, M. (2001). Internet strategy for nonprofits. In T. D. Connors (Ed.), *The nonprofit handbook: Management* (3rd ed., pp. 199–222). New York: Wiley.

Frankenberg, R. (1993). *White women, race matters: The social construction of whiteness.* Minneapolis: University of Minnesota Press.

Franklin, U. M. (1992). *The real world of technology.* Concord, ON: Anansi.

Freeman, B. (2007). Indigenous pathway to anti-oppressive practice. In D. Baines (Ed.), *Doing anti-oppressive practice: Building transformative politicized social work* (pp. 95–109). Halifax: Fernwood.

Freeman, B., & Lee, B. (2007, March). Towards an aboriginal model of community healing. *Native Social Work Journal*, 6, 97–120.

Frey, G. A. (1990, March). A framework for promoting organizational change. *Journal of Contemporary Human Services*, 142–147.

Freyd, W., & Carlson, D. M. (1997). Telemarketing. In J. M. Greenfield (Ed.), *The nonprofit handbook: Fund raising* (2nd ed., pp. 317–328). New York: Wiley.

Friere, P. (1973). *Education for critical consciousness.* New York: Seabury.

Friesen, J. (2009, August). Contentious landfill put on hold: One year moratorium of Site 41. *Globe and Mail*, p. A11.

Galabuzi, G.-E. (2006). *Canada's economic apartheid: The social exclusion of racialized groups in the new century.* Toronto: Canadian Scholars' Press.

Galabuzi, G.-E. (2009). Social exclusion. In D. Raphael (Ed.), *Social determinants of health: Canadian perspectives* (pp. 252–268). Toronto, Ontario: Canadian Scholars' Press.

Gatewood, E. (1994). *Do it yourself: A simple approach to neighborhood improvement.* Tacoma WA: City of Tacoma.

Geever, J. C. (2001). The *Foundation Center's guide to proposal writing* (3rd ed.). New York: Foundation Center.

Geever, J. C., & McNeill, P. (1997). *The Foundation Center's guide to proposal writing* (Rev. ed.). New York: The Foundation Center.

George, P., Coleman, B., & Barnoff, L. (2007). Beyond providing services: Voices of service users on structural social work practice in community based social services agencies. *Canadian Social Work Review*, 24(1), 5–23.

George, P., Moffatt, K., Alphonse, M., Kanitkar, A., Anand,V., & Chamberlain, J. (2009). Strategies of resistance in the context of marginalization and globalization in India. *Social Development Issues*, 31(3), 1–14.

George, S. (1986). *How the other half dies: The real reasons for world hunger* (Rev. ed.). Harmondsworth, Middlesex: Penguin Books.

George, U., Moffatt, K., Lee, B., & McGrath, S. (2003).Exploring citizenship in contemporary community practice. *Journal of Community Practice* 11(3), 71–85.

Ghorayshi, P., Graydon, H., & Kliewer, B. (2007). Towards a social theory in community economic development in the era of globalization. In J. Loxley (Ed.), *Transforming or reforming capitalism: Towards a theory of community economic development.* Winnipeg: Fernwood Publishing.

Gindin, J. (2006). Chavistas in the halls of power, chavistas in the streets. In V. Prashad & T. Ballve (Eds.), *Dispatches from Latin America: On the frontlines against neo-liberalism* (pp. 89–92). Cambridge, MA: South End Press.

Goffin, S. G., & Lombardi, J. (1988). *Speaking out: Early childhood advocacy.* Washington, DC: National Association for the Education of Young Children.

Goldberg, G. S. (1980, June). New directions for the community service society of New York: A study of organizational change. *Social Service Review*, 184–219.

Golden, S. L. (2001). The grant-seeking process. In J. M. Greenfield (Ed.), The *nonprofit handbook: Fund raising* (3rd ed., pp. 666–691). New York: Wiley.

Gottleib, N. (1992). Empowerment, political analyses, and services for women. In Y. Hasenfeld (Ed.), *Human services as complex organizations* (pp. 301–319). Newbury Park, CA: Sage.

Greenfield, J. M. (2002). *Fundraising fundamentals: A guided to annual giving for professionals and volunteers* (2nd ed.). New York: Wiley.

Guerra, L. (1999). *Technical assistance and progressive organizations for social change in communities of color: A report to the Saguaro Grantmaking Board of the Funding Exchange.* New York: The Funding Exchange.

Gummer, B. (1978, September). A power-politics approach to social welfare organizations. *Social Service Review*, 349–361.

Gutiérrez, L. M. (1995). Working with women of color: An empowerment perspective. In J. Rothman, J. L. Erlich, & J. E. Tropman (Eds.), *Strategies of community intervention* (5th ed., pp. 204–212). Itasca, IL: Peacock.

Gutiérrez, L. M., & Lewis, E. A. (1994). Community organizing with women of color: A feminist approach. *Journal of Community Practice*, 1(2), 23–44.

Gutiérrez, L. M., & Lewis, E. A. (1995). A feminist perspective on organizing with women of color. In F. G. Rivera & J. L. Erlich (Eds.), *Organizing in a diverse society* (2nd ed., pp. 95–112). Boston: Allyn & Bacon.

Hagebak, B. R. (1982). *Getting local agencies to cooperate.* Baltimore: University Park Press.

Hall, H. (1996). Direct mail: Can it still deliver? *The Chronicle of Philanthropy*, 8(10).

Hall, M., Lasby, D., Gumulka, G., & Tryon, C. (2006). *2004 Canada survey of giving, volunteering and participating.* Ottawa: Minister of Industry.

Hallman, H. W. (1984). *Neighborhoods: Their place in urban life.* Newbury Park, CA: Sage.

Hart, M. (2002). *Seeking Mino-Pimatisiwin.* Halifax: Fernwood.

Hartcastle, D., & Powers, P. (2004). *Community practice: Theory and skills for social workers.* New York: Oxford University Press.

Harwood Group. (1999). *Community rhythms: Five stages of community life.* Bethesda, MD: The Harwood Group and the Charles Stewart Mott Foundation.

Haynes, K. S., & Mickelson, J. S. (2000). *Affecting change: Social workers in the political arena* (4th ed.). New York: Longman.

Health Canada. (2007). *Canadian Community Health Survey, Cycle 2.2, Nutrition-income-related household food security in Canada.* Ottawa: Office of Nutrition Policy and Promotion, Health Products and Food Branch.

Healy, K. (2000). *Social work practices: Contemporary perspectives on change.* London: Sage.

Healy, K. (2005). Under reconstruction: Renewing critical social work practices. In S. Hick, J. Fook, & R. Pozzuto (Eds.), *Social work: A critical turn* (pp. 219–230). Toronto: Thompson Educational.

Heintze, T., & Bretschneider, S. (2000). Information technology and restructuring in public organizations: Does adoption of information technology affect organizational structures, communications, and decision making? *Journal of Public Administration Research and Theory,* 10(4), 801–830.

Herbert, W. (1996, January 29). The revival of civic life. *U.S. News & World Report,* 63–67.

Hick, S. (2002). *Social work in Canada: An introduction.* Toronto: Thompson Education Publishing.

Hick, S., Fook, J., & Pozzuto, R. (2005). *Social work: a critical turn.* Toronto: Thompson Educational Pub.

Hicks, J. (2001). Grass-roots fund raising. In J. M. Greenfield (Ed.), *The nonprofit handbook: Fund raising* (3rd ed., pp. 920–947). New York: Wiley.

Hill, M. (2009). Young people fight poverty from grassroots. Retrieved September 14, 2009, www.vancouversun.com/lif/young+people+fight+poverty+from+grassroots/1745869/story.html.

Hodiak, D. (2001, May 11). Cultivating your donors on the Internet [Online]. Available: http://www.onphilanthropy.com/op2001-09-10h.html.

Hofford, R. A. (2001). Seven tips for effecting legislative change: Getting involved in state and local politics is another way you can care for your patients and community. *Family Practice Management,* 8(4), 35–37.

Holloway, S. (1987). Staff-initiated organizational change. In National Association of Social Workers (Ed.), *Encyclopedia of social work* (18th ed., pp. 729–736). Silver Spring, MD: National Association of Social Workers.

Home, A. L. (1991). Mobilizing women's strengths for social change: The group connection. In A. Vinik & M. Levin (Eds.), *Social action in group work* (pp. 153–173). New York: Haworth.

Hope, A., & Timmel, S. (1992). *Training for transformation: A handbook for community workers, Book 2.* Gweru, Zimbabwe: Mambo Press.

House of Commons Procedures and Practice. (2009). Compendium of the House of Common, Procedure: The Legislative Process [Online]. Available: www.parl.gc.ca/compendium/web-content/c_g_legislativeprocess-e.htm.

Howe, F. (1985, March/April). *What you need to know about fundraising.* Harvard Business Review, 24.

Hrebenar, R. J., & Scott, R. K. (1982). *Interest group politics in America.* Englewood Cliffs, NJ: Prentice-Hall.

Huang, Y. (2001). Women's contradictory roles in the community: A case study of the community development project in Taiwan. *International Social Work,* 44(3), 361–373.

Hum, D., & Simpson, W. (2007). The legacy of immigration: Labour market performance and education in the second generation. *Applied Economics,* 39(15), 1–25.

Hunt, A. (1986, July/August). Strategic philanthropy. *Across the Board,* 23–30.

Hyde, C. (1992). The ideational system of social movement agencies: An examination of feminist health centers. In Y. Hasenfeld (Ed.), *Human services as complex organizations* (pp. 121–144). Newbury Park, CA: Sage.

Iglehart, A., & Becerra, R. (1996). Social work and the ethnic agency. *Journal of Multicultural Social Work,* 4(1), 1–20.

Ilcan, S., Basok, T. (2004). Community government: Voluntary agencies, social justice, and the responsibilization of citizens. *Citizenship Studies*, 8(2), 129–144.

Institute for Community Economics. (2002). The community land trust model [Online]. Available: http://www.iceclt.org/clt/

Isin, E. F., & Wood, P. K. (1999). *Citizenship and identity*. Thousand Oaks, CA: Sage Publications.

Janis, I. L. (1982). Groupthink: Psychological studies of policy decisions and fiascos (2nd ed.). Boston: Houghton Mifflin.

Jansson, B. S. (1994). *Social welfare policy: From theory to practice* (2nd ed.). Belmont, CA: Wadsworth.

Jansson, B. S. (1997). *The reluctant welfare state: A history of American social welfare policies* (3rd ed.). Pacific Grove, CA: Brooks/Cole.

Jansson, B. S. (2002). *Becoming an effective policy advocate: From policy practice to social justice* (2nd ed.). Pacific Grove, CA: Brooks/Cole.

Jeffery, D. (2007). Radical problems and liberal selves:Professional subjectivity in the anti-oppressive social work classroom. *Canadian Social Work Review*, 24(2), 125–139.

Johnson, D. W., & Johnson, F. P. (1997). *Joining together: Group theory and group skills* (7th ed.). Englewood Cliffs, NJ: Prentice-Hall.

Johnson, D. W., & Johnson, F. P. (2003). *Joining together: Group theory and group skills* (8th ed.). Englewood Cliffs, NJ: Prentice-Hall.

Johnson, L., & Yanca. S. J. (2001). *Social work practice: A generalist approach* (7th ed.). Boston: Allyn & Bacon.

Johnson, L. C., & Schwartz, C. L. (1997). *Social welfare: A response to human need* (4th ed.). Boston: Allyn & Bacon.

Johnson, M. (2001). Fundraising on the net. In J. M. Greenfield (Ed.), *The nonprofit handbook: Fund raising* (3rd ed., pp. 518–536). New York: Wiley.

Join Together Online. (2000, March 29). Sports franchises commit to helping communities [Online]. Available: http://www.jointogether.org/sa/resources/fuing/reader.jtml?Object_ID=262546.

Jones, M. (2000). Hope and despair at the front line: Observations on integrity and change in the human services. *International Social Work* 43(3), 365–380.

Julian, J. (1973). Social problems. Englewood Cliffs, NJ: Prentice-Hall.

Jungk, R., & Mullert, N. (1996). *Future workshops: How to create desirable futures.* London: Institute for Social Inventions.

Kagan, S. L. (1999) Using a theory of change approach in a national evaluation of family support programs: Practitioner reflections [Online]. Available: www.aspenroundtable.org/vol2/kagan.htm

Kahn, S. (1970). *How people get power: Organizing oppressed communities for action.* New York: McGraw-Hill.

Kahn, S. (1991). *Organizing: A guide for grassroots leaders* (Rev. ed.). Silver Spring, MD: National Association of Social Workers.

Kahn, S. (1994). *How people get power* (Rev. ed.). Washington, DC: NASW Press.

Kaminski, A. (2001). Women as philanthropists: A new approach and a new voice in major gifts. In J. M. Greenfield (Ed.), *The nonprofit handbook: Fund raising* (3rd ed., pp. 361–381). New York: Wiley.

Kaner, S., Lind, L., Toldi, C., Fisk, S., & Berger, D. (1996). *Facilitator's guide to participatory decision-making.* Gabriola Island, BC: New Society.

Kanyoro, M. (2000, March). Braced for change [Online]. Available: www.worldywca.org/common_concern/mar2000/bracedchange.html

Keller, S. (1968). *The urban neighborhood.* New York: Random House.

Kennedy, D. M. (1996, August). Neighborhood revitalization: Lessons from Savannah and Baltimore. *National Institute of Justice Journal*, 13–17.

Kettner, P. M., Daley, J. M., & Nichols, A. W. (1985). *Initiating change in organizations and communities: A macro practice model.* Pacific Grove, CA: Brooks/Cole.

Kettner, P. M., Moroney, R. M., & Martin, L. L. (1999). *Designing and managing programs: An effectiveness-based approach* (2nd ed.). Newbury Park, CA: Sage.

Kibel, B., & Miner, W. (1996). *The basics of results mapping.* Bethesda, MD: Pacific Institute for Research and Evaluation.

Kindervater, S. (1983). *Women working together for personal, economic, and community development.* Washington, DC: Overseas Education Fund.

King, M. A., Sims, A., & Osher, D. (2000). How is cultural competency integrated in education? Centre for Effective Collaboration and Practice. Retrieved December 16, 2009, http://cecp.air.org/cultural/Q_integrated.htm#def.

Kinsmen, G. (1996). The *regulation of desire: Homophobia and the hetero sexualities.* Montreal: Black Rose Books.

Kirst-Ashman, K. K., & Hull, G. H. (2001). *Generalist practice with organizations and communities* (2nd ed.) Chicago: Nelson-Hall.

Kitchener-Waterloo Multicultural Centre. (2009). Welcome to the Kitchener-Waterloo Multicultural Centre. Retrieved September 26, 2009, www.kwmc.on.ca.

Klein, K. (1992, December). Budgeting for fundraising. *Grassroots Fundraising Journal*, 3–5.

Klein, K. (2000). *Fundraising: For the long haul.* Berkeley, CA: Chardon Press.

Kondrat, M. (1999). Who is the self in self-aware? Professional self awareness from critical theory perspective. *Social Service Review*, 73(3), 451–477.

Konopka, G. (1983). *Social group work: A helping process* (3rd ed.). Englewood Cliffs, NJ: Prentice-Hall.

Kotler, M. (1969). *Neighborhood government: The local foundations of political life.* Indianapolis: Bobbs-Merrill.

Kramer, R., & Specht, H. (1983). *Readings in community organization practice* (3rd ed.). Englewood Cliffs, NJ: Prentice-Hall.

Kretzman, J. P., & McKnight, J. L. (1993). *Building communities from the inside out.* Chicago: ACTA.

Kretzman, J. P., & McKnight, J. L. (1997). *A guide to capacity inventories: Mobilizing the community skills of local residents.* Chicago: ACTA.

Krueger, R. A., & King, J. A. (1997). *Involving community members in focus groups* (Focus Group Kit, Vol. 5). Thousand Oaks, CA: Sage.

Kublick, R. (2009). Multicultural association goes 25th anniversary. Retrieved October 2, 2009, www.multifest.ca/new.html.

Kumsa, M. (2007). A resettlement story of unsettlement: Transformative practices of taking it personally. In D. Baines (Ed.), *Doing anti-oppressive practice building transformative politicized social work.* Halifax: Fernwood.

Kwon, O., & Wen, Y. (2010). An empirical study of the factors affecting social network service use. *Computers in Human Behaviour*, 26, 254–263.

Laboucane, R. (2009). Apology offers glimmer of hope for Aboriginal Canadians. Retrieved December, 5, 2009, www.troymedia.com/?p=2190.

Lamiell, R. (1984). The people's lobby. In L. Staples (Ed.), *Roots of power: A manual for grassroots organizing* (pp. 188–197). New York: Praeger.

Langton, S. (1982). Networking and community education. In J. M. Brandon & Associates (Eds.), *Networking: A trainers manual* (pp. 212–213). Amherst, MA: University of Massachusetts, Community Education Resource Center, School of Education.

Latting, J. K. (1990). Motivational differences between Black and White volunteers. *Non-Profit and Voluntary Sector Quarterly*, 19(2), 121–136.

Lautman, K. P. (1997). Direct mail. In J. M. Greenfield (Ed.), The *nonprofit handbook: Fund raising* (2nd ed., pp. 254–277). New York: Wiley.

Lautman, K. P. (2001). Direct mail. In J. M. Greenfield (Ed.), *The nonprofit handbook: Fund raising* (3rd ed., pp. 456–479). New York: Wiley.

League of Women Voters. (1976). *Making an issue of it: The campaign handbook.* Publication No. 613.

League of Women Voters Education Fund. (1977). How to plan an environmental conference. In F. Cox, J. L. Erlich, J. Rothman, & J. E. Tropman (Eds.), *Tactics and techniques of community practice* (pp. 111–152). Itasca, IL: Peacock.

Lechte, R. (1983, October 27–29). *Report of the world YWCA workshop on development and social change.* Singapore.

Lee, B. (1999). *Pragmatics of community organization* (3rd ed.). Toronto: Common Act Press.

Lee, B. (2008). Will the real community research please stand up? *Canadian Social Work Review*, 25(1), 5–22.

Lee, B., McGrath, S., Moffatt, K., & George, U. (1996). Community practice education in Canadian schools of social work. *Canadian Social Work Review*, 14, 221–236.

Lee, B., McGrath, S., Moffatt, K., & George, U. (2002). Exploring the insider role in community practice within diverse communities. *Critical Social Work*, 2(2), 69–87.

Lee, B., McGrath, S., Moffatt, K., & George, U. (2006). Community practice with traumatized populations. Paper presented at the Canadian Association of Schools of Social Work Conference.

Lee, B., & Todd, S. (2007). *A Casebook of community practice: Problems and strategies.* Toronto: Common Act Press.

Leher, M. (2000, April-May). Endowment building: Myth and reality checks. *PhilanthropyWorks AZ,* 1(2), 9.

Lepishchak, B., & Moffatt, K. (2007). Supporting our youth: Development of a community-based response to risk and marginalization. In B. Lee & S. Todd (Eds.), *A casebook of community practices: Problems and strategies.* Toronto: Common Act Press.

Lessa, I. (2006). Single motherhood in the Canadian landscape: Postcards from a subject. In A. Westhues (Ed.), *Canadian social policy: Issues and perspectives* (4th ed., pp. 291–309). Waterloo, ON: Wilfrid Laurier University.

Lewin, K. (1951). *Field theory in social science.* New York: Harper.

Lewis, J. (2002). *Welcome to the grants collection Tucson-Pima Public Library, Main Library.* Tucson, AZ: Tucson-Pima Public Library.

Lewis, J. A., Lewis, M. D., Packard, T., & Souflée, F., Jr. (2001). *Management of human service programs* (3rd ed.). Pacific Grove, CA: Brooks/Cole.

Lewis, R. (2009). 2006 Census Housing Series: Issue 3—The adequacy, suitability and affordability of Canadian housing, 1991–2006. Research Highlight, February 15, 2009, doi:https://www03.cmhc-schl.gc.ca/catalog/productDetail.cfm?lang=en&cat=150&itm=1&sid=7a6d0bf85de04636a68f91abf856ec99&fr=1274791163125.

Liamzon, C. (1997). An overview of the concept of empowerment. In *People's empowerment: Grassroots experiences in Africa, Asia and Latin America* (pp. 1–32). Rome, Italy: IRED Nord.

Lipsky, M. (1984). Bureaucratic disentitlement in social welfare programs. *Social Service Review,* 58(2), 3–27.

Litwak, E., Shiroi, E., Zimmerman, L., & Bernstein, J. (1970). Community participation in bureaucratic organizations: Principles and strategies. *Interchange,* 1(4), 44–60.

Lloyd-Jones, E. (1989). Foreword. In D. Roberts, *Designing campus activities to foster a sense of community* [New Direction for Student Services, 48]. San Francisco: Jossey-Bass.

Lofquist, W. A. (1996). *The technology of development: A framework for transforming community cultures.* Tucson, AZ: Development Publications.

Longres, J. (2000). *Human behavior in the social environment* (3rd ed.). Itasca, IL: Peacock.

Lotspeich, M. L., & Kleymeyer, J. E. (1976). How to gather data about your neighborhood. *Neighborhood Technical Information Service,* 1(10). Chicago: American Society of Planning Officials.

Loxley, J. (2007). *Transforming or reforming capitalism: Towards a theory of community economic development.* Halifax: Fernwood Publishing.

Luchuk, L.C. (2008, November 25). Hosting a "giving circle": Finding new donors and new dollars. www.charityvillage.com/cv/archive/acov/acov08/acov0838.asp.

Luke, T. W. (1989). *Screens of power: Ideology, domination, and resistance in informational society.* Urbana: University of Illinois Press.

Lumsden, G., & Lumsden, D. (2000). *Communicating in groups and teams: Sharing leadership* (3rd ed.). Belmont, CA: Wadsworth/Thomson Learning.

Lundy, C. (2004). *Social work and social justice: A structural approach to social work.* Peterborough, ON: Broadview Press.

Lynn, K., & Lynn, D. (1992). Common cents fund raising. *New Designs for Youth Development,* 10(2), 34–39.

Magliocca, L. A., & Christakis, A. N. (2001). Creating transforming leadership for organizational change: The CogniScope system approach. *Systems Research and Behavioral Science,* 18(3), 259–282.

Makhoul, A. (May 2009). Saint John Neighbourhood assistants inspire hope. Vibrant Communities Community Snapshot. Caledon Institute. www.caledoninst.org/Publications/PDF/781ENG.pdf

Male, R. (1993). The politics of thriving as well as surviving. In R. L. Clifton & A. M. Davis (Eds.), *Grassroots administration: A resource book for directors, staff, and volunteers of small community-based nonprofit agencies* (2nd ed., pp. 83–95). Pacific Heights, IL: Waveland Press.

Mamphiswana, D., & Noyoo, N. (2000). Social work education in a changing sociopolitical and economic dispensation: Perspectives from South Africa. *International Social Work,* 43(1), 21–32.

Mancoske, R. J., & Hunzeker, J. M. (1994). Advocating for community services coordination: An empowerment perspective for planning AIDS services. *Journal of Community Practice*, 1(3), 49–58.

Martí-Costa, S., & Serrano-García, I. (1995). Needs assessment and community development: An ideological perspective. In J. Rothman, J. L. Erlich, & J. E. Tropman (Eds.), *Strategies of community intervention* (5th ed., pp. 257–267). Itasca, IL: Peacock.

Martin, P. Y. (1980). Multiple constituencies, dominant societal values, and the human service administrator: Implications for service delivery. *Administration in Social Work*, 4(2), 15–27.

Martinez-Brawley, E. A. (2000). *Closer to home: Human services in the small community*. Washington, DC: NASW Press.

Marx, J. D. (2000). Women and human services giving. *Social Work*, 45(1), 27–38.

Mason, J. L. (1988). Investing for results: Corporate philanthropic activities. *Vital Speeches of the Day* (Vol. LIV, No. 12, pp. 379–381). New York: Press Group.

Mason, R. O., & Mitroff, I. I. (1985). A teleological power-oriented theory of strategy. In W. G. Bennis, K. D. Benne, & R. Chin (Eds.), *The planning of change* (4th ed., pp. 215–223). New York: Holt, Rinehart & Winston.

Massaquoi, N. (2007). Crossing boundaries to radicalize social work practice and education. In D. Baines (Ed.), *Doing anti-oppressive practice: Building transformative politicized social work* (pp. 176–190). Halifax: Fernwood.

Mathbor, G. (2008). *Effective community participation in coastal development*. Chicago: Lyceum.

Max, S. (1980). *Making a first contact with a potential member*. Chicago: Midwest Academy.

Mayer, N. S. (1984). *Neighborhood organizations and community development: Making revitalization work*. Washington, DC: The Urban Institute Press.

Mayer, R. R. (1985). *Program planning: A developmental perspective*. Englewood Cliffs, NJ: Prentice-Hall.

McClenaghan, P. (2000). Social capital: Exploring the theoretical foundations of community development education. *British Educational Research Journal*, 26(5), 565–582.

McCreight, M. (1984). Lawsuits for leverage. In L. Staples (Ed.), *Roots to power: A manual for grassroots organizing* (pp. 181–187). New York: Praeger.

McGrath, S., George, U., Lee, B., & Moffatt, K. (2007). Social justice: The goal of community practice in diverse communities. *Social Development Issues*, 29(2), 77–91.

McGrath, S., Moffatt, K., George, U., & Lee, B. (1999). Community capacity: The emperor's new clothes. *Canadian Review of Social Policy*, 44, 9–23.

McGrory, B. (2006). Nothing done about injustice: Aboriginal problems left festering for more than 100 years. *Toronto Star*, A 17.

McKay, S. (1988, November). The manager: Profile artistic director. *Canadian Business*, 193–196.

McKillip, J. (1987). *Needs analysis: Tools for the human services and education*. Newbury Park, CA: Sage.

McKnight, J. (1995). *The careless society: Community and its counterfeits*. New York: Basic Books.

McKnight, J., & Kretzman, J. (1988). (1988). Mapping community capacity. In M. Minkler (Ed.), *Community organization and community building for health* (pp. 157–172). London: Rutgers University Press.

McLean, C. (1980). The lobbying process and the community service agency. In R. L. Clifton & A. M. Dahms (Eds.), *Grassroots administration: A handbook for staff and directors of small community-based social service agencies* (pp. 133–140). Pacific Grove, CA: Brooks/Cole.

Mediratta, K., & Smith, C. (2002). Up from the grassroots: Ideology, identity and movement building in India. *The Ark: Newsletter of the National Organizers Alliance*, 18, 33–39.

Meenaghan, T. M., & Gibbons, W. E. (2000). *Generalist practice in larger settings: Knowledge and skill concepts*. Chicago: Lyceum.

Melanesian Council of Churches. (1977). *Lilik Buk: A rural development for Papua New Guinea* (English ed.). Wewak, PNG: Wirui Press.

Mendoza, M. (2005). Social work in Mexico: Toward a different practice. In I. Ferguson, M. Lavalette, & E. Whitmore (Eds.), *Globalization, global justice and social work* (pp. 11–21). London: Routledge.

Meyer, A. E. (1945, June 5). *Washington Post*.

Midwest Academy. (2001). *Organizing for social change: Midwest Academy manual for activists.* Santa Ana, CA: Seven Locks Press.

Miehls, D., & Moffatt, K. (2000). Constructing social work identity based on the reflexive self. *British Journal of Social Work*, 30(3), 339–348.

Minkler, M., & Wallerstein, N. (1997). Improving health through community organizing and community building: A health education perspective. In M. Minkler (Ed.), *Community organizing and community building for health.* Brunswick, NJ: Rutgers University Press.

Mirazo, C., Hicks, T., Taylor, C., & Ferlazzo, T. (2001). Small is not beautiful. *Social Policy*, 32(2), 39–43.

Mirkin, H. R. (1978). *The complete fundraising guide.* New York: Public Service Materials Center.

Mitchell, A., Lightman, E., & Herd, D. (2007). Work First and immigrants in Toronto. *Social Policy and Society*, 6(3), 293–307.

Mitiguy, N. (1978). *The rich get richer and the poor write proposals.* Amherst, MA: University of Massachusetts, Citizen Involvement Training Project.

Mizrahi, T., & Rosenthal, B. B. (2001). Complexities of coalition building: Leaders' successes: Strategies, struggles, and solutions. *Social Work*, 46(1), 63–78.

Moerschbaecher, L. S., & Dryburgh, E. D. (2001). Planned giving: Gift vehicles. In J. M. Greenfield (Ed.), *The nonprofit handbook: Fund raising* (3rd ed., pp.788–823). New York: Wiley.

Moffatt, K. (1996). Teaching social work practice as a reflective process. In N. Gould & I. Taylor (Eds.), *Reflective learning for social work: Research, theory and practice.* Aldershot: Ashgate.

Moffatt, K. (2001). *A poetics of social work: Personal agency and social transformation in Canada, 1920–1939.* Toronto: University of Toronto.

Moffatt, K., Barnoff, L., George, P., & B. Coleman, B. (2009). Process as labour: Struggles for anti-oppressive/anti-racist change in a feminist organization. *Canadian Review of Social Policy*, 62, 34–54.

Moffatt, K., George, U., Lee, B., & McGrath, S. (2005). Community practice researchers as reflective learners. *British Journal of Social Work*, 35(1), 89–104.

Mondross, J. B., & Berman-Rossi, T. (1992). The relevance of stages of group development theory to community organization practice. In A. Vinik & M. Levin (Eds.), *Social action in group work* (pp. 203–221). New York: Haworth.

Morgan, G. (1997). *Images of organization* (2nd ed.). Thousand Oaks, CA: Sage.

Morrison, J. D., Howard, J., Johnson, C., Navarro, F. J., Placheta, B., & Bell, T. (1997). Strengthening neighborhoods by developing community networks. *Social Work*, 42(5), 527–534.

Morrissette, V., McKenzie, B., & Morrissette, L. (1993). Towards an Aboriginal model of social work practice. *Canadian Social Work Review*, 10(1), 91–108.

Morth, M., & Collins, S. (1996). The *Foundation Center's user-friendly guide: A grantseeker's guide to resources* (Rev. ed.). New York: The Foundation Center.

Mullaly, B. (2002). *Challenging oppression: A critical social work approach.* Don Mills: Oxford University Press.

Mupedziswa, R. (2001). The quest for relevance: Towards a model of developmental social work education and training in Africa. *International Social Work*, 44(3), 285–300.

Mutz, J., & Murray, C. (2000). Fundraising for dummies. Foster City, CA: IDG Books.

Napier, R. W., & Gershenfeld, M. K. (1989). *Groups: Theory and experience* (4th ed.). Boston: Houghton Mifflin.

Napier, R. W., & Gershenfeld, M. K. (1999). *Groups: Theory and experience* (6th ed.). Boston: Houghton Mifflin.

Nash, J. (2006). Towards pluricultural states: Indigenous movements challenge neo-liberalism. *Latin American and Caribbean Ethnic Studies*, 1(1), 125–140.

National Center for Economic and Security Alternatives. (2002). Models and innovations: Community development financial institutions [Online]. Available: http://www.ncesa.org/html/comdevfin.html

Nelson, G. M. (2000). Self-*governance in communities and families.* San Francisco: Barrett-Koehler.

Nelson-Jones, R. (1992). *Group leadership: A training approach.* Pacific Grove, CA: Brooks/Cole.

Netting, F. E., Kettner, P. M., & McMurtry, S. L. (1998). *Social work macro practice* (2nd ed.). New York: Longman.

Neuber, K. A., Atkins, W. T., Jacobson, J. A., & Reuterman, N. A. (1980). *Needs assessment: A model for community planning*. Newbury Park, CA: Sage.

New, C. (2001). Grants from the government. In J. M. Greenfield (Ed.), *The nonprofit handbook: Fund raising* (3rd ed., pp. 692–712). New York: Wiley.

New Brunswick Health and Wellness. (October 2002). New Brunswick Community Health Needs Assessment. www.gnb.ca/0601/pdf/CHCNBNeedsAssessmentEngNov201.pdf.

Nichols, J. (2001). *Pinpointing affluence in the 21st century: Increasing your share of donor dollars*. Chicago: Bonus Books.

Nonprofit Counsel. (1986, March). Planned giving: It's for all: The ten steps for beginning. *Nonprofit Counsel*, 4–9.

Nutt, P. C. (1985). The study of planning process. In W. G. Bennis, K. D. Benne, & R. C. Chin (Eds.), *The planning of change* (4th ed., p. 198). New York: Holt, Rinehart & Winston.

O. M. Collective. (1971). *The organizers manual*. New York: Bantam Books.

O'Brien, C. (1999). Contested territory: Sexualities and social work. In A. Chambon, A. Irvin, & L. Epstein (Ed.), *Reading Foucault for social work* (pp. 131–156). New York: Columbia University Press.

Oliver, D. (2002, April). *Promoting asset based community development in the UK*. North East England: Scarman Trust.

Olney, P. (2001). A vital contribution to community building. *Social Policy*, 31(4), 44.

O'Looney, J. (1993, December). Beyond privatization and service integration: Organizational models for service delivery. *Social Service Review*, 501–534.

Ontario Women Health Network (OWHN). (2009). Inclusion Research. Retrieved December 3, 2009, www.owhn.on.ca/inclusionhandbook.htm.

Osten, M. (2001). Technology and strategy for organizational effectiveness. In T. D. Connors (Ed.), *The nonprofit handbook: Management* (3rd ed., pp. 319–347). New York: Wiley.

Palmer, P. (1993). *The promise of paradox*. Notre Dame, IN: Ave Maria.

Panas, J. (1989). *Research shows eight reasons why philanthropists make major gifts*. Chicago: Panas, Linzy, & Partners, Inc.

Parada, H. (2004). Social work practices within the restructured child welfare system in Ontario: An institutional ethnography. *Canadian Social Work Review*, 21(1), 67–86.

Parada, H. (2007). Regional perspectives from Latin America: Social work in Latin America history, challenges and renewal. *International Social Work*, 50(4), 560–569.

Parada, H., Barnoff, L., & Coleman, B. (2007). Negotiating professional agency: Social work and decision making within child welfare. *Journal of Sociology and Social Welfare*, 4, 35–56.

Parsons, R. J. (1989). Empowerment for role alternatives for low income minority girls: A group work approach. In J. A. B. Lee (Ed.), *Group work with the poor and oppressed* (pp. 27–42). New York: Haworth.

Parsons, R. J., Gutiérrez, L. M., & Cox, E. O. (1998). A model for empowerment practice. In L. M. Gutiérrez, R. J. Parsons, & E. O. Cox (Eds.), *Empowerment in social work practice: A sourcebook* (pp. 3–4). Pacific Grove, CA: Brooks/Cole.

Patti, R. J. (1974). Limitations and prospects of internal advocacy. *Social Casework*, 55(9), 537–545.

Patti, R. J. (1980). Internal advocacy and human services practitioners: An exploratory study. In H. Resnick & R. J. Patti, *Change from within: Humanizing social welfare organizations* (pp. 287–301). Philadelphia: Temple University Press.

Patti, R. J., & Resnick, H. (1975). Changing the agency from within. In R. M. Kramer & H. Specht (Eds.), *Readings in community organization practice* (2nd ed., pp. 65–74). Englewood Cliffs, NJ: Prentice-Hall.

Patton, C. V. (1987). Citizen input and professional responsibility. In F. M. Cox, J. L. Erlich, J. Rothman, & J. E. Tropman (Eds.), *Strategies of community organization: Macro practice* (4th ed., pp. 343–350). Itasca, IL: Peacock.

Peck, M. (1987). *The different drum: Community making and peace*. New York: Simon & Schuster.

Pendleton, N. (1981). *Fund raising*. Englewood Cliffs, NJ: Prentice-Hall.

Perlman, R., & Gurin, A. (1972). *Community organization and social planning*. New York: Wiley.

Pertschuk, M. (1986). *Giant killers*. New York: W.W. Norton.

Piccard, B. (1988). *Introduction to social work: A primer* (4th ed.). Pacific Grove, CA: Brooks/Cole.

Picker, L. A. (1997). The corporate support marketplace. In J. M. Greenfield (Ed.), *The nonprofit handbook: Fund raising* (2nd ed., pp. 372–395). New York: Wiley.

Picker, L. A. (2001). The corporate support marketplace. In J. M. Greenfield (Ed.), *The nonprofit handbook: Fund raising* (3rd ed., pp. 615–637). New York: Wiley.

Pincus, A., & Minahan, A. (1973). *Social work practice: Model and method*. Itasca, IL: Peacock.

Poley, J. (2001). Management implications and opportunities of global communications: "Hawken-Kraks Howl" and Global dot com: Storm, norm, form. In T. D. Connors (Ed.), *The nonprofit handbook: Management* (3rd ed., pp. 162–177). New York: Wiley.

Portes, A. (1998). Social capital: Its origins and applications in modern sociology. *Annual Review of Sociology* 24(1), 1–24.

Portes, A., & Landolt, P. (1996). *Unsolved mysteries: The Tocqueville Files II*. The American Prospect 7(26).

Power, E. (2001). Coping with change: A primer for developing human resources. In T. D. Connors (Ed.), *The nonprofit handbook: Management* (3rd ed., pp. 716–725). New York: Wiley.

Prentice, J. (2009). 2006 Census Housing Series: Issue 2—The Geography of Core Housing Need, 2001–2006. February, 2009. doi:https://www03.cmhc-schl.gc.ca/catalog/productDetail.cfm?lang=en&cat=150&itm=3&sid=06419d5027784745a47190180ca2c2b7&fr=1274790986890.

Pretty, J. (2000). Towards sustainable food and farming systems in industrialized countries. *International Journal of Agricultural Resources, Governance, and Ecology* 1(1), 77–94.

Pruitt, D. (1981). *Negotiating behavior*. New York: Academic Press.

Putnam, R. D. (1993). The prosperous community: Social capital and economic growth. *The American Prospect*, 35–42.

Putnam, R. D. (1995, January). Bowling alone: America's declining social capital. *Journal of Democracy*, 6(1), 65–78.

Putnam, R. D. (1996). The strange disappearance of civic America. *The American Prospect*, 24, 34–49.

Putnam, R. (2000). *Bowling alone: The collapse and revival of American community*. New York: Simon & Shuster.

Quarter, J., Mook, L., & Armstrong, A. (2009). *Understanding the social economy: A Canadian perspective*. Toronto: University of Toronto Press.

Quick, J. A., & New, C. C. (2000). *Grant winner's toolkit: Project management and evaluation*. New York: Wiley.

Quick, J. A., & New, C. C. (2001). Grant seeker's budget toolkit. New York: Wiley.

Rahman, T. (2008). Darfur—a lost cause? How you can make a difference. Retrieved October 9, 2009, www.youthcanada.ca/article/darfur-%E2%80%93-lost-cause-how-you-can-make-difference.

Raphael, D. (2007). *Poverty and policy in Canada: Implications for health and quality of life*. Toronto: CSPI.

Raphael, D. (2009). *Social determinants of health: Canadian perspectives* (2nd ed.). Toronto: Canadian Scholar's Press.

Reeves, R. A., Macolini, R. M., & Martin, R. C. (1987). Legitimizing paltry contributions: On-the-spot vs. mail-in requests. *Journal of Applied Social Psychology*, 17(8), 731–738.

Regan, D. T. (1971). Effects of a favor on liking and compliance. *Journal of Experimental Social Psychology*, 7, 627–639.

Reinhart, P. C. (1990, July). Forecasting the 1990's: The art of fund raising for the next decade. *Fund Raising Management*, 42–48.

Resnick, H. (1978). Tasks in changing the organization from within (COFW). *Administration in Social Work*, 2(1), 29–44.

Resnick, H., & Menefee, D. (1994). A comparative analysis of organization development and social work, with suggestions for what organization development can do for social work. *Journal of Applied Behavioral Science*, 29(4), 432–445.

Rich, R. C. (1979, Fall). The roles of neighborhood organizations in urban service delivery. *Urban Affairs Papers*, 1, 81–93.

Richan, W. C. (1992). *Lobbying for social change.* New York: Haworth.

Riley, J. (2000, July 17). Charitable work sells at a number of firms. *Arizona Daily Star*, pp. D1–3.

Rivera, F., & Erlich, J. (1998). *Community organizing in a diverse society* (3rd ed.). Boston: Allyn & Bacon.

Roach, M. J., & O'Brien, D. J. (1982). The impact of different kinds of neighborhood involvement on residents' overall evaluations of their neighborhoods. *Sociological Focus*, 15(4), 379–391.

Robinson, A. (1996). *Grassroots grants: An activists guide to proposal writing.* Berkeley, CA: Chardon Press.

Robinson, A. (2002). *Selling social change: Without selling out.* San Francisco: Jossey-Bass.

Robinson, B., & Hanna, M. G. (1994). Lessons for academics from grassroots community organizing: A case study—the industrial areas foundation. *Journal of Community Practice,* 1(4), 63–94.

Robinson, D., & Williams, T. (2001, December). Social capital and voluntary activity: Giving and sharing in Maori and non-Maori society. *Social Policy Journal of New Zealand*, 52–71.

Roloff, M. E., & Paulson, G. D. (2001). Confronting organizational transgressions. In J. M. Darley, D. M. Messick, & T. R. Tyler (Eds.), *Social influences on ethical behavior in organizations* (pp. 53–68). Mahwah, NJ: Erlbaum.

Ronnby, A. (1995). *Mobilizing local communities.* Brookfield, VT: Avebury.

Ronnby, A. (1996). Local development and new cooperatives in Sweden: A grassroots approach. In Bauhaus Dessau Foundation & European Network for Economic Self-Help and Local Development (Eds.), *People's economy, wirtschaft von unten: Approaches toward a new social economy in Europe* (pp. 69–81). Dessau, Germany: Bauhaus Dessau Foundation.

Ronnby, A. (1998). Mobilizing the local community. In P. Saukkonen & H. Vihinen, (Eds.), *Rural and regional development* (pp. 65–80). Helsinki, Finland: University of Helsinki, Mikkeli Institute for Rural Research and Training.

Roper Center for Public Opinion Research. (1999, February). *Ethnic patterns in attitudes to philanthropy: A special report to the W. K. Kellogg Foundation.* Storrs, CT: Roper Center for Public Opinion Research, University of Connecticut.

Rose, S. (2000). Reflections on empowerment-based practice. *Social Work*, 45(5), 403–412.

Rossiter, A., Blocki-Radeke, C., Daley, A., & Eisenstat, M. (2006). An investigation into youths' perceptions of their experience of wraparound. *Canadian Social Work Review*, 23(1/2), 21–40.

Rothman, J. (1968). Three models of community organization practice. In F. Cox, J. Erlich, J. Rothman, & J. Tropman (Eds.), *Strategies of community organization: A book of readings* (pp. 3–26). Itasca, IL: Peacock.

Rothman, J., & Tropman, J. (1987). Models of community organization and macro practice perspectives: Their mixing and phasing. In F. M. Cox, J. L. Erlich, J. Rothman, & J. E. Tropman (Eds.), *Strategies of community organization: Macro practice* (4th ed., pp. 3–26). Itasca, IL: Peacock.

Rubin, H., & Rubin, I. (1986). *Community organizing and development.* Columbus, OH: Merrill.

Rubin, H. J., & Rubin, I. S. (2001). *Community organizing and development* (3rd ed.). Boston: Allyn & Bacon.

Ruby, J. F., & O'Brien, M. A. (1978). *United Way-Tucson: Communications kit.* Tucson, AZ: United Way-Tucson.

Saad-Filho, A. (2005a). From Washington to Post-Washington consensus: Neo-liberal agendas for economic development. In A. Saad-Filho & D. Johnston (Eds.), *Neoliberalism: A critical reader* (pp. 113–119). London: Pluto Press.

Saad-Filho, A. (2005b). The political economy of neoliberalism in Latin America. In A. Saad-Filho, Johnston, D. (Ed.), *Neoliberalism: A critical reader* (pp. 222–229). London: Pluto Press.

Sachs, J. (1991). Action and reflection in work with a group of homeless people. In A. Vinik & M. Levin (Eds.), *Social action in group work* (pp. 187–202). New York: Haworth.

Sagasti, F. (1990). Interview in Against the odds [Videotape]. Visions in video series. (Available from South Carolina Educational Television Network, Columbia, SC.)

Sakamoto, I. (2007). An anti-oppressive approach to cultural competence. *Canadian Social Work Review*, 24(1), 105–114.

Sakamoto, I., & Pitner, R. (2005). Use of critical consciousness in anti-oppressive social work practice: Disentagling power dynamics at personal and structural levels. *British Journal of Social Work*, 35, 435–452.

Saulis, M. (2006). Program and policy development from a holistic Aboriginal perspective. In A. Westhues (Ed.), *Canadian social policy: Issues and perspectives* (pp. 115–130). Waterloo, ON: Wilfrid Laurier University Press.

Scheie, D., Williams, T., Mayer, S. E., Kroll, B. S., & Dewar, T. (1997a). *Building support for neighborhood action: Lessons from the community foundations and neighborhoods program, 1991–1995.* Minneapolis: Rainbow Research.

Scheie, D., Williams, T., Mayer, S. E., Kroll, B. S., & Dewar, T. (1997b). *Helping neighborhood groups and leaders grow stronger: Lessons from the community foundations and neighborhoods program, 1991–1995.* Minneapolis: Rainbow Research.

Schelling, T. C. (1963). The strategy of conflict. Cambridge, MA: Harvard University Press.

Scherch, J. (2000). Riverton: Envisioning a sustainable community. In D. P. Fauri, S. P. Wernet, & F. E. Netting (Eds.), *Cases in macro social work practice* (pp. 157–171). Boston: Allyn & Bacon.

Scheuring, J. (2002). The magic of community development in action: Case from Upper Volta 1972. Unpublished manuscript.

Schindler-Rainman, E. (1977). Goals to action. In E. Schindler-Rainman, R. Lippitt, & J. Cole (Eds.), *Taking your meetings out of the doldrums.* La Jolla, CA: University Associates, Inc.

Schmolling, P., Jr., Youkeles, M., & Burger, W. R. (1997). *Human services in contemporary America* (4th ed.). Pacific Grove, CA: Brooks/Cole.

Schneider, M. (1997). Pride, prejudice and lesbian, gay and bisexual youth. In M. T. Schneider (Ed.), *Pride and prejudice.* Toronto: Central Toronto Youth Services.

Schon, D. (1983). *The reflective practitioner: How professionals think in action.* New York: Basic Books.

Schon, D. (1987). *Educating the reflective practitioner: Toward a new design for teaching and learning in the professions* (1st ed.). San Francisco: Jossey-Bass.

Schumacher, D. (1992). *Get funded: A practical guide for scholars seeking research support from business.* Newbury Park, CA: Sage.

Schwab, W., & Ringel, B. (1991). An evaluation of the utility of five models of neighborhood change: The case of Cincinnati, Ohio. *Free Inquiry in Creative Sociology*, 19(2), 125–133.

Schwirian, K. P. (1983). Models of neighborhood change. *Annual Review of Sociology*, 9, 83–103.

Seltzer, S. (2001). *Securing your foundation's future: A complete guide to fundraising strategies.* New York: The Foundation Center.

Senge, P., Kleiner, A., Roberts, C., Ross, R., & Smith, B. (1994). *The fifth discipline fieldbook.* New York: Currency Doubleday.

Shamai, M., & Boehm, A. (2001). Politically oriented social work intervention. *International Social Work*, 44(3), 343–360.

Shapcott, M. (2009). Housing. In D. Raphael (Ed.), *Social determinants of health* (pp. 221–234). Toronto: Canadian Scholars' Press Inc.

Sharp, G. (1973). *The politics of nonviolent action: Part two: The methods of nonviolent action.* Boston: Porter Sargent.

Shaw, S. C., & Taylor, M. A. (1995). *Reinventing fundraising: Realizing the potential of women's philanthropy.* San Francisco: Jossey-Bass.

Shebib, B. (2007). *Choices: Interviewing and counselling skills for Canadians.* Toronto: Pearson Canada.

Sheldon, K. S. (2000). *Successful corporate fund raising: Effective strategies for today's nonprofits.* New York: Wiley.

Sherman, W. R., & Wenocur, S. (1983, September–October). Empowering the public welfare workers through mutual support. *Social Work*, 375–379.

Shmyr, Z. (2003). Recognition of prior learning (RPL) within the newcomer community: A needs assessment. Retrieved January 9, 2010, www.aeel.gov.sk.ca/adx/aspx/adxGetMedia.aspx?DocID=579,195,178,169).

Shragge, E. (2003). *Activism and social change: lessons for community and local organizing.* Peterborough, ON: Broadview Press.

Shulman, L. (1991). *Interactional social work practice: Toward an empirical theory.* Itasca, IL: Peacock.

Siglin, D. (1999). How to win the advocacy game: Rarified air. In R. B. Smucker (Ed.), *The nonprofit lobbying guide* (2nd ed., pp. 121–124). Washington, DC: Independent Sector.

Simpson, D., & Gentile, A. (1986, Spring). Effective neighborhood government. *Social Policy*, 25–30.

Sinnock, B. (1995, August). Fundraising trends move towards more choice, fewer dollars. *The Nonprofit Times*, 27–30.

Six Nations Reclamation. (nd). Welcome to Six Nations Reclamations. Retrieved September 23, 2009, http://reclamationinfo.com.

Smith, C. (2006). Racial profiling in Canada, the United States and the United Kingdom. In C. Tattor & F. Henry (Eds.), *Racial profiling in Canada: Challenging the myth of a "few bad apples."* Toronto: University of Toronto Press.

Smith, D. (1979). In our own interest: A handbook for the citizen lobbyist in state legislatures. Seattle: Madrona.

Smith, S. C. (1989). *Reflections on grantseeking.* Vancouver, WA: M. J. Murdock Charitable Trust.

Smucker, R. B. (1999). *The nonprofit lobbying guide* (2nd ed.). Washington, DC: Independent Sector.

Smylie, J. (2009). The health of Aboriginal peoples. In D. Raphael (Ed.), *The social determinants of health: Canadians' perspectives* (pp. 280–300). Toronto: Canadian Scholars' Press.

Snyder, L. (2006). Workfare: Ten years of pickin' on the poor. In A. Westhues (Ed.), *Canadian social policy issues and perspectives* (4 ed., pp. 309–330). Waterloo, ON: Wilfrid Laurier University.

Speeter, G. (1978). *Playing their game our way: Using the political process to meet community needs.* Amherst, MA: University of Massachusetts, Citizen Involvement Training Project.

Splain, M. J. (1984). Negotiations: Using a weapon as a way out. In L. Staples (Ed.), *Roots to power: A manual for grassroots organizing* (pp. 166–170). New York: Praeger.

Srivastava, S. (2007). Troubles with "anti-racist multiculturalism". In S. Hier & B. Bolaria (Eds.), Race *and Racism in 21st century Canada: Continuity, complexity and change* (pp. 291–312). Peterborough, ON: Broadview Press.

Staples, L. (Ed.). (1984). *Roots to power: A manual for grassroots organizing.* New York: Praeger.

Statistics Canada. (2006). Census: www12.statcan.gc.ca/census-recensement/2006/as-sa/index-eng.cfm

Statistics Canada. (2008). Table 202-0801 low-income cut-offs before and after tax for rural and urban areas, by family, size, current dollars, annual. Retrieved September 7, 2009, http://cansim2.statcan.gc.ca/cgi-win/cnsmcgi.exe?Lang=E&CNSM-Fi=CII/CII_1-eng.htm.

Stein, M. (2001). Nonprofit success on the Internet: Creating an effective online presence. In T. D. Connors (Ed.), *The nonprofit handbook: Management* (3rd ed., pp. 223–243). New York: Wiley.

Steptoe, A., & Feldman, P. J. (2001). Neighborhood problems as sources of chronic stress: Development of a measure of neighborhood problems, and associations with socioeconomic status and health. *Annals of Behavioral Medicine*, 23(3), 177–185.

Strega, S. (2007). Anti-oppressive practice in child welfare. In D. Baines (Ed.), *Doing anti-oppressive practice: Building transformative politized social work* (pp. 67–82). Halifax: Fernwood.

Suchman, D. R. (1993). Recreating Vermont Avenue. *Urban Land*, 52, 20–24.

Suchman, D. R. (1994). *Revitalizing low-income neighborhoods: Recommendations from ULI advisory series panels.* Washington, DC: The Urban Land Institute.

Suchman, D. R., & Lamb, M. I. (1991). West Dallas poised for change. *Urban Land*, 50, 10–16.

Sun, A-P. (2001). Targeting women donors: A response to "Women and Human Service Giving." *Social Work,* 46(1), 79–81.

Swift, K., & Callahan, M. (2009). At *risk: Social justice in child welfare and other human services.* Toronto: University of Toronto Press.

Tenbrunsel, A. E., & Messick, D. M. (2001). Power asymmetries and the ethical atmosphere in negotiations. In J. M. Darley, D. M. Messick, & T. R. Tyler (Eds.), *Social influences on ethical behavior in organizations* (pp. 201–216). Mahwah, NJ: Erlbaum.

Thomas, J. C. (1986). *Between citizen and city: Neighborhood organizations and urban politics in Cincinnati.* Lawrence, KS: University of Kansas Press.

Todd, S. (2005). Unfinished fictions: Becoming and unbecoming feminist community organizers. In

S. Hick, J. Fook, & R. Pozzuto (Eds.), *Social work: A critical turn* (pp. 137–152). Toronto: Thompson Educational Publishing.

Trebesch, L., & Robinson, T. (2007). Six unique online fundraising techniques for your nonprofit—Social Networking. Retrieved January 3, 2010, www.charityvillage.com/cv/research/rofr44.html.

Tropman, J. E., Johnson, H. R., & Tropman, E. J. (1979). *The essentials of committee management.* Chicago: Nelson-Hall.

Tucker Rambally, R. E. (1999). Field education in a developing country: Promoting organizational change and social development. *International Social Work*, 42(4), 485–496.

Tuckman, B. W., & Jensen, M. A. C. (1977). Stages of small group development revisited. *Group and Organizational Studies*, 2(4), 419–427.

Tungasuvvingat. (2009). A place where all Inuit are welcome. Retrieved October 14, 2009, www.tungasuvvingatinuit.ca/eng/ti.htm.

Ulin, S. B. (1997). Benefit event enhancements. In J. M. Greenfield (Ed.), The nonprofit handbook: Fund raising (2nd ed., pp. 299–316). New York: Wiley.

Ulin, S. (2001). Benefit event enhancements. In J. M. Greenfield (Ed.), *The nonprofit handbook: Fund raising* (3rd ed., pp. 500–517). New York: Wiley.

United Way of Greater Toronto and the Canadian Council on Social Development. (2004). Poverty by postal code: The geography of neighbourhood poverty 1981–2001. Retrieved March 25, 2010, www.unitedwaytoronto.com/downloads/whatWeDo/reports/PovertybyPostalCodeFinal.pdf).

Valente, M. (2002, March 25). Argentina's new neighborhood assemblies: The seed of a new form of citizen participation [Online]. Available: www/commondreams.org/headlines02/0325-06.htm.

Von Hoffman, N. (n.d.). Finding and making leaders. Unpublished manuscript.

W. K. Kellogg Foundation. (2001). Using logic models to bring together planning, evaluation, and action: Logic development guide [Online]. Available: http://www.wkkf.org/pubs/Pub3669.pdf

Wagner, A. R. (1995, February 25). Hope for the American neighborhood: Creating a fourth sector—the community sector. Paper presented for the Nobel Prize Forum at Augsburg College, Minneapolis.

Warheit, G. J., Bell, R. A., & Schwab, J. J. (1984). Selecting the needs assessment approach. In F. Cox, J. L. Erlich, J. Rothman, & J. E. Tropman (Eds.), *Tactics and techniques of community practice* (2nd ed., pp. 41–55). Itasca, IL: Peacock.

Warner, T. (2002). *Never going back: A history of queer activism in Canada.* Toronto: University of Toronto Press.

Warren, R. B., & Warren, D. I. (1977). *The neighborhood organizer's handbook.* Notre Dame, IN: University of Notre Dame Press.

Warren, R. B., & Warren, D. I. (1984). How to diagnose a neighborhood. In F. Cox, J. L. Erlich, J. Rothman, & J. E. Tropman (Eds.), *Tactics and techniques of community practice* (2nd ed., pp. 27–40). Itasca, IL: Peacock.

Waterfall, B. (2006). Native people and child welfare practices. In A. Westhues (Ed.), *Canadian social policy: Issues and perspectives* (pp. 223–244). Waterloo, ON: Wilfrid Laurier University Press.

Weaver, L. (2009). A law to enshrine a poverty reduction strategy. The Hamilton Spector. Retrieved December 15, 2009, doi:http://poverty.thespec.com/2009/04/a-law-to-enshrine-a-poverty-reduction-strategy.html.

Webb, C. (1982, May). Communications in fundraising. *Fund Raising Management*, 13, 60.

Wehbi, S. (2008). Teaching international social work: A guiding framework. *Canadian Social Work Review*, 25(2), 117–132.

Weinbach, R. W. (1984, May/June). Implementing change: Insights and strategies for the supervisor. *Social Work*, 282–285.

Weinbach, R. W. (1990). *The social worker as manager: Theory and practice.* New York: Longman.

Wenocur, S. (1992). Should community organization be based on a grassroots strategy? Yes. In E. Gambrill & R. Pruger (Eds.), *Controversial issues in social work* (pp. 289–293). Boston: Allyn & Bacon.

Wernet, S. P. (1994). A case study of adaptation in a nonprofit human service organization. *Journal of Community Practice*, 1(3), 93–111.

Wesley-Esquimaux, C. (2009). Trauma to resilience: Notes on decolonization. In G. Valaskakis, M. Dion, & E. Guimond (Eds.), *Restoring the balance: First Nations women, community and culture*. Winnipeg: University of Manitoba Press.

Westhues, A. (2006). Becoming acquainted with social policy. In A. Westhues (Ed.), *Canadian social policy: Issues and perspectives* (pp. 5–26). Waterloo, ON: Wilfrid Laurier University Press.

Wharf, B. (2002). *Community work approaches to child welfare*. Peterborough, ON: Broadview.

Wharf, B., & Clague, M. (1997). *Community organizing: Canadian experience*. Toronto: Oxford University Press.

White, D. E. (2001). Why do people donate to charity? In J. M. Greenfield (Ed.), *The nonprofit handbook: Fund raising* (3rd ed., pp. 347–360). New York: Wiley.

Whitzman, C. (2008). *The handbook of community safety gender and violence prevention practical planning tools*. Sterling VA: Earthscan.

Wiborg, A. (1998). Changing women in rural areas in change: New challenges for rural development. In P. Saukkonen & H. Vihinen (Eds.), *Rural and regional development*. Helsinki, Finland: University of Helsinki.

Wickramaratne-Rebera, R. (1998, September). Organizations and structures: A case study [Online]. Available: www.worldywca.org/common_concern/sept1998/organizationsandstructures.html.

Williams, M. R. (1985). *Neighborhood organizations: Seeds of a new life*. Westport, CN: Greenwood Press.

Williams, M. R. (1989). *Neighborhood organizing for urban school reform*. New York: Teachers College Press.

Wilson, W., & Beresford, P. (2000). Anti-oppressive practice: Emancipation or appropriation. *British Journal of Social Work*, 30, 553–573.

Wireman, P. (1984). *Urban neighborhoods, networks, and families: New forms for old values*. Lexington, MA: Lexington Books.

Wolff, T. (2001). Community coalition building—contemporary practice and research: Introduction. *American Journal of Community Psychology*, 29(2), 165–173.

Wolpert, J., Mumphrey, A. J., & Seley, J. E. (1972). Metropolitan neighborhoods: Participation and conflict over change [Resource Paper No. 16]. Washington, DC: Association of American Geographers.

Women at Work. (2002). Women at work background [Online]. Available: www.womenngo.org.yu/sajt/english/sajt/women_groups_directories/women_at_work/index.htm

World Health Organization. (2002). *Children in the new millennium*. Geneva: World Health Organization.

Wortley, S., & Tanner, J. (2003). Data denials and confusion: The racial profiling debate in Toronto. *Canadian Journal of Criminology and Criminal Justice*, 45(3), 367–390.

Wrong, D. (1995). Power*: Its forms, bases and uses*. New Brunswick, NJ: Transaction.

Yee, J., & Dumbrill, G. (2003). Whiteout: Looking for race in Canadian social work practice. In A. Al-Krenawi & J. Graham (Eds.), *Multicultural social work in Canada: Working with diverse ethno-racial communities* (pp. 98–121). Toronto: Oxford Press.

Zastrow, C. (1999). *The practice of social work* (6th ed.). Pacific Grove, CA: Brooks/Cole.

Zastrow, C. (2001). *Social work with groups* (5th ed.). Chicago: Nelson-Hall.

Zippay, A. (1992, May). Corporate funding of human service agencies. *Social Work*, 37, 210–214.

# INDEX

Figures and tables are denoted by *f* or *t*, respectively, following page numbers.